THE NEW CAMBRIDGE MODERN HISTORY

VOLUME I

THE RENAISSANCE
1493-1520

EDITED BY

G. R. POTTER

CAMBRIDGE UNIVERSITY PRESS

CAMBRIDGE

LONDON · NEW YORK · MELBOURNE

Published by the Syndics of the Cambridge University Press
The Pitt Building, Trumpington Street, Cambridge CB2 1RP
Bentley House, 200 Euston Road, London NW1 2DB
32 East 57th Street, New York, NY 10022, USA
296 Beaconsfield Parade, Middle Park, Melbourne 3206, Australia

ISBN 0 521 04541 X hard covers
ISBN 0 521 09974 9 paperback

First edition 1957
Reprinted with minor corrections 1961
Reprinted 1964 1967 1971
First paperback edition 1975
Reprinted 1976 1978 1979

Printed in Great Britain at the
University Press, Cambridge

CONTENTS

CONTENTS

PREFACE TO THE PAPERBACK EDITION

THIS book was planned and written well over twenty years ago. The Introduction, to which this is an addendum, was written, somewhat hurriedly, in 1956.[1] In what ways would it have been different if written in 1975? The book itself would, of course have been different. Professor Potter's team of authors was the team then at his disposal, and there were doubtless writers he would have liked to enlist had he been able[2]. But I suspect that the very chronological limits of the volume and its place in related series imposed severe limitations on available choices. As Sir George Clark writes below (p. xxxiv), Lord Acton had produced the masterly design of the *Cambridge Modern History*; the *Medieval History* came out of the same Press (1911–36) and then there was a reversion to the beginning, as one might say, with the *Ancient History* (1923–39), quite apart from other works on the *British Empire* and other areas. Hence a fresh *Cambridge Modern History* had to be tailored to fit existing models. Its first two volumes had surely to be called 'Renaissance' and 'Reformation' respectively.

Of all the changes that have overtaken historical scholarship in recent times, it may be suspected that a desire to jettison the old hard-and-fast division between 'medieval' and 'modern' has pride of place. This yearning is frequently satisfied by the device of using the word Renaissance to mean primarily not a cultural crisis spread over a period, but a period itself. In the U.S.A. indeed Renaissance conveniently covers the centuries between Petrarch and Vico; and in this volume the 'Renaissance' of the title covers a survey of the main developments in most aspects of European History within an era over-precisely described in the title as running from 1493 to 1520. Such a use of the word to denote an epoch, however long or short, obliterates the ideological sense of the word. Everything that happens within the time span can be labelled 'Renaissance', just as anything that happened in Victorian Britain can be labelled 'Victorian'. This is quite a reasonable way out of the difficulty, provided one does not confuse the two interpretations of the word. As explained below (p. 2) the harbingers of what a later age would regard as the physical sciences were in no way humanist in their interests. In the new school curriculum, the major innovation of the Renaissance (along with

---

[1] When Professor Potter was appointed cultural attaché in Germany the present writer undertook to provide an introduction and see the volume through the Press.

[2] Professor Potter writes: 'The planning of this volume was influenced by wise editorial "instructions" from Sir George Clark and by the inability of two distinguished authors to write chapters originally allocated to them. Renaissance scholarship in 1950 when the first invitations were sent out was in an unusually transitional state.'

vii

parallel developments in the fine arts), there was naturally a small place allowed to the gentlemanly subject of mathematics. But the time-table was overwhelmingly devoted to Latin. Latin was no longer treated as necessary because one needed it to read the Scriptures and the Missal, but because it was the language of Cicero and Vergil, of truth and beauty in their own right. By means of Latin one might attain the supreme ability—the ability to communicate. Of course such communication was often not in Latin, although a surprising amount of it was. But even when people wrote or spoke in Italian, French or the other vernaculars, those of them who were literate, who were important, had all been to the same sort of grammar school; they all knew the basic Latin classics and the Bible. Even those who had no interest whatever in learning, but only an appropriate place in society, had had the ablative absolute instilled into them, often at a heavy price: what Ascham was later to call 'beating nature'.

The use of the word 'Renaissance' as a period, then, should encourage us to transcend, as contemporaries perforce had to, those frontiers of convenience adopted by historians as temporal divisions. It has been by neglecting such artificial boundaries that much new light has been thrown, for example, on Thomas More and Luther. It is clear from Professor Elton's preface to the paperback edition of the second volume of the *N.C.M.H.* the degree to which current Reformation research has begun to emphasize the medieval antecedents and influences in much sixteenth-century religious thought.

One change which has certainly affected Renaissance studies (as also and *a fortiori* classical and medieval studies) has been the dramatic decline in the amount of Latin taught in the schools of at any rate the English-speaking world. This is admittedly a process which began a long while back, but until the Second World War most boys or girls proceeding to read any kind of Arts at the university would have been given some kind of training in Latin. In the last quarter of a century the scene has been dramatically transformed in Britain and the Commonwealth; in the countries of North America the decline has been less pronounced, but only because Latin had never been so generally taught in the secondary schools. The results of this change are manifold. One is the difficulty many students experience in reading the older canonical works which, although written in their own language, have a fair amount of quotation and allusion in 'the obscurity of a learned language'. Text-books and even monographs must now provide translations or at any rate ample clues for the interpretation of such material. This may or may not be all loss: it is occasionally no bad thing for a scholar to make up his mind exactly what his text means. Further, there has been a quite remarkable increase in the quantity and quality of Renaissance texts available in translation. Writers like More and Erasmus were, of course, translated more or less in their own day, so far as their more popular books were concerned. But 'Tudor translations' are notoriously unreliable, and in any event involve the comprehension of archaic or obsolete words and phrases. Later translations, especially those produced in the nineteenth century, were all too frequently hack works, debased 'modernisations' of earlier and erratic versions, devoid of literary merit and innocent of any pretence at scholarship. (A good example of this can be found in the English versions of Platina's *Lives of the Popes*.) But in the last couple of decades a quite new standard has been attained. Two enterprises are so ambitious and impressive that they must be instanced.[1] In 1963 there appeared the second volume (but the first to be published) of the Yale edition of the complete works of Thomas More: *The History of King Richard III*. More had himself produced an English version of this which was printed on facing pages by the Yale editor, R. S. Sylvester. The next volume to appear (vol. 4, 1965) was *Utopia*, with a scrupulously revised text and translation by Edward Surtz S.J., and a long and authoritative introduction by J. H. Hexter. The series continues. Meanwhile an even more staggering programme has been initiated in Toronto, a complete English version of the works of Erasmus. Of this the first volume to appear contains his early letters (nos. 1–141 in P. S. Allen's enumeration): this section of the *Correspondence*, translated by R. A. B. Mynors and D. F. S. Thomson, is edited by Wallace K. Ferguson and was published in 1974. The editorial board cautiously avoids stating how many volumes the scheme will ultimately entail.

Many other lesser examples can be found in all modern languages of texts printed with translations, or of translations treated with the care and precision which enable the reader to rely on them with confidence and with a learned commentary which goes much of the way to dispense the scholar from recourse to the original. It would naturally be absurd to imply that the preparation of critical editions of Renaissance texts without translation has stopped. Erasmus is again a case in point. An international team has embarked on a new and revised recension of the Leyden *Opera omnia* of 1703–6. The first instalment of this appeared at Amsterdam in 1969.

Another development, not unique to Renaissance studies, but most prominent in that area, is the publication of collections of essays by different authors, organised round a theme. Three such works have proved influential: *Renaissance Studies*, ed. E. F. Jacob (1960), *Florentine Studies*, ed. N. Rubinstein (1969), and *Renaissance Venice—Essays*, ed. John Hale (1973). The emphasis on Florence and Venice reflected in the titles of these books not unfairly represents the direction of most Italian

---

[1] It is fair to say that in medieval history the trail was blazed long ago with 'Les classiques de l'histoire de France au moyen âge' and the Columbia 'Records of Civilization'. The 'Nelson's Medieval Texts', now continued as the 'Oxford Medieval Texts', began in 1949.

research, at least by British and American scholars; other centres have been relatively neglected, despite (for example) the exciting prospects suggested by the relevant volumes of the 'Treccani degli Alfieri' *Storia di Milano*. Rome in the early Renaissance awaits its historian, although there are some excellent works now available in the fields of *urbanistica* and the fine arts: one may instance T. Magnuson's *Studies in Roman Quattrocento Architecture* (1958) and L. D. Ettlinger's *The Sistine Chapel before Michelangelo* (1965). This concentration of research, especially in English, on Florence and Venice, reflects traditional sentiment of a non-scholarly kind and also library facilities well above the Italian average. And of course both towns have remarkable archives, often nowadays exploited by scholars anxious to bridge the gap between sociology and history. The shadow of the computer lies over the Renaissance.

Down to the 1520's, when this volume has its formal terminus, the new humanities and the new arts were more actively pursued in Italy than elsewhere. As yet only Erasmus, Budé and More had attained the stature of the greater Italian scholars and men of letters, and they have been accorded due recognition in recent years. Other questions remain without any answers, other authors with only partial treatment. Far too little attention has been paid as yet to northern cultural influences in Italy during the *quattrocento*, and much more light could be thrown on the Italian contributions to trans-Alpine 'prehumanism'. Of most countries it is true that our knowledge is still very much what it was a quarter of a century ago. France, however, has been very much better served. The energy of Franco Simone has resulted in a number of important books, and notably his *Il Rinascimento Francese* (1961); more recently we have been presented by Eugene F. Rice with his fundamental edition of the *Prefatory Epistles of Jacques Lefèvre d'Étaples and Related Texts* (1972): '...the efforts of Lefèvre and his circle to reform instruction in the faculty of arts during the last decade of the fifteenth century and the first decade of the sixteenth mark the critical stage in the adaptation of the cultural program of Italian humanism to the educational tradition of the University of Paris'. Lefèvre was a clear case of the old or medieval mingling with new ideas, and the same interesting amalgam can be seen in the German Abbot Johannes Trithemius, to whom Klaus Arnold has devoted a welcome study (1971). And, if much awaits investigation, specialists in the period now at last have their own *Bibliographie internationale de l'humanisme et de la Renaissance*, an annual which first came out at Geneva in 1966 with a survey of works published in 1965.

The present volume of the *N.C.M.H.* is entitled *The Renaissance* and in the preceding paragraphs some account has been taken of changing influences on and new contributions to the study of Renaissance civilisation. Many more remarks might have been made under this head. There is, for example, a new and stimulating interest in rhetoric, and an attempt to see how the assumptions deriving from classical and medieval rhetorical theory have to be mastered if we are properly to understand what humanists were trying to say. There is a new and lively activity to be seen in the history and achievements of humanist historians. For the period covered in the following pages original reflections are expressed by Felix Gilbert in his study of *Machiavelli and Guicciardini* (1965), the two historians who, from Ranke onwards, have dominated the interpretation of the Italian and European background of this epoch. Some valuable work has also been devoted to the rich interaction, just beginning at this time, between law and history; see, for instance, Donald K. Kelley's *Foundations of Modern Historical Scholarship* (1970), and compare too the perceptive remark below at p. xx.

It would be beyond the present writer's competence and the space allotted to these brief additional remarks to indicate even the most important works in all the subjects covered in the following chapters which have materially added to our knowledge since this book first came out. The attempt would in any case produce a list even more idiosyncratic than the handful of titles in cultural history already given. What may be indicated in conclusion are one or two of the ways in which our general assumptions may have altered in the interval.

One oppressive experience to which we are all at present exposed on an unprecedented scale is inflation. Nowadays this exercises a distinct restraint on discussions of what used to be called 'The Price Revolution of the Sixteenth Century'. Economists now freely admit that they cannot explain, let alone control, our predicament; likewise economic historians are more reticent when dealing with the milder upheavals of the mid-1500's, whose beginnings in foreign exploration and exploitation are touched on below.

Another closed episode was reopened when the late Pope John XXIII convoked the Second Vatican Council in 1962. Or rather a whole range of attitudes and actions, formerly regarded as irreversibly incompatible with the doctrines and practices of the Roman Catholic Church, once again emerged as possibilities. The role and authority of an ecumenical council was one such matter. Church historians of the medieval and Renaissance periods had accepted that the efforts of conciliarists at Constance and Basle had been frustrated by Trent and finally annihilated by the subservience of Vatican I (1869–70), which saw the proclamation of papal infallibility as a dogma. Now once again the place of the bishop in church government may be re-examined historically; 'head and members' has taken on renewed actuality. Beyond that the question of a married priesthood, of the endowment and financial control of the Roman Church even in areas where it is 'official', of the Cup for the laity (already an issue in Bohemia as Hus lay in prison at Constance), all these burning topics may now freely be debated by Roman Catholic historians, and for others have lost their confessional bitternesses. They went with simplification of the Roman liturgy and the use in it of the vernacular (a further blow for Latin!). In these and other ways what had seemed final paragraphs may become the beginnings of new chapters.

The spiritual life of pre-Reformation Europe is another field which is somewhat neglected in this volume, for the reason that historians interested in it had not yet published their work, save for the scholars who had dealt with the German mystics and the Brethren of the Common Life. Even the parish clergy, dealt with severely below, often had a worthwhile social role in the many confraternities and guilds of the period, themselves in many aspects 'religious' in the largest sense of the term. Charity and good works were a prominent part of the living and the dying of ordinary people everywhere, as W. K. Jordan has shown for England in his many writings, and as Brian Pullan has shown for Venice. The iconography of such spirituality was the subject of that fine study: Alberto Tenenti, *Il senso della morte e l'amore della vita nel Rinascimento* (1957).

An equally serious ambiguity surrounds many of the political solutions which used to seem fixed and certain not so long ago. It is now far from easy to ignore the fact that our world may change out of recognition. The old truths seem to have less force: England and Scotland joined by marriage in 1503 led ineluctably to the later United Kingdom; the even more famous marriage of Ferdinand and Isabella in the end produced a kingdom of Spain. (I notice with some shame that on p. 5 below I wrote of the 'final emergence of a pattern of international relationships'.) The dislocations resulting from the Second World War, it seemed twenty-five years ago, would sooner or later be cancelled out: there would again be— to take a case in point—one Germany, just as France, Spain, the U.K. would remain unchanged. In our own day devolution has everywhere powerful advocates and there is no state large or small which can be sure that its past will determine its future. 'Nothing is inevitable until it has happened.' The consequences of any public event are quite incalculable. All of this is a further reminder that 'definitive history' is no longer on the agenda (see below pp. xxiv–xxvi), despite the authoritative appearance and the continued viability of the Cambridge Histories.

January 1975   D.H.

GENERAL INTRODUCTION: HISTORY AND THE MODERN HISTORIAN

By Sir GEORGE CLARK

THE original *Cambridge Modern History*, to which the present series of volumes is the successor, was planned by the first Lord Acton in the year 1896, and its publication was completed when the atlas volume appeared in 1912.[1] It has been familiar ever since as a standard work, both a book of reference and a book to read, and it was the most influential survey in the English language of the history of the five previous centuries as they appeared to the scholars of that time. In British universities history, as a subject for examinations, was then attracting considerable, and growing, numbers of candidates. The same interest spread downwards into the schools and outwards through the ranks of educated men and women, bringing with it a demand for historical books and for new kinds of historical books. This change in the content of education was due to many changes in the public mind. One body of educational reformers promoted the teaching of history, while another promoted that of natural science, as alternatives to the more established subjects, especially the Greek and Latin classics; but the propaganda within the educational world echoed opinions which were current outside it. There was a utilitarian demand for more knowledge of history, appropriate enough at a time when British governments were assuming new functions at home and becoming more closely involved in international politics, so that the public had to discuss many issues which could scarcely be explained except in their historical setting. There was also an enthusiasm for history as a literary study, enlarging the mind, training political judgment and even confirming moral character. The imposing figures of the two historians who had become bishops, Stubbs and Creighton, stood among the eminent Victorians. The imperialistic mood of the time had but recently lost its historian, Sir John Seeley. Above all there was a belief that a new science of history, more impartial and more exact than anything previously practised, had provided a key to the past and the future. Samuel Rawson Gardiner was demonstrating what the method could do for English history, and a number of historians were available who had trained themselves in the same arduous technique. Yet there was a shortage of recent English books on continental history. There were few, if any, on a large scale worth mentioning except Creighton's

[1] An account of the planning and editing, fuller than that which follows here, is in the *Cambridge Historical Journal*, VII (1945), pp. 57ff.

History of the Papacy and Seeley's *Life of Stein*. For ordinary purposes it was still necessary to use older writers like Robertson, Coxe, Prescott, Motley and even Carlyle.

Some of these things must have been in the minds of the Syndics of the Cambridge University Press, one of whom was the great historian Maitland, when in 1896 they invited Lord Acton to consider undertaking the general direction of a History of the World. Acton had entered on his office as Regius Professor of Modern History in the previous year, and he had not decided what work to do in addition to giving his lectures. Of all men he had the strongest faith in the new scientific history. It was for this that he had stood up in the controversies of his younger days when, as an editor of periodicals, he had tried to show that his Church would further her own ends if she encouraged those of science 'which are truth' and those of the State 'which are liberty'. He did not hesitate for long before accepting the Syndics' invitation. 'Such an opportunity', he wrote, 'of promoting his own ideas for the treatment of history has seldom been given to any man.'

Among the adjustments of the plan which preceded Acton's final acceptance was one which must be noticed here. The Syndics cut down their original scheme, so that now it was to include 'Modern History only, beginning with the Renaissance'. There had already been writers before this time who maintained that this familiar, or even customary, division of history into two chapters in or about the fifteenth century was less appropriate to the subject-matter than a division at a later point, perhaps somewhere in the seventeenth. This view attracts historians who wish to minimise the importance of the earlier and emphasise that of the later changes; but for two reasons it seems not to merit much discussion here. In the first place it implies that the divisions of books and chapters belong to the nature of things and not merely to convenience in writing and teaching. Secondly, the *Cambridge Medieval History* has been published, ending where the *Modern History* began, and therefore when the present series of volumes was planned the date for its beginning was no longer an open question. Something may, however, be said about the wider and more substantial problem, whether there is a difference of kind between modern history and other, earlier, sorts of history.

Such a difference between the more and the less remote is implied in many of our habits of thought and speech. More than one Roman author of the first century A.D. discussed the question where it is proper to draw the line which separates the ancients from the moderns. Most people still assume that one or more such lines ought to be drawn, if only to divide up the past into manageable units; but their reasons for thinking so reveal endless disagreements. Some of them give the name of modern to the history of any periods recent enough to have left answers in writing to such questions as we are disposed to ask about them. Ancient or medieval history, on this view, relates to ages in which men's minds worked differently from ours: for instance they were blind to the advantages of digesting their experience into statistical or even chronologically accurate statements. Some people, however, believe that human nature never changes. They are content to distinguish the remoter ages, which it is hard to understand because our information about them is scanty, from the nearer, which it is equally hard to understand because our information about them is too voluminous. Writers of this latter complexion have, to be sure, looked more favourably on later than on earlier periods, because, as one of them remarked 'Historical science...is always becoming more possible; not solely because it is better studied, but because, in every generation, it becomes better adapted for study'.[1] Unhappily, however, there are some who maintain that the mere notion of modern history is absurd. On the one hand there is the proposition that 'modern history' is a contradiction in terms. History, we are told, is in its essence the reverse of modern; what makes it history is that it is different from our knowledge of the present, so that, unless they start from the assumption that the past is finished and done with, historians cannot be historians at all. However we define it we must recognise that history deals with the past; whatever we may mean by 'modern' we must mean something closely related to the present. The more anything belongs to history, it would seem, the less modern it must be, and conversely the more modern it is, the less it can be historical. If we do not like this, we may turn to the opposing proposition, equally plausible, equally sparkling with paradox, if, perhaps, equally shallow, that 'modern history' is a tautology. All history is modern, or in more familiar words, 'every true history is ideally contemporary',[2] for if there were no continuity between past and present; if the historian, living as he must live in the present, could not assimilate the past into his present, then he could not know it or write anything about it that was either true or intelligible to his contemporaries.

Although we are so far from agreeing about what they are doing or why they do it, a very large number of men and women, larger than ever before, spend some or all of their working time on research into modern history. A few of them work by themselves, but, since they use books or manuscripts prepared by other people, even the research of these hermits is a social activity. The great majority belong to organisations of various kinds, research institutes, universities, academies, publishing societies, national or international associations of historians or of students of special branches of history. They contribute to journals, reviews, and research periodicals. Librarians, archivists and museum officials, many of them highly expert, collect, arrange and make available for them an immense

---

[1] J. S. Mill, 'Additional Elucidations of the Science of History' in *System of Logic* (1843).
[2] This is the form of the phrase in B. Croce, *Storia, cronaca, e false storie* (1912), p. 2, reprinted in *Teoria e storia della storiografia* (1917), p. 4.

apparatus comprising both raw and half-finished materials and the finished products of earlier investigation. By correspondence, conferences and other contacts these organisations are linked with one another and with other component parts of the world of science and learning. Those who work in and for them think of research in modern history as a going concern, an immense organisation of workers.

Systematic instruction in methods of historical research has become a settled part of the routine of universities, and there are many text-books setting out its technique. Some are general; others deal with what are portentously called 'auxiliary sciences', such as chronology, bibliography, palaeography, diplomatic, and the study of seals, which is sometimes called sigillography and sometimes, even less gracefully, sphragistics. It has, however, been held that, just as most historians are eclectic in the general ideas which they apply in their work, depending for them on non-historical writers, so most of the actual operations carried out in the course of historical research have been derived from other studies which would not ordinarily be called historical. They are applications of the habits of mind which distinguish scholarly from unscholarly work. Some of these were familiar to lawyers long before they were thought to be necessary for historians. It was not lawyer-like in the sixth century to give an opinion on one particular section of a law without looking through the whole;[1] now it is also not historian-like. In the fifteenth century the jurists of Europe in general were skilful in deciding on the authenticity of old documents and establishing their purport. Ecclesiastics were at work on the relationships of different systems of reckoning time. Classical scholars were improving the emendation of corrupted texts, and in the course of time historians availed themselves of all these older and newer kinds of skill, just as they followed the general movement of thought by eliminating miracles and the influence of the stars from their narratives. In later centuries they took over from natural science the ambition to frame general laws, and to explain particular events or the broader course of history by some evolutionary principle. Along with these governing ideas, they borrowed many devices of detail. Recently they have busied themselves with graphs and curves and statistical tables. Beginning in economic history these have come to be used in such different fields as bibliographical and ecclesiastical history. Some historians regard their task as a special kind of inductive reasoning, distilling the truth from an exhaustive examination of all the available evidence. They aim at 'total cover' of their subject-matter, and this in spite of an uneasy suspicion that the subject-matter even of a narrow, particular history may be in some way inexhaustible. No historian hitherto has had at his command all the sources which might be relevant to his subject; none has ever completed

---

[1] *Digest*, I, 3, 24: Celsus Lib. VIII digestorum. Incivile est nisi tota lege perspecta una aliqua particula eius proposita iudicare vel respondere.

his work so that no newly emerging source could invalidate it. However limited the subject, and however few the aspects from which it could be approached, the bulk of the relevant materials will be so great that the historian who tries to acquaint himself with all of them must give up the attempt to handle them all for himself. He may trustingly accept what other scholars tell him about this or that outlying field. He may be content to make his contribution to the joint research of some great organisation which provides somewhere for the co-ordination of his discoveries with others. In any case the nearer we come to 'total cover', the further we move from the primitive historian-like exactness. It seems that historians have adopted a miscellaneous collection of other people's tools.

These appearances are deceptive. There is a method or technique or approach which is distinctive of history, and by which historians make their own contribution to thought. All their subjects belong to the study of human life in the framework of time, and their speciality is to treat their subject-matter as organically related by successiveness, by sequence in time. Any investigator who sets out to digest a confused mass of evidence needs some means of distinguishing what is relevant to his purpose from what is not relevant. He must be able to sift his evidence so that, once he finds a sufficient proof, or the best available proof, for a conclusion, he can discard all the rest as superfluous. He aims at extracting from each item that and only that which it and it alone can contribute to the knowledge of his subject. Lawyers are guided by rules about what kinds of evidence are admissible; scientists plan their experiments so as to yield the answers to set questions. Historians have to sort out their evidence from all the books and manuscripts and material objects which may include relevant information. Among these there may be written or printed documents or material things which actually were parts of the events or times which the historian studies. There are also all the contemporary or subsequent writings, pictures and other objects which give information about former events without having formed parts of them. It may happen that nothing has survived from the event itself, and yet we may have abundant means of knowing about it. There is a general presumption that the historian can make a first rough grading of his materials by trusting his evidence more the earlier it is in time. Many historians distinguish original or primary from secondary authorities. This ceases to be a sharp distinction as soon as anything is included in the primary class besides the materials actually surviving from the events. A report of a speech, in a newspaper or a diplomatic dispatch, may be written immediately after the speech is delivered, but it is not so completely primary as a tape-recording: in however subordinate a way, another personality intrudes and may bring in errors or even falsifications. A summary written afterwards, even by the speaker himself, is still further away. For many kinds of occurrences over long stretches of time memoirs and histories afford the best evidence we have, but this is not only more remote; it is tinged with the personalities of the writers. All interpretation rests on the selection of evidence, and whenever evidence has been selected, whether by chance or deliberately, the selection governs any possible interpretation. Since, either intentionally or by accident, all our authorities have been selected, this means that they must all be examined in the light of all that we can know about their lost context.

The distinction between primary and secondary authorities is thus neither as simple nor as useful as it appears at first sight. Historians who regard their work as the answering of questions, even when they know that its progress must change the form of the questions themselves, are disposed to approach the primary authorities through the secondary. There are obvious advantages in doing this. If a historian confined himself to studying only the first-hand authorities or the nearest that he could get to first-hand, he might spend hours in deciphering manuscripts which had already been printed and could be read in as many minutes. If, among printed works, he read only the original documents, he would have to do over again for himself whatever his predecessors had done that might lighten his task. Strictly speaking it is impossible to derive historical knowledge only from primary authorities. Merely by knowing that such authorities exist and where he is to find them, the historian knows something about them from outside. The disputes of the sixteenth and seventeenth centuries about the authority of scripture and tradition in ecclesiastical matters turned on similar issues, and John Selden annihilated the argument that belief and practice should or could be founded on the authority of scripture alone. He said: 'Say what you will against tradition, we know the signification of words by nothing but tradition... take these words, *In principio erat verbum.* How do you know those words signify, *In the beginning was the word,* but by tradition, because someone has told you so.'[1] As history cannot be founded on knowledge of primary authorities alone, the best way not to be misled by the errors and accretions or omissions of later writers is to study these later writers and then work back from them to their sources.

It does indeed often happen that a historian sets out to correct an authorised version but fails to free himself from its assumptions and adduces new evidence without seeing that it is decisive. Others who, for any reason, are free from his assumptions, see the effect of this evidence more clearly, and it is natural to infer that the way to see everything clearly is to empty the mind of all assumptions whatsoever. This is one, but only one, of the reasons why some historians exalt primary and despise secondary authorities. Another is that the approach from secondary authorities involves the temptation to read history backwards. Some eminent historians condemned the imperfections of one age by comparison

[1] *Table Talk*, ed. S. H. Reynolds (1892), p. cxxvii.

with the successes of another or judged by results, or judged by the standards of their own time. Others may avoid these errors and yet may unconsciously see the earlier period through the eyes of their own, or of some intermediate time. It has been said, for instance, that Johan Huizinga, in spite of all his learning and sympathy, saw the age of Erasmus too much from the point of view of the eighteenth century; and indeed scholars who value lucidity of thought and expression must always find it hard to depart from the judgments of the eighteenth century. To study history forwards would be to plunge into the moving stream of events, identifying oneself in imagination with the time, knowing and feeling only what could be known and felt then. This is what Samuel Rawson Gardiner tried to do: he worked through mountains of contemporary books, pamphlets, statutes, dispatches, and letters, day by day and year by year, not looking ahead into the next batch of materials to see what the outcome of anything was going to be. And any historian may be overtaken by the feeling that he has left and forgotten his own circumstances and become one with the world of the old book or parchment in his hand. This feeling comes most perfectly to those who are very learned and yet keep alive the poet in them; but there are many more to whom it seems to be an end worth pursuing in itself, and worth transmitting by the magic of good writing to every reader who can receive it. Nor is this only a question of emotional experience: the scientific historian also will prize the authenticity of the best sources. If he can reconstruct the past, and eliminate from his mind everything that came to pass afterwards, he will have isolated the pure object of his study. Many teachers of historical method, therefore, advise their pupils to go straight to the original authorities and to master them first. The most austere adherents of this doctrine give no references in their footnotes to the works of previous historians, or to any of their contemporaries except the compilers of such monographs as approximate to the character of mere précis of materials. They do indeed use dictionaries, catalogues, and works of reference of many other kinds; but these too appear to be impersonal, as innocent of bias or interpretation as the *Nautical Almanac*. The technique of using them, the application of auxiliary sciences, has its own innocent delights, and 'pure history' seems to be an end in itself, an aesthetic activity, untroubled by utilitarian aims or pressure from the outer world.

This was not the attitude of the historians who created the *Cambridge Modern History*. There were, of course, many varieties of method within their school, and no convenient name has been found for describing their highest common factor. They are sometimes called liberal historians; but the word 'liberal' has many meanings. On the Continent it often carries an implication of unfriendliness to churches or even to religion; but in England among the great writers of this school were the bishops, Stubbs and Creighton, and the zealous Roman Catholic Lord Acton. In some respects they carried on the eighteenth-century attitude, especially in rejecting as untrue what seemed inherently improbable; in others, from the early days of their greatest master Leopold von Ranke, they were influenced by the romantic movement, which emphasised the differences, insuperable as it was supposed, between races, or nationalities, or times. What they had in common is most easily seen from their relation to their sources. During the nineteenth century the sum of historical knowledge received enormous additions from the opening of archives. Governments had for a considerable time admitted approved persons to read among their accumulated papers, and had even spent large sums on printing selections of documents relating to earlier times. Now, one by one, they opened their repositories more freely. All of them still kept some papers under lock and key, and drew a line between the older papers which were open to search, and those so close to the present that they must be reserved; but well before the end of the century it was normal for a civilised capital to have some virtually public search-rooms where official historical records were accessible. Most of the historians who used them were learned in the printed literature of their subjects, and most of them worked either alone or with the help of at most a few copyists. Confronted by enormous masses of papers most of which had been unread from a time soon after they were written, they had no temptation to try to read every word that bore on their subjects. That had to wait until inventories and catalogues were much improved not only in the official archives but in the great libraries as well. They could only pick out the plums, and these were the records from which the accepted version could be corrected, or a decision made between conflicting versions. Nineteenth-century historians, like nineteenth-century scientists, prided themselves on their discoveries: to Acton Ranke was first and foremost a pathfinder. The advance of historical studies appeared as the detection of error by the touchstone of accurate knowledge. Much importance was therefore attached to emending texts so as to restore the authentic words of documents which had been garbled or misread. Next, the ranking of authorities was studied. Like the classical scholars who studied the derivation of manuscripts, the historians invented systems for tracing back historical statements to their sources, and so were able to reject the derivative and draw their own conclusions from the primary. They looked with little favour on probabilities or corroborative evidence. They scored so many successes in disposing of lies or legends by the confrontation of crucial facts that they came to think of facts as the indestructible atoms by the adding of which together true history could be composed. With something of this sort in mind they looked forward to a future when it would be possible to write 'definitive history'.

Historians of a later generation do not look forward to any such prospect. They expect their work to be superseded again and again. They consider that knowledge of the past has come down through one or more human minds, has been 'processed' by them, and therefore cannot consist of elemental and impersonal atoms which nothing can alter. They do not even ascribe these qualities to the material objects which form the evidence for archaeology in all ages. A flint implement, however durable, and a pyramid, however large, have not yielded all their testimony until we have examined them in their context, until, for instance, we know how they and not others like them have survived until our time. The exploration seems to be endless, and some impatient scholars take refuge in scepticism, or at least in the doctrine that, since all historical judgments involve persons and points of view, one is as good as another and there is no 'objective' historical truth.

The nineteenth-century cult of facts was intended, among other purposes, to guard against this relativism. Few of the historians were speculative enough to inquire what facts are. It appeared sufficient that they were not fancies, nor theories; the adjective most commonly applied to them was 'hard'. Whatever else might be open to question, they seemed real. They seemed to be components of a real past which was implied by the study of history itself. When we set out to restore a damaged inscription, we act on the assumption that it was once complete, and that the words it then included were there and were what they were whether we succeed in recovering them or not. In the same way when we set out to discover any missing fact, or to correct any historical statement, we assume that both a known and an unknown past exist. Some such assumption indeed is built into the structure of our Indo-European languages: the tenses of the verbs imply time and change, and some of them imply degrees of continuity and discontinuity between the past and the present. We know some of the past and we may know more. In moving through the past from the known to the unknown, we apply our customary tests for distinguishing true knowledge from opinion. One of these is coherence. If a pretended new fact is inconsistent with our knowledge of the past, one or the other must be amended or rejected. The real past, known and unknown, forms a coherent whole; but it is not merely a whole of which every single component may be challenged by some new discovery. Besides being coherent, it is in some way fixed. Nothing can undo it, and that is a significant statement, not a mere commonplace. There is an old saying that God himself cannot cancel the past, cannot unmake the facts:

> Hoc namque dumtaxat negatum etiam Deo est
> Quae facta sunt, infecta posse reddere.[1]

Research workers whose methods imply that there is a real past with a coherent structure, and who are constantly becoming more skilful in

[1] This is Casaubon's translation in his edition of Aristotle (1590) of the fragment quoted in the *Nicomachaean Ethics* 1139 b 9, from the dramatist Agathon.

learning more about it, easily forget that only an infinitesimal fraction of that whole can ever be known. Most of the past has vanished and can never be recovered by the means at our disposal. Out of the millions upon millions of men, women and children who have lived on the surface of the globe, there are indeed some few millions of whom something is recorded; but it would require many volumes to set down all that passed through the consciousness of any one of them in an hour, and, in comparison with such a record as that, the whole of our historical knowledge is proportionately less than a single comma surviving from a lost encyclopaedia. This does not only mean that we must make the best of what little we can know. It also means that the collector's notion of total cover must be inappropriate to history. It means, further, that the function of the historian is not to be compared with that of the map-maker, who reproduces on a smaller scale the proportions and lay-out of a piece of ground. The map-maker, to be sure, displays the gaps in his knowledge: where there is an unexplored desert or an uncharted sea, he leaves a blank. Another kind of blank in his map indicates a featureless area, a part of the earth's surface where there is nothing that he wishes to indicate. For the historian there is a third kind of blank, which cannot be filled by exploration but does not indicate that there never was anything there. If this were a comparatively small matter, it might be overcome by reasonably inferring from the known course of events what the lost events must have been like. Sometimes and in a small way historians do this, as statisticians interpolate figures; but when their task is looked at as a whole, it appears that they must allow that there are many differences of kind between the known and the unknown. Their ignorance is an essential element in their knowledge. They work with materials which have already been fortuitously or deliberately selected; they carry the process of selection further; but they are not merely abstracting from a mixed mass of data. They are carrying out a kind of selection which involves more than taking some parts and rejecting others.

If historical writing were simply putting facts together, it might be not ordered construction but mere shapeless heaping-up. Many writers about history have maintained that one distinction between a history and a mere quantity of information about the past lies in the constant exercise of judgment by the historian. This may indeed be called the classical view. Edward Gibbon, for instance, the author of *The Decline and Fall of the Roman Empire*, who is sometimes regarded as a literary man rather than a serious thinker, specified 'civil prudence' as 'the first and most essential virtue of an historian'. His phrase 'civil prudence' has a long and curious history.[1] Even if its early occurrences were not in his mind when he wrote,

---

[1] It occurs in Milton's *Civil Power in Ecclesiastical Causes* (1659), in the dedicatory letter. In Latin Cicero has it, and it occurs in J. J. Becher, *Psychosophia oder Seelenweisheit* (1678). Grotius, *Briefwisseling*, ed. Molhuysen, no. 402 (1615) has 'civilis sapientia'.

Gibbon was in essence repeating the opinion of Lucian, who regarded good sense in relation to public affairs as the born gift of the good historian.[1] Civil prudence, or political judgment, is not a purely intellectual quality; it is the capacity to judge concrete situations well, in the sense in which we commonly speak of a good judge of a man, or a horse or a picture.

This classical view of the historian's procedure consorts well with the formula that history is the consciousness of continuity, *das Bewusstsein der Continuität*.[2] It may indeed be true that, however little the past could be known in earlier ages, when historical knowledge was scanty and was confined to the few literate people, the past nevertheless penetrated, informed and governed the present even more than it can nowadays. History never supersedes but only reinforces and elucidates other older, underlying continuities. The lowest stratum is the physical continuity of the universe. A second underlying continuity is biological. Genealogy is a primitive kind of history, but it did not arise from thought about given data, namely the facts of marriages and births. The knowledge of these facts arose in and with the knowledge of their genealogical framework as a crystallisation within a complex experience which was instinctive, biological and social. Heredity is still one of the factors of social continuity everywhere, and the family is still one of the fundamental institutions even in societies where its character and functions have most changed; but the continuity provided by the family has always been defined and stabilised by conscious knowledge, by what we may call traditional continuity. The successive and overlapping generations pass on acquired aptitudes. Oral tradition, however, is not the only means by which continuity with the past is maintained intentionally. Words, even when they are used with the most expert skill, can never revive the whole of any experience, and so in addition to traditional words, and sometimes in association with them, there is another way of fixing events in memory so that they can be called up again. This is ritual. For the ordering of society it is necessary that only those who are properly entitled, only those in due succession to the past, should enjoy the majesty of a king or the status of a wife, should exercise a priest's office or a scholar's right to teach, a landlord's right to the services of his tenants, or a tenant's right to the produce of the soil. Of old, therefore, these titles were affirmed and fixed in the memory of witnesses by ceremonial, as some of them still are. Not every registry-office marriage is symbolised by a ring, but our newspapers announce actual coronations, consecrations, ordinations, investitures, degree-givings, institutions to benefices. These are performed not because there is any danger that the *London Gazette* or the legal documents relating to such occasions may perish or be disputed; but because there is something in

---

[1] *Quomodo Historia Conscribenda sit*, 34.
[2] J. G. Droysen, *Grundriss der Historik* (1868).

each of them which cannot be put into words. In earlier times, even when there was a document to embody a legal act, there was also a ritual, and the ritual rather than the document was the act. We retain the ritual when we distrust the efficacy of words to record the essence of the event.

Written history does indeed provide us with our surest knowledge of the past. Written words are more precise and easier to work with, if less expressive, than spoken, but writing has not rendered oral tradition useless. There are stresses and intonations which can be taught but not written and written history is still embedded in the deeper continuities, physical, biological, ritual and traditional. They are less clear and explicit, but they have their independent value and sometimes they can interpret what survives in writing. All these continuities are organically connected; all alike are means by which the present carries its past along with it, so that history is not the continuity of human life, but the continuity made conscious.

There is indeed one respect in which history provides a continuity quite unlike the others. Once any of these others is interrupted it can never be put together again. When a family has no heirs that is the end of it; when the last minstrel dies his unwritten ballads die with him. But history can be neglected and forgotten for centuries and yet begin afresh. Perhaps the most striking of all historical discoveries are those made by scholars who read lost languages. Even where the language of the sources is well known, their nature may be forgotten. A document may appear to mean something quite different from what it meant to its writer. Thus an eminent English historian accused the English queen, Catherine of Aragon, of being still loyal to her nephew Charles V because she ended a letter to him in Spanish with the words, before her signature, 'who kisses your hand'. He could have found from an elementary Spanish grammar that this is still, as it was then, an ordinary formula for ending a letter. And if historical research can recreate continuities by interpreting documents, in the same way it renews them on the largest scale by bringing every kind of relevant knowledge to bear on every aspect of the past.

The purposes of the historian are as wide as the purposes for which a knowledge of continuity with the past may be desired. A man may wish to draw out the continuity of some village or town or nation, of some institution or practice or belief with its past for one or more of an immense number of reasons. At one extreme a writer of genius like Michelet may proclaim his own version of the grandeurs and miseries of the national past. At the other extreme there are simple practical reasons. A town clerk may trace the ownership of a ferry through old deeds in order to discover who has the right to fix the toll. Lawyers constantly have searches made to provide proofs of the claims of litigants. Political parties set up research departments to provide materials for their decisions on policy and for their propaganda. Lord Allenby read the campaigns of the Old Testament and the ancient Romans when he planned his conquest of Palestine. There are equally simple emotional or aesthetic reasons. The owner of an ancient castle, or a citizen of an ancient borough may delve into its records from a mere sense of wonder and curiosity. Simply as an adventure-story, a book on Napoleon's campaigns may absorb the attention of a man who has no interest in strategy or tactics. But in practice it is exceptional for the historian's interest to be simple. Usually in the mind of any one writer different lines of interest run side by side: many military historians write romantically, and many romantic historians are surprised into studying the technicalities of tactics. There are, indeed, innumerable branches of history which isolate some special interest. In the larger universities there are specialists in legal, military, literary, ecclesiastical and economic history as well as in the history of certain countries and regions; some universities also make special provision for the history of the arts and sciences and of philosophy. These special branches are, however, taught and studied in connection with general history, which may pay more or less attention to some of them, but somehow provides an introduction or groundwork, if not a final summing-up, for all. This is how the current work of the great going concern of historical research and teaching is organised now; and the shape of this organisation corresponds to the demands of a collective opinion among the historians. Commonly it is this collective opinion which dictates the choice of subjects. From time to time attempts are made to show that one or other branch of history is more truly historical than the others, or is fundamental to them; but, if we remember that all historical research implies a real past, we shall be content to believe that any historical investigation which is undertaken to discover truth will lay bare part of this real past. We shall not be tempted to say that one branch of history is more legitimate than another, that its historical character depends on its choice of subject within the infinite field of the past.

What historical subjects are studied and for what reasons depends on many seemingly unrelated circumstances of human society; and the same is true of the other activities which precede historical study and on which it depends. First there are the recording activities. These make provision beforehand for those who may need knowledge of what will then have become the past. In our literate world a private individual whose affairs are simple may keep no records except a bank pass-book and a few letters and receipts, but a rich man may need muniment-rooms with a staff of clerks. Businesses, even small businesses, are embarrassed to find room for the records that accumulate in their offices. Government departments and local authorities often employ trained archivists, who follow elaborate regulations in deciding what to preserve and what to destroy among the papers deposited with them. There are experts, whether professional or belonging to voluntary societies, who give advice to firms on the selecting and preservation of their records and on the disposal of those which deserve to survive but for which they have no room. Keepers of records must understand difficult technical questions of registration and storage and such considerations as safe custody and secrecy. But, in spite of all this organisation and skill, the quantity of records increases beyond the point where there is any prospect that any large proportion of them will be useful. One after another new means of recording have been called into use by the immediate needs of an increasingly complex society. Shorthand, the typewriter, sound-recording, photography, and the cinema all leave behind from the day's work their heaps of material.

During the period, roughly the last sixty years, when this plethora has spread from office to office all over the world the scope of historical studies has been broadening. The numbers of those engaged in them has multiplied many times; the variety of calls on their services has grown equally quickly; they study more aspects of life and more periods; in particular they have begun to examine the very recent past. The physical multiplication of materials seems for these purposes to be a gain. If they are hard to manage, co-operative research can apply the principle of the division of labour. It is impossible to be sure that any piece of paper may not supply the answer to some question which no one can foresee now, or fill a gap in a picture which no one has yet wanted to draw. We therefore constantly hear appeals for the preservation of records; but sooner or later, and more cheaply and easily soon than late, enormous masses of records must be destroyed. Recording has indeed reached a point at which it can only with difficulty be made to serve the less immediate of the purposes of the historian. It has even reached a point where the mass of records clogs the wheels of administration. Every day thousands of committeemen sit down before piles of paper which they cannot read through. However good their summaries and indexes and tables of contents may be, superfluous thousands of words will prevent some of them from reading the few words that matter. It has therefore become a problem for administrators to find methods of limiting the output of official papers, in other words of selecting records, for the short-term purposes of current business rather than with an eye to the long-term needs of historians. The same man sometimes exercises both kinds of selection as he goes along. A statesman who intends to write his memoirs may keep a file for tit-bits which might easily become submerged in the ocean of a departmental registry. But the two kinds of selection, normally two successive stages in winnowing, are essentially different even when they are carried on simultaneously by one man.

Historians naturally try to ensure that their interests are considered when any selection is made, and administrators may be willing or reluctant to comply. In the same way they may or may not allow the students easy access to the records once they are selected. For centuries past there have been classes of records which members of the public had a legal right to consult for certain purposes: the wills of deceased persons are shown because it is desirable that those entitled to benefit under them should know their rights. The general public also has a legal right to know about certain kinds of proceedings, for instance those in the British parliament. This particular right was conceded after long and bitter disputes. The modern States are the owners of the records which form the main data of some of the social sciences; but they have only granted access to them on their own terms. They have also asserted their rights of ownership over official papers which have been carried away into private possession, partly in order to provide themselves with the historical knowledge which they may need, but partly also in order to withhold it from other States or from individuals who may use it against them. Since in earlier times they succeeded only imperfectly in maintaining control over the materials to which they had a legal right, and since complementary materials were, lawfully or unlawfully, in private ownership, it was a natural completion of the opening of the public archives for States to encourage the opening of private archives, for instance by having them catalogued and publishing parts of their contents, and by controlling or subsidising libraries which collected manuscripts. As historians thus came to know more about these collections they applied to their owners for permission to work in them, not always successfully. Every improvement of transport and photography made access to documents physically easier and so made any failure to see a document seem the more regrettable. At the same time, since history has become the basis of the education of large numbers of people, and a favourite way of studying and explaining public affairs, the writing of history ranks as a public, or at least a socially valuable, function, and it is inferred that the historian, as a servant of the public, has a right of access to his materials.

The relation of historians to the State is so many-sided that this claim to access is sometimes made by the State on their behalf, but in other cases it is a claim of theirs against the State. It is almost a necessary consequence of the nature of historical writing that all those who engage in a contest for power or who attempt to control opinion should wish to be served by historians. The Burgundian princes of the fifteenth century had official chroniclers and official historiographers, the distinction being perhaps between those who dealt with current and those who dealt with former events. From the seventeenth century or earlier princes published large extracts from their own records in order to enable historians to write history. With the growth of popular education in the nineteenth century, and with the increase in the size and cost of libraries and museums, States applied their resources to maintaining huge institutions for research and education. The enjoyment of works of art and of historical monuments spread through all classes, and so access to historical materials has come to be claimed as part of a general claim of the public to enjoyments which used to be denied or restricted by owners of property. This claim has gathered strength when property-owners have made voluntary concessions to it. The State has reinforced it and taken advantage of it by extending its functions as a universal cataloguer and organiser of access. The National Portrait Gallery collects information about all British historical portraits; the National Register of Archives catalogues all ancient documents, whoever owns them. Catalogues exist to be used; they promote and assist the will to see the catalogued objects. Departments of State may make lists for their own use, as the Ordnance Survey did of ancient cadastral maps, but once they are known to exist they can scarcely be withheld from use for the wider purposes of research.

The desire of public authorities to survey and collect and use historical information bearing on their functions thus stimulates the desire of members of the public to look at it for themselves. This in turn is separated by a very short distance from the demand of the public for knowledge of the proceedings of government. There is a perpetual pulling and pushing between journalists and elected representatives who want to unearth buried treasure of information and men in office who want to work undisturbed. Most of the historians in the present-day Europe are either civil servants of the State, like the professors in most of the continental universities, or members of universities which are subsidised and partly controlled by the States; yet this subordination to the machinery of organised society need not hamper their freedom as scholars. There are infinite varieties in the pressure which society may exercise upon the historian. It may be as crippling when it is exercised by a foundation or a board of trustees or the highest authority in a self-governing university as when it is exercised by a minister. Fortunately there are equally varied and adaptable defences by which the historian can protect his right and duty to seek and disseminate the truth. These are a social right and a social duty: they cannot exist except in the context of other rights and duties which also are valid. They may therefore be involved in conflicts with other rights and other obligations. Freedom of thought, like any other freedom, implies responsibility. It is sometimes right and it is sometimes a duty for a statesman or an official or a private man to maintain secrecy. The historian serves society by his judgment, and, as we have seen, he cannot divest himself of his responsibility by acting like a copying-machine and leaving it to others, his readers, to judge after he has merely transcribed.

The social function of historians has always varied and will always vary with the changing social scene; but there is always tension between the historian's standards in his craft and the demands of his readers. Whether he writes for an individual patron, or for a government department or for such members of the general public as he can induce to read his book, he must to some extent supply a demand. Even if this is merely a demand for true information about a subject or true answers to questions, he must be prepared to face the problem of the missionary, who must state his new message at least in the old language, if not in the old thought-forms to which his hearers are accustomed. The fewer of their beliefs he wishes to challenge, the easier will be his task of transposition. When the original *Cambridge Modern History* was planned it seemed to Acton that, without challenging beliefs, it could be a 'chart and compass for the coming century'. The chart and the compass are products of science. They are completely impersonal; the least element of bias or interested misrepresentation would spoil them. So far the metaphor admirably expresses the nature of modern history. But the navigator must understand something of their scientific nature if he is to use these aids, and they will not decide his destination for him. The metaphor does not show what corresponds to his training and his sailing-orders if history or any other social science is a chart and compass. Half a century ago it was still natural for a European thinker to assume that, in spite of their diversities, the states of the civilised world were all more or less effectively controlled by educated elements and in accordance with more or less generally accepted opinions as to the ends of government. The idea of the social sciences, and in particular of history, appropriate to this view was the 'liberal' view that it was a scale-reduction of the facts, with the necessary compass-like specific interpretations. In our altered world this view is no longer tenable. Many social scientists have found that they cannot pursue their inquiries unless they discuss their purposes: they prepare charts but they also compare one destination with another. For the historian the principle that his work is the exercise of judgment implies that he may have to engage in the choice of ends. If he accepts the limitations of the court historian, the patriotic historian or the writer of any kind of commissioned or sponsored history, he either renounces his function of judging or consciously proceeds on the hypothesis, which he or his reader remains free to reject, that the end prescribed by his employer is good. The historian may judge it to be his duty to obey the law regarding the disclosure of the contents of the public records. He may judge it to be his duty to disobey; but in either event he forms a judgment. Whatever he conceals and whatever he discloses, whether to the general public or to a government or an employer, whatever lines of investigation he follows and whatever lines he avoids, he is making decisions in which society has an interest, actual or potential. If there could be social knowledge entirely free from the factor of judgment, then, on the one hand, there could be an impersonal and mechanistic science of society and, on the other, an unqualified right to freedom in constructing it. Social policy could then be separated from social science. The division would be like that which, in some systems of government, is supposed to distinguish policy from administration. The latter distinction is indeed often, if not always, conventional, arbitrary and illusory; the former might well be like it in that too. It is outside our present scope to discuss this question as it affects the social sciences in general, but so far as history is concerned we may affirm that, if it is a science, it is a science of values.

This new issue of the *Cambridge Modern History* has been planned neither as a stepping-stone to definitive history, nor as an abstract or a scale-reduction of all our knowledge of the period, but as a coherent body of judgments true to the facts. Over a great part of the field its aims will coincide with those which Lord Acton formulated for its predecessor; but it is necessary to recede from one of Acton's principles. He expected his contributors to suppress or conceal their individual convictions, and we know on the high authority of his pupil Dr Gooch that 'he never wrote or uttered a word as Regius Professor which revealed him as a member of one church rather than another'.[1] In the triumphant phase of liberal historiography this kind of impartiality seemed attainable; but even for Acton there were limits to the application of the principle. In his central concepts of freedom and progress he asserted opinions which were not above controversy even then. With no weakened devotion to truth, historians in our self-critical age are aware that there will not be general agreement with their conclusions, nor even with some of the premisses which they regard as self-evident. They must be content to set out their own thought without reserve and to respect the differences which they cannot eradicate.

In Lord Acton's plan for the History there were some impressive and characteristic sentences about the concept of general history.

Universal history [he wrote] is not the sum of all particular histories, and ought to be contemplated, first, in its distinctive essence, as Renaissance, Reformation, Religious Wars, Absolute Monarchy, Revolution, etc. The several countries may or may not contribute to feed the main stream, and the distribution of matter must be made accordingly. The history of nations that are off the line must not suffer; it must be told as accurately as if the whole was divided into annals. But attention ought not to be dispersed, by putting Portugal, Transylvania, Iceland, side by side with France and Germany. I wish to speak of them when they are important, and not, whether or not, according to date.

When a country first came into 'the line', as Russia did under Peter the Great, there was to be 'a sufficient and connected retrospect' of its former history; when one dropped out, as Venice did early in the seventeenth century, there should be 'a prospective sketch'. He acknowledged that there would be difficulties in putting all this into practice, as indeed proved to be the case when, after his untimely death, his plan was executed by other hands; but his governing conception remains as that of this second *Cambridge Modern History*. It has not indeed been possible

---

[1] *History and Historians in the Nineteenth Century*, 2nd ed. (1913), p. 387.

merely to revise the original fourteen volumes and bring them up to date. Not only has research added much to our knowledge of almost every country and period; new methods are applied and new questions are asked. There are far more books in the English language about every department of modern history than there were fifty years ago, so that the new *Modern History* need not satisfy all the requirements which the old tried to meet, but it can fulfil a more specific purpose as a standard general history, adapted to the needs of study and teaching in our time.

The purpose is to set out the ascertained results of research into the history of that 'civilisation' which, from the fifteenth century, spread from its original European homes, assimilating extraneous elements as it expanded, until it was more or less firmly planted in all parts of the world. The civilisation is to be treated in all its aspects, political, economic, social, 'cultural' and religious. Whenever it is possible to combine these aspects, or some of them, in a single presentation, this will be the plan; but there will be no forced synthesis or artificial simplification. Where the different factors are interdependent they will be brought together, and where they are not, they will be treated separately. When there is a common process affecting a number of states or nations, this will provide the theme; but where necessary there will be separate chapters or sections for the affairs of nations or groups of nations which diverge too markedly to be treated along with others.

The History will not give separate continuous accounts of all the separate states; it will neither be nor include a collection of separate national histories bound together in the same covers. It will not try to serve the purpose of a handbook to the history of each vernacular literature or each regional school of art. Events which are international will be dealt with from the international point of view. Thus each war will be described as a whole: the battle of Waterloo will not be treated (apart from minor allusions to it) three or four times over, as an event in the history of France, of Great Britain, of Prussia and of the Netherlands.

The course of events will not be described without reference to the structure of society. Thus the narratives of campaigns will be in close relation to the accounts of the art of war, and of its usages and its social and economic aspects. The history of diplomatic negotiations will be kept in touch with the social forces behind them. There will be links between the political narrative and the chapters on political thought: questions like nationality, toleration and so forth will be handled not in the abstract but so as to convey an idea of the changes in the actual foundations of government.

The New Cambridge Modern History follows the precedent of the older series in not giving footnote-references for the statements in the text except on occasions when they seem to be specially called for. This is a well-established practice in works which give brief surveys of very wide fields, but another difference between the old series and the new, not unrelated to this practice, should perhaps be mentioned here. Each volume of the old series included bibliographies for the separate chapters, sometimes with information about unpublished manuscript sources. These bibliographies were not intended to show what authorities the writers of the chapters had actually used; they were to serve as guides for students of the subjects. They were so full, and at the same time they offered so little comment, that they proved more useful to advanced students than to general readers or beginners in research. That in the fourth volume, to take the extreme example, occupies 161 pages and includes a full catalogue of Lord Acton's collection of pamphlets on the Thirty Years War, now in the University Library at Cambridge. At the time when the *Cambridge Modern History* was published there were comparatively few historical bibliographies in the English language. It was still advisable to insist that compilations of this kind were necessary tools for the historian. That is no longer the case. So many bibliographies, general and special, are available that additions to their number can only be justified if they are appropriate, both in their contents and in the places where they appear, to specific needs. Many, indeed the great majority, of those who read or consult a general history, do not require such bibliographies as the older series presented. The editors will consider, in the course of their work, what kinds of bibliographical publication will best suit the needs of the present time; but it is not intended that such matter should be contained within the covers of this series of volumes.

Each volume is to cover roughly a chronological period, but the divisions of time will not be rigid, for each volume will be a self-contained whole, carrying each subject from a real beginning to a real halt. Within the volumes the chapters are to be divided not chronologically but by subjects. Within each chapter the author will decide whether to follow a chronological or a systematic plan, or a combination of the two. The writers of the separate chapters and the editors of the separate volumes are not bound by detailed instructions but only by their agreement in the guiding principles which have been stated here. They represent many schools of thought and many specialised branches of research; but so great is their common inheritance that they hope, by means of all this diversity, to create an articulated history.

CHAPTER I

INTRODUCTION

THE fall of Constantinople in 1453 and the identification at about the same time in Italy of a *medium aevum* separating the ancient from the contemporary world were in themselves sufficient to account for the subsequent adoption of the Renaissance as a turning-point in the history of western society. Bacon claimed further that printing, gunpowder and the magnet 'have changed the whole face and state of things throughout the world'. The political historians of the nineteenth century, led by Ranke, saw in the late fifteenth and early sixteenth centuries the emergence of phenomena regarded as characteristically 'modern', nation-states, bureaucracy, secular values in public policy, and a balance of power. On top of that came the acceptance in Europe at large of the views of Burckhardt on the civilisation of the Renaissance in Italy. First published in 1860, Burckhardt's analysis gave aesthetic and psychological conviction to the same attitude: the cultural achievements at this time of the Italians form the pattern of western values in the centuries to come. By 1900 the current view of the break between modern and medieval had hardened into a pedagogical dogma, and historians in each western nation had found a convenient date round which to manipulate the universally accepted categories. For France the invasion of Italy (1494), for Spain the union of the Crowns (1479), for England the establishment of the Tudors (1485), for Germany the accession of Charles V (1519) were plausible and readily accepted lines of demarcation.

Flaws in this imposing simplification have always been discernible. Whatever was important in Italy, for instance, had happened before the end of the fifteenth century, both in the fields of culture and politics; had happened, indeed, long before 1453. If Dante may be relegated to the Middle Ages, Petrarch cannot be, and in the Florence of the generation of Coluccio Salutati (d. 1406) nearly all that was unique in the Italian world had been adumbrated. Even in the northern world the old divisions have lately come to be scrutinised more sceptically. In Germany one can call Maximilian more irresponsible than his grandson, but in his attitude to dynasticism or German patriotism and letters can one call him more medieval? Are not Charles VII and Louis XI of France more modern than Charles VIII or Francis I—in their attention to administration, domination of the Church, repression of franchises? In England the conventional importance of the battle of Bosworth has been disputed by those who wish to see Thomas More (d. 1535) as the last representative

I

of an ecumenical Christendom, by those who argue that Thomas Crom-well inaugurated a profoundly new approach to government, and by others who claim that the new monarchy begins not with the Tudors but with the Yorkists.

Even more telling arguments have been advanced to throw doubt on the importance of the older concepts. If the Renaissance ushers in the modern world, we should find in it the roots of that most characteristic feature of the modern world—a preoccupation with physical science. Yet it can be shown that humanism neglected science; advances in this field in the fifteenth century are confined to a handful of old-fashioned nomi-nalists in Paris and Averroists in Padua. The architects of Renaissance Italy were no better engineers than their Gothic predecessors: no wave of mechanical inventions characterises the rebirth of learning. Ergo, because there was no renaissance in the sciences at this time, there was no Renaissance at all.[1] And as for the 'discovery of the world and of man', with its realism and its consequent cynicism, its desire for 'fame' and its cultivation of personal talent and *virtù*, what may we make of an Abelard, a Jehan de Meung, a Commynes or the sculptors who took (from the life) the sentimental virgins in Rhenish cathedrals or the botanical illus-trations at Southwell Minster? Is not *Le Petit Jehan de Saintré* a more astringent portrayal of a new society than anything in the *Decameron*? Is not the painting of the van Eycks incomparably more concrete, prac-tical, realistic than the dreamy, academic romanticism of Botticelli or the learned allegories of his contemporaries in Italy? Burckhardt, besides at-tributing unique discoveries to the Italians, attributed to them also unique penalties—the darkly painted irreligion, cynicism and immorality which he saw as the shadows of his bright world. Here, too, a glance at northern Europe suggests qualifications: the brutality of the Visconti can be paralleled in the Burgundian court; in the fourteenth and fifteenth cen-turies no fewer than four English kings (to descend no farther down the social scale) were deposed and murdered by successful rivals and another was killed in battle; the Borgias were Spaniards by origin, not Italians.

As for the geographical discoveries of the Renaissance, there is now less confidence that they were in any genuine sense a product of the new thought of the period. A fresh interest in the text of Ptolemy may have been influential—but less so, we may suppose, than the writings of Marco Polo. The motives behind Portuguese exploration (ch. xv, I) were, to say the least, mixed; scientific cartography, a disinterested wish for geographical knowledge were certainly there, but were equally certainly subordinated to a programme determined by politics, religion and (in-

---

[1] Dana B. Durand, 'Tradition and innovation in XV century Italy', *Journal of the History of Ideas*, IV (1943), pp. 1–20; Lynn Thorndike, 'Renaissance or pre-Renaissance', *ibid*. pp. 65–74.

creasingly) commercial advantage. Nor was the discovery of America important at the time. It is, in fact, argued elsewhere in this volume (ch. xvi) that the impact of the New World on Europe as a whole was not marked until the last decade of the sixteenth century. The population of Europe, recovering maybe from the demographic disasters of the fourteenth century, was in no state to lend men to colonial activity; in view of Ottoman pressure, the Conquistadores could ill be spared; the first effects of the exploitation of America were due to the importation of gold and silver, and upsetting they were for all but some lucky members of the merchant class.

Nor can one accept uncritically the diffusion of interest in classical antiquity and the revival of classical Latin as in themselves constituting an unequivocal break with the past. The very remarkable spread of the new scholarship is described below in some detail (ch. v) and if the names of many of the *érudits* there assembled have all but fallen into oblivion, sufficient of them remain as stars in the galaxy of western scholarship and literature to make the era notable; while the cumulative effect of the revival of letters was to produce an attitude to education the consequences of which are with us today. One must, however, be chary of attributing too much to the humanists, and particularly to the latter-day humanists. Latin grammar was no novelty at the Renaissance: it was the only grammar that had been taught for a thousand years in the West; and the methods —indeed the text-books themselves—were for long the same. The new grammar admittedly had a precision and an authority which were different (and more difficult), and conversational dialogues gradually evicted dialectic as the technical method of instruction. Texts of Latin authors became purer; a greater range of authors was read; Cicero was viewed as a man of affairs and not as a recluse, and Virgil ceased to be a magician; a little Greek entered the curriculum of school and university and a handful of scholars turned to Hebrew. But just as to oppose these advances to a static medievalism is to falsify them, so if one makes the diffusion of the new Latin the sole criterion of a changed view of the world one neglects what is, perhaps, the more significant aspect of the Renaissance outside Italy—its reflection in vernacular literature (ch. vi, 4). The Italians of the *quattrocento* had, in fact, two admirations in literature, two groups of 'classical' models. Beside Cicero and Virgil we must set Dante, Petrarch and Boccaccio. By the early sixteenth century Italian was the most mature of the 'modern' languages and it was to be through the Italian writers of the first half of the sixteenth century that northern Europe was to acquire all that it could most easily digest in the moral qualities evolved in the peninsula. It was in the vernacular that these were to be most truly expressed. Castiglione's *Courtier* was soon translated into the vernaculars; the serious works of Bruni or Valla naturally did not lend themselves so readily to vulgarisation. It is in Rabelais rather than in

2-2

Erasmus that we find most faithfully displayed most of the attitudes we regard as essentially 'Renaissance'.

New points of view and old points of view were broadcast during the second half of the fifteenth century by printed books,[1] and this has often been regarded as constituting a watershed in western history. But the importance of the printing press is analogous to the discovery of America: it took many generations to affect men in any material way. The books printed by the early printers were the books manufactured by hand by the scriveners, not only the writings of contemporary authors but the old texts which were the established classics of education, science and literature. 'An analysis of the published output of the printers, who we must assume knew something of the demands of the reading public, clearly demonstrated that a great proportion of the surviving writings of the Middle Ages were not only known but in current use and circulation continuously till about 1600; though to a diminishing degree in the latter half of the sixteenth century.'[2] Nor can it confidently be argued that it needed printing to cure illiteracy. It is as clear that the invention of printing by moveable type was the result of a rising demand for books as it is obvious that the greater quantity of books thus made available encouraged literacy still further. The number of schools multiplied everywhere in the fifteenth century, a process which was not seriously interrupted (and then only for a short time) by the Reformation; four times as many students were attending German universities in 1500 as had been attending them in 1400 and by the end of the fifteenth century the majority were in the arts faculties, did not complete even a first degree and came only to learn what would now be taught in a secondary school. Thomas More estimated that three out of five persons in the England of his day could read—a soberingly high proportion, even if it is limited to reading as opposed to writing and to London rather than the country as a whole, but one which a few scraps of evidence suggest may have been almost as true a century earlier.[3]

The criticisms advanced above do not, however, dispose of the 'Renaissance'. It is not sufficient to find in other periods evidence for behaviour or institutions generally regarded as peculiar to a later age: one must also determine the degree to which particular attitudes flourished at any given moment. Viewed in this way there is no doubt that Abélard, for instance, is an exceptional figure in the twelfth-century scene; the cultivation of personality is rare and intermittent before the Renaissance. And so with other fields of human activity. What is termed below in connection with

[1] A brief discussion of the rise of printing will be found in vol. II of this *History*, ch. XII.
[2] E. P. Goldschmidt, *Medieval Texts and their First Appearance in Print* (Bibliographical Society of London, 1943), p. 2.
[3] Sylvia Thrupp, *The Merchant Class of Medieval London* (Chicago, 1948), pp. 156–8; and in general J. W. Adamson, *The Illiterate Anglo-Saxon* (1946), ch. III.

architecture an 'anthropometric' view (p. 129) cannot be denied to the Renaissance in Italy as a whole and to its later manifestations elsewhere in Europe. This measurement of problems, aesthetic and moral, by a scale of human achievement, was admittedly not as 'pagan' as many (for example Burckhardt) have supposed: it was, indeed, characteristic of the most religious phase of all in Italy—the Platonic and Neoplatonic thought of Florence at the end of the fifteenth century; it assumed that man's intellectual and his physical proportions were part of the divine structure of the universe. Furthermore, the rapidity with which Italian educational, economic, artistic, and political inventions were communicated to trans-Alpine countries suggests that forces were at work outside Italy which justify extending the term Renaissance to Europe as a whole; the peoples of the peninsula, and in particular of the centre and north, were, in this sense, pioneers exploring territories which were to be occupied by the French, the Germans and the rest in the course of the sixteenth and seventeenth centuries.

Aside, however, from these subjective categories, the period covered by this volume had for contemporaries a natural coherence and inevitability which it is also the historian's duty to analyse. In certain spheres of public life developments were on foot which were both regarded as important at the time and were to be significant in the retrospect of later ages. The gradual recovery of Europe from the disastrous economic regression of the fourteenth century is clearly central, but the chronology of this is doubtful as yet and its effects on agrarian and commercial life cannot therefore be briefly discussed (chs. II, XVI). Another matter of common concern was the exploration and occupation of the New World by 'professional' explorers, soldiers and sailors: it is sufficient to call attention to the discussion of this below (chs. XV, XVI). Four characteristic aspects of the period are, however, worth examining further both for their inherent interest and because they are discussed in more than one of the following chapters. These are: the consolidation of princely government and the decline of rivals to monarchy; the final emergence of a pattern of international relationships based on dynasticism; the progressive instability in, and the loss in ecumenical authority of, the Church; and the growth of novel spiritual attitudes, both secular and religious. These points are further examined in what follows.

Medieval treatises on government dealt with what kings should do in order to be good. Commynes in his *Mémoires* (finished by 1498, first published 1524) and Machiavelli in his *Prince* (written 1513, published 1532) tried to deal with something different, what kings found it most advantageous to do in order to be effective rulers. The notion that efficient government was as worthy of investigation as the moral principles of Christian dominion naturally took time to develop, for it involved

5

abandoning sentiments inculcated in the most influential books and pulpits for a thousand years, sentiments, moreover, which had been in complete sympathy with the decentralised, feudal society of the early Middle Ages: a Machiavelli or a Commynes would have been inconceivable if there had not been for several generations, and over much of Europe, practical demonstrations of the thesis which they were to expound. The experience they were digesting was, of course, vividly illuminated by contemporaneous events, but these served merely to confirm the past, not to deny it. In France, England and Italy in particular relatively strong kings repeatedly emerge from the late thirteenth century onwards: Edward I, Edward IV, Richard III in England; Philip IV, Charles V, Charles VII, Louis XI in France; in Italy, let alone the precocious government of Frederick II in Naples before 1250, the 'tyrannies' of more than local significance of the Este at Ferrara, the della Scala at Verona and the Visconti at Milan. These periods of active monarchy are, of course, not without moments of weakness due to the resentment and obstruction of a class of magnates for whom the situation represented decline; the strong kings of France and England had to face internal trouble; and between times of strong government came long and debilitating periods of recession, as in England under Edward II and Henry VI, or in France for nearly two generations after 1392. Even within a single reign monarchical power could fluctuate enormously; Richard II of England and Charles VII of France must figure both as effective and as ineffective rulers. In Italy an even more precarious situation existed: the Visconti, for instance, faced not only disintegrating forces from within, but a slowly hardening resistance from Venice and Florence. Yet as the fifteenth century proceeds the momentum of monarchy noticeably increases. From the 1460's in both England and France the structure of government, one might say, is no longer in doubt: the *coups d'état* in England from 1483–5 already appear as exceptional, just as the War of the Common Weal (1465) seems painfully anachronistic. The reason for this is in part the evolution of government machinery.

Spain offers a singular example of these processes at work. The peninsula had a long tradition of divided races, divided governments and divided languages, the expression of the divisions imposed by its mountainous geography. In spite of these factors Aragon (itself a three-fold country where Catalonia, Valencia and Aragon itself were often drawn in contrary directions) was joined with Castile by the marriage of Ferdinand and Isabella. Alone the marriage might not have effected a permanent union; that it did so was partly accidental (ch. XI). But the consciously aggressive policy of the Catholic kings also played a part: the conquest of Granada and later the occupation of Navarre; a resolute and skilful control over the military orders and the Church in general; a firm insistence on central organs of government as against provincial cortes. In both Castile and Aragon the royal councils were professionalised and largely staffed by lawyers; to them were added the councils of the Inquisition, of finance, of the military orders, of the *Hermandad*. Such a structure could be expanded as the need arose, as when the council of the Indies hived off from the royal council of Castile. Local government was provided for by viceroys, by a careful control of municipal politics through the *corregidor* appointed to the council of each Castilian city after 1480, and, in the countryside, by lending royal authority for a time to the *Hermandad*.

In France and in England the Crown had embarked earlier on the extension of its powers so that parallel developments there do not appear so striking. Yet the late fifteenth century in both countries ushered in an era of self-conscious royal activity which was critical. This is the period in France (ch. x) which saw the Estates General sink finally into moribund insignificance, when the standing army achieved coherence, when king and ministers even went beyond the Gallican position of the Pragmatic Sanction of Bourges (1438) in their determination to master the Church. The hazardous policy of the *appanages* was triumphantly justified as they fell in to the Crown, working concerns modelled on the royal system at the centre, capable of rapid integration into a hierarchy of provincial administration depending as never before on the king. Taxation was largely a matter of royal discretion. In England administrative reforms were also in the air, great islands of immunity and privilege were being joined to the monarchical mainland: the northern borders are no longer a Percy preserve; the sanctuaries crumble; and by avoiding foreign war the Crown acquires a financial independence no less significant than that of the French sovereigns, and one less dangerous for further constitutional development. The English parliament, unlike the Estates General in France, survives and grows as an instrument of royal government. As in Spain, so in France and England the conciliar structure develops and the royal secretaries begin to take the place of older officials of the Crown.

Events in the political evolution of Germany and Italy are usually contrasted with those in the monarchical countries touched on above. Italy had her *Prince* only in the pages of Machiavelli. With the French invasion of Italy (ch. xII), above all with the union of Spain, the Empire, Naples and Sicily under Charles V, the peninsula entered a period of foreign intervention which effectively stopped any native process of unification, and which ensured for the next 350 years the existence of half a dozen principalities and the decaying republic of Venice. As for Germany, the efforts at reform of the imperial constitution undertaken in the reign of Maximilian (ch. vII) were as ineffective as those which had been attempted by earlier emperors and as those which were to be tried by Charles V. There was a German empire; a few tenuous institutions, like the *Reichskammergericht*, were instituted; a diet survived usually as the focal point of disagreement and opposition. These were factors which kept alive a sense of German unity. But there was virtually no imperial army, no imperial taxation, and no imperial church.

At a level below that of the national monarchy, however, the emergence of the prince was as rapid as it was in the countries of the Atlantic seaboard. This may be less clear in Italy, where the Papacy had an elaborate administration but a policy which suffered a revolution after every conclave, and where the shadow of Habsburg and Valois lay across every palace. But it is not obscure in Germany. There a few great houses and a number of smaller ones were consolidating their power despite the emperor, the towns and the knights. The Habsburgs may have been ineffective in ruling Germany as a whole, but even Maximilian was a respected and aggressive prince as far as his Austrian and other dynastic domains were concerned (p. 219). In Germany notably, and to a lesser degree elsewhere, the precepts of civil law did much to buttress the prince, whose feudal rights and duties were now prudently reserved for his relations with the emperor (p. 198): the king of the Romans benefited not at all from this reception of the Roman law; like the Italian town of the post-glossators, the German potentate was *sibi princeps*.

It is customary to ascribe the absence of effective resistance to the monarchy in France and England to the consequences of fifteenth-century foreign and civil war. There is much truth in this. The magnates of both countries suffered seriously in wealth and in blood: in England the Wars of the Roses doubled the natural rate at which noble families were extinguished. Aside from these catastrophes, however, there were at work pressures which made the peer more amenable to the Crown than he had been of old. Though land was still the possession most coveted by all classes, great territorial possessions by the early sixteenth century did not alone confer political and economic security or social prestige. Cash and influence were both more readily secured by a courtier than a grandee living in a remote castle, and the courts of England, France and Spain were thronged by the greatest men in the land. Pensions, commands, offices flowed from the king; to be near the fountain of honour put a magnate in a favourable position for helping his clients in their ambitions, in return for their support, material and moral. In France and Spain nobility conferred immunity to taxation and the doctrine was encouraged which justified the gentleman's fiscal privilege by his military service. And in gravitating to the royal army the *noblesse de l'epeé* were still further strengthening the hands of the king and thus indirectly lightening the bonds of other classes in society.

The prevailing trend to monarchial absolutism which distinguished western Europe at this time is far from being characteristic of eastern Europe (ch. XIII). The internal politics of Poland, Hungary and Bohemia are the very opposite of monarchical. In each country the sovereign was more or

8

less in a state of subservience to the nobles—a numerous class in both Poland and Hungary, and one in which the minor nobles found it possible to consolidate their position. Even in Bohemia, 'in all but name, an aristocratic republic' (p. 390), the knightly class made an effort to share power with the few great families who formed an hereditary and superior caste. Though not legally separated from the lesser nobles, the great magnates of both Poland and Hungary formed the dominating cliques which strove to exploit the dwindling resources of the Crown. In all these countries a depression in the status of towns and peasantry is very marked, and again contrasts with western developments.

Two countries on the eastern perimeter of Europe were, in their very different ways, more akin in political tone to the West than the states just mentioned. Russia was emerging as a state in which the princes of Moscow were to endure no rivals (pp. 368–70). And on the ruins of Byzantium the Ottoman Turks (ch. XIV) were developing an autocracy, which (like the Russian) owed a good deal to the example of the expropriated empire of East Rome. Many a western prince must have envied a ruler who was legally empowered to execute his rivals at his accession (p. 396).

In two areas of the West the pattern of strong government was absent or less evident: Switzerland and the Low Countries. The Swiss at this period were at the apogee of their brief military supremacy. Regarded with distaste by gentlemen who disliked their tactics while learning from them, and by humanists who looked upon them as the very essence of all the worst vices—bloodthirstiness, covetousness and barbarism, the Swiss were not yet aware of the uniqueness of their political institutions. As for the Low Countries (ch. VIII), where within a century a second republic was to emerge, the ghost of the Burgundian State, with its confused traditions of regionalism and centralisation, its growing oligarchy and the shift in economic importance from Flanders northwards to Holland, also concealed the importance of those constitutional checks on the prince which were to be significant in the future. Republicanism had, in fact, a slender enough basis in theory in a Europe where only in Italy was there any awareness of its political justification. And even in Italy the romantic and futile gestures in this direction (p. 97) were inspired rather by literature than by an active interest in political reform. Only Venice was to survive in the end as an independent republic, and the Venetian oligarchy of 'noblemen' offered no programme to the bourgeoisie of the North.

Kings had become masters of their kingdoms. As a result, dynasticism determined the pattern of international relations. In a sense this was not new, for the feudal king had furthered his interests in the main by marriage: the Angevin 'empire' was an accidental product of this; the interlocking princely families of Scandinavia and East Europe, the Luxemburg emperors, the kings of Castile, Aragon and Portugal all provide many medieval examples. But in France and England royal marriages were normally not calculated to produce major political changes, at any rate before the marriage of Henry V and Catherine in 1420: it was rather the magnates who followed this line as a means of advancement—the Angevins in Naples, Orleans in Milan, Gaunt in Spain and Gloucester in Hainault. The carefully contrived Habsburg alliances changed all this. In so far as one can plan anything which depends on the hazards of heredity, one can say that the empire of Charles V was deliberately created: it was the result of one of those double marriages (Philip to Juana, Margaret of Austria to the Infante, 1496–7) which distinguished the house of Habsburg (p. 341). By the end of the period with which this volume deals, Maximilian's grandson was ruler of the Netherlands, Spain, Germany, part of Italy, and part of the New World. Soon Valois and Habsburgs were seeking further marriages to consolidate their rival positions and the whole network of sixteenth-century diplomacy was to turn on the results. While these relationships dominated European politics, others, different in scale but not in kind, were produced by the marriage of Margaret Tudor to King James IV of Scotland (1503).

This is all well-known. It gave scope for the development of those instruments of international political contacts—ever-growing diplomatic machinery, armies which were increasingly professional—which are so pronounced a feature of sixteenth-century history. The ambassador is still often a prince or prelate specially sent to seek an alliance or conclude a treaty; but the shabbier residents grow more numerous, and the volume of diplomatic despatches which survives from the fifteenth century is very large (ch. IX). Italian experience set the pace in the evolution of diplomatic technique. And it is only in Italy that we meet the professional general before the sixteenth century. Thereafter the armies of the Powers, increasingly composed of infantry not cavalry, and with artillery becoming more important, were entrusted to experts whenever possible.

Although the reality of politics was princely aggrandisement, the ruins of Christendom can be descried behind the rising walls of Europe. The Crusade was dead but its name and some of its magic lived on. Until 1492, when Granada fell, the crusade had some meaning in Spain; defence against the Ottoman Turk was equally a genuine problem in the Balkans and East Europe. But in the West the invocation of a 'crusade' was only a preliminary to more immediate depredation. From the pope downwards, Christian kings were prepared to come to terms—at any rate over short term issues—with the infidel. Most statesmen must in their hearts have accepted as properly detached, Commynes's approving references to the 'saige et vaillant' Mehemmed II.[1] Though Christians affected to be shocked, there was nothing inherently surprising in the acceptance by Innocent VIII of a pension from the sultan in 1490 (p. 78).

[1] *Mémoires*, ed. Calmette, vol. II, p. 337.

Chief symbol of the rise of Christendom, the pope was now a symbol of its decline. The panoply of universal monarchy hung awkwardly on the shoulders of Alexander VI and Julius II. Their policies were princely, not to say dynastic, and limited to Italy. This kind of behaviour in a pope roused contempt and indignation in northern Europe. Erasmus's *Julius Exclusus* (1513), directed specifically at Julius II, held its accusing finger at all popes of the time: 'nunc regnum est ac tyrannis'.[1] For this state of affairs the character of individual popes was in part responsible. But even more was due to processes which were divorcing the Papacy from the Church, compelling popes to become princelings. These processes were all intimately interconnected, but for convenience they may be considered under three heads: the internal disintegration of the Church, the rise of national churches, and the pressure by the laity on the landed endowments of the clergy.

By the internal disintegration of the Church is meant the decline in uniformity of obedience which characterises the fifteenth century. For this the schism of 1378 was only partly responsible, though the effects of that were grave. The existence of rival hierarchies split the international religious orders, which were already showing fissiparous tendencies. The credit of the cardinals, who had caused the schism, was permanently lowered, for far from mending their position at Pisa and Constance, they recreated a Papacy determined at all costs to prevent them ever again assuming power. Above all, as a result of the schism and its aftermath the popes of the fifteenth century were terrified of councils. At Constance decrees, which, to all appearances, received a papal confirmation, laid down both the supremacy of general councils and the machinery by which they were to be summoned every ten years. It became the consistent policy of Eugenius IV (who had to endure the Council of Basle) and his successors both to prevent the actual summoning of councils and positively to affirm that the doctrine of conciliar supremacy was anathema. The Lateran Council of 1512 was held solely to counteract the French-sponsored 'conciliabulum' of Pisa (ch. IV).

This refusal to hold a general council, in which the reform of the Church could be undertaken, resulted in the further development of heresy, near-heresy and indifference. It may be suspected that the problem of real heresy was the least important. Heresy had been endemic in parts of western Europe from the twelfth century, but the Church had at least contained it, where it had not wiped it out altogether. The heresies of the fourteenth century met a similar fate: the Lollards were (after 1417) restricted to a handful of uninfluential Englishmen; the Hussites, though important in Bohemia, were no threat to Christendom generally. The popular mysticism which coloured so much trans-Alpine thought in the fifteenth century was a far more insidious danger to religious uniformity.

---

[1] *Opuscula*, ed. Ferguson, p. 83.

Groups of mystical associates, beghards and beguines, were particularly numerous in western Germany and the Low Countries; sometimes they were encouraged by the local ordinary, sometimes they were persecuted. The laity who more and more took the lead in such associations were largely urban, and shared that traditional hostility to the religious to which literary sources are a regular witness, from the *Decameron* and the *Canterbury Tales* to the *Cent Nouvelles Nouvelles* and the *Colloquies* of Erasmus. The more serious critics, from Gerson onwards, combined personal devotion with a contempt for much of organised religion which gave a lead to those anxious to make trouble for monks and friars. To this kind of criticism only an impeccable and industrious Papacy could have answered. The popes after Pius II stimulated suspicions which could only be dispelled by conciliar methods they would not countenance.

The emergence of national churches was naturally encouraged by the weakness of the Papacy. Even before the fourteenth century princes had been disinclined to allow the Church the liberties it demanded. Prelates were royal nominees wherever and whenever kings were powerful. In the later Middle Ages some control over the Church in their dominions passed even to relatively minor rulers, while the greater sovereigns of Europe pursued ecclesiastical policies which enabled them to become masters of their clergy. The history of the English kings' truculent attitude to the clergy during the whole course of the fourteenth century is familiar: it was justified then by the Papacy being at Avignon, but it continued in even more marked fashion after the schism ended in 1417. The concordat of the English nation with the Papacy after Constance was a formal document, the real basis of royal power being the statutes of Provisors and Praemunire as re-enacted by Richard II's government. In France the concordat was a genuine reflection of a monarchy asserting its control over the Church. The adoption by the French clergy of the anti-papal legislation of the Council of Basle (Pragmatic Sanction of Bourges, 1438) was merely the first explicit formulation of regalian as against papal rights over the French Church. Later kings were able to modify it; and Louis XII in particular had to temporise for a while (p. 302); but whatever the outward promises of the king to the pope may have been, his practical mastery over the Church was not in doubt. The most remarkable example of royal power in the ecclesiastical field was, of course, the Inquisition in Spain (1478) which put at the disposal, not of the Church but of the Crown, an instrument which was both efficient as a control over opinion and as a promoter of unification, and also highly profitable (p. 336).

Nowhere were these developments more congenial than in Germany. There a prolonged hatred of popes was a sentiment that occasionally could even bind the emperors and the princes together. The Germans, both lay and ecclesiastical rulers, were naturally amongst the warmest supporters of the conciliar reform programme, which promised them the greatest possible independence in ecclesiastical matters. Here (as in the case of the reception of Roman law) the conciliarism of the Germans redounded to the advantage of the prince, not the emperor. As many of the German prelates were also temporal rulers (p. 195), their attitude is hardly to be distinguished from that of the secular princes, to whom they were frequently related; indeed, the bishops had even more to gain than the lay lords from a reduction in papal power.

On the basis of a church locally controlled by the prince ecclesiastical politics were naturally often conducted provincially with a cynical ambition truly papal in extent. The career of Cardinal d'Amboise, which is told elsewhere in this volume (pp. 302–3) is significant. It was logical that his plunder of the Church should lead on to his desire to become pope and to his being given the consolation of a legatine commission: Wolsey's story in the next generation was to be not dissimilar. Equally significant of the future was Maximilian's naïve plan to occupy the throne of St Peter in 1511, during the illness of Julius II (p. 215). It was, indeed, bizarre, but had it been conceived on a national level it would have merely anticipated Henry VIII's action when he became 'Supreme Head on Earth'.

The aspect of papal policy which most disturbed the trans-Alpine Christian was financial. That hardly any money was going to the Curia from England, and not much from other non-Italian provinces of the Church, was beside the point; indulgences were growing in importance if more regular sources of revenue were in decline (p. 87); and any payment at all roused passions which were deep and found in all branches of society. Papal 'fiscality' was unendurable because of the wealth of the Church and the desire of the laity to recover, or at any rate share in, the enjoyment of the vast endowments which lay in mortmain. Legislation against mortmain is found practically everywhere in the later Middle Ages. And so are devices by which the laity participated in the landed wealth of the Church: stewardships, wardenships, corrodies, pensions of all kinds were awarded to the laity by the possessioners. Even more significant was the extensive use in certain areas of grants *in commendam* to persons who were not in any true sense religious, and the promotion to high ecclesiastical office of the children of great men. In Scotland the illegitimate progeny of the Stewarts occupied archbishoprics, bishoprics and abbeys: sometimes papal compliance impressed even the royal impetrant, as when James IV himself described as 'a hard matter scarcely to be hoped for' the successful promotion of his eleven year old illegitimate son Alexander to the archbishopric of St Andrews in 1504.[1] Under the successors of James IV the spoliation of the Scottish Church by the royal family and the magnates continued unabated, and when the

---

[1] *Letters of James IV 1505–13*, ed. R. K. Hannay, R. L. Mackie A. Spilman (Scot. Hist. Soc. 1953), p. xxxvi.

Reformation came to Scotland there was no need formally to dissolve the monasteries: there were in practice no monasteries left to dissolve.

The confiscation of church lands in Scotland was the work of king and pope acting in collusion. In Italy it was no less thorough and no less 'legal', though it was accomplished in a different way. The astonishing conveyance of lands from clergy to laity in northern Italy was a long process.[1] The clergy there were cruelly taxed—by pope, towns and tyrants; they were further impoverished by commendation; they were ill-placed to take advantage of the opportunities of improving their estates; the rapid devaluation of the currency after 1300 put them in an even worse position. When these pressures began to be obtrusive a great deal of land was already leased out, much of it at a low rent to creditors, *potentes*, relatives of the abbot, who were able to sublet at an advantageous rate. In the mid-fifteenth century the 'pillage of ecclesiastical property went to unheard-of lengths'; profits of sub-letting now ran as high as 700 per cent and were far more certain as well as larger than the profits of trade. Leases of this kind (*fictalicia*) were for a fixed period; but the Church had to reimburse the tenant for improvements effected during the tenancy or else renew on the same disadvantageous terms (*eodem ficto*); as the Church could not in practice compensate the tenant, the second alternative was adopted so that, though on paper still a vast landed proprietor, the Church drew no profits from her estates. The final stage came when the favoured tenant (*fictabilis*) was allowed, first of all a perpetual lease at a higher rent, and then the right of enjoying the estate *pleno iure* if he provided in exchange the equivalent *value*, not extent, of land. Hence great estates, which the impoverished Church could not maintain in good condition, passed into lay hands in return for small ones. The new style of architecture and ecclesiastical decoration which became *de rigueur* as the fifteenth century progressed has left many monuments of lasting value, but it is no indication of the wealth of the Church, for it was often financed by selling lands and by neglecting the upkeep of the remaining property.[2] In northern Italy by the mid-sixteenth century the Church was proprietor of only 10 per cent or 15 per cent of the land, compared with a holding in the south of 65 per cent or 70 per cent. At least one motive for a reformation of the Church was thus largely absent in Italy.

The period covered by this volume saw the first real contacts between the Renaissance in Italy and the northern world (chs. III, V, VI). The delay in the effective diffusion of the attitudes associated with Italian thought from Petrarch to Leonardo Bruni is a matter which has properly received much attention in recent years. Where so much in the north seems dis-

[1] C. M. Cipolla, 'Comment s'est perdue la propriété ecclésiastique dans l'Italie du Nord entre le XI et le XVI siècle', *Annales*, II (Paris, 1947), 317–27.

[2] Cipolla, p. 323 n.

posed to a reception of humanism—the bourgeois values of the Low Countries, the progress to realism in much of northern art, a hostility among some mystics to the pedantries of the schoolmen—it seems odd that there is no humanism to speak of in fifteenth-century England (p. 55), hardly any in France and in Germany little till the end of the century. What the north for long saw in the *trecento* and *quattrocento* was only the integument of humanism, not its spirit: a fondness for Latinising and for classical motifs, not an understanding of the moral values of antiquity which had inspired the main humanists in the peninsula. There were, however, good reasons for this slowness in apprehending the Italian world.

At the material level, Italy had a wealth which was great by comparison with the north and which was predominantly urban. An interest in art, literature and moral philosophy needs ample resources to develop and in northern Europe these were tied up more closely than in Italy with a conservative Church; theology dominated the universities of France, England and Germany, but was practically absent in the universities of Italy. There had always been a homogeneity about Tuscan and Lombard society which contrasted with the feudal North: the magnates were town-dwellers and, despite Guelf and Ghibelline political traditions, the *grandi* lived the same life as the *grassi*; even the tyrants of the fourteenth century were urban in origin, and shared to a great extent the values of their subjects. In taste and inclination the Italian prince was very different from the ruler of the north; equally the republics of Italy were different from the Flemish or German towns.

Nevertheless the humanist in Italy must not be regarded as an immutable type reflecting a unified society. One difficulty in seizing on Italian values was that they were by no means consistent: the humanist could speak with several voices. Petrarch had been essentially a product of an exile from Florence spent in the courts of the northern tyrants: his attitude to letters was one of detachment. Only in an *otium* provided most easily by a princely patron could the man of letters fulfil his appointed task. This attitude could have its political complications, for the disciples of Petrarch at Milan argued that Italy itself was only to be saved by the intervention of their Visconti master. At Florence republicanism gradually emerged, very much as the result of the threat of Giangaleazzo Visconti, so it has been argued.[1] Whatever its causes, the attitude of Bruni was diametrically opposed to that of Petrarch on other issues besides that of republicanism. For Bruni rejected Petrarch's whole attitude to the active life, accepted Cicero's political activity as a fulfilment, not a negation, of his moral teaching, and regarded Dante—head of a family and politician

---

[1] Hans Baron, *The Crisis of the Early Italian Renaissance*, 2 vols. (Princeton, 1955). See the bibliographical references in vol. II and especially Dr Baron's other writings in *History*, *Speculum*, and *Bulletin of the John Rylands Library*, all for 1938.

as well as poet and philosopher—as an ideal citizen. Soon the Florentine circle of humanists was to take the even more surprising step of challenging the condemnation of wealth and establishing the doctrine that poverty was not the only way of appearing virtuous in the eyes of God. We may choose to regard these developments as characteristic of the Renaissance in Italy, because they are sympathetic to our own outlook. But they never lacked critics in Italy at the time. There was, for example, always a princely tradition as well as a republican one: because Michelangelo idealised Brutus when Dante had put him in the nethermost pit, we should not therefore assume that Caesar had no devotees. Indeed, the Italian who reflected on the political needs of his country was forced into the uncomfortable position of advocating what seem contradictory policies: Machiavelli is a republican and an advocate of strong monarchy at the same time, a republican for Florence, and for Italy an impassioned defender of the Prince.

By the time of Machiavelli we thus have some sort of junction in the opposing traditions in Italian political thought. Such an amalgamation took place in Italian thought in general in the late fifteenth century. It entered, as we read below (p. 69), upon a religious phase in the late fifteenth century, when Platonic and neo-Platonic ideas began to attract attention. Marsilio Ficino and Pico della Mirandola tried to find a synthesis, far broader than earlier Italian humanism had been capable of, for aspirations towards that 'wisdom' which had often in earlier days been lost sight of in 'eloquence'. That Pico did not even try to meet the demands of contemporary good Latin style indicates how far this syncretism was taken, and puts latter-day humanism into as contradictory a position (viewed in the light of previous scholarship in Italy) as that found in Machiavelli. Such a religious preoccupation was, it must be added, not solely found in the Florentine circle. The humanist was not a pagan: nor was the Italian artist. We read elsewhere in this book (p. 135) that there is truth in the Michelet-Burckhardt 'thesis of the "discovery of man" in the age of the Renaissance, but it is man conscious of his individual role in the great plan of redemption'; in its theological implications Michelangelo's ceiling in the Sistine chapel is of 'unequalled profundity' (p. 139).

Looked at merely from the viewpoint of patronage, a stage had again been reached in Italy where contrary tendencies were drawing together. The earlier patrons of literature and the arts demanded works diverse in range and even opposed in spirit; the court of the Visconti, the merchants of Florence, the friars of Assisi had very different tastes. The late fifteenth century saw Medici influence dominant in Florence, and soon it was to be dominant also in Rome and in the Church. The courts of Italy, small ones like Montefeltro Urbino, and the largest one of all in Leonine Rome, talked a common language, the 'illustrious Italian', and patronised the same craftsmen and scholars in much the same mood: an 'inter-Italian medium' in architecture (p. 131) and Ciceronianism in scholarship are signs of the new uniformity.

Northern Europe meanwhile had acquired time to expand and to experiment. The early fifteenth century had been a period when lavish patronage had hardly been possible in England, France or Spain: the duke of Gloucester and the duke of Berri are far more important as patrons than their kings; but the only northern magnates who really had time and money for the graces of life were the dukes of Burgundy, so long as they could trim economically between the English and the French. By the end of the century, however, England and Spain were under centralising monarchies anxious to impress the outside world, and France was engaged on that invasion of Italy which was to produce, in the cultural field, an occupation of France by the ideas and attitudes of Italy. The adoption of much that Italy had to offer was easier than it had been: the concentration of Italian civilisation in an atmosphere of princes and their courts made it easy for northern princes and northern courts to assimilate what had earlier proved inaccessible. The humanist became a necessity to northern kings; Latin secretaries were needed for foreign correspondence; men capable of rhetorical Latin were needed for embassies; the humanist historian could put his country's case before the international world in what Camden, almost a century later, was still to call the 'universal language'. Called from Urbino or Rome, the Italian artist or writer was more completely at home in England or France than he had been two generations earlier. The northern scholar or painter who visited the peninsula—and for both this was becoming a regular part of their training (p. 155)—moved in an atmosphere not greatly different from what he was used to at home.

Nowhere at first was the response to Italian values more rapid than in Germany (p. 68). This was somewhat paradoxical, for there hostility to the Roman Church was strong and most of the country had an even slenderer historical connection with Rome than Gaul, Britain or Spain. Yet there were good reasons for it. The German vernacular presented more difficulties for the writer than French or English, and all the attractions of humanist Latin, all the optimistic hopes of Italian educational programmes, were correspondingly enhanced. Besides, the German king had a traditional connection with the *regnum Italicum*; the reality of this was dead, but it had a certain sentimental value, and Italian humanists of the first rank, like Aeneas Sylvius Piccolomini, had taken service for a time in Germany. More important perhaps were the interest of Germans in the civil law, which took them to Bologna; the receptivity to new ideas of the new universities; and the commercial relations of south Germany with urban Italy: in Augsburg the burgesses were to be early patrons of the new style in art (p. 156). Above all, the German humanist cultivated his past antiquities in the new Italianate manner and found, of course, much in Tacitus' *Germania* to give his interest in the classics something of the patriotism which inspired Italian students. Maximilian actively promoted these developments. Their best monument is Ulrich von Hutten's brief dialogue *Arminius*, in which the primacy of the German hero over Alexander, Scipio, and Hannibal is asserted.

There were, however, aspects of the northern movement which are not in any profound sense Italian or humanist (p. 64). From the most significant of these derives the attraction exerted in certain quarters by the 'religious' thought of late-fifteenth-century Italy. That this appealed in different ways to Colet and Lefèvre d'Étaples is not sufficient to make the latter 'humanists' if the word is to be taken as meaning something more than merely a synonym for scholar or man of devotion. Our study of these men is clouded by the Reformation which so soon swamped their particular kind of evangelism. We lack adequate biographies even, let alone complete evaluations of their place in the world of ideas. It is, however, abundantly clear that Colet was 'an ascetic reformer of the type of John Standonck and the Brothers of the Common Life, he was an educator of importance, he was profoundly Christian; but he was not a humanist'. Erasmus's biographical letter to Jodocus Badius has misled generations of critics. In fact Colet was utterly opposed to the kind of *docta pietas* of the contemporary humanist, and the Augustinian *sapientia* he revered excluded not only the contemptible logic of the schools, but also the philosophers and the poets.[1] If this is humanism, then Thomas à Kempis also must be enrolled among the humanists.

Erasmus's position in relation to northern mysticism and evangelism and to Italian humanism is central in all senses. More than any other scholar he displays characteristics from both camps: like Holbein, who made such fine portraits of him, his work has elements in it which are Gothic and others which are Italian (p. 155). He represents all the optimism of the southern tradition, its conviction that letters were the noblest expression of a noble mind, its relish for eloquence. At the same time he is desperately concerned with the reality of religion and the need to strip it of all that can distract and confuse the devout. The revival of letters was for him one aspect of the revival of Christianity; the republic of letters a facet of the *respublica Christiana*; scholarship led to God. Nothing is more instructive than the publication by Erasmus in 1505 of the *Adnotationes in Novum Testamentum* of Lorenzo Valla. Valla, an enigmatic figure certainly, but surely not an active Christian, had been preoccupied with philology: for Erasmus the work was the prolegomena to a 'Biblical Humanism' where philology was a servant, not a master (p. 115). This approach, which owes as much to the *nova devotio* as it does to the revival

[1] See the important article by Eugene F. Rice, Jr., 'John Colet and the annihilation of the natural', *Harvard Theological Review*, XLV (1952), pp. 141–63.

of letters, is sometimes to be discerned only with difficulty, for Erasmus was also a writer, and his meanness, suspicion, cantankerousness are often obtrusive, while his impulse to satire was often indulged in almost for its own sake.

The Erasmus of the period covered by this volume could sting and tease without qualms. The first twenty years of the sixteenth century is the halcyon period of the northern Renaissance. Thereafter Luther and the Roman Church could legitimately demand of Erasmus a plain yes or no. His attempt to continue his *via media* after the Lutheran schism brings into clear relief that doctrine of the 'philosophy of Christ' which was not philosophy or theology as they were understood by his contemporaries: a concept which not only offended the reformers, but which 'could satisfy neither Thomist rationalism, the fideism of Ockham, nor the intuitionism of the mystics, and which was rejected by rationalists, fideists and mystics at the Council of Trent'.[1] 1520 was, in fact, a key year.[2] The papal bull *Exsurge, Domine* of June was a terrible blow to good letters as Erasmus saw them and to the policy of conciliation he advocated: in December Luther burnt the bull and this destroyed all chance of reason prevailing. Dogma was thereafter the order of the day in both camps and the undogmatic approach of Erasmus was condemned to isolation. The Renaissance made way for the Reformation.

[1] A. Renaudet, *Érasme, sa pensée religieuse et son action...1518–21* (Bibliothèque de la Revue Historique, Paris, 1926), p. 11.

[2] *Ibid.* pp. 87–103.

CHAPTER II

THE FACE OF EUROPE ON THE EVE OF THE GREAT DISCOVERIES

'IF we would study with profit the history of our ancestors, we...must never forget that the country of which we read was a very different country from that in which we live.' Lord Macaulay's dictum is certainly true of Europe on the eve of the Great Discoveries. Could the landscapes of that time be set before our eyes, we should find them very different from those of today. The countryside, although tamed by the pioneering activity of the Middle Ages, would still look wild to our eyes —or much of it would. If the great forests had been reduced, much of the marsh and heath still remained untouched. The medieval city had risen to prominence, yet most of the towns and cities would appear small to us, and their industrial and commercial activities limited.

But although much has changed, the bold facts of physical geography have remained much the same. Europe is a peninsula of peninsulas; and on either side of the great peninsula itself lie, and lay, the two maritime worlds of the Mediterranean and of northern and western Europe, with their contrasting histories and climates and commodities. Towards the broad base of the peninsula, where it is attached to Asia, Europe loses its identity. Vast plains replace the variety of mountain and lowland, and the temperatures on these plains fall below freezing point for most of the winter.

But the human geography of Europe in the fifteenth century must be considered not only against the variety of its physical setting, but also in the framework of its time. One of the most notable achievements of the Middle Ages was the clearing and reclamation and draining by which the countryside was tamed and transformed. But this great expansive movement did not continue uninterruptedly right up to the dawn of modern times. In places it slowed down; in some places it ceased; in yet other places the frontiers of cultivation even retreated. Certainly over most of the Continent, agricultural effort had passed its maximum by 1300, and the great age of expanding arable was succeeded, in the fourteenth and fifteenth centuries, by one of stagnation and contraction. During the hundred years between 1350 and 1450 the decline was especially marked. What was true of agriculture was true of trade and mining and industry. It was also true of town growth, although local fortunes complicated the general picture. The causes for this recession are involved and obscure, and among the agencies invoked to explain it are the destruction of war, great pestilences, falling prices and a basic decline in population. Towards the end of the century there are signs of a recovery which was to lead on to the new prosperity of the sixteenth and seventeenth centuries. It is against this background of space and time that first the countrysides and then the cities of Europe must be considered.

In the east, the triple division into coniferous forest, deciduous forest and steppe reflected itself in ways of living. The deciduous area was the home of the Muscovite State. Clearings in the land drained by the Oka, the upper Volga and their tributaries provided an agricultural base for the early principality of Muscovy, and gave it some advantage over the other principalities of the deciduous lands; rye was the main crop, but barley, oats and some wheat were also grown. From this centre, consolidated by Ivan the Great (1462–1505), expansion to the north and south was to create the Russian State of modern times.

Northwards to the White Sea stretched the coniferous forest, sparsely peopled by Finnish and Lapp tribes, and providing a reservoir of fur— sable, marten, fox and, of lesser value, beaver, squirrel and otter. Fur led the traders northward and eastward along the great rivers, linked one to another by portages. Along the White Sea shores, and elsewhere, salt making was important; so were fishing, sealing and whaling. Agriculture was subsidiary, except possibly along the upper courses of the Dvina River. The trade of the area drained to Novgorod near the Baltic coast, a Hanse centre and a market of high renown. Into the northern region had come not only merchants but missionaries. Between 1340 and 1440 there had been a great development of monasticism, and the monks had sought the untamed wilderness. Byelozero (founded in 1397) and Solovetsky (founded in 1436) became important economic as well as cultural centres. There were also other towns to the north of Moscow, e.g. Yaroslavl, Vologda, Rostov and Troitsa. All these were to gain a new importance with the opening of the White Sea route to the west by Elizabethan adventurers in 1553. By this time the subjection of Novgorod by Ivan the Great in 1478 had brought her rough trading empire within the sphere of Muscovy, and the new gains of the sixteenth century were to fall to Moscow.

Southwards from Moscow lay the steppes. By the fifteenth century their role as a passage-way from Asia was over. The last great nomadic horde to ride across them was that of the Tartars in the thirteenth century, and for over two centuries the Golden Horde of Kipchak were the overlords of their Russian neighbours to the north. But by the fifteenth century dissensions had weakened the Horde, and in 1480 Ivan refused to pay tribute. The way was now open for the colonists of his successors to advance out of the forest into those steppelands described by Gogol as 'a green-yellow ocean, besprinkled with millions of spring flowers'.

The latter years of the fifteenth century, with the subjugation of Novgorod in 1478 and the repulse of the Golden Horde in 1480, marked the end of a chapter and the beginning of modern Russia. It was, in the eighteenth century, for Peter the Great to carry its frontiers to the Baltic and for Catherine the Great to bring them to the Black Sea.

Across the Baltic Sea lay Scandinavia. By the eleventh century its political geography had taken the form it retained right through the Middle Ages. The territory of Denmark stretched across the entrance to the Baltic; it included not only the peninsula of Jutland but the more fertile islands of Fünen and Zealand and a strip of what is now Sweden. Here, off the coasts of Skania, were some of the richest fishing grounds in Europe. Fishing, especially for the herring, was important in all the northern waters. Beyond Skania, to the north of the barren upland of Småland, lay the centre of the Swedish kingdom—in the lowland that runs south-westward from Stockholm around the lakes of Wener and Wetter; here, tillage and stock raising were important on land cleared of its wood. Northwards stretched the great forests of Norrland, sparsely inhabited. In the twelfth and thirteenth centuries Sweden had occupied Finland, and to this day Swedish speech persists along parts of the coast, a memorial of that period of colonisation. To the west, Norway faced the Atlantic and the North Sea; the greater part of its mountainous surface was not suitable for agriculture or for permanent settlement.

We are fortunate in having a remarkable picture of these Scandinavian lands in the map that was produced in 1539 by Olaus Magnus.[1] This map, richly embellished by many small sketches, gives us some of the main facts about the contemporary geography. The great forests are indicated, and also the various fur-bearing animals of northern Sweden and Finland; the limits of winter ice in the Baltic Sea and in the inland lakes are marked; the rich mines of Kopparberg and elsewhere in the broad lake-filled plain of Sweden are indicated, and separate symbols show iron, copper, silver and gold. Some of the sketches illustrate incidents in the daily life both on land and at sea. The map extends south to include the Baltic coasts of the German realm to which we must now turn.

The Russian plain continued into that of northern Germany across the Pripet Marshes that covered a substantial area nearly one-half the size of England. These enormous swamps, traversed by an intricate network of streams and relieved by sandy islets, were to remain in their amphibious condition until the nineteenth and twentieth centuries. This countryside is usually regarded as the homeland of the Slav peoples, whence they spread east and south and west to cover such an immense tract of Europe. They moved westward across the Vistula and the Oder into the lands abandoned by the Teutonic peoples who had entered the Roman Empire.

---

[1] Edward Lynam, *The Carta Marina of Olaus Magnus, Venice 1539 & Rome 1572* (Tall Tree Library, Jenkintown, Pa., U.S.A., 1949).

By A.D. 600 the line of the Elbe-Saale had become the frontier between the German and Slav worlds, but this frontier was not to last, for, between 900 and 1250, the Germans recovered much of this territory. The German advance eastward took place under the impetus of economic and missionary motives, and there arose a contrast between the new east colonial Germany and the old west feudal Germany. Analogy has been drawn between this advance and the expansion of the American people westward from the Atlantic seaboard. What the new west meant to Young America in the nineteenth century, that the new east had meant to Medieval Germany. Although historical analogies are often misleading, this comparison does emphasise the colonial character of much of Germany during and towards the end of the Middle Ages.

The surface of the German plain is covered, almost everywhere, with deposits brought by the great ice-sheets which spread out from Scandinavia in Quaternary times. Much of the clay is hummocky and on its ill-drained surface lay marsh and shallow lakes of curious shape; many of the river valleys were also marshy. Elsewhere, stretches of infertile sand and gravel, derived from the glacial deposits, form a type of country known as 'Geest'. The landscape that confronted the German settlers was one of wood and marsh and heath. The wood, or most of it, fell before the axe of the pioneers. Place-names that end in *wald* and *holz* indicate the former character of the countryside, and those ending in *rode*, *schwend* and *hagen* bear witness to the activity of the pioneers. They came from the older parts of Germany, 'with horses and oxen, with ploughs and wagons' to transform the countrysides of what are now Brandenburg, Mecklenburg, Pomerania and Silesia. They were accompanied and followed by Dutch, Flemish and Frisian colonists who embanked streams and drained marshes. Between the Elbe and the Oder they transformed the inland marshes into productive countrysides along the Mark of Brandenburg. Into the dry soils of parts of the Geest they cut irrigation canals, and they gave their name to the district of Fläming that lies to the east of Magdeburg. The changes were urban as well as rural. The dates of the founding of the cities of north Germany mark the success of the advance. Behind the achievement of the Hanseatic cities in the fourteenth and fifteenth centuries lay a background of some centuries of colonial effort.

By the end of the thirteenth century the advance had spent itself. Poland was penetrated by German colonists and civilisation, but only to a limited degree. Yet in two outlying eastern areas German missionary zeal and colonising impulse had found fruitful fields of activity. Early in the thirteenth century the Military Order of the Brethren of the Sword had planted the country around the Gulf of Riga with German fortified towns, and to this the German Balts mainly owed their origin. Later in the century, between this northern outpost and the homeland, a second

Military Order, the Teutonic Knights, more thoroughly occupied the land. The consequences were fateful for the affairs of Europe because this new sphere of German colonisation, later known as East Prussia, was separated from the main body of German settlement by what was to become known as the Polish Corridor.

The total result of this eastward expansion was that the main outlines of the frontier between German and Slav had been drawn before the end of the Middle Ages. The countryside of the north German plain had also been transformed. But we must not endow this countryside with a prosperity it did not possess in the fifteenth century. In places, it was only with assiduous labour that the sands could be made to yield their crops of rye and oats, and the improvement of great stretches of Geest had to wait for the scientific agriculture of a later age. Much of the land, too, remained in its boggy condition for many centuries. Even the modern map shows large numbers of shallow lakes in Mecklenburg and Pomerania.

While the eastward march was in progress, colonists also achieved a more intensive use of land in the older settled districts. Woods were cleared and wasted lands were once more reoccupied. In Germany, between the Rhine and the Elbe, daughter houses of the great Rhineland monasteries contributed much to transforming the countryside of Thuringia and Saxony into arable and pasture. Similar work was accomplished elsewhere. New fields were carved out to lie alongside those already cultivated, and, where soil and aspect were suitable, the newly cleared lands were planted with vines. The opportunity and success of cultivation varied from region to region. They were at their highest along the northern edge of the central highlands. Here lies a belt of gently sloping fertile country with a characteristic covering of 'loess' or 'limon', easily worked and fertile. The belt, it is true, is of varying width and is broken by embayments from the plain. The Börde and Hellweg regions of Germany stretch from Magdeburg to Westphalia, and their characteristics are prolonged across the Rhine into the low uplands of Hesbaye, Brabant and Hainault. Limon also covers great terraces in the Rhine valley. These loess or limon lands are the most tractable to the plough in Europe, and the effort of the Middle Ages left them closely settled and well cultivated. On the other hand, attempts to improve the hungry sands, that cover much of this older settled region, had only limited results. The Lüneburg Heath, the Geest of Hanover, and the Kempenland defeated the efforts of medieval colonists to bring them satisfactorily into cultivation. In later centuries, as at the close of the Middle Ages, they stood out as empty and neglected areas; some wealth was brought to the area by the salt springs around Lüneburg.

Along the shores of the North Sea there was loss and gain, and perhaps more loss than gain. Between 1377 and 1421, in the Low Countries, the sea had swallowed up many townships and increased the size of the

Zuider Zee; the Bay of Jade had also been enlarged by storms. But lords and abbeys and peasants had formed themselves into associations for dyking and draining (*wateringen*), and under the shelter of their dykes fertile polders were coming into being from Flanders to Frisia. The inundated and marshy lands of Schleswig and Holstein, too, were rescued from the sea.

This activity along the polders of the North Sea was not typical of the general trend of European agriculture in the fifteenth century. Agricultural expansion had long reached its limit, and recession had left its mark upon most countrysides. Abandoned holdings, depopulated and deserted villages were to be found not only in the 'old lands' of the south and west but also in Mecklenburg, Pomerania, Brandenburg and Prussia. In the south and west, the acreage of these *Wüstungen* has been placed as high as about one-half of the area at one time cultivated; and the statistical mode for Germany as a whole has been estimated at about 25 per cent. These figures probably over-emphasise the contraction, because some abandoned holdings may represent no more than temporary withdrawals or changes in the use of land; but when all reservations are made, the facts are striking enough. The old prosperity had departed and the new prosperity of the sixteenth century had not come, although there seem to have been signs of it before 1500.[1]

Westward lay the kingdom of France, which between 1050 and 1300 had also known its heroic period of reclamation. Great inroads had been made upon the woods. The work, carried on by lay lords, ecclesiastics and peasants, resulted sometimes in new villages and semi-urban settlements (*villes neuves*, *bastides*, *bourgs*), sometimes in extension of the old. Northern France, in the Paris basin, had some of the most favoured agricultural lands in Europe; the limon-covered uplands of the Pays de Caux, Picardy, Beauce and other districts were famous for their fertility. The coastal marshes near St Omer, and those along the estuaries of the Somme, the Seine and the Loire, and also the Marais Poitevin, had been drained, at any rate in part. Some of these flooded areas along the west coast of France formed natural salt pans; those of the Bay of Bourgneuf to the south of the Loire, for example, were particularly important and attracted traders from distant ports. It is true there were exceptions to this tale of conquest. The forests and swamps of the 'Wet' Champagne, in the east of the Paris basin, had been greatly reduced, but it still remained a waterlogged countryside with pools of standing water; and again, little change of any kind had been wrought in the lakes and marshes of the Sologne in the south of the basin. In the west, in Celtic Brittany, compact enclosures replaced the large open fields of the rest of northern

---

[1] For a discussion of these phenomena see: (i) W. Abel, *Die Wüstungen des ausgehenden Mittelalters* (Jena, 1943); (ii) H. Pohlendt, *Die Verbreitung der mittelalterlichen Wüstungen in Deutschland* (Göttingen, 1950).

France; there had been clearing and draining as elsewhere, but the soils of the ancient rocks of the peninsula were poor. Yet, in any general view, the prosperity of northern France in the Middle Ages had been outstanding. It had outstripped all the lands of the West, and Froissart, writing early in the fourteenth century, could well declare it to be 'the fairest kingdom of the world after the kingdom of heaven'.

The Hundred Years War changed all this. France became, in the words of Petrarch (1360), 'a heap of ruins'. Thomas Basin, bishop of Lisieux, writing about 1440, said that between the Loire and the Somme 'all was a desert. A few patches of cultivated land or a vineyard might here and there be seen, but only rarely, and never save in the immediate neighbourhood of a castle or a walled town.' The country had become a prey to wolves and to unemployed mercenaries known under the expressive name of *routiers*. Population fell to one-half, even in places to one-third, of its former level. The marshes of Poitou reverted to their natural condition. Woods reappeared on the untilled fields, and in Saintonge the people for a long time said 'the forests came back to France through the English'. Some of the accounts may have been exaggerated, but the fact of desolation is borne out by the legal instruments of the time which tell a story less embroidered but hardly less impressive; there were contracts that dealt only in wasted land.

But before the end of the fifteenth century, recovery was in sight. If we can believe Claude Seyssel, one-third of the kingdom was brought under cultivation between 1480 and 1510; certainly there was an outburst of activity and by 1565 Bodin could testify to the flourishing state of the countryside. Mining activity was also encouraged. Louis XI, in 1471, created a bureau of mines with powers to grant concessions and to prospect for ore. German miners were brought in to assist in some enterprises. Small iron centres were to be found in many localities—in the Bocage and Perche districts of Brittany and Normandy, and also in the Champagne country and in Nivernais and elsewhere. In 1455–6 Charles VII employed Saxon and Bohemian miners to work the silver-bearing ores of Beaujolais and Lyonnais. But in general the soil of France was poor in metal ore.

The southern half of France had shared in many of the fortunes of the north. A period of clearing had been followed by one of devastation, but these changes had taken place in a different setting. Roughly south of latitude 46° N. was a different language, Provençal or *Langue d'Oc* as opposed to the *Langue d'Oïl* of the north. The south, too, was the land of 'written law' (*droit écrit*) where Roman law, modified by local usage, was the general rule; the more Frankish north was the land of customary law (*droit coutumier*). In this southern country stands the great upland of the Central Massif, well over 1500 feet above sea level. Its circumstances varied, as today. There are fertile valleys of long-established agriculture, and elsewhere the fertility of stretches of volcanic soil is such that they are cultivated well above the usual limits. But there are also great limestone tracts (*causses*) that are little better than stony deserts; and, in the south-east, the massif rises into the rugged Cévennes where isolated villages are to be found amidst chestnut woodland. Much of the massif is occupied by great pasturelands that nourished sheep and cattle, and exported cheeses. Records from the Middle Ages show the movement of transhumant flocks and herds from the lowlands around.

To the west, the agricultural plain of Aquitaine included, amongst others, two distinctive and contrasting localities. One was the rich vine-growing area of Médoc and Bordelais around the marshes of the Gironde estuary, linked through its wine trade with England; its ruined vineyards were recovering, like the rest of France, from the Hundred Years War. The other locality was the sandy expanse of the Landes, virtually a waste widely covered by swamps and lakes behind a belt of coastal dunes; this fever-haunted region had to await the eighteenth and nineteenth centuries for some effective amelioration of its surface. On the other side of the Central Massif was the Rhône valley, and here, across the plateau of Langres, the plain of Europe descends into a different world. The mulberry is encountered at Lyons, the evergreen oak at Vienne, the olive farther south still, near Valence. A local saying has it 'A Valence le Midi commence', for the olive is a good index of Mediterranean conditions. And these, in the fifteenth century as today, were quite different from those in the Paris basin and all that plain of Europe stretching back into Russia.

The difference between the climate of the Mediterranean basin and that of the rest of Europe is striking. The rainfall of the three summer months (June, July and August) rarely exceeds six inches, and in many areas it is less than two. The vine and the olive can withstand this drought and, while the vine can be grown as far north as England, the limits of the olive follow very closely the margin of the 'practically rainless summer'. The winter rain, on the other hand, is sufficient for grain to be grown. Corn, wine and olive oil have been called 'the Mediterranean triad', and they have always formed the basis of Mediterranean subsistence.

To what extent the Mediterranean lands were once covered by forest is uncertain, but it is clear that by the fifteenth century the greater part of the original cover had disappeared. The characteristic Mediterranean forest grows in open formation, is largely evergreen in character, and is quite unlike the dense deciduous woodlands of central and western Europe. It easily degenerates into scrub, and this process has been aided by human agency—by clearing for cultivation or fuel, by fires, and by the grazing of animals. The names given to this scrub in all its variations are many— *maquis, macchia, matorral, garrigue, monte bajo, phrygana*—and among its constituents are such aromatic shrubs as lavender, myrtle, rosemary and thyme. Developed on thin soils, and varied by dwarf evergreens, this scrub is encountered from Portugal to the Dardanelles; and with its associated pastures, it provides grazing for sheep and goats. One effect of clearing has been to accelerate erosion. The soil is swept away by torrential showers, and carried in swollen streams to form deltaic plains such as those of the Ebro, the Po and the Eurotas; hence the predominance of bare rock in many upland areas.

Evergreen scrub has been described as 'the standard vegetation of the Mediterranean world, common to all its shores'. But there is much local variation in land use as in climate, varying from steppe to deciduous forest, and depending upon relief and history. The Iberian peninsula, the coastlands of France, Italy and the Balkans, each area had its special characteristics in the fifteenth century as it has today.

The closing years of the fifteenth century in the Iberian peninsula saw the last phase of the reconquest against the infidel. The Moslems had swept into Spain in 711 and within a few years had over-run all the peninsula up to the Cantabrians and the Pyrenees. From these strongholds in the north, the reconquest had begun almost immediately, and had been marked by the rise of the Christian kingdoms—Castile-Léon, Aragon, Navarre and Portugal. Their progress had been such that, by the middle of the thirteenth century, Moslem power was limited to the kingdom of Granada in the south-east, but it was not until 1492 that this southern strip was conquered and Moslem rule obliterated from the peninsula. In the meantime (1469) marriage had prepared the way for the union of the two crowns of Castile and Aragon; and early in the next century Navarre was acquired (1512). With the completion of the reconquest and the union of the kingdoms, the peninsula emerged, at the dawn of modern times, divided between Spain and Portugal.

The long years of Moslem occupation had left many marks both on life and landscape. Some of the great intellectual centres of medieval Europe were in Spain where Arab learning was made known to the West. Furthermore, many tangible expressions of Moorish influence were, and are, to be seen in Spanish architecture. Agriculturally, the Moors made great contributions both to the development of pastoral activity and to the extension of cultivation, and thus did much to alter the appearance of the countryside.

The scarcity of rain on the enormous tableland of central Spain gave it vast stretches more suitable to pasturage than to cultivation. Sheep-rearing had long been important here, so had the practice of semi-annual sheep migrations. But during the Moorish period the rearing of sheep was greatly extended and its migratory character emphasised. The fact that the greater part of Spanish pastoral terminology was Arabic is indicative of Moorish influence. What is more, the Moors in the twelfth century introduced the merino sheep, although the word 'merino' itself does not seem to have been used until the middle of the fifteenth century. As the reconquest proceeded, the expenses of rehabilitation and of agriculture were clearly heavier than those involved in the hiring of shepherds and the use of natural pastures; and the pastoral industry therefore developed in the new Christian kingdoms in a very marked manner.

The existence of large-scale migratory flocks necessitated organisation, and in 1273 Alfonso the learned brought 'all of the shepherds of Castile' into one association, and, in giving it a title, used a word already connected with the meetings of herdsmen and sheep-owners—the 'Honorable Assembly of the Mesta of the Shepherds'. This organisation grew in importance and by the fifteenth century its activity and influence was one of the outstanding facts about the economic life of the peninsula. A prominent feature of the organisation was the system of special highways for the use of flocks; they were known by different names, the *cabañeras* of Aragon, the *carreradas* of Catalonia, the *azadores reales* of Valencia, and, above all, the *cañadas* of Castile. These great routeways were, in effect, elongated grazing grounds connecting the summer pasturages of the north, around Léon, Soria, Cuenca and Segovia, with the winter homes of the south in La Mancha, Estremadura, Alcantara and the lowlands of Andalusia. The highways were protected by elaborate regulation, and along them the sheep travelled for distances up to 350 and 450 miles. The movement south began in September, and the end of October found the sheep grazing in their winter homes. The return movement began about the middle of April and the sheep were clipped at stations on the way until they were back in the north by the end of May or early June. The wool was taken to the great fairs, especially that of Medina del Campo, or to the north-coast ports for shipment to France, England and Flanders. By the latter years of the fifteenth century, the number of sheep on the move was over two and a half millions. Similar regulations, though not as centralised, were to be found in Aragon. Nor were Spanish sheep the only animals upon the road in Spain, for the ordinances of the town league of Daroca, south of the Ebro, show us 'French, Gascon, Basque and foreign' herdsmen coming over the Pyrenees and down the Ebro valley to winter in Aragon.

These migrating flocks inevitably caused a clash between pastoral and agricultural interests. Attempts were made to limit cultivation in order to preserve grazing grounds, and the policy of the Mesta, supported by royal authority, was one among other factors that brought agrarian decay to Spain. Furthermore, the Castilian forests suffered greatly from the frequent passage of migrating sheep, but various conservation measures, adopted in the thirteenth century, seem to have had some effect and substantial forests were still to be seen in the fifteenth century.

The influence of the Moors upon cultivation was perhaps even greater than on sheep rearing. Coming from an even drier land, they knew well the value of water, and they regarded it as the property of the community to be used as seemed best for all. Irrigation had been practised in Spain in Roman and Visigothic times, but, in the years following 711, it was developed and extended in a remarkable manner. The Moors introduced the *noria*, a bucket-and-chain device driven by animals, for raising water from wells. They also, with labour and ingenuity, cut canals and conveyed water in aqueducts down to the lowlands where they constructed complicated irrigation systems—on the river flats and coastal plains of the southern and eastern shores, along the Ebro and in Valencia and Murcia, and also in the Guadalquivir valley. These luxuriant *huertas* and *vegas* were scenes of intensive cultivation and prosperity. New olive trees are said to have been brought from Africa; the cultivation of the olive became widespread in the south-east; and despite the injunction of the Prophet, the vine was also much cultivated. Not only were the older crops of the peninsula tended but new ones were introduced—sugar cane, cotton, saffron, rice and the mulberrry. Fruit-growing was also extended with a wide variety of fruits—oranges, apricots, figs, lemons and pomegranates. Moslem writers on agriculture were many and they testify to an intense interest in the problems of cultivation. Nor did this achievement come to naught in areas from which the Moors were driven out, for their work was preserved and its harvest reaped by Christians. By the time of the completion of the reconquest in 1492, these two developments, intensive agriculture in the south-eastern plains and valleys and extensive sheep grazing on the tableland, gave Spanish rural life its distinctive character. But we must not forget that side by side with these more distinctive activities along the *cañadas* and on the *huertas*, the Spanish peasant struggled with an ungrateful soil in many other areas, and, as the proverb went, made bread out of stones.

There was also a little exploitation of minerals. Thus the silver mines of Guadalcanal and the quicksilver mines of Almadén were productive. So were the iron mines of the Basque provinces. Salt was produced at Cardona in Catalonia and at other places in the peninsula. But the sum total of this mineral activity was small.

Mediterranean France had been raided by Moorish pirates but, apart from one temporary outpost at Fraxinetum near Cannes, it had never been occupied. Yet, in a milder form and on a smaller scale, it had some features that recalled conditions in Spain. Here was transhumance, and immense flocks made their way between plain and mountain along sheep-ways called *carraïres*, but there was no organisation to correspond with that of the Mesta and the sheep-owners never had the prerogatives of those of Spain; the agriculturalists were better able to hold their own and restrict the movements of flocks. Here, too, was cultivation not only of the vine and olive but also of fruits such as the orange, the lemon and the apricot. The Spanish *huertas* served as models for small irrigated areas, and the cultivation even of sugar cane was attempted. The mulberry had been introduced and was spreading in the Rhône valley and the foundations were being laid for the development of a silk industry in the seventeenth and eighteenth centuries. Salt was produced in the coastal marshes of Languedoc and Provence; some drainage had been undertaken in Languedoc; and the lower Rhône had been dyked by associations of *levadiers*; but the delta itself remained a windswept solitude of marsh and lagoon. It is to Italy that we must turn for closer parallels with Spain.

In the fifteenth century, as in the nineteenth, Italy was merely a geographical expression. In the south, in Naples and Sicily, there had been many changes of dynasty but hardly any changes of frontier. Moslem, Norman, Angevin and Aragonese had succeeded one another, and at the end of the fifteenth century the two kingdoms of Naples and Sicily were held by Spanish princes. In the north, the cities had built territorial domains around themselves; and Milan, Venice, Genoa, Florence and Siena were the chief political units. Between north and south, the papal states stretched across the Apennines from Rome to Ravenna and along the old *Via Flaminia*. No mantle of political unity covered the diversity of Italy at the end of the Middle Ages. But if it thus differed politically from Spain, the rural economies of both lands had a good deal in common.

Since the earliest times migratory flocks had ascended from the coastal plains up into the hill country of the Apennines. Under Frederick II (1194–1250) the regulations governing these various movements were codified and brought under a central authority, and restriction was placed upon the sale of lowland for agricultural purposes in order to preserve it for winter pasturage. When the kingdom of Naples passed to the house of Aragon in the fifteenth century, it was only natural that the new rulers, with their homeland in mind, should make further changes designed to support the pastoral industry, and, incidentally, to increase the tolls derived from the migrating sheep. Merino sheep were imported from Spain; no part of the Tavoliere, or lowland around Foggia near the eastern coast, was allowed to be cultivated; the sheep-ways were organised into *tratturi delle pecore*; further regulations were instituted to control the movement of flocks; and pastoralists were given privileges reminiscent of those of the Mesta. The regime thus inaugurated remained substantially the basis of the pastoral economy of southern Italy until the nineteenth century.

In the interior highlands, rough grazing and brushwood merged into chestnut groves and forests of fir, beech, oak and other trees. The coastal plains varied. Some, like the Roman Campagna, the Pontine Marshes and the Tuscan Maremma, provided pasture for winter grazing, but were malarial and deserted; and these retained their solitary aspect from medieval until recent times. Other plains were more fertile. Much of the Campania was productive and a part of it, the Terra di Lavoro to the north of Vesuvius, was one of the most intensively cultivated parts of Italy in the fifteenth century; the plain of the lower Arno was another. The traditional and basic crops were cereals, olives and vines; Apulia and Sicily exported grain at this time despite the summer droughts. But among the crops there were also newcomers. Arab civilisation had brought sugar-cane, rice, cotton and the mulberry; and southern Italy and Sicily also vied with south-eastern Spain in the production of fruit—oranges, apricots, figs and the like.

One unusual element in the economy of the western coastlands of the peninsula was the manufacture of alum at Tolfa near Città Vecchia. Alum deposits were discovered here in 1462, and long before the end of the century the output was very considerable and greatly added to the income of the papal states. A little iron was also worked in Tuscany, and there were salt pans along the shores of the Maremma.

To the north, in the plain of Lombardy, the essential Mediterranean characteristics mingled with those of continental Europe. Here, during the Middle Ages, much effort had been expended on taming the River Po. Dykes had been built in the twelfth century as a protection against floods, and irrigation channels had been constructed to provide water to improve hitherto barren land. The Cistercian house of Chiaravalle, near Milan, had an irrigation canal at work in 1138; and La Muzza, Milan's great irrigation canal, was completed in 1239. The famous *marcite*, or irrigated water meadows, were already productive by the fourteenth century. Many other irrigation canals were built between the twelfth and fifteenth centuries to sustain the agriculture of the rich alluvial plain; the plans for the Martesana canal between Milan itself and the River Adda are said to have been made by Leonardo da Vinci (1452–1519). The lagoons of the Adriatic coast, especially those of Comacchio, produced salt.

The mulberry spread widely over the hill slopes, and today the plain is the main mulberry area in Italy. Rice, known for some centuries in the south, did not appear in northern Italy until late in the fifteenth century. We hear of it in 1468 on the plain around Pisa, and in 1475 on the plain of Lombardy. Its cultivation was promoted by Lodovico Sforza, duke of Milan, whose model farm won much praise from his contemporaries. But soon this 'garden of Europe', as the plain of Lombardy was called, was to be plunged into destructive war.

To the east, the Balkan peninsula was entering upon a new phase in its history. The Ottoman Turks made their first permanent settlement in Europe in 1354, and in 1361 they not only captured Adrianople but moved their capital thither from Brusa in Asia Minor. From this base in Thrace the Turkish conquest of south-eastern Europe was begun. The desperate resistance of the Slav peoples to the north was broken on the field of

Kossovo in 1389, and by the middle of the next century the Slav states had become part of the Turkish empire in name as well as in fact—Bulgaria in 1382, Serbia in 1459, Bosnia in 1463; the northern frontier of the empire stretched east-west along the Danube and the Save. To the south, the curious Latin-Frankish states that had occupied the Greek peninsula since the Fourth Crusade also fell one by one into Turkish hands until by 1461 the Turks were in complete control over the whole area, apart from some scattered points held by the Venetians. The islands of the Aegean were more difficult to acquire, and over a century was to elapse before Turkish control was effective (1566). In the meantime, a seal had been set upon the Turkish dominion in Europe by the capture of Constantinople itself in 1453.

The Frankish occupation of medieval Greece left many traces upon the countryside in great castles and towers, and their ruins are still to be seen, but it made little mark upon the Greek population. The medley of Italians and Frenchmen, Catalans and Navarrese, remained to the end a series of garrisons in a foreign land. 'New France' passed away for ever before the advance of the Turk, leaving not much more than archaeological remains to recall a brilliant interlude of western chivalry. The Turkish occupation from the fifteenth century onwards likewise contributed no appreciable ingredient to the population of the Greek peninsula itself, but to the north, in the valleys and lowlands of Macedonia and Thrace, there were substantial tracts of Turkish settlement which lasted until the exchanges of population after 1923; and, in addition, there were considerable areas of Turkish-speaking peoples in Bulgaria. Turkish influence was also apparent in the *tchliflik*, or large estate, worked by a servile population of Christians and characterised by a low efficiency; it was, for instance, widespread on the plains of Thessaly and was to be found all over Bulgaria and southern Serbia as far as a line roughly connecting the Gulf of Drin and the Iron Gate on the Danube. Other indications of Turkish influence may still be seen today in the large number of Albanian Moslems in Albania itself and in Montenegro and southern Serbia, and also in the Bosnian Moslems who present the curious spectacle of a people Slav in language and race, and yet Mohammedan in religion. Believers in the Bogomil heresy, 'they had preferred to be conquered by the Sultan than converted by the Pope'.[1] Other consequences of the Turkish advance in the fourteenth century were the numerous Slav migrations northward, and these were to continue in one form or another for five centuries or so.

There is much that is obscure about the condition of the Balkans under its new masters in the fifteenth century, but the main lines of its economy cannot be in doubt. Only a part of the area was typically Mediterranean in climate and products—the coastal fringe of Dalmatia hemmed in by

[1] W. Miller, *Essays on the Latin Orient* (Cambridge, 1921), p. 494.

the upland of the interior, Greece itself (and especially the Peloponnese), and the islands of its seas. Here, life was dominated by the triad of 'corn, wine and olive oil'. The fig and various citrus fruits were also characteristic. Since the sixth century A.D., when the silk-worm was smuggled from the East into the Byzantine empire, the cultivation of the mulberry had spread. So much of the Peloponnese was planted with the mulberry that, according to one view, it became known as 'the Morea' from the Greek name of the tree (*moréa*); the plain around Thebes was called 'Morokampos', and Thebes itself was famous for its silk. But the thin soil of much of Greece is infertile; such alluvial areas as those of Thrace, Macedonia, Thessaly and Thebes were famed as granaries and as cattle areas, yet much of their surface was still ill-drained and marshy and had to await the improvements of recent times. Furthermore, maize and tobacco had not yet come to add variety to the agricultural economy. The agricultural achievement of the Balkans in the fifteenth century did not match that of parts of Italy and Spain. Nor, with the coming of the Ottoman Turks, did the future hold much promise.

The typical landscape of much of Greece has always consisted of small cultivated plains above which rise arid foot-hills covered by olive trees or by scrub that provides pasture for sheep and goats. The foot-hills in turn rise into mountains forested in part, but also with brushwood and summer pasture of varying quality. The seasonal migration of flocks was a feature of the whole of Greece, but it was particularly developed in the mountainous interior to the north of the Gulf of Corinth. Here were the nomad shepherds known as Vlachs. The name 'Vlach' or 'Wallach', applied to them by their neighbours, is identical with the English 'Wealh' or 'Welsh' and means 'stranger', but the Vlachs call themselves 'Aromani', i.e. Romans. Their origin is obscure, but it is now generally admitted that they are descended from Roman colonists and latinised provincials, and that, as their language suggests, they are akin to the Roumanians. Their presence may be inferred from records as early as the sixth century, but the first definite mention of them was not until the year 976. During the next two centuries reference to them becomes frequent, and their mode of life seems to have been much the same in the eleventh as in the nineteenth century. From April to September they lived with their flocks in the mountains and they descended to the plains only in winter. Northward, in this mountain interior, summer rainfall and winter cold increase; the characteristic Mediterranean vegetation gives way to deciduous forest and to the deciduous brushwood known by the Serbian name of *shiblyak*. Its affinities are with central Europe and not with the south.

Set between the Mediterranean basin and the plain of Europe lies a mountainous tract for the most part over 1500 feet above sea-level; much of it is over 5000 feet and it has many heights above 13,000 feet. It is a tract of great variety, ranging from the flat upland surfaces of ancient worn-down mountains to the irregular array of glittering Alpine peaks, and from narrow valleys to the great expanse of the Hungarian plain. In the west was the meeting-place of French, Italian and German speech. All three languages came to be represented in Switzerland which had grown up from the union of three cantons around Lake Lucerne in the thirteenth century. Other cantons joined the union until by 1513 it had reached a form which it was to retain until the wars of the French Revolution. In the valleys of eastern Switzerland and southern Tyrol a number of Romance dialects survived from remote times, and these formed a wedge of Romansch speech set between German and Italian.

In the eastern Alps the rise of the Mark of Austria, established as an outpost against the Magyar in the tenth century, was accompanied by an advance of German-speaking peoples comparable to that across the northern plain. The advance took place not only down the Danube but also south and south-east into the lands of the Slovenes and the Croats. Beyond the main frontier of German speech, isolated German settlements appeared as islands in Slav or Hungarian territory. Thus in 1347 Bavarian settlers came to Gottschee in Carniola which was described at the time as a wilderness.

The economy of this central mountainous tract displayed a wide variety and many differences of detail associated with climatic and geographical conditions. Yet the area as a whole had gone through an agrarian history roughly analogous to that of the northern plain. Widespread clearing had changed the face of the countryside. Thus in the Tyrol, in the early Middle Ages, only the fertile slopes of the valleys of the Inn and the Etsch had been settled, but by the fifteenth century, colonisation had spread up the side valleys. As in the north, the fifteenth century was a period of recession and the desertion of farms, particularly those at a high level. In many alpine areas, the peasants had two homes—a permanent winter settlement surrounded by cultivated fields in the valley itself, and a summer hut near high-lying pastures or alps set amid woods and snow and peaks. Very complicated forms of transhumance resulted from these arrangements. Some indication of this pastoralism is provided by the fact that before the end of the Middle Ages butter and cheese were being sold from the Swiss Alps, and Swiss cattle were being exported northwards into Germany and southwards into upper Italy.

The upland of Bohemia, clearly bounded by high mountain barriers, formed a distinct unit in central Europe. The immigration of German colonists into the Slav lands of Bohemia began on a large scale towards the end of the twelfth century, and was encouraged by the Bohemian rulers in order to counteract the power of the native aristocracy. The Germans came as merchants, clergy and miners, and as peasants clearing the land. Whole districts along the borders were settled by Germans and this German element has remained a prominent feature of the ethno-graphic map of Bohemia until recent times. But in spite of this varied influx and in spite of the importance of German culture, the Bohemian Slavs never lost their identity as did those of Silesia and Brandenburg to the north. Furthermore, an internal slavonic colonisation went on by which the Czechs themselves reclaimed the wilderness and founded new villages. In Bohemia there are over 300 place-names that include the element *lhota*, and there are eighty more in Moravia. The word, roughly speaking, means 'freedom' and it was used, in this connection, to denote the exemptions from render that were sometimes granted to settlements made on waste or empty land. Its widespread distribution can be taken as some index of the transforming activity of the Czechs. The word, in the form of *lehota*, occurs more than forty times in Slovakia farther east, but there it seems to have been associated with German and not Slav activity. The cultivated land thus brought into being in Bohemia was very adversely affected by the Hussite Wars (1419–36). It has been estimated that one-sixth of the population perished. Many people left the country to seek new homes in the west. These Bohemian exiles were often confused with the gipsies that first appeared in central and western Europe about this time, and the French word for gipsy (*bohémien*) still recalls this fact.

In addition to Bohemia, there is a second distinctive unit to be con-sidered. The great plain of Hungary, enclosed by the Carpathian arc, is as separate racially as it is distinctive geographically from the lands around. The Magyars in the ninth century had moved westward from the lands beyond the Don, and their arrival on the plain about the year A.D. 900 was followed by a series of devastating raids that reached even into France and southern Italy. They were defeated, at Lechfeld near Augs-burg in 955, and the years that followed saw the transformation of a predatory horde of nomadic horsemen into a European state, Roman Catholic in allegiance: the tent was given up for the village, the castle and the church. The arrival and consolidation of the Magyars had permanent consequences for the political geography of Europe, for they formed a wedge separating the northern from the southern Slavs and greatly com-plicated the affairs of the Danube basin. The flat plain upon which they settled was far from uniform. Much of it was covered by fertile loess soils rich in agricultural possibility, but the streams of the Danube and the Tisza were bordered by wide marshes, and elsewhere, especially between the two great rivers and in the north-east, there were great stretches of grass and sand where the so-called *puszta* was especially characteristic; the word *puszta* in Slavonic means solitude.

The colonising activity so characteristic of Europe between 1000 and 1350 was also manifest here. Benedictine monks not only fostered con-version but promoted colonisation and the extension of western methods of agriculture. Arable farming and immense cattle ranches on the *pusztas* changed the economy of the area. Immigration was encouraged by successive Magyar kings, and German settlers appeared in country and town alike. The destruction wrought by the Mongol raids in 1241 was repaired with the help of German colonists. Thus the population of Vács (Waitzen) to the north of Budapest, on the left bank of the Danube, was entirely destroyed and had to be replaced by Germans. Other immigrants were Slavs fleeing before the Turks, especially after the complete fall of Serbia in 1459. In 1483 Matthias Corvinus wrote to the pope that 200,000 Serbs had setttled in the south of his kingdom in four years, and there is also other testimony to the large Serb element in the Voivodina at this time.

To the east of the plain were the mountains of Transylvania. Its Latin name indicates its forested nature, and its Magyar name, Edily, comes from *Erdö*, a forest. This land of mountains and forests seems to have been appropriated by the Magyars in the tenth and eleventh centuries, and many settled in the western valleys, notably in that of the Someş. Apart from the Magyars, Transylvania in the fifteenth century included three other groups. One was a people of mysterious origin—the Szeklers —possibly akin to the Magyars themselves and certainly speaking their language; another was the Roumanians whose arrival in these parts has been hotly debated by Magyar and Roumanian historians. But the origin of the third group—that of the Germans—is not in dispute. They came from the Rhineland, mostly in the twelfth century, at the invitation of the early kings of Hungary, to fell the frontier forests and to become farmers and miners; the presence of German speech in the area today is some memorial to their activity. In 1224 they were granted a remarkable charter which gave them a measure of autonomy.

Thus by 1500 some of the main elements in the later ethnic problems of Hungary were already apparent. Further settlement and further complication were to come as a result of the arrival and then the withdrawal of the Turk. During the fifteenth century the Magyars had played a great part in resisting the Turkish advance, but in 1526 they were defeated at Mohacz on the banks of the Danube, and all but a western strip fell into Turkish hands until 1699.

One of the characteristic features of the mountain belt as a whole was the mining activity that was to be found throughout it. At many places, seams of ores containing iron, copper, lead, silver, gold, zinc and tin, as well as coal, lay near the surface or broke through it, and the origins of the exploitation of many of these seams stretch back into remote times. The vicissitudes of mining during the Middle Ages culminated towards the end of the fifteenth century in a boom, particularly in silver. 'Between 1460 and 1530', writes J.U.Nef, 'the annual output of silver in central Europe increased several times over, perhaps more than five-fold.'[1] What

[1] *The Cambridge Economic History of Europe*, ed. M. Postan and E. E. Rich (Cambridge, 1952), vol. II, p. 470.

was true of silver was true, in varying degrees, of copper and iron; and there was also an increasing interest in coal seams. If the amounts appear small to us, and the technology primitive, we must consider them in the context of their time. In 1523 Charles V placed the number of people employed in mining and metallurgy in his empire at about 100,000.

Coal mining was never important in the Middle Ages. Coal was dug in many places, but only around Liège and at Mons to the west had it attained any prominence by the fifteenth century; Liège coal competed in the Channel ports with 'sea-coal' from Newcastle. Iron-working was scattered in the nearby forests of the Condroz and the Ardennes. Iron mining and smelting were also widespread in the plateaus of Rhineland-Westphalia and especially in the uplands of Siegerland and Sauerland between the Ruhr and the Sieg. Not far away, the discovery of calamine (the ore of zinc) at Moresnet near Aachen during the fifteenth century led to the manufacture of brass and to a demand for copper. Some silver as well as iron was mined in these and other highlands of the Rhine basin—in the Siegerland, the Spessart, the Black Forest and the Vosges. Deposits of low-grade iron ore were also worked in Lorraine, and there were salt works here around the rich brine springs at Dieuze. Salt, too, was manufactured at the great establishment at Salins in Franche Comté. There were also mines of silver-bearing lead and copper ores in the Lyonnais and Beaujolais districts of the Central Plateau of France. Across the Channel, iron, lead, silver and copper were being mined in England; and tin from Cornwall and Devon entered the European market.

But it was in the east that medieval mining reached its highest development. Ores of silver mixed with lead or copper were widely distributed, and their exploitation was greatly stimulated by the discovery, about 1450, that silver could be effectively extracted from argentiferous copper ores with the aid of lead. One of the main mining centres since the tenth century had been the Harz mountains. The great silver and copper deposits of the Rammelsberg, near Goslar, were actively worked and the fame of Goslar as a mining centre was widespread. There were other centres in the Harz area, and not far to the east there were mines at Mansfeld where Martin Luther's father worked as a miner. Nearby at Halle, in the valley of the Saale, there were salt works. Silver-bearing ores were discovered during the second half of the twelfth century in the Erzgebirge, and on the Saxon slopes of these mountains mining camps grew into towns; Freiberg was founded in 1171, and there were other mining centres at Annaberg, Marienberg and Schneeberg. Tin was mined around Altenberg and also around Zinnwald on the Bohemian side of the Erzgebirge. Farther east still, in Silesia, there were silver centres at Tarnowitz, Gottesberg and Waldenburg; Reichenstein yielded gold as well as silver.

To the south of Saxony and Silesia lies Bohemia, which has been described as 'the Nevada of Europe at the end of the Middle Ages'. German mining camps grew into towns in an area hitherto Czech in population. Joachimstal, Kuttenberg, Iglau, Deutschbrod and other mining towns were German in origin. This mineral wealth explains much of the importance of Bohemia in the later medieval history of Europe. The Hussite Wars (above, p. 36) left some of the mining towns in ruins, but they had recovered before the end of the century. Eastwards, in Slovakia, there were important copper and silver mines around Neusohl, Kremnitz and Schemnitz, exploited for centuries with the aid of German miners; and at Wieliczka in Poland there were salt mines. Other mining centres for copper, silver and lead lay to the south, in the eastern Alps: in the Tyrol (particularly around Schwaz, near Innsbruck); to the south of Salzburg; and in Styria, Carinthia and Carniola. Salt was also worked at a number of places in the Tyrol and elsewhere; Styria contained some of the leading iron centres on the Continent, and their production quadrupled between the 1460's and the 1530's. Calamine was discovered in the Tyrol and in Carinthia during the fifteenth century, and quicksilver was mined at Idria in Carniola. The coming of skilled German miners into eastern Europe was part of the general eastward movement of the Germans during the Middle Ages. Small isolated groups of Saxon miners were to be found, for example, at Srebrenica in Bosnia (*srebro* means silver) and at Novo Brdo in Serbia. Ragusans also aided in the exploitation of the Serbian silver and copper deposits. Much more important were the so-called 'Saxons' of Transylvania who had come from the Rhineland as early as the twelfth and thirteenth centuries to be farmers and miners. The minerals included silver, lead and copper, some gold and also salt.

This mining activity at the close of the Middle Ages is epitomised in the activity of the great merchant family of the Fuggers of Augsburg. At the end of the fifteenth century they controlled silver, copper and iron mines in Silesia, Slovakia, Bohemia, Tyrol, Carinthia and also in Spain. The progress of much of European mining was bound up with the extraction of silver from copper and lead ores, and the discovery of rich silver ores in the New World, especially those of Potosi in Bolivia about 1546, was to deal a blow not only to European silver mining but to European mining in general.

If the fifteenth-century countryside was largely the product of the pioneering activity of the Middle Ages, the fifteenth-century town was the result of medieval trading activity. Most towns owed their sites to local and particular causes; they grew around fortified centres, or about cathedrals, or at the nodal points of roads and waterways, or near harbours. Nor were those towns that had been deliberately planted, particularly in colonial Germany, without advantages of local topography.

But if the origins of individual towns are bound up with local circumstances, we must look elsewhere for an explanation of that general manifestation of urban growth that had characterised eleventh- and twelfth-century Europe. That explanation lies in a revival of commerce which brought distant lands closer together and made possible an exchange of products between districts that differed in climate and in stage of development. Expanding cultivation, growing industry, productive mining and increasing population are bound up one with another and with reviving trade. It is difficult to separate cause and effect, but we can at any rate discern symptoms, and one of the most marked symptoms of a new economic order had been the growth of cities, large and small.

But the so-called commercial revolution of the twelfth century did not continue without a break into the expanding economy of the sixteenth century. Just as arable cultivation contracted in the late fourteenth and early fifteenth centuries, so did commercial activity. Wars, epidemics, the interruption of the eastern trade, and perhaps other and obscure causes resulted in a lessening of production, in a diminution of cargoes and in the stagnation and even decline of towns. It has been estimated, for example, that the population of the north German cities decreased during the fourteenth and fifteenth centuries by some 20 per cent. But, in general, the statistical evidence is far from certain, and one must always remember that within the general contraction there were local shifts. Thus the golden age of the Catalan merchant was over when the French seaports were reviving, and when the Portuguese were pioneering along the west African coast and opening up new vistas of expansion.

Broadly speaking, medieval Europe comprised two commercial worlds —that of the Baltic and the North Sea, and that of the Mediterranean. They were connected by land and by sea. By land, Italian traders had found their way across the Alpine passes in the twelfth and thirteenth centuries, and the fairs of the Champagne district had provided convenient meeting places for southern and northern merchants. But long before the early fourteenth century, when the fairs started to decline and to shrink to provincial markets, the Italians had established contacts with other centres in France, England, Flanders and also in Germany, Hungary and Poland. By sea, the galleys of Genoa and Venice had reached the ports of the North Sea before the end of the thirteenth century, and in succeeding centuries these contacts grew into considerable proportions. For long, the chief meeting place on these northern shores had been the port of Bruges; but in the fifteenth century, partly because of the silting of the Zwin which connected the port with the sea, and partly because of political complications, Bruges was succeeded by Antwerp as a terminus of routes. Yet, spectacular though they were, these numerous contacts between south and north, by land and sea, were not the most important feature of medieval trade. This was the separate activity that went on within each of the two worlds of the Baltic-North Sea and the Mediterranean. We are fortunate in having two English views of European commerce in the fifteenth century. *The Libelle of Englyshe Polycye*, by an anonymous author, appeared in 1436,[1] and Sir John Fortescue's *Comodytes of England* was written about the same time.[2]

The characteristic commodities of the northern trade, unlike those of the south, were not luxuries but necessities. A prominent item, and an important one to Catholic Europe, was fish. The waters around Iceland yielded stockfish, but the main sources of fish lay nearer at home. The herring which now ranges mainly on the western side of the North Sea, was then abundant in the eastern parts and especially in the southern Baltic. The fisheries of Skania, in southern Sweden, had long been the most important in Europe, and the trade in dried and salted fish formed one of the chief branches of northern commerce. During the course of the fifteenth century the fisheries of Skania came to be rivalled and replaced by those of the North Sea as the main source of supply. The disappearance of summer herring shoals in the Baltic is obscure,[3] but before the fisheries of Skania had finally ceased to be productive, the Dutch were building up their herring trade in the North Sea. The distribution and marketing of the herring catch gave opportunities for return cargoes, and, in the words of a Dutch contemporary, 'The herring keeps Dutch trade going, and the Dutch trade sets the world afloat.' Set midway between the northern and southern seas, Amsterdam, Flushing, Rotterdam and other ports of the Netherlands were well placed for developing large-scale entrepôt trade, but the finest flowering of this was yet to come.

The salt involved in the preparation of the fish came from a variety of sources, from Lüneburg, for example, and especially from the estuaries of the western coast of France; there, the Bay of Bourgneuf was frequented by the salt fleets of all the northern peoples. Another important item of food was grain. It was exported from the fertile lands of northern France, from England and the Rhineland, and, more recently, from the newly colonised lands of eastern Germany. Upon such sources did the dense population of industrial Flanders rely. Another commodity was wine, and by the fifteenth century the commercial production of wine had become concentrated in a few specialised areas—Poitou, Gascony, Burgundy and the lands along the Moselle; the connection between Gascony and England was particularly close.

But foodstuffs do not exhaust the list. From the fourteenth century onwards, the vast coniferous forests of Poland, Livonia, Russia and

[1] G. Warner (ed.), *The Libelle of Englyshe Polycye* (Oxford, 1926). The author seems to have been Adam Moleyns, afterwards bishop of Chichester.
[2] Printed in *The Works of Sir John Fortescue*, 2 vols. (London, 1869).
[3] Otto Pettersson, 'The connection between hydrographical and meteorological phenomena', *Quarterly Journal Royal Meteorological Society*, vol. 38 (London, 1912), pp. 173–91.

Scandinavia began to assume an importance in the water-borne commerce of the north, especially as the woodlands of the west had retreated before the plough. Not only timber itself, but the miscellany known as 'forest products'—pitch, tar, potash—were important. From these northern lands also came some luxuries—amber for ornaments, wax for candles and, not least, furs for warmth as well as for appearance. Yet another commodity was wool, and it was upon imported wool that the most highly specialised industrial regions of fifteenth-century Europe were based. The chief exporting area had long been England, and the chief receiving area included the Low Countries and northern France. By the thirteenth century, Flanders and the neighbouring districts had become the principal manufacturing area of north-western Europe. The stream of textiles flowing south and east had been augmented before 1400 by English cloth, and in the fifteenth century England became mainly an exporter of manufactured woollens rather than of raw wool. The development of the fulling mill on streams not only produced changes in the location of cloth-making in England, but gave the country as a whole an advantage over Flanders. That the cloth centres in the west of England, in East Anglia and in Yorkshire were growing rich is testified by the magnificence of some of their Perpendicular churches. By the end of the century, English cloth was a very prominent item in the international trade of Europe and, if Erasmus is to be believed, it was finer in quality than any other.

Nourished by this trading activity and by these industries, the towns of northern and western Europe flourished. In Flanders and Brabant, according to one estimate, the urban population was as great as, and perhaps greater than, the rural population. Nowhere on the Continent, save in northern Italy, were the towns so numerous, so large and so active. The medieval buildings of the Flemish towns, especially their Cloth Halls and their *Hôtels de Ville* tell a story of prosperity. Many towns had their specialities. Arras gave its name to the hanging curtain called arras; Cambrai to cambric; Lille to lisle thread; Valenciennes manufactured valence; the diaper pattern came from Ypres. Then again, some cities excelled in metal work, especially Liège in iron, and Dinant in copper. Other towns producing cloth included Brussels, Malines, Louvain, Douai and Amiens; a complete list would be a long one. It is difficult to be certain about the size of these towns, and estimates have varied greatly.[1] There certainly cannot have been many towns with over 20,000 inhabitants; the population of Arras, for example, seems barely to have exceeded 20,000. But the most such figures can do is to give us some rough idea of the order of magnitude involved.

England had nothing to compare with this constellation of towns. At the end of the century, London itself seems to have had not more than

[1] For a convenient summary of some of the problems see *IX Congrès international des sciences historiques, Rapports* (Paris, 1950), pp. 55–80.

60,000 inhabitants. Far below it came Norwich with about 12,000 and Bristol with perhaps 10,000 people. Bristol had grown rapidly in recent years as a result of trade with Ireland and the Continent. Below these came a dozen or so towns with populations of between 5000 and 10,000. The average size of most market towns, that served the surrounding countryside, seems to have been well below the 2000 mark.[1] In France, on the other hand, was the queen of all the western cities. Paris, apparently, had a population approaching 200,000, and its size and beauty evoked the admiration of traveller after traveller. Lyons, well placed on the Saône, was a notable trading centre with widespread connections; its *bourse*, opened in 1506, is the oldest in France; its silk and printing industries were well known. Along the west coast, there was a stirring of life after the Hundred Years War. Bordeaux and Bayonne shipped wine; and La Rochelle, Nantes, Rouen and Dieppe likewise grew rich by trade.

To the east of France, the long-established cities of the Rhineland stood out prominently. It is an intrinsically fertile area and its rivers provide arteries for trade. Cologne, set between Flanders and southern Germany, was well placed for commerce, and its linen cloth and metal industries were important; yet its population has been placed at not more than 35,000. Upstream were well-known centres like Coblenz, Mainz, Frankfurt-am-Main, Worms, Strassburg, Freiburg, Basle and a host of others that were seats of industry as well as foci of local life. Estimates of their size vary; Strassburg may have had 25,000 inhabitants, but the others were considerably smaller, and the usual range of population seems to have been between below 10,000, and sometimes considerably so.

In southern Germany, a group of cities was sustained in part by the trade across the Alpine passes—Nürnberg, Ulm, Regensburg, Passau, Vienna, Zürich, Augsburg, Munich, Salzburg, Innsbruck; to them must be added the mining towns of Bohemia and elsewhere. All these, and others in the region, enjoyed a remarkable prosperity in the latter part of the fifteenth century, yet none of them seems to have contained more than 20,000 inhabitants, and many little more than 10,000. The Fugger family of Augsburg built up enormous mining interests in Germany, Hungary and Spain, and their commercial interests were even more widespread, extending in the next century into America and Asia. The Fuggers have been described as the financiers of the Habsburgs and they were able to interfere decisively in the international politics of the age. All this influence stemmed from the initiative of Johannes Fugger, a linen weaver of Augsburg in the fourteenth century. The house of Fugger was not the only merchant dynasty of these south German towns. The merchants of Nürnberg had agents in Lübeck and connections in East Prussia and Livonia; they had contacts with the Rhineland cities and interests in

[1] W. G. Hoskins, 'English provincial towns in the early sixteenth century', *Trans. Roy. Hist. Soc.* 5th series, V (1956), 1–19.

north Italy. They brought Baltic herrings to Salzburg and Polish oxen to Frankfurt-am-Main, and they sold eastern spices and western textiles in the markets of central Europe.

In the north, between the Rhine and the Elbe, was another group of towns—Dortmund, Soest, Münster, Goslar, Brunswick, Magdeburg and others less notable. Serving local markets and sustained by local industry and by distant connections, they grew up to a modest size, mostly, it seems, below the 5000 mark. Hamburg and Bremen, as ports, shared in the activities of the northern seas and exported, amongst other things, grain and salt. Beyond the Elbe was the great array of new towns that had been deliberately founded between 1200 and 1400, on virgin sites or on sites of earlier Slavonic settlements several times destroyed. Their carefully laid-out rectangular streets formed a contrast with the tortuous ways of the western cities. Many of these towns served as local market centres for the new villages around. Some grew into prominence as foci of administration or, more particularly, as links in the wider commerce between East and West. Lübeck, founded as a German town in 1143, became an emporium of northern trade and one of the most important centres around the Baltic; its population seems to have been just over 20,000. But there were other prominent centres in this new colonial area: Rostock, Wismar, Leipzig, Dresden, Berlin and Stettin were familiar names, and beyond lay such centres as Danzig, Marienburg, Elbing, Thorn and Königsberg. Farther east still, in Livonia and Estonia, were Riga (founded as long ago as 1201), Dorpat, Reval and many other German fortified centres. The new foundations east of the Elbe numbered between one and two thousand. From the Baltic shores, German merchants reached out to establish a 'Kontor' or settlement at the great centre of Novgorod and subsidiary factories at Pskov, Polotsk, Vitebsk and Smolensk. Elsewhere in the Baltic lands the same motivating force can be discerned. Towns as economic centres appeared in Sweden between 1200 and 1400, particularly in the Mälardalen region that stretches west of Stockholm, and Stockholm itself grew as a terminus of the trans-Baltic trade with Lübeck. On the island of Gotland, Wisby was well placed as a centre for German merchants. On the other side of the peninsula, Bergen stood out, with connections not only to the south but westward, by way of the Shetlands and the Faroes, with Iceland.

Different in size, different in appearance, with varying constitutional histories and divergent activities, all these towns bore a family resemblance. Their inhabitants—or at any rate many of them—were engaged in trade and industry. The life-blood of a town was trade, and consequently the townsfolk were always at the mercy of political disturbance and heavy tolls, to say nothing of robber barons and river pirates. It is not surprising therefore that many cities, in the thirteenth and fourteenth centuries, had formed leagues for mutual protection; there had been, for example, a league of the Rhineland cities and another of the south German cities. The greatest and most enduring of all these associations was the Hanseatic League, and it serves more than anything else to epitomise the trading activity and the town development of the northern economic realm of Europe. Two circumstances made it possible. One was the development of a network of commercial relations extending from the English Channel to the Gulf of Finland, from London to Novgorod, and from Cologne to Bergen. It is difficult to say how many towns belonged to the League, for the number was constantly fluctuating, but the usual estimate at the height of its power is eighty. These lay not only along the coast but also along the waterways of the north German plain. It was organised into four 'circles' with centres at Lübeck, Danzig, Brunswick and Cologne; Hamburg and Bremen were prominent members.

But by the fifteenth century the power of the League had passed its zenith. There were divergencies of interest and political difficulties; and the decline of the Baltic herring industry was a blow to individual members. Amsterdam was to gain what Lübeck lost. As the fifteenth century drew to a close, Dutch and English maritime enterprise was competing with that of the Hanse, so that even before the oceanic discoveries, 'most of its teeth were out and the rest loose', as one English observer in Germany put it. The earliest returns of the toll-stations at the Sound date from 1495, and they show that the shipping bound for the Baltic was predominantly Dutch. Thus was the stage set for an even greater expansion of Dutch shipping out into the wide ocean.

The activity in the north was rivalled, and indeed exceeded, by that around the Mediterranean. The southern peninsulas of Europe stretched forth to meet not only fresh continents, fresh climates and fresh products, but also a different civilisation that extended far behind the Mediterranean coastlands. 'Muslim merchants', it has been said, 'could travel from Spain to India without feeling that they were going to foreign lands',[1] and not only to India but well into Africa and the oases of the Sahara. The trade of these far distant lands brought to Europe exotic goods of many kinds. Spices figured prominently and included pepper, ginger, cloves, cinnamon, nutmeg and mace. Among other rare commodities were such drugs as cubebs, cardamoms, camphor and tragacanth together with perfumes, sugar, precious stones, dyestuffs (indigo, madder, saffron), alum and carpets. And in return went western woollens and linen together with some raw wool, metals and hides. These and other commodities entered and left the Mediterranean world through the Red Sea or the Persian Gulf or overland from the Black Sea across Central Asia. It is easy, therefore, to appreciate the importance of such ancient centres as

[1] *The Cambridge Economic History of Europe*, ed. M. Postan and E. E. Rich (Cambridge, 1952), vol. II, p. 283.

Constantinople and Alexandria. Constantinople, in particular, stood out as one of the great cities of the world. Benjamin of Tudela, in the twelfth century, had described it as 'a great business centre whither merchants come from all countries of the world'; travellers were struck by its industrial enterprises—its silk industry, its metal-work in gold and silver, and its armament factories. It still remained a very considerable commercial centre in the fifteenth century, and in the East too there were other great trading cities like Tarsus, Ephesus, Antioch, Smyrna, Trebizond and Salonica. The coming of the Turk, and in particular the fall of Constantinople in 1453, interrupted but did not permanently block the immemorial trade routes.[1]

In the meantime the glittering prizes of Mediterranean trade had been won by the Italian cities. It was they who provided the connecting links between the trade routes of the Near East and those of transalpine Europe. Their merchants sought oriental wares in the termini of Egypt, the Levant and the Black Sea, and then distributed them across the passes of the Alps or by sea through the Straits of Gibraltar. And of these Italian cities the greatest was Venice. Set upon a cluster of islands amid marshes and lagoons at the head of the Adriatic, the Venetians had exploited their advantages of location with shrewd policy. That they could undertake the transport of the Fourth Crusade in 1204 was a measure of their maritime strength, and, as a result of that Crusade, the Byzantine empire was replaced by a congeries of Latin states around the Aegean; and Venice, in her own phrase, received 'one-fourth and a half of the Greek empire'. In the centuries that followed, the Venetians increased their colonies in the Aegean and elsewhere by conquest or by purchase. 'Never', we are told, 'was there a state so completely dependent upon the sea.' Structurally, the Venetian empire had come to consist of a series of strategic points, calling stations, islands and merchant quarters in cities, all strung along the greatest of medieval trade routes. This maritime state was not without its weakness, and during the fourteenth century a policy of expansion overland had been reluctantly initiated. The guiding considerations were two—the need of grain- and meat-producing areas which the empire of fragments did not provide, and the necessity of securing the alpine approaches to the northern markets. Successive advances brought Padua, Verona, Brescia and Bergamo under Venetian control, and Venetian territory in the latter part of the fifteenth century extended westward almost to Lake Como. The population of the city itself at this time has been placed at nearly 100,000; Philippe de Commines could well describe it as 'the most triumphant city I have ever seen'.

Rivalling Venice in the eastern waters was Genoa, a city of about one-half its size, but the great struggle was long over by the fifteenth century,

---

[1] A. H. Lybyer, 'The Ottoman Turks and the routes of oriental trade', *Eng. Hist. Rev.* vol. xxx (London, 1915), pp. 577–88.

and it had left Genoa in a position of inferiority. Even so, the Genoese were far from inactive; their commercial depots were many and extended to the Crimea where Caffa, lost to the Ottomans in 1475, had become a city as large as, or larger than, Genoa itself, a cosmopolitan mart where Turks, Tartars, Russians, Poles, Armenians and Greeks mingled. The Genoese were also exploiting the alum mines of Phocea and the rich mastic plantations of Chios, and they exercised control of varying duration over Lesbos, Thasos, Samos, Icaria and other islands of the Aegean. With the coming of the Ottoman, and the fall of Constantinople in 1453, there were many oscillations in Venetian and Genoese suzerainty over the Aegean islands, but Venice was able to keep Crete and in 1489 to acquire Cyprus.

The great arteries of trade in the eastern Mediterranean had been supplemented long before 1400 by regular convoys from Venice and Genoa to the ports of Flanders and England, and there were Venetian and Genoese agents in many western cities. Merchants from both cities also visited the ports of North Africa, and in 1447 a Genoese agent, Antonio Malfante, travelled into the heart of the desert, and from the large oasis of Tuat he wrote a report about the caravan trade with the rich countries along the Niger whence came gold and ivory in exchange for copper and other merchandise.

There had been other Italian competitors for the eastern trade. Amalfi had lost its glory in 1343 when a large part of the town was destroyed by an inundation of the sea. Pisa had been hampered by the opposition of Genoa and by complications within Tuscany. Salerno, Gaeta, Leghorn and many a smaller port had shared in the crumbs from the Venetian table. Naples, with some 100,000 inhabitants, was a metropolitan city as well as a port. Another important centre was the great cosmopolitan city of Palermo where Greeks, Latins, Moslems, and Jews occupied separate quarters of the town.

But trade was not the only sustaining force of the Italian cities; industry was also important. Venice was an important glass-making centre, and also wove silk and woollen cloth. Elsewhere in Lombardy, the woollen industry, although it had arisen later than in the north, had become important in a variety of cities—Bergamo, Bologna, Brescia, Como, Cremona, Mantua, Padua, Parma, Verona and Vicenza. Among these, Milan, with a population of perhaps 100,000, stood out as a metallurgical as well as a textile centre. Another cluster of textile towns was in Tuscany. The silk industry of Lucca, although it had lost some of its greatness, was still important. Pisa was another textile centre. But overshadowing all was Florence, with 50,000 people; her industry was built upon imported wool from England and, by this time, more particularly Spain. Machiavelli had been born in the city in 1469, and his *History of Florence*, which carries the story up to 1492, shows the importance of commercial rivalry in shaping the policy of the Italian cities. Not all cities emerged as triumphantly from the economic circumstances of the time. Some, like Siena, Pavia, Ferrara and Ravenna, took second place. Others were still farther behind and remained little more than market centres for their surrounding countrysides.

Prominent though the Italian cities were, they were not the only active agents in the commerce of the Mediterranean. Southern France was beginning to recover from a century of disorganisation. Thus the city of Montpellier, greatly reduced at the beginning of the fifteenth century, was stimulated into new activity by the enterprise of Jacques Cœur about 1440; the French competed against the monopoly of Venice and re-established contacts with Egypt, Syria and North Africa. The story of Jacques Cœur has become legendary, but it is only one indication amongst others of French activity. Louis XI (1461–83), immediately after the occupation of Roussillon, began work on the harbour of Collioure. Towards the end of his reign, he at last obtained possession of Marseilles, and announced that it was to become the emporium at which merchandise from the East would be unloaded, to be distributed to all the countries of the West. He planned the building of a great Mediterranean fleet, and, although he died before his project could be realised, he had given an impetus to French activity in the Mediterranean.

Another competitor in the Mediterranean was Aragon, which, amid the complicated politics of the western basin, had acquired the Balearic Islands and Sardinia and had extended her sway over Sicily and Naples. But these were not the only markets for Catalan wool and woollens. Catalan merchants traded with Ragusa and other ports of the Adriatic, with Egypt and the Levant generally, with the Barbary Coast, and, beyond the Pillars of Hercules, with Flanders and England. But owing to internal politics and to Italian competition, Catalan influence was in decline in the fifteenth century; it is doubtful whether Barcelona had as many as 35,000 inhabitants, and Valencia was even smaller. We have a memorial of earlier activity in the remarkably fine portolan charts of the Catalan seamen.

The interior of the Iberian peninsula had nothing to rival the cities of Italy, but, even so, its bare monotony was relieved by small centres of vivid life. 'Toledo the rich', ran the old Spanish tag, 'Salamanca the strong, León the fair, Oviedo the divine, and Seville the great.' But there were also many other centres of industry, of marketing and administration and of learning, Córdoba with its leather, Jaen with its silk and paper, Saragossa with its cloth; and besides these there were Burgos, Valladolid, Segovia, and the last stronghold of the Moors in Spain, the beautiful city of Granada. Madrid was but a small agricultural town and did not become the capital of a united Spain until 1560. In the north, the small Biscayan ports traded with Gascony and Normandy and with England and Flanders, particularly in iron and wool.

On the west lay Portugal, slow in developing a maritime trade but with possibilities. From its harbours, and especially from Lisbon and Oporto, ships carried wine and dried fruits and olive oil northwards, and there was a Portuguese agency in Bruges before 1400. But its destiny lay to the south. In the fifteenth century, with the encouragement of Prince Henry, generally known as 'the Navigator', successive expeditions sailed along the west African coast, and, incidentally, many Genoese sailors took part in these. Cape Verde was reached by 1445, and in 1461, a year after Henry's death, the Portuguese sailed into the Gulf of Guinea. In 1487 Bartolomeu Dias succeeded in rounding the Cape of Good Hope. Meanwhile, a Portuguese expedition under Covilhã had been sent out to the Near East, and had reached India by sea from Egypt. His reports encouraged further effort and, on 8 July 1497, an expedition under Vasco da Gama sailed from the Tagus river. In the following year, on 23 May, it anchored off Calicut on the Malabar Coast of India. When asked what they wanted, the Portuguese replied 'Christians and spices'. Laden with ginger, cinnamon, pepper, cloves and the like, the first ships of the return voyage reached Lisbon on 10 July 1499.

In the meantime, a Genoese sailor, Christopher Columbus, had settled in Lisbon in 1477; but, finding little response to his schemes, he left for Castile in 1484, and after a long struggle for recognition, he began his famous voyage on 3 August 1492. There is much that is obscure about our knowledge of Portuguese endeavour down the African coast, and even more controversy surrounds the aims and beliefs of Columbus. But one thing is clear. These Portuguese-Spanish achievements came not only at the end of a century but marked the end of an age. The trade of the marginal seas of Europe was now to be extended into the great oceans beyond. The life of Europe, its economic circumstances and its political character, and also its human geography, took on a new aspect.

CHAPTER III

FIFTEENTH-CENTURY CIVILISATION AND THE RENAISSANCE

IN the history of the events which changed the face of Europe around 1500, we must distinguish two interlocking developments. Besides the cultural transformation from which the term 'Renaissance' has been borrowed to describe the whole period, there was the emergence of the states-system of modern Europe. During the last decades of the fifteenth century, England, France, and Spain, after long and complex preparation, had attained national unification under strong monarchies. In addition, a bilingual state had grown up in the rich border-lands of France and Germany—the State of the dukes of Burgundy. Since France, with an estimated fifteen million inhabitants, was potentially far superior to any of her competitors and, indeed, represented a type of Great Power not yet realised elsewhere (there were only about three million inhabitants in England, six million in Spain, and hardly more than six million in the State of Burgundy with the inclusion of industrial Artois, Flanders, and Brabant), France's neighbour-states of necessity combined their resources. The German empire, France's only equal in population, could not serve as a piece on the new European chess-board because it was a loose federation of territorial states and half-independent cities under the Habsburgs, who had little power as German emperors. In its Austrian and Alpine dominions, however, this house possessed the largest and strongest of the territorial states, and so the anti-French counterpoise was built upon a system of princely marriage alliances, first (1477) between Habsburg and Burgundy, and subsequently (1496) between Habsburg-Burgundy and Spain. The years around 1500, therefore, saw the encounter of two gigantic Powers or power combinations such as had not been known to the medieval world; and when, beginning with the early 1520's, England endeavoured to become the moderator of the balance between France and Habsburg-Spain, the modern pattern of an equilibrium of states had been established on the European scene.

It was the same generation from about 1490 to 1520 which experienced the ascendancy of Renaissance art, humanism, and a new historico-political science. (The growth of natural science did not reach a comparable phase of maturity until half a century later.) However, there exists a basic difference between this cultural revolution and the political transformation. It would be difficult to contend that outside Italy the new aesthetic values in art and literature, or the fresh views opened up in education and humanistic learning, had gradually matured in interrelation with the political development. Their roots were not in the soil of the west European countries; rather they lay in a part of Europe which had not shared in the process of large-scale political integration, but was to become the helpless object of the power politics of the new giant states: the Italian peninsula. This is not to say that Renaissance culture north of the Alps was merely an importation from the south. The art of France, Flanders, and Germany in the fifteenth century leaves no doubt that there was everywhere in the air a fresh realism; not only in Italy, but also in the northern countries, a growing individualism was striving for expression. Moreover, after contact with Italy had been made, the art and literature which finally emerged showed in every European nation a different texture, according to the native traditions. Yet the Renaissance artists, writers, and scholars outside Italy, from the late fifteenth century onward, were persuaded that the new era in art, literature, education, and scholarship had had its first and model phase in Italy; that their own inherited ways were hopelessly outdated; and that no future progress was possible in any field without deliberate efforts to absorb the best that had been attained south of the Alps. What were the factors in late medieval civilisation, especially during the fifteenth century, that had produced this situation?

For many of the aspirations of the Middle Ages a turning-point was reached when the Church Councils of Constance (1414–18) and Basle (1431–49) succeeded in ending the schism, which had torn the unity of the Church but failed to satisfy the long-sustained hopes for religious reform and a moderation of the strictly monarchical fabric of the Church. The programme then frustrated had chiefly been elaborated by the medieval universities; the leaders of the party of reform had been the foremost minds of those great centres of scholastic learning which had earlier been productive of bold political philosophies and had incessantly explored and adapted to changing conditions the fundamental questions of the relation between Church and State and of the mutual obligation between ruler and people. The intellectual vigour of scholasticism in this whole area of thought was sapped when the outcome of the Church Councils put an end to all attempts at constitutional reform within the Church and made nearly absolute the power of the pope, who, as the ruler of the papal state in central Italy, was soon to be drawn into the whirlpool of the politics of the Italian tyrant states. Nor were the considerable achievements of fourteenth-century scholasticism in the natural sciences followed by comparable results after the middle of the fifteenth century. Life and teaching in the universities became characterised by lack of originality and by sterile traditionalism[1]—the accusation which is so

[1] After much debate, this is still the picture, as found for Oxford in H. Rashdall, *The Universities of Europe*, ed. Powicke and Emden (1936), vol. III, pp. 270 f.; for Paris,

often levelled by later humanists against the learning of the Middle Ages as a whole.

By the fifteenth century it was true that the day of medieval knighthood had also passed. The military service of the vassal was nearly obsolete; and the economic position of the landed noblemen, dependent as it was on easy availability of agricultural labour, had been greatly weakened by the destruction of a third or more of the European peasant population through the Black Death and the lasting economic decline that ravaged most countries in the fourteenth century. Yet it would be erroneous to think that the foremost place on the European scene was henceforth left to the bourgeoisie. The strengthening of monarchy in building up the new great European Powers created fresh opportunities for the nobility, which, side by side with the burgher class, was indispensable in the new armies and administrations, and moreover could provide splendour to the princes' entourage. The balance between burghers and noblemen and between urban and chivalric culture, during the fifteenth century, was largely to depend on the existence and the influence of central princely courts; the outcome was entirely different in each European country.

In terms of social and constitutional history, the greatest strides beyond medieval feudal conditions were made, except for Italy, in the English monarchy. The English knights had been the first to lose the status of an armed military caste; in the course of the fifteenth century they merged into a gentry no longer separated by a gulf from the commercial world of the burgher class. They intermarried and socially intermingled with the leading London merchant families, and in the House of Commons the 'Knights of the Shire' sat side by side with the burgesses from the boroughs—a mark of social equality inconceivable in the meetings of most continental estates. It would be wrong, however, to presume that, in this association, the balance of influence was equal or even gradually turned against the knightly element. Since the first decades of the fifteenth century, a growing number of the smaller parliamentary boroughs returned gentlemen to the Commons, instead of the merchants or members of the burgess class proper who had been sent during the fourteenth century; the social composition of the English parliament was changing in favour, not of the bourgeoisie, but of the gentry until, by the time of Elizabeth, there were four gentlemen to every townsman among the members.

We find a corresponding survival and even recrudescence of the traditions of gentility in the cultural life of fifteenth-century England. As Dr G. M. Trevelyan characterises the situation: if Chaucer's ghost had returned to

in A. Renaudet, *Préréforme et Humanisme à Paris* (2nd ed. 1953), pp. 98ff., 158f.; for the German universities, in G. Ritter, 'Via antiqua und via moderna auf den deutschen Universitäten des XV. Jahrhunderts', *Sitzungsberichte der Heidelberger Akad. der Wiss.* Philos.-Hist. Klasse, 1922, Abh. 7, pp. 95–9, 113–15.

the English scene in the late fifteenth century, he would have felt entirely at home although a century had passed. No fundamentally new ideas or literary tastes had emerged; the works of Chaucer were still read as if they had been contemporary productions. One might go even farther and judge that English literature had not yet fully assimilated Chaucer's best achievements. His had been a development in taste and interest from the days when he translated into English the *Roman de la Rose* and acclimatised in England the allegorical style of French knightly love poetry, to the time of the fresh realism of his *Canterbury Tales*. Literary production in fifteenth-century England did include a realistic trend, expressing itself chiefly in satirical and didactic writings; but the elaborate literary works which expressed the intellectual climate of the period between 1400 and 1500 rather continued the 'aureate diction' of the allegoric and chivalrous love-poetry of the early Chaucer. The favourite subject-matter remained the knightly epic which transformed past history into a web of legendary tales of the descent of England's knighthood from Troy, Rome, and the 'Round Table' of King Arthur.

To be sure, the century saw significant innovations and inventions. New schools were founded—among them Eton and Winchester—where the descendants of gentle and even noble families were educated along with the best talent from lower circles; as elsewhere in Europe, the period was at hand when a scholarly education became a normal part of the preparation for the man of the world. For the first time, letter writing was common in the higher strata of lay society. But wherever, as in the correspondence of the Pastons (yeoman farmers who rose into the gentry), these letters allow us to observe prevailing cultural trends, we find, besides an active interest and participation in tournaments, that the medieval bookshelf was yet unchanged, comprising epics of knightly exploits, some religious works, and a few translations (not the original texts) of ancient authors. The coming of the printed book did not immediately produce substantial changes in taste and outlook. When William Caxton, after a long life as a London merchant and representative of English commercial interests in the Low Countries, was engaged (during the 1470's and 1480's) in running the press which for England initiated the era of printing, the core of his book production, in addition to Chaucer's works, was the publication, in English versions, of the vast literature on the knights of Troy, Greece, Rome, Charlemagne, and King Arthur, the reading-matter at late medieval courts. In translating and publishing a French work entitled *The Order of Chivalry or Knighthood*, Caxton, mouthpiece of the sentiments of the London merchant patriciate, did not hesitate to comment that this was a timely book to remind forgetful England of the rules accepted in all periods of the past when English knights were known for true chivalry—especially in the memorable days of King Arthur's, Tristan's, and Percivale's noble 'manhood, courtesy and gentilness'.

The historiography of fifteenth-century England proves that a glorified knightly past was indeed the spiritual world in which the contemporaries of Caxton lived. To be sure, instead of clerics writing in Latin, wealthy merchants now composed English chronicles of their cities, especially in London; and, as a consequence, many everyday events from the burgher's life were realistically observed and recorded in every small detail. But if the composition of the vernacular *London Chronicles* emancipated the burgher from his dependence on clerical writers, this change did not mean emancipation from the standards and prejudices imposed by the predominance of chivalrous culture. Among the scenes of city life found in the *London Chronicles*, none are described with greater zest than knightly tournaments and royal processions in the town; and no attempt is made as yet to look beyond external facts and pageantry, to consider causes and effects, the value of sources, the need for selection and proportion—the features of the historiography which was to rise in the sixteenth century. In general historical works, such as the *Chronicles of England* published in final form in 1480, the background remains the fantastic tale, as told by Geoffrey of Monmouth in the twelfth century, about Brutus, grandson of Aeneas, who after his victories over aboriginal giants founded the British kingdom; the chivalrous deeds of King Arthur and the knights of his Round Table are still accepted as historical facts and used as yardsticks in all judgments on past and present. These deeds were also the theme of the greatest imaginative work of fifteenth-century England, Malory's *Morte d'Arthur*. When Caxton first published it in print, he urged his readers to believe that the stories of Arthur were not mere fiction; Malory's descriptions, he said, had given a glorified account of the greatest age in England's history.

This inability and unwillingness to break away from the world of medieval chivalry must be explained largely by social facts. From the fourteenth to the end of the fifteenth century, England, like many parts of Europe, passed through an extended period of economic stagnation. Although this was the time which saw the emergence of the figure of the clothier, the woollen manufacturer who built up capitalistic industry in a country-side unhampered by medieval city-guild regulations, the output of the English cloth industry remained almost unchanged until the great upsurge of England's economic life in the course of the Tudor era; the day of the industrial middle class still lay far in the future. The only social group of the bourgeoisie whose impact on culture could be significant in the fifteenth century was the London wholesale merchant class, which wielded the government of England's only metropolitan city and controlled her trade with the Continent. But the exclusive and privileged 'livery companies' of these merchants were by their nature less a harbinger of modern society than an epilogue to the history of medieval merchant guilds; nor did they represent a group keenly aware of its differences from the nobility, but rather formed a social stratum regularly passing into the landed gentry by intermarriage. Having acquired property in the country, the merchants merged into a half-feudal environment. Even as late as the time of Elizabeth, gentlemen of social and political importance led a seignorial existence in their counties, surrounded by a crowd of retainers, and in their turn gathering round a patron in the higher nobility. If by that time the culture of the gentry and the nobility had largely outgrown the medieval chivalrous tradition, in many respects this was due to the influence of the new aristocratic education which had first flowered at the Italian courts.

It was not until the end of the fifteenth century, however, that any serious contacts between England and Renaissance Italy were made. Up to then, journeys to Italy had not formed a part of the education of the sons of the gentry or of the London merchant aristocracy. Before 1490, English travellers to Italy had been as a rule clergy, or officials travelling in the king's service. Although these men occasionally acted as pioneers in that they brought home rare humanistic manuscripts and a love for the new learning, humanism was not to them a new education of man or a new world of ideas. On returning to England, they did not found new intellectual movements, or groups opposed to scholasticism. As a consequence, in spite of the stimulus of such pioneers, and in spite of the patronage of individual members of the English high nobility who persuaded some Italian humanists to come to England to serve as secretaries or teachers, the only tangible result was the addition of a substantial number of humanistic manuscripts to English libraries and the inclusion of some Greek in the curriculum of the old schools and universities.

Before humanism could mean more to late medieval England, the growth of humanism in Italy had to reach the stage where the classicists' enthusiasm for ancient literature and art was balanced by renewed thoughts of religion, and by endeavours to reconcile the classical legacy with the Christian tradition. After Lorenzo Valla, the great Roman humanist, had given the first example of a critical revision of the text of the New Testament, it was in the school of Neoplatonic philosophy revived in Florence that Italian scholars, foremost among them Marsilio Ficino and Pico della Mirandola, drawing upon the religious literature of classical antiquity, set to work upon a new theology in a half-classical and half-scholastic framework—a deepening of religious interest in Florence that was enhanced when the preaching of Savonarola for a while after 1490 caused a widespread estrangement from the secularism of the early Renaissance. It was in this religious-minded phase of the Renaissance that English scholarship established contacts with Italy. After a two-year visit to Italy, John Colet delivered in Oxford, from 1496 onward, public lectures on the epistles of St Paul that represented a decisive break with the methods of scholastic learning. Along paths also followed by Ficino in those years,

Paul's teaching and missionary work was here interpreted historically against the background of the pagan and early Christian period. As was the case with Ficino, Colet's was a new perspicacity in psychological insight and an understanding springing from a loving intimacy with the human personality of Paul as a biblical teacher. In his exegesis of Paul's doctrine Colet was guided by a simple kind of piety and a confidence that faith in divine grace and the right spirit were of greater account than any letter or rite. From this confidence sprang a striking unconcern for most of the abstruse problems of the theology of the schoolmen.[1]

Once this first bridge to the intellectual world of Renaissance Italy had been built, humanism in England quickly became a movement which could spread beyond the walls of the universities. In metropolitan London, owing to Colet and Thomas More, there formed a circle of men whose minds, having been shaped by the new religious learning, were soon spurred on to social and political concerns, until after the 1520's, in the latter part of Henry VIII's reign, Renaissance ideas on history and politics, on social problems and human conduct, were reaching England in an uninterrupted stream. When shortly after 1500 an Italian humanist residing in England, Polydore Vergil, detected the fantastic note of medieval legend in the accepted accounts of Brutus and King Arthur, and reconstructed the history of England in humanist fashion, his criticism was still greeted with indignation and unbelief. Yet the seeds of doubt once sown would unfold, and from the 1530's onward the world of Geoffrey of Monmouth was gradually replaced by the historical vistas created by the Renaissance in Italy.

Across the Channel, the fifteenth-century balance between monarchy, nobility, and bourgeoisie had been different. The performance of monarchy in promoting political integration was more spectacular in the French-speaking countries than anywhere else in fifteenth-century Europe. In the darkest hours of the Hundred Years War (1337–1453) and during the subsequent period of reconstruction, the Crown had been the rallying point and the salvation of France; similarly, the State of the dukes of Burgundy was a creation solely of the efforts of a younger branch of the French royal house. In France, royal power was already becoming absolute;

---

[1] That Colet's studies were influenced by Ficino is obvious from the similarity of their approaches and has been accepted as a fact ever since F. Seebohm's *The Oxford Reformers* (1867). However, as very little is known about the details of Colet's Italian journey, evidence of personal relations between the two men has been lacking. Direct contacts have now been proved by the discovery of two intimate letters of Ficino to Colet: see R. Marcel, *Bibliothèque d'Hum. et Renaiss.* XIV (1952), pp. 122 f. Another difficulty in inquiries about Colet's debt to Ficino is the late date of Ficino's commentary on Paul's epistles—between 1496 and 1499, according to P. O. Kristeller's *Supplementum Ficinianum* (1937), vol. I, p. lxxxii. But since the commentary had been preceded by lectures, its date is no obstacle to the assumption that Ficino was already engaged in his biblical studies, or was even giving his lectures, at the time when Colet stayed at Florence.

the *États Généraux* had practically lost the right of consent in matters of taxation, and the supreme judicial court, the *Parlement* of Paris, exerted only occasional checks on the omnipotence of the king. If royal centralised administration could not yet be extended to every province of the vast kingdom, its place in Orleans and Anjou, Brittany and Burgundy was taken by the princely courts and regional administrations of branch lines of the royal family, or of members of the high nobility. The work of reconstruction carried out by king and princes in the second half of the fifteenth century depended on the co-operation not only of the nobility but also of the bourgeoisie. Yet, although royal policy highly favoured the industry and commerce of the towns, the urban element in France was not so much a respected ally as a submissive favourite, closely supervised by royal officials. The leading ranks of the townsmen did not represent a commercial or industrial class with a national horizon; they rather formed wealthy local aristocracies with merely provincial interests. Their most successful elements were eager to purchase landed estates and associate themselves with the provincial noblemen. At the French courts, therefore, the forms of social life and the spirit of literature and art remained almost untouched by urban influences; the legacy of medieval chivalry continued to be the dominating factor.

To be sure, within the framework of the princely courts we meet with still another element of cultural significance. Studies of the classical authors had always flourished among the clerks in the French chancery, and in these circles, during the later Middle Ages, there existed a strong affinity of mind with the Latin classicism of Italian humanists. Frenchmen, like Italians, spoke a Romance language, and interest in surviving Latin literature had spread more widely in medieval France than in any other European country, including Italy before the coming of Petrarch. In the fourteenth century, the residence of the Papal Curia at Avignon on the banks of the Rhône had brought the two countries into close intellectual contact; Petrarch had spent his formative years in a mixed Italian-French environment at Avignon, and during the first part of his life may have found better classical texts and information among his French friends than in his native Italy. In the first two generations after Petrarch (roughly the years 1360–1420) we find the typical social life of humanists among the secretaries of the royal chancery: classical manuscripts were eagerly transcribed; letters and poems imitating ancient models were exchanged. But after the 1430's these exercises declined, apparently leaving no permanent effects.[1] The explanation is not far to seek. A chiefly rhetorical trend of studies, confined to the narrow world

---

[1] See A. Coville, *Gontier et Pierre Col et l'Humanisme en France au temps de Charles VI* (1934), esp. pp. 229–34. The decline of this early French humanism after 1430 has been disputed by F. Simone in *Convivium* (Turin, 1951), pp. 189, 193 ff., for reasons which in the present writer's opinion are not strong enough to destroy the picture drawn by Coville.

of the chanceries and lacking serious significance for contemporaneous French learning or for the values of those who were socially important, could not result in anything comparable to the organic development of Italian humanism.

Although a mature humanistic movement could not develop on so slender a basis, the long influence of classical studies on France, as well as the proximity of Italy, caused interest in some favourite ancient authors to hold its own in the culture of the French courts. From the middle of the fourteenth century, the library of the kings added to its treasures of religious and chivalrous literature a number of manuscripts of Greek and Roman works translated into French at royal request. Livy's Roman history, Cicero *On Old Age* and *On Friendship*, as well as the Aristotelian *Ethics*, *Politics*, and *Economics*, thus became available to courtiers ignorant of Latin and Greek; there were also some products of the early Italian humanists, especially Petrarch and Boccaccio. But these French versions made for princely libraries were very different from humanist translations bent on reproducing the exact text, the literary form and the historical atmosphere of the translated works; they were rather paraphrases and adaptations made up in such a way that the contents could be readily understood and borrowed as subject-matter by readers and writers eager to find an antidote against the decay of present-day chivalry in the hardiness, patriotism, and warrior virtues of the Roman 'knights'. At the court of Burgundy, cultural centre of the French-speaking countries in the latter half of the fifteenth century, the legendary history of the knighthood of ancient Troy, Greece, and Rome became the framework of all ideas on conduct, education, and even politics. Ducal secretaries collected in beautifully illuminated manuscripts all available sources on Alexander the Great, translations of the ancient historical accounts and medieval tales alike; the fabulous splendours of Alexander's court in war and peace served as a model and reflected image of social life at the Burgundian court. The knightly world of King Arthur's Round Table, still seen through the eyes of Geoffrey of Monmouth, and every available bit of information on Troy, whether wholly fictitious or from an ancient source, remained accepted parts of the picture of the past. Duke Philip the Good personally took a hand in the preparation of the *Hystoires de Troye*, the most splendid manuscript book among these collections; it was one of the continental works on chivalry later translated into English and published by Caxton.

In this atmosphere, ancient elements and Italian influences proved powerless to modify traditional ideals and the conduct of life. In the earlier development of chivalry, the knightly orders, the crusades, and the rise of the love-poetry of the minstrel had been the crowning events; they had sprung naturally from the necessities of medieval conditions. Now these memories of the past were kept alive by being turned into parts of an elaborate system and ceremonial at the courts. The knightly orders of the Middle Ages had been free associations of knights devoted to the fight for Christianity in the East. In the late fourteenth and the early fifteenth centuries new knightly orders appeared, creations of the new monarchies which, with the help of the old chivalrous symbols and social forms, endeavoured to integrate the nobility of many far-flung provinces into the new State and provide new outlets in the princely service for the ambitions of noblemen. The first of these courtly orders had been the English Order of the Garter; it was followed by the Burgundian Order of the Golden Fleece, the most magnificent and sumptuous of these foundations, continued as a Spanish institution after the union of the Low Countries with Spain. The rise of a French counterpart founded by Louis XI, the *Ordre de Saint-Michel*, and the subsequent creation of similar orders in countries as distant from each other as Savoy, Denmark, and Hungary shows the significance of the Burgundian example for courtly society all over Europe.

In these new orders, the pomp and distinction of the ceremonial were intended to keep aloft the old standards of caste and honour. At least in Burgundy, the memory even of the crusades continued to play a vivid part. Plans for a new crusade were widely made in Europe after the Turkish conquest of Constantinople in 1453; in Renaissance Italy the humanist pope, Pius II, spent all his energies and resources on futile efforts. In the atmosphere of Burgundy the plans for the crusade assumed the appearance of a thrilling courtly event—a fascinating chapter to be added to the old epic of chivalry. At the end of a ducal banquet in 1454, famed in the annals of the period for its luxury, a symbolic figure representing the Church in her humiliation appeared praying for salvation from the infidels; whereupon the duke, in a scene meant to revive the spirit of knightly valour, vowed not only his personal participation in a crusade, but even his readiness for single combat with the sultan—an oath outdone by many of the vows of the knights of the Golden Fleece. Chivalrous love and poetry, too, were turned into a planned and organised institution at the French courts. From the end of the fourteenth century, *cours d'amour* were set up among the courtiers, who in formal meetings judged delicate problems of chivalrous behaviour and love, and recited the poems they had composed in the traditional manner of knightly love-poetry. These institutions were intended to shape the minds of all the members of the court in the same mould, from the prince down to his secretaries of bourgeois descent; they all were joined together, and yet carefully differentiated one from the other, in a solemn hierarchy of princes, *grands conservateurs*, ministers, counsellors, secretaries, and many other distinct grades, of the *cour amoureuse*.

This background readily explains the spirit of the *Rhétoriqueurs*, the school which in the fifteenth century dominated French and Burgundian literature—such traits as the ostentatious rhetoric and the scorn of these writers for the vulgar world below the level of nobility; their delight in archaic forms; their clinging to the allegories and symbols of medieval poetry; and their deep pessimism and melancholy caused by the knowledge that knighthood and chivalrous love, outside the beautiful conventions of the courts, were everywhere contradicted by the realities of life.[1] There were, it is true, a few great writers of the fifteenth century who, for various reasons, were able to break loose from the pervasive influence of the school of the *Rhétoriqueurs*; in their works realistic observation and psychology gained more ample scope and produced masterpieces of literature. But since the social structure of the period so strongly favoured adherence to the outlook and the conventions of the age of chivalry, we find no literary schools determinedly opposing the dominant trend; even masters in the presentation of realistic detail did not develop into conscious rebels against the traditional ways, or become pioneers of the tendencies of the Renaissance. A great French poet of the period, François Villon, known for his blunt self-revelation, could free himself from many conformities with his time only because he led the erratic life of a vagabond; in his attitude to life and society he was a late successor of the wandering scholars of the early Middle Ages rather than a precursor of the Renaissance. Another well-known writer, Antoine de la Sale, who has been called one of the pioneers of the modern novel, shows that the realism and psychological experience of the period could well result in a satirical critique of chivalry; but his intention remained to castigate abuses and human frailties, not to propose new ways. Although La Sale had seen humanistic Italy, his hero's education, of which he gives so masterly an analysis, remains the training of a young knight through tournaments and courtly love.

In historical writing, realism and psychological penetration reached toward the end of the century a climax with Philippe de Commynes, the historiographer of Louis XI. In Commynes, condemnation of chivalry as an antiquated illusion is definite; he echoes in this attitude the spirit of Louis XI's reign (1461–83), when for a while sober concern for the political and economic reconstruction of France had overshadowed the royal patronage of traditional culture. In a measure, Commynes's ruthless probing into human motives, his maxim that success alone, not honour, counts in politics, and his pessimistic view of human nature are northern parallels to the thought of his younger Italian contemporary, Machiavelli. Yet there remains an important difference. In Commynes's historiography, these fruits of fifteenth-century realism are not used for a new causal theory in interpreting historical and political life—the ultimate attainment

[1] For the preceding and following characterisations of Burgundian culture, cf. J. Huizinga's *Der Herbst des Mittelalters* (6th ed. 1952; Engl. version, *The Waning of the Middle Ages* (1924)), *passim*, and his *Im Bann der Geschichte* (1943), pp. 326–36; for the French parallels, R. L. Kilgour, *The Decline of Chivalry as shown in the French literature of the late Middle Ages* (1937).

of Machiavelli and the Italian Renaissance. The framework in which Commynes's discerning description of detail is placed remains a naïve attribution of the causes of wars and defeats, of all historical changes, to divine intention to punish or educate. It is in the light of observations like these that the era of Louis XI falls into historical place. The realistic tendencies of his reign did not result in any permanent changes in the life of the French court and the direction of the royal patronage. Except for the modifications gradually brought about by Italian influence, the French court of the Renaissance was to continue in the chivalrous traditions of the court of the fifteenth century. And even in Louis XI's own reign one notes that among the few measures of the cool diplomat with a cultural bearing there was, as we have seen, the foundation of one of the new courtly orders. Moreover, when the history of France was written by Louis's secretaries, these *Grandes Chroniques de France* embodied all the legendary medieval traditions which were to give way to a new type of historiography only in the course of the sixteenth century, after the historical criticism of the humanists had done its work.

In the Burgundian area, a unique cultural role devolved upon the bourgeoisie of the Flemish and Brabantine cities. In an account of the art of the fifteenth century, no region north of the Alps would be represented by so many leading names as Flanders and Brabant. Indeed, the story of the growth of sensitivity to nature and the realisation of human individuality in fifteenth-century painting is to a large extent the story of the Flemish school, beginning with Hubert and Jan van Eyck. In a chapter on the rise of the new spirit in plastic art, the names of the greatest pioneer, Claus Sluter, and many of his followers would take us again to Flanders-Brabant or to the neighbouring regions. Yet, to determine the historical place of these attainments in art, we must remember also some other facts. The new trend did not originate as a genuine creation of the cities of the Low Countries; even the paintings of the 'Flemish school' were not strictly products of workshops in Flemish towns, executed in an urban atmosphere to suit the taste of bourgeois patricians. The social background of the art of the Low Countries was different from that of the art of the early Italian *Quattrocento* which arose in the civic domain of Florence and other Tuscan city-states. In Flemish-Burgundian art, the seeds were sown in an urban milieu, but the growth took place in the world of the dukes of Burgundy. Jan van Eyck and most of the other leading painters and sculptors lived, and created many of their major works, in the employment of the chivalrous ducal court, surrounded by its princely atmosphere. Their sensitiveness for minute detail in portraying man and scenery had been anticipated largely not in any urban art, but in the work of the miniaturists of the precious manuscripts produced for the libraries of the French kings and princes of the fourteenth century. In many respects the character of these medieval surroundings left its mark on the realism of the

Flemish school. As in the historiography of Commynes, the skill achieved in reproducing realistic detail was not matched by the power of organisation according to rules and laws derived from nature; the total view of the world and man's place in it remained religious, spiritual, and symbolic in the medieval manner. As a consequence, the still imperfect grasp by the Flemish artists of the human organism and of perspective did not develop into a systematic, scientific study of anatomy and optics—an indispensable contribution of the art to the mind of the Renaissance—as we find it in Italy.

The influence of the Burgundian court made itself strongly felt even inside the walls of the Flemish cities. The finely adorned town halls of Ghent, Bruges, Louvain, and other cities, built at the time, have, as a recent historian of Burgundian culture has said, an appearance more of jeweller's work than architecture; they resemble graceful shrines for relics, executed in the ornamental style characteristic of the ducal court.[1] Nothing could be farther removed from the organic simplicity which distinguishes the simultaneous architecture of the early Italian Renaissance. As for literature and poetry, the cities of Artois, Flanders, and Brabant possessed a singular type of institution: the *chambres de rhétorique* (*Rederijkerskamers* in the Germanic-speaking provinces), a secularised sequel to the medieval associations for the performance of religious miracle plays. The *chambres* in the fifteenth century served two major purposes: the training of a troupe for the performance of plays—now often moral-allegorical in content—and the constant exercise of all members in the 'art of rhetoric'. For education in this art, meetings were held in formal sessions, with a strict social ceremonial, where everyone present, in a prescribed time, had to compose and recite compositions in verse on a common theme assigned by the chairman, often a high-ranking member of the Burgundian nobility. With this emphasis on etiquette and the teachable elements of literary expression, the *chambres* were a bourgeois counterpart to the *cours d'amour* of the nobility; in both institutions the preservation of socially accepted forms and traditions far outweighed in value individual originality. A few generations later, during the sixteenth century, the *chambres* were to provide a social forum for the dissemination of new ideas, first of Erasmian humanism, and subsequently, in the northern provinces of the Netherlands, of the Reformation. But to discover the channels through which new intellectual forces first gradually spread, from the latter half of the fifteenth century onwards, we must turn our attention away from the cities of Flanders and Brabant, to cultural centres outside the sphere of Burgundy.

There were in continental western and central Europe three focal points, or areas, that kept aloof from the overpowering influence of the French

[1] J. Huizinga, *Im Bann*, p. 332.

and Burgundian courts. One was the University of Paris, the old international meeting place of European scholars. There we observe conditions which closely resemble the course of the development in the universities of England. In spite of France's proximity to Italy, the Parisian schoolmen scorned serious Italian influences and any major changes in their curriculum until the last decades of the fifteenth century. True, after 1450 a few Italian humanists had been admitted by the faculty of arts as teachers of Greek; some humanistic text-books had replaced medieval Latin grammars; and the Parisian printing presses, from their inception in 1470, produced some books of humanist interest. But these were minor innovations which did not influence the trend of studies in any of the faculties; the centre of the life of the university remained the bitter controversies between the schools of Aquinas, Scotus, and Occam, and the discussions, varying but little, of the traditional logical and metaphysical problems. Students who searched for more nourishing food in their spiritual education found satisfaction in reading the works of the late-medieval mystics. In Paris, as in Oxford, a cool reserve towards Italian humanism did not change until the latter had begun to apply the interpretative methods of classical scholarship to the Scriptures and explore humanist avenues for theology by turning attention to the mystical and religious elements in the legacy of antiquity. In Paris, too, the ice was broken about the middle of the last decade of the fifteenth century. Like Colet in Oxford, Lefèvre d'Étaples (Faber Stapulensis) in Paris at that time brought home from a journey to Italy the enthusiasm for a new learning which offered at once a training in the methods of classical scholarship, an eager interest in Plato and Neoplatonism, a fresh theological start, and the warmth of a new piety penetrating all studies. Lefèvre differed from Colet only in that the aspect of Florentine Neoplatonism chiefly grasped by him was not the interest in the epistles of St Paul, but the attention paid by Ficino and Pico della Mirandola to the ancient works on mysticism and occult sciences, on astrology and the symbolism of names—a late-classical corpus of writings which allowed a glimpse of pre-Christian piety. The interest in this body of literature was to become almost as influential as was the humanist interest in the Scriptures.

As for the later course of the relations between the French humanist movement and Renaissance Italy, in France as in England it was only after these contacts in religious sentiment and theological scholarship had been made that Italian humanism was embraced as a new attitude toward contemporary life and toward the traditions of the past. Even then the change did not come about suddenly. When Paolo Emilio, an Italian humanist in the employ of the French king, writing the early history of France about 1500, rejected the legend of the Trojan origin of the knights of France, the results of his scholarship failed to impress French writers. Not until the generation of Jean Bodin, in the second half of the sixteenth century, did the historical criticism of the Renaissance definitely begin to do away with the fantastic world of French knightly legend.

The second focal area outside the sway of French-Burgundian courtly culture was the galaxy of towns on the eastern flank of Brabant-Flanders and Burgundy, spread through the vast valley of the Rhine from its northern mouths in the lands around the Zuider Zee to Switzerland in the south. Compared with the phenomenal concentration of the cloth industry and international trade in Ghent and Ypres, Brussels and Antwerp, this eastern area was more remote and provincial, of moderate wealth, and the home of the greatest mystics in the fourteenth century; in the fifteenth, it saw the spread of a pietist movement, the *Devotio moderna*, which during the preceding century had originated in the quiet districts between the Rhine and the Zuider Zee. Among the most interesting fruits of this 'new devotion' were the 'Brethren of the Common Life', associations of men (occasionally also of women) who, though not taking irrevocable monastic vows, gave up their private property and lived a chaste and strictly regulated life in common houses, devoting each waking hour to divine service, labour, reading, and preaching of sermons, according to a prescribed schedule, the common meals being accompanied by readings from the Scriptures. Judged from the ascetic discipline and intention of this life, it had few features which distinguished it from life in a monastery; occasionally members joined a convent of the Windesheim Congregation of reformed Augustinian Canons, another reflection of the 'new devotion'. Yet even though the Brethren lived in the shadow of the monastery, the existence of associations of men who laid down their own rules for religious life without seeking guidance and supervision by any of the established orders was something new; and the consequences were felt in the Brethren's attitude towards church, theology, and education. Their confidence that a spiritual discipline similar to that of the monk was possible without binding vows, combined with their emphasis on conduct, produced a tendency to value character and piety more highly than strict adherence to rite and doctrine. To a degree, the brotherhood had this tendency in common with the mystics of the fourteenth century, but unlike them were no longer seeking the essential nourishment for the soul in mystic rapture; in the regulated life of brotherhood houses, the spirit was to be fortified by a persistent and methodical reading of the Scriptures and of devotional works of a practical educational nature. The book and the common library, therefore, were the centre of life in the houses; and even the manual labour prescribed for certain hours of day was preferably done by making careful and reliable copies of manuscripts, the sale of which would contribute to the expenses of the common life and, at the same time, help to disseminate the books in which the Brethren had found their spiritual guides.

To be sure, the books thus read and circulated by the Brethren had little in common with the intellectual interests of humanism. Nevertheless, the Brethren's dislike of abstruse theological discussions had some resemblance to the humanists' opposition to the intellectual subtlety of scholasticism; their love of books that gave spiritual and moral guidance could serve as a bridge to the humanists' love of classical poets and moralists who educate the reader's mind; and their insistence on honesty and faithfulness as an aim in manuscript copying could be a preparation for the humanists' philological accuracy in the reconstruction of ancient texts. This is not to say that the Brethren developed into humanists or on their own account produced any new secular culture; the intellectual independence and the experience of life needed for the growth of humanistic scholarship would have been difficult to find in these brotherhood houses. But the affinity to some essential aspects of humanism went far enough for the Brethren to recognise in humanist pedagogy something of their own intentions, and readily associate themselves with schools run by men who had pursued studies in Italy, or had elsewhere made contact with humanism. In such cases, the Brethren founded and supervised dormitories connected with their houses, for the pupils of the school; they thus were able to imbue the pupils' lives with their religious earnestness and methodical discipline. Indeed, so widely did they engage in this work of educational assistance that the Netherlands, Brabant, and Flanders, and even large parts of Germany, were eventually strewn with humanist schools whose unusual size and pedagogical excellence largely derived from the co-operation of a brotherhood house and the availability of dormitories under the Brethren's supervision.

As early as the beginning of the fifteenth century we find in Nicholas of Cusa a great philosopher whose mind was formed first by an education in the school connected with the Brethren at Deventer near the Zuider Zee, and afterwards by university studies at Heidelberg and in Italy; out of the marriage of northern and southern elements in Nicholas's thought emerged the first philosophy in which the spirituality of mysticism and of the 'new devotion' was fused with the mind of the Italian Renaissance. During the last decades of the fifteenth century, the leading figure bred in the atmosphere of the Netherlands was Erasmus. He did not visit Italy in his formative years, but he had as a boy in the school at Deventer found himself under the twofold influence of the Brethren and of teachers influenced by Italian humanism. Early in his life, he met Colet in Oxford. By this meeting the humanism of the Low Countries, already tinged with the spirituality and the biblical interest of the Brethren, was put in contact with the new theology and approach to the epistles of St Paul which Colet, only a few years earlier, had brought home from Italy and continued in England. Thus at the cross-roads of various northern and southern influences there emerged a biblical humanism, a school of studies which gained a foothold also at Paris, where Lefèvre became a great biblical scholar during his later years. Between 1500 and 1520, under Erasmus's leadership, biblical humanism was to be the most significant trend of humanism outside Italy.

Spreading to the Upper Rhine and south Germany, Erasmian and biblical humanism entered into a region which had been in close contact with Italy for several generations—the third major area of important cultural developments north of the Alps outside the sphere of the French and Burgundian courts. This area, too, had a marked urban character. South Germany, indeed Germany as a whole, had not produced a centralising monarchy; and the courts—or centres of administration—of the rising territorial states were still too provincial in outlook and composition to exert a decisive influence on German culture. The German lower nobility found little opportunity in princely service during the fifteenth century. It was not until the second half of the sixteenth century that the German noblemen as such began to play a predominant political and cultural role in the greater states; from then on the glamorous life of the nobility of the western courts became an object for imitation at every princely seat.

In the two centuries from 1350 to 1550 many factors had conspired in favour of the German cities and urban classes. In industry and commerce the baneful effects of the fourteenth-century epidemics were more than counterbalanced by the advantages of the country's geographic position. From the late fourteenth century onwards, the progress of long-distance inland transportation linked more and more of the east-European countries in inter-European commerce. Large eastern resources of food and raw materials supplied a substitute for German agricultural losses caused by the depopulation of the Black Death. The need for industrial goods to be used in exchange resulted in a rapid growth of new handicrafts and industries in the German cities; at the same time new mines were opened, with the consequent establishment of highly-skilled metal arts and crafts. In addition, the German cities had not yet ceased to be the centre of a network of trade spreading between England and the Scandinavian countries to the north and Italy to the south.[1]

German life in the fifteenth century, therefore, was characterised by a sharp contrast between the vigour of countless small communities—among them many half-independent imperial towns—and the weakness of all uniting and integrating forces that might have fused these teeming energies on a regional, if not national, level. The political consequences were strife among the cities and territorial states, revolutionary stirrings

---

[1] For German fifteenth-century economic history, many aspects of which still defy generalisation, cf. the chapter on 'the pre-eminence of the city' in F. Lütge's *Deutsche Sozial- und Wirtschaftsgeschichte* (1952), pp. 142 ff.; on the role of the German nobility, *ibid.* pp. 149 f.

in many social groups, and a dissatisfaction with the out-dated medieval structure of the Empire. In sculpture and painting, no modern school comparable to that of Flanders in singleness of purpose and freedom from provincialism emerged; but a new grasp of the material substance of things, and the growing ability to represent human character realistically, appeared in the art of many German provinces and towns, independently producing counterparts to the Flemish achievements. In literature and intellectual culture, too, the lack of centres with more than merely local influence was fatal to the rise of broad, let alone national, trends. But because there was so little courtly life to uphold medieval conventions and traditions, the German scholar and writer, in many provincial places, had an open mind and looked for new discoveries in the humanistic world beyond the Alps long before western scholars and writers.

In the southern parts of Germany, it early became customary for students of jurisprudence and medicine, as well as for the young patricians of Nürnberg, Augsburg, and Ulm, to attend the universities of Bologna and Padua, whence they might bring home the recent products of humanistic literature. At the same time this literature continuously reached south Germany through Italian visitors. During the earlier part of the fifteenth century, the church councils of Constance and Basle had caused a great number of Italian secretary-humanists to spend years on the Upper Rhine; Aeneas Sylvius Piccolomini (later Pope Pius II), one of the most effective humanist writers of the century, who was at one time a secretary in the imperial chancery, then played a vital role in the dissemination of new interests. Before the middle of the century, the German public had received from his pen not only a vast Latin correspondence and elaborate programmes for the *studia humanitatis* and the humanist philosophy of life, but also a pioneer psychological novel and exemplary descriptions of Germany's geography and history. Thus educated in their tastes, translators of Latin literature into the German vernacular soon took an interest in the writings in which Italian humanists of the early fifteenth century had first proposed the new ideas of humane studies and civility, of human nature, of the role of women, of public and family life; almost none of these pioneering works, made available in German by the 1470's, became accessible to French, Burgundian, and English readers in fifteenth-century translations. Equally swift among German writers was the influence of the new historiography. A semi-humanist chronicle of the city of Augsburg as early as 1456 repudiated the customary city legend that the early settlers were descended from Trojan fugitives. Thirty years later a similar criticism was applied to the history of Nürnberg, and by about 1500 the critical study of Germanic origins, based on data in Caesar and Tacitus, and of the medieval history of Germany had become a widely explored field among German scholars.

The acclimatisation of university instruction of a humanistic type was

4-2

easier in this atmosphere than at the old centres of scholasticism in Paris and Oxford. New universities whose arts faculties showed definitely humanistic interests were founded: the first, in 1460, at Basle where the influence of Aeneas Sylvius coincided with the stimulus left by other visitors to the council. Humanist beginnings such as these blended with another new tendency. The mathematical and astronomical studies which had flowered in the Occamist school of scholasticism during the fourteenth century were early revitalised in this area of cross-fertilisation between Italian influences and practical experimentation in the workshops of the German industrial towns. It was in the University of Vienna, during the 1450's and 1460's, that Peuerbach and Regiomontanus initiated the association of humanist studies with mathematics, astronomy, and mechanics that was to become an essential trait of the later Renaissance, particularly in Germany. The great part which in Dürer's day Nürnberg was to play in these fields of Renaissance science was prepared as early as the 1470's when Regiomontanus, through patrician patronage, received the observatory and the workshop he needed for his astronomical and mechanical researches. By that time Nürnberg, along with its leadership in many other arts and crafts, had also established its great place in the new art of printing with moveable types, invented on the middle Rhine by 1450.

Although the road to the Renaissance had been opened earlier in Germany than in the western countries, one must, nevertheless, not overlook the fact that those who travelled the new route were for a long time chiefly students who had spent some of their formative years in Italy, or had made contacts with Italians in south Germany; their influence remained restricted to scattered places and small circles during the fifteenth century. In Germany, as in the West, humanism did not take roots in the native soil until, towards the end of the century, it became allied to the religious interests without which no lasting effect on late-medieval lay society was possible. In the time of Erasmus, the expectation that the new studies would bring about a spiritual as well as cultural reform was crucial in giving rise to the optimism with which men faced the great intellectual changes of their own time and looked forward to the future. There had been no trace of this optimism in German literature during the fifteenth century, except in the small groups connected with Italy. German didactic poetry of the fifteenth century reveals at every turn the fact that even in Germany, where we find no magnificent courts still displaying knightly conduct, new standards had not as yet sufficiently matured to compete with the respect paid to the time-honoured virtues of the knight. Since these virtues had all but disappeared in urban society, the critics, burghers themselves, expressed the melancholy conviction that the world had become old and disjointed and was heading towards demoralisation and decay—a note sounding through all late-medieval literature. And just as Renaissance optimism and faith in new values had not as yet emerged, so

Renaissance pride in originality and unconventionality was in the fifteenth century still foreign to German urban culture. In the associations of the *Meistersinger*—the counterpart among German artisans of the *chambres de rhétorique* of the bourgeoisie of Flanders and Brabant—the traditionalism of late-medieval guild society decreed that no competing member in reciting his poems could use a tune which was not ascribed to one of the 'twelve great masters', the legendary authorities of the singers; to try to go beyond the forms once fixed smacked of presumption. It is in the humanistic milieu of Nürnberg at the turn of the fifteenth and sixteenth centuries that the singer's right to individual creation was first recognised; soon a singer was called a master only after he had invented at least one tune of his own. During the early sixteenth century, this principle—proof that growing individualism was at last breaking down traditionalism in all urban classes—became the rule for the German *Meistersinger* in all German towns.

In every European country outside the Italian peninsula we have, then, found a similar situation at the beginning of the last decade of the fifteenth century. Everywhere—Spain, which space does not permit us to include in this survey, would be a less pronounced example, but no exception—minds turned toward Italy. This contact of the north with the south was made at the point where citizens and scholars in the northern countries, having begun to free themselves from the traditions of scholasticism and chivalric culture, searched for a type of education which was at once humanist and religious; hence the key position, in the process, of Florentine Neoplatonism, the phase of the Italian development in which humanistic culture, more than in any other, seemed capable of providing a religion-motivated approach to antiquity and a devout philosophy of life. The European recourse to Italian civilisation coincided with the invasion of Italy by French armies; from then on the northern portion of the peninsula was to be an annex alternately of the French and Habsburg monarchies. Thus, from the 1490's onward, Italy became an object of incessant attention, not only for travelling clerics and scholars, but also for the diplomats and courtiers of all the European countries; and it was soon realised that religious philosophy and the critical study of the Bible, brought home from Italy by Christian humanists like Colet and Lefèvre, had been but one late phase of a much more diversified political, social, and cultural development.

A major cause of the peculiar evolution of Italy had been the history of her nobility. From the early Middle Ages, large parts of the peninsula had not known the feudal separation of the burgher class from a knighthood monopolising political, military, and cultural leadership. At least in northern and central Italy, where emperor and pope were the sole but weak overlords, most cities at an early date had developed into city-states, practically, if not legally, independent—the only republics in the western world before the seventeenth century, except a few rural and city-state cantons of Switzerland. The landed nobility had been forced to move into the adjacent cities whose ruling commercial class in most metropolitan centres, and especially in Florence, was engaged by the thirteenth century in both long-distance trade and the manufacture of woollen cloth, Europe's earliest major export industry. Through this gathering of important sections of the Italian nobility and the leading commercial and industrial groups within the same city walls there was formed, earlier than anywhere else in Europe, a relatively integrated civil society in which the balance gradually swung away from the knightly element and the chivalric tradition.

The love-poetry of the Provençal troubadours, when taken over and adapted by this Italian town patriciate, began to lose its conventionality and assumed a simpler, more personal, and more natural note; this was the trend of Italian literature at the time of Dante, about 1300. By the middle of the fourteenth century, we find in Italy a conscious reaction against the form and content of chivalrous poetry as well as of scholastic learning—a change of taste and judgment which gave to classicism, in the humanist movement led by Petrarch, aggressive power. The cultural ideals of the ancient Roman patriciate, as handed down in Cicero's writings, began to furnish a new standard; Ciceronian *humanitas* became the watch-word for an education which claimed to free man from social conventions and professional narrowness by trying to make his conduct, speech and writing a genuine expression of his own self, his moral and intellectual individuality. In Virgil's epic, it was thought, there was at hand a model of poetry echoing simple human loyalties and passions and the Roman's love of his country—a national epic free from the bizarreness of the knightly code which dominated medieval poetry. Livy seemed to fulfil a similar function for historical literature, providing a standard for the dramatic portrayal of the growth of a nation and showing, by contrast, how barbarous was delight in external pomp and irrelevant detail.

Enjoyment and considerable knowledge of the ancient poets, orators, historians, and moral philosophers had not been lacking in the Middle Ages; their study had been widespread among French and English clergymen before the rise of scholasticism, especially during the twelfth century. The novel element in Petrarch's humanism was his singleness of mind in using the Ciceronian idea of *humanitas* as a guide in the interpretation of antiquity. In spending the larger part of his life at the courts of tyrants, who by the middle of the fourteenth century had replaced republican government in many cities of northern Italy, Petrarch did not become unfaithful to his ideals. The dictator of the city-state, the *signore*, was essentially a strong, self-made personality capable of attracting an entourage of unusual men in politics and culture whom he befriended and with whom he could have informal intercourse; hardly ever was he the centre of a ceremonial built on courtly customs and the differences of caste. The intellectual climate in the tyrant-state was, indeed, initially almost as congenial as that of the city-republic to a type of culture that knew of only one form of humane contact between man and man and of only one kind of liberal education; and the triumph of Petrarch's humanism greatly helped to retard until late in the fifteenth century the slow, though eventually inevitable, transformation of the Italian tyrants' seats into new centres of courtly culture. During the greater part of the period stretching from 1400 to 1500—the *Quattrocento*—and especially at its beginning, Renaissance humanists, building on the foundations laid by Dante, Petrarch, and Boccaccio, were busy creating a culture and literature intended as the common property of educated men in all social classes—laymen as well as clergy. In the famed boarding-schools of humanist educators like Guarino da Verona in Ferrara and Vittorino da Feltre in Mantua, the same curriculum of classical studies and physical exercises was required from every pupil, even from the sons of princes.

A corollary to the feeling that a new and more valuable culture had replaced the medieval pattern was the changed perspective, in *Quattrocento* works, of the historical past and of the relationship of the past to the present. Through Dante and Petrarch—so it was argued—genuine poetry and ancient wisdom had been 'reborn' after a death-like sleep of a thousand years, just as true art had again risen as if from a grave; the subsequent resurgence of the *studia humanitatis*, the recovery of some major Latin works, among them Tacitus and Cicero's letters, and the access, facilitated by refugee scholars from Byzantium, to the authentic texts of Greek literature, seemed to introduce an age which, if it did not equal antiquity, marked the beginning of fresh achievements in all fields of culture. It should be noted that this confidence grew in Renaissance Italy at the very time when in those countries which still accepted the code of chivalry we find widespread a melancholy feeling of decay.

To be sure, had the freedom of the city-state been replaced everywhere in northern and central Italy by dictatorial *signorie* and all Italy become an area of monarchic rule, the strongly urban and civic strain in Italian culture could hardly have survived far into the Renaissance. But during the two generations from 1390 to 1450, the bourgeois element in the Italian republics—although the time of its greatest industrial power and predominance in European trade had then already passed—gained buoyancy and prestige by the defence of city-state independence and civic freedom in a crucial struggle with tyranny. At the close of the fourteenth century, the strongest tyranny, that of the Visconti of Milan, had by incessant expansion reached the point where it was threatening to transform northern and central Italy into one absolute monarchy. If this had happened, *Quattrocento* Italy would not have become an area of great, stimulating variety within small compass, a civilisation with a city-state basis in some respects akin to the pattern of ancient Greece; and the Italian Renaissance would not, by her own experience, have been uniquely prepared for the historical rediscovery of the ancient world. Owing to a determined Florentine-Venetian resistance, however, Milan by the middle of the century was restricted to the region of Lombardy; and meanwhile the republics of Florence and Venice had built up regional states of their own while, as a consequence of the establishment of a balance of power, a number of minor free cities and tyrannies had also managed to survive. Upon these foundations there emerged in the second half of the fifteenth century a system of five major states differing greatly from each other by their histories and institutions (the republics of Venice and Florence, the duchy of Milan, the kingdom of Naples, and the Papal States): the first modern example of an interrelated family of states guided by the idea of equilibrium through continual readjustment of the balance of power.[1]

The political struggle of the early *Quattrocento* and the resultant pre-servation of republican freedom side by side with tyranny left lasting marks on humanistic thought. By studying the constitutional life of the ancient city-states from Greek sources, now read in their original texts, and by appraising against this background the history of the modern Italian city-states, the humanists of the early *Quattrocento* paved the way for the political science and the historiography of the Renaissance. In their endeavour to understand the natural causes of the emergence of the Italian system of states out of the dying body of the Empire, they came to question the basic assumptions of medieval historiography—the faith in the divine ordainment of a universal empire, heir of Rome, and the hap-hazard methods by which the cities and noble families of medieval Europe had traced their pedigrees to Troy or Rome, to Aeneas or Caesar. In Italy these legends were in the early *Quattrocento* replaced by a realistic reconstruction of the historical roles of the republic and the monarchy in ancient Rome; the genesis of Florence, Venice, and Milan was conceived in the framework of the pre-Roman civilisations, Rome's colonisation of Italy, the later decay of the Roman empire, and the cataclysms of the

---

[1] For this estimate of the political situation, cf. N. Valeri, *L'Italia nell'età dei principati dal 1343 al 1516* (1950), esp. pp. 189ff., 260ff., and H. Baron, *The Crisis of the Early Italian Renaissance: Civic Humanism and Republican Liberty in an Age of Classicism and Tyranny* (1955), esp. pp. 7ff., 315ff., 379ff. L. Simeoni, *Le signorie* (1950), attempts to make a stronger case for the Visconti, and the tyrant-state in general.

Interpretations of the *Quattrocento* emphasising social-economic rather than social-political factors are numerous, but, until now, have resulted in a confusing variety of views. Besides the older theories of W. Sombart (*Der Bourgeois*; in Engl. trans. *Quintessence of Capitalism*) and A. v. Martin (*Sociology of the Renaissance*), cf. F. Antal's *Florentine Painting and Its Social Background* (1947), together with the criticisms by T. E. Mommsen, *Jour. Hist. Ideas*, XI (1950), pp. 369ff. and M. Meiss, *Art Bulletin*, XXXI (1949), pp. 143ff. For the divergence of viewpoints see also C. M. Cipolla, *Economic Hist .Rev.* (1949), pp. 181ff.; A. Sapori, *Atti del III. convegno internazionale del Rinascimento, 1952*, pp. 107ff.; R. S. Lopez and H. Baron, *American Hist. Rev.* LXI (1956), pp. 1087ff.

Germanic migrations. Thus the histories of the regional states of *Quattro-cento* Italy became the early models of the new historiography which, in most cases not until a whole century later, superseded the medieval myths of the past in all European nations.

Another mark left by the early *Quattrocento* on the humanistic mind was produced by the values which determined the citizen's outlook on life. Petrarch and his contemporaries had read the classical writings on moral conduct with the eyes of devout late-medieval laymen; ancient wisdom and Christian persuasion appeared to them at one in giving pre-ference to the contemplative life, and in teaching renunciation of material goods and the need to free the mind from passion. It was because of this interpretation that Petrarch's treatises on moral questions immediately became so popular all over Europe. In Italy after 1400, however, the citizen's pride in his own way of life, and the increasing knowledge of antiquity, combined to bring on a revolt against such concessions to the ascetic view. Nature, so it was argued, had equipped man for action and usefulness to his family and fellow men; the culture of the humanist was not to lead man into seclusion. Also, material possessions must not be viewed merely with suspicion; for they provide the means for virtuous deeds, and the history of man has been his progress in becoming lord of the earth and its resources. Passion, ambition, and the striving after glory are springs of action for a noble mind; they must be encouraged in a humanistic education. There was no branch of humanist literature in early fifteenth-century Italy where some of these ideas did not play a part, and even in the later phases of the Renaissance, when movements dif-ferent in spirit had risen in philosophy and literature, the early humanist philosophy of life remained a spreading and transforming influence. The views of human nature, history, and politics, found in the generation of Machiavelli and Guicciardini, were still substantially moulded by this influence.[1]

By the time of Machiavelli, however, Italy had gradually reverted to some of the social conditions and cultural trends from which Renaissance civilisation had been turning during the first hundred years after Petrarch. But, though from the second half of the *Quattrocento* onwards certain

---

[1] For these interpretations of humanist *Quattrocento* culture and its relations to the society and the politico-historical ideas of the Renaissance, see E. Garin, *Der italienische Humanismus* (1947; Ital. version, *L'umanesimo italiano: filosofia e vita civile nel Rinasci-mento*, 1952); H. Baron, *The Crisis*, and R. v. Albertini, *Das florentinische Staatsbewusstsein im Übergang von der Republik zum Prinzipat* (1955). Cf. also A. Renaudet, 'Le Problème Historique de la Renaissance Italienne', *Bibliothèque d'Hum. et Renaiss.* IX (1947), pp. 21 ff., R. Spongano, 'L'umanesimo e le sue origini,' *Giorn. stor. della lett. ital.* CXXX (1953), pp. 289 ff.; and the chapter 'The Early Humanist Tradition' in W. K. Ferguson's *The Renaissance in Historical Thought* (1948). A different appraisal of early Italian humanism —seen basically not as a new philosophy of life and history, but as continuation, on a higher level, of the work of 'medieval rhetoricians' in grammar, poetry, and eloquence— has been given by P. O. Kristeller, 'Humanism and Scholasticism in the Italian Renais-sance', in his *Studies in Renaissance Thought and Letters* (1956).

medieval traditions were resumed, they reappeared transformed by the spirit of the Renaissance. One of these regressions was a marked change in the character of the Italian courts. During the period of a stabilised states-system after 1450, a new courtly society and nobility developed in some of the monarchical states, particularly in Milan where the influence of France was strong, as well as in the Ferrara of the Este family and in the Mantua of the Gonzaga, both of whom had risen as vassals of the Empire and had preserved a certain air of feudal lordship even through the early Renaissance. It was especially in these courtly circles that the knightly themes of the medieval epic and the ideals of chivalry were revived. Until about 1450, the legends of the knights of Charlemagne and of King Arthur had been used in Italy as popular entertainment by wandering singers; during the second half of the century they were admitted to literature as an alluring subject for romantic poetry—even in Florence, in the circle of Lorenzo de' Medici. Before the invading French armies appeared on the peninsula, Matteo Boiardo at the court of Ferrara wrote his *Orlando Innamorato*, the work which introduced a new phase in the history of medieval epic traditions. Yet this resumption of long-discarded themes meant a revival merely on the plane of artistic imagination; neither the medieval faith in the historicity of the glorious knightly feats nor the medieval mingling of legend with historical truth were really renewed. A measure of irony pervaded the resurgent admiration for chivalrous bravery, loyalty and love, revealing a state of mind no longer medieval. It is in a similar light that we must view the late Renaissance recasting of the ideal of the perfect courtier, which was to find its most mature expression in Baldesar Castiglione's *Il Cortegiano*, published in 1528, but begun as early as about 1510. In contrast to the civic character of early humanistic education, the new idea of the 'courtier' appears to be a throw-back to the standards of a noble class. Yet, as conceived by Castiglione, the *cortegiano* was the *uomo universale* of the Renaissance; in substance, this notion of the courtier had not grown from the soil of medieval knighthood, but was a transformation of the humanistic programme for the culture of a rounded personality, built on the training of the body and the mind as well as on encouragement of ambition and every noble passion befitting human nature.

In late *Quattrocento* philosophy, the secularism of the early Renaissance was thrust into the background through both the re-emergence of Neoplatonism and a religious reinterpretation of Aristotle's thought. The Englishmen and Frenchmen who felt a kindred spirit in Ficino were correct in thinking that Italy, after long concentration on the problems of the temporal life, had returned in many respects to spiritual interests and a devout attitude of mind. From the beginning of his career as a philosopher, Ficino had rejected some of the basic tenets of the early humanists: their insistence on the inseparable unity of soul and body, their high esteem for material goods, their preference for the active life and neglect of the values of contemplation. The basic ideas of Ficino's and Pico della Mirandola's metaphysical speculation, their abstract logical arguments, the very structure of their writings did, indeed, testify to a reversion to medieval and partly even to scholastic thinking. Yet, within this framework, Ficino as well as Pico conceived the position of man in the universe, his dignity and creative powers, in terms that were the language of the Renaissance. Ficino's Neoplatonism, in spite of its ascetic and scholastic elements, was moulded by the humanistic spirit of Plato's dialogues more profoundly than any medieval philosophy had been. And if Ficino's view of life reflected a waning of the early *Quattrocento* civic spirit—a waning ultimately caused by the rise in Ficino's day of a disguised *signoria* in Florence under Lorenzo de' Medici—still the relationship of Lorenzo, the first Florentine citizen, to artists and men of letters bore little similarity to the patronage at late-medieval princely courts. Social contact in Lorenzo's circle was the fulfilment of the ideals of human companionship that had guided Italian humanists since Petrarch: a conscious attempt to revive the ancient forms of cultured association as they were found in Cicero's and Plato's dialogues and letters. Some of Ficino's northern visitors during Lorenzo's last years could still attend the informal meetings of friends in the 'Platonic Academy' whose members, emulating Plato and his disciples, gathered in Lorenzo's villa at Careggi for philosophical discussion and a social life in which art and music played a foremost part. It was in these gatherings, and through the work of Ficino, that the Platonic philosophy of love obtained the central position in Renaissance thought that it continued to occupy in European literature, philosophy, and art during the sixteenth century.

The meeting in the 1490's of northern scholarship with the Italian humanistic Renaissance, then, was fraught with potentialities for the future of European culture. Although the 'new learning', which was rising at Oxford, London, Paris, in the Low Countries, in the Rhinelands, and in Spain, was meant to give direction to religious studies, its actual effect was like the opening of a window looking out on the wide new world that in the course of two centuries had emerged in Italy. Thenceforth the assimilation and adaptation of the Italian achievements in education and politico-historical thought, in literature and art, in social intercourse and in the philosophy of man, became a basic task of all cultural life. The performance of this task was mainly the work of the period from 1490 to 1520 when the Renaissance issued forth as a movement European in scope; but the process was to go on until the seventeenth century, during the long years in which the Reformation, the overseas discoveries, and the beginnings of modern natural science gradually reversed the cultural balance between Italy and the rest of Europe.

CHAPTER IV

THE PAPACY AND
THE CATHOLIC CHURCH

AFTER the long period of strife brought about by the Great Schism, the Church had at last become reunited. Rallying round Nicholas V (1449), it seemed as though, in a less troubled atmosphere, it would now pursue its unchanging ideal. There resounded once more the two words which symbolised its twin aspirations: at home, reform; abroad, crusade. Both were of pressing necessity. Perspicacious minds in every country were calling for a far-reaching reform of the Church and hoping —somewhat vaguely, it is true—for something of a return to the purity of earlier times. As far as the crusade against the Turks was concerned, events which moved daily more rapidly were enough to prove, even to the most indifferent, that it had become inescapably necessary. From then on, and for a long time to come, reform at home and crusade abroad were to occupy a prominent place in papal speeches—in speeches and bulls rather than in deeds.

Indeed, by the middle of the fifteenth century, the Renaissance was already to some extent bursting upon Italy, and the brilliance with which it was spreading was to dazzle the Papacy itself no less than the nations. Nicholas V, a first-rate scholar (he it was who founded the Vatican Library), was to be the first 'Renaissance Pope', and his decision to pull down the old basilica of Constantine and put up in its place a building in keeping with the spirit of the new age was a sign of his propensities and tastes. His decision, it should be added, has been criticised as an act of vandalism. The brilliance of the Renaissance was to be so intense as to blind the pope to every other ideal and lead the Holy See into a course where temporal glory and artistic splendour pushed spiritual matters into the background. Even an event as spectacular as the capture of Constantinople by the Turks (1453) could not rouse the already lukewarm fervour of the Christian world, nor did it effectively tear the Papacy away from preoccupations primarily concerned with earthly glories—or even, more sordidly, from mere family ambitions.

Calixtus III, a fiery Spaniard, appeared for a time as the prophet and champion of the crusade: the papal fleet—the first amazing venture of the Papacy in this sphere—was a bold but short-lived achievement. On the other hand, with this pope—the first of the Borgias—nepotism, the curse of his and the succeeding century, began to poison the atmosphere of Rome. Pius II (Aeneas Sylvius) was the perfect example of a humanist pontiff. An engaging personality, this pope left an extensive literary production: in addition to a novel, *Euryalus and Lucretia*, and a comedy, *Chrysis*, both written moreover before he took orders, mention may be made of the voluminous correspondence in which his discerning mind is often in evidence, and his *Commentaries*, which are still of great historical interest, even if they are not always completely objective. Circumspect and adaptable in diplomacy, this pontiff seemed to be marked out for great undertakings, and especially to organise at last the crusade which had been so dear to his predecessor. But the results of his activities were disappointing in the extreme. He was doubtless sincere in appealing for a crusade, but could he really believe that such an enterprise would succeed? His famous bull *Exsecrabilis*, a clear affirmation of pontifical absolutism, was to re-echo for many a year. Europe was already irretrievably split up and torn apart; the old common ideal had been abandoned little by little: these were not encouraging factors, and the pontiff soon realised it. Because of his assertion, tinged though it was with despair, of the traditional Christian ideal of universality, he is to our minds, as has been said, the last great pope of the Middle Ages.

After him, the decline of the Papacy became more marked. Paul II, a luxury-loving Venetian, was certainly not the man to restore an unstable situation. And what can we say of the three 'evil geniuses of the Church', Sixtus IV, Innocent VIII and Alexander VI? The shameless nepotism of Sixtus IV, and his violent and extortionate policy are damning to his memory. He can, of course, be regarded as a great figure of the Renaissance scene, a typical Maecenas, but was not that characteristic in his day of many an Italian princeling, with whom he has all too close a resemblance by virtue of his territorial ambitions and aggressive absolutism? Already the nations, and the Germanic world in particular, were about to give vent to their bitterness and rancour and to cast their vehement *gravamina* in his face. Already cracks were showing in the Christian edifice, symptomatic of the split to come. Nor were the pitiless methods and plundering cruelties of the Spanish Inquisition likely to enhance the prestige of the Papacy, whatever may be thought in other respects of such a variously judged figure as Torquemada. More ominous still, if that is possible, were the eight years of the pontificate of Innocent VIII: it was then that nepotism and financial exaction reached their evil height. 'The Lord desireth not the death of a sinner', said his vice-chamberlain, 'but rather that he may live and pay.' To this pontificate the bull *Summis desiderantes* belongs: sinister in its renown, it was to give a powerful stimulus to trials for witchcraft (1484). Shortly afterwards, the fearful *Malleus maleficarum* (1487) was to become a manual for inquisitors. This pontificate touched a baseness unheard-of until then: internal reform, which had been scarcely tackled, marked time; as for crusade, no one believed in it any longer. If the masses persisted in their trusting submission to the Holy See, the *élite* and the rulers themselves were either lacking in deference or openly rebellious, and the example of George Podiebrad, the king of Bohemia, was not easily forgotten. For a long time to come, the threat of an appeal to a general council was to be a constant bugbear to the popes.

While the Papacy, forgetful of the great part it ought to have been playing, was becoming involved in paltry family intrigues and weakening its authority by agreeing to unfortunate compromises, the first official Turkish embassy arrived at Rome at the end of November 1490. The astonishing story of Jem, son of Mehemmed II and brother of Bāyezīd (p. 398), symbolised papal policy towards the Turks, a venal policy lacking in perception. Meanwhile, tremendous events were taking place, among them the discovery of the New World. The year 1492 saw Christopher Columbus landing in America and at the same time Rodrigo de Borgia, thanks to agreements notoriously tainted with simony, ascending the throne of St Peter. By a curious mockery, the widening of the world's horizons coincided with the accession of the man least worthy of the supreme pontificate.

It would be difficult to be better endowed by nature than was Don Rodrigo de Borgia, elected pope in 1492 as Alexander VI, but it would be almost impossible to make worse use of such remarkable gifts. Consequently, this disconcerting pope has been most severely judged. There can be no question here of pleading for such a man, still less of sketching out any kind of rehabilitation as certain historians have somewhat unsuccessfully tried to do. It is true that he typified, to the highest degree, Renaissance man: he had a versatile intelligence, extraordinary energy, boundless ambition, but he was also completely unscrupulous. There is no need to dwell upon the excesses and crimes, exaggerated even further by legend, of a family always treated by the pope with unpardonable weakness. Many of his contemporaries, accustomed though they were to the scented scandals and sumptuous horrors of the Italian courts of the time, cried shame.

The tragedy of the Savonarola affair was due above all to the violent contrast between this reforming friar and the unworthy pontiff. Prompted by ardent zeal and sincere piety, the friar from Ferrara, Girolamo Savonarola, like so many others, was consumed with a desire to reform the Church, restore it to its early purity and wrest it from the hands of questionable pastors. Like so many preachers of that time, Savonarola liked to make the crowds tremble with his impassioned and vaguely prophetic sermons. The pope, for long indifferent, was roused only when he himself was personally attacked with extraordinary violence. Furthermore, the astonishing dictatorship which Savonarola for several years exercised over a Florence he held in subjection, had brought hatred upon his authority, which had at first been easily accepted. The excesses in which Savonarola's partisans unhesitatingly indulged have often been described;

similarly, the festivals and ceremonies established by the dictator enjoyed long-lasting fame and still seem a strange phenomenon. It is difficult to imagine that the Florentines enjoyed those dances of old men or burgesses garlanded with flowers, those masquerades which, far from ennobling it, made a laughing-stock of religious feeling. To be sure, together with these childish things, more serious and comparatively new ideas might be discerned, even if only the relatively democratic conception of his 'popular government', but in that too the extravagances of a few fanatics ruined everything. In an atmosphere of extreme nervous tension—as also amid a strange tangle of obscure political intrigues—Savonarola did not perceive that Florence would soon slip from his grasp and that events were turning in the pope's favour. The historian is bound to record, with some regret, that the reformer's excellent intentions, warped by an obvious lack of balance, were leading to a frankly intolerable régime: vexatious dealings worthy of the Inquisition coupled with grotesque ceremonies were scarcely capable of restoring morals! Events followed each other in quick succession once Savonarola had been excommunicated—a punitive weapon whose edge was not yet blunted in the eyes of public opinion. The absurd tragi-comedy of trial by fire, which revived the atmosphere of real scenes of ordeal from the later Middle Ages, was fatal to the reformer and hardly allows him to be considered as a forerunner of modern ideas. Soon afterwards, he was executed (May 1498) and, in the unwonted seething of passions and din of war, he was quickly forgotten. Much later, Savonarola was to be claimed as one of the precursors of the Protestant Reformation, an opinion widely held, but ill founded.

For all its bewildering character, this episode was as nothing compared with other events that were taking place, and as yet it shook the prestige of the Papacy less than might have been expected. Clear proof of this is to be found in the pope's celebrated arbitration between Spain and Portugal in the matter of the immense territories discovered by Columbus and his successors.[1] Admittedly, it was believed that it was a question of a few islands rather than a whole continent, and that is perhaps why they were treated in a series of bulls as being within the jurisdiction of papal suzerainty over 'islands', a theory which had long been put forward. Hence the six 'Alexandrine Bulls', spread over the years 1493–1501, the most important of which was that of 28 June 1493 (*Inter cetera*), called the 'bull of demarcation'. This partition of newly-discovered lands was perhaps purely medieval in conception: it was certainly already an anachronism whose stupidity the Maritime Powers of the future, England, France and the Low Countries, were later to show.

In their turn, the pope's constant efforts to establish the redoubtable members of his family firmly on Italian soil were not destined to be any

[1] L. Weckmann, *Las bulas alejandrinas de 1493 y la teoría política del Papado medieval, estudio de la supremacia papal sobre islas* (Mexico, Instituto de Historia, 1949).

more successful. In the European imbroglio resulting from the development of the wars in Italy, in which the kings of France experienced illustrious triumphs no less than crushing defeats, the machinations of a pope like Alexander VI could only bring feeble repercussions in their wake. Discredited because he had toadied too much to the French king Louis XII (in the matter of the latter's divorce, an insolent farce that had shocked public opinion), dishonoured by his private life and the infamies and cruelties of his family, would the pope yet lead Christendom on a Turkish crusade? The Turks, assuredly, still constituted a threat, but in a Europe torn asunder Alexander VI was the last man to awaken the enthusiasm needed in such undertakings. He was much more liable to enter into tortuous intrigues with the infidel, intrigues such that it has been said that his policy was Turcophil.[1] So it was not surprising that the show of force made by the Christian fleets in the Aegean Sea in 1501–2 did not produce brilliant results. The crusading idea was dead indeed.

In almost every state, on the other hand, the tendency towards the establishment of a national Church was becoming more and more marked, and this disruptive movement was all the more serious because at that time the signs of incipient nationalism were making their appearance. Maximilian in Germany and Louis XII in France were dreaming, one of a German national Church, the other of a Gallican Church, each strictly subject to its respective sovereign. In France, the kings boldly made play with the Pragmatic Sanction (below, p. 302) in the face of an irresolute Papacy. The same tendencies, with slight differences, were to be seen in Spain, in England and even in Italy. The Papacy reacted only half-heartedly, satisfied with day-to-day settlements and compromises.

As for the question of internal reform of the Church, which was still being debated, no real progress could be discovered: while enlightened opinion persisted in demanding it, the Papacy never succeeded in drawing up a coherent programme of reforms. It was thus only a question of a few isolated attempts inconsistent in method. For this reason, the Fleming Jean Standonck (1443–1504) deserves to be remembered. His ideal of austerity and asceticism, belonging therefore to the Middle Ages, was not always very much appreciated, and his already out-of-date ideas earned the gibes of Erasmus. On the other hand, the spiritual exercises recommended by Jean Mombaer (1460–1501) hardly sufficed to bring about a revival of piety. On the whole, in spite of the zeal of these reformers and their disciples, its effects were most insignificant, except perhaps in the Iberian peninsula where, notably as a result of the efforts of Cardinal Jiménez de Cisneros, the seeds of the great mystical movement of the sixteenth century were beginning to grow.

If the pontificate of Pius III, which lasted a mere three weeks, deserves

[1] H. Pfeffermann, *Die Zusammenarbeit der Renaissancepäpste mit den Türken* (Winterthur, 1946).

to be mentioned only in passing, we must, on the other hand, dwell at length upon that of a pope who was an exceptionally powerful figure, Julius II. The life of this nephew of Sixtus IV had been eventful, and in the course of a brilliant career he had shown indomitable energy and vigorous administrative ability. A passionate, warlike spirit, better fitted for violent activity than for meditation, thus it is that this pope appears in Raphael's famous picture which has been so often reproduced and interpreted: tight lips, flashing, deepset eyes, 'terrible' as his contemporaries averred.

His undeniably successful domestic policy led to a secure restoration of papal power in the states of the Church which, until then, had been devastated by constant anarchy. Within a short time, Julius II had removed the redoubtable Caesar Borgia, who had been so powerful a few years earlier, made the most turbulent of the feudal nobles see reason, and put down brigandage. Making bold to pursue a policy of his own, this pope, endowed with the gifts of a warrior, did not hesitate to lead in person more than one expedition, to the stupefaction of a Europe which was nevertheless accustomed to spectacles that would appear scandalous today. His rapid conquest of Perugia, then of Bologna, gave the pope the opportunity of celebrating his successes with a ceremonial which was rather too vivid a reminder of the triumphal processions of Roman emperors (1507). From then on, Julius II was to be at the centre of every diplomatic manœuvre. It was he who organised the struggle against Venice, which was quickly crushed thanks to the support he received from France (1509); then it was he who, unscrupulously changing his policy, restored that same Venice whose humiliation had been too great, and took steps to create the Holy League against the French, whose ambitions he dreaded and whom he wished to drive out of Italy. The most spectacular episode of these wars was the siege and capture of the fortress of Mirandola in midwinter: the pope, helmeted, directed the operations in person, in exceptionally cold weather. Naturally, his prowess earned the admiration of some, Machiavelli for example, but it scandalised enlightened people, and rightly so. His was undoubtedly a bold policy, fruitful in its immediate consequences, but fraught with tremendous risks for the future. Finding it necessary to play off the principal sovereigns one against the other in succession, Julius II turned Italy into a battlefield for a long time and drew down upon his country those 'barbarians', as he termed them, whom he earnestly desired to destroy. All that was gained from these things, for civilisation if not for the Church, was that the new principles of the Italian Renaissance spread through a Europe that was still very medieval.

This unleashing of acts of violence by a pope was ill-received by those who were still able to preserve sound judgment. Suffice it here to recall the celebrated passages directed by Erasmus against the pope who filled him with horror. In the *Praise of Folly* (1511) the humanist wrote these lines in which Julius II, though not expressly named, could not fail to be recognised:

Although in the Gospel the Apostle Peter says to his divine Master: We have left all, and followed Thee, yet the popes call His patrimony lands, cities, tribute, principalities; for which, being enflamed with the love of Christ, they contend with fire and sword, and not without loss of much Christian blood, and boast that they have then most apostolically defended the Church, the spouse of Christ, when the enemy, as they call them, are valiantly routed....Here you'll see decrepit old fellows acting the parts of young men, neither troubled at their enormous cost nor wearied with the labour involved..., becoming, in short, the scourges of the human race.

The allusion was transparent, and no one mistook it. The same criticisms were to be found in the *Querela Pacis* of 1517:

What have the helmet and mitre in common? What connection is there between the crozier and the sword? between the Holy Gospel and the buckler? How, O bishop standing in the room of the Apostles, dare you teach the peoples the things that pertain to war?

Lastly, the pamphlet entitled *Julius exclusus a coelis*, attributed to Erasmus without altogether conclusive evidence, gives expression in bitter terms to the indignation felt by the enlightened section of the Christian world at conduct which was far indeed from being evangelical.

The pontificate of Julius II also witnessed one of the most conspicuous episodes in the struggle between conciliar trends and papal absolutism, a struggle whose progress, since the Great Schism, had been marked by resounding events. Already in the middle of the fifteenth century, Pius II had most clearly and solemnly expressed papal doctrine in his bull *Exsecrabilis*, but the conciliar movement favoured the sovereigns' interests too much to disappear quickly. The end of the fifteenth century indeed saw the popes still asserting their absolutism, but it also witnessed the revival of conciliar doctrine by certain princes. Louis XI, the king of France, for example, had used and abused this threat in his dealings with Sixtus IV, and he was not alone in doing so. Later, Alexander VI had for long feared that he might be deposed by a council. Under Julius II the struggle was resumed with extraordinary intensity. In 1509 the pope had solemnly reaffirmed the terms of the bull of Pius II; for his part, the king of France, Louis XII, whom the policy of Julius II had just isolated on the level of international politics, attempted to bring about a signal victory for the conciliar thesis by prevailing upon a few cardinals who were zealous in his service to call a general council at Pisa (16 May 1511). To this Julius II retorted by calling a council himself—also a general one—for 19 April 1512 at the Lateran. It is impossible to imagine the two opposing theories confronting each other more vigorously: in the sight of contemporary opinion, the test was to be decisive.

The beginnings of Louis XII's attempt, which was in any case wavering, augured badly. Only a very small number of cardinals consented to go to Pisa, and no one could believe that this small group of dissentients represented the Universal Church. It was quickly realised that the members of this council were merely the unenthusiastic instruments of French policy. So this council—or rather this 'conciliabulum', as its adversaries called it—could only drag on a languishing existence, knowing that it was in a false position and doomed to failure from the start. A few prelates devoted to the service of the king of France tried in vain to stage an impressive manifestation; they went as far as arraigning the pope and promulgating a decree of suspension against him (21 April 1512). But this produced practically no effect. The pope then contemplated making a counterstroke which proves that the papal claims of the time of Gregory VII and Innocent III were not yet forgotten: the throne of the king of France would be declared vacant and the crown transferred to Henry VIII of England! However, the pope no doubt realised that such a decision was out of date and that it would be impossible to carry it out, for the brief which he prepared on it was never more than a draft, and most of his contemporaries knew nothing of it, while for us it is only a curiosity of history, though rich in implications.

The period of the 'council' of Pisa witnessed on both sides the birth of a polemical literature which is one of the first modern examples of the use of propaganda in politics. The pope and the king of France exerted themselves in its use whole-heartedly and with equal violence. But, in the long run, these innumerable pamphlets and the theatrical performances in which the pope was shown with ludicrous or hateful characteristics succeeded only in confusing and dismaying public opinion which, almost exclusively, disliked the idea of setting up the council against the pope. It was all too easy for the supporters of the king of France and the Council of Pisa to stigmatise the machinations of Julius II, his warlike frenzy, his tortuous political manœuvring and his neglect of the traditional role of the church as peacemaker. But, in spite of the veritable profusion of methods used, there was scarcely any response from the masses. It must not, indeed, be forgotten that the people on the whole still respected the papacy, even though it might be represented by an Alexander VI or a Julius II. From many points of view, the general atmosphere was still very much that of the Middle Ages, and it was not to change for at least two generations. French opinion was weary of quarrels to which it could see no solution, weary also of the Italian expeditions which it vaguely felt to be futile in the political sphere. When news of the military disasters of 1512 was spread abroad, everyone realised that the days of the Council of Pisa were numbered. On the other hand, the Fifth Lateran Council, solemnly opened by Julius II on 3 May 1512, appeared more and more clearly to be winning over the majority of prelates. The spiritual sanctions it decided on against the king of France and his supporters made a great impression, and the king himself, wavering even before then, was very much shaken. From then on, it became clear that the Council of Pisa would have an inglorious end: soon afterwards, its members dispersed.

And so it was a triumph for the pope. Indeed, in January 1513 a real 'Roman triumph' was given to Julius, the 'liberator of Italy'. This was proof enough that the pope had acted much more as an Italian prince than as head of the Universal Church. One can imagine the pope's immeasurable satisfaction at seeing himself depicted in the guise of an emperor wielding an earthly sceptre. It was not to be his to enjoy for long. A few weeks later, this extraordinary pope lay dying: he had been, for but a short space, it is true, the 'arbiter of the whole world'.

Severe judgment must be passed on this pope who was admired by Machiavelli. Many of his contemporaries were greatly distressed by the methods he so brazenly made use of and which were unworthy of the leader of Christendom. The Florentine historian, Guicciardini, in a very objective judgment, wrote:

He would have been a pope worthy of the highest renown if he had been a secular prince or if the care and diligence he showed in glorifying the church in the temporal sphere and through the art of war had been used to glorify it in the spiritual sphere through the arts of peace; yet he was worthier than any of his predecessors to be honoured and held in illustrious remembrance.

This exceptional man, born for pomp and war, a protector of the arts and a military commander, had the soul of a founder of empires, but was not cast in the mould of the leader of a church whose aim was to be universal.

The sixteenth century was formerly often called the 'Age of Leo X'; one may at least say that the personality of the successor of Julius II is not to be disregarded. Giovanni de' Medici, son of the great Florentine Lorenzo the Magnificent, was elected, while still very young, on 11 March 1513, and his election was favourably received. The Christian world had grown weary of the warlike exuberance of the late pope: the new pontificate seemed likely to be more peaceable.

The new pope, Leo X, bore no resemblance to his predecessor, for whom, by the way, he had no liking. Of a most refined and cultured mind, a protector of humanists, scholars and artists, there was no longer anything medieval about him: on the contrary, he was the very personification of the Renaissance. His pontificate seemed to herald the advent of an era of tolerance and generosity, just as his round, plump face, somewhat slothful of aspect, contrasted markedly with the savage countenance of Julius II. Settlements by diplomacy rather than declarations of war could be expected of a man like this. This became evident in matters affecting relations with France.

The new policy of flexibility was revealed almost immediately when the disturbing affair of the Council of Pisa was wound up: instead of treating them harshly as some demanded, Leo X extended a free pardon to those lost sheep who gave evidence of their repentance by going through a real ceremony of recantation. Having dressed this internal wound, he had to find a way of concluding the Italian wars which had received fresh impetus from the accession of Francis I, the new king of France. In this matter also, a flexible policy had become indispensable.

The time was well chosen. Each of the two adversaries desired an interview which might put an end to a situation in which everyone was awkwardly placed. At Bologna (11–15 December 1515) king and pope laid the foundations of an agreement which they had long felt to be necessary. For almost a century the Church in France had been without authority, torn between two masters both equally inclined to absolutism. The Pragmatic Sanction had not brought to the French Church the liberties it was intended to give. On the contrary, indeed, that Church had passed through grievous times, when bishoprics and monasteries, regarded merely as spoils, had been wrangled over in the most pernicious way. Hardly anywhere were elections held in due form, for the king succeeded in foisting his own candidates upon the electors by every conceivable means, not excluding the most ruthless: there are accounts of episcopal elections which tell of dealings disgraceful in the extreme. Even if there was no struggle *vi et armis*, there was a lawsuit before the *Parlement* or *Grand Conseil*: the picture one feels bound to paint is deplorable, and the body of the faithful groaned, not knowing which pastor to obey. This situation could not go on. By common consent, a sincere agreement between king and pope was a matter of the greatest urgency. It was achieved, but not without difficulty, by the Concordat of Bologna.

This concordat took credit to itself for putting an end to all these evils and abuses, and the settlements it proposed had the appearance of reasonableness. The following is a brief summary of them. With regard to benefices, nomination was reserved to the king, canonical institution to the pope, a logical division of prerogatives, but one which involved discontinuance of elections. This seemed to be an innovation of the utmost seriousness, but was only apparently so: in point of fact, as we have seen, elections had long been no more than a myth. Further, the king's choice was not to be purely arbitrary: he had thus to abide by rules respecting the candidates' age and suitability. Otherwise, the pope was empowered to reject any candidate he deemed unworthy. In the matter of jurisdiction, the pope made considerable concessions—inevitably, because the Paris *Parlement* had always rebelled against the claims of the court of Rome. As for the very delicate question of taxation, which lay at the heart of the problem, it was not tackled altogether without equivocation, and it was soon thought that the king had yielded a good deal of ground. The possibility of a tax on benefices to the advantage of the Roman treasury was still a menacing contingency. Naturally—and this was an enormous success for the pope—the Pragmatic Sanction was abolished, and in terms such that those close to the king dared not make them public. Finally, the concordat contained a few articles concerning reform of the Church; but they were rather faint-hearted and were never seriously regarded as efficacious. At bottom, the concordat left many problems still unsolved.

This being so, it was not accepted in France without some lively displays of opposition, encouraged by the king's hesitancy. The *Parlement* and university showed determined hostility to the idea of accepting the papal bulls, and engaged throughout the country in a campaign of agitation which forced the king and his chancellor, Duprat, to take stern measures. The *Parlement* agreed to register the concordat only on 22 March 1518, and two days later it protested vigorously yet again against the decision which had been forced upon it. For several months longer, in university circles and those of the *Parlement*, the restlessness continued. But in spite of this opposition, the concordat was enforced.

The fiscal exactions of the Papacy, treated with too much circumspection in the concordat, were still one of the black spots of the situation. For two centuries, these exactions had given rise to much agitation: every government had censured their excesses, which grew daily more oppressive. At the end of the fifteenth century especially, it was all too clear that the financial needs of the Papacy—sometimes for the meanest ends—governed the entire policy of the Roman See.

While as yet the most hot-headed protesters did not think of eventually breaking with Rome, a few voices were nevertheless heard here and there, pillorying the hated excesses of these exactions and drawing the pope's attention to the dangers of such a policy. The feeling of being robbed through taxation largely explains the anti-Roman attitude perceptible in certain episodes, in Germany more seriously than elsewhere, though they occurred everywhere to some extent. The notoriously inadequate attempts to reform the Church, and the deplorable pontificates of the end of the fifteenth century, provided the foundation for that genuine 'anticlericalism' which we observe at that time, not only among certain sections of the aristocracy or the common people, but above all among the wealthy taxpaying burgesses of the larger cities. Hence the wide circulation of the *gravamina*, for example, which persisted for several generations. Moreover, these tendencies were not at variance with a faith that was still deeprooted and, in some cases, quite medieval. Indeed, it was in the most profoundly religious nations of the time that this state of mind, combined with pained indignation and rebellious nationalist feeling, was most sharply apparent. This was particularly the case in Germany, where this movement provides a partial explanation for Luther's success, and in England, where it was later to lead to the creation of a national church disunited from Rome. A spark would be enough to set everything on fire: the affair of the 'indulgences' was to be that spark.

Frequently misunderstood as it has been, a reminder of what an indulgence was is not out of place here. It was a remission, plenary or partial as the case might be, of punishment for sin which still had to be suffered, on earth or in purgatory, even after the sacrament of penance had given the sinner absolution for his lapse. To be in a state of grace was an indispensable preliminary condition. In addition, prayer, fasting and self-denial were ordained, as well as the performance of such good works as giving donations and alms, visiting churches, paying for pilgrimages, carrying out works of charity or even of general utility, such as building churches, bridges, roads or dykes. Understood in this sense, indulgences had been variously applied, often to the benefit of the community. As for applying indulgences to the dead, this had been long in dispute but was at that time authorised and enjoyed considerable favour. Unfortunately, the practice was too much open to abuse. By a strange lack of vigilance, charlatanism was rife: a whole host of more or less official alms-collectors and scores of 'indulgence preachers' went about promising all too easily absolution for any crime in exchange for money. For this reason, these things were bitterly and justifiably criticised, often by people who were sincere in their devotion to these practices, and in particular in regard to indulgences for the dead. Ignorance and bad faith conspired together to bring into disrepute an institution which, moreover, seemed too obviously to be a shameful expedient accepted by the Church as a means of increasing its wealth. Whereas it ought to have helped in promoting spiritual advancement, it was in fact one of the many methods used in the exaction of money for the Church. At that time, indeed, the end of the Middle Ages, it must be admitted that the popes had a most unfortunate tendency to increase the number of indulgences granted for purely fiscal purposes. The moral effect of this was deplorable, and was condemned by men of enlightened views. Erasmus was doing no more than expressing the feelings of a large section of the public when he wrote, in a well-known passage of the *Praise of Folly*:

What should I say of them that hug themselves with their counterfeit pardons; that have measured Purgatory by an hour-glass, and can without the least mistake demonstrate its ages, years, months, days, hours, minutes and seconds, as it were in a mathematical table? And now suppose some Merchant, Soldier, or Judge, parts with some small piece of ill-gotten money. He at once conceives all that sink of his whole life quite cleansed; so many perjuries, so many lusts, so many debaucheries, so many contentions, so many murders, so many deceits, so many breaches of trust, so many treacheries bought off, as it were, by compact; and so bought off that they may begin upon a new score....

Now it happened that, from the day of his accession, Leo X needed considerable sums of money in order, in particular, to carry on with the erection of the basilica of St Peter in Rome. To collect funds, the pope had the unhappy inspiration of granting an indulgence (October 1513) for the continuation of work on this historic building, and made the mistake of entrusting the preaching of this indulgence to men who did not hesitate to bring any kind of pressure to bear and who were apt to make use of methods befitting fairground mountebanks. One of these preachers, Tetzel, behaved in such a way in Germany as to arouse the indignation of Luther, and it was he who provided Luther with the opportunity, at Wittenberg, of presenting his famous ninety-five theses on the value of indulgences (31 October 1517). The consequences were therefore incalculable. This is not the place to describe them, but rather must we give a picture of the state of the Papacy and Christendom, as well as of public opinion, in the years 1515-20.

As yet, the influence of the Renaissance had not been felt with general force. Italy was well in advance of the rest of Europe, and everywhere the medieval world resisted to some extent the encroachments of the new ideal. If, in Italy, the movement may be regarded as something of a return to a glorious past, it was not the same in other countries whose national traditions were very different. Fundamentally, the Christianity of Renaissance Italy was unlike that of other Christian nations, particularly with regard to the outward forms and appearance of devotion. The Italian mind, accustomed as it was to a sometimes disconcerting blend of 'inner paganism and emotional mysticism', quite readily accepted the new conventions that were arising. Among the masses the most unfortunate superstitions were current, but on the other hand these same masses were not shocked by the rather theatrical attitudes struck by certain representatives of the upper classes whose incredulity was somewhat affected. And one may doubt whether deliberately out-of-date conspirators, like those who were members of the Roman Academy in the time of Paul II, were really taken seriously. The influence of men such as Lorenzo Valla or Pomponazzi or even Machiavelli on the common people was naturally insignificant; likewise, souls as tormented as those of Pico della Mirandola and Botticelli were few and far between. Generally speaking, the peoples of Italy could scarcely be aware of such uneasiness of conscience, still less of the schisms of world-wide concern or the national heresies that were soon to be observed on their borders.

Almost everywhere else, the situation was more dangerous to the Papacy. To begin with, it should not be forgotten that the end of the fifteenth century and the start of the sixteenth witnessed a great upsurge of nationalism, especially in Germany and France. In the Germanic empire, a genuine national awakening can be sensed in the reign of Maximilian. Doubtless this sovereign was not cut out to be a great statesman; besides, he was sadly lacking in the material resources needed for any large-scale enterprise. But his chivalrous personality was such that a Germanic patriotism of a sort became crystallised around him. Maximilian would have had no objection to the establishment of a Germanic national church with only the loosest of ties with Rome—even if he never seriously thought (as some have averred) of becoming in reality its pope! But on whom could he rely for support? He could not count on the higher clergy who appear on the whole to have been very second-rate, more interested in increasing their temporal revenues or hunting than in raising the religious or moral standards of the nation. As for the people, they were, as in other countries, deeply religious, fervent to the point of causing new churches to be built, and so liberal as to maintain innumerable charitable foundations. And yet they evinced feelings hostile to Rome, of which the Papacy was to become aware only when it was too late. The national genius of Germany was charting for the influential classes in the nation a route very different from that followed by the *élite* of Italy. Of course, German opinion took no small interest in the Renaissance movement in Italy, but it was with keen anxiety that it watched certain practices of the court of Rome to which the Italians were accustomed, if not indifferent. This same attitude may be seen in the mistrust of accepting Roman law shown by the German people: for Roman law was also considered to run counter to their national aspirations and traditions. These feelings were aggravated by the blundering and vexatious fiscal measures of the Papacy. Charles V went so far as to say that Rome levied more money in Germany than did the emperor himself. In such an atmosphere, Luther's revolt could not fail to find ample support. The few weeks—at the end of 1510 and beginning of 1511—which the German monk spent in Rome served only to intensify his dislike of the kind of life led by the pope and his intimates which was depicted for him in the blackest hues. Having no understanding of the peculiar characteristics of devotional practices in Italy, which shocked him profoundly, he returned to Germany embittered and disillusioned. He doubtless experienced great spiritual uneasiness, but failed also to understand a civilisation different from his own. In the same way—also in 1510—the English ambassador, Richard Pace, expressed his intense disgust with the corruption of the court of Rome.

In England, the situation in general presented obvious similarities to that which has just been described. Among the masses there was deep and sincere piety, displayed in ways as numerous as they are undeniable, also a feeling of mistrust towards the fiscal and judicial organisation of the Church. Despite all that has been said on the subject, the people as a whole had in no wise abandoned traditional practices. On the contrary there was much fervour, which gave rise to a real flowering of church building and religious foundations. It has rightly been pointed out that more than half the books printed in England between 1468 and 1530 were religious works, two-thirds of these being devotional treatises. This was so, one should add, all over Europe, where the proportion of religious works to the total number of books printed was the same. In England, as everywhere else, the liking for religious literature was very pronounced, and the taste of the public for the innumerable small volumes of popular piety was insatiable. It is not surprising to discover this in a country which was still to all intents and purposes more medieval than the Continent, in its art as well as in its literature. Some significance may be attached to the fact that John Mirk's old *Liber festivalis*, a collection of sermons and religious legends composed before 1415, ran through no less than nineteen editions between 1483 and 1532. As for manuals devoted to preaching, and even to asceticism and mysticism, the first thirty years or so of the sixteenth century swarmed with them. In contrast to these displays of enthusiasm, the national consciousness of England at the same time gave evidence of unmistakable anti-clerical feeling, particularly—as in Germany—among the wealthy and cultured middle classes. Although they were no longer a dangerous body, the Lollards had certainly not disappeared.

Such were the faithful. What, compared with them, was the state of mind of the clergy? It is indeed dangerous and futile, in dealing with such problems as this, to try to offer a solution which might be valid for all countries and at every moment in any given period. In the light of recent research, however, a few general impressions can be specified.

Let us look first at the higher clergy. They could easily be crushingly condemned if one mentioned the numerous cases of prelates who were warriors rather than pastors. Particularly in Germany, there was the kind of bishop, stigmatised by Thomas Mürner and Erasmus, who was also a great feudal lord. In France, too, it is undeniable that a few disturbing personalities stand out. Others were less warlike, and prepared to cut a figure as humanists or patrons of the arts: they, too, lost the 'spiritual understanding of their mission'. In order to be quite objective, it is well to remember that one should not draw false generalisations from a few individual cases which were perhaps exceptional. Yet it must be agreed that one's general impression of the higher clergy is not very inspiring.

As for the lower clergy, it is also extremely difficult to form an opinion, owing to the absence of studies which make a careful analysis of the situation in a given region and are not mere collections of anecdotes. It is clear that in many places the lower secular clergy could not rise to their task, and their lack of education, their vulgarity and even their violence have long been criticised. Born of the people to whom they were still very close, the lower clergy had too often continued in their uncouth, good-natured customs, taking part in their pleasures and even in their games, dances and quarrels. Sometimes, perhaps, this attitude was misplaced, but it did make the lower clergy really popular in the best sense of the word. More serious, however, was the problem of the swarms of clerics on the very threshold of holy orders, without any recognised ties with a congregation, sometimes of no fixed abode, and always on the watch for mischief. These pseudo-clerics were a thorn in the flesh, and caused the authorities much anxiety. We must also admit that in general the intellectual qualities of the lower clergy left much to be desired: the 'manuals for the use of priests' were at that time inadequate means to intellectual advancement. The humanists of the Renaissance flung gibe after gibe at these unprententious works. Yet they had long been quite adequate to sustain the zeal of the lower clergy as well as the humble faithful in country districts. It must also be admitted that there were reprehensible practices among the country clergy: too many of them lived in concubinage, for example. These facts come down to us not only through the fiery sermons that were preached—these may sometimes be suspected of exaggeration —but also through the registers of the ecclesiastical courts. There is no question of concealing these undoubted blemishes. But attention should also be drawn to the dire poverty of these country priests: the *Epistola de miseria curatorum* was no mere literary exercise.

The same imperfections prevailed among the regular clergy, who showed clear signs of decline. Antagonism between the various orders, and bitter rivalries between the regular and secular clergy brought to them all considerable loss of prestige and influence. As for the material wealth of the monasteries, published research gives very contradictory impressions. As regards both England[1] and Germany, exhaustive studies would have to be made before one could give an opinion on this problem, and in all probability it would reveal marked regional differences.

In view of all this, what was becoming of that reform of the Church which was, as we have seen, one of the leitmotives of the Papacy? It has to be granted that the Papacy was unable to give the reforming movement any strong impetus or even a rudimentary coherence. That is why the praiseworthy endeavours of the Bursfeld Congregation, like those of the Dutch Congregation, produced only insignificant and, above all, short-lived results. As for the methods adopted by the Congregation of Montaigu or the canons of Windesheim, they were unlikely to be effective and, what is more, they met with insuperable opposition. With the possible exceptions of Spain and England the situation had scarcely improved, and yet, now more than ever, people everywhere were genuinely athirst for reform. Occasionally, a sovereign made a show of taking the long-desired reform into his own hands: he would summon assembly after assembly and have plans and programmes drawn up, but not without ulterior motives—and it was in this way that the king of France called a reform commission at

[1] A. Hamilton Thompson, *The English Clergy and their Organization in the later Middle Ages* (Oxford, 1947)—a work which perhaps generalises rather too much.

Tours in November 1493. While the results produced should not be disregarded, they did not lead to any real change for the better.

The whole undertaking should have been initiated by the Papacy and prosecuted with indomitable tenacity. At one time it seemed as though Rome had realised that this was so. In fact the Lateran Council opened by Julius II in 1512, in very troubled times, announced in the course of sessions held in a calmer atmosphere that it intended to tackle this redemptive work. There was much to be done in every sphere and at every level of the hierarchy, from the Roman *Curia* down to the lowliest country cleric.

An emphatic bull issued on 5 May 1514 took some sensible measures, particularly in regard to the frequently criticised abuses of the *Commendam*, a running sore in the Church: the *Commendam* was to be granted only in quite exceptional circumstances and those to whom it was granted were to be subject in their stewardships to certain fixed rules. These were excellent clauses, but were unfortunately hardly ever put into practice. Other parts of the bull were an attempt to restrain the cardinals from their tendency to make a show of their ever-increasing extravagance, but one can well see how difficult it was for a pope as prodigal as Leo X to enforce provisions of this kind. There were also a few sound clauses on the reform of morals and in favour of a more enlightened kind of devotion: these provided for severer penalties for the blasphemy, sorcery and superstition which were rife everywhere. But belief in magic was widespread: the *Malleus maleficarum* characterises the spirit of the times. The vast majority believed in witchcraft, and this attitude was to persist for many years. It was realised that it was necessary to instruct not only the faithful, but first of all the clergy themselves. Until then the education given to most of the clergy, particularly the lower clergy, was very poor, despite local endeavours which were noteworthy in some cases. For example, the end of the fifteenth century saw in England, and particularly at Cambridge, the foundation of theological colleges and institutions to promote the education of preachers. Printing, which had been in use since the middle of the fifteenth century, was of course called into service, but it was a two-edged sword, since it could also be used to disseminate questionable ideas. The council realised this, and forbade the printing of any book not sanctioned by the officially appointed ecclesiastical authorities. In short, these clauses attacked the problem piecemeal and were far from courageous.

The council was also disturbed by a fresh outbreak of the old struggle between the bishops and the regular clergy and especially between the bishops and the mendicant orders, which had shown great vitality in days gone by. The opposing parties were never short of arguments and in their dispute words sometimes ran high: but the regular clergy eventually agreed to a reduction of a few altogether inordinate privileges, some of which had been granted during the pontificate of Sixtus IV. If this had not come about, episcopal order in its entirety would have been perilously weakened, as public order was disturbed by the abuse of prophecy of which far too many preachers were guilty. On many occasions, these preachers had been undoubtedly courageous and remarkably sensitive to the needs of society: in France, for example, the outspoken Olivier Maillard had not bowed to the most overbearing kings, and in every country there were men who emulated him. But side by side with such powerful figures there were many harmful individuals: preachers, and even pseudo-preachers, poured out unorthodox ideas and predicted appalling disasters in order to terrorise those who listened to them—dangerous words which ran away with their speakers and often led to panic and rioting. A close watch had to be kept on these popular orators, and this the council realised.[1]

On 16 March 1517 there took place the last session of that memorable council which had lasted five years, and was a kind of sudden awakening for the Church at a critical moment in its history. Had the Papacy, heedful of the voice of Christendom, done what was needed towards the long-awaited reform? Had it regained its prestige? Had it recovered, and did it enjoy a high reputation at a time when Luther was about to come on the scene? In concluding this chapter, we shall try to give a clear answer to these questions.

Bad pontificates following each other in seemingly endless succession, the warlike passions of Julius II, the extravagance of Leo X—these were hardly propitious factors in the situation. Even if the masses still had some regard for it, the moral reputation of the Papacy was nevertheless shaken. It was all the more severely shaken on account of the low esteem into which the court of Rome had fallen. Even if allowance is made for the prevailing spirit of the age, it must be admitted that this court abounded in disgraceful conduct; the frequently inordinate luxury enjoyed by certain cardinals, some of whom, by reason of their age and bearing, were incapable of inspiring respect, served only to accentuate the poverty of the lower clergy in every country. Political intrigue, nepotism beyond all measure, unscrupulousness in all things, simony that was often blatant—these are things which, from a distance, become rather dimmed by the dazzling radiance of the Renaissance; but for the people of the time, they were unbearable. The thirst for earthly pleasures displayed by the most prominent members of the papal court necessitated the spending of ever larger sums. Hence the adoption of oppressive fiscal measures and the most dangerous financial expedients; hence, too, the importance of the bankers who were constantly in the background of the policy of Rome. Except in Italy, of

[1] The great influence these preachers exerted upon the masses is brought to light by a number of recent monographs devoted to particular preachers.

course, the humbler classes had little knowledge of all these matters or could only hazard a vague guess at them through allusions made by preachers, but the more advanced sections of society did not remain in ignorance of them. The wealthy, educated middle classes gladly read pamphlets and satires written by the humanists who were to be found everywhere. Very few, no doubt, of the writers were unbelievers and very few went to the limits of boldness, but their criticisms struck home hard and everyone could see that they were perfectly justified. The rulers, leaning on the earliest nationalist feelings, which were hostile to Rome, were to try to turn this widespread rancour and bitterness to good account. It would be easy for them to show that the two goals the Church intended to attain at the time it rallied round Nicholas V—crusade abroad and reform at home—not only had not been attained but seemed to be retreating farther away.

Indeed, there could no longer seriously be any question of a crusade. It is true that in 1518–19 Leo X was still talking of a crusade, trumpeting forth the Brotherhood of the Holy Crusade, estimating its resources and drawing up plans; but few people believed that he was sincere. The Turkish threat had not disappeared—far from it—but the Turks were no longer regarded with the abhorrence of earlier times. The popes themselves had dealings with them—sometimes in connection with the meanest haggling, as for example over the unfortunate Djem affair—and the Christian kings followed suit. And the tithes destined for the Crusade had been too often appropriated for any and every object for public opinion to be enthusiastic. The Crusade was dead indeed.

What was more serious still was that the Church gave the impression of being unable to achieve the reform that was on every lip and in every heart. The pope had indeed overcome the supporters of conciliar ideas, but his absolutism, which was henceforth blazoned abroad, did not afford him complete protection from criticism. And what may be said of the College of Cardinals? The selection of nominees in the time of Leo X was on the whole almost as deplorable as in the reign of the worst of his predecessors. In truth, Rome was completely absorbed in the building of St Peter's: as we have seen, the preaching of indulgences was instituted to provide the necessary money, while many more urgent tasks awaited attention. In the midst of this feverish building and this sumptuous, refined way of life, how could serious thought be given to reforming the morals of the clergy and their flocks? At a time when the religious feeling of the masses was still intense, the neglect and indolence of the court of Rome were bitterly resented. The indifferent would have shrugged their shoulders, but there were none—or very few—who were indifferent at the beginning of the sixteenth century.

CHAPTER V

LEARNING AND EDUCATION IN WESTERN EUROPE FROM 1470 TO 1520

WHATEVER its ultimate origins, it is undisputed that the intellectual movement which eventually blossomed into the Renaissance began to be first noticeable in Italy during the fourteenth century. Its real development occurred, however, during the fifteenth century. By 1450 humanism had already been dominating Italian culture for some time, and during the second half of the century it began to penetrate north of the Alps. Outside Italy, however, humanist development followed different lines from those pursued in its country of origin. This was only natural, since whereas in Italy humanism had gradually grown out of medieval learning, in the other countries of western Europe it was suddenly brought to bear upon the structure of different traditions. Inevitably, there were occasional clashes between the followers of the new ideas and the upholders of the older ones. Humanism was to prevail, and by 1520 it had considerably changed the intellectual life of western Europe.

The political structure of Italy made humanism take pronounced local characteristics in its various centres. At Naples, Urbino, Mantua, Ferrara, and Milan, humanism assumed a courtly complexion. In Rome humanism naturally found inspiration in the ancient ruins, showed little interest in Greek before the days of Leo X, and gravitated towards the papal court, just as in Florence the patronage of the Medici drew the leading scholars within their orbit. In Venice, on the other hand, the pursuit of the humanities, which incidentally showed a strong bias in favour of Greek studies, was confined to some members of the nobility, to some scholars engaged in school teaching, and to the learned men assisting Aldus with his publications. The development of humanism in fifteenth-century Italy had been made much easier by the greater accessibility of books. Many new libraries were founded at Florence, Naples, Cesena, Urbino, Venice and elsewhere, while some of the older ones (the Vatican collection of books is a notable example) were completely reorganised and brought up to date. Such a considerable library development had been made possible by the favourable economic climate, and also by the improved methods in the mass producing of manuscript texts. Just when these methods had reached their highest efficiency, the invention of printing brought about a revolution in book production. An important result of this invention was a spate of editions of the ancient classics; over two hundred editions of Cicero and seventy of Virgil were printed in Italy before 1500. Thanks to printing, the leading humanists were now able to release the texts of the ancient writers as they had already corrected and emended them, as well as preparing texts especially for the printers. This was a field in which the highest standards were reached in Venice at the very end of the fifteenth century, when Aldus's press began to pour out a steady stream of Greek and Latin classics edited by the best humanist skill available.

The classical emphasis in education introduced by the humanists did not lead to a sudden weeding out of medieval handbooks. Even as late as the early sixteenth century, the manuals by Everard of Béthune and Alexander of Villedieu were still in use, though by then they had been replaced in most schools by the new grammars by Perotti, Sulpizio, and Mancinelli. The simultaneous presence of medieval and new elements, so noticeable in school teaching, was also to be found at the universities. At the beginning of the sixteenth century the organisation of Italian universities was still that of the Middle Ages. At Bologna, for instance, the arts faculty still followed the divisions of the *trivium* and *quadrivium*, and both there and at Padua Aristotle was supreme, while the writings of the Greek and Arabic natural philosophers had lost none of their old prestige with the physicians. Yet side by side with a good deal of traditional learning, one could also find at the universities the new values of humanism. Politian at Florence, Beroaldo, Codro Urceo and Bombasio at Bologna, Leonico Tomeo and Romolo Amaseo at Padua, taught side by side with theologians and canon lawyers scarcely affected by the new intellectual fashions. What actually happened at the universities was a working compromise, by which the old and new traditions were able to work together in harmony for a long time and without too much rivalry. The organisation of the universities made it easy for humanist ideals to percolate *via* the arts faculties into law, medicine, and theology. It was left to the academies to provide the humanists with opportunities for discussions and exchanges with their fellow-scholars and patrons. The earliest humanist academy had been started informally in Naples by Antonio Panormita in the days of Alfonso V (d. 1458), in order to discuss all kinds of subjects, mostly connected with classical antiquity. On the other hand, the Florentine or Platonic Academy led by Marsilio Ficino (1433–99) and his Medici patrons, was inspired by the cult of Plato and was responsible for many of the peculiar features in the intellectual life of Florence during the late fifteenth and early sixteenth centuries. A role similar to that of Ficino in Florence was played in Rome by Pomponio Leto (1425–98), whose *Accademia Romana* was entirely dominated by archaeological interests. Sent 'underground' in 1468 by Paul II (1464–71), who saw a threat to Christianity in its harmless paganising, Leto's academy came into the light again under Sixtus IV (1471–84), when the leading officials of the Curia belonged to it. Its heyday was, however, in the days of Leo X (1513–21), when it enjoyed the pope's patronage. Somewhat different from the other Italian academies, the one at Venice presided over by Aldus proved particularly interested in Hellenism and quickly achieved a great reputation and connections throughout Europe.

One effect of humanism was that classical antiquity could occasionally continue to be also a source of inspiration in politics and political thought as it had during the Middle Ages. It was the ancient world as seen through Livy and Polybius that lay underneath Machiavelli's treatises, in which ancient history suggested rules of conduct in contemporary affairs. Romantic memories of republican Rome could, moreover, still prove quite efficacious, in a very few cases, in arousing feeling against despotic rule. Thus the humanist teaching of Cola Monatano led directly to the murder of Galeazzo Maria Sforza, duke of Milan, in 1476, while the haunting example of Brutus was among the causes which encouraged Pier Paolo Boscoli and his associates to conspire against the Medici in 1513. But the great majority of humanists were definitely on the side of their rulers, indeed some of them, such as Jacopo Antiquario in Milan, Gioviano Pontano in Naples, and Bartolomeo Scala in Florence, reached very high state office. These activities are certainly not surprising, particularly when we recall not only the frequent employment of humanists for political propaganda, but also their position in the disputes about the advantages of the active and the contemplative life. This had been one of the issues dominating philosophical speculation in fifteenth-century Florence, which found its fullest statement in Cristoforo Landino's *Disputationes Camaldulenses*, a work completed about 1475. Another subject arousing as much interest in late fifteenth-century humanist circles was the position of man. It was thus left to Pico della Mirandola (1463–94) to bring forth a revaluation of man's intellectual freedom and the relevance of his position in the universe, further contributions to the discussion being furnished by Pomponazzi and Ficino.

This exaltation of human dignity was not meant to be an attack against religion. Both Pico della Mirandola and Ficino were men of deep piety, and most humanists had genuine religious feelings. It was certainly not unusual for the scholars meeting in the academies to take part in the pious exercises of lay religious brotherhoods, and throughout the Age of Humanism the study of the Fathers was certainly not neglected. Hence the reaction of Savonarola against classicism was above all a revivalist movement striving to establish a narrow Puritanism in a climate which was obviously favourable to the new learning and what it stood for. Savonarola's failure was not a failure of Christianity; and even those humanists who opposed him were certainly not hostile to the Church. If there was one thing towards which some of them felt definitely ill-disposed, this was rather the vernacular language or, more exactly, its use in literature. Politian and his patron Lorenzo de' Medici (better known as the Magnificent, 1449–92) had not been amongst them; in fact their literary remains include some of the best Italian verse written during the fifteenth century. Moreover, during the early sixteenth century this hostility to the vernacular had already narrowed down to a small though very vocal clique, and just when Pietro Bembo (1470–1547) was showing how to express the spirit of humanism in both Latin and Italian, Castiglione (1478–1529) was drawing his unforgettable picture of the ideal Renaissance man in the language spoken daily at the Roman court, while Ariosto (1474–1533) was giving poetic life to what was best in humanism in his *Orlando Furioso*.

The struggle between the followers of Latin and those of Italian was just one aspect of the battle between the ancients and moderns. Another issue was to split the classicists themselves into Ciceronians and Anti-ciceronians, and came to a head with Angelo Ambrogini surnamed Poliziano or, as we call him, Politian (1454–94). Endowed with very great critical powers, exquisite taste, a powerful imagination, and high poetic gifts, Politian proved easily the greatest poet and classical scholar of his age. It was Politian who really initiated the channelling of classical scholarship into more modern lines, and, as if such an achievement was not enough, he also displayed a mastery of Greek far superior to that of any Byzantine refugee then in Italy. He was also the first to show (in his *Rusticus*, an inaugural lecture in Latin verse to his course on Hesiod and the *Georgics*) an appreciation of Virgil's *Georgics* and of late classical Latin literature, and to consider the ancient writers from the aesthetic as well as the antiquarian point of view. That Ciceronianism was ultimately a subordination of one's own personality to the principle of imitation, in fact the very negation of style, was vigorously put forward by Politian, who absolutely refused to worship at the Ciceronian shrine. Such a stand was not an isolated one. Ermolao Barbaro also assumed a position hostile to Cicero, while Filippo Beroaldo chose the meretricious prose of Apuleius as his own model. Of course all this aroused opposition at once. Politian's stand was openly censured by Bartolomeo Scala and was the subject of a spirited attack by Paolo Cortese. Despite the great prestige of some of the Anticiceronians, Ciceronianism was still supreme as late as 1520. Its greatest exponent in Italy at the time, Pietro Bembo, went even as far as formulating its rules during his controversy with Gian-francesco Pico on the subject of imitation, which took place in 1512–13. All the same Politian's views were eventually to be vindicated by Erasmus in the *Ciceronianus*, that devastating satire on Cicero's devotees, first published in 1528.

Among the most lasting achievements of Italian humanism between 1470 and 1520, three are particularly worth noting. They are its contributions to textual criticism, classical archaeology, and Greek studies. Some striking advance in the criticism of texts had already been achieved by Lorenzo Valla during the first half of the fifteenth century. It was nevertheless with Politian that the scholarly examination of manuscripts, attention to palaeographical evidence, orthography and the 'usus scribendi', were first conducted in a thorough and systematic way. Modern textual criticism really started with Politian, and his methods may be seen at their best in his *Miscellanea*. They were made even more scientific by his pupil Pietro Crinito. In archaeology the real pioneer had been Biondo Flavio (1392–1463), who had attempted in his *Roma instaurata* to supply a topographical reconstruction of ancient Rome, while classical epigraphy had been considerably advanced in Biondo's time by the researches of Ciriaco d'Ancona and Giovanni Marcanova. The achievements of these early epigraphists found many continuators between 1470 and 1520, among whom Felice Feliciano and Fra Giocondo of Verona are worth mentioning. Biondo's labours were taken over by Pomponio Leto and several members of his academy, thanks to whom the study of Roman remains acquired new strength. Further stimulus to archaeological research was given by the discovery of such important masterpieces as the Apollo of Belvedere during the pontificate of Innocent VIII and the Laocoön in 1505. The writings of Francesco Albertini (e.g. his successful *Opusculum de Mirabilibus Novae Urbis Romae*, 1510) and Andrea Fulvio (e.g. his *Antiquaria Urbis*, Rome, 1513; *Illustrium Imagines*, Rome, 1517; *De Urbis Antiquitatibus*, Rome, 1527) reflect the antiquarian outlook of early sixteenth-century Rome, an outlook also responsible for the ambitious schemes of excavation outlined by Raphael in his report to Pope Leo X in 1519. The assembling of collections of ancient objects and particularly works of art, not unknown during the early fifteenth century, became almost a mania in Florence, Rome and Venice by the first decade of the sixteenth century. The best of these collections were naturally owned by popes and princes; yet even private scholars like Pietro Bembo and Angelo Colocci were able to assemble very impressive numbers of antiques, which aroused the admiration and envy of their contemporaries.

Renaissance archaeology was prevalently Roman. The study of Greek remains, so vigorously initiated by Ciriaco d'Ancona during the first half of the fifteenth century, was quickly brought to a standstill by the Turkish conquest of the Greek world. One of the effects of this conquest was also the pouring of crowds of refugees into Italy, many of whom were gifted scholars anxious for academic employment. The view that these refugees brought Greek back to western Europe can of course no longer be accepted. It is nevertheless undeniable that several of them made valuable contributions to Greek studies in Italy and elsewhere. By 1470 these pursuits had already reached a considerable development in Italy, though even then knowledge of Greek was not as widely spread as one might think, and not every large centre could offer facilities for its study. For instance, Pietro Bembo had to go to Messina in 1492 to secure a good knowledge of the language at the school of Constantine Lascaris. Nevertheless Greek was rapidly becoming a recognised university subject, and the available refugee talent was employed in university and other teaching activities. Greek refugees such as Johannes Argyropoulos, Andronicus Callistus, the two Lascaris, and Marcus Musurus, taught in Italian universities side by side with Italian hellenists such as Politian and Codro Urceo. The greatest translating achievement of the second half of the fifteenth century, the Latin version of the *Corpus Platonicum*, first printed in Florence in 1484, was none the less the work not of a Byzantine but of an Italian, the Florentine Marsilio Ficino. It was shortly after 1470 that the lack of efficient instruments for learning Greek began to be felt particularly acutely and was eventually remedied. Even Politian and Pico della Mirandola had been forced to learn their Greek with bilingual texts, since no proper grammars and dictionaries existed. Accordingly the publication of a Greek grammar written in Latin by Urbano Bolzanio in 1497 and of a Graeco-Latin dictionary by Giovanni Crestone about 1478 proved decisive in the history of Renaissance Greek. At the same time the comparative rarity of Greek manuscripts became much less irksome, thanks to the growth of Greek printing, which made possible the issue of editions of the principal Greek classics by the presses of Milan, Florence and, above all, Venice.

One result of the pursuit of Greek learning by the Italians was an interesting development in philosophical thought. The humanist interpretation of Aristotle and the new discovery of Plato were principally responsible for the new trends in philosophical speculation which were followed at Padua, Bologna, and Florence. The supremacy of Aristotle in the first two of these towns was natural in such prominent university centres. At Florence, on the other hand, Platonism predominated, thanks to Ficino and his associates. Controversy between Platonists and Aristotelians had been raging since about 1450–60. Cardinal Bessarion's spirited defence of Plato published in Rome in 1469 gives a good picture of what was at stake. The struggle had, however, been mainly fought among humanists rather than professional philosophers, the latter preferring to follow the principles laid down by the schoolmen. Thus what prevailed in Padua until the very end of the fifteenth century, and to some extent even after, was an Averroist and naturalist tradition, contrasting strikingly with the spiritual approach of the Florentines. An attack on the very heart of this tradition was delivered by Politian's friend, the Venetian patrician Ermolao Barbaro (1454–93), whose hostility to scholasticism found expression in the belief that it was essential to study Aristotle directly from the Greek original and not from old translations. The efforts of Barbaro, who was also responsible for very important work on the text of Pliny the Elder, were successful, so much so that lectures on the Greek text of Aristotle were already being delivered in the University of Padua by Leonico Tomeo in 1497. The strongest efforts to dislodge the medieval Aristotle came, however, not from Barbaro but from Platonist Florence. Broadly speaking, Ficino's Platonism was ultimately a re-valuation of moral problems in opposition to the prevailing naturalism, as well as a humanist interpretation of Christianity. As such, this Christian Platonism was not without influence upon contemporary and later theology. The writings of Egidio da Viterbo (1465–1532), the great Augustinian theologian, show the influence of Florentine Platonism on divinity, while even so conservative a Thomist as Cardinal Tommaso da Vio, better known as Cajetan (1468–1533), found it imperative to take into account the intellectual tendencies of his own time in interpreting the thought of Aquinas. The impact of humanism upon scholasticism appears perhaps at its best in the strange and pathetic figure of Pico della Mirandola. The outlook of Pico, his tastes, his very terminology, belong to scholastic tradition, and equally medieval are his love of allegory and interest in the Jewish Cabbala. Yet for all this, his encyclopaedism had at the same time a true humanist range, just as his extremely ambitious attempt to reconcile the basic harmony of all religions and philosophies went well beyond the wildest dreams of the schoolmen.

Barbaro, Ficino, and Pico were, though in different ways, all rebels against the speculative trends fashionable at Padua and Bologna, where the naturalistic approach to Aristotle had dominated philosophical specu-lation during most of the fifteenth century. What was pursued at Padua was, however, not so much the genuine Aristotelian thought as rather the travesty of it supplied by the medieval commentators. Thus it was not Aristotle but Averroes's materialist interpretation of his doctrines that supplied foundations for the theories of Nicoletto Vernia (1420–99), who held a chair at Padua from 1468 to 1499. It was Vernia who, by stressing that physics ought to be separated from metaphysics, really came to uphold for the first time the absolute autonomy of science. He lacked, however, the humanist sympathies of Alessandro Achillini (1463–1512), whose independent Averroism allowed nevertheless some room for human individuality. It was left instead to Pietro Pomponazzi (1462–1525) to show a novel approach to Aristotle through Alexander of Aphrodisias in a Renaissance climate. Deeply convinced of the dialectical irreconci-lability between faith and philosophy, Pomponazzi even dared to conclude that it was impossible to prove that the human soul was immortal, and that one could only say at most that it was absolutely mortal and only relatively immortal. Yet at the same time he shared with Ficino a lively interest in the ultimate destiny of man, a subject to which he dedicated much of his thought. Pomponazzi was doubtless the most acute philo-sophical mind of his time, and though his sympathies were on the whole humanistic, he really represents the logical development of that Paduan naturalist Averroism which was to dominate philosophy in Padua until the end of the sixteenth century.

Another field that aroused particular interest in Padua from the last quarter of the fifteenth century was Hebrew philosophy, thanks chiefly to Elia del Medigo, the Jewish scholar who exerted so great an influence upon Pico della Mirandola. Pico was also instrumental in stimulating an interest in Hebrew and Oriental languages. Among these, Arabic was particularly studied by Pico's friend Girolamo Ramusio (1450–86), while the study of Egyptian hieroglyphics also attracted the interest of some humanists, particularly within the circle of Ficino, and stimulated some of the forgeries by Annio da Viterbo (published in Rome in 1498) and eventually also a treatise on hieroglyphics by Pierio Valeriano (completed in 1556). On the other hand, the study of Roman law only ceased to be pursued on medieval lines after 1520, in spite of the fact that both Lorenzo Valla and later Politian had also given their attention to the text of the Pandects. This may be explained by the conservatism of the lawyers and by the traditional hostility of most humanists to legal studies, which made them look with distaste at anything connected with law.

French humanism developed comparatively late. It is true that as early as the last quarter of the fourteenth century intellectual fashions from Italy had found a few followers in France. But the promising efforts of Nicholas de Clémanges, Jean de Montreuil, Gontier and Pierre Col, and their friends were soon forgotten during the desolation brought about by the final stages of the Hundred Years War. Thus until the second half of the fifteenth century the new conceptions of scholarship fashionable in Italy failed to attract the French mind again. The traditional scholastic approach to knowledge was good enough to satisfy the intellectual appetite of the country, while the French genius preferred to express itself in the spoken tongue, in the poems of Villon and the euphuistic compositions of the *rhétoriqueurs*. Even when a humanist outlook developed in France, it only affected at first a very small though admittedly a far from insignificant group. Throughout the period 1470–1520 school teaching clung tenaciously to the old traditions, old text-books like the *Graecismus* and the *Doctrinale* losing none of their former popularity. An old-fashioned outlook prevailed also at the universities, although some room for the new ideas was provided. Paris, for instance, was then still very much an international centre of learning and the leading theological school in Europe, with a great majority among its regent masters showing hardly any interest in intellectual novelties. What divided the university during the last quarter of the fifteenth century was not whether the new studies should be accepted or not, but the struggle between Nominalists and Realists. In 1474 the long campaign of the Realists against their opponents had led to an official condemnation and prohibition of Nominalist doctrines. Yet the defeated party had not given up the struggle, with the result that in 1481 the interdict was finally lifted, and Nominalism was henceforth to enjoy a real supremacy in Paris until scholasticism was finally laughed out of the universities in the days of Rabelais. The Nominalists strenuously opposed Platonism as well as Realism, scarcely showing any greater readiness to compromise than their opponents. The atmosphere was by no means liberal. Astrology, for instance, was formally condemned by the university in 1494, while during the reign of Louis XII the royal policy against freedom of thought was felt to such an extent in academic circles, that even the orthodox Jean de Standonck, the re-founder of the Collège de Montaigu, was banished in 1499 for some opinons he had been rash enough to utter. By then the humanist influence had been at work for some time in the university, particularly in the faculty of arts. The Paris teaching of Gregorio Tifernate in 1456–8 had shown some aspects of the humanism of Italy to the schoolmen, and more emphasis on this subject had been given by Filippo Beroaldo while in Paris in 1476–8. Such opportunities were certainly not lost on Robert Gaguin and some of his friends, and that this was so is also evident from the nature of the books issued from the printing press installed in one of the cellars of the Sorbonne in 1470 by the university librarian Guillaume Fichet and his associate Jean Heynlen. Characteristically enough, their series of publications started with the Latin epistles of an Italian humanist, Gasparino Barzizza, this first volume being followed by other classical and humanist texts, such as Barzizza's *Orthographia*, Sallust, Florus, and Fichet's own *Rhetorica*. In short, humanist enthusiasm was responsible for the beginnings of printing in France, and nowhere in the whole country was this enthusiasm higher than among Robert Gaguin and his friends. An old pupil of Gregorio Tifernate, Robert Gaguin (1433–1501) was a keen Ciceronian who envisaged a union of knowledge and eloquence leading to the advancement of theology. This he strove to achieve not only with his numerous writings, in which he tried to conform to his Italian models, but also through his personal influence, which proved very powerful indeed. Little wonder, then, that Gaguin's circle was the cradle of French humanism, a humanism which was not opposed to, but rather within the orbit of, scholasticism and showing a definite flair for grammar and rhetoric.

In view of Gaguin's prominent academic position in Paris, it is scarcely surprising that many of the foreign scholars who resorted there (the young Erasmus and many Italians were among them) should eagerly have sought his favour. Another person they tried to ingratiate themselves with was the Italian-born archbishop of Vienne, Angelo Cato (*c.* 1440–96), a most influential member of Gaguin's circle, who stood high in the king's favour. It was to Cato that Domenico Mancini addressed from Beaugency, on 1 December 1483, a highly dramatic account of the usurpation of Richard III, and it was only natural, in view of his exalted position, that Cato should have been chosen to arbitrate in 1487 in the dispute between Guillaume Tardif and Gerolamo Balbo. Balbo had appeared in Paris about 1484, intending to set up a monopoly of humanist teaching on Italian lines. His scandalous conduct against Tardif and later against his Italian colleagues Andrelini and Vitelli made it imperative for him to leave Paris in haste in 1491, to the relief of his fellow teachers. Cornelio Vitelli, after lecturing on the humanities for a few months in 1488-9, also preferred to leave for England. It was left instead to Fausto Andrelini (*c.* 1462-1518) to settle in France, where his popularity as a humanist lecturer was only surpassed by that of Gerolamo Aleandro (1480-1542), whose Paris courses on Greek and Latin authors started in 1508. Another Italian scholar who exerted some influence and found success in France during this period was Paolo Emilio of Verona (*c.* 1460-1529) who, after arriving in 1483 in order to read theology in Paris, took up the study of French history and antiquities, becoming eventually royal historiographer and the author of a history of France published in 1517 and written in accordance with the principles of humanist historiography.

The success of Italian scholars like Andrelini, Aleandro, and Paolo Emilio, speaks clearly for the appreciation of humanist values in late fifteenth- and early sixteenth-century Paris. This is confirmed by the kind of books then appearing in print. Although French publishers (among whom should be particularly noted the scholarly Jodocus Badius, who had studied in Italy) issued a large number of volumes dealing with scholastic learning, devotion, and literature in the vernacular, they also published a very considerable number of classical and humanist texts. Strangely enough, the Italian wars begun by Charles VIII did not at once lead to closer links between the two countries. On the other hand, these wars did bring a considerable increase in the number of books available in France, through the wholesale removal to France of the Sforza library from Pavia. Another result was the arrival of the Greek refugee scholar Johannes Lascaris, who also proved invaluable to Louis XII as a diplomatic agent, and of the humanist poet Jacopo Sannazzaro, who found some reward for his exile in the discovery of some long-forgotten poems by Ovid and Nemesianus. It was just on the eve of the Italian wars that the humanist study of Greek became noticeable in France. Gregorio Tifernate's teaching in Paris had included some instruction in that tongue, but his teaching came too early to leave a deep mark. Gaguin, who had been Gregorio's pupil, certainly did not go very far with his Greek. It was in fact only from 1476 that Greek was taught again in Paris, thanks to the presence there of the Greek refugee George Hermonymos. Hermonymos was admittedly an incompetent teacher. All the same he left a large number of distinguished pupils— Budé, Reuchlin, and Erasmus among them—whom he had introduced, however badly, to Greek learning. A further step in the teaching of Greek in France was the courses held in Paris in 1507-9 by François Tissard, who also had several Greek texts especially printed by Gilles de Gourmont during these years for use among his pupils. The regular teaching of Greek in the University of Paris was, however, only started in 1508, when Gerolamo Aleandro, the future cardinal and papal representative at Worms, started his courses there.

Among those Frenchmen who took up the study of Greek with enthusiasm one should certainly mention Jean de Pins, who had studied at Bologna under such accomplished masters as Beroaldo, whose life he had written, and Codro Urceo. Another who drew much inspiration from Greek learning, though he never had a thorough mastery of the tongue, was Jacques Lefèvre d'Étaples (c. 1450–1536). Lefèvre's links with Politian, Ermolao Barbaro and Pico della Mirandola had acquainted him with what was best in Italian humanism. He remained, however, to the end not so much a classical scholar as a humanist theologian, whose intellectual interests did not exclude the schoolmen and whose works also included editions of Nicholas of Cusa, Richard of St Victor and medieval Flemish mystics. He was also capable of following the new approach to Aristotle, doubtless inspired by Ermolao Barbaro, which was openly against the traditions of the medieval schools. His aim here was to enable people to know the real Aristotle and not the one deformed by medieval commentators, an aim which is already evident as early as 1493 in his *Paraphrasis in Aristotelis octo physicos libros*. At a later stage in his career he tried to do for the whole of divinity what he had done for Aristotle. What he envisaged now was nothing less than a thorough reform of theology and, in addition, the placing of the early Fathers at the disposal of those who had no Greek. It was with these goals in view that he issued a Latin version of Damascene in 1507 and an edition of the Psalms one year later. It was with his commentary on the Pauline epistles, published in 1512, in which he still defended the authenticity of the spurious correspondence between Seneca and St Paul, that Lefèvre revealed his theological thought in all its depth and originality, as well as his enthusiastic approach to biblical criticism.

Lefèvre d'Étaples was undoubtedly the most brilliant French thinker of the early sixteenth century. Yet as a scholar he certainly fell far behind Guillaume Budé (1468–1540), particularly in Greek studies. A lawyer by training, Budé had studied civil law at Orleans and had started to learn Greek under Hermonymos about 1494. His real Greek teachers were, however, Johannes Lascaris and Gerolamo Aleandro, two very great names in contemporary humanism. In 1502–5 Budé had already turned some of Plutarch's treatises into Latin. But his real gifts were disclosed in full only in 1508, when there appeared his *Annotationes in Pandectas*, where he did not hide his contempt for the medieval interpreters of Roman law. The *De Asse* published in 1515 shows Budé's scholarly qualities and his grasp of classical antiquity at their highest. It placed its author at once among the foremost scholars of his day. In this amazing work, which supplied for the first time a scholarly and reliable account of the Roman monetary system, the choice of sources and the critical insight are particularly astounding, when we consider the author's background and upbringing. Less surprising is the contempt for the vernacular, which Budé shared with so many Italian humanists of his time. But then his heart was entirely with the ancient classics. It was, therefore, quite characteristic of his enthusiasm for scholarship, that upon hearing in 1517 that Francis I had it in mind to found the college of learned men which eventually became the Collège de France, he should have set himself at once to make sure that the idea was not given up, and it was thanks to him that the king's scheme came into being in 1530.

In late fifteenth-century England, as in France, learning and education still conformed to the medieval pattern. Throughout the Middle Ages, the English monasteries had played a prominent cultural role. A general picture of English monastic life during the last quarter of the fifteenth century shows, on the other hand, how many of the learned and educational functions previously performed by the monasteries had now been taken over by schools and universities. It was just during this period that new methods in grammatical teaching began to be followed at two of the grammar schools, at Banbury and at the school attached to Magdalen College, Oxford. The spirit behind these innovations was also noticeable at the universities. True, the theological faculties still continued to dominate academic life at Oxford and Cambridge. The supremacy of the theologians had not, however, prevented the rise of a taste for some aspects of humanist learning, brought over by Italian scholars and Oxford and Cambridge graduates who had studied in Italy. The introduction of printing naturally led to a revolution in the production of books. What is noticeable in the beginnings of printing in England is that the earliest printers, Caxton, Rood, and the mysterious 'St Albans Schoolmaster', were not without some humanist sympathies. Most of their productions were naturally meant for a wide public: nevertheless they also published a few works linked with the New Learning, and Rood in Oxford even went as far as issuing Aristotle's *Ethics* in the Latin translation of Leonardo Bruni in 1483 and the epistles of the Pseudo-Phalaris in that by Francesco Aretino in 1485. Both Caxton and Rood made use of the advice of Italian scholars resident in England, which suggests that by the last quarter of the fifteenth century Italian humanism had made a niche for itself. In England this new conception of learning at once manifested itself in many ways. With John Rous (*c.* 1411–91) and William Botoner (of Worcester, 1415–82?) it gravitated towards antiquarianism and an enthusiasm for British antiquity. On the other hand, with Robert Flemmyng, dean of Lincoln (d. 1483), it also led to the learning of Greek and the writing of indifferent Latin verse which was inspired by contemporary Italian fashions. Such also were the scholarly activities of John Gunthorpe, dean of Wells (d. 1498), whose formal Latin orations were modelled on the conventional humanist oratory which he had learnt at Ferrara.

Latin grammar was one of the first branches of learning to feel the impact of humanist influence. The new grammatical handbooks by the Italians which were reaching England proved so popular, that they soon aroused a feeling that the manuals used until then in school teaching were no longer satisfactory. An intention to improve the study of Latin grammar is obviously behind the books on this subject by John Anwykyll (d. 1487), Master of Magdalen College School, Oxford, whose example was followed by John Stanbridge and by Robert Whittinton in treatises which enjoyed considerable vogue. These Latin grammars by Anwykyll, Stanbridge, and Whittinton definitely established new ways of grammatical teaching in England. Little wonder then, that when Colet founded St Paul's School in 1510 he should also have taken steps to have a Latin grammar especially written for it by Linacre, and appointed the well-known grammarian William Lilly, who incidentally was also an accomplished Greek scholar, as its first High Master.

The spread of humanist learning in England also made its impact felt at court. The rise of a taste for polished Latin in courtly circles had been mainly due to Italian influence, exerted through papal officials and scholars trying to attract the king's notice. The way adopted by these scholars to win favour was to submit fulsome panegyrics in Latin verse and to dedicate treatises in the same language either to the king or to persons closely linked with him. Thus Pietro Carmeliano (1450–1527) started by sending some laudatory Latin verses to Edward IV and was still doing so in Henry VIII's time. Similar activities were pursued by Giovanni Gigli, the papal collector who eventually became bishop of Worcester in 1497, and by other Italians in London, such as Michele Nagonio, Filippo Alberico of Mantua (who addressed a Latin poem to Henry VII and another to Richard Fox) and Giovanni Opicio. All these writings and the careers of Gigli and Carmeliano show the existence of some appreciation of polite letters under the Yorkist kings. A direct outcome of this was an even greater recognition of the political value of good Latin. Not only did Henry VII establish the post of Latin secretary, he also appointed Carmeliano to the new office. Under this same king a French scholar, the Augustinian Bernard André, was acting as poet laureate, and although his Latin was deservedly criticised by Erasmus, his flattering panegyrics certainly pleased his employer. It is accordingly not surprising to find that when Robert Gaguin issued an insulting Latin epigram against Henry VII during a visit to England in 1489, he became immediately the target of a shower of abusive Latin verse from the various humanists hanging about the court. Naturally this courtly humanism was primarily rhetorical and restricted to panegyric, formal oratory, and the writing of fine Latin epistles. At Oxford and Cambridge, on the other hand, it assumed a more academic outlook, though even there it began by first manifesting itself through rhetoric. The teaching of this subject on modern lines appears to have been initiated at Cambridge by the Italian Franciscan Lorenzo da Savona, whose lectures were already being delivered in 1478. Lorenzo's *Rhetorica Nova* was published by Caxton in 1479 and by the 'St Albans Schoolmaster' in 1480. Caxton also published an abridgement in 1480, which suggests that the work was popular. He was followed there by another Italian, Caio Auberino, who besides holding classes on Terence was also employed by the university to write formal letters in Latin. It was, moreover, a Cambridge scholar who had studied in Italy, John Doget, provost of King's College from 1499 to 1501, who prepared an extensive commentary of Plato's *Phaedo*, in which Italian influence is certainly not absent. The greatest development of the new cultural values during the last quarter of the fifteenth century was to take place not at Cambridge but at Oxford, where the Italian Stefano Surigone had already been teaching rhetoric from about 1465 to 1470. Surigone may also have taught some Greek; but whether he did or not, the presence in Exeter College from 1490 of another Italian humanist, Cornelio Vitelli, proved undeniably stimulating to Oxford learning and particularly to Greek studies. Greek was certainly known in fifteenth-century England before Vitelli. Robert Flemmyng had secured some knowledge of it at Ferrara, and William Sellyng, prior of Christ Church, Canterbury (d. 1494), not only turned a tract of St John Chrysostom into Latin in 1488, but was already teaching the rudiments of Greek, which he had learnt at Bologna, in his monastery about 1472. Greek studies had also been cultivated in the household of George Neville, archbishop of York, until his exile to Calais in 1472; and Neville's secretary, John Shirwood, who became bishop of Durham in 1484, was an accomplished Greek scholar, while a Byzantine refugee, Emanuel of Constantinople, actually copied a Demosthenes (now at Leiden) for Neville in 1468 and probably other texts too. Nor is it surprising to find that both Neville and Shirwood were in touch with another Greek, namely that George Hermonymos who eventually settled in Paris as a teacher. The extant manuscripts copied in England by Emanuel and his fellow scribe Johannes Serbopoulos, who was active in this country from 1484 to 1500, indicate quite plainly a demand for such texts (and particularly for Greek grammars) at Oxford, where William Grocin and Thomas Linacre were almost certainly among their patrons.

The career of William Grocin (*c.* 1446–1519) was remarkable in many ways. Although he wrote very little and with extreme reluctance, he exerted a deep influence on his contemporaries. Colet, Linacre, and More owed much to him, and even Erasmus could not but admire the fine quality of his scholarship. The classical learning secured by Grocin in Italy was matched by his critical powers. This was particularly shown by his discovery, during a course of lectures he delivered on the subject in St Paul's Cathedral in 1501, that the *De Ecclesiastica Hierarchia*, hitherto attributed to Dionysius the Areopagite, could not possibly be by him. This bringing of humanist scholarship to bear upon theological studies was not unique in England at the time. John Colet (1466?–1519), who had studied in Italy, where he had absorbed the doctrines of Ficino and Pico and developed an enthusiasm for Plato and Plotinus, had also introduced humanist learning into theological studies. This is evident not only in his treatises, but also in his courses on the Pauline epistles delivered in Oxford about 1496–7, where he struck a new note in biblical exegesis by replacing the fashionable literal and allegorical interpretation with the Italian method of considering the text as a whole. The humanist conception of religion was indeed so powerful in Colet that it made him not only reject the schoolmen in favour of the Fathers, but also envisage a school aiming at the formation of learned Christians, a scheme he was able to realise in 1510 with the foundation of St Paul's School.

Compared with Grocin and Colet, Thomas Linacre (1460–1524) offers a striking contrast. Although he shared their enthusiasm for Latin grammar, his chief interests lay not in theology but in medicine. From Oxford Linacre had gone to study medicine and the humanities in Italy, where his Greek learning impressed those who came into contact with him. Linacre's Latin translation of Proclus' *De Sphaera* was published in Venice by Aldus in 1497. His real achievement lay, however, in his study of the Greek physicians, a study which led to his turning several of Galen's treatises into Latin.

Grocin, Colet, Linacre, and most of their humanist friends were in Holy Orders. It was a layman, Sir Thomas More (1478–1535), who became the most striking figure in the English humanism of his time. As a scholar, More was really an amateur who never taught and whose profession was the law, but he was endowed with exceptional gifts. Brought up in the cultured atmosphere of Cardinal Morton's household, he had later quickly learnt Greek from Linacre. His Latin versions from Lucian and the Greek Anthology and his study of Plato show the complexion of his hellenism. Nevertheless More was far from uninterested in theological matters; he took, for instance, a firm stand in favour of Erasmus's version of the Greek New Testament, and also did everything in his power to help the study of Greek at Oxford, when it was threatened by the more conservative schoolmen. As with Colet, so with More it was the Neoplatonist side of the Renaissance that proved most congenial to him. Characteristically, he was also a warm devotee of Pico, whose life and some of whose letters he turned into his vigorous English prose. This was a field in which he had no rivals in his day, just as his Latin poetry and prose are the best produced by English humanism. It is in the *Utopia*, that charming and so often misunderstood satire on the ways of the world, that More's humanism appears at its best, in a Latin prose where wit, urbanity, and lightness of touch are happily matched by a distinguished intellect.

The *Utopia* shows that in More's time it was no longer essential for an Englishman to study in Italy in order to become an accomplished humanist. One reason for this was that by this time some of the intellectual climate of Italy could be recaptured in London, thanks to the presence of several learned Italians at court. For these scholars, the death of Henry VII in 1509 was a calamity. A group of them failed to find favour with Henry VIII: André, the poet laureate, had to withdraw into obscurity, while Carmeliano was replaced in 1511 as Latin secretary by another Italian, Andrea Ammonio, whose official duties alternated with Latin versification and an intensive correspondence with Erasmus. Those Italians who definitely suffered from the change of ruler included Polydore Vergil (*c.* 1470–1555), who had started about 1506, with Henry VII's encouragement, a Latin history of England, the aim of which was to justify the Tudor monarchy to Europe. It was Polydore who introduced into England the broad conceptions of humanist historiography and stimulated the study of British antiquity with his edition of Gildas. Unfortunately for him he also incurred the enmity of Cardinal Wolsey, with the result that he suffered imprisonment in 1515 and only succeeded in publishing his *Historia Anglica* in 1534.

Despite the humanist activity going on in London and at the universities, the latter continued to remain a scholastic preserve until the Reformation. The real issue at Oxford and Cambridge was between the syllogistic and allegorical methods and the new criticism of the Bible, together with a return to the early Fathers; but at Oxford it narrowed down to a choice between Duns Scotus and all he stood for and Greek. The reaction of the old-fashioned divines, who regarded Greek as the very language of heresy, broke out violently at Oxford in 1518, and it was only the great prestige of John Fisher that averted a similar outbreak at Cambridge, where Richard Croke inaugurated his teaching of Greek in 1518. Yet the last two decades which witnessed the last stand of reactionary scholasticism in the universities, saw also some significant developments in school and university education. Colet's founding of St Paul's School was really a successful compromise between the ideals of the Renaissance and those of the Christian Middle Ages. The activities of Fisher at Cambridge and Richard Fox at Oxford were directed to meet new needs at the universities. What Fisher wanted was to raise Cambridge to the level of Oxford. Hence having secured the patronage of Henry VII's mother, the Lady Margaret (Margaret Beaufort, countess of Richmond and Derby, 1443–1509), he was able to induce her to found Christ's College in 1505 and provide in her will for the founding of St John's College. The need for trilingual colleges, where instruction in Latin, Greek, and Hebrew was given for the advancement of theological studies, had been felt since the end of the thirteenth century, but nothing was done about it until the sixteenth. Fisher saw to it that St John's College, Cambridge, was trilingual, through the establishment of fellowships in Latin, Greek, and Hebrew. This was no doubt one of Fisher's great achievements. Another one was his persuading his patroness to establish chairs of divinity at the two universities. He was very probably also responsible for Erasmus coming to teach in Cambridge from 1511 to 1514, which naturally proved invaluable to humanist and biblical learning in that university.

Fisher's example was followed a few years later at Oxford by Richard Fox, bishop of Winchester (1448?–1528), whose foundation of Corpus Christi College in 1517 gave Oxford a place where the humanities and particularly Greek held an exalted position. Here also the ultimate aim was to give new life to theology. It is, however, significant that the first president of Fox's college, John Claymond, was a keen classical scholar. He was just the man to preside over a college where the reader in Latin was expected to do his utmost to extirpate barbarism, and the reader in divinity to lecture not on Aquinas or Duns Scotus, but on the early Fathers.

The influence exerted by humanism upon English learning did not extend to Wales, Scotland, and Ireland. In Wales and Ireland no change occurred in the traditional learning of those countries between 1470 and 1520. In Scotland, despite the foundation of three universities during the fifteenth century, at St Andrews, Glasgow, and Aberdeen, learning and education remained rigidly medieval and so did university curricula until the Reformation. The many students from Scotland who went to Italian universities during the fifteenth and early sixteenth centuries remained utterly unaffected by the new values. The only Scotsman who succumbed to the attractions of humanism, Hector Boece (1465?–1536), a friend of Erasmus in Paris whose Latin history of Scotland modelled on Livy was published in 1527, became, it is true, principal of the College of the Holy Virgin in the Nativity at Aberdeen (later King's College) in 1505. Yet even Boece, despite his prominent academic position, failed to exert any immediate influence upon his fellow countrymen.

During the last quarter of the fifteenth century the Low Countries displayed a cultural scene of some interest. There was the flashy and rather superficial learning of the Bruges court of the Burgundian dukes and their Habsburg successors; there was the intellectual movement drawing its inspiration from the pious ideals of the *Devotio Moderna*; and finally there was the traditional scholasticism of the Louvain theologians. Intellectual activity at the Bruges court found its favourite expression not in the imitation of classical models, but in the superficial rendering in French of classical themes conditioned by an obvious taste for mythology. Some translating from the classics was not unknown, but it was not the turning of Greek authors into Latin but rather of Latin texts into French. Books printed at Bruges during the last quarter of the fifteenth century provide a reliable picture of the prevailing taste, a taste which appears at its most typical in the tortuous and meretricious writings of Jean Lemaire de Belges (c. 1473-1516?). On the other hand, outside the court, intellectual vigour was found in the clergy, not the laity; it came, however, not from scholastic learning, but from the sober piety of the *Devotio Moderna*. What the two branches of the *Devotio Moderna* (the congregation of Austin Canons at Windesheim and the Brethren of the Common Life) had ultimately in view, was to do for religion what humanism was doing for learning. Deeply influenced by mystics like St Bernard and the writers of the school of St Victor, they opposed to the dry formalism of medieval scholasticism that intellectual humility which found its best expression in the pages of the *Imitatio Christi*.

As educators, the Brethren proved outstanding and successful. In fact their schools, which by the end of the fifteenth century had spread as far as Alsace and south Germany, were responsible among other things for the education of such leading figures in the intellectual history of northern Europe as Nicholas of Cusa and Erasmus. The great success of the Brethren's schools was due to many things: to their efficient organisation and sensible syllabus, to their introduction of religious instruction, to their boarding arrangements, and above all to their employment of up-to-date methods of teaching. The greatest of their schoolmasters, Alexander van Heek, or Hegius (1433-98), who taught at Deventer from 1483, was a great believer in the cultural value of Greek and in the desirability of modelling one's style on the best classical and humanist examples. The Brethren's cultural activity did not stop at education: they were also very active in the writing of devotional literature and in the transcription of manuscripts. Once printing started they were quick to see its significance and to establish printing presses, which turned out not treatises on scholastic theology, but devotional works, grammars, and classical and humanist writings suitable for school teaching. The interest in humanist works taken by the Brethren of the Common Life is certainly not surprising, in view of the many cultural and trade exchanges between the Low Countries and Italy. Throughout the fifteenth century students from Flanders and the Netherlands had gone to study at the principal Italian universities, including Rudolf Husmann surnamed Agricola (1444-85), whose humanist learning aroused admiration in Germany and Italy as well as at home. It was to the Italians that Agricola owed his conception of *eloquentia*, and it was in Italy that he formed his excellent Latin style and mastered Greek. In the *Inventio Dialectica* Agricola showed an approach to rhetoric which harmonised the new and the traditional views, while in the *De Formando Studio* he put forward a conception of education full of refreshing common sense. Despite his humanist leanings, Agricola never wavered in his respect for Aristotle and his Thomist interpreters. Nevertheless, up to his death he remained above all a very gifted rhetorician, fascinated by the formal side of humanism. Now an assimilation of the new values as shown by Agricola was certainly exceptional in a man with his background. His countryman John Wessel of Gansfort (*c.* 1420–89), for instance, never faltered in his allegiance to William of Occam, the *Venerabilis Inceptor* of the Nominalists. It is true that he was indebted for his Greek and his Hebrew, both of which he also taught, to his Italian masters. Yet this puritan so much admired by Luther was utterly unimpressed by the Florence of Marsilio Ficino and the Rome of Pomponio Leto, and remained to the end a theologian strongly imbued with mysticism, enthusiastic for reform and the advancement of biblical knowledge.

On the whole, the followers of the *Devotio Moderna* had been hostile to traditional scholasticism. A stronghold of scholasticism in the Low Countries was provided by the University of Louvain, which was dominated by Realist theologians and was eventually to become a powerful fortress of the Counter-Reformation. The teaching in Louvain of the humanist rhetorician Stefano Surigone about 1480 left no appreciable signs and was quickly forgotten. Not forgotten, however, were the activities of Adrian Florents of Utrecht, who ended his life in 1523 as Pope Adrian VI. The brilliant academic career of Adrian of Utrecht shows also how the old syllogistic methods were still being pursued at Louvain during the second decade of the sixteenth century. Yet even in so conservative a university, humanist ideas were not by-passed altogether. Greek printing started there about 1515, and it was thanks to the imaginative generosity of Jerome Busleiden that a trilingual college was established at Louvain about 1517, with the result that Greek and Hebrew began to be taught regularly there from 1518. As might have been expected, such innovations were not unopposed. Jacobus Latomus (1475–1544), the formidable controversialist who attacked both Luther and Erasmus, and Martin van Dorp or Dorpius (1485–1525), now chiefly remembered for his hostility to Erasmus, took up a definite position against Greek. Dorpius is also known to have replied in some of his Louvain lectures to the attacks which Lorenzo Valla had delivered against the schoolmen a couple of generations earlier; he held that the Greek text of the gospels was utterly useless for the study of the Bible, an attitude which was but typical in view of his suspicions of the new trends in biblical scholarship.

Among classical scholars who hailed from the Low Countries, we must also include Christopher de Longueil, better known as Longolius (1488–1522). A native of Malines, he had been brought up in France, but his scholarly activity took place in Italy, where his ability and uncompromising devotion to Ciceronianism soon placed him among the best followers of that fashion. As a scholar Longolius aroused both envy and admiration among the Italians; even Erasmus, for all his hostility to Ciceronianism, appreciated his many good qualities.

In due course Erasmus (1466–1536) became the most significant figure in the intellectual life of Europe of his time. Yet this truly international scholar never shook off completely all traces of the learning in which he had been brought up. He remained to the end a typical child of the *Devotio Moderna* in his desire to serve God by advancing knowledge and in his passion for sacred letters, which he intended to free from the prevailing *barbaries*. It is true that he soon gave up many of the views held by Alexander Hegius and that he was indifferent to mysticism; all the same his humanist evangelism, with its strong emphasis on a return to the Bible, as well as his hostility to Lutheran determinism, certainly place him within the tradition of the *Devotio Moderna*, just as his distaste for scholasticism also links him with this tradition.

Erasmus's Greek learning and contacts with Italian humanism proved invaluable for his biblical and patristic studies. His critical approach to the text of the gospels—culminating in his edition of the Greek New Testament, which first appeared in 1516—was clearly conditioned by Valla's work in this field. (Erasmus was responsible for the first edition of Valla's *In Novum Testamentum Annotationes*, printed at Paris in 1505.) Erasmus's textual criticism followed the lines recommended by Politian and his pupils for the editing of classical writings. The anticiceronian revolt initiated by Politian was also taken up by Erasmus; his opinions on the subject were given full expression in 1528 in his *Ciceronianus*, where ridicule is mercilessly poured upon Cicero's devotees. Altogether, Erasmus's literary output was prodigious. His numerous writings include biblical exegesis, versions from the Greek, doctrinal treatises, apologies, and editions of the classics and the Fathers. For all its greatness, his learning had some limitations. As a hellenist he paid no attention to Homer, Sophocles, or Aeschylus, probably because they were too difficult for him rather than because Euripides, Libanius, and Lucian were really more congenial to his tastes. In Latin he was not particularly impressed by Virgil and his own poems were undistinguished. But then Erasmus's gifts did not include a real feeling for poetry or literary beauty. His approach to the classics was in some ways still medieval, particularly in his regarding them ultimately as repositories of ethical principles, moral wisdom, and fine phrases, rather than expressions of a great civilisation. As a thinker he was admittedly neither profound nor very original, and abstract speculation was clearly distasteful to him. Yet he could surmount such deficiencies thanks to his extremely sharp eye for the significant, his massive erudition, and his gift for persuasive writing, which made his views often appear well-nigh irresistible. His influence upon his contemporaries was immense, chiefly because of his admirable common sense, and yet his name is not linked to any great movement or event. Erasmus was well aware of his powers, but instead of becoming a papalist like Aleandro or a reformer like Melanchthon, he chose to remain a private scholar, mostly engaged in the editing of ancient writings. A survey of Erasmus's labours will make it appear quite clear that his best-known works are not really those which form his real and lasting contribution to learning. His real achievement is not to be found in his brilliantly entertaining Latin dialogues, nor in the *Praise of Folly*, nor in his handbooks on education and practical piety, but in his work as an editor of texts. It was definitely with him that the critical study of the early Fathers had its beginnings; he carried Valla's New Testament criticism a stage farther, showing eventually that the Vulgate was far from infallible. An interesting aspect of all this editorial and critical activity lies in the results which Erasmus expected it to yield. Once accurate texts of the Fathers and above all of the New Testament were available, religious contention was in his opinion bound to come to an end, since with the relevant texts freed from ambiguities and interpolations, no misunderstanding as to their real meaning would be possible. It was perhaps in the *Adagia*, first published in 1500, that admirable collection of classical quotations fully commented, that Erasmus's gifts and learning appear at their best, just as it is above all from the pages of this book that there emerges the real Erasmus, displaying his tolerance, his wit, his amazing learning, and the astonishing range of his intellectual powers.

Italian influence on late fifteenth-century German culture was inevitable. Some of the most significant figures in the intellectual history of the century, such as Nicholas of Cusa (*c.* 1401–64), Gregor Heimburg (1410–72), and Albrecht von Eyb (1420–75) had studied in Italy, where they had been influenced by humanism. Such an influence upon German scholars had been steadily increasing as the fifteenth century went on, to such an extent that by the end of it some of them had assumed some of the methods and mannerisms of their colleagues south of the Alps. Printing was a German invention: hence it is not surprising that this art should have spread more rapidly at first in German lands than anywhere else. The number of books published in the imperial territories and Switzerland between the days of Gutenberg and 1520 is most impressive and, as might be expected, most of these volumes treated subjects linked with traditional studies, religious practice, or professional use; but side by side with them there appeared also a substantial number of publications dedicated to classical and humanist literature. Indeed, by the beginning of the sixteenth century more than one publisher had started to cater especially, or at any rate mostly, for a clientele with humanist sympathies: the leading example being at Basle, where first the Amerbachs and then Froben, Erasmus's own publisher, established traditions similar to those which Aldus had in-augurated in Venice. It was also during the last quarter of the fifteenth century that school teaching began to be affected by the new values. Schools like the one established by Rudolf von Langen at Münster, or the one at Schlettstadt headed by Ludwig Dringenberg, conformed to the emphasis on the ancient classics traditional in the teaching of the Brethren of the Common Life, yet displaying also a more liberal concep-tion of education than had hitherto been the case. This favourable attitude towards the humanities was also to be found at the universities. Even the oldest German universities had only been founded during the second half of the fourteenth century; but once they had been started their develop-ment was so swift, that by the beginning of the fifteenth century Vienna, Erfurt, and Heidelberg were already flourishing seats of learning. The rise of humanism at the German universities met with little opposition at first, partly because no dangers were seen in it, but also because academic attention was too much absorbed by the strife between Realists and Nomi-nalists. So deep was this feud that at some universities, at Heidelberg and Ingolstadt for instance, it led to the arts faculties splitting into two, each section with deans, teachers, and halls of its own, one following the *via antiqua*, that is to say Realism, and the other the *via moderna*, that is to say Nominalism. Far from opposing them, the theologians actually welcomed the humanists at first because of the assistance which their studies could give to divinity. The real difficulties facing the introduction of humanist teaching were administrative, as there was no financial provis-ion for it and the existing curricula were not elastic enough to admit new subjects. These difficulties were not insuperable: lectures on humanist topics were gradually fitted in without unduly upsetting the curricula, while the funds required to pay the teachers were somehow raised. Thus Peter Luder was able to lecture on the Latin poets at several German universities until his death about 1474, and his is not the only example. Among those who introduced humanist studies into the German uni-versities there were also some of those Italian wandering scholars who were so frequently to be found throughout Europe during the fifteenth century. One of them, the Florentine rhetorician Jacopo Publicio, taught with some success at Erfurt, Leipzig, Cracow, and Basle in 1467–70. Another, the Milanese Stefano Surigone, pursued similar activities at Strassburg and Cologne, while Cinzio da Borgo Sansepolcro was active in Vienna in 1487. Cinzio's role in Vienna was, however, dimmed by that of Gerolamo Balbo, who proved to be undoubtedly the most influential Italian teacher in the imperial territories. The greatest contributions to the new conceptions of learning came even in the early stages from the Germans themselves, and particularly from those who had studied in Italy. Among other things, these German scholars were instrumental in creating an interest in Italian humanist writings, those by Pico della

Mirandola, Ficino, Valla, and Battista Mantovano being clearly the most popular. Another scholar from abroad whose writings proved both popular and influential was Lefèvre d'Étaples, thanks chiefly to Beatus Rhenanus, who had been his pupil in Paris, and also to Peutinger, Reuchlin, and the Amerbachs, all of whom were in touch with him. Lefèvre's many German admirers actually assumed the name of 'Fabristae', and as such claimed, in opposition to the Occamists, that they and they alone were the true representatives of Aristotelianism.

In such a world as that of German learning amateurs were also able to exert a vigorous influence. A scholar like Peter Schott, canon of Strassburg and the author of Latin poems and a treatise on prosody (1458–90), impressed his own town with his example: Hermann Schedel (1410–85) and Hartmann Schedel (1440–1514) left a mark on the intellectual life of Nürnberg. But by far the most influential of these amateurs was Johannes Trithemius (1462–1516), abbot of Sponheim and later of Würzburg. The literary output of Trithemius, which ranged from theology to practical piety and from bibliography to history, is impressive, and his *De scriptoribus ecclesiasticis* published in 1494 is still useful to scholars today. His greatest achievement is, however, to be sought in the powerful influence exerted by him upon those scholars from all parts of the Empire who either corresponded or came into contact with him. Because of the geographical and political structure of German-speaking Europe, it was inevitable that humanism should flourish simultaneously in various towns of those regions. A result of this lack of centralisation was the presence of circles of scholars, for instance those who gathered around Pirckheimer at Nürnberg or Wimpfeling at Strassburg during the early sixteenth century. Another result was the foundation of literary societies or academies, some of which owed their existence to the enthusiasm of Conrad Celtis (1459–1508). One of these societies founded by Celtis was the *Sodalitas Literaria Rhenana*. Another, the *Sodalitas Danubiana*, was established by him after he had settled in Vienna in 1497 at the invitation of the Emperor Maximilian I, and it continued to flourish under Celtis's successor, Johannes Cuspinianus (1473–1529), the antiquary who initiated the study of Roman chronology. And while in Vienna Celtis was also able to induce Maximilian I to found a *Collegium Poetarum et Mathematicorum*, which was duly placed under Celtis's headship and drew its main strength from his enthusiasm. All these academies were chiefly mutual admiration societies with a bent for antiquarian pursuits and Latin versification. This latter was certainly a most popular activity among German humanists. Albrecht von Eyb and Peter Luder had above all been rhetoricians with a taste for poetics, and so had Wimpfeling, though he also had other interests. Celtis thought primarily of himself as a poet, and his poems, though commonplace enough, secured for him the laurel crown and the title of laureate from the emperor Frederick III at

Nürnberg in 1487. The poems by Celtis and Eobanus Hess (1488–1540), who held a chair of rhetoric at Erfurt from 1517 to 1526, show how very mediocre was even the best that German humanism could offer in this respect. Equally mediocre were the Latin poems of Sebastian Brant, whose most successful work, the *Narrenschiff*, was written in German.

Rhetoric and versification may have been the most showy, but were certainly not the most important activity of German humanism. Those scholars who chose to edit ancient texts gave a more solid contribution to learning, even though many of their emendations were purely fanciful. It is to the astronomer Johann Müller, better known as Regiomontanus (1436–76), that we owe the *editio princeps* of Manilius published in 1472. Celtis edited two of Seneca's tragedies in 1489 and Tacitus' *Germania* in 1500, Cuspinianus was responsible for editions of Florus and Avianus, while Virgil found an editor in Sebastian Brant. But the most important German editor of classical texts was Beatus Rhenanus (1485–1547), whose work includes the first edition of the Roman history by Velleius Paterculus, a work which he himself had discovered in 1515 at Murbach. Another important activity of German humanism was the outcome of the belief, fostered by the new conceptions of learning, that the German past had a greatness of its own by no means inferior to that of ancient Rome. This romantic notion was responsible for Celtis's publication of Tacitus' *Germania*, for the editing of medieval texts reflecting Germany's past glory and also for research into its early history and antiquities. In medieval studies Celtis proved a pioneer with his editions of Hrotswitha's plays in 1500 and of the *Ligurinus* by Gunther the Cistercian seven years later. Stimulated by the example of Biondo Flavio's *Italia Illustrata*, Celtis planned also a *Germania Illustrata*, which was to show Germany in its true light. Only part of it, the *Germania Generalis*, was completed and published in 1500. In the following year appeared the *Germania* of Jacob Wimpfeling (1450–1528), in which it was claimed with a wealth of historical documentation that Alsace was German: a thesis which naturally caused much controversy. Wimpfeling's *Epitome Rerum Germanicarum*, published in 1505, gave a history of Germany from the earliest times; this was followed in 1518 by Franciscus Irenicus's survey of German medieval history. The best work of the kind was, however, the *Annales Boaiorum* by Johann Turmair surnamed Aventinus (1477–1534), which constituted also a definite landmark in the development of German historiography. Interest in the German past was also responsible for the commentary on Tacitus' *Germania* by Beatus Rhenanus, published in Basle in 1520: its fullest glorification is, however, to be found in the writings of Ulrich von Hutten (1488–1523) and particularly in his Latin dialogue *Arminius*, written in 1520, but only published in 1528, where Arminius is set up as a national hero and a symbol of German resistance to Rome throughout the ages.

During the late fifteenth and early sixteenth centuries some German antiquaries developed a taste for epigraphy, which proved of some value. Classical and medieval inscriptions had been collected by Hartmann Schedel, whose large corpus is now at Munich; Thomas Wolf (1457–1509) had also indulged in similar pursuits. It was Konrad Peutinger of Augsburg (1465–1547) who proved the most distinguished epigraphist and antiquary of his time in Germany. His collections included coins, medals, sculptures, manuscripts, and, of course, the famous *Tabula Peutingeriana*, which he had obtained from Celtis. He was nevertheless more than a mere collector of antiques; besides editing some classical and early medieval authors he was also responsible for the publication in 1505 of an important series of Roman inscriptions found in the Augsburg Diocese. Like many of his contemporaries, Peutinger knew Greek, was interested in Hebrew, and extended his investigations to medieval remains. Now the value of Greek had already been realised in German-speaking Europe during the fifteenth century. It must, however, be noted that here Greek studies were mostly directed towards securing a better knowledge of the Bible and the Fathers; this was an obvious outcome of the close connection between early German humanism and scholasticism. During the last quarter of the fifteenth century some teaching of Greek had been given at Heidelberg by Agricola, and at Basle by the Byzantine refugee Andronicus Cantoblacas, who numbered Reuchlin among his pupils. At a later stage Greek was also taught at Basle by Johann Kuno (d. 1513) and another Greek scholar in the same town was Johann Oecolampadius (1482–1531), whose assistance proved invaluable to Erasmus in editing the Greek New Testament. Meanwhile at Cologne and Leipzig some considerable advance in Greek studies was achieved thanks to the teaching of an Englishman, Richard Croke (c. 1489–1558), a former pupil of Aleandro, who continued lecturing until 1517, when he returned home. A successor for him was, however, found in 1518 in the person of Peter Mosellanus, thanks to whom the traditions initiated by Croke were continued in Leipzig. During this same year Melanchthon (1497–1560), in his inaugural lecture at Wittenberg, stressed the importance of classical languages and particularly Greek, and published a handbook on Greek grammar. Yet although by 1520 Greek had been for some time a recognised university subject, it had not been easy for Germans to secure a knowledge of the language before the sixteenth century except abroad. Nicholas of Cusa, Regiomontanus, Peter Schott, Johann Kuno, and Beatus Rhenanus had learnt the language outside Germany, and the last of them had started Greek in Paris under George Hermonymos, while Reuchlin, besides receiving instruction from Cantoblacas and Hermonymos, had also spent some time in Italy in the lecture-rooms of Argyropoulos and Chalcocondylas. The version of a Latin homily of Proclus made by Reuchlin in 1488 indicates his proficiency in Greek at an early stage; his later erudition in this field was particularly shown in the tract in which he defended the traditional pronunciation of Greek in opposition to Erasmus's views on the subject. A competent grasp of Greek is also evident in the translation of two sermons by St Gregory of Nazianzus by Beatus Rhenanus, whose activity also included the occasional writing of letters in a Greek much superior to that of those pitiful epigrams in which Celtis had proudly meant to advertise his Greek scholarship.

Theological studies were responsible for a lively interest in Hebrew. Celtis, Trithemius, and Peutinger had certainly been interested in this language. It was, however, Johann Reuchlin (1455–1522) who became the first German humanist to rank also as a competent Hebrew scholar. Hebrew was Reuchlin's great passion. He had started to study it about 1493 with the assistance of Jacob Jehiel Loans. What attracted Reuchlin towards Hebrew studies was his desire to study the Old Testament in the original, and to master cabbalistic literature as Pico della Mirandola had done before him. The *De Arte Cabbalistica*, published in 1517, was one of the results of these studies; others were his works on Hebrew grammar issued in 1506 and 1518. By then Hebrew had also secured other non-Jewish devotees in German lands, including Conrad Pellican (1478–1556), who taught himself the language, and Oecolampadius, Erasmus's friend and collaborator at Basle. The name of Reuchlin is for ever linked with the controversy about Hebrew books, which eventually became a struggle between scholasticism and the humanities. His fight with the Cologne Dominicans, who had secured a ban on Hebrew literature in 1509, led to a permanent split between humanism and scholasticism in Germany. Not only the reactionary Thomism of Cologne, but also the other traditional manifestations of theological thought, were now violently attacked by the supporters of Reuchlin, to whom this ban was a threat against the very values of humanism. In the *Epistolae Obscurorum Virorum*, that striking expression of the feelings of the humanist side, ridicule is pitilessly poured upon the methods of the schoolmen. Ultimately these fictitious letters aim at its methods in order to strike at the very core of scholastic learning. The condemnation of Hebrew books had been a spark, which had precipitated a crisis which was in any case bound to occur. By the second decade of the sixteenth century German secular culture had reached such a stage in its development that no compromise with the traditional learning of the schoolmen was any longer possible. The tendency now was no longer to bring the humanities into the theological orbit but rather the opposite, which partly explains also why so many German humanists sided with the Reformation.

Whereas in Germany humanism was already fully developed by the end of the fifteenth century, the Scandinavian countries were still unaffected by it even as late as 1520. This is not surprising in Norway and Iceland, but it is so in Sweden and Denmark, when we consider their many exchanges with the rest of Europe. In Sweden no university had existed until 1477, when a bull of Sixtus IV sanctioned the foundation of one at Uppsala. Teaching in the arts and theology started there at once, but it was conducted on strictly medieval lines. Books issued by the early Swedish press between its inception in 1478 and 1520 confirm the conservative nature of the country's learning. The situation in Denmark was the same. The university established at Copenhagen in 1478 was hardly more progressive than Uppsala, while the evidence of books printed in Denmark between 1482 and 1520 shows no wider range of intellectual interests than in Sweden. It was only with the Reformation that the New Learning penetrated into Scandinavia.

The swift development of Spain during the half-century 1470–1520 was also reflected in the intellectual sphere. A new interest in the humanities was already evident there shortly after 1470, being mainly the outcome of humanist influence from Italy. All the great early Spanish humanists, Nebrija and Hernan Nuñez among them, had attended Italian universities, and it was chiefly through their enthusiasm that the new values were established in the Castilian kingdom. Scarcely less valuable than the efforts of these scholars was the role played by those Italian men of learning who had come over to teach during the last quarter of the fifteenth century. The first of them, Pomponio Mantovano, was already lecturing on the Latin poets at Salamanca in 1473; a more important contribution to Spanish learning was given by two former pupils of Pomponio Leto: Lucio Marineo Siculo (c. 1446–c. 1533), who reached Spain in 1484, and Pietro Martire d'Anghiera (1459–1526), who arrived there some three years later. Both Marineo and Martire proved invaluable as teachers of the humanities. Yet their greatest achievement was in the field of history, for Marineo, whose interest in Spanish antiquities is already evident in his *De Hispaniae Laudibus* issued in 1495, wrote also the history of his royal master in accordance with the principles of humanist historiography; it was left to Pietro Martire to become with his *Decades de Orbe Novo* the historian of the New World and of Columbus's achievement.

The humanist interest so evident at the court of Ferdinand and Isabella and at Salamanca was bound to influence school teaching. This influence was particularly obvious in the school attached to the court, where Italian scholars were especially appointed as instructors in order to improve the scholarship of members of the royal household. Antonio Geraldini, for instance, was acting as tutor to one of the princesses until his death in 1488, and both Marineo and Martire were among those who taught at this court school. The post of secretary for Latin letters, a position which had been held under Henry IV (1454–74) by Alonso Hernandez de Palencia (c. 1423–92), a scholar trained in Italy, where he had assimilated some of the ideals of humanism, was occupied for some time under Ferdinand and Isabella by Pietro Martire, this being yet another sign of the official appreciation of good Latin. The humanist teaching so evident at court extended also to Salamanca, then the most important university in the whole kingdom. In 1484, that is to say after Pomponio Mantovano had been lecturing on the Latin poets at Salamanca for eleven years, similar courses were given there by Marineo Siculo and from 1488 by Pietro Martire. This humanist lecturing was by no means an Italian monopoly. One of the chairs of grammar at the university was occupied by Antonio de Nebrija, the foremost Spanish humanist of the age, and towards the very end of the fifteenth century a former pupil of Politian in Florence, the Portuguese Arias Barbosa, gave public instruction in Greek. What counted most at Salamanca was Thomist theology, no room being allowed there for rival doctrines, such as Scotism and Occamism. It was as a reaction against the old-fashioned conservatism of Salamanca that Cardinal Francisco Jiménez de Cisneros, archbishop of Toledo and primate of Spain (1437–1517), founded a university at Alcalá de Hénares in 1508. His intention in doing this was not to found a home for the New Learning in Spain, but to establish an institution dedicated to ecclesiastical teaching and the philosophy of Duns Scotus. The enlightened outlook of the founder led nevertheless to its soon becoming the headquarters of Christian humanism in the country. The establishment of Scotist and Nominalist teaching at Alcalá was no doubt a striking innovation. But besides this, Jiménez had also provided for the study of Greek and Oriental languages to the advancement of biblical knowledge: and when it is added that the greatest early sixteenth-century Spanish humanists were invited to Alcalá by the founder, one can hardly doubt the ultimate nature of his intentions.

Further proof of the enthusiasm for humanism in the Castilian kingdom is given by the nature of some of the books printed there up to 1520. These included several texts of the Latin classics, starting with the Sallust of 1475, and also some humanist writings from Italy. Equally significant is the number of grammatical treatises published during the late fifteenth and early sixteenth centuries, which show the growing interest in this field since the introduction of printing in the peninsula. The main innovations in grammatical teaching came from Antonio de Nebrija who, having assimilated Valla's precepts in Italy, started a vigorous campaign against barbarous Latin after his return home in 1473. Nebrija's *Introductiones Latinae* quickly supplanted the old-fashioned Latin grammars in schools and universities. Nor was his example an isolated one, for Andreas Gutierrez issued his *Grammatica* in 1485 and Juan de Pastraña his popular *Compendium Grammaticae* in 1492. About this same year came out Nebrija's Latin–Castilian dictionary as well as one by Alonso Hernandez de Palencia, these being followed in 1499 by the *Vocabularium Ecclesias-*

ticum of Maese Rodrigo de Santaella (1444–1509), which aimed to explain the terminology of the Church to those who had no Latin.

The position of Elio Antonio de Nebrija (1444–1522) in the early history of Spanish humanism is very significant. Ten years in Italy gave him mastery of the humanities, and a determination to introduce Italian cultural values at home. He achieved this by teaching and personal influence and by his writings. As a scholar his interests were many-sided. Besides grammatical and lexicographical work, he edited and commented on several Latin classics and was the first Renaissance scholar to set down definite rules for the pronunciation of Greek. He also left important work on Spanish antiquities and the ancient geographers and was interested in Hebrew. His historical work, the *Decades*, where he gave the events of their reign up to 1485 in the manner prescribed by humanist tradition, justified his appointment as historiographer royal by Ferdinand and Isabella. But his great passion was the study of the Bible, where he struck an original note by holding that the real Vulgate could only be established by a critical examination of the most ancient manuscripts and through submitting several of its passages to a searching critical examination. This attitude towards Holy Writ was obviously too revolutionary for the Salamanca divines; after teaching for many years at that university, Nebrija was eventually forced to give up his chair about 1512. He was promptly rescued by Jiménez, who had him appointed to a chair at Alcalá where, besides lecturing on the classics, he also assisted in the preparation of the Greek sections of the Complutensian Bible.

Greek studies had been started at Salamanca during the last years of the fifteenth century by Arias Barbosa, whose best pupil, Hernan Nuñez (1471–1522), was to become the most prominent hellenist of his time in Spain. Other Greek scholars in the country during this period were Fernando de Córdoba (1425–86), whose main preoccupation was the reconciling of Aristotle's doctrines with those of Plato, and Maese Rodrigo de Santaella, who translated a letter by St Basil and another one by the Emperor Julian into Latin and Spanish. These versions were printed at the end of the first edition of his *Vocabularium* and are probably the first versions from the Greek made by a Spaniard during the Renaissance. One thing that appears from these early Greek studies in Spain is that Greek was valued not so much on account of its classical literature, as because it was the tongue of the New Testament and many of the early Fathers. This was actually also the view of Jiménez who held that no one could be a good theologian without a knowledge of Greek, which explains of course his anxiety to make Alcalá the leading centre of Hellenic studies in the country. Thus the Cretan Demetrius Doukas held a chair of Greek at Alcalá from 1512 to 1518, the same chair being filled in 1519 by Hernan Nuñez. The activities of Doukas at Alcalá included the publication in 1514 of two Greek works, Lascaris's grammar and the poem on Hero and Leander by Musaeus, for the use of students. These two books were printed in one volume at Alcalá in 1514. This example was followed later by Hernan Nuñez, who in the year of his appointment issued there two short Greek texts with an interlinear Latin version. About this same period Jiménez's secretary, Juan de Vergara, was busy turning three of Aristotle's treatises into Latin. The main achievement of the Alcalá hellenists was, however, their collaborative edition of the Greek New Testament, an edition which was already in print in 1514, that is to say some two years before Erasmus's text was published at Basle.

The enthusiasm for biblical scholarship at Alcalá was also responsible for the study of the other languages of the Bible: Hebrew and Aramaic. A converted Jew, Alfonso de Zamora, was already teaching Hebrew there in 1512, and both he and his fellow convert, Pablo de Coronel, were also engaged on the Hebrew and Aramaic sections of the Complutensian Polyglot Bible, which derived its name of Complutensian from the Latin name for Alcalá (Complutum). It was a splendid achievement inspired by Jiménez's enthusiasm and carried out at his expense. As early as 1502 Jiménez had started to take steps to publish the whole Bible in its original languages as well as in the Vulgate text. Soon after founding the university at Alcalá, he had gathered there a group of eminent scholars entrusted with the editorial side of the venture, and even a printer for producing the actual volumes. The first part, which consisted of the New Testament, was already printed in 1514, though not issued. This was followed one year later by a lexicon of Greek, Hebrew, and Aramaic, after which there came in 1517 four more volumes with the Old Testament. Jiménez was, however, fated never to see the publication of this monumental work, since he died in 1517 and it was only in 1520 that Pope Leo X finally licensed it for publication.

Without doubt the Complutensian Bible was the greatest achievement of early Spanish humanism. Another and hardly less ambitious project of Jiménez, the publication of all the works of Aristotle both in the original and in a new Latin translation which was to supersede all the earlier ones, was interrupted by the Cardinal's death, when only three works had been turned into Latin by Juan de Vergara. Equally unsuccessful were the efforts made by Jiménez shortly before his death to attract Erasmus to Spain. Instead Erasmus, whose influence had proved so strong in that country, was to become in 1520 the target of an attack by Diego Lopez Zuñiga, whose work on the Complutensian Bible had not prevented him from developing a fierce hostility towards Erasmus (in his *Jacobi Lopidis Stunicae Annotationes contra Erasmum*, Alcalá, 1520) and Lefèvre d'Étaples (in *Annotationes Jacobi Lopidis Stunicae contra Jacobum Fabrum Stapulensem*, Alcalá, 1519), hostility being aroused above all by a fear of their views.

The Christian humanism which had aroused so much interest and controversy in the Castilian kingdom found much less response in Aragon. Despite its close links with south Italy, and with Rome under the two Borgia popes, Calixtus III (1455–8) and Alexander VI (1492–1503), education in Aragon had remained thoroughly medieval throughout the fifteenth century. The activities of Jeronimo Amiguet, whose *Synonima* appeared in 1502 and whose *Isagogicon sive introductoria ad artem grammaticam* came out in Barcelona in 1514, show, however, how the approach to Latin grammar, which had been fashionable in Castile for some time, had by then also reached Aragon. What were not to be found, on the other hand, were scholars like Nebrija or Hernan Nuñez. The first exponent of the New Learning in Aragon, Cardinal Joan Margarit i Pau, bishop of Gerona (d. 1484), was primarily a diplomat who wrote also on politics and moral philophy. Humanist influence is, however, undeniably present in his *Paralipomena Hispaniae*, where the author is obviously conforming with the humanist conception of historiography inaugurated by Leonardo Bruni in the early fifteenth century, as well as showing an attitude to Spanish antiquities which is not too dissimilar from that held by Nebrija. The cardinal's attraction for humanist learning was shared by his nephew, Geroni i Pau, who besides securing a sound knowledge of Greek and preparing a Latin treatise on the rivers and mountains of Spain, obviously inspired by Boccaccio's *De Montibus*, became also the librarian of Pope Alexander VI. The foundation of a university at Valencia in 1500 was meant to stimulate humanist studies, as is evident from the terms of its foundation bull, which made provision for the teaching of Greek and Latin letters as well as for the traditional subjects. Yet even this did not succeed in arousing that kind of popularity for the humanities which was so evident at Salamanca and above all at Alcalá.

Not so dissimilar from the cultural situation in Aragon was that prevailing in Portugal, where some links with Florentine humanism had already been established during the last decades of the fifteenth century. The Florentine rhetorician Jacopo Publicio had taught in Portugal during his wanderings through Europe between 1465 and 1480, and later Politian had been in correspondence with King John II of Portugal (1481–95), while his pupils had included Arias Barbosa, who became the first teacher of Greek at Salamanca. A former teacher of rhetoric at the University of Pavia, Cataldo Parisio, taught at Coimbra until 1495, when King John II called him to his court. The Latin oration addressed to this king by Ludovico Texeira, printed at Coimbra in 1502, is already quite humanist in outlook. So is the *Prosodia Grammaticae* by Estevan Cavaillero printed at Lisbon in 1505, four years after an edition of the Latin grammar by Pastraña had appeared in that town. All the same, it would be an exaggeration to say that humanism had become an essential part of Portuguese culture by the year 1520. Until then both learning and education had strayed very little from the old standards, and it was only during the subsequent decade that Portugal was able to provide in Damião de Góis a scholar of European reputation.

An account of western European culture between 1470 and 1520 shows how humanism gradually succeeded in becoming an integral part of it during this half century. Outside Italy, humanism was admitted into the structure of scholasticism, thus becoming a Christian humanism, and still keeping many traditional features of the medieval schools in a Renaissance attire. Whereas in Italy humanism had remained fundamentally secular, it could not be said that this was so in the other countries of western Europe on the eve of the Reformation. What existed north of the Alps was a Christian conception and adaptation of humane studies, whose ultimate goals were the advancement of theological and biblical knowledge. Scholars like Budé in France or Linacre in England were certainly not typical of their environment. It was left rather to Colet, Lefèvre d'Étaples, Beatus Rhenanus, and Nebrija to show the approach to humanism in their countries at its most typical. If there was in fact one person who may be said to have personified the various trends and ideals of non-Italian humanism, it was Erasmus. With him northern humanism reached its peak, just as during the period which was justly called his Age western European humanism succeeded in achieving a successful compromise between the excessively rhetorical preoccupations of the Italians and the limited horizons of northern piety. The Reformation was in a way both the culmination and the ruin of humanism. Although scholars and divines continued even after then to cultivate the humanities, classical antiquity came less and less to be felt as a living thing and a real source of inspiration. The end of religious unity in western Europe was also the end of humanism.

CHAPTER VI

THE ARTS IN WESTERN EUROPE

I. IN ITALY

THE period of Italian art with which these pages are concerned is usually called 'High Renaissance'. In the course of the fifteenth century a long chain of 'Early Renaissance' artists, mainly of Florentine descent, had concentrated on a visual as well as theoretical conquest of nature. Their work formed the basis for a great idealistic style which began to emerge from about 1490 onwards and was nearing its end at the time of Raphael's death in 1520. It was given fullest expression during the decade 1500 to 1510, and the names of Leonardo, Michelangelo, Raphael, Bramante, Giorgione and Titian, round which legions of minor stars of considerable brilliance revolve, indicate its climax. Modern interpreters have excellently analysed the truly classical qualities of this style which combines, like Greek art of the fifth and fourth centuries B.C., a spiritual and formal dignity, harmony and equipoise never before or after equalled in the history of post-classical art. It is easier to describe this phenomenon than to explain it; nor can an explanation be offered here. But while older writers regarded it mainly and too simply as a revival of the pagan art of antiquity, more recent studies have begun to throw light on the complexities of the style by investigating the intentions of its creators. In following this line of approach, stylistic appreciations, biographical details and chronology have on the whole been dispensed with in what follows.

Renaissance architecture is usually described as a 'rebirth' of ancient architecture. This statement finds support in the writings of contemporary architects themselves, who all professed that they were returning to the 'ancient manner of building', after a long period of decline. However, if one compares a Roman temple with the highest class of centrally-planned Renaissance church such as Bramante's design for St Peter's (1505), S. Maria della Consolazione at Todi (1508 ff.), perhaps also designed by him, or Antonio da Sangallo's Madonna di S. Biagio at Montepulciano (1518 ff.), it needs real sophistication to discover points of contact between these buildings. It is true, that during the fifteenth century the Gothic structural system was superseded by a 'language' of forms derived from classical antiquity, to mention only the five classical orders, Roman types of vaults and ceilings with coffers, and decorations reminiscent of antique floral and animal motifs. But these elements had to be adapted to architectural tasks unknown to antiquity; neither for the planning and elevations of churches nor for communal and private buildings did there exist classical models which could be used without considerable trans-formation. In addition, Renaissance architects freely reinterpreted the classical grammar. Leon Battista Alberti used classical pilasters to ar-ticulate the rhythmic alternation of narrow walls and large openings in S. Andrea at Mantua (1470–93), and this very un-Roman arrangement became of the greatest importance for the further course of Renaissance architecture after Bramante had incorporated it in his Vatican buildings (after 1503).

Furthermore, important motifs of Renaissance architecture are late antique, medieval and Byzantine. Arches over columns, first introduced by Brunelleschi in S. Lorenzo, Florence, and later to be found in Biagio Rossetti's S. Francesco, Ferrara (1494–1516), Alessio Tramellio's S. Sisto, Piacenza (1499–1511), and in many other churches, in courtyards and loggias, came to them directly or indirectly from Early Christian basilicas which, in turn, depended on late classical buildings. Centrally-planned churches with cylindrical exteriors opened in tiers of galleries, a type common in northern Italy (most notable: Giovanni di Domenico Battagio's S. Maria della Croce, Crema, 1490–1500), continue the tradition of medieval baptisteries (twelfth-century Parma baptistery). Similarly, in the wake of the same tradition, Lombard Renaissance domes were regu-larly encased by galleries recalling romanesque architecture. Bramante's dome of S. Maria delle Grazie, Milan (1492 ff.), is the principal example. The palace façade in the early Florentine phase of the Renaissance was no more than a systematisation of the medieval rusticated front. Although, beginning with Alberti's Palazzo Rucellai, Florence (1446), new and more classical types of palaces were slowly evolved, the simple rusticated front had a long progeny: Benedetto da Maiano's Palazzo Strozzi (1489–1536), Giuliano da Sangallo's Palazzo Gondi (1490–4), both in Florence, the Palazzo Piccolomini, Siena (1469–1509), Biagio Rossetti's Palazzo dei Diamanti, Ferrara (1492–3) and many others are proof of it. In Venice the traditional medieval palace front was modernised by applying a veneer of classical forms, as Mauro Conducci's Palazzi Corner-Spinelli (before 1500) and Manzoni-Angaran (after 1500) exemplify.

The most important type of Renaissance vaulting, the high dome with or without drum above pendentives, which effect the transition between the square crossing and the circular shape of the dome, had a Byzantine pedigree. It was via Venice (St Mark's, eleventh century) that the type found entry into Italy. Many of the finest Renaissance domes, culmi-nating in Michelangelo's dome of St Peter's, therefore point back to Constantinople rather than Rome. A Greek cross plan for churches, consisting of a dominating dome in the centre, erected above lofty piers, four short equal arms in the main directions and four satellite domes in the diagonals, was also of Byzantine derivation. The type was resuscitated by Mauro Conducci in S. Giovanni Crisostomo, Venice (1497–1504), and, transformed into a longitudinal plan by aligning three such Greek cross units, in Giorgio Spavento's masterpiece, S. Salvatore, Venice (1506–34). In his design for St Peter's Bramante combined the Byzantine Greek cross plan with massive piers deriving from the sixth-century church of S. Lorenzo in Milan. Finally, the ruins of Roman architecture which Renaissance architects studied were uniform in colour. Following Florentine Gothic usage (S. Maria Novella, S. Croce), Brunelleschi differentiated in his buildings between dark structural or articulating features in stone and light-coloured walls; and an endless number of Renaissance architects followed him in this respect.

If, genetically speaking, Renaissance architecture combines antique, Early Christian, medieval and Byzantine elements, and if buildings of the period under review show little similarity to the architecture of ancient Rome, Renaissance architects could still rightly claim that they revived the ancient manner of building. Like ancient architecture, and even more so, Renaissance architecture is anthropomorphic or, better, anthropometric. Anthropomorphic, because these architects, thinking in terms of a new organic conception of nature, claimed that the parts of a building must be related to each other and to the whole like the members of the human body; and anthropometric, because it was the metrical relationships of the human body on which their interest was focused. The Bible taught them that man was created by divine will in the image of God, and Neoplatonism that perfect proportions in man reflect something of the harmony of the universe. Man's proportions, therefore, should be the norm for man-made buildings. This was no mere metaphor. The classical column with its clear division in base, shaft, capital and entablature lent itself to an interpretation in terms of the human body; and surviving drawings by Renaissance architects show to what length the anthropometric interpretation of the orders was carried. It is probably correct to say that the importance attached to the orders in Renaissance architecture was due to their supreme place in the metrical organisation of buildings rather than to the wish to use them as structural elements. By making the diameter of column or pilaster the unit of measurement ('module') for all dimensions in a building, and by multiplying and dividing this unit, architects welded details as well as whole buildings into metrically related organisms. Herein consists their main achievement, and it is this 'humanist' principle of metrical integration of all the component parts (like fingers and toes, feet and hands in the human body) that they found in ancient architecture but in none of the post-classical styles.

Vitruvius' work, the only surviving ancient treatise on architecture, contained what they were looking for. Here they found the most general principle, first repeated by Alberti and reiterated a hundred times, that beauty consists in interrelating the size and shape of all the parts so that nothing could be added or taken away without destroying the harmony of the whole. Here they found a detailed discussion of the orders and their proportions, of the module and the anthropomorphic character of architecture. Moreover, Vitruvius demonstrated that a well-built man fitted with extended arms and feet into a square and circle, and they took this as proof of the mathematical sympathy between the microcosm of man and the macrocosm of the universe. Following an old tradition, they saw in the circle, which has neither beginning nor end, a symbol of God; and concluded that the centralised church with the crowning dome assured the fullest union of man with God. In addition, the metrical perfection of centralised churches, in which unity, balance and uniformity are absolute, appeared to these men as the most adequate earthly realisation of cosmic order and harmony. No wonder then, that after Brunelleschi's S. Maria degli Angeli, Florence (1434), centralised churches were erected in quick succession until there is in the decades before and after 1500 hardly a year without the foundation being laid of one of these great and beautifully poised buildings. No wonder that Bramante planned the new St Peter's, greatest church of Christianity, as a centralised building surmounted by the mighty hemi-sphere of the dome. While little of this plan was executed, and while Leonardo's passionate studies of centralised churches remained on paper, High Renaissance aspirations found fulfilment in such perfect creations as Giuliano da Sangallo's S. Maria delle Carceri, Prato (1485–91), Bramante's Tempietto, Rome (1502), S. Maria della Consolazione at Todi (1508), Raphael's S. Eligio degli Orefici, Rome (1509) and Zaccagni's Madonna della Steccata at Parma (1521–39).

Vitruvius' influence grew rapidly in the course of the fifteenth century, and by 1500 familiarity with, and interpretation of, his work had become every architect's peremptory duty. This is evidenced by the fact that Raphael as well as Antonio da Sangallo was engaged on an Italian edition, and that Fra Giocondo, who shortly before his death in 1515 shared responsibility in the planning of St Peter's, published in 1511 the first illustrated Latin text; followed a decade later by Cesariano's magnificent edition which reflects Bramante's and Leonardo's occupation with the ancient author. The study of Vitruvius was accompanied by the methodical copying and measuring of the remains of ancient architecture. Again a climax was reached in the early years of the sixteenth century with Baldassare Peruzzi's vast corpus of drawings and Raphael's appointment in 1515 as conservator of Roman antiquities. But these untiring efforts were not of a primarily antiquarian nature: just as the empirical method of measuring human figures led Renaissance artists to the ideally proportioned figure, so the measuring and comparing of ancient architecture was the acknowledged method of combining the most harmonious proportions and the most perfect forms. Architects also regarded the ancient ruins as visible evidence of Roman *virtus* which had made Rome the mistress of the world and, in copying them, performed an almost magical act of identification through which they hoped to recapture something of the greatness of bygone days.

Filippo Brunelleschi (1377–1446) was the father of the new style in architecture. While he and his younger contemporaries, above all Michelozzo and Alberti, began to transform Florence into a Renaissance city, the rest of Italy remained Gothic. Florentine architects, painters and sculptors spread the new gospel; but outside Florence the new manner was assimilated slowly, and in the north and south of Italy its victory was not complete until the latter part of the fifteenth century. Regional differences remained strongly marked; for instance, the love for colourful incrustation in Venice, and for rich brick and terracotta detail in Lombardy. At the end of the century Renaissance architecture throughout Italy had many facets, as a comparison of such diverse buildings as the severe Palazzo Strozzi, Florence (1489), the refined Cancelleria (1486–98) and Palazzo Giraud, Rome (1496), which combine rustication and orders, Conducci's gay and elegant façade of the Scuola di San Marco, Venice (1485), and the finical and over-decorated façade of the Certosa di Pavia (1490's) aptly shows. In spite of such divergencies, all these buildings are equally informed by anthropometry.

When Bramante (1444–1514), coming from Milan, settled in Rome in 1499, this city, barren of native artists and of trifling importance as an artistic centre, rose to the distinguished position which it maintained for the next 200 years. The artistic and cultural primacy shifted for good from Florence to Rome. It is difficult to account for the reasons; they lie as much in the strengthened authority of the papal court and the overpowering personality of Julius II as in the commanding genius of Bramante and the unique and inspiring task offered by the rebuilding of St Peter's. Under Bramante's guidance Renaissance architecture entered a new austere and monumental phase: the 'grand manner' of the High Renaissance came into its own. The increasing stress on Vitruvian studies, together with the looming scale of ancient ruins permanently before the architects' eyes, led to a more decisive assimilation and codification of the classical vocabulary. Next to Bramante, it was Fra Giocondo, Peruzzi, Raphael, Giuliano and Antonio da Sangallo who gave the style its perennial character in Rome.

Although regional differences never entirely disappeared, they were now, on the authority of the imposing Roman classicism, superseded by an inter-Italian idiom. Bramante's Palazzo Caprini and Raphael's Palazzo Vidoni-Caffarelli (1515), both with a rusticated ground-floor and a compact arrangement of double columns in the *piano nobile*, were solutions of compelling logic, simplicity and grandeur. This new type was amplified and modified by Sansovino, Sanmicheli, Palladio and others, and left its mark not only in Italian towns throughout the sixteenth century, but on European architecture well into the nineteenth century.

Architectural theory of the Renaissance was much concerned with the internal organisation of palaces, the arrangement, size, proportions and decorations of rooms. Many attempts at evolving absolutely regular plans, analogous to Vitruvius' description of the ancient house, remained theoretical exercises on paper. The symmetrical plans of the Palazzo Strozzi and of Raphael's unfinished Villa Madama near Rome are rather exceptional. Not until the post-Renaissance period (after 1550) did symmetrical plans become the rule (Palladio).

The origin and development of the Renaissance villa, a type of building unknown during the Middle Ages, was stimulated by the suburban villa of classical antiquity. As Pliny the Younger retired after the day's work to his villa at Laurentinum, so the wealthy Florentine of the fifteenth century sought peace in rural solitude. The early Medici villas were simple and informal buildings; but Giuliano da Sangallo's villa of Poggio a Caiano near Florence, built between 1480 and 1485 for Lorenzo the Magnificent, is a stately house with a classical portico. From then on villas were given a more formalised and outwardly antique character. The most magnificent early sixteenth-century suburban villa, the Farnesina in Rome, designed by Raphael and Peruzzi in 1509 for the rich banker Agostino Chigi, contains the finest flowers of High Renaissance art. With Raphael's late work, the villa Madama, begun for the future pope Clement VII, the extension of the planning, the sophistication of the decoration, the blending of the main building with the large terraced formal garden, a climax was reached which was followed up in the 1520's and 1530's by such vast enterprises as Giulio Romano's Palazzo del Tè at Mantua and Girolamo Genga's Villa Imperiale near Pesaro.

Renaissance theorists envisaged their ideal city with straight roads following a geometrical configuration and with every building in its appointed place. Alberti compared the city to a large house adapted to the needs of the inhabitants. Francesco di Giorgio, writing after 1482, explained that all the parts of the city must be proportionate to the whole, 'just as the members of the human body'. But most of the Italian towns, cities like Florence and Siena, Verona, Piacenza and Perugia, had been given their centres of communal life, their spacious squares, town halls and public buildings, between the twelfth and fourteenth centuries when the politically powerful city-states flourished. The Renaissance hardly interfered with the organic patterns of these medieval towns. It was mainly the Renaissance palace, each one individual with regard to size, planning and decoration and erected along the existing thoroughfares, that changed the character of the old cities. The creation of large and coherent units, like Biagio Rossetti's new quarters at Ferrara, the laying-out of St Mark's Square at Venice (1496 ff.), Bramante's design of the centre of Vigevano near Milan (1475–85), his building of new straight streets in Julius II's Rome (Via Giulia), Antonio da Sangallo's symmetrical organisation of the Piazza SS. Annunziata in Florence (1516 ff.) remained somewhat isolated. The great period of town-planning begins in the late sixteenth century.

The Renaissance ideals of symmetry and regularity, of simple geometrical shapes, integrity of isolated masses and clarity of articulation were relatively short-lived. After 1520 there is hardly a pure Renaissance building. Between 1520 and 1530 the great men of the Renaissance themselves, Michelangelo, Peruzzi, Antonio da Sangallo, Giulio Romano, reversed the old values and began to disintegrate the balanced and harmonious style of the High Renaissance.

The development of sculpture and painting follows a parallel course to that of architecture. This is not to be wondered at, since specialisation in the modern sense hardly existed. None of the great Renaissance architects had a professional training: Bramante began as a painter, and so did Francesco di Giorgio (1439–1502) and Leonardo, both equally accomplished in the theory and practice of all three arts; for Raphael architecture remained a side-line; and Michelangelo was forty-one years old when he made his first architectural design, the façade of S. Lorenzo, Florence (1516), which was never executed. As in architecture, so in sculpture and painting a change in the interpretation of antiquity was coming about at the end of the fifteenth century. The preciousness and grace of fifteenth-century art was replaced by a heroic and lofty ideal of vaster scale and nobler proportions, which had its roots in classical art. In 1477 Botticelli represented in his *Primavera* the Three Graces as ethereal dancers united by a beautiful linear rhythm. In about 1500 the young Raphael painted a small picture of the same subject (Chantilly) in which he recaptured the very essence of the celebrated ancient marble group, its composure and poise. Rome, and not Florence, was the obvious place for this style to mature; and there Michelangelo's and Raphael's achievements in sculpture and painting vied with Bramante's in architecture. But whether the new standards were set by the Three Graces or the Laocoön, enthusiastically hailed by artists when found in 1506, by the Belvedere Apollo, the Vatican Torso or the Grotesques of the Golden House of Nero, under the impression of which Raphael perfected a new mode of decoration (Vatican Loggie, 1515–21), these classical works were as a rule no more than representational formulas for an entirely new content.

This will be evident to anyone who studies the history of Renaissance tombs; funerary art is at all times a measure of the beliefs of the living. Although classically dressed up, Florentine tombs of the Early Renaissance continue the medieval tradition of placing recumbent effigies on sarcophagi in arched recesses under religious symbols of redemption. In one way or another every Renaissance tomb remains focused on the idea of salvation. This is also true of Antonio Pollaiuolo's tomb of

Innocent VIII, erected in St Peter's between 1492 and 1498, on which the splendid realistic likeness of the pope appears twice, recumbent and seated in the act of blessing, following the tradition of the Angevin tombs at Naples. And it is true of Michelangelo's tomb of Julius II, which would have been the most gigantic sculptural enterprise of the High Renaissance, if completed according to the original design. Michelangelo's biographer Condivi talked of this work that occupied him intermittently for fully forty years (1505–45) as the 'tragedy of the tomb'. Instead of the more than forty huge marble figures placed round a freestanding structure to be erected in three tiers in a specially built chapel adjoining St Peter's, only a much reduced version found a permanent home as a wall-tomb in the church of S. Pietro in Vincoli. In the first scheme classical ideas of a burial chamber, of apotheosis and triumph (Victories and Slaves) were interwoven with the concept, derived from medieval funerary art, of separating a lower terrestrial from an upper celestial sphere where the Pontiff would have been seen supported by angels. An intermediary zone with the statues of active and contemplative life, of Moses and St Paul would have prepared for the catharsis of the soul which ascends triumphantly to eternal life. It has been convincingly shown that the unifying concept of the intricate programme was Neoplatonic,[1] but there is disagreement amongst scholars on many minor points. To the second considerably altered phase of the tomb after the pope's death in 1513 belong the two Slaves in the Louvre and the Moses, active leader and contemplative thinker in one, who found a place in the final arrangement of the tomb. During a much later phase (1532) Michelangelo executed the Victor and the four unfinished Captives in Florence, the most powerful and most tragic of his works.

Michelangelo realised more fully his dreams as a sculptor in the Medici Chapel at Florence. Only the initiated know that this work too is a fragment of a much more extensive scheme (1520–34). Two relatively unimportant members of the Medici family, Giuliano, duke of Nemours, and Lorenzo, duke of Urbino, are shown seated in niches above the sarcophagi on which lie the mighty figures of the four Times of the Day. The dukes are dressed in Roman armour and many classical concepts are incorporated in the overall design, but the spiritual centre of the chapel remains the third wall with the statue of the Virgin between the patron saints of the Medici. No other monument has given rise to so many and so contradictory interpretations[2] and, while it cannot be doubted that it is charged with Neoplatonically coloured Christianity, the precise meaning of the single figures remains conjectural.

Michelangelo was the only great sculptor during the period under

---

[1] Best survey in E. Panofsky, *Studies in Iconology* (1939).
[2] Charles de Tolnay, *The Medici Chapel* (1948); Panofsky, *Iconology*; F. Hartt, 'The Meaning of Michelangelo's Medici Chapel', *Essays in Honor of Georg Swarzenski* (1951).

discussion. Compared with the timeless greatness of his genius, every-thing else fades into insignificance. At a time when he harnessed classical antiquity to the creation of his turbulent, highly personal, grand manner, Venetian sculptors evolved a classicising High Renaissance idiom, some-what dry and almost academic, which is best exemplified by Antonio and Tullio Lombardi's large reliefs with the Miracles of St Anthony in the Santo at Padua. While Michelangelo was engaged on the superhuman plans for the tomb of Julius II, the talented Andrea Sansovino created in the Basso and Sforza tombs in S. Maria del Popolo, Rome (1505–7), the most successful High Renaissance wall tombs. He revised the established form of the Florentine wall tomb by placing the figures in a setting derived from triumphal arches. Christian virtues and emblems of salvation point to the spirit in which these triumphs should be understood. From then on the triumphal motif in tombs became of ever increasing importance.

During the Middle Ages the greatest cycles of sculptural decoration are to be found on the portals and tympanums of cathedrals. This tra-dition almost entirely ceased with the rise of the Renaissance. It is not by chance that, instead of the older encyclopaedic programmes, the two greatest sculptural enterprises of the High Renaissance, the Julius tomb and the Medici Chapel, are devoted to mortals, their glorification, transi-toriness and salvation. This shift proves, if proof were needed, that there is truth in Burckhardt's thesis of the 'discovery of man' in the Age of the Renaissance, but it is man conscious of his individual role in the great plan of redemption. The only important Renaissance monument with a sculptural programme analogous to those of the cathedrals is the façade of the Certosa near Pavia. Reliefs, statues, groups and medallions cover the whole front like a colourful carpet. The leading masters until 1499, Giovanni Antonio Amadeo and Antonio Mantegazza (d. 1493), and there-after Benedetto Briosco, who finished the decorations of the main portal in 1506, were supported by a whole army of sculptors; and whoever wants to study Lombard Renaissance sculpture, in which classical detail is peculiarly submerged in late Gothic emotionalism, must turn to this façade rather than to Milan Cathedral. The lowest tier of the decoration shows oriental sovereigns and Roman kings and emperors together with mythological and historical figures of antiquity, gleaned from classical coins and gems. The figures of the classical world appear here as historical precursors of Christianity, representatives of the empires which preceded the empire of Christ to which all the decorations of the upper tiers are devoted.

Connection between architecture and sculpture was not discontinued during the Renaissance, but it differed from the Gothic method of subordinating sculpture to architecture. Now the niche instead of the statue was made part of the architectural structure. By removing a statue from a French cathedral, a structural vacuum is created. As early as the thirteenth century Italian artists began to reject the merging of sculpture and architecture. This native sense for the individuality of three-dimensionally conceived sculpture was in line with the monumental Roman tradition. The autonomous figure in the niche gained in importance and became one of the main themes of Renaissance sculptors. In northern countries artists rejected the antique-Italian autonomous figure until they came under the spell of the Italian Renaissance. From here it was a short step to a revival of free-standing commemorative statuary in public squares, a familiar practice in antiquity. On a few rare occasions the Middle Ages had anticipated this Renaissance development, which came into its own when in the year 1504 Michelangelo's giant David, nude like an ancient hero, was placed in front of the Palazzo Vecchio, a mighty symbol of the Florentine commune. Verrocchio's Colleoni (1479–88; finished 1496) was —in contrast to Donatello's earlier Gattamelata—the first commemorative equestrian monument placed in a public square (SS. Giovanni e Paolo, Venice), reviving the tradition of the equestrian statue of Marcus Aurelius which enjoyed legendary fame in post-classical Rome. Leonardo's equestrian monuments to Francesco Sforza, made as a clay model in 1493, and to Marshal Trivulzio, designed after 1506, were never executed. As his many studies show, they would have emulated all previous equestrian statues, but they were to form part of tombs and continued, therefore, the tradition of the medieval tombs of the Scaligeri at Verona.

Compared with the great mass of religious works, pagan themes play a small part in Renaissance sculpture. Michelangelo's career is typical; there are only the early relief of the Battle of the Centaurs, made at the time of the Virgin at the Staircase (1490–2), and the life-size drunken Bacchus at Florence dating from the period of the Pietà in St Peter's (1497–1500); a few other classical themes followed in works of the 1520's and 1530's. The bulk of classical subject-matter is to be found in small objects, medals, plaquettes, bronze reliefs and bronze statuettes. On the one hand, these objects were regarded as suitable repositories for emblematical mysteries which appealed to a humanistically trained clientèle; on the other, they served as fashionable decorations of sitting-room and study. In antiquity bronze statuettes were placed in the *lararium*, the sanctuary of the Roman house where the inhabitants performed their devotions. While the small Italian bronze derived from classical models, which were often directly copied, it had acquired an entirely new meaning: it had become the hallmark of refined taste. The demand for these objects grew steadily. Ghiberti's Florentine foundry was the cradle from which it all started. Donatello, while in Padua, set the north Italian production in motion; and the Venetian Andrea Riccio (1470–1552), fired by an unlimited imagination, poured out of his studio an endless number of small classical bronzes; their immense popularity was due to his activity.

It has become apparent that it would be wrong to assume, as is often done, that the Renaissance produced a predominantly worldly art, that the Gods of Olympus replaced Christ and the host of Saints. On the contrary, Renaissance art is first and foremost a religious art.

Raphael's career begins with a series of representations of the Virgin and Child, and the most spiritual works of his brush throughout his life were devoted to this subject. His teacher Perugino (1445–1523) was the painter of Madonnas *par excellence.* Leonardo's *Virgin of the Rocks* (Louvre and London), his *Virgin and St Anne* (cartoon, Royal Academy) and, above all, his *Last Supper* (Milan), Fra Bartolomeo's (1475–1517) monumental representations of holy scenes, Andrea del Sarto's (1486–1531) sensitive Holy Families, Correggio's (1494–1534) great altars of Madonnas and Saints, Giovanni Bellini's (1430?–1516) endless series of beautifully poised variations of the Madonna theme, Titian's religious paintings, numbering well over a hundred—all these show that, as during the Middle Ages, the interest and activity of painters was still mainly focused on the religious theme. But different from the often awe-inspiring medieval cult image, different also from the often somewhat pedestrian realism of fifteenth-century painters, these artists of the High Renaissance imbued religious subjects with a humane and idealised quality, a sublime vision of God become Man, which is without parallel. Raphael achieved the most perfect realisations of this ideal in pictures of his maturity, such as the *Madonna Alba* (c. 1511, Washington) or the *Madonna della Sedia* (1514–15, Florence).

The range of religious painting was extremely wide. An endless number of small easel pictures had to be produced for private devotion in house and palace; rich families, the higher clergy and public bodies competed in adorning churches with altarpieces and cycles of frescoes. Every one of these large paintings and cycles was worked out in collaboration with the patrons or even with the help of theological advisers; and although the High Renaissance continued the venerable tradition of Christian iconography, there is always an element of personal devotion, of local or theological imponderable elements which cannot be understood without precise historical scrutiny. Thus Titian's *Pesaro Madonna* (S. Maria dei Frari, Venice, 1519–26) is a thanksgiving of Jacopo Pesaro for his victory over the unbelievers; and while the unfurled standard of the church and a captive Turk allude to this, St Peter, St Francis and St Anthony of Padua intercede with the Virgin to procure divine grace for the assembled Pesaro family.

Much more difficult to follow are the allusions and thematic complexities in the bigger cycles, of which some of the more important may be mentioned. In the choir of S. Maria Novella, Florence, Domenico Ghirlandaio turned the scenes from the lives of the Virgin and St John, painted 1486–90 for the rich banker Giovanni Tornabuoni, into a colourful chronicle of contemporary Florentine life. It was this kind of typical *Quattrocento* painting that Savonarola stigmatised a few years later as irreverent and irreligious. In the same church, Filippino Lippi painted between 1487 and 1502 for the Strozzi family fantastic scenes from the life of St John the Evangelist and of the Apostle Philip in which reflections of the hypertrophic religious climate of Savonarola's revolution may be sensed. A similar spirit of religious urgency and fervour will be found in Luca Signorelli's dramatic, apocalyptic wall paintings in Orvieto Cathedral (1499–1502) which cannot be deciphered without a learned commentary. By contrast, Sodoma's stories from the life of St Benedict, painted between 1505 and 1508 in the cloisters of the great Benedictine house of Monte Oliveto Maggiore near Siena, are unsophisticated narratives, perfect illustrations of the peace and dignity of simple monastic life; while Gentile Bellini's (1429–1507) and Vittore Carpaccio's (c. 1455–1526) series of religious paintings for the oratories of Venetian brotherhoods mirror the glamour and splendour as well as the homeliness of life in this wealthiest Renaissance state. The tendencies of Florentine painting between 1510 and 1520 can well be studied in the frescoes of the entrance court to SS. Annunziata. Here are scenes by Andrea del Sarto from the life of S. Filippo Benizzi, founder of the order of Servants of Mary; and scenes from the life of the Virgin by Franciabigio, Pontormo, and Giovan Battista Rosso, to which Sarto contributed the *Nativity of the Virgin* (1513). A comparison with the same subject by Ghirlandaio in S. Maria Novella illustrates the development of Florentine painting in the intervening twenty-five years, away from preciousness and elegance and from the wealth of narrative and decorative detail towards a great and noble rhythmic style with a few carefully placed accents. Moreover, the later painting reveals a new visionary approach to religious subjects: instead of a ceiling, the sky opens and an angel with a censer on clouds testifies to the miracle of this birth.

The ascetic and mystic qualities of Savonarola's religious teaching and the force of his personality had a passing but immensely stirring influence on a limited group of artists. None succumbed more completely to this influence than the sensitive Botticelli (1444–1510), as the ecstatic and passionate style of his late works shows (*Nativity*, National Gallery, London, 1500). The new religious enthusiasm was of a different and less esoteric kind; it spread after 1510 from the centre of Catholicism, the papal court, and was intimately connected with a reforming zeal which found expression in the Lateran Council. Raphael, then working in the Vatican, registered in his works the changing mood like a seismograph. While his *Madonna under the Baldachin* (Palazzo Pitti, Florence) was painted between 1506 and 1508 in the representative classical style, with figures completely balanced in expression and composition, his *Madonna di Foligno* of only three years later (1511–12, Vatican) is a document of the new visionary style. The Virgin is no longer on a throne surrounded by quiet philosophical saints—the customary way of representing this subject since the fifteenth century—but sits on clouds like an apparition from heaven, and is adored with deep ardour by the donor and attending saints. Raphael's later *Sistine Madonna* (1513, Dresden) is the grandest single work showing this visionary interpretation of a religious theme.

The most progressive artists throughout Italy were remarkably swift to follow the lead given by Raphael. A study of the development of Sebastiano del Piombo (*Pietà*, Viterbo, *c.* 1520), Lorenzo Lotto, and Gaudenzio Ferrari, amongst others, proves it. Correggio (1494–1534) changed from his early, classically poised *Virgin with St Francis* (Dresden, 1514) to the sweeping compositions and the bold use of light of the Parma *Madonna della Scodella* and the Dresden *Nativity* (1522 ff.), in which sky and earth merge; his cupola decorations of S. Giovanni Evangelista at Parma (1520–4) are the first monumental example of an illusionism which makes supernatural events a powerful, realistically-felt experience. Even Venice, in spite of her long independent political, mercantile and cultural tradition, followed the general trend. Titian's *St Mark* (Venice, *c.* 1510), showing a peaceful assembly of saints symmetrically arranged in the manner of the well-established type of the *sacra conversazione*, is soon followed by such dynamic and visionary works as the *Assumption* in S. Maria dei Frari (1516–18) and the altarpiece at Ancona (1520), where in the unreal gloom of the evening inspired saints are deeply moved by the mirage of the Virgin on clouds.

Michelangelo's ceiling frescoes of the Sistine Chapel, the epitome of Renaissance religious imagery, painted between 1508 and 1512, are also theologically speaking of unequalled profundity. Along the walls of the chapel, erected under Pope Sixtus IV between 1473 and 1481, there existed frescoes representing scenes from the life of Moses and Christ. In keeping with the old-established concordance between the Old and the New Testament, events of the former prefigure those of the latter. These frescoes, which have therefore not only a literal but above all a symbolic meaning, were painted by the most celebrated artists of the day—Botticelli, Ghirlandaio, Perugino, Signorelli, and the less eminent Cosimo Rosselli. Historically, the reign of law, beginning with the life of Moses, was followed by the reign of grace, beginning with the life of Christ. Michelangelo completed the historical cycle of the walls by painting on the ceiling nine scenes illustrating the period before the reign of law. He rendered the story from the Creation to Original Sin, and further from the ensuing great catastrophe, the Flood, to the mocking of the drunken Noah by his sons. The central panels end pessimistically with the humiliation of the ancestor of the new race of mankind. Under these principal scenes are the enthroned figures of prophets and sibyls; and above their thrones are seated nudes of extraordinary beauty, holding up bronze-coloured medallions with scenes from the Book of Kings. These, like the large liberation scenes from the history of the Jewish people in the four corner spandrels, represent different prefigurations of Christian salvation. Finally, the ancestors of Christ in the eight spandrels and fourteen lunettes of the walls show the physical succession from Noah down to Christ. Thus the spiritual link between the pre-Christian and the Christian era represented by the prophets and sibyls finds a parallel in the physical link of the ancestors.

The history of Bible exegesis from Early Christian times onwards shows that the literal reading of the scriptures must be supplemented by symbolical interpretation. During the thirteenth and fourteenth centuries, vast illustrated compendia of this nature were produced, which still had very wide currency in printed editions throughout the fifteenth and sixteenth centuries. The conclusion must therefore be drawn that, just like the corner spandrels and the medallions of the Sistine ceiling, the central panels also adumbrate revealed truth. In fact, an intricate web of theological allusions proves that these scenes illustrate symbolically the mysteries of Christ's Passion.[1] It is precisely this that, in the view of Renaissance interpreters, the prophecies of Hebrew and classical seers implied. On the symbolical level, therefore, the entire ceiling forms a coherent whole, while the central panels continue the story of the older wall paintings which ended with the Last Supper. The language of religious symbolism is no longer understood, and one example of its handling should therefore illustrate it. Exactly in the centre of the ceiling is painted the Creation of Eve. Since the time of the Fathers of the Church, this event was regarded as a symbol of the Church. St Augustine compares Adam's sleep with the death of Christ; and, as Adam's side was opened and Eve extracted from his rib, so from Christ's side on the Cross flowed the blood, the sacrament on which the Church was built. The creation of Eve as a simile of the creation of the Church was so generally accepted that most printed bibles of the sixteenth century show this scene as frontispiece without any further comment.

At a first glance, the Sistine ceiling appears to be stylistically homogeneous. This, however, is not the case. There is a gradual change of scale from the (original) entrance towards the altar. The more one approaches the creation scenes, starting with the Mocking of Noah, the more colossal grow the figures and the more unreal is the space in which the scenes are set. In the Creation of Eve the figure of God the Father transcends the frame of the picture. Hereafter, this figure absorbs the entire interest, and everything is concentrated on the dynamic act of creation. It is this God the Father storming through empty spaces who has kindled the imagination of later generations perhaps more than any other painted figure, for never before or since has the mystery of primeval creation been rendered with such supernatural power. The crescendo which can be followed from the east to the west end of the chapel reaches its climax in

[1] For controversies about the symbolism of the ceiling, see: Charles de Tolnay, *Michelangelo*, vol. II (1945); E. Wind, 'Sante Pagnini and Michelangelo', *Gaz. d. Beaux-Arts*, LXXXVI (1944); *idem*, 'The Ark of Noah', *Measure*, I (1950), p. 411; *idem*, in *Art Bulletin*, XXXIII (1951), p. 41; F. Hartt, 'Lignum Vitae in medio Paradisi', *Art Bulletin*, XXXII (1950), pp. 115ff., 181ff. and 239; *idem*, in *Art Bulletin*, XXXIII (1951), p. 262.

these creation scenes. The early parts of the Sistine ceiling display the balance and poise characteristic of the situation of about 1510; while the later more heroic, dynamic and visionary parts go with the general change of style which has been discussed. In fact, it was the Michelangelo of the Sistine ceiling who set the pace of the new development, and even influenced Raphael.

Profane history painting in the modern sense, as an accurate rendering of past events, was unknown during the Renaissance. And yet history painting played a vital part in artistic theory as well as practice. The pictorial treatment of historical subjects shows many different facets, and no simple formula for their interpretation can be given. But two general observations are worth making: first, that painters regarded it as obligatory to stress the permanent rather than the passing and accidental characteristics of an event; and secondly, that the great majority of works of this class is devoted to ecclesiastical history, or in some way or other linked with it. Leonardo's and Michelangelo's battle-pieces, commissioned in 1503 and 1504 by the Signoria for two walls of the hall of the Great Council in the Palazzo Vecchio, Florence, are rather exceptional. But even these idealised commemorative representations of Florentine victories over the Pisans and Milanese would have existed under the shadow of a great statue of the Saviour, the ideal centre of the hall, if the political situation had favoured completion of the programme. The murals, too, never reached the stage of execution. In spite of this, the spectacle of these two giants of the Renaissance competing in this unusual task made a profound and lasting impression. Leonardo's cartoon of the *Battle for the Flag* remained the unsurpassed model of later battle-scenes, while Michelangelo's *Bathers* set the standard for the study and interpretation of the nude.

Pinturicchio's ten large frescoes in the library of Siena Cathedral (1503–8), illustrating in a retrogressive style with light-hearted *naïveté* the life of the Piccolomini pope Pius II, come perhaps nearer to a straightforward historical narrative than any other historical cycle. But the precious characterisation and the imaginary setting of these stories, studded with classical detail, reveal the painter's intention to render the rarefied atmosphere of super-personal events. Ten years earlier, the same Pinturicchio had painted in the Vatican Palace for Pope Alexander VI a series of rooms, in one of which he displayed in great detail the story of the sacred Egyptian bull Apis. A bull figured in the Borgia coat of arms, and Alexander implied by the painted programme that he traced the origin of his family to Apis himself. There is clearly a magical element in this story; for although the bull is shown bowing before the successor of Christ, he has imparted his vitality and strength to the Borgia family, and is thus the mainspring of Alexander's rise to the highest position in Christendom. This somewhat barbarian 'totemistic' story is yet a link in the unbroken Euhemerist tradition according to which the gods and heroes of antiquity were mythical ancestors of great families and founders of towns and communities.

By far the greatest historical cycle and, taken as a whole, the most sublime creation of the High Renaissance are the frescoes of Raphael's Stanze, decorations of some interconnected papal rooms in the Vatican Palace, hardly a stone's throw from Michelangelo's Sistine ceiling. Raphael finished the first stanza ('Stanza della Segnatura') in the course of three years (1509–12) almost single-handed, concurrently with Michelangelo's frescoes. It is probably correct to say that the murals of these four walls represent the fullest Renaissance revision of the medieval encyclopaedia; no more than the barest outline can be given of the accretion, abundance and subtlety of ideas, to the expression of which Raphael's idiom was singularly congenial. Vividly acting groups of historic figures personify the constituent forces of human society: the domain of the spirit is shown in the theological disputation over the miracle of the Eucharist, known as the *Disputa*; that of thought, opposite, in the philosophical disputation—led by Plato and Aristotle—of the *School of Athens*. Rational and metaphysical knowledge—'acquired and revealed science' in thomistic language—are the pillars on which cognition of truth rests. The third wall illustrates the domain of *Justice*, which makes the moral order of human affairs possible; and the fourth, the *Parnassus*, that of imagination and enthusiasm—an exposition of the Platonic concept that without the experience of inspired rapture, which musicians and poets express in their songs, no individual soul, no society, and not even the universe can exist. In this stanza Raphael brilliantly translated abstract thought into visual language. The great and simple form, the unsurpassed dignity of his serene and lucid style, and the compositional device of carefully balanced contrasts combine to raise the literary programme, prepared by learned advisers of the papal court, into the sphere of high ideality.

Between the summer of 1512 and the summer of 1514 Raphael executed the frescoes of the Stanza d'Eliodoro with the help of pupils. The programme changed from learned speculations of a general character to direct reflections on the exciting political events of the day. However, the four paintings, representing the *Expulsion of Heliodorus* from the Temple, the *Mass of Bolsena*, Pope Leo's meeting with Attila, and the liberation of St Peter from prison reveal their meaning only to the initiated. Pope Leo I in the meeting with Attila bears the features of the reigning Pope Leo X; as his great forerunner miraculously delivered Rome from the Huns, so Leo X by his victory at Novara cleared Italy of the French invader. The other frescoes, too, depict modern events through the medium of venerable stories from history and legend. Not only is the recent event ennobled by the parallel with the past one, but more than this: by expressing one event through the other, each painting becomes a symbol of the eternal greatness of the Church. These paintings are thus visual symbols of an exalted mystery which could only be conveyed by this particular form of allegorical history painting. Raphael adjusted his style to this new task; in all these frescoes, those who have faith and are protected by God are characterised by calm verticals, while the fear, terror and surprise of the unenlightened is expressed by rapid, diagonal movements and physical contortions.

In the third room, the Stanza dell'Incendio, painted under Raphael's direction mainly by pupils between 1514 and 1517, the relation between contemporary occurrences and time-honoured ecclesiastical history is somewhat modified. All four frescoes show the reigning Pope Leo X impersonating his forerunners Leo III and Leo IV. But these paintings disclose no parallels between similar historical situations; they allude to the proceedings of the Lateran Council, and must be understood as metaphors expressing fundamental dogmas of the Church. The *Borgo Fire*, showing the pope quelling a catastrophe in the year 849 by making the sign of the Cross, confirms the miraculous power of the Church; the *Battle of Ostia*, illustrating Leo IV's victory over the Saracens, extols her all-embracing character, the *Coronation of Charlemagne* the supremacy of Papacy, and the *Oath of Leo III* the responsibility of the clergy to God alone.

The four large frescoes of the Sala di Constantino, begun after 1517, but carried out after Raphael's death between 1523 and 1524, tell the tale of how Christianity was raised to its status of world religion. The programme logically starts with the appearance of the Cross to Constantine, followed by his battle against Maxentius, his baptism and the foundation of the papal state by Constantine's donation. Although the programme of the four stanze was in no way devised as a whole, it still expounds a uniform cycle of ideas. The Segnatura frescoes show the Church in relation to the other fundamental forces in human life, the Stanza d'Eliodoro glorifies the triumph of the Church, the Stanza dell'Incendio propagates her articles of faith, and the Sala di Constantino relates the story of her origin.

With each of the first three stanze Raphael set a stylistic example of the greatest importance. The Segnatura frescoes will always be regarded as the high-water mark of 'classical' Renaissance aspirations. In the dramatic style of the Stanza d'Eliodoro he developed principles which, characteristically, were taken up a hundred years later when painting reflected the religious enthusiasm of the Catholic Restoration, and with some justification the style of this stanza has occasionally been labelled 'proto-baroque'. With the style of the Stanza dell'Incendio, perfectly adapted to the dogmatic programme, Raphael inaugurated the two main trends of sixteenth-century mannerism. The *Fire in the Borgo* and, above all, the *Battle of Ostia* lead to the discordant style of which Vasari's mid-sixteenth-century elaborate schemes are typical; the *Coronation of*

Charlemagne and the *Oath of Leo III* find a continuation in the consciously simplified dogmatic style of masters like Federigo Zuccaro in the second half of the century.

The border-line between history painting, allegorical and mythological pictures is not easy to draw. History painting, it appeared, was given an allegorical cloak, while allegory may be represented through the veil of history or mythology, and mythology may have an allegorical meaning. Pictorial language is more ambiguous than words; and Renaissance artists, continuing a long tradition, rarely made representation and meaning coincide. Thus when Raphael's teacher, Perugino, was commissioned in 1496 to represent twelve life-size ancient heroes on the walls of the assembly hall of the wealthy guild of money-lenders, the *Cambio*, at Perugia, their quasi-allegorical character was made evident; for they are shown in groups of three under the personifications of the cardinal virtues which they are meant to exemplify. Ever since Petrarch wrote his work about famous men of antiquity, their courage and justice, their warlike and civic qualities were regarded as models for the moderns to follow. It is for this reason that the ancient exemplars fitted perfectly into the world of Christian ethics.

The representation of classical mythology was not due to a sudden pagan revival, as older writers on the Renaissance believed. More recent studies have revealed how tenaciously the ancient gods survived the ages.[1] The Middle Ages infused new life into them, and the Renaissance administered that heritage, as is shown by the fact that Boccaccio's *Genealogy of the Gods* remained the principal source book. After the first printed edition of 1472, four further editions were necessary during the fifteenth century, and innumerable more in the course of the sixteenth. Corresponding to the traditional Bible exegesis, Boccaccio maintained that a myth has four layers of meaning—literal, moral, allegorical and metaphysical. In considering mythological Renaissance pictures this must not be lost sight of, although every case should be approached on its merits, and will only reveal its meaning if the salient circumstances have been fully investigated.

When Isabella d'Este, one of the most avid collectors and discriminating patrons of the Renaissance, decided to have her private study in the Palace at Mantua decorated with a coherent cycle by great masters, she chose mythological scenes, but wrote in a letter: 'We desire to have in our study paintings of allegorical subjects by the best painters in Italy.' Amongst the paintings was Mantegna's *Parnassus* (1497, now Louvre), one of the most beautiful and accomplished works of allegorical mythology. While this picture seems to glorify the civilising influence of poetry and music, a counterpart painted by the same master and finished in 1502, showing as main

[1] See, above all, the writings by A. Warburg, F. Saxl and E. Panofsky, all quoted in J. Seznec, *La survivance des dieux antiques* (1940), Eng. translation (1953).

protagonists Athena and Venus, teaches the lesson, translated into pedestrian language, that Vice must be expelled by Virtue. These and other mythologies of the same cycle are embellished with an infinite variety of learned allusions. This cycle is of particular interest because the programme for one of the pictures, written by Isabella's humanist adviser, Paride da Ceresara, and bristling with weird erudition, has survived. Pallas and Diana had to be shown fighting Venus and Cupid, symbolising the *Battle of Love and Chastity*. The painter, Perugino, was tied down to the minutest detail, and expressly forbidden to introduce anything of his own invention. The picture reached Mantua in 1505. It aroused no enthusiasm; clearly this formidable task went beyond the capability of the tame painter of sweet Madonnas.

Isabella's brother, Duke Alfonso of Ferrara, stimulated by his sister's enterprise, decided to have a room of his castle similarly decorated. In the refined intellectual atmosphere of Alfonso's court, which counted Ariosto amongst its luminaries, the programme differed from that of Isabella; it was entirely devoted to the humanist interpretation of Love. The aged Giovanni Bellini began, shortly before his death, a strange, somewhat burlesque and not yet fully explained *Feast of the Gods*, later to be finished by Titian (Washington), and the latter contributed three *Bacchanals* (1516–23) now in Madrid and London, two of which are precise illustrations of scenes described by the Greek writer Philostratus. No more accomplished north Italian Renaissance interpretations of a classical text exist; they translate the literary concept into free, infinitely rich and harmonious painterly compositions. But again, they are more than pure illustrations. Philostratus himself had pointed the moral of the *Bacchanal of Children*. Love, he explained, symbolised by the play of the cupids, governs all that is mortal. The love over which Venus presides is sensuous love, and yet these cupids show all the stages of love 'from its first dawning to eternal duration'. One is reminded that eternal love in Christian terms is Charity, and it is likely that Titian and his advisers endeavoured to blend in these pictures Christian conceptions with current Neoplatonic theories of love.

This may be supported by reference to Titian's so-called *Sacred and Profane Love* (c. 1515, Rome), one of the happiest of his creations, breathing an atmosphere of peace and beatitude. It has been, we think, correctly argued[1] that the nude Venus represents the higher principle; for celestial Beauty, that beauty which is eternal and unchangeable, is as naked as Truth. Her counterpart, adorned with all the worldly charms, is the principle of visible, tangible and perishable terrestrial beauty. But these two forms of Platonic beauty adumbrate the two principles of Christian love—the love of God and the love of one's neighbour—which together inform the highest Christian virtue, Charity. The attributes of

[1] Panofsky, *Iconology*.

Titian's twin Venuses resemble closely those given to traditional representations of Charity. It is not easy nowadays fully to grasp the overtones or
undertones of Renaissance mythological and quasi-mythological pictures.
However, this class of picture was always exclusive, painted for a clientele
which had imbibed current philosophical and humanist ideas. With regard
to pictures like Leonardo's *Leda*, only preserved in copies, Giorgione's
Dresden *Venus*, or Titian's later representations of Venus (Florence,
Madrid), we are groping more or less in the dark. But this much can be
said—that these works established the High Renaissance ideal of female
beauty; a sublime, noble and infinitely delicate beauty which could not
have been developed without the almost religious Neoplatonic yearning
for the beautiful soul in the beautiful body. It is the same spirit which
made Michelangelo represent the Virgin of his Pietà in St Peter's in a
state of eternal youth, and which informed the bodily perfection of the
nude youths of the Sistine ceiling.

Correggio's decoration of a room of the former convent of S. Paolo at
Parma (1518–19) is perhaps the most fascinating document of the use of
mythology and allegory serving a Christian content. Here are shown
Diana and her *cortège*, Faun and Vestal, sacrifices and libations, the
Graces and Fates, Venus and Juno, together with allegories of simplicity
and virginity, nature and immortality. This was the dining-room of the
abbess Giovanna Piacenza, the patroness, who, immortalised in the large
painting of Diana, remains for ever the vigilant custodian of chastity. Its
triumph was here expressed by the medieval allegorical method, while the
learned antiquarian detail and the classical and sensuous pictorial language
are typical of the High Renaissance.

Raphael's *Cupid and Psyche* cycle in the Villa Farnesina, begun *c.* 1518,
is the monumental Roman counterpart to Titian's *Bacchanals*. The
painter chose twelve episodes from Apuleius' charming story to decorate
the spandrels and ceiling of the once open loggia. Raphael died on
6 April 1520, five days before his patron Agostino Chigi, and left the
frescoes to be finished by pupils. The cycle not only constitutes a climax
of the High Renaissance reconciliation of the textual and formal tradition
of antiquity, but this eloquent and serene hymn to love also recaptures
the fairy-tale spirit of its source. By thus feeling and revealing the poetical
quality of the ancient myth, Raphael opened new avenues of approach
to classical antiquity. In these frescoes, as well as in the earlier fresco of
Galatea's Triumph (1514) in an adjoining room, stimulated perhaps by
some verses in Politian's *Giostra*, Raphael's style is classical and sculptural,
and individual pieces of ancient statuary served as models for some of the
figures. A comparison with the style of his contemporary religious imagery
and the later Stanze shows that, at the summit of his power, this great
master changed his idiom to suit the subject-matter.

The decoration of the Farnesina as a whole gives an unequalled insight into certain 'pagan' aspects of the High Renaissance. Agostino Chigi's bedroom on the first floor is suitably decorated with Sodoma's free interpretation of Lucian's (second century A.D.) description of the wedding of Alexander and Roxana; and other rooms contain Peruzzi's mythological friezes of the loves of the gods after Ovid. But in the Galatea room there is also Peruzzi's ceiling, which illustrates in mythological terms a precise celestial chart of the northern sky on 1 December 1466. This was the date of Agostino Chigi's birth. The ceiling therefore illustrates a monumental horoscope of the patron. It reflects the enormous vogue of astrology at this period. It was the power of the classical gods as planets and constellations that had for long invested them with a sinister vitality. The antagonism to Christianity expressed in these frescoes is revealed by the belief in a fatalistic determinism as opposed to divine providence, rather than in the familiar contrast of paganism and Christianity.

In order to understand the full breadth of Agostino's princely patronage, it should not be forgotten how much the Church profited from his liberality. Amongst other things, Raphael's frescoes of prophets and sibyls in S. Agostino, Rome (1514), and the sepulchral chapel of the family in S. Maria del Popolo, designed by Raphael and decorated by him and Sebastiano del Piombo, will for ever be connected with his name.

Since Dante had described his vision of the Church riding on 'a car triumphal' and Petrarch written his allegorical epic *Trionfi*, triumphal arches and triumphal processions *all'antica* played an ever-increasing part in the festive life of the Renaissance. Mythological, allegorical and historical triumphs were acted and represented for the celebration of weddings, the receptions of honoured guests or victorious commanders. And it is characteristic of the spirit of the Renaissance that the classical triumph could be harnessed to the services of the Church. In 1491 Lorenzo the Magnificent had the Triumph of Aemilius Paulus from the description of Plutarch represented to celebrate the feast of St John; in 1506 Julius II entered Bologna on a triumphal car; the triumph of Camillus was shown at Leo X's entry into Florence. Titian's woodcuts of the *Triumph of Faith* (1510) showing Christ in a car drawn by the Doctors of the Church, preceded and followed by the patriarchs and sibyls, martyrs and confessors, is evidence that the classical conception was well suited to glorify the Church triumphant, implying at the same time that the triumphs of Christianity had superseded those of antiquity. Similarly pagan sacrifices, common in religious imagery of the Renaissance, were meant to foreshadow the sacrifice of Christ that had superseded them.

Just as Andrea Riccio's bronze candlestick in the Santo at Padua and his reliefs for the Della Torre tomb (Louvre) show archaeologically accurate sacrifices, so Mantegna in the nine large cartoons of the *Triumph of Caesar* (c. 1485–94), now at Hampton Court, made it a point of honour to emulate antiquity itself. Nobody before him had developed the triumphal theme either in such a monumental way or with such archaeological erudition. Here are the trophies and statuary, the sacrificial vessels and prisoners, all studied and gleaned from ancient monuments and descriptions of classical triumphs as found in Appian, Suetonius and Josephus. The north Italian approach to antiquity was always more archaeological than that of central Italy, and in this respect his *Triumph* reflects the particular character of northern humanism. But the erudition noticeable in this work is not pedantic; it is a highly personal, imaginative and even fantastic creation, in which classical detail has been assembled to form something quite new—a typical Renaissance entity. Mantegna's *Triumph*, painted for Marchese Francesco Gonzaga, was later arranged by his son Federigo in a room of the Mantuan palace in such a way that its panels framed a picture by Lorenzo Costa (1522), which recorded Federigo's own triumph on the occasion of his victorious participation in the battle of Pavia. Thus, by linking his career with the great Roman imperial tradition, Federigo gave lustre to his own military success.

In contrast to Mantegna's antiquarianism, Perugino's ancient heroes in the *Cambio* at Perugia are clad in fanciful dress which ultimately derived from the Burgundian court style, fashionable in Italy throughout the fifteenth century. While in this as in many other cases the rich and strange costume was meant to indicate historical distance rather than historical fidelity, at the beginning of the sixteenth century—simultaneously with the cogent classicism to be found in all the three arts—compliance with archaeologically established facts became the rule. Indeed, anything else would then have appeared as perverting the truth. From then on, such fidelity belonged to the requirements of 'propriety', one of the pillars of Renaissance art theory (p. 151).

From the birth of art theory as a proper aesthetic discipline, that is, from the beginning of the fifteenth century onwards to the end of the eighteenth century, portraiture as an imitative art ranked lower than the subjects from history, mythology and the Scriptures. It would, therefore, seem logical to infer that portraiture should have been shunned by patrons and artists alike. However, the reverse is true. From the first half of the fifteenth century onwards, the new type of self-contained easel portrait occupied an important position in artistic production, and the demand for portraits steadily grew. The greatest artists during the first quarter of the sixteenth century, Leonardo, Raphael, Giorgione, Titian, Lotto—with the one memorable exception of Michelangelo—produced portraits in considerable numbers. It was these High Renaissance artists who solved the contradiction between a theoretical refusal and the actual practice of portrait painting. Leonardo's *Mona Lisa* (1502, Louvre) is the first great example of a veritable revolution in portraiture. While the formal elements of this portrait—half-figure, three-quarter view, eyes meeting the beholder, distant landscape—reveal Italian fifteenth-century and, in addition, Flemish prototypes, the earlier customary realism was here replaced by a vision of an inscrutable physical and spiritual perfection of the sitter, before which the world has always bowed in admiration. Raphael's early portraits of *Angelo and Maddalena Doni* (Florence), painted shortly after he had settled in Florence in 1504, show the impact of Leonardo's new approach. But Leonardo's spiritualisation and idealisation of the sitter is still missing. Raphael's change from the *Maddalena Doni* to the *Lady with the Veil* (Palazzo Pitti, Florence) or from *Angelo Doni* to the portrait of *Baldesar Castiglione* (Louvre) must be seen not only as a stylistic development towards broader, fuller and more rhythmical forms, but above all as a development towards the spiritual ideal of refined humanity which Leonardo had established in his *Mona Lisa*. Raphael's portraits of about 1515 express the new conception of man, temperate, noble and dignified, to which his friend Castiglione himself erected a lasting literary monument in his immensely influential *Courtier*.

Nobody rendered this humane ideal more fully than Titian. In many of his portraits he dispensed entirely with accessories. The heads embody the ideal of the well-groomed, controlled and perfectly balanced personality. Often he replaced the traditional half-length by the three-quarter length, for the graceful deportment of the figure, the simple and careful elegance of the dress—all this was now important for the characterisation of the sitter; while the warm colours of his broad painterly brushwork facilitate human contact between sitter and spectator.

The idealisation attempted by, and demanded from, the painter was not to undermine realistic likeness. No finer character studies exist than Raphael's portraits of Julius II and Leo X, or Titian's likeness of his friend Aretino and of many a humanist of his day. It is in this reconciliation of idealised vision and realistic appearance that the subtle task of the portrait painter consisted. Only when he surpasses nature by forming an inner vision of his sitter—that is, only by a process of idealised sublimation—is he able to raise portraiture, according to the Plato-inspired Renaissance theory, from mere imitation to the level of 'high' art.

The new type of Renaissance man longed for a retreat into a happy Utopia. What the chivalrous romances and the love poetry of the troubadours had been for the Middle Ages, Arcady became for people from the Renaissance onwards. Theocritus' pastoral idylls and Virgil's bucolic poetry found their Renaissance apogee in Sannazzaro's *Arcadia* (1502). And while Politian in Florence, Boiardo and later Tasso at Ferrara, and Molza in Rome poured forth their elegiac songs, while pastoral plays and masques became fashionable about the year 1500, Lorenzo de' Medici resurrected Arcady in his Fiesole villa, for which Signorelli probably painted his nostalgic *Pan* (destroyed, formerly Berlin, c. 1490), and Giorgione created a pictorial vision of arcadian innocence.

Giorgione is probably the most evasive genius of the Renaissance.

When he died in 1510 he was about 33 years old. Considering his enormous reputation amongst contemporaries, he must have left a fair number of paintings, but nowadays opinions differ widely over the attribution of pictures to him. One would be inclined to say that an artist about whose work experts cannot agree is not a clearly defined personality. And yet, the opposite is the case. The name Giorgione evokes quite definite associations, for which Walter Pater in his famous essay found beautiful words. It was precisely the singular poetical quality of Giorgione's art which captivated other masters to such a degree that their work appears like an extension of his. Giorgione set his figures in a wide landscape, and made figures and landscape express the same mood. The landscape itself, with its clumps of dark trees, its peaceful undulating movement and its mysterious golden light, has the emotive quality of the elegiac melancholic paradise that is Arcady. To translate thus the Arcady of the poets into visual language was an achievement of first-rate importance; and this explains why Giorgione's art appeared to his contemporaries as a fascinating revelation. Giorgione brought to perfection tendencies which had a home in Venice. Venetian artists had always tried to express moods by colour, in contrast to artistic trends in Florence, where colour remained accessory to line and design. In the work of some older artists, particularly in the landscape backgrounds of pictures by Giovanni Bellini and Vittore Carpaccio, one can trace how the ground was prepared for Giorgione's genius. In addition, Francesco Colonna's *Hypnerotomachia Poliphili*, printed by Aldus Manutius in 1499 and embellished with many woodcuts, helped to spread a dreamland romanticism. But Giorgione's art must not be regarded as expressing a vague lyrical and elegiac sentiment. In accordance with the requirements of his time, the paintings always relate definite stories. It remains one of the mysteries of the mysterious Giorgione that the exact meaning of some of his most important pictures, like the *Tempest* (Venice), the *Magi* (Vienna) and *The Concert* (Louvre) still defies interpretation.

More than once in these pages reference has been made to the creation of art theory as a discipline in its own right. Ever since Renaissance artists introduced the dogma of art as a science—ever since Alberti and Leonardo propounded that practice must be based on theory—the status of the artist in society, his relation to his patrons and the conception of his own calling began to change. It was theory that equipped the individual artist for his struggle with reality.

Art theory was concerned with two principal problems—that of representational correctness and that of beauty. The former was achieved through the theory and practice of perspective, the study of bodies and of anatomy, of botany, zoology and the wide field of natural phenomena. Hence Alberti's demand: 'First draw the figure nude; then show it dressed'—an advice accepted by the great Renaissance artists, as can be seen in innumerable preparatory drawings by Leonardo, Raphael and others; hence the passionate study of anatomy and the dissecting of bodies, pursued most indefatigably of all by Michelangelo and Leonardo. Seven hundred and seventy-nine sheets of Leonardo's planned 'Anatomy' were still extant at the end of the sixteenth century. Hence also Leonardo's infinite labour in trying to decode the secrets of nature by a strictly empirical method of observation and experiment. Beauty, on the other hand, an echo or reflection of divine order, could only be achieved by using those proportions on which the harmony of the universe is based. 'Proportion', Leonardo exclaimed, 'is found not only in numbers and measures, but also in sounds, weights, times, and places, and in every force. . . .' A theory of expression and propriety had to be allied to that of proportion to guarantee beauty in a work of art. Leonardo, in particular, on the basis of Alberti's findings, demanded that the artist must convincingly express the passions and emotions, and that these must be precisely related to the dramatic content of the story. His *Last Supper* provides an object-lesson in the application of his theory. Since these artists believed in the moral purpose of their work, the theory of expression held a place of special importance. Again using Alberti's definitions, Leonardo explained that propriety or decorum consisted in the appropriateness of gesture, dress and locality. Thus propriety was equivalent to historical truth, and in classical circles the demand for it never abated. When Raphael designed the *Feast of the Ancient Gods* for the ceiling of the Farnesina, propriety required that the participants should lie on triclinia or couches, the antique fashion of taking meals.

In all the discussion about expression, decorum and historical truth, the comparison with poetry was ready at hand. If one could prove that painting and poetry were two realisations of the same thing, then painting would be raised to the noble rank of poetry. Horace's phrase from the *Ars Poetica*: 'ut pictura poesis'—'as is painting, so is poetry'—supplied the classical verdict. From the end of the fifteenth to the end of the eighteenth century the affinity between poetry and painting was indeed regarded as being very close. Like poetry, it was argued, painting is concerned with the imitation of human action, and like the poet the painter should choose his themes from sacred and profane history and from the great exemplars of the past. Like the poet, he must express human emotions, and not only please but also inform—arouse emotions in his audience and impart wisdom to mankind. Like the poet, finally the artist ascends through knowledge to inspiration, 'that divine power which transforms his mind into the likeness of the divine mind' (Leonardo).

Although in theory Alberti had raised the profession of an artist from a craft to 'high art', it took a long time even in Florence until the new attitude had results in practice. Throughout the fifteenth century artists were still recruited from the lower middle class. It was rare for sons of intellectuals, civil servants or of the aristocracy to become artists. If a boy from a good family insisted on an artist's career, it was more honourable to apprentice him as a painter than as a sculptor, for painters belonged to the guild of the apothecaries, whereas sculptors ranked as stonemasons with the bricklayers. A well-authenticated anecdote from Michelangelo's life shows that in his days the old notions were thrown overboard, at least in the progressive Florentine circles. His family belonged to the old burgher-nobility of Florence, and the father, therefore, opposed the son's determination to become an artist. In the end he consented to apprentice him to the painter Ghirlandaio (1488). When Lorenzo the Magnificent discovered Michelangelo's gift as a sculptor, the father declared that he would never permit a son of his to be a stone-cutter; he consented only after Lorenzo had explained to him the difference between a stone-cutter and the modern conception of a sculptor.

It was at this period that the medieval craftsman-employee developed into the modern artist and the employer into the patron. Lorenzo the Magnificent, a great Maecenas and collector and altogether the quint-essence of the modern patron, inaugurated with his venture in the garden of S. Marco the new type of artistic education. Here young artists, among them Michelangelo, worked under the supervision of the aged sculptor Bertoldo; and although the precise character of the enterprise, which only existed for about three years until Lorenzo's death in 1492, is unknown, it can yet be said that for the first time traditional apprenticeship was re-placed by a free and liberal education in which the first germs of later academies of art may be found.

During the fifteenth century, it was still common for artists, even of the first rank, to be prepared to accept any occasional work. They undertook designs not only for such transient occasions as festivals, but also for chests and curtains, pennons and trappings of horses. In the beginning of the sixteenth century, all this changed. It throws a light on the new social position of artists and the respect for their genius that Vasari in the *Lives of Artists*, published in 1550, constantly returns to the slur cast on the dignity of the profession by requests for this kind of low-class work. With the new freedom, the artist himself as a type began to change, and from the end of the fifteenth century onwards one begins to discern those special characteristics which are still often associated with artists. We now hear of their extravagant tastes and habits. Artists like the sculptor Gianfrancesco Rustici (1474–1554), for a time Leonardo's collaborator, and, it seems, the first example of a nobleman who practised art for his own satisfaction, the painter Sodoma (1477–1549), Piero di Cosimo (1462–1521) and Pontormo (1494–1556) were all notoriously eccentric. Piero di Cosimo lived as a recluse in dirt and squalor; his strange and abstruse pictures of primeval life (New York and Oxford) seem to reveal something of his troubled mind. Pontormo completely cut himself off from the world. It is perhaps not accidental that it was this melancholic, above all, who in the years around 1520 headed the revolt against the equipoise of the High Renaissance.

It is a sign of the new era that artists insisted more and more on creating in solitude. Michelangelo never allowed anybody to see the work in hand. Many of them also began to work spasmodically; furiously creative periods alternated with long pauses. The continuity of the medieval workshop tradition was irrevocably broken. It needed a new type of patron to tolerate the new type of artist; one who recognised and admired genius, and was therefore prepared to put up with eccentricity and artistic temperament. The legend that the Emperor Charles V showed his reverence for Titian's genius by stooping to pick up a brush characterises the new relationship.

Pope Julius II's treatment of Michelangelo epitomises the change that had come about. Julius, the greatest patron of his day, the man who had gathered round him Bramante, Raphael and Michelangelo, in a resolve to make Rome the artistic centre of the world, was tied by strong bonds of sympathy to Michelangelo, whose daemonic powers, so similar to his own, he fully appreciated. Once the pope refused to see the master on matters concerning the tomb, whereupon Michelangelo wrote: 'Most Holy Father: this morning I was driven from your Palace by Your Holiness's orders; I give you to understand that from henceforth, if you desire my services, you must look for me elsewhere than in Rome'— and departed for Florence. Julius patiently tried to induce him to return. 'Michelangelo the sculptor,' he wrote to the Signoria of Florence, 'who left us without reason and in mere caprice is afraid, as we are informed, of returning; though we for our part are not angry with him, knowing the humours of such men of genius.' This surely was a new language.

No other artist did an equally great service to the profession as a whole. Michelangelo was the herald of the artists' ambitions, of their aspirations of autonomy and sovereignty. When he began his career, his family thought he was stepping down the social ladder. Long before he died, he was venerated as super-man, as *divino*. The Portuguese painter Francisco de Hollanda voiced the change that had come about when he wrote: 'In Italy one does not care for the renown of great princes; it's a painter only that they call divine.'

2. IN NORTHERN EUROPE

THE period between 1490 and 1520 was one of great efflorescence in the arts of the north, when men like Dürer, Grünewald and Holbein were active in Germany and the workshops in the Netherlands were still prolific. It was at this time that artists in these countries became aware of the Italian Renaissance and also felt the first tremors of the Reformation.

In the spring of 1494 the young Albrecht Dürer was recalled by his father from the 'bachelor journey' which had taken him west to some of the big towns on the Rhine. Obediently, he came home to Nürnberg to marry and set up his own workshop, but a few months later he left again, this time, however, going south to Italy. These two journeys are symptomatic of the crisis which the artists of the north had to face at the turn of the century. Dürer, born in 1471 as the son of a goldsmith in whose workshop he received his first training, had been apprenticed to the leading Nürnberg painter Michael Wolgemut (1434–1519). This master, like most German painters of his generation, had been strongly influenced by Roger van der Weyden (d. 1464) in whose work traditional Gothic design and the new delight in depicting the outward appearance of the world are perfectly merged. During his 'Wanderjahre' Dürer tried to meet the painter and engraver Martin Schongauer (1445?–91) who was looked upon almost as a pupil of Roger. But the sudden journey to Italy speaks of very different interests. During his stay in Basle (about 1491) Dürer had been in close touch with humanists and publishers for whom he had been working; there he may well have seen Italian books and engravings. Back in Nürnberg we find him copying Italian engravings with care and accuracy. In his copies after Mantegna and Pollaiuolo Dürer's preoccupation with the beauty and proportion of the human form becomes at once obvious. It was this interest which drove him to Italy, first in 1494 and again in 1505: he entreated the Italian painter Jacopo di Barbari, who came to Nürnberg probably in 1500, to tell him his 'secret' of figure construction and when the Italian showed himself uncommunicative he began to study Vitruvius. In 1504 Dürer published an engraving, *Adam and Eve*, which embodied the first fruits of his researches in proportion; further investigations were carried out with the help of measured drawings and resulted finally in two large panel-paintings of the same subject (1508, Madrid). A little later he tackled the problem once more in a different way and the famous engraving *Knight, Death and Devil* was the result. By now Dürer was also preparing a comprehensive treatise on art, but characteristically he completed no more than the books on perspective and proportion. At the end of his life he demonstrated his views again in the *Four Apostles* (1526, Munich), this time with a grandeur and conviction that came from life-long study.

Once Dürer began to pursue these questions he had to turn to Italian art for help. Fifteenth-century artists of the north had been well aware of the world around them, but their pursuit of visual beauty had been purely empirical. The Italians, having studied nature, applied mathematics to picture-making. Yet these Italian artists meant to do no more than to return to their own past; for them the study of ancient monuments, the study of the rules of Vitruvius and the study of nature were but facets of one and the same problem. Dürer's case was different. He never went to Rome, or Florence; he was content to visit Venice, the nearest centre where artists were practising what he was trying to learn.

By about 1500 most northern artists had to take note of the developments which had occurred in Italy during the previous seventy years. Dürer's journey as a 'student' may have been one of the first of its kind, but soon afterwards such travels were to become more common. The 'bachelor journey' which a generation earlier used to take young artists to the fountain-heads of Flemish realism now took them south. Hans Burgmair, a painter from Augsburg, visited Venice just before 1500, the Nürnberg sculptor Peter Vischer the Younger went to Italy in 1508 and Hans Holbein was in Milan in 1518. Even artists from the Low Countries now went south; Mabuse was in Rome in 1508 and Jan van Scorel must have been there about 1520.

Yet the purpose of these journeys varied a good deal. Dürer alone among his German contemporaries seems to have understood one of the main problems of the Renaissance: Leonardo's construction of the microcosm by means of number and proportion. Dürer wrote: 'For truly art is embedded in nature; he who can pull it out will hold it. If you can get the better of art, you will not make mistakes in your work. Through geometry you can prove much of your work.'[1]

His contemporaries received the lessons of the Renaissance on an altogether lower level. Hans Holbein (1497–1541) certainly had little of Dürer's depth or searching mind, but he was perhaps gifted with a much more immediate artistic perception, which enabled him to weld the experiences of an Italian journey perfectly into his work. For he too grew up in a late Gothic workshop—that of his father, Holbein the Elder, in Augsburg—and he too had to come to terms with the new art of Italy. In Milan he must have seen Leonardo's *Last Supper* and the *Virgin of the Rocks*; he may have met Luini and he certainly saw something of Bramante's early works. Holbein's façade decorations on the *Haus zum Tanz* (1519) and the frescoes in the Town Hall (1522) in Basle are full of Italian motifs, particularly in their Bramantesque architectural settings. However, his style cannot be explained by pointing out the borrowing of motifs; the results of his encounter with Italian art were much more profound. From his beginnings he made up for a certain lack of imagination and poetry by an overwhelming sense of reality and scrupulous matter-of-factness. Contact with Leonardo's circle can only have helped to sharpen his eyes. The unsophisticated late Gothic realism became an unremitting recording of observations controlled by more austere principles of form. The great series of portraits with their almost brutal faithfulness and their simplicity of composition are the outcome of this intermingling of German and Italian elements.

In Augsburg, an important centre of the arts, we can study yet another

[1] E. Panofsky, *Albrecht Dürer*, 1943, pp. 242ff., esp. p. 279.

aspect of the clash between north and south. Augsburg, like Nürnberg, was a rich commercial city engaged mainly in trade between Germany and Italy and ties with Venice were particularly close. In fact, the German merchants had their own settlement in Venice, the *fondaco dei Tedeschi*. The Italianate taste of this German colony was so strong that two Italian masters, Giorgione and his young assistant Titian, were commissioned in 1508 to decorate the façade of the *fondaco*, and Dürer's altarpiece for the German chapel, the *Virgin of the Rosaries* (1506, Prague) owes perhaps more to Giovanni Bellini, whom Dürer greatly admired, than to northern tradition. It is therefore hardly astonishing that the merchants of Augsburg wanted from their leading painter, Hans Burgmair (1473–1531), the kind of painting that was being done for their colleagues in Venice. In Burgmair's portraits in particular, but also in his altarpieces, elements of composition and the rich glow of colour can easily be traced back to Venetian influence. It was the taste of his patrons which made the pupil of Schongauer into a follower of the Venetians. The stronger such external pressure became, the more superficial the reception of the Italian Renaissance was likely to be.

We can observe this phenomenon in many instances but nowhere more clearly than in the work of Lucas Cranach (1473–1553), who in some respects was one of the most important innovators of the age. From 1505 until his death Cranach was employed by successive electors of Saxony and he had a flourishing workshop in Wittenberg which was patronised by many German princes. His immense output includes a number of curious mythological pieces with such subjects as *Nymph by a Spring* (Leipzig), *Venus and Amor* (Rome, Gal. Borghese), and *The Choice of Hercules*. All these are subjects in which Renaissance patrons naturally demanded 'classical nudes'. Cranach is true to these demands of taste even if his figures retain much of Gothic linear flow and grace and it is not this stylistic peculiarity which makes them look so unclassical. They are not nude, they are merely undressed. Venus wears nothing but a large hat, the Graces display shining golden necklaces and Cupid has draped round his middle a tiny—and transparent—veil. Many of these pictures still exist in two or more versions for they were choice collectors' pieces. This amusing amalgam of Gothic survival and classical revival is little more than licence made respectable through art.

In the Netherlands artists experienced the same clash of the two traditions. The power of the school of Roger van der Weyden was ebbing; Hans Memling, one of his most influential and popular pupils, died in 1494. Gerhard David (*c*. 1460–1523) and Geertgen tot Sint Jans (working *c*. 1490–1510) continued the tradition of Gothic realism for some time. Once patrons and artists became aware that this manner was really outmoded, Dürer's woodcuts and engravings began to exert a considerable influence, as is most clearly seen in the works of Lucas van Leyden

(1494–1533). When Dürer himself visited the Netherlands in 1520 he was greeted everywhere with the utmost deference and hailed as the greatest living artist in the north. Direct and important contacts with Italian art had existed throughout the second half of the fifteenth century, but it was largely a one-way traffic. The Medici adorned their palace with Flemish tapestries, Tommaso Portinari commissioned an altarpiece from Hugo van der Goes for a Florentine church, yet Dutch and Flemish artists were hardly shaken in their own traditions by such works of their Italian contemporaries as they saw. The paintings of Roger van der Weyden hardly reveal that he undertook a journey to Italy in about 1450. The work of an artist living some fifty years later usually betrays at once whether he has been to Italy, even without supporting documentary evidence. Mabuse is perhaps the most characteristic example of a painter whose style was shaped by his experience of Italian and classical art. Here the classical tradition which we saw so curiously distorted in Cranach's painting flows much more purely. The study of Dürer must have played an important part in Mabuse's training, though the characteristic style for which his contemporaries esteemed him was acquired only through his sojourn in Rome in 1508 which was suggested by his patron, the highly cultured Philip of Burgundy. In 1484 a Bruges publisher had brought out an edition of the medieval allegorised version of Ovid's *Metamorphoses*, the *Ovide Moralisé*. It is illustrated with a number of woodcuts showing the heroes of classical antiquity in heavy medieval armour and the nymphs and goddesses dressed like ladies of the day. Some twenty years later Mabuse painted *Neptune and Amphitrite* (1516, Berlin) for his patron. The two life-size nudes owe their existence first and foremost to a close study of classical statues and reliefs; equally the setting, an enormous aedicula, is purely classical in character. Vasari tells us that Mabuse was the first artist to introduce mythological subjects, properly treated, into Flanders.[1] Even in the north these legends had never been quite forgotten and the Italian Renaissance now helped artists and patrons to reintegrate once more form and content. In this 'revival' we can again discern a strong sociological impetus, for it was the kind of art demanded by a well-educated *élite*.

For Dürer the problem of the classical revival was quite different. In his youth, he was attracted by strange mythological subjects, such as the *Rape of Europa*, the *Sea Monster*, *Hercules* or the *Dream of a Scholar* into which he introduced a nude classical Venus. But with growing maturity and self-assurance it became a certainty to Dürer that he could best express his ideal of beauty through works of a religious, specifically Christian character. At times of great mental stress, as in the years preceding the Reformation, he occasionally returned to what were for him dark pagan powers (*Abduction on a Unicorn*, 1516), but if we take

[1] Vasari (ed. G. Milanesi), vol. VII, p. 584.

Dürer's work as a whole the absence of any mythological subjects after his second Italian journey of 1505–6 is remarkable and hardly fortuitous. Dürer himself makes it quite clear in his theoretical writings that religious art must take precedence over all other art. The search for laws of beauty is valid only within limits. Dürer was at one and the same time a painter and engraver of traditional religious subjects, and the first German artist to outgrow the modes of late Gothic art.

France remained relatively free from Italian Renaissance influence until the advent of Francis I in 1515. The Maître de Moulins, so called after his most important work, an altarpiece in the cathedral of Moulins, is a typical artist in the conventional Gothic style; 'clarity, limpidity, dignity' are the chief characteristics of his art.[1] Jean Perréal (c. 1455–1530) accompanied Louis XII to Italy, but remained nevertheless true to tradition, as his portrait of the king (Windsor) shows. At most one may see weak reflections of Milanese painting in some of his works. Bourdichon (c. 1457–1521) seems to have come under the influence of Perugino. But on the whole French painting was remarkably stagnant at the end of the fifteenth century.[2]

German sculptors show awareness of the same problems which beset the painters, though to a lesser extent. Tilman Riemenschneider (1468–1531), working mainly in the Rhine-Main region, successfully continued the tradition of Gothic sculpture. The anatomy of the human figure, whether draped or not, is never taken too seriously, the stance is uncertain and heads are rarely expressive of true emotion. But the outline of figures is always lively and draperies and hair are arranged to give the maximum effect to the play of light and shade. The charming figures of Adam and Eve (Würzburg) are good examples of his rather delicate art.

Veit Stoss's monumental altarpiece of 1493 (Cracow cathedral) also remains wholly within the Gothic tradition. Here Flemish realism, a treatment of draperies derived from German sculpture and a marked interest in expressive gestures and heads combine to create a personal and highly dramatic style quite uninhibited by any Renaissance rules and restraints. Stoss's other works, most of them in and around Nürnberg, where he had his workshop, show similar characteristics.

It is once again in Nürnberg and Augsburg that we find workshops catering for an Italianate taste. The workshop of Peter Vischer (the Elder, c. 1455–1529) experienced the full impact of the Italian Renaissance, since two of his sons, Peter (the Younger, 1487–1528) and Hans (c. 1490–1549) spent some time in Italy. The most important work of the family foundry, the monumental tabernacle over the relics of St Sebaldus (1508–17, Nürnberg, Sebalduskirche) is still Gothic in general conception and follows a traditional shape. It is, however, decorated with over one

[1] G. Ring, *A Century of French Painting, 1400–1500* (1949).
[2] A. F. Blunt, *Art and Architecture in France, 1500–1700* (1953), p. 18.

hundred statuettes many of which clearly betray Italian models. What could be a better illustration of this odd mixture of heterogeneous styles than the appearance of nymphs, tritons and satyrs of truly classical shape at the foot of a Gothic shrine? The Augsburg sculptor Adolf Daucher (c. 1465–1524) decorated a tomb for a member of the Fugger family with mourning satyrs and putti riding on dolphins, which may have been derived from Venetian models.

There was at the time little activity in church building, resulting in a dearth of monumental commissions, and the Reformation was soon to make all but an end of carved altar shrines. Lavish tombs, however, were constantly commissioned in a period so preoccupied with thoughts of death and disaster, and Renaissance ornament plays an ever greater part in their decoration. Fountains too were sometimes fashioned in the new style; in 1532 Hans Vischer placed a figure of Apollo on top of a fountain in the courtyard of Nürnberg Town Hall. In this case the design may have been inspired by the famous Belvedere Apollo in Rome. But the sculptors devoted most of their energy to the creation of small decorative works and collectors' pieces. These had to conform to contemporary taste since they were produced for wealthy and educated patrons, who had usually been to Italy themselves, and Renaissance sculpture became known in Germany mainly through such small figures.

Not only classical mythology was treated in the new manner. When Conrad Meit of Worms (c. 1475–c. 1550), who for many years was employed by Margaret of Austria, made a little alabaster statuette of Judith (Munich, Bayrisches National-Museum) he showed her completely nude, modelled like a classical Venus and imbued with a strong sensuality. Hans Daucher (c. 1485–1538) placed a Virgin with Child and angels, conceived in a purely Gothic fashion, into an airy Bramantesque hall which would pass muster in the eye of the most critical Italian (relief, dated 1518, Vienna).

The same transitional style is also to be found in French sculpture of this period. Michel Colombe's tomb of Francis II, duke of Brittany, (Nantes cathedral, 1502–7) is the most characteristic example. The recumbent effigy and the little angels kneeling by the head are traditional, but the decorative details, particularly the scallop-shells and the allegorical figures at the four corners of the tomb, tell a different story. In France, unlike Germany, there are a number of Italian sculptors active throughout this period. While the tomb of Charles VIII by the Lombard sculptor Mazzoni has not survived, that of Louis XII (1516–1531, Saint-Denis) by a member of the Giusti family, which settled in Tours and called itself Juste, shows what was fashionable in France. The individual forms are Italian but the tomb is still Gothic in type.

In the Netherlands the influence of the Italian Renaissance on sculpture can scarcely be discovered until the late 1520's and there is no really important example before the richly decorated carved mantelpiece by Lancelot Blondel in the Palace of Justice at Bruges (1529–31).

Architecture in northern Europe was hardly affected by what had happened in Italy during the fifteenth century. The architect even more than the painter or sculptor depended on pattern books and theoretical treatises when he wished to absorb a new style, and nothing of the kind existed as yet. Alberti's *De Re Aedificatoria* was published in 1485, but it is obvious that after reading this unillustrated text no architect could possibly have constructed any building even vaguely resembling the Palazzo Rucellai. Furthermore, work on some of the great cathedrals, such as Ulm, Cologne and Tours, was still in progress and the masons' lodges with their strict traditions were still the nurseries for young architects. If masons did go to Italy, they went not as students of the art of Brunelleschi or Bramante, but to work on the great Gothic structures of S. Petronio in Bologna or Milan cathedral. It is for these reasons that the Gothic tradition survived longest in architecture. The Annenkirche in Annaberg (Saxony), begun in 1499, and the Liebfrauenkirche in Halle, begun in 1518, are Gothic hall-type churches, but the ribs under the vault no longer have any functional character and the octagonal piers with their concave sides seem curiously unrelated to the vault. Gothic forms were still in use, but the logic which had pervaded the whole of the great Gothic cathedral now seems lost. The same holds true to a lesser degree for France, where the flamboyant style remained sufficiently vigorous to produce the richly decorated screen masking the fourteenth-century façade of Rouen cathedral or the façade of Troyes cathedral designed by Martin Chambiges in 1507. In fact, Charles VIII's Italian enterprise of 1494 seems to have been as little influential in the arts as it was in the realm of politics. Fra Giocondo and Giuliano da San Gallo, both of whom were in France for a while after 1495, have left no traceable works, and the wing of Blois castle built during the reign of Louis XII shows no Italian influence at all. Not until Francis I came to the throne was a strongly italianising court style created. The wing which he added to Blois castle, while Gothic in structure, displays many Renaissance decorations not unnaturally derived from Milanese architecture. Even Chambord, begun in 1519, is still an intriguing mixture of styles. Certain of Leonardo's designs, made whilst he was living in France (1516–19) were to influence palace architecture. However, most of the buildings which showed marked Italian influence fall outside the period under discussion.

During the first two decades of the sixteenth century architects as a rule were content to borrow decorative motifs from the south and put a thin Renaissance veneer over an essentially Gothic structure. The palace which was built for Margaret of Austria at Malines between 1507 and 1526 (now the Palais de Justice) is a typical example. The main door is decorated in Renaissance fashion, the windows are crowned with segmental arches, but the steep roof remains Gothic.

This hybrid style also prevailed in Germany. Once more the best early examples are in Augsburg. The rich Fuggers, protagonists of the Italian Renaissance, employed Italian workmen for the building of a chapel in the church of St Anne (1509–18) and tried to give their town house (1512–15) the appearance of an Italian *palazzo*. The most characteristic product of a mixture of forms and styles in the north is the model of the church *Zur schönen Maria* in Regensburg (1519). Here an almost correct Italian centralised ground plan is combined with a nave and a late Gothic elevation.

The patronage of the time clearly mirrors this uncomfortable transitional stage. Enough has been said of the role of the French kings to make this plain. Two typical German examples may be discussed here. The Emperor Maximilian (1493–1519) appears as an embodiment both of the medieval and of the renaissance spirit. The 'last knight', who himself was the author of a traditional romance, *Der Weisskunig*, who loved jousts and tournaments, who put King Arthur among his ancestry, also liked to see himself as a true Roman emperor riding in triumph under an arch commemorating his great deeds; he surrounded himself with scholars and humanists and took part in their antiquarian and literary studies; he liked personally to supervise the designs of artists working for him. Yet it was all only a paper dream. The triumphal arch was never actually built, but like the procession remained only a series of woodcuts designed by a great number of German artists of whom Dürer was the most prominent. In these woodcuts the two worlds once more meet. The wisdom of the ancients, culled from the pages of Horus Apollo's *Hieroglyphica*, first printed in 1505, intermingles with motives from medieval bestiaries and Italian putti ride alongside the German Landsknecht. The *Triumphal Arch* uses Italian decorative elements applied to a quite unclassical Gothic structure. But the oddest of Maximilian's enterprises is perhaps the tomb he planned for himself at Innsbruck (from 1502 onwards) which, like so many of his undertakings, was never finished. The best German sculptors were called in, among them Veit Stoss and Peter Vischer the Elder. The central feature was to be the bronze figure of the emperor kneeling on a sarcophagus and he was to be surrounded by some 140 statues and statuettes representing his ancestors, his prominent courtiers, the subjugated provinces and so forth. Michelangelo's tomb for Julius II comes to mind, but we immediately realise the enormous difference between the two schemes. Michelangelo strove hard to maintain the formal unity of his monument and, moreover, every detail is subservient to a general philosophical concept (p. 134). Maximilian's tomb might at best have been a conglomeration of good statues, since the iconographic programme is lacking in unity. Pride, a craving for eternal glory, the unique position of the emperor, all these worldly ambitions may be read from this tomb. Like any Italian of his age Maximilian wanted to be worthily commemorated; he wished for a visible symbol of survival, but he remained a knight in medieval armour like his ancestors who surround his effigy.

If Maximilian cast himself in the role of a Roman emperor, Cardinal Albrecht of Brandenburg, archbishop of Mainz, Magdeburg and Halberstadt attempted to emulate contemporary Italian princes. He was both a leading ecclesiastic and a territorial ruler, besides being one of the electors. He was ruthless, vainglorious and yet a highly educated man of taste. He imitated Italian patronage of the arts on a grand scale and Dürer, Grünewald, Cranach and many others were called upon to work for him. Grünewald, in fact, held an official position at his court for many years. When he painted the cardinal as Saint Erasmus (c. 1518, Munich) the fashionable classical form of allegorical portraiture must have been suggested by the patron, but in composition and design the picture remained unmistakably northern.

German historians have often tended to deplore the clash between north and south as a kind of calamity for German art which, they claim, fell victim to a foreign invasion. This is not the place to rebut such a nationalistic theory. Two factors, however, should be borne in mind. It will have become evident that by the end of the fifteenth century Gothic art was showing signs of exhaustion. What had been a style was by now in danger of becoming a mannerism. Furthermore, the 'Renaissance' was a European and not a limited Italian movement, even if the beginnings were to be found in Italy. Jacob Burckhardt, in a celebrated passage, has spoken of the 'discovery of the world and of man' as the chief characteristics of the movement. Though we tend to modify this claim today, it remains fundamentally true. If in Italy the 'discovery of the world' culminated in the all-embracing work of Leonardo, in Germany, or to be precise in Austria, it found artistic expression in pure landscape painting. Even the Greeks, with all their awareness of natural beauty, had never treated landscape as a subject in its own right. In the Middle Ages landscape elements were no more than symbolic props in religious narratives. Not until the late Middle Ages was exact observation applied, for instance, to render correctly plants in herbals. Flemish artists of the fifteenth century and their German followers had given much attention —and space—to landscape, though it was never more than a distant background. When Lucas Cranach, while working in Vienna, painted a *Crucifixion* (1503, Munich) he showed no unusual interest in nature, but he introduced in his composition two innovations of the utmost consequence: the whole scenery is rendered with the greatest possible geological and botanical accuracy and at the same time the viewpoint is taken so low that we seem to be looking into these forest glades and meadows and are thus drawn right into the landscape. Also the landscape element began to grow in proportion to the whole picture. In the *Rest on the Flight into Egypt* (1504, Berlin) the setting appears to be as important as the Holy Family. Albrecht Altdorfer (*c.* 1475–1538), who may have met Cranach personally, was certainly fully acquainted with these innovations and carried them yet a step further. His *St George and the Dragon* (1510, Munich) is really a landscape with figures. Moreover, it seems that Altdorfer was the first European artist to paint landscapes without figures (*c.* 1532, Munich), and there are pure landscapes among his drawings and etchings. Wolf Huber (*c.* 1490–1553) continued in this manner, probably after personal contact with Altdorfer.

The three artists just discussed, together with some minor painters, are sometimes referred to as the 'Danube School', though there was no school in the accepted sense of the word, nor were the landscapes of this group unique. Dürer on his two journeys to Italy produced some of his finest and most delicate water-colours of alpine scenery and even later he occasionally worked in this genre. In the beginning this new branch of painting seems to have been appreciated by artists and connoisseurs only. Dürer regarded his water-colours as mere sketches; drawing, etching and water-colour were the media employed and the few extant paintings are on a small scale. Being painted on vellum they can hardly be called easel paintings, but retain the character of miniatures. Whatever the medium, all these works share a deep feeling for the poetry and beauty of nature, at times expressing a kind of awe for the strange vastness of the world as is the case in some of the late drawings by Altdorfer.

This feeling for nature also pervades the religious paintings of the same master. In his great altarpiece of St Florian (1518) the stories of St Sebastian are in landscapes which enhance emotional participation, most moving in the scene of the finding of the Saint's body by the banks of a river depicted in eerie twilight.

The intensity of religious feeling expressed in this way is characteristic of much that was done by German artists before and during the Reformation. In the course of the fifteenth century German and Flemish artists had fashioned one particular tool for religious imagery which was to be of material assistance to the reformers: the print. By refining the techniques of both woodcut and engraving Dürer produced works in these media unrivalled in Europe, and even Italian artists pirated his prints. Dürer's *Life of the Virgin*, his several series of the Passion, his innumerable individual prints, the prints of his school at Nürnberg, those of Pencz, the Beham brothers, Hans Baldung Grien and many others, all testify to the productivity and virility of this branch of art. In his lifetime Dürer seems to have been esteemed even more for his graphic work than for his paintings and even after his death Erasmus spoke of him in elegant humanistic style as the 'Apelles of black lines'.[1]

[1] E. Panofsky, *Jour. Warburg and Courtauld Inst.* XIV (1951), pp. 34ff.

Hans Holbein's *Dance of Death*, designed 1523–6 but published in 1538, and Dürer's *Apocalypse* of 1498 remind us of the more sombre side of religious meditation during the period under discussion. The haunting fear of the millennium and the morbid preoccupation with torment and suffering are predominant in the work of two of the greatest painters of the period, Bosch and Grünewald. Hieronymus Bosch (*c.* 1450–1516) still belongs to the fifteenth-century tradition of his native Holland, but with the help of a late Gothic vocabulary he developed an imagery which is as yet largely unexplained. A recent attempt to make Bosch into the painter of an abstruse Adamite sect is unconvincing.[1] The horrifying fabulous monster threatening St Anthony (Madrid) and the appallingly cruel representations of Hell, which Bosch liked to paint again and again, are part of the mental pattern of the age. These horrors are all the more frightening since Bosch skilfully and paradoxically applied the utmost realism to their representation.

Matthias Grünewald (*c.* 1480–1529), whose real name was Mathis Nithart Gotthart, gave tangible expression to the religious intensity of late medieval mysticism. He fashioned his powerful religious imagery out of German tradition, admitting Italian Renaissance elements only to a limited degree. His greatest work, an altarpiece executed for the Antonite House of Isenheim (completed *c.* 1512, now in Colmar Museum) is one of the most monumental of all Gothic altarpieces. It consists of a shrine with carved figures by Niclas Hagenauer and two pairs of movable painted wings. The panel with the *Temptation of St Anthony* has a nightmarish quality of unequalled power and a spirit akin to the most frightening works of Bosch. The *Crucifixion* is no longer a *tableau vivant* in a religious drama, as artists of the fifteenth century had frequently painted it. By bringing together the Lamb and the Baptist under the Cross he stressed the symbolic meaning of the sacrifice. The visionary intensity with which the suffering of Christ is rendered invites the beholder to that *imitatio Christi* which inspired much of the religious thought of the age.

Here we can sense the same religious troubles which are mirrored in Dürer's works and discussed in his letters.[2] The way in which both Dürer and Grünewald reacted to Luther's writings has an importance far beyond their individual experiences. Grünewald seems to have become deeply involved in the religious and social upheavals which accompanied the Reformation and it seems that he took an active part in the Peasants' Revolt. In any case he must have ceased painting in the early 1520's and thereafter he made a living by such menial work as soap-boiling. There was no longer room for his deeply mystical approach to art. Dürer, on the other hand, had found a new language through the study of Italian art; on his own testimony, he was greatly helped in his torment by the writings

---

[1] W. Fraenger, *The Millennium of Hieronymus Bosch* (1952).
[2] H. Rupprich, *Dürer, Schriftlicher Nachlass*, vol. 1 (1956), pp. 85 ff.

of Luther. Soon after 1520 Protestant imagery appears in his woodcuts and he abandoned a large altarpiece of which the central panel was to represent the Virgin and Child to devote all his energies to his 'Bekenntnisbild', the *Four Apostles* (1526, Munich), which as a significant gesture he gave to his native Nürnberg in 1526. This was not just the act of a self-conscious artist, eager to perpetuate his fame, it was even more the act of a modern artist conscious of his responsibility. All that Dürer had ever pondered and studied was now brought into play to paint four preachers of true Christianity, warning his fellow human beings less against the failings of Rome than against the excesses of over-zealous reformers. Here indeed was an attempt to find a new dynamic mean between old and new, both in art and religion. Many of the German artists provided Luther with powerful pictorial weapons in his fight, but it was given to Dürer alone to find a perfect fusion between Renaissance and Reformation, the two great forces which overshadowed artistic creation in the north about 1520.

3. IN SPAIN

ONE of the many fruits of national activity in Spain during the age of Ferdinand and Isabella was a new and widespread stimulus to the arts. If by European standards Spanish art of the period under consideration was only of minor importance, it was in many respects distinctive in character and it was to have a far-reaching effect in Spain's possessions in the New World. Whilst artistic production was still largely religious in purpose, royal patronage now played a major role in fostering it. Isabella herself built and endowed monasteries, churches and public institutions; the yoke and arrows, emblem of the Catholic sovereigns, and their escutcheon appear as decorative motifs on her buildings as they do in the margins of her manuscripts. Moreover, by adorning her residences with tapestries and paintings, mostly acquired from abroad, Isabella laid the foundations of the Spanish royal collection. The other chief patrons of art were the nobles and rich and powerful prelates, such as the Mendozas, Fonseca and Jiménez, who built palaces, chapels, hospitals and universities and followed the royal fashion for having themselves commemorated by monumental tombs. Newly acquired wealth and power nourished a taste for lavish decoration, inspired by the example of the Moors, in which the minor arts—woodwork, goldsmith's work, ironwork, etc.—played an important part.

Until the end of the fifteenth century Spanish art continued to be governed by northern influence which survived, moreover, well into the sixteenth century, when the style chosen for the cathedrals of Salamanca and Segovia was still pure Gothic. Echoes of the Italian *Quattrocento* first appeared in painting and sculpture during the last quarter of the fifteenth century, but they were confined for the most part to architectural features and ornamental details, which modified rather than transformed the prevailing Hispano-Flemish and Gothic styles. A long-standing liking for northern art and an innate taste for Mudéjar (the art of subject Muhammadans, which still survived in architecture and the minor arts) made Spain slow to adopt the innovations of the Italian Renaissance. Furthermore, pagan subjects, though familiar in literature, had little appeal for patrons who were the militant champions of Christianity dedicating their achievements to the Church. Painting was confined almost exclusively to altarpieces and easel paintings of religious subjects; fresco paintings and even portraits were rare. Sculpture was devoted chiefly to altarpieces, sepulchral monuments and architectural decoration and there was little demand for portrait busts, civic monuments or any other kind of free-standing statuary.

Despite a close dependence on foreign models and the intervention of many foreign artists, in one particular field, that of architectural sculpture, Spanish art developed a peculiar character of its own. Thus the Spanish version of Flamboyant Gothic, which flourished during the reign of the queen, has been termed Isabelline; and the following phase, marked by the introduction of Italian influence, is also denoted by a special term, Plateresque, a term derived from *platería* (silverwork) and coined in the seventeenth century in criticism of artists who violated the rules of Roman (Renaissance) architecture with 'plateresque fantasies'.[1] The chief and common features of Isabelline and Plateresque, a profusion of ornament in low relief covering large surfaces and the screen-like application of this ornament, with little regard for the underlying structure, are strongly reminiscent of Moorish art. The repetition and mixture of motifs, which range from conventional Gothic or Renaissance forms to emblems, heraldry, inscriptions and arabesques, produce an effect that is invariably extravagant, often bizarre and exotic. The close association of architecture and sculpture (many artists followed both professions) makes the terms Isabelline and Plateresque applicable to altarpieces and sepulchral monuments as well as to the decoration of architecture proper—walls, doorways, arches, windows, etc. Whilst the sculptured façades of S. Gregorio and S. Pablo in Valladolid look like enlarged stone retables, the enormous polychrome altarpieces of Gil de Siloe and his followers almost fill the apses that they adorn; both free-standing tombs and wall-tombs are similarly elaborate in structure and monumental in scale.

The monastery of San Juan de los Reyes, Toledo, begun by order of Ferdinand and Isabella in 1476 to commemorate their victory over the Portuguese at Toro, is one of the first and most characteristic examples of the Isabelline style, although Juan Guas, the sculptor-architect who designed it, was probably of French origin. The inside of the Gothic

---

[1] Cf. D. Ortiz de Zúñiga, *Anales eclesiásticos* (Madrid, 1677), p. 546.

church, originally intended for the burial-place of the king and queen, is covered with decorative carvings—figures, ornament, a frieze of inscriptions in large Gothic letters—the whole dominated by the huge motif of the royal escutcheon, accompanied by the yoke and arrows, repeated round the transept.

The sculptured decoration of portals and tympana, which survived in ecclesiastical architecture from medieval times and became the main feature of Isabelline and Plateresque façades, was now extended to domestic architecture, where decoration was for the first time lavished on the exterior as well as the interior. Windows, galleries, cornices, balustrades, and the arcades of the *patio*—the inner court, characteristic of Spanish houses since the Middle Ages—were also richly carved. Façades were often studded with faceted stones, and that of the Casa de las Conchas, Salamanca, is covered with scallop shells, referring to the owner's title of Knight of Santiago. Profusion and complexity of ornament made the Infantado Palace, Guadalajara, built by Juan Guas and assistants (1480–92, largely destroyed 1936), the most sumptuous example of a nobleman's house. An arcaded gallery, stalactite cornice and the Mendoza escutcheon supported by 'wild men' contributed to the adornment of the façade; in the *patio* Tuscan columns supported trefoil arches with spandrils filled with heraldic animals, shields and scrolls; and the ceilings were of elaborate Mudéjar construction.

The infiltration of Italian influence at the end of the fifteenth century did not restrain the taste for ostentation shown by the victors over Muhammadanism and the discoverers of the New World; it provided the artist with a further repertoire of decorative motifs. There was, too, no hesitation in mixing the new style, called 'obra á la antigua', with 'obra moderna' or Gothic, nor did they follow any clear chronological sequence. Enrique de Egas who, after the fall of Granada, built the Royal Chapel there in Gothic style (1506) was also the foremost exponent of early Plateresque. The Royal Hospice for Pilgrims, Santiago (begun 1501), which he built for Ferdinand and Isabella and the Hospital de Santa Cruz, Toledo (begun 1504), designed by him for Cardinal Mendoza, have typical Plateresque portals in which Italian ornamental motifs predominate, though mixed with Gothic forms. Renaissance ornament was also frequently blended with Mudéjar, as in the painted stucco decoration of the entrance to the Chapel of the Annunciation in Sigüenza cathedral (1510). The portal of Salamanca University (completed 1529), where the arms of the Emperor Charles V appear beside those of Ferdinand and Isabella, is thoroughly Italianate in detail, with portrait medallions and copies of antique statues; but it is still confined in a Gothic frame and applied like a screen to the façade. Plateresque, as a style of decoration, whether composed of Italian and Gothic, Italian and Mudéjar, or purely Italian features, continued to be applied to both Gothic and Renaissance buildings throughout the reign of Charles V; and many of its features found an echo in the Baroque age.

The first wave of Italian influence that inspired Plateresque decoration was stimulated by the importation of sculpture and by the arrival of Italian artists in Spain. Felipe Vigarny (de Borgoña), a Frenchman who was in Burgos by 1498, also did much to spread the new style, particularly through his adaptations of Renaissance design to the traditional Spanish polychrome altarpiece; and his activities extended from Burgos to Granada. But the chief source of Italian influence in the first quarter of the sixteenth century was the new fashion for commissioning sepulchral monuments in Italy; and the most important Italian artist to visit Spain was the Florentine Domenico Fancelli, who went to Seville in 1510 to set up the tomb of Archbishop Mendoza, which he had carved in Genoa. This led to a series of royal commissions including the tomb of the Infante Juan in S. Tomás, Ávila (1513) and the tombs of Ferdinand and Isabella themselves in the Royal Chapel, Granada (1518); all three inspired by Pollaiuolo's tomb of Sixtus IV in St Peter's and in accordance with the tradition for free-standing tombs which was still popular in Spain. As in the case of architecture, Italian influence on monumental sculpture was at first confined to ornamental detail and it was not until after Fancelli's death (1519) that it really bore fruit. When Renaissance forms finally ousted Gothic survivals this was largely due to a new generation of artists like Ordoñez, Machuca, Alonso Berruguete and Diego de Siloe—the four Spaniards named by Francisco de Holanda, the Portuguese enthusiast of Italy and the antique, in his list of 'eagles' or famous modern artists (1548); they were trained in Italy and took back to Spain the mature fashions of the High Renaissance. It was not until 1526 that the first classical building in Spain, Machuca's unfinished palace of Charles V in Granada, was begun and the first work on classical art to be published there, Diego de Sagredo's *Medidas del Romano*, based on Vitruvius, appeared in Toledo in the same year.

In painting as in architecture and sculpture the taste for northern art lasted well into the sixteenth century and Queen Isabella's patronage did much to perpetuate it. The inventories of her collection of over two hundred paintings and the work that she bequeathed to the Royal Chapel, Granada, show her predilection for Netherlandish artists: van der Weyden, Memling, Bosch, David. She also employed several northerners as court painters—Melchior Alemán, Michel Sittow, Juan de Flandes—though her chief painter was Francisco Chacón of Toledo, who also held the office of censor, whose duty it was to prevent any Jew or Moor from daring to paint the forms of Christ, the Virgin or any of the Saints. But Isabella also possessed some Italian paintings, including a Botticelli and a Perugino (?), and some of the Flemish artists that she favoured had had contact with Italy. Thus, whilst the Hispano-Flemish style flourished at the court and with artists like Gallegos in Castile and Bermejo in Aragon, Italian elements were beginning to make their appearance in much the same way as they did in the plastic arts and as they did in many Flemish paintings of the period; they were due as much to the influence of these paintings as to direct influence from Italy.

Pedro Berruguete, one of the few Spanish artists to visit Italy in the fifteenth century, was in Urbino in 1477 with Melozzo da Forlí and Justus of Ghent. He returned to Spain with a taste for narrative, realistic detail and Renaissance ornament and with a knowledge of perspective. But as he worked chiefly on small panels for the large altarpieces that were popular in Spain, his style comes closer to that of Italianising Flemings than to that of any Italian artist. In Andalusia, Alejo Fernández (d. 1543) was the chief artist to combine Italian and Flemish influences and, more than any other Spanish painter of his time, his idealised types recall those of older Italian contemporaries, such as Pinturicchio. But what gives the works of even the more Italianate artists like Berruguete and Alejo Fernández a peculiarly Spanish character is the archaistic use of gold and patterned background and costume.

The first direct influence of the Italian High Renaissance on painting came in Valencia, the birthplace of Pope Alexander VI, and the city that had the closest cultural ties with Italy. As early as 1472 the future pope, as cardinal, had brought three artists there from Italy, one of them Paolo da San Leocadio from Reggio, who painted frescoes in the cathedral. Local artists, like Rodrigo de Osona, father and son, soon began to introduce Italian architecture and ornament into their Flemish-style compositions. In 1507–10 Fernando Yañez and Fernando Llanos, one of whom had assisted Leonardo in the hall of the great council in Florence, implanted his influence in Valencia with their paintings for the retable in the cathedral. Some years later Vicente Juan Masip became the founder of a school, based on sixteenth-century Italian painting, which was continued by his son Juan de Juanes and survived until the end of the century. But it was decidedly provincial; for nowhere in Spain did Italian influence inspire a distinctive style of painting, even to the extent that earlier Flemish influence had; and though Charles V's patronage of Titian was important for the development of court portraiture, it was not until the seventeenth century that a truly national school of painting emerged.

4. VERNACULAR LITERATURE IN WESTERN EUROPE, 1493–1520

THE end of the fifteenth century and the beginning of the sixteenth saw Europe at a crossroads, cultural as well as political and religious. The medieval traditions were failing, though not yet dead, and for many years 'modern' literature was still to feel influences which had informed the writings of the Middle Ages. The most striking of these were the spirit of free and often licentious realism embodied in *fabliau*, *novella* or farce, a realism which in one or other of its many forms was to enliven the work of a Machiavelli, a Folengo, a Rabelais and a Cervantes; the spirit of chivalry, courtesy and gallantry which, although chivalry itself was dying or dead, continued to find an increasingly artificial expression in lyric and romance until it was given new life by the influx of Platonic notions; and the moralising spirit with its inescapable concomitants of allegory and symbol. But other phenomena which were appearing in different parts of Europe deserve notice. Not unconnected, at any rate as a parallel mental tendency, with the decline of the scholastic philosophy into formalism was the reduction of poetry to conformity with highly complex rules. In some countries poetry was frankly regarded as a 'second rhetoric' and hence subject to similar rules; the ideal became the skilful and ingenious manipulation of words to fit a complicated structure of phrase, metre and rhyme which all but killed poetry. This formalism was to be seen not only in the lesser Petrarchans of Italy, the *Grands Rhétoriqueurs* of France and the Netherlandish *Rederijkers*, but also in the decaying *Minnesang* and the developing *Meistergesang* of Germany and the bardic developments of later fifteenth-century Wales. This regrettable development had, however, its more honourable origins in the growth, in the last two centuries, of a spirit of individual craftsmanship which, while it reduced the number of anonymous works devoted to the greater glory of God and increased the proportion of signed works to the greater glory of the author, imbued the artist with the desire to perfect his work according to his lights and the fashions of the time. So the writer placed technique above matter and above emotive intensity. At the same time the objective, and so the matter, of writing might be narrowed. The Middle Ages had been interested, in their own way, in great general matters: Christianity and Christendom, the virtues and vices of man, man's relation to God; these had found expression in works which, while perhaps particular in manner, were nevertheless of universal application, as the wide diffusion of the Charlemagne and Arthurian matters showed. Now, however, the growth of writing as a means of livelihood brought with it the need of patronage and reward, to be sought if possible in kingly or princely courts, if not, in the houses of the local nobility or wealthy bourgeoisie. On the humblest level this might lead to purely local literature; on the higher to 'national' literature, whether the nation was the city-state or the expanding royal realm. The movement coincided in time with that very development in political history which forced upon the attention of writer and patron alike the nature and claims of the 'nation' as a separate and easily identifiable unit having its own interests and no longer merely a part of a greater European community. Yet a Leonardo or an Erasmus was constantly crossing these boundaries which the latter, at all events, could see solidifying around him.

The name of Erasmus brings us to a consideration of the highest importance: the co-existence and cross-fertilisation at this time of vernacular
literatures and of a flourishing and renovated Latin literature, of the more
significance in that it was still thought necessary to write serious works in
that language. Except in its most popular kinds, vernacular literature was
more and more influenced by neo-Latin, so that any strict dichotomy
between the two is, in the last resort, artificial. The influence of Erasmus's
Adages on literature generally, the impact of neo-Latin plays on the development of the new 'regular' theatres in the vulgar tongue are but two
instances of a complex revitalising of vernacular literature by classical
antiquity through the writings of the humanists. Many authors, it must
be remembered, wrote both in Latin and in their native idiom. Inevitably
the question arose: could not the vernaculars take the place of Latin even
in learned works? It was no new problem in Italy, but at this time it
became acute once more and in other countries it was destined, at a
somewhat later date, to be diligently studied and argued. To these considerations add the new attitude to ancient letters fostered by the Italians
and the humanists in general, the study of Latin and Greek authors not
merely for their content (often a misunderstood or invented 'moral'
content) but also for their aesthetic merit and the adaptation of their
formal beauty to the matter expressed; the juxtaposition of classical
mythology with Christian matter and even the substitution of the former
for the latter; the revelation not only of a 'new' antiquity but also of a
whole New World; and the development of printing which speeded and
consolidated the diffusion of these elements. Such factors, in varying
degree, affected all the important vernacular literatures of Europe.

The political disunity of Italy was reflected in the localisation of literary
and artistic activity around a number of centres: the Papacy, the principalities or republics of Florence, Ferrara, Venice, Urbino or Mantua.
The use of mercenary troops liberated the citizens for the acquisition of
wealth and influence or for the pursuit of arts and letters; the potentates
themselves indulged in literary creation and felt their glory real when it
was reflected in the magnificence of their courts and the number of their
literary hangers-on, but if there were scores of scribbling parasites there
were also serious thinkers and superior writers. The strange thing is that,
though the political chaos attracted the vultures, the invasion of Italy by
Charles VIII of France and all the marchings and countermarchings that
ensued left the Italian states relatively prosperous, their writers productive.
Most Italian centres had their academies, which, though originally devoted in the main to the fostering of the classical humanities, encouraged
—albeit indirectly—the development of vernacular literature.

To attempt to describe the varied literature of Italy in these decades
within the framework of these local centres would be to destroy the unity

of the impact which it had upon succeeding generations elsewhere; to proceed chronologically would be to confuse the developments which the divers genres underwent. We shall attempt therefore to survey the main achievements in lyrical poetry, in the different kinds of prose and in the theatre.

The Italian courts swarmed with rhymers good and bad, vying with each other in the production of all manner of poems: the by now sancrosanct *canzone* and sonnet, traditional forms like ballads and carnival songs, relatively new forms like the *stanza* or *ottava rima*. Others busied themselves with the rehandling of romances, mainly French in origin and unceasingly popular with all ranks of society, but the main preoccupation was in the imitation of Petrarch. Lorenzo de' Medici himself was no mean adept in all kinds of verse. Repetition stales good matter and concentrates upon manner; a reaction was inevitable. Pietro Bembo, purist and severe self-critic, set up in face of this debased Petrarchism a loftier conception of the lyric. Like Malherbe's verse in France a century later, his *Rime* (first collected edition 1530) excelled in formal perfection but lacked warmth; he had a host of imitators and became a 'canonical' model; it is interesting that he should have been one of the patterns chosen by the *Pléiade* in France, whom Malherbe was to condemn as extravagant! The exaggerations of the Petrarchists were pilloried also by Francesco Berni (1497–1535), who like Bembo dwelt much in the papal court, but his parodying of them was but part of his humorous and satirical output, in the tradition of Pulci and Burchiello, ridiculing the follies of society with such vividness, such linguistic skill and such a keen sense of the absurd that he gave his name to a whole genre of humorous satire. He had his forerunners not only in Pulci and Burchiello but also in Il Pistoia (1436–1502), whose satirical poems even include one on the French invasion of Italy! Nor must we forget that some of the powerful sonnets of Michelangelo may well date from our period in stark contrast to the Petrarchising of the smaller fry. Nor was didactic poetry lacking, as witness *Le Api* of Rucellai, based on Virgil's *Georgics*. But if the lyric flourished, the most important achievements of the age were to be found in romance and epic.

Long before the end of the Middle Ages the distinction between epic and romance had been lost; or rather a fusion of the noble exploits of Charlemagne and his peers with the amazing adventures and the chivalrous courtesy of the *roman d'aventure* and the Arthurian matter had produced a somewhat indeterminate genre, now in verse, increasingly in prose, but subject to infinite rehandling. In Italy in the 1480's Sannazaro's *Arcadia*, a pastoral romance in prose with verse interludes, emphasised the courteous element with vague and usually pathetic or emotional situations against a clearly drawn background compounded of an imagined Arcadia and an idealised Campagna. With its elegant and often inflated diction, it was to be much imitated in the future, not only in Italy.

Nearer, however, to the traditional romance was the *Morgante Maggiore* of Luigi Pulci (1432–84), an intimate of Lorenzo. This burlesque epic of the Charlemagne matter has been variously judged: as sheer buffoonery or as the fooling of a cultured bourgeois: as possessing a wealth of imagination or as commonplace and never rising to pure fantasy: as concealing a sinister scepticism or as merely parodying popular taste: as having in Astarotte, the devil, a powerful representation of contemporary man with his problems, or as failing even to see that this was so. The rapid and boisterous work was destined to influence many, Rabelais included. On the very threshold of our period and under the influence of the Ferrara court appeared the *Orlando Innamorato* of Boiardo (c. 1440–94), an unfinished poem in complete contrast with Pulci's. Its title indicates the fusion of epic and romance and the story is treated with the imagination and dignity of courtly chivalry; adventures and tales told by the personages embellish and complicate the structure and these episodes, sometimes of normal romantic type, sometimes akin to the *novelle*, are rich in invention and skilfully narrated. The style, however, was harsh and graceless. Early in the sixteenth century Niccolo degli Agostini wrote an ending to it, but this, and indeed Boiardo's poem, were overshadowed by Berni's rewriting of the *Orlando Innamorato* in polished Tuscan. Before passing to Ariosto, we may mention the *Mambriano* of Francesco Bello (Il Cieco), a poem of similar spirit published posthumously in 1509; it was not well constructed and never enjoyed much favour.

Lodovico Ariosto (1474–1533) was undoubtedly the greatest of them all. Like Boiardo he belonged to the Este circle, though his relations with some members of that family were not comfortable. His early lyrics need not detain us, but in his *Satires* the gentle irony of an easy-going and humorous nature can be seen; some of them were composed during our period, intensely personal poems, perhaps not intended for publication and cast in the general mould of the Horatian satire or epistle. His comedies will be dealt with later. The *Orlando Furioso*, on which Ariosto's fame chiefly rests, was conceived as a continuation of Boiardo's poem. It was begun in the first decade of the century, but the first edition of forty cantos did not appear till 1516 at the expense of his patron, the Cardinal Ippolito d'Este; a second edition of 1521 was followed by a definitive edition of forty-six cantos in 1532. Once again epic and romantic elements are fused, the background to the main events of the story being the epic struggle between Christians and Saracens. The madness of Orlando, its progress and cure, are interrupted by a succession of highly varied episodes, heroic, pathetic and even comic, involving a multitude of personages. A secondary plot, the loves of Roger and Bradamante, imagined as the founders of the Este house, spoils some passages for the modern reader with flattery, but this and other flaws—occasional lapses into impropriety, exaggerations in imagery or affectations in expression

—matter little against the ease, clarity and smooth movement of the narrative, the perfection of style and the purity of the language. Ariosto is not only a greater artist than Boiardo, but his attitude and tone are different. He does not take his knights and their chivalry with the same seriousness; indeed he seems to write, in places, with his tongue in his cheek. He does not eschew satire nor even, as in the portrait and exploits of Astolfo the English knight, caricature and burlesque. He blends a little Pulci with a polished Boiardo. The man himself comes through, urbane, humorous, ironical, gentle and clear-sighted, in the lively, picturesque flow. No great profundity is to be found or even expected, but, superficial in some sense as the poem may seem, it helped to establish the literary language of Italy and it exercised upon posterity a great and lasting influence.

It would seem to be the man Teofilo Folengo (1496–1544) who comes through, too, in the rumbustious *Baldus*. Already in 1490 Tifi Odasi of Padua had used macaronic jargon, a mixture of Italian and Latin, in his *Macaronea* to mock epico-romantic matter. It was this medium which Folengo, an unfrocked monk who later returned to his monastery, chose as a comic weapon wherewith to batter the same victim. His other work was in much the same vein: the *Moschaea*, relating a war between the flies and the ants, was imitated from the *Batrachomyomachia*; the *Zanitonella* parodied the Petrarchan and Arcadian love-poems in a rustic setting; the *Orlandino*, not published till 1526, continued the parodic vein in literary Italian. The *Baldus* or, as it is better known with a variety of spellings, the *Macaronea*, was published in twenty-five books in 1519, its author using the pseudonym of Merlin Cocai. The amazing mock epic seized the public fancy and had six editions in four years. The beginning closely resembles the *Orlandino*, but the names are changed and soon the personages are off into a succession of wild adventures which end in hell, where, finding himself in congenial company with all the frauds and deceivers, including astrologers and poets, the author bids us goodbye with a final poke of fun at his hero, at himself and at his own artistic hotchpotch. The vigorous mock-epic style clothes the most vulgar matter, but there are charming sketches and there is a deeper satirical vein, as if he were determined, earnestly if at times obscenely, to destroy by his buffoonery the hollow art, the social graces and conventions, the literary posturings and the worship of a dead chivalry, the scholasticism and the religious shams of his age. He saw futility around him, but he is basically moral. Evil is not made attractive in his stark realism. The importance of this lively parody was not lost on Rabelais nor on Samuel Butler.

At the end of the fifteenth century the Italian theatre was already showing some signs of classical influence, but though Seneca, Plautus and Terence were known to the scholars and in some of the noble courts, they were not yet capable of transforming the drama. The old farces were still popular, as they were to be for some time to come, while in the serious vein the dominant kind was the *sacre rappresentazioni*. These plays had not only literary merit sometimes, but were the occasion of magnificent spectacles, for their performance was a craze, chiefly at the courts but also sometimes at the expense of a municipality. The humanist Poliziano had used the *sacra rappresentazione* form for his *Orfeo* at Mantua in 1471, but had infused into it a profane subject and an elegiac tone. Lorenzo il Magnifico himself wrote a *Rappresentazione dei SS. Giovanni e Paolo*, performed in 1489 and exhibiting the same lyrical elegance as his shorter poems. The further development of this genre was, for literary purposes, stifled eventually by the growing vogue of Seneca, whose tragedies had been printed and some translated before the end of the fifteenth century. Senecan traits may be detected in a few vernacular pieces, but the reign of Senecan tragedy was not to be fully established until after 1540, with the plays of Cinthio. In the meantime Pistoia's *Panfila* (1499) took a story from the *Decamerone*, changed the names and presented Seneca himself as Prologue. The insipid *Sofonisba* of Caretto (1502) was followed by the *Sofonisba* of Trissino (1515), an attempt at a 'classical' tragedy divided into acts, with choruses in lyrical metres; but it was not printed until 1524 nor performed again till 1562. Rucellai's *Rosmunda* (1515), though not without some Senecan influence, escaped from the actionless lyrical drama by reason of its horrific plot based on an incident in Lombard history.

Comedy (as in France half a century later) was more lively and produced more notable works, partly no doubt because comedy had behind it a living farce, partly because it could draw upon the collections of *novelle*, but principally because, when all is said, it is nearer to life, especially to the artificial, vicious and extravagant life of contemporary Italy. About 1508 Cardinal Bibbiena's *Calandria* was performed at Urbino and then in Rome, lavishly produced with hidden musicians and ballet-like intermezzi on classical themes. The ingredients of the comedy are those of a *novella*; a doltish husband, an astute and cynical go-between who tricks and fools the husband, a brother and sister so alike that confusing disguises produce equivocal situations, all this in an outward shape imitated from Latin comedy, yet unmistakably Italian and alive. There is no psychological profundity, no underlying liaison of events; it is the events themselves which matter, the complication of incident. Machiavelli's *Mandragola*, written at some time between 1504 and 1513, but not printed until 1524, was not the author's only dramatic work; he had translated Terence's *Andria*; his *Clizia* adapted the form of Latin comedy to a portrayal of the life of a Florentine family. The *Mandragola* might seem to be more remote than the *Clizia* from the ordinary business of the citizen, but it had far more profound qualities. A bare summary of the plot (Callimaco with the aid of a parasite outwits the foolish Nicia and enjoys Nicia's wife) would appear to place the comedy in the same class as Bibbiena's, but a closer examination reveals two features which make it not merely far superior to the *Calandria* as comedy, but the cleverest comedy of the Cinquecento. In the first place, the plot is extraordinarily tightly constructed, every move carefully calculated and subtly produced; in the second place this calculation is based upon a penetrating, if cynical, observation of human nature. All the characters are vivid, but two in particular impress themselves on the memory: Nicia the foolish and pompous husband, strong in the conceit of his own wisdom but whipped by the author from situation to situation, each revealing his colossal stupidity, and Fra Timoleo, the venal and cynical confessor, painfully aware of the shamefulness of his conduct but (like Parmeno in Terence's *Eunuchus*) easing his conscience by explanations to himself, and becoming the chief instrument in bringing Callimaco to Lucrezia's bed. Machiavelli laughs at human folly and corruption, but he does not appear to be indignant; he dissects and analyses them unemotionally and dispassionately. Incidentally, too, he reveals the attitude of mind which pope and prince seem to have adopted towards the iniquities which he portrays. At the same time he fuses into one great, if immoral, work the comedy of intrigue and the comedy of character. The comedy is written in lively dialogue which carries the action along without hitch and is always admirably suited to the personages concerned, so that the fantastic plot carries conviction.

Ariosto too made his contribution to the Italian stage. He was made superintendent of the ducal theatre at Ferrara, where, ever since 1486, Plautus and Terence had been performed in Latin; it is not surprising if he turned to these models for his own comedies, five in number, the last of which, *Gli Studenti*, remained unfinished. The first, the *Cassaria*, was purely imitative; its personages, taken from the Plautine and Terentian stock, dubbed with Italian names, revolve in a complex intrigue according to recipe; the play was a success because it repeated in the vernacular what was familiar to its audiences in Latin. The *Suppositi* (1509) made a better comedy, with substitution as the theme, but kept to the pattern and, like the *Negromante* (1520) was to serve as a model for French comedy in the latter half of the century. This last-named play has more lively action and dialogue, but lacks the reality of Machiavelli's comedy; the astrologer of the title is not a real astrologer, whose art could then be ridiculed, but an ignorant and bumptious charlatan who is continually revealing his own stupidity and being taken down by his own servant. The intrigue is conventional and complicated, but Ariosto has his moments when he infuses into the Terentian pattern snatches of satirical observation of his own; yet this comedy and the *Lena* (1529) remain inferior to the *Mandragola* and to Aretino's *Cortegiana*. The energetic and licentious Aretino (1492–1556) poured into his comedies (most of which lie strictly outside our period) the personages of his own dissolute world: harlots, panders, hypocrites and ruffians; he disregards, when it pleases him, the 'rules' of the genre and often gains vigour by his neglect of 'regularity' and if his works lack the tight construction of the *Mandragola* they have their own merits of gusto, of the uninhibited reproduction of a shameless, cynical, debauched but comic society. It is interesting that Ariosto wrote his earlier comedies in prose, but rewrote them later in *sdruccioli* which he regarded as nearer to his models and as representing adequately the freedom of ordinary dialogue.

Prose indeed flourished at this time. To pick out some significant works, we may turn first to Bembo, who was the author of two prose works of some interest. The *Asolani* (composed about 1500–2, printed in 1505 and dedicated to Lucrezia Borgia), a work of vulgarisation in the good sense, explained in Platonic dialogue form the principles of Platonic love, a task for which Bembo, who was editing Petrarch at about this time for Aldus, was well fitted. The dialogues are eloquent, if rather long-winded and languid. A similar form was used for the *Prose della volgar lingua*, begun in the early years of the century, perhaps perfected between 1506 and 1512 and circulated in manuscript, but not printed till 1525. In them the much debated question of literary language is discussed and largely settled; Bembo comes down on the side of the vernacular as against Latin and, among the vulgar tongues available, on the side of Tuscan. His elegance, his judicious arguments, his authority as scholar and poet did much to make the Tuscan victory complete. In another field, the *Cortegiano* of Baldesar Castiglione (1478–1529) had a similar influence. This writer too was the author of graceful letters, of polished poems in Latin and Italian and of a dramatic eclogue, *I Tirsi*. The *Cortegiano* was begun at Urbino in 1507 or thereabouts and was printed in 1528; in dialogue form it examined the nature of the gentleman, and the ideal reached in this perhaps idealised picture of the Urbino court and its interests had in France and in England as well as in Italy an enormous and lasting influence. The accepted ideal of the hidalgo was a successful rival in Spain.

In this age of diplomacy, intrigue and war, letters, diaries and memoirs were many. 'Serious' annals and the like were still written in Latin, but the vernacular does appear. Bisticci (1421–98) left his *Vite d'uomini illustri del secolo XV* and a companion work on illustrious ladies. In vernacular history proper, however, the names of Machiavelli (1469–1527) and Guicciardini (1483–1540) are the most eminent, though the dates of publication of their major works sometimes fall into a later period. We have already met the former as a dramatist, but he had no mean repute as a poet for his sonnets, *stanze*, burlesque and satirical *capitoli*, carnival songs, rhymed chronicles (the *Decennali*, 1506–9) in *terza rima*, as a tale-teller for his *Belfagor arcidiavolo* (1515), a traditional story enriched by his raciness, as a writer on language in the dialogue *Della lingua* (1514) and as the observant and cool author of various reports on political and administrative matters which range from 1499 onwards. Some of the works by which he is best known, the *Principe* (1513), the *Discorsi* (1512 onwards) and the *Arte della guerra* (1519–20), were composed or begun while he was in temporary retirement at San Casciano and his great *Istorie fiorentine*, commissioned in 1520, was published only in 1525. The *Principe* was a kind of excursus from his discourse on Livy; it treated, succinctly and unsentimentally, the nature of princeship and how it was to be maintained and developed. It has aroused violent judgments, particularly on moral grounds, but it is not primarily a work of cynical 'machiavellianism'; it is an appraisal of an existing and possible situation; it looks beyond Italian disunity to the ideal of a strong and united Italy and to the means whereby that ideal could be achieved. This achievement was, for Machiavelli, of more immediate importance than accepted morals or traditional law. With this book, as with *Discorsi* and the *Vita di Castruccio* (1520), the portrait of the Machiavellian ideal of man, and with the *Istorie fiorentine*, the author not only set up a purely intellectual and amoral attitude to public affairs but also gave the example of a prose style to match, clear, concise, calm and even meditative, orderly and remarkably modern. Guicciardini really belongs to a later generation, one affected by Machiavelli's thought as by the increasing and chaotic corruption of Italian politics, and we need mention here only his early work, the *Storia fiorentina* of 1508, a lively record of Florence in the strange days of Savonarola written with insight and a remarkable sense of the concatenation of events.

The other important prose genre of medieval and Renaissance Italy, the *novella*, had no remarkable fortune in our period except as a source. The collections of Masuccio Salernitano and Giovanni Sabbadino were all completed in the 1470's and 1480's, while Bandello's works, perhaps already being collected, were not published until long afterwards, as were the significant writings of Firenzuola, Pietro Aretino, Benvenuto Cellini and others.

In the Spanish peninsula and Spanish Italy, our three decades were a time of promise and of achievement. The union of Castile and Aragon and the growth of the joint realm as a Great Power in Europe and overseas, the development of Portugal into an imperial Power, gave the inhabitants of these lands a sense of strength and destiny. The long struggle with the Moors delayed the end of the Middle Ages, but the new and glorious epoch stimulated activity in arts and letters as well as in conquest. The full impact of classical and Italian humanism was still to be felt, in spite of the close contact between the two Mediterranean peninsulas, and in many respects Spanish literature was for long to bear strongly marked individual traits. Even in the most advanced works of our period a strong medieval flavour was to be found, though new models were sought and followed. It is not merely convenient, but necessary, to avoid any strict separation of this literature into Castilian, Portuguese and Catalan. Not only was Castilian advancing steadily to the status of 'Spanish' and gradually eliminating dialect literature, but more than one author wrote in more than one language, while works in Portuguese and Catalan were often translated into Castilian. In 1492 the first grammar of Castilian was written by the humanist Nebrija and three years later the same scholar issued his Latin-Spanish, Spanish-Latin dictionary. At the same time, here as in other lands, new universities were being founded, libraries collected, translations of classical and Italian literature made. Yet the general background would not at first sight appear conducive to literary or artistic production; the activities of the Inquisition, the expulsion of Jews (1492) and of the Moors (1502) may well, however, have helped to prevent the growth of cynicism, luxury and *virtù* which abounded in Italy, as the advent of the Reformation inhibited these excesses in France, Germany and England. Popular literature had its ballads, its rehandling of old romances, like *El Baladro del sabio Merlin* (1498) or *La Demanda del Sancto Grial* (1515), its religious *rapresentaciones* and *autos*, its *églogas* and its farces. The major works themselves are so bound, in general, to older works that reference backwards in time is inevitable; especially as works of considerable importance now printed for the first time had already been written, read and known for years.

The two great events in the realm of lyrical poetry were the printing of the *Cancionero general* of Hernando del Castillo in 1511 and of the *Cancioneiro geral* of Garcia de Resende in 1515. The former, containing nearly a thousand pieces mainly of earlier composition but including a number of contemporary poems, ran into many editions during the century; it had a section of *obras de burla* which in 1529 developed into a separate collection of burlesque and frequently obscene poems. The Resende collection consisted mainly of poems in Portuguese but significantly included a number of pieces in Castilian. In both collections the majority of the writers were skilful versifiers in the courteous tradition, artificial, uninspired, but elegant and highly polished; and both bring to an end, to all intents and purposes, the tradition of these song-books. New fashions were soon to take their place, for already in the contents were signs of Petrarchan influence and of classical antiquity. Few, however, of the poets writing before 1520 can be placed very high, though Pedro Manuel Jiménez de Urrea, whose Castilian works appeared in 1513, wrote to his wife and his mother personal poems which are generally acknowledged to be pleasing, while his re-handling of the end of the *Celestina* in an *égloga* and of its whole matter in his prose *Penitencia de Amor* (1514) testify to his interest in that remarkable work, to which we shall come later. Satirical verse was not unknown, but, like the abounding religious and devotional verse, it need not detain us.

The most important writing of the time was in prose. Alfonso Martínez de Toledo, archpriest of Talavera, wrote a work called *Reprobación del amor mundano* but better known as the *Corbacho* (after Boccaccio's

Corbaccio); it was finished in 1438, but not printed till 1498. It was a satirical and didactic treatise on morals, male and female, calling for its material on Catalan and Italian sources as well as on the author's own experience; its style was exuberant, its imaginative qualities fertile, its satire energetic and its language popular. To this half-didactic, half-novelistic literature Diego de San Pedro contributed his *Tratado de Amores de Arnalte y Lucenda* (1491), which contained letters and reflections on love and, the following year, his *Carcel de Amor*, a better-known work which combined in a somewhat confused but stimulating array personal recollections, psychological analysis, wonderful adventures and subtle allegories. Continuing and developing the tradition of the *Fiammetta*, it was immediately popular and was frequently reprinted and widely translated. It was imitated in the *Cuestión de Amor*, composed in Naples, where the action takes place, between 1508 and 1512, and attributed to Vásquez, the author of a similar work, the *Dechado de Amor* (c. 1510). The *Tratado de Grimalte y Gradissa* was another continuation of the *Fiammetta*; it dated from the closing years of the fifteenth century and was still being read in the 1520's, when it took a new title. The narrative prose masterpiece of our period was, however, undoubtedly the *Amadis de Gaula*, destined to play a great part in the history of the European novel. Its matter had been known in the peninsula for a couple of hundred years and derives ultimately from the French Arthurian romance tradition. Garci Rodríguez de Montalvo claims to be merely the editor of older material, but the fourth and fifth books are almost certainly his own. The first four books were printed in 1508, though they seem to have been set down some fifteen years earlier. Enormously popular, frequently reprinted and translated into almost all the languages of Europe, it expounds the most refined chivalrous ideals of the time, giving examples of feudal loyalty and knightly conduct and thus embodying, though its setting was not Spanish, a typically Spanish spirit of romantic chivalry in an easy and colourful, though occasionally redundant, style. It influenced the development of the prose romance outside as well as inside Spain, though the genre often degenerated into the foolish and artificial forms which Cervantes was to scarify. The author of *Don Quixote*, however, found something to approve in the earlier Catalan burlesque romance *Tirant lo Blanch* of Johanot Martorell, which was translated into Castilian in 1511. The years that followed saw many imitations and continuations of the Amadis matter and the formation of a similar group in the Palmerin romances, one of which, *Palmerín de Inglaterra*, first appeared in a Portuguese version.

The only work which can be compared in importance with the *Amadis* was the *Tragicomedia de Calisto y Melibea*, or *La Celestina*, a work difficult to classify. In spite of its title of 'tragicomedy', it is perhaps better described as a prose narrative in dramatic form. The oldest known edition (Burgos, 1499) contains sixteen 'acts', but later editions intercalate new acts bringing the number to twenty-two. The authorship has been much disputed, but it is now generally agreed that the author of all but the first act was a converted Jew, Fernando de Rojas. He constantly insists upon his moral intentions in composing this story of the ill-fated loves of two young people against a background of crime and corruption displayed with stark realism which contrasts effectively with the idyllic and pathetic love-story. The popularity of the secondary title is due to the amazing and horrifying portrait of the procuress Celestina, whose cynical intrigues are covered by a specious pietism. The literary sources are many, from Terence and Ovid to medieval tales, but the work remains highly original and in its realistic psychology far superior to the *Amadis*. For more than a hundred and fifty years the *Celestina* profoundly influenced the Spanish novel and drama and, through its numerous translations, the novel and drama of other European countries.

A number of vernacular chronicles composed in earlier years were first printed in our period, among which must be mentioned the *Generaciones é Semblanzas* of Fernán Pérez de Guzmán, a useful series of contemporary biographies incorporated around 1450 in the *Mar de Historias*, which was printed in 1512 and imitated in Alonso de Toledo's *Espejo de las Historias*. Other historical works were Diego de Valera's *Crónica* (1482) and *Memorial de diversas hazañas*, a rehandling of Alfonso de Palencia's earlier *Décadas*; Enríquez de Castillo's *Crónica de Enrique IV*, over-eloquent and partial, but showing powers of observation; Hernando del Pulgar's *Claros varones* (1500) and his panegyric *Crónica de...los Reyes Católicos*, not printed till 1565, but translated into Latin by Nebrija. The main interest of such works is biographical, but other aspects of history are not neglected. The more ambitious works on history and philosophy were, of course, still written in Latin, but a vernacular work which deserves mention as influential during our period, though written before it, was the *Visión deleitable de la Filosofía y de las sciençias* by Alfonso de la Torre; it was one of the last of the medieval encyclopaedias and, as the title suggests, had as its framework an allegory in which Reason, Wisdom, Nature and similar personifications sum up the knowledge of the period.

The theatre (apart from the *Celestina*, if that work can count as drama) has few names of note. Juan del Encina (c. 1468–c. 1529) contributed both in Spain and in Spanish Italy to the developing theatre by enriching and secularising existing forms, until then traditionally religious; he infused a lyrical manner (his conception of poetry, based on the teachings of Nebrija, is expounded in his *Arte de la poesía* of 1496) and was the better able to do so as he was a skilled musician; and he introduced pleasing and fruitful peasant types to the stage. The *Propalladia* (1517) of Bartolomé de Torres Naharro contained pieces produced in Italy and showing Italian and Latin influence in the complexity of their intrigue and their division into prologue and five 'jornadas', a kind of transition from the 'days' of the mystery to the five acts prescribed by Horace. The greatest dramatist of the age was, however, the Portuguese Gil Vicente (*c.* 1465–*c.* 1536), a versatile poet and silversmith of whose forty-four plays sixteen are in Portuguese, eleven in Castilian, seventeen in mixed language. His earlier dramatic works were mainly religious, connected with the great festivals, but from 1508 he turned to the secular and humorous kind; his greatest work, in his later years, included both farces and his three eschatological 'autos' *Inferno, Purgatório* and *Glória.* His lyrical inspiration, his keen insight into human nature, his range of humour make him the most interesting figure of this time of transition in two languages.

In France too this generation of writers exemplifies perhaps even more clearly the decay, but not death, of the medieval tradition and the first effects of Italian and humanist influence. The *Roman de la Rose* with all that it entailed by way of allegory, eroticism and didacticism, was still a dominant influence. The works of Villon were being printed and read; between 1489 and 1533 a score of more or less defective editions of his poems saw the light. Dante had been known to earlier centuries and the *Inferno* was translated into French tercets towards the end of the fifteenth century. Direct and stimulating contact with Italy was made when Charles VIII invaded it in 1494; the invasion was the discovery of an exciting country. Intercourse became continuous; Frenchmen like Budé and Lazare de Baïf travelled or studied in Italy; Lefèvre d'Étaples met Ficino, Pico della Mirandola and Poliziano; Italian soldiers, diplomats, scholars, artists came to France. The great city of Lyons with its industries, its printing presses, its authority as a former capital and its wonderful strategic position not only gave shelter to Italian exiles but built up twin traditions of humanist and Italian culture. Italian literature was revealed to France by translations: of the *Decamerone* in 1485, of the *Trionfi* of Petrarch in 1514; of the *Paradiso* between 1515 and 1524; of Pulci's *Morgante* in 1519 and so on. At the same time were being printed editions of ancient authors, translations, commentaries. Vérard printed a Terence in prose and verse about 1500; Octovien de Saint-Gelais translated the *Aeneid* in 1509; Marot the first eclogue of Virgil in 1512, and there were many more. Charles VIII brought the hellenist Lascaris back with him to France. Erasmus studied at the Collège de Montaigu and published his *Adages* in Paris in 1500. Budé, Erasmus's great rival, was hard at work. But the full fruits of this activity were to be reaped later. The three great names of this generation were Jean Lemaire de Belges, Commynes and Gringore; they have a ring of the medieval about them, but all point forward in their different ways.

This was the Age of the *Grands Rhétoriqueurs*, versifiers and often historiographers who were the feeble if verbose offspring of the bourgeois lyrical tradition of the past two centuries. They flourished first in the courts of Burgundy and Flanders, around the person of Margaret of Austria, and only gained notable positions in the French court when the death of Louis XI opened the gates to them. The subjects of their poems, as of their prose, were many and varied: love and chivalry, statecraft and history, religion and morals, science and art, but their treatment was flat and didactic, with rarely a real personal note to enliven it. These matters they smothered in allegory, mythology, personifications. Their language was stilted, full of verbal ingenuities, inflated with ill-digested Latinisms, while their versification was vitiated by the conception of verse as a 'second rhetoric'. They excelled in the fixed form, infinitely complicated with elaborate rhyme schemes and exaggeratedly rich rhymes. Yet some have left their names not without credit: Meschinot (c. 1420–91), whose allegorical *Lunettes des Princes* in prose and verse had over twenty editions between 1493 and 1539; Molinet (1435–1507), chronicler in the Burgundian service and author of a prose *Roman de la Rose* with appended moral commentaries; Coquillart (d. 1490) who is remembered for some forcible satire; Chastellain, the doyen of the Burgundians; Crétin (d. c.1525), a Parisian with such a reputation that even Clément Marot could call him a 'sovereign poet'; Jean Marot (c. 1465–1526) who taught his more celebrated son the art of versification which he was to use so skilfully. For all their shortcomings, these craftsmen did make some contribution; they tried to wed poetry to learning; they drew, according to their lights, on ancient Latin literature; they insisted on the value of technique. But they were interested too closely in superficial form and they were ignorant of their own national heritage except through late rehandlings in debased form. Clément Marot, who was to liberate himself from the bonds of rhetoric but yet employ some of its skills in the creation of a new and lively personal poetry, was at this time still writing in the fashion of his mentors, as his earlier work like the *Temple de Cupido* (1515) bears witness. But in 1519 he was to enter the service of Marguerite d'Alençon, later of Navarre, there to receive the first elements of his real poetic education before he passed to the service of Francis I and emancipation.

Apart from the younger Marot, Jean Lemaire de Belges (c. 1473–c. 1515) was the greatest, because the most emancipated, of the *Grands Rhétoriqueurs*. After serving the duc de Bourbon and Louis de Luxembourg, he entered the train of Margaret of Austria and then that of Anne of Brittany and distinguished himself as poet, historiographer, diplomat and traveller; he was a man of independent judgment and wide interests. His official poems were ingenious, but his three main works have other qualities. The *Epistres de l'Amant Vert* (printed 1511), supposedly written by Margaret of Austria's pet parrot, recounted in graceful verse and lively diction the bird's suicide in his distress at his mistress's absence and his journeyings to the beasts' Hades and Elysium, not, of course, without the display of considerable erudition. The *Concorde des deux langages* (composed 1511, printed 1513 and frequently afterwards) takes triple allegorical form: the poet visits the temple of Venus, which he describes in decasyllabic *terza rima*, but finds no peace; a prose interlude brings him to the temple of Minerva, which he deals with in alexandrines. There Honour and all virtues are to be found. He confronts French and Italian, not linguistically as the title would suggest, but on the plane of letters and learning, where they are equal and should collaborate in fruitful and noble rivalry. The *Illustrations de Gaule et Singularitez de Troye* (in three books, composed and printed 1510–13) develops the medieval legend of the foundation of France by Francus, a son of Hector, in a kind of universal history from the Flood to the establishment of Francus in Gaul. Classical antiquity is freely plundered, while passages of charming description and lush imagery show at once an advance in the appreciation of ancient literature and a feeling for the suggestive value of words; show also why Ronsard was later to take this legend for the framework of his epic failure, the *Franciade*. Lemaire was still a *Rhétoriqueur*, sometimes pedantic and uncritical especially in the earlier allegory-laden work, but as he progresses his erudition becomes more alive, his sensibility more acute, his taste in verse and his command of words more fruitful of harmony and clarity.

French prose is old-fashioned, represented by a mass of chronicles, treatises and discourses written by *Rhétoriqueurs*, by translations, by the vigorous and essentially popular sermons of a Michel Menot (1450–1518) or an Olivier Maillard (*c.* 1450–1502), by prose rehandlings of romances and romanticised epics and by tales or collections of tales like the *Quinze Joyes de Mariage*, the *Petit Jehan de Saintré* of Antoine de la Sale or the *Cent nouvelles nouvelles* which, though it claims descent from the *Decameron*, has borrowed nothing but the superficial 'nouvelle' form. All of these were composed well before our period.

Only one name approaches first-rank greatness: that of Philippe de Commynes (*c.* 1447–1511). This highly intelligent and practical man of Flemish descent was an astute psychologist, a skilful politician and diplomat, who passed from the service of the duke of Burgundy to that of Louis XI, in whom he found not only an appreciative master but a kindred spirit. His later fortunes were not so happy. His *Mémoires* are in two parts, of which the first, composed in the years around 1490, dealt with events between 1464 and 1483 and first appeared in print in 1524; the second, composed towards the end of his life, narrated the Italian expeditions of Charles VIII and was printed in 1528. Written as material for a Latin life of Louis XI which was to be undertaken by the archbishop of Vienne, the *Mémoires* make no claim to literary merit, of which, however, they are not devoid. Commynes was concerned with events and he disdained the stylistic acrobatics of the *Rhétoriqueurs* and wrote in a plain, unadorned style, sometimes heavy, but often possessing admirable precision and appositeness. His perceptive powers, his skill in analysis, his penetration into the relationship of events, his devotion to the interests of king and state, his coolness and apparent detachment from moral considerations have given rise to a conception of Commynes as a fore-runner of Machiavelli. He certainly believes in diplomacy and its arts, but he prefers, when he can, to have morality and public opinion on his side and, in his reflections on the progress of events, he perceives a force which may intervene and bring about an unforeseeable upshot. This force he sees as the will of God and not the mere play of hazard, for, in spite of superficial appearances, Commynes was a Christian. His intellectual approach to events and the operation of cause and effect, his powers of abstraction and generalisation make him the first really modern historian, whose work might indeed have been injured for us by a greater attention to stylistic adornment.

The history of the French theatre at this time is almost devoid of landmarks; few works are dateable with precision and these are but part of a general movement which stretches from 1450 to 1550 and beyond. The great mystery-plays date mainly from about the middle of the fifteenth century and were still being played; they rarely leave the religious field and may deal on a large scale with the principal events of biblical history or with the lives and miracles of individual saints. They might involve a whole village or town and last for weeks, or merely a small confraternity and last one day; they might be performed for a great festival or be played for the cessation of a plague or in the hope of a good harvest. They are essentially popular, which accounts for their general lack of literary worth, though successful passages are to be found, and for their mixture of serious and comic scenes, the latter of which were to degenerate into mischievous pranks on which authority frowned. In Paris the *Confrérie de la Passion* was chiefly concerned with their pro-duction until in 1548 a decree put a stop to it. Other bodies were con-cerned with dramatic production in both Paris and the provinces. The clerks of the Paris *Parlement*, for instance, were organised into a veritable corporation, the Basoche, which played mysteries, moralities and farces; the clerks of the Chatelet had their own Basoche, those of the Cour des Comptes their *Empire de Galilée*, while similar bodies existed in Dijon, Rouen, Lyons and other important towns. Another Parisian body was the *Enfans sans Souci* or the *Sots*, with their *Prince des Sots* and *Mère Sotte*, who organised *soties*, farces and moralities, usually on Shrove Tuesday. It is not easy to draw a clear line between these various kinds of play, but some general distinctions can be made. In general the morality was a dramatised allegory, employing personifications for didactic pur-poses, but comic moralities were frequent, like that of André de la Vigne who attached to his *Mystery of Saint Martin* an amusing morality in which a blind man and a lame man are cured of their infirmities against their wish and react to the situation in well-imagined different ways or the

Condamnation de Banquet (about 1507, by Nicholas de la Chesnaye) where a comic treatment is used to condemn gluttony. It is interesting to note that in 1548 Sebillet, discussing tragedy and comedy, found parallels for both in the morality. The farce, which survived well into the seventeenth century, was normally a brief and robust dramatisation of a situation illustrating the inconstancy of women, the vulnerability of a man's skin or purse, indeed any common human weakness. Like the earlier narrative *fabliau*, which it resembled in tone, it varied from skilful if summary psychological portrayal to depths of obscenity. Its octosyllabic verse was rapid and effective. The famous *Pathelin* (1470) is an exception in its length, in its organisation and its continuously high level of observation and literary skill. The *sotie*, often played along with a farce and a morality, sometimes had topical application. The *Nouveau Monde*, perhaps by André de la Vigne and played by the Sots in 1508, deals with the Pragmatic Sanction; Gringore's *Prince des Sots* (1512) attacked the Pope Julius II and was reinforced by a morality, *Peuple françois, Peuple italique, l'Homme obstiné*, on the differences between the pope and Louis XII, the 'obstinate man' being, of course, the pope. The *sotie Le Monde, Abus, les Sots* (about 1514) is of more general import and shows that the world, in spite of those who wish to rebuild it on folly and corruption, will remain what it was. It will be noted that allegory plays an important part in these *soties*. Pierre Gringore was outstanding; he was *Mère Sotte* in 1511–12 and his bold *Prince des Sots* must have been written with the connivance, if not at the instigation, of the king or his ministers. Gringore must have been something of a public figure; he was certainly versatile, though much of his work falls within the *Rhétoriqueur* tradition; his *Vie de Monseigneur Sainct Loys* (*c.* 1514) shows what appears to be real religious sentiment. But it is doubtful if he deserved the idealisation which the Romantics accorded him in the nineteenth century.

Provençal literature was by this time in a state of decay. Southern French writers were composing almost entirely in French, though religious drama in Provençal has left a few traces, but the pieces are of French derivation. It is significant that a literary competition like the Jeux Floraux of Toulouse opened its lists to French compositions in 1513 and that the last works crowned by such 'academies' at the end of the fifteenth century show formalism taking the place of inspiration.

A similar movement in German lyric poetry is, in the light of the general history of German verse, a most significant phenomenon: the decay of the *Minnesang* and its replacement by the increasingly flourishing *Meistergesang*. The delicate love-songs of the early poets gave way in the fourteenth century to the formal virtuosity and ostentatious learning of the 'Master' poets (for example Frauenlob), this in its turn to the work of the guild-organised verse-smiths of the south German cities—the *Meistersinger*, with their grades of proficiency and codified rules. Few poets escaped from the prevalent mechanical conception of verse-making. Much of the work of the outstanding *Meistersinger*, Hans Sachs (1494–1576), falls outside the *Meistergesang* genre, most of it indeed outside our period. His chief significance lies perhaps in his exploitation of the *Fastnachtspiel* or Shrovetide play, developed from the primitive mumming play under the influence of the comic scenes in religious drama, which Germany possessed in abundance for Christmas and Easter. The plays of Hans Rosenplüt and Dietrich Schernberg's *Spiel von Frau Jutta* (1480) had already shown the way to the utilisation of comic anecdotes for dramatic matter, a practice found in the works of Hans Folz who flourished in Nürnberg around 1510. Pamphilus Gengenbach wrote moralising plays of this kind between 1515 and 1518, and later Niklas Manuel of Berne was to use the form to attack Catholic doctrine and practice. In the meantime folksongs appear to have flourished, the traditional allegorical poetry based on the *Roman de la Rose* tradition was still popular but becoming more and more artificial, while the chivalric romances became the object of parody or were appearing more and more in debased rehandlings, like Füetrer's *Buch der Abenteuer*. It is interesting therefore to see the Emperor Maximilian entering the lists and directing the composition of the *Theuerdank* (1517), an allegorical account, with magnificent woodcuts, of his exploits in the wooing of Mary of Burgundy.

Apart from the development of the *Schwänke*, comic anecdotes, the main revivification of old matter is in the satirical vein, which produced the masterpieces of the period. The first, in date of printing, was the *Narrenschiff* (1494) of Sebastian Brant (1457–1521), a jurist and civic magnate of Strassburg who had also to his credit Latin poems, legal works, the editing of traditional jest-books and of a popular thirteenth-century didactic work, Freidank's *Bescheidenheit*. The *Ship of Fools* tells in stinging satire and in lively memorable couplets the follies of mankind; the form is allegorical, the framework being a ship manned and steered by fools, with fools as passengers, sailing to a fools' paradise. It ran into many editions with its exciting and amusing woodcuts, was translated into many languages (including Latin) and everywhere exercised an immediate influence. It was translated twice into English before 1509. In Germany it gave rise to sermons like those of Geiler von Kaisersberg (1500, printed in Latin 1511) and to dependent satires like Thomas Murner's *Narrenbeschwörung* (1512). It was beloved by humanists and unlearned alike. The Low German *Reinke de Vos* (Lübeck, 1498) put into print matter which had already had a long history in the Netherlands, Germany, France and elsewhere; it appears to have been based upon a Flemish version which also served for Caxton's *Reynard the Fox* of 1481. In various rehandlings, this satirical beast-epic has never lost its popularity and innumerable editions and adaptations have been published. *Till Eulenspiegel* (1515) is connected with the *Schwänke* tradition; it is a collection of pranks and jests attributed to a peasant of the early fourteenth century and represents the revenge of the rustic mentality on the more sophisticated townsman. Earlier collections had been made but have not survived; the 1515 Strassburg collection was translated into many languages and for long served, in spite of its coarseness and because of its ebullient energy, as a source-book and model for satirists. Among the German satirists Thomas Murner (1475–c. 1527) is eminent; the 1515 *Till Eulenspiegel* has indeed been attributed to him on insufficient grounds. He led an agitated wandering life, and was at one time Maximilian's poet laureate, but he could not settle down. In some works in the tradition of the *Narrenschiff* he berated social follies and vices; of these the most notable were the *Gäuchmatt* (composed 1515, printed 1519) on the follies of lovers, and the self-explaining *Von dem lutherischen Narren* of 1522. The *Meistersinger* Gengenbach (1470–1524) also composed a *Gäuchmatt* in 1518. In the meantime translation of ancient literature had been going on: the fable was popular and a number of collections, including both Latin and German material, had appeared, notably that of Strassburg (1508) edited by Johann Adelphus; another collection by Martinus Dorpius was several times reprinted. A complete Terence in German appeared in 1499. Nor must it be forgotten that the whole period was one of great activity in the neo-Latin theatre, which, while falling strictly outside our rubric, must be mentioned as having contributed much to the growth of the vernacular drama, especially comedy, outside as well as inside Germany. In this connection the name of Reuchlin is important; his comedies were printed in 1496.

Reuchlin's most important influence lay, however, in the contribution which, as scholar and humanist, he made to the creation of the atmosphere in which Luther was to succeed. Other influences were, of course, at work. In 1498 the sermons of Johannes Tauler, the fourteenth-century mystic, were printed, while from before the beginning of the sixteenth century the bold sermons of Geiler von Kaisersberg (1445–1510), the 'German Savonarola', were being taken down by his friends and published, it would seem, without his consent; he used all that came to hand, including, as we have seen, the *Narrenschiff*. Already before 1520 Luther was in action; his ninety-five theses date from 1517 while in 1520 his three famous 'Reformation treatises' appeared: *An den christlichen Adel deutscher Nation*, *Von der babylonischen Gefangenschaft* and *Von der Freiheit eines Christenmenschen*, treating respectively the duty of the German nation to resist Roman exactions, the sacramental system and justification by faith. It was on 10 December 1520 that Luther invited the people of the university and town of Wittenberg to witness the burning of the bull of excommunication and other 'Roman' matter. A landmark was passed and the rest of Luther's work, including his Bible (finished 1534, New Testament issued 1522), the influence of which on the Reformation, and on the evolution of standard German prose style was enormous, belongs to a new age. It may be remembered, however, that his was not the first German translation; to mention only the main stream, the 1466 edition printed in Strassburg by Mentelin, itself based on an earlier version, was the source of at least thirteen other High German editions up to 1518 and of four Low German editions up to 1522. These versions were dull and lifeless, were full of errors and had relatively little influence.

The literature of the Low Countries at this time was, apart from medieval survivals such as romances and religious and devotional writings, the work of the flourishing Chambers of Rhetoric or *Rederijkerskamers*, guild-like corporations with fanciful names and devoted to poetry and learning. While the abundant religious drama of the fifteenth century was dying (*Het Spel van de heilig Sacramente* attributed to Smeeken, but claimed by some for Anthonis de Roovere, a *rederijker* of Bruges, and played at Breda in 1500 seeming to be one of the last), the *rederijkers* were developing the morality. The most notable morality was the *Elckerlijke*, attributed to Peter Dorlandus, written about 1470, performed in Antwerp about 1485 and printed in 1495; it may have been the original of the English *Everyman*. These moralities, *abele spelen*, chiefly on themes of courtly exploits of gallantry, and broad farces were presented by the Chambers of Rhetoric, along with an occasional miracle such as the *Mariken van Nieumeghen*, probably composed by a *rederijker* from Antwerp about 1500. These dramatic works and some rhetorical lyrics appear to represent the chief Netherlandish contribution to literature at this time, but little of it (unlike some medieval matter like the *Reinaert de Vos*) reached what might be called European stature.

The relations of English scholars with Erasmus and other continental humanists are well known and some flavour of humanism is to be seen in some of the English vernacular literature of the time. The main tradition, however, is still medieval; in poetry the spell of Chaucer and that of allegory were not yet to be shaken off. It is hard to believe that the world of chivalry in which he moves is at all real for Stephen Hawes (1475–1530), the dull didactic allegorist; his *Example of Virtu* (composed c. 1503, printed 1512) and his *Pastime of Pleasure* (composed c. 1505) are tedious moral adventures, marred by a latinised diction and a complicated style. Alexander Barclay (1474–1552), a pious Franciscan, adapted Brant's *Ship of Fools* in 1509. He had earlier imitated Mantuan's eclogues rather stiffly for educational purposes. John Skelton (c. 1460–1529), who earned the praise of Erasmus as a humanist but who was an unsatisfactory parish priest, was for a time tutor of the future Henry VIII. He established a reputation for himself as a vigorous satirist and incorrigible joker. In his satirical allegories he abandons the traditional heroic verse and adopts a ragged irregular rhythm with repeated rhymes which, in his own words, 'hath in it some pyth'. In his *Bowge of*

Court (1499) he satirises court life in Chaucerian stanzas. His *Colin Clout* (1519) attacked the clergy and even Wolsey himself, an attack repeated in most scathing terms in *Why come ye not to Court?* (1522). His earlier *Boke of Phyllyp Sparowe* was a lament on the death of Jane Scroupe's pet, based on Catullus but packed and stretched with reminiscences and digressions. He also had a morality to his credit. This curious figure, who recalls Rabelais and who possessed abundant invective, an exuberant style, much pugnacity and some inklings of humanism, still belongs on the whole to the medieval rather than to the Renaissance tradition. The Scottish poets too retain a medieval tang. Robert Henryson (*c.* 1425–1500) moved in a Chaucerian world. He gave a (to him) more satisfying end to the tale of Troilus and Cressida in his *Testament of Cresseid*; his *Fabilis* (fables) are well told and there is pathos and lyrical movement in his *Orpheus and Eurydice*, ingenious rustic realism in his *Robene and Makyne*. Of the whole Scottish group the most deservedly famous was William Dunbar (*c.* 1460–*c.* 1520), though his output was not large and his poems are usually short. But there is virtuosity in his allegories like the *Thrissel and the Rois* (Thistle and Rose) written to welcome Margaret Tudor to Scotland, or his *Dance of the Sevin Deidly Synnis*, and in his satirical poems like the *Tua Mariit Wemen and the Wedo*, remarkable for its realism, and the *Fenyeit Freir of Tungland*. It is his linguistic and metrical skill that distinguish him rather than any originality of thought or sentiment, even in his *Lament for the Makeris*, a melancholy lyric on death, reviewing the poets of his country's past. Gawin Douglas (*c.* 1475–*c.* 1522) seems at first sight to have moved towards something less medieval, though his early allegories, the *Palice of Honour* (1501) and *King Hart*, better for its brevity, are still in the old tradition. He is best remembered for the first translation (apart from some fragments) into English of the *Aeneid*; it is done in rhyming decasyllables and aims at exactness, but the Virgilian poetry hardly comes through, so that it is the poet's own prologues to each book which, written with spontaneity and colour, are most prized. For all his medieval form and traditional framework, the writings of Sir David Lyndsay fall outside our limits. There can be little doubt that popular verse in the shape of ballads was circulating on both sides of the Border, but it is impossible to pin them down to dates. It is as difficult to date with precision as to composition or performance many of the plays, religious and secular, which were played up and down the country. The town-cycles were still popular and were to remain so. A number of moralities date from the fifteenth century and follow the normal pattern. The merits of *Everyman* are known to all. The *Four Elements*, printed *c.* 1519, but surviving only in incomplete form, takes an interest in science and the new discoveries.

There is little prose to mention strictly within our period. Serious writing was still mainly in Latin; the old romances circulated in chapbooks;

the lively translation of Froissart's *Chronicles* by Lord Berners (1467–1533) and the same translator's *Huon de Bordeaux* fall into a later decade, though they look back to the Middle Ages. We must remember the popularity of Malory's *Morte d'Arthur*, printed in 1485 by Caxton, whose other publications, like those of Wynkyn de Worde, kept alive much that was best in the available literature of their time and, in translation, of classical antiquity.

In the Scandinavian countries, as elsewhere, there was a background of popular literature: folksongs and ballads, collected at a later time; narrative poems on heroic, supernatural or amusing themes or, like the Icelandic *Ballad of Tristan*, going back to the widespread 'Breton' matter; and in Iceland too the *rímur*, verse stories from the saga stock. The first Danish book to be printed was the *Rimkrönicke* (1495) attributed to the monk Niels of Sorö. Swedish chronicles produced at about the same time were the *Nya Karlskrönikan* and the *Sturerkrönikorna* (c. 1500). The traditional narrative poems were also being rehandled in prose in Iceland. Religious poetry was not lacking and produced new work like the three sacred poems of Mikkel of Odense, *The Rose Garland of Maiden Mary*, *The Creation* and *Human Life*, which appeared in 1514; while in Iceland the last Catholic bishop of Holar, Jon Arsson, set up the first printing press and wrote poems of piety, patriotism and polemic before he was beheaded in 1550. In 1506 was printed a collection of Danish proverbs, attributed to Peter Laala. In Sweden the *Love Letters* (1498) of Ingrid Persdotter, a nun of Vadstena, to a young noble, are a touching departure from current types. There is little precise evidence, but it is difficult to believe that mysteries and moralities of the type so universal elsewhere were not to be found in these countries.

Gaelic literature in Ireland and Scotland remained true to its ancient traditions. The collection of texts went on in Ireland, together with continuations of the Ulster and Finn cycles, sometimes in ballad form; chronicles, religious and devotional literature persisted, as did the translation and adaptation of stories taken in the Middle Ages from the classical stock. In Scotland, where the literary language proper remained Irish, like the basic verse technique, the outstanding document was the *Book of the Dean of Lismore*, compiled in the early decades of the sixteenth century by Sir James Macgregor and his brother; it contained poems by old and recent poets including Campbell of Glenorchy (d. 1513) and some satire on women. 'Ossianic' ballads were also collected. But the great period of Scottish Gaelic dates from the Forty-Five.

Brythonic Celtic literature shows more advance. Brittany was under French influence and French works were translated and adapted. In 1499 appeared the first book printed in Breton, the *Catholicon* of Jean Lagadeuc, who had compiled this Breton-Latin-French dictionary some thirty years earlier. In 1519 the *Mellezour an Maru* (Mirror of Death) was composed, a long poem of over three thousand verses, on Death and the Last Things; it was not printed till 1575. From the early sixteenth century come two verse mysteries, the *Buhez Santez Nonn* (Life of St Non), adapted from a Latin life and localised in Brittany, and the *Burzud Bras Jezuz* (Great Miracle of Jesus), which is in the line of the French mysteries. Devotional literature drew on the *Golden Legend* for matter. In Cornwall religious drama continued. The *Pascon Agan Arluth* (Passion of Our Lord) was a tedious play based on gospels canonical and apocryphal. It dates from the fifteenth century as do the *Ordinalia*, three religious plays, in varied metres, on the Creation, the Passion and the Resurrection; in spite of some comic scenes, the general effect is poor, the dialogue inert. Of the same general type is the *Beunans Meriasek* (Life of St Meriasek), which runs to nearly 5000 lines, varied in metre and in tone, full of anachronisms and loose in structure; this play, of Breton origin but interlarded with English words, was written down, if not composed, by 'Dominus Hadton' in 1504. In Wales, as in Ireland and Scotland, the Age of the Bards was by no means over. The Welsh bards proper were highly respected, proud of their craft and of their position in society, but there existed a rabble of self-styled bards who were little better than wandering beggars and who had become a menace, social, political and artistic. The great Carmarthen Eisteddfod of 1451 tried to deal with the situation but only succeeded in tightening the rules of versification into a strict code with the usual results. While disciples of the freer style of Dufydd ap Gwilym were still found, the more formal poetry prevailed at the end of the century with Dufydd ap Edmwnd (d. *c.* 1480) and his disciples, particularly Tudur Aled, whose sententious verse was long remembered. A number of poets sang the praises of Henry Tudor even before he won the English throne, while the topicality of this lively Welsh verse has an example in the bitter satire by Lewis Glyn Cotti (d. 1490) against the men of Chester. Outside the continuation of the gnomic triads, prose appears to have been at a standstill. The first book in Welsh was printed only in the middle of the sixteenth century.

Outside western Europe proper, the Renaissance as we know it had little effect, though young Polish nobles were sometimes educated in Italy. The general tradition in the Slav world remained that of Byzantium and of local matter. There is one notable exception, the Catholic Slavs of western Serbia and Dalmatia, who formed, particularly in Ragusa, a society which looked to Venice and Italy, and to which, earlier, Greek scholars had fled from Constantinople. Sisko Menćetić (1457–1527) and Djordje Drzić (1461–1501), in their love-poems and elegies, were in the line of Ovid and of Petrarch. These poets at any rate should be included in our survey.

To summarise this complex account is not easy, but in the welter of promise and accomplishment, backwardness and conservatism, the unique position of Italy shines out. Italy indeed was to serve for many years as a pattern and guide. Nowhere else, in spite of the achievements of a Rojas or a Brant, a Dunbar or a Lemaire de Belges, a Commynes or a Montalvo, were the Middle Ages so far outstripped and left behind. The full impact of the revival of ancient learning (even in Italy itself) and of the Italian example was yet to reach the rest of Europe and then usually modified and in some cases limited by the effect of the Lutheran and Calvinist Reformations.

CHAPTER VII

THE EMPIRE UNDER MAXIMILIAN I

O N 19 August 1493 the old emperor Frederick III died. His long reign, ever since 1440, had been marked by a rising consciousness of German nationality. This had been nourished by the controversies of the conciliar period, stimulated by the invention of printing amongst an increasingly wealthy and German-reading public in the courts and towns, and expressed in the newly current phrase 'The Holy Roman Empire of the German Nation'. But the reign had witnessed territorial losses on all sides. The estates of Holstein had accepted the rule of the Danish king (1460). The Teutonic Order had come under the control of Poland (1466). The Austrian duchies were overrun at intervals by the Turks. The Swiss had ceased to regard themselves as having duties to the *Reich*. On the collapse of the Burgundian power (1477) the French monarchy resumed its efforts at eastward expansion; and French diplomacy stimulated centrifugal movements from the Netherlands to the Alps. Frederick's son, Maximilian, took over a *Reich* diminished and threatened.

Indignation was felt at the helplessness of the *Reich*. But what could be done? Machiavelli wrote truly 'Of the power of Germany none can doubt, for it abounds in men, riches and arms. ...But it is such as cannot be used'.[1] The supreme authority was the king acting with the advice and consent of the *Reichstag*, the assembly of his estates or direct tenants. At full strength it could consist of the six electors, some 120 prelates, about thirty lay princes and 140 counts and lords, and eighty-five towns. But the list was confused and untrustworthy; and from any *Reichstag* many estates were absent. Others were represented by envoys who might prove not to have full powers to bind their principals. Many towns, nobles and the subordinate rural population were unrepresented. Certain points of *Reichstag* procedure had been established. The king made his proposals and then withdrew. Electors, princes and towns separated for discussion. The elector of Mainz then presided over a joint session and conveyed an agreed answer to the king. An agreement of king and estates became law. But the medieval principle that new obligations could not be imposed on a man without his own consent died hard. Moreover, those who had assented to a proposal at a *Reichstag* often postponed its fulfilment till the need for it had passed. *Reichstag* after *Reichstag* had met during Frederick's reign. Schemes for settling disputes and maintaining the peace for limited periods had been drawn up and pompously

---

[1] *Ritratto delle cose della Magna*; see Machiavelli's Works, ed. G. Mazzoni and M. Casella (1929), pp. 740, 742, or ed. M. Bonfantini (1954), pp. 487, 491.

announced. They had produced little effect beyond stimulating thought and demands for order. Germany remained a mass of greater and smaller powers. Her people looked to their local ruler as the last word of power. But only in the greater principalities and larger towns could they have confidence that their ruler's power would normally suffice to uphold order and provide defence.

In France and England the Church inculcated obedience in temporal matters to the royal authority and often acted as an instrument of royal policy in spiritual affairs. But over a hundred German prelates, from the three Rhenish archbishop-electors of Mainz, Cologne, and Trier, down to abbots and provosts, especially in the south and west, were themselves temporal rulers, mostly members of princely families and sharing the princely political outlook. Such prelates habitually accumulated benefices. Thus Count George of the Palatinate, on becoming bishop of Speyer, obtained from the Holy See in 1513 permission to remain dean of Mainz, a canon of Cologne and of Trier, provost of St Donatian at Bruges, parish priest of Hochheim and of Lorch am Rhein. Albert von Hohenzollern, brother of the elector of Brandenburg, on his election to the archbishopric of Mainz in 1514, was allowed to retain another archbishopric, Magdeburg, with the see of Halberstadt. Preoccupied with matters of wealth and power, such prelates were little concerned with the spiritual welfare of their flocks. Some of them rarely performed any sacerdotal functions. An extreme case was that of Rupert von Simmern, who, as bishop of Strassburg from 1440 to 1478, never once said mass, and received the sacrament once a year, like the laity.

Nevertheless, the Church was fulfilling a great task of civilisation, of spreading among the Germans the virtues of duty, goodwill and humility. Her stability appeared imposing. Her courts administered her law and their decisions were effective. Education was still almost wholly in her hands. The piety of the Germans overflowed lavishly into charitable and religious foundations. Artists and craftsmen adorned her cathedrals, churches and religious houses. Pilgrimages attracted many thousands, eager to venerate relics or to gain indulgences, the proceeds of some of which supported various forms of social service.

But the general acceptance of tradition was accompanied by the rising indignation of many orthodox reformers at the lack of discipline and education among the clergy, and by the impatience of much bourgeois opinion with ecclesiastical power. There was also much discontent among the clerical 'proletariat'. Thousands of the secular clergy were miserably paid vicars of beneficed superiors occupied elsewhere, or had no cure of souls and lived by saying masses at particular altars or picking up other pious jobs for small fees. Attached to two parish churches of Breslau there were, at the end of the fifteenth century, 236 clergy.[1] Despite

[1] J. Lortz, *Die Reformation in Deutschland*, vol. I, p. 86.

repeated and partially successful efforts at reform, there were many inefficient and unspiritual religious houses; and there was a horde of wandering mendicants, some of them impostors belonging to obscure or non-existent brotherhoods. And the country was filled with wealthy monasteries, and with collegiate foundations whose members, mostly not in priest's orders and drawn exclusively from noble families (*Gottesjunker*, as they were called), were indistinguishable from their fighting, hunting elder brothers, except for their unmarried status. An orderly, peaceful, Christian society could not develop while so many persons with no Christian aspirations were included in the clerical order. There were no seminaries. Only clerks in search of benefices and regulars attended the universities. Few of the clergy received any theological, pastoral or devotional training. And no bishop took the fundamental problem of clerical education in hand.

In these circumstances the great demand for books of popular religion and the score of editions of the Bible printed in German, before Luther's time, were viewed with not unnatural concern. The numerous publications in defence of human free will, the foundation of the Church's doctrine of man, show that it was being questioned. The great preacher of Strassburg, Geiler von Kaisersberg, said that it was as dangerous to leave the common man to make what he could of the Bible as to put a carving knife into the hands of a small child and tell him to cut the bread. Archbishop Berthold of Mainz's prohibition of the unauthorised printing and sale of vernacular works on religion was caused by similar misgivings. If revolt against the Church's teaching remained, outside Bohemia, on a very small scale, being either obscure or confined to a few virtually pagan humanists, the way for that revolt was being prepared.

Such reform as was authoritatively imposed came not from the indifferent prelates but from lay rulers. Earnest reformers among the clergy, losing confidence in their own order and in distant Rome, and fearing the growth of anti-clericalism, turned to their prince for support. It became not unusual for princes to issue instructions on ecclesiastical matters, and to reform or suppress ecclesiastical foundations. And towns were increasingly taking over activities hitherto the province of the clergy, such as hospitals, schools, the control of morals, even the control of churches and abbeys. It is noticeable that of the twenty pre-Reformation German universities, eighteen were founded either by lay princes or by town councils; whereas only two, and those the least considerable, Mainz and Würzburg, were founded by spiritual authorities.

This process of increasing lay control of the Church could, however, only be applied by the powerful. It helped to consolidate the increasing power and wealth of the few great princely families which in the decade 1495–1504 aspired to share the control of the *Reich*, and of the more numerous principalities which, together with a few great towns, also emerged as virtually independent states in the sixteenth century.

Economic changes were breaking the medieval rhythm of German life. German merchants learned Italian methods of large-scale capitalism. The generation before Luther saw the rise of the new power of the great capitalists, organising the production of the precious metals and industrial material and controlling prices. Rulers pursued dynamic policies of expansion, by purchase, by bribing ministers of other Powers or by war. And war was being increasingly waged with mercenary professional soldiers, who would desert if their pay was not punctually forthcoming. Cash was in great demand, and the capitalists would provide it, in return for productive monopolies which they could turn to advantage. A remarkable example of monopolistic power is afforded by the arrangement, towards the end of Maximilian's reign, between the firms of Fugger, then the controllers of the Hungarian copper mines, and of Höchstetter, who dealt largely in Tirolese copper. By it the copper markets of north Italy and south Germany were to be supplied exclusively from Tirol, while the Netherlands were to be supplied from Hungary. Among the results of the general economic disturbance were the depression of the old corporations of small-scale producers, increased specialisation due to new inventions, the growth of an industrial proletariat of wage-earners, and a rapid increase in wealth and culture amongst the more successful bourgeoisie. This in turn stimulated the smaller rural nobility to increase the burdens on their unfree tenants and to deprive them of common rights, as the only means, in addition to robbery with violence, of enabling themselves to emulate the style of life of the wealthy townsmen. No decade passed without a serious peasant revolt somewhere in southern Germany; and the resultant repression often added to the authority of a neighbouring territorial prince, when he proved to be the only power capable of dealing with the outbreak.

Another influence making for change was the diffusion of the Roman law, a victory of the intellectuals at the expense of the people. German laws were local and various. There was no central source of German law. The Roman law cut a clear and consistent path, favourable to authority and wealth, through the jungle. Its prestige was high at a time when Roman antiquity was almost worshipped in humanistic circles. Civilian lawyers, trained in the universities of Italy and Germany, were increasingly used by princes as administrators, judges and arbitrators. In the *Reichskammergericht* (the supreme court of the Empire), established in 1495, half of the judges were to be civilian lawyers. Thereafter the foreign, authoritarian law, which treated the monarch as the source of all rights, flowed more rapidly into the justice and administration of the territories, to the advantage of regular, systematic government. But the central authority derived no benefit therefrom. The princes, while concerned to be, each in his own territory, the Roman law's sovereign source of authority, insisted on their feudal, traditional, relation to the emperor.

At the close of the fifteenth century the triumph of the greater princes was as yet by no means assured. The larger towns, the chief centres of wealth, were still strong enough to defend themselves and, if they had to choose, preferred effective imperial government to princely rule. In the south-west the Swabian League of princes, prelates, counts, knights and towns, with regular meetings, tribunals and a minimum common force of 12,000 foot and 1200 horse, did much to maintain the peace and defend the existing order in an area where the idea of the *Reich* was strongest, but the division of actual power was greatest. Brought into existence in 1488 by the alarm of the Swabian estates at the growing 'revolutionary' power of the Swiss and the aggressive policy of the Wittelsbach dukes of Bavaria, the League provided an example of a union which demanded considerable sacrifices of autonomy from its members. Maximilian and Berthold of Mainz both adhered to the League and each tried to gain its support for his conception of the *Reich*. In its earlier years the League did support Berthold's efforts for reform, but after the peace of 1499 with the Swiss and the defeat of the Wittelsbachs in 1504, the original purpose of the League, the maintenance of the *status quo* in the south-west, was achieved. By that time the reform movement was dead. And after the death of Eberhard of Württemberg (1496) the League enjoyed no purposeful and generally accepted leadership. It was still strong enough in 1519 to overthrow the ambitious Ulrich of Württemberg, whose territory it sold to Charles V. But its members tended to claim the benefits of the League, without vigorously fulfilling its obligations. The religious revolution further divided it, and gradually it broke down.

Ecclesiastically, economically, politically, socially, Germany was in confusion and undergoing rapid change. There was a great longing for order, peace and security, and for a leader who should fulfil this longing; for an emperor who, according to a widespread apocalyptic tradition, would appear and restore the Golden Age. And to large circles of German opinion Maximilian, king of the Romans since 1486 and, with his father's death, sole ruler of the *Reich* and of the Habsburg dominions, appeared to be the God-given leader. For Maximilian had qualities that appealed to all classes of his people. He was 34 years of age; of magnificent appearance; a great gentleman, genial and at his ease with all, princes, churchmen, knights, ladies, merchants, peasants; an athlete and a mountaineer, superb in the lists and in the chase; a scholar and a poet, the patron of humanists and artists; a skilful commander in war, the organiser of the German infantry, the *Landsknechte*, and expert in the technicalities of artillery. He had beaten off the French from the Netherlands in 1479, and as recently as January 1493, with inadequate forces, he had delivered western Germany from the prospect of French invasion by his victory at Salins, followed by the Peace of Senlis in May. Three years before, by acquiring Tirol and ejecting the Hungarians from Lower Austria, he had reunited all the Habsburg lands under his father and himself. At the moment of his succession to sole rulership, he was covered with glory and popular approval.

But Maximilian had already had experience of the baffling difficulties which beset a German king, and these, together with his own inability to estimate realistically the possibilities open to him, made his reign one of frustration, disappointment and failure. In an age of growing armed autocracies, France, Spain, the Ottoman empire, he rightly perceived the dangers to which a disunited Germany was exposed. 'Unite under your king, defend Germany against France and the Turks, or perish' was his constant theme, eloquently propounded to the *Reichstag*, to the leading princes, or to assemblies of towns. He failed to persuade the estates, and the history of Germany for the next three centuries confirmed his warnings.

In opposition to Maximilian's efforts to create a strong monarchy, free to impose taxation and maintain a standing army, support for an alternative reform of the *Reich* was organised by Berthold of Henneberg, archbishop of Mainz, arch-chancellor of the empire and chairman of the Electoral College. It is evidence of his great abilities and tenacity of purpose that he was able to convert his electoral colleagues, and such good friends of Maximilian as Albert of Saxe-Meissen and Eberhard of Württemberg, to his views; so that for about a decade they presented a more or less united front. Berthold represented the aristocratic constitutionalism of the later Middle Ages. He and his colleagues demanded effective organs of central government as the essential remedy for the anarchy in Germany. But the supreme central authority must be composed of a group of the greater princes, in which the electors, with their tradition and experience of co-operation, should take the lead as the councillors of the Crown. The reformers' aim amounted to a federal *Reich*, in which the great princes, each autonomous in the affairs of his own territory, should act with the Crown as a government for common affairs. And whatever armed forces the *Reich* might have should be used for the maintenance of domestic order. Foreign war must be avoided, to give the new institutions the possibility of acceptance and growth during a period of peace. Accordingly they refused to entrust Maximilian with the discretionary control of troops and money, and with the decision of war and peace, which he maintained to be his right. They had seen his adventures on the periphery of the *Reich* in quest of objects that might increase the power of Habsburg, but seemed remote from central German interests. As regent of the Netherlands for his son Philip, he had exasperated the Flemish towns with his French war, and an imperial army had had to deliver him from imprisonment by the burghers of Bruges (1488). Two years later he had secretly married Anne, duchess of Brittany, by proxy, a mad scheme intended to enable him to attack France from the rear, just when he was fully occupied, with inadequate resources, in asserting his family's claim to the contingent succession in Hungary. Neither his father nor the *Reichstag* had supported him in either project.

In the summer of 1493 Maximilian's mind was turned once more to the east. The Turks had appeared in Croatia and southern Styria, and Maximilian went to Graz to organise defence. The west was calm, after the Treaty of Senlis. Maximilian's *Statthalter* in the Netherlands, Albert of Saxe-Meissen, had reduced the Flemish towns to obedience—so successfully that for 300 years they remained loyal to Habsburg—and in August 1494 he handed over his authority to the young Duke Philip. A gateway for French advance into Germany in the lower Rhineland seemed to have been closed. Indeed Charles VIII of France seemed to share Maximilian's dream of a united European crusade against Islam.

In September 1494 came the French invasion of Italy. Maximilian did not oppose it. On the contrary, it seems certain that his negotiations with Charles included an arrangement that, in return for his acquiescence in the French conquest of Naples, Charles would support him against Venice, the constant object of Maximilian's resentment, the filcher during the past century of much imperial territory. In this early rehearsal of the League of Cambrai of 1509 the two kings would divide the control of Italy.[1] To further this project of imperial revival in Italy, Maximilian entered into close relations with Ludovico il Moro, regent of Milan, investing him with the dukedom and marrying his niece, Bianca Maria Sforza, in return for 440,000 very welcome ducats. With French and Milanese support he would expel the Serene Republic from the mainland, which should be restored to the *Reich*. And then from the Adriatic for a great Balkan expedition for the deliverance of the east. He was still indulging these hopes when, on 24 November 1494, he summoned the *Reichstag* to meet, with armed contingents, at Worms on 2 February 1495. His immediate purpose was the journey to Rome, accompanied by a German host, for his imperial coronation. In the summer the Turkish crusade might follow.

But the complete and unexpected French success in Italy spread general alarm. Spain, Venice, the pope and Milan quickly drew together in resistance. Maximilian resented Charles's disregard of imperial rights in central Italy and the rumour that Charles proposed to reform the Holy See and even to obtain the imperial crown. Nevertheless it was only earnest warnings from Ferdinand of Spain of the danger of a French domination of Italy and the offer of a double marriage of Maximilian's

---

[1] Such is the view of Ulmann in his *Kaiser Maximilian I*, vol. 1, p. 271; and of Kaser, *Deutsche Geschichte, 1486–1519*, p. 55.

children, Philip and Margaret, to Juana and Juan of Spain, that induced Maximilian, by February 1495, to join the League of Venice for the expulsion of the French from Italy.

The League's half-hearted performance against the French army at Fornovo in July 1495 was weakened by the absence of the German contingent. Why was not Maximilian there, and in command of the League's forces? He was held down at Worms by the *Reichstag*'s resistance to his demands for supply. He had expected the assembly to last for a couple of weeks. It lasted for twenty-six. For Maximilian wanted a considerable force. Berthold of Mainz and the reformers saw their opportunity to insist on those constitutional reforms which Maximilian in 1489 and 1491 had promised to promote—a supreme court of justice and the permanent prohibition of private war—and to add further measures. Maximilian eloquently addressed the estates on the dangers of a French control of Italy, of French attacks from the south as well as the west, in addition to the constant threat of Turkish invasion. He demanded the money for an Italian campaign forthwith and further sums for the maintenance of an army for ten or twelve years. Each side admitted the strength of the other's argument. It was a question of priorities. The reformers argued that a coherent, working system of law and order was Germany's first necessity. They presented a scheme. It included the former demands, but also a permanent supreme executive council (*Reichsrat*) of seventeen, without whose consent royal acts would be invalid, to provide for defence and internal peace, to carry out decisions of the court and to control royal revenue. The king should be represented by the president, each of ｜the six electors should nominate one councillor, the spiritual princes four, the temporal princes four, and the towns two. Matters of importance, including foreign relations and new taxes, would be referred to the king (if he were available) and the electors.

Moved by the news of the virtual French victory at Fornovo, the *Reichstag* agreed to a scheme of general taxation, the Common Penny, to provide an army for defence, and an immediate loan from the towns of 150,000 *gulden* and a further sum of 150,000 *gulden* from those who were prepared to make an advance payment on account of the Common Penny. But the argument over the other measures went on till August. There was even a proposal for a German Church, not controlled from Rome. The great point of difference was the *Reichsrat*. The king would not consent to being reduced to the status of an executive officer of a commission controlled by the electors. Few of the estates liked it. Some, like the Wittelsbachs, openly opposed it. So the *Reichsrat* was dropped. But Berthold insisted that some representative organ of executive government was essential. So it was finally provided that to the *Reichstag* itself, meeting annually or in extraordinary sessions, should be entrusted the ordering of measures for the maintenance of the peace, the expenditure of the Common Penny, the conduct of foreign policy, the decision on war and peace. Thus an institution of long-proved incapacity for decisive action was made the supreme executive power.

The Public Peace was declared permanent. That was something achieved. The effectiveness of the Peace, indeed, depended on the princes' support of collective security. It was still violated—some princes could not be restrained, and the knightly highwaymen (*Raubritter*) could not for a generation be brought to abandon their gangster way of life—but it was less so than before. And the principle had been proclaimed that private war was a crime. The *Reichskammergericht*, sitting at Frankfurt (in Rhenish, electoral Germany, far from the Habsburg sphere of power), was to apply the rule of law. The king was to nominate its president, who would be assisted by eight nobles and eight doctors of law, approved by the *Reichstag*. Maximilian duly inaugurated the court on 31 October, and it was the one permanent institutional outcome of the *Reichstag* of Worms. But it began feebly. It could not discipline the mighty. The judges could not obtain their salaries, payable out of the Common Penny. Suitors complained that without bribery they could get no attention. In May 1497 the court moved to Worms, where life was cheaper.

The financial provision was a failure. The Common Penny, voted for four years only, was to support an imperial army and the *Reichskammergericht* and other expenses of government. It was to be paid to seven treasurers, nominated by the king and the estates and stationed at Frankfurt. These treasurers were to submit accounts annually to the *Reichstag*, which would allocate expenditure. The great innovation, which stressed the unity of the *Reich*, was that the tax, $2\frac{1}{2}$ per cent of income or 0·1 per cent of capital, was to fall directly on all persons over fifteen and capable of paying and to be collected by parish priests, since it was primarily intended for the Turkish crusade. It was a step towards true federal taxation, although the estates were responsible for seeing that it was collected. It was not a mere confederate demand addressed to rulers, who could raise it as they pleased. But the money did not come in. Many princes, counts and towns considered the tax an outrage. Many refused to take orders from a *Reichstag* at which they had been neither present nor represented. An assembly of Franconian knights declared that their duty was to fight, not to pay, for the *Reich*. After two years only Mainz (of course) and two other bishops, the elector of Brandenburg and two lesser princes, and some towns of the south-west had paid up. Without money, without coercive authority, the reforms of Worms were unworkable.

For the next four years Maximilian was engaged upon various enterprises, whose connecting thread was his continual contest with France. The rumour that Charles VIII would shortly return to Italy seemed confirmed when some French troops crossed the Alps early in 1496. Ludovico of Milan, upon whom the blow might fall in the first instance, persuaded the Venetians to join him in offering Maximilian a monthly subsidy to become their *condottiere* and bring a German army into Italy. To show the imperial flag in Italy, to eject the French, and then together with Spain to invade France from the south, while the English should invade it from the north, was now his grandiose plan. But his summons of an imperial host to join him in July met with little response. No prince of the empire came or approved of the expedition. He must, therefore, have money with which to hire troops. The house of Fugger agreed to pay 121,600 *gulden* for a silver mining monopoly in Tirol. But that sum was almost entirely swallowed by old debts and payments to his Tirolese officials. Despite the Edict of Worms, he collected as much as possible of the Tirolese share of the Common Penny, and crossed the Alps with a small force of 4000 horse and foot, vainly hoping with the Italian subsidies to hire an imposing contingent of Swiss. But it was now clear that there was to be no French invasion of Italy, and the Venetians advised Maximilian that he would do well not to proceed farther. He was not to be restrained, however; and he appeared in Italy as the angel of deliverance —whom nobody now wanted. Ludovico invented a task for him, the deliverance of Pisa from Florentine attack. Maximilian accordingly laid siege by sea and land to the Florentine port of Leghorn. Defeated there by the autumn weather, and finding that the Venetian subsidy was not forthcoming, Maximilian hastily abandoned his Italian plans and hurried back to Germany, pursued by the mocking laughter of all Italy.

Yet while Maximilian was cutting so ridiculous a figure in Italy, there occurred at Antwerp, on 21 October 1496, an event destined in the future to raise the house of Habsburg almost to that European monarchy of which he dreamed; the marriage of his son, Philip of Burgundy, to Juana of Spain.

From the summer of 1496 to that of 1498 Berthold of Mainz kept the *Reichstag* in almost continuous session at Lindau, Worms and Freiburg-im-Breisgau, struggling to persuade such estates as attended to abandon their particularism in the common interest. Maximilian remained aloof, engaged in organising the administration of his Tirol. The *Reichstag* discussed and agreed on sumptuary and temperance regulations. At last, in June 1498, Maximilian appeared at Freiburg. Charles VIII had died suddenly, and Louis of Orleans was king of France. Maximilian was already organising a preventive war, before Louis could be secure on his throne. Ducal Burgundy should be recovered and France's satellites along the Rhine prevented from defying the *Reich*. Bitterly he broke out to a group of princes: 'By the Lombards I am betrayed. By the Germans deserted. But I will not let myself again be bound hand and foot as at Worms....I must and will make war....This must I say, even should I have to throw the crown at my feet and stamp upon it.'[1]

---

[1] Kaser, *op. cit.* p. 77; cf. Ulmann, *op. cit.* vol. I, p. 592.

The *Reichstag* could see no sense in the war. But king and estates came to terms. The Common Penny had been coming in better, and a small amount was appropriated for the war. Maximilian confirmed the Edict of Worms. But Maximilian's war petered out. Louis, preparing for the conquest of Milan, was content to remain on the defensive in Burgundy, while he skilfully dissolved the Italian League and established friendly relations with Venice and Spain, made a treaty of friendship with Maximilian's son, Philip, at Brussels, negotiated with the Swiss, and stimulated Charles of Egmond, the deposed, but defiant, duke of Guelders, to activity. Maximilian was engaged in dealing with Guelders in February 1499, when he heard that all along the Swabian-Swiss border war had broken out.

The Swiss Confederation then consisted of the original forest cantons, Uri, Schwyz and Unterwalden; two other rural cantons, Zug and Glarus; the town-dominated cantons of Berne, Lucerne and Zürich; and the post-1477 accessions of Fribourg and Solothurn. There were also areas under the joint lordship of two or more cantons, as well as associated Alpine communities and allied towns. Annual or more frequent diets of representatives of the ten peasant and burgher republics provided some central control and common policy.

Guicciardini described the Swiss as 'fierce and rustic; pastoral rather than agricultural, because of the barrenness of their country.... This fierce and primitive people have won great renown by their union and feats of arms, for by their natural ferocity and military discipline they have always bravely defended their own country and won great fame fighting in foreign service.'[1] During the transition from feudal to professional armies, from the dominance of the mounted knight to the new power of fire-arms, the disciplined valour of the Swiss made war their national industry. Apart from the modest returns on their cattle-breeding, the Swiss derived some profit from the transit of goods through their centrally-placed territory and from the industries of Zürich and Berne. These resources they augmented by pay and loot in foreign military service, which the young men enjoyed. Other motives also, a threat to their independence, the defence of the Church, the arguments of leaders who knew something of Europe and had been adequately bribed, would suffice to send a force of these magnificent fighters into action. Of foreign Powers the best paymasters had been the kings of France, so that in the later fifteenth century Swiss troops had been an almost permanent instrument of French policy, to the indignation of German opinion. On occasions the response of the Swiss could be embarrassing; as when Charles VIII sent agents from Turin to recruit 12,000 Swiss in August 1495. Double that number came, and the passes had to be manned to prevent women and children from coming to earn French gold.

The weakness of the Swiss was disunity, the mutual distrust of the

[1] Guicciardini, *Storia d'Italia*, book x.

rural and urban cantons, the rivalries of Berne, Zürich and Lucerne, family and personal feuds. The Burgundian wars and their aftermath had increased the hegemony of Berne, brought a considerable French-speaking population under Swiss control, and given rise to disputes over the profits. Only by long negotiations and compromise was civil war avoided in 1481. A period of peace followed, during which Hans Wald-mann, burgomaster of Zürich (1483–9), with the help of the artisans' guilds, became virtual dictator of his canton and aimed at a closer Swiss union in resistance to what he considered the Habsburg danger from the east. His arrest and execution by his opponents left the Swiss with no unifying control.

A permanent bond between the Swiss and their associated communities to the east was hatred of Habsburg. Arising from memories of past struggles, it was kept alive by the Habsburg possession of Tirol and many lands in Swabia, Alsace and Burgundy. And ever since 1438 the head of the *Reich* had been a Habsburg. The *Reich*'s authority had indeed been allowed to lapse. And the Swiss were quick to resent any revival of it, for behind it would lie Habsburg interests and the feudal conceptions from which they had successfully liberated themselves. The creation of the Swabian League was ill received by the Swiss, who saw in it a Habsburg-contrived barrier to their own expansion. Insults and opprobrious epithets were habitually flung to and fro across the Rhine and the situation on that border was always explosive.

The reforms of the *Reich* agreed at Worms in 1495 might have received Swiss approbation, if the reforming oligarchs had given the well-organised Swiss republics a place in their councils. As it was, the Swiss would have none of them. What did they care for a *Reichstag* in which the voice of the peasant was not heard? They, whose arbitral tribunals operated satisfactorily, had no use for the *Reichskammergericht*. As for paying the Common Penny, to be used by a Habsburg king and the electors, it was out of the question. The reformers of the *Reich* were trying to convert a long inoperative suzerainty into effective sovereignty. The Swiss not only rejected it, but magnet-like attracted to their system one neighbour after another, who wished to avoid imperial obligations.

In October 1496 an adverse sentence of the *Reichskammergericht* against the Swiss town of St Gall was angrily rejected. During 1497 the Swabian League and the Swiss began to sharpen their swords and pikes. In 1498 Louis XII's agents were active among the Swiss, distributing money and arguments against the *Reich*, so that Ludovico of Milan should receive no support from north of the Alps. The spark that exploded the accumulated powder was an obscure dispute between Tirol and the *Grauer Bund*, a community of the high Alps round the Engadine. The *Graubündner* summoned Swiss help, Tirol appealed to the Swabian League. In February 1499 war flared up along the Rhine from Basle to

Feldkirch. It was a savage, shapeless war of small, heroic fights and much plunder and destruction. To defend their liberty the Swiss fought with a solidarity and loyalty that was lacking on the Swabian side, where some knights refused to fight the 'contemptible bumpkins'.

The Swiss explosion was highly distasteful to Maximilian. It was not *his* war. The Swiss were the finest soldiers in Europe and he constantly needed their services. If only he could get their military support, their *de facto* independence might well be ignored. This civil war could bring little gain and must cause the loss of much German manpower. However, he could not avoid his duty as head of the *Reich*. He nominated his brother-in-law, Albert of Bavaria, as temporary commander-in-chief, to the disgust of many Swabian knights who would not serve under a Bavarian. He himself came slowly south to the lake of Constance, and worked out a plan for the encirclement of the Swiss. Before it could be carried out, disaster occurred. The German right wing, a force of 16,000 men, was surprised and wiped out at Dornach, near Basle, on 22 July. The Swiss victory was decisive. The war, estimated to have cost 20,000 dead and 200 castles and villages destroyed, was ended by negotiation and the Peace of Basle, 22 September 1499.

The peace effected no change in the territorial *status quo*; and the main issue, the claims of the *Reich* to authority over the Swiss, was passed over in silence. But actions begun in the courts of the *Reich* against the Swiss were to be abandoned. Maximilian thus accepted the fact of Swiss independence. And in 1508, when bargaining for Swiss troops, he formally emancipated the confederation and its members from the jurisdiction of the courts of the *Reich*.

After the war the Swiss further consolidated their position. In 1501 Basle and Schaffhausen, key positions on the Rhine, were admitted as full members of the confederation. It was perhaps as an offset to this increase of the urban element that the rural district of Appenzell was admitted as a sovereign canton in 1513. The achievement of security was also followed by expansion southwards. In 1500 Ludovico Sforza recovered Milan from the French with the help of 8000 hastily recruited Swiss. But a French army, with a larger force of Swiss, recruited with the approval of the Swiss diet, appeared in Lombardy. The two bodies of Swiss met at Novara. Ludovico's Swiss, already disappointed of immediate payment and plunder, refused to fight their countrymen and marched off home; and Milan was once more in Louis's hands. Disputes, however, arose between the French king and his Swiss allies over freedom of trade with Milan and the possession of Bellinzona, long promised to the forest cantons. Early in 1503 a Swiss force crossed the St Gotthard, and Louis, preoccupied with Naples, surrendered the coveted district to the forest cantons, which thus acquired permanent control of an Italian-speaking area.

Meanwhile some of the soberer leaders of the confederation had become convinced of the dangers of foreign military service to the true interests of their people. A diet of all twelve cantons agreed at Baden, on 21 July 1503, to renounce foreign military service and the acceptance of pensions and other inducements to recruiting. But the diet had imperfect control of the cantons, as the cantons had of their citizens. The act of renunciation remained an aspiration.

Till 1510 the Swiss held more or less consistently to their French alliance. But Pope Julius II determined to use them for the expulsion of the French from Italy. His agent, Matthias Schinner, owed his elevation to the bishopric of Sion to his prominence in the German, anti-French party in the Valais. The military service of the pope appeared highly respectable, and on 14 March 1510 a diet of all the cantons at Lucerne authorised a treaty, by which for five years the Swiss should provide 6000 men, on demand, for the service of the Holy See, and each canton should receive 1000 *gulden* annually. The treaty was soon more than fulfilled. Swiss indignation was aroused by Louis XII's refusal of an increase in his regular payments to the Swiss, by his enlistment of German *Landsknechte* and by his schismatic Council of Pisa. In the summer of 1512 over 12,000 Swiss came down the Adige and swept the French out of Italy. It was the supreme moment of the Swiss in power politics. All the Alpine passes from the St Bernard to the Stilfserjoch were now under their control. Lugano and Locarno were held by the forest cantons; Chiavenna and the Valtelline by the *Grauer Bund*. The restoration of the Sforza to Milan, with a Swiss guarantee, suggested that the great Lombard duchy was coming under a Swiss protectorate.

Further triumphs followed in 1513. Louis XII's effort to recover Milan was decisively defeated by the Swiss at Novara in June. While the English invaded northern France, a large Swiss army advanced into ducal Burgundy. Dijon capitulated on terms which included the definitive evacuation of Lombardy by the French and a payment of 400,000 crowns to the Swiss. Exultantly the mountaineers returned home, without waiting for the ratification of the treaty; which Louis repudiated.

Francis I made it his first business in 1515 to recover Milan. Massimiliano Sforza appealed to his guarantors. Swiss counsels were divided. The francophiles and the neutralists reasserted themselves. The western cantons marched indeed, but allowed themselves to be bought off by Francis. The army of the eastern cantons, in a bad tactical position at Marignano, was completely defeated (13 September). The history of the Swiss as a military Power came to an end. In 1516 some of the cantons still sent men to serve Maximilian and the Sforza. But their pay was soon in arrears; the French army included some of their countrymen; and Francis was prepared to let the Swiss keep their acquisitions south of the Alps. Accordingly the arguments prevailed that mercenary service bred avarice and led to disputes and habits of violence and was too costly in casualties for a small community, and that the better policy would be neutrality with a powerful supporter. On 29 November 1516 the confederation entered into a 'perpetual peace' with France. Swiss forces were never to be used against France; and the king of France was authorised to enlist up to 16,000 Swiss for defence only. The confederation also received valuable economic preferences. Thus France became the 'first friend' and adviser of the confederation. Thereafter the rarity of civil war among the Swiss and the total absence of foreign war bear testimony to the skill of French diplomacy. The Swiss were irretrievably lost to the *Reich* and created their tradition of permanent neutrality.

During the Swiss war of 1499 Louis XII had crossed the Alps and annexed the imperial fief of Milan. Would the *Reichstag* tolerate this injury? It met at Augsburg on 10 April 1500, the day of Ludovico's final capture by the French. A much chastened Maximilian appeared. Since 1495 he had repeatedly disregarded the Edict of Worms and tried to commit the *Reich* to war. He had fought Florence, France, Guelders and the Swiss; and without success. He could argue that his failures were due to lack of support from the estates, rendered more disastrous by a constitutional experiment that did not work. The result was what he had foretold in 1495, the French power to the south as well as the west of Germany. While the French, Venetians and Turks pressed in on the *Reich*, the German king had to cope with confusion, disobedience and treachery. But the reformers were still strong and determined. To disarm his opponents Maximilian himself proposed what he had rejected at Worms, the appointment of a representative supreme Executive Council, a *Reichsregiment*. Berthold and his colleagues went to work and produced a scheme to be applied for the next six years. The *Reichsregiment* should be composed of twenty-one members. The king or his deputy should preside; two councillors would represent Austria and Burgundy; each elector should appoint one councillor; and the remaining twelve would be elected by the estates according to their ranks and representing six areas (*Kreise*) other than the Habsburg and electoral lands. Provision was made for the inclusion of burghers, knights and doctors of law. One elector should attend in person during each period of three months. He would vote first, and countersign decisions. The seat of this Government was to be Nürnberg. Its members would be paid out of taxation approved by the *Reichstag*. If neither the king nor his deputy appeared, the *Regiment* should proceed with the business nevertheless. And the *Regiment* was to take over virtually all the functions of the monarchy. Administration, the management of finance, the reform of justice, the maintenance of order, the conduct of foreign policy, the raising and even the command of the armed forces, were all attributed to it. Its orders would go out in the name of the king and with his seal. The *Regiment* would report annually to the *Reichstag*, to which, at the end of six years, supreme power would revert.

To meet the needs of defence a new expedient was adopted. All should contribute. The nobility would provide cavalry, while the princes would tax their non-noble subjects for the provision of a militia. The expenses of the *Reichsregiment* and *Reichskammergericht* would be met from the contributions of the clergy and towns, who might be trusted to understand the needs of these institutions. The scheme was a step back from federal to confederate organisation, in that to the individual estates was left the entire responsibility for raising the tax and the armed forces.

Thus Maximilian's desire for an army of the *Reich* was to be fulfilled. But at what a price! He was no longer king in any sense of the word that he could admit. He had sunk into the formal president of a commission dominated by Berthold and his electoral colleagues. In the affairs of the *Reich* he had no veto and no freedom of action. Even the military command was transferred from him to Duke Albert of Bavaria. Maximilian bowed to necessity. But he warned the *Reichstag* that, if things did not now improve, he would not wait to be dethroned, but would take the crown and smash it to pieces. Before the *Reichstag* dissolved he went off to hunt chamois in Tirol.

The reformers were no more successful in conducting central government than Maximilian, who now gave them no assistance. They would not make peace with France by the surrender of Milan to Louis. But, as they would not embark on war, they made no impression on Louis. And the militia remained unformed. Berthold's health was beginning to suffer. The estates gave him little support. The sessions of the *Regiment* were always badly attended. So little taxation came in that its members could not recover their expenses, and in 1501 they tried, unsuccessfully, to persuade Cardinal Peraudi, the papal legate, newly arrived to organise the collection of alms in connection with the jubilee indulgence, to turn over to them part of the proceeds. The *Regiment* was no more than a fifth wheel, turning in the air.

And Maximilian was not slow to recover from his humiliations and resume his freedom of action. He did his best to secure the payment to him, as the commander of the coming crusade, of as much as possible of the proceeds of the jubilee indulgence. In his own lands, he ordered the retention of the indulgence monies pending his further instructions. In defiance of the *Reichsregiment* he summoned the German princes to join him, with armed contingents, on 1 June 1502, for the crusade. Berthold responded by summoning a meeting of the electors to consider the king's violation of the edicts of Worms and Augsburg. In March 1502 Maximilian demanded from Berthold, arch-chancellor of the empire, the surrender of the imperial seal. That was virtually the end of the *Reichsregiment*. The *Reichskammergericht* also ceased to function, since its members remained unpaid and Maximilian had restored his own royal court with judges nominated by himself. The electors assembled at Gelnhausen on 30 June and undertook to meet four times a year and to act as a government of the *Reich* in disregard of the king. While Maximilian exchanged a heated correspondence with Berthold, whom he openly accused to the town council of Ulm of being in the pay of the king of France, Germany sank into even greater than usual confusion and disturbance.

Maximilian was now engaged not in expensive operations of war, but in tortuous diplomacy concerned with the dynastic possibilities of future Habsburg greatness. His son, Philip, had become, through his wife, Juana, the prospective ruler of Spain; and the complete victory of Spain over France in southern Italy during 1503 strengthened the position of Spain's ally, Maximilian. On the other hand, Philip and his Flemish councillors maintained friendly relations with France and Maximilian was induced to be a party to a series of treaties with Louis XII, which differed in various respects but repeatedly provided for the marriage of Philip's baby son, Charles, with Louis's baby daughter, Claude. Although the French and German kings trusted each other not at all, it appeared possible that the Archduke Charles might one day become the ruler not only of Spain, but of some, at least, of Louis's possessions. By the Treaty of Blois, in September 1504, Louis was to have Milan, for 200,000 ducats, and undertook to interfere no more in the affairs of the *Reich*. If Louis died sonless, Charles and Claude were to succeed to Milan, Blois and Brittany. The following April Cardinal d'Amboise, on behalf of Louis, did homage to Maximilian for Milan at Hagenau and was solemnly invested. Despite the anarchy in Germany, Maximilian's dreams of a future universal monarchy of Habsburg were receiving encouragement.

Maximilian was also engaged in developing the monarchical administration in his own lands. He often said that he would prefer to be duke of Austria, which meant something, rather than a helpless German king. While the reformers were reducing his authority in the *Reich* to nothing, he sought the roots of power in Habsburg soil (p. 219).

He was also patiently, diligently active in building up support for himself among the princes. His royal functions and dignity gave him much influence over chapters, princely families and towns. He had successfully arranged that many bishoprics should be filled with his supporters. Among the secular princes he had been able, by grants of fiefs, tolls and other rights, to create a party of adherents, in addition to those whose tradition it was to support the emperor.

And Maximilian's greatest asset was his personality. He was expert in all the pursuits that appealed to the young, fighting, hunting nobles; his praises were sung by writers, artists, preachers; he was a welcome guest in the towns where he fascinated burgher society by his geniality, eloquence and wide interests.

Finally his chief opponent, Berthold, without whose energy and devotion to principle the movement for constitutional reform could have had no success at all, was sinking in health and died on 21 December 1504.

The episode which suddenly changed the situation and gave Maximilian a short period of triumph in the *Reich* was the war of the Landshut succession. Duke George 'the Rich' of Bavaria-Landshut died without a male heir on 1 December 1503. He had made a succession agreement with his cousins, Dukes Albert and Wolfgang of Bavaria-Munich. But by his will he bequeathed all his possessions to his daughter, Elizabeth, wife of Rupert, son of the Elector Palatine. The will defied not only the previous agreement, but also the imperial rights over an escheated fief. And Maximilian could not willingly permit so considerable an accession of strength to the Palatinate, the habitual satellite of France and his own enemy. Accordingly Maximilian presided over his own royal court (*Hofkammergericht*) at Augsburg, found legal flaws in the arguments of both claimants to the succession and proposed partition. But the young Rupert tried to effect a *fait accompli* by seizing the town of Landshut. It was essential for Maximilian to suppress and punish this defiance of his royal authority; and in the process he could retain some pickings for Habsburg. He therefore pronounced the ban of the empire upon Rupert on 23 April 1504. The Swabian League and many enemies of the Palatinate took up arms for the king, and south Germany was devastated by war. No support for the Palatinate was forthcoming from France, which Maximilian's diplomacy had, for the moment, succeeded in neutralising. The decisive engagement was Maximilian's defeat of the Palatinate's Bohemian mercenaries near Regensburg on 12 September. He then turned to protect his own interests in Tirol and besieged the fortress of Kufstein, which held out for Rupert. After three weeks it surrendered. The commander and seventeen of the garrison were hanged, as a warning to rebels. And Maximilian had a valuable stronghold, at the northern gate of Tirol, in his hands.

Victorious in the Bavarian war, Maximilian summoned the *Reichstag* to Cologne for June 1505. It was his moment of glory. The electoral opposition had dissolved. Mainz and Trier were now his supporters. Cologne had never been personally unfriendly to Maximilian, nor active in reform. The young Elector Joachim of Brandenburg was himself arranging to spend a year in Maximilian's service. The defeated Philip of the Palatinate was in no position to assert himself. Of the electors, who three years before had proposed to conduct the government of the *Reich*, only Frederick of Saxony remained to offer cautious resistance to any attempts at monarchical power. Maximilian, on the other hand, enjoyed immense popularity and respect. In April 1505 the Venetian envoys reported home that 'His imperial majesty is now a true emperor of the empire and ruler of Germany'.[1]

> [1] *Archiv f. österr. Gesch.* vol. 66 (1885), p. 77.

The Landshut succession was again submitted to Maximilian's judgment. He accorded the smaller part, north of the Danube, to Rupert's three sons, whose father had fallen in the course of the war; and the larger share, south of the Danube, to the house of Munich; an arrangement calculated to leave a permanent source of discord between the two branches of the Wittelsbach family. The victor and judge took an ample reward for his services. Maximilian rounded off his Tirol by annexing to it Kufstein and the valleys south of it, while the Elector Palatine had to surrender many towns and districts to Habsburg.

At Cologne Maximilian took up the task of providing the *Reich* with organs of central government. Instead of floundering in the bog of attempted government by discussion among the oligarchs, Germany should have a strong monarchy. He brought forward proposals much like those with which he had opposed Berthold's suggested *Reichsrat* at Worms in 1495. There should be a permanent *Reichsregiment* at Nürnberg for the next six years. It should consist of twelve members elected from the six *Kreise* and invested with all the powers of the *Reichstag*. But the king should at any moment be entitled to summon it to himself, and in important matters of policy it was to carry out his orders. As some provision that this executive council should not be the mere instrument of the royal will, which it was evidently intended to be, Maximilian undertook that in all cases of difference between himself and the council he would call in the electors and other princes to share in the decision. Maximilian also proposed to provide the *Reich* with what it had never had, permanent armed contingents for the enforcement of the law. There should be four marshals, for four areas of Germany, each commanding a posse of twenty-five knights as a form of imperial police. This plan of setting thieves to catch greater thieves was ingenious. The knights might be expected to be glad of such employment and of the chance of disciplining some princes; though it may be doubted whether such small forces of knights would have been effective. The plan was not unnaturally rejected by a *Reichstag* of princes.

Indeed the estates, if immensely respectful to their king, were in no mood to reopen the discussion on reform. They were weary of the efforts at constitution building. Courteously they assured Maximilian that he had ruled nobly, honourably and well, and would know how to continue doing so. They therefore did not wish to limit or define his powers. In fact they had become aware that plans for the creation of a German state were unrealistic. The princes would not accept the status of subjects of a state however constitutional; the king would not sink to the level of a president of a federal republic. There was nothing for it but to go on with the existing muddle rendered worse than ever by uncertainty on how much of the *Reichstag*'s legislation of recent years could be supposed to be still valid.

Maximilian's usual request, for money for war, this time to assert the Habsburg claim of succession to the Hungarian Crown, should King Wladislaw die without a male heir, against a movement of nationalistic Magyar nobles (to be followed by the expedition to Rome for the imperial coronation), was moderate and well received. He only asked for 4000 men from the *Reich*. He would supply 10,000 from his own lands. There was no question of reviving the Common Penny in any form. A return was made to the traditional and obsolete list (*matricula*) of the money and men owed by each estate to the *Reich*.

The appearance of Maximilian's almost entirely Austrian army in Hungary, but much more the birth of a son, Lewis, to Wladislaw in July 1506, led to an inconclusive peace (19 July). The hostile Magyar nobles did not withdraw their oath to reject any non-Hungarian claimant to the Crown (p. 222); but the Habsburg contingent right of succession, should the Jagiello line fail of male heirs, was included in the settlement.

After Hungary, the coronation at Rome and the revival of the empire in Italy. But while Maximilian's fortunes in the *Reich* had improved, the foreign situation had deteriorated. Louis XII had denounced the Treaty of Blois, with its marriage of Charles and Claude, as was to be foreseen. Louis and Ferdinand of Aragon were now allies, each dominating his share of Italy. And in September 1506 the Archduke Philip, who had succeeded Isabella as king of Castille, died. Ferdinand, who had married a French wife, Louis's niece, was once more ruler of all Spain and might have a son, who would cut out Philip's son, Charles, from the Spanish succession. Maximilian was without allies, and the entrance to Italy was blocked by France and Venice. He must appeal to a *Reichstag* for adequate support.

At the *Reichstag* of Constance, in May 1507, Maximilian's prestige was still high. The apparent failure of his dynastic hopes in France and Spain increased his popularity by relieving the estates of the fear of an international Habsburg monarchy. Eloquently he invited the estates to support the *Reich*. He asked for supply for 30,000 men and promised that Lombardy and Venetia, when recovered for the *Reich*, should become imperial domain, the empire's treasure-house, to the great financial relief of Germany. But the estates could only be moved to half measures. On a serious war against France and Venice they would not embark. For the Roman expedition they agreed to 3000 horse for six months and 120,000 *gulden* for 9000 foot, on the *matricula* basis—a wholly inadequate provision for an undertaking that was sure to be vigorously opposed. On their side the estates asked for the effective restoration of the *Reichskammergericht* inaugurated in 1495. This was agreed. The king should nominate the president and two assessors for Austria and Burgundy; each elector one assessor; the estates of the six *Kreise* the remaining eight assessors. Two princes, as visitors, should annually inspect the court's work and report to the *Reichstag*. The great weakness remained the lack of sanctions. Should the court's sentence be defied, the court and visitors were to discuss suitable measures of enforcement and report them to the king. That was all. So at Constance the two highly unsatisfactory imperial institutions, which lasted for the next three centuries, the *matricula* and the *Reichskammergericht*, were definitely established.

Once more Maximilian's grandiose plans for Italy came to nothing. Early in 1508 he was at Trent. But of the promised troops there was hardly a sign, and only a quarter of the money had come in. He had to abandon the journey to Rome, and instead, on 6 February 1508, he announced in the cathedral at Trent that, with Pope Julius's consent, he assumed the title of 'Emperor-elect'.[1] But, if Rome was unreachable, the insolent, bourgeois republic of Venice must be forced to surrender some of the territory which she had filched from the Empire. So Maximilian embarked on a struggle with Venice which continued intermittently for eight years. For that war the *Reichstag* would not vote the necessary supplies. And the German towns resented the interference with their commercial relations with Venice. Maximilian had to operate with such subsidies as he could raise from foreign allies and his own long-suffering lands, and by pledging all his capital resources till he was ultimately reduced to poverty.

In the spring of 1508 the Venetians not only defeated Maximilian's small forces, but overran and annexed the Habsburg territories of Gorizia, Trieste and Istria. Maximilian had to make a truce, accepting the situation. But chastisement awaited Venice. Louis resented the republic's cessation of hostilities against Maximilian, and in December 1508 the emperor's daughter, the wise and skilful Margaret, regent of the Netherlands, negotiated the League of Cambrai for united Franco-Imperial action against Venice. The League was joined by Spain and the pope. All four powers were to fall upon Venice and no peace was to be made until each had obtained what it claimed from her. The emperor's share was to be all the mainland from Verona and Padua eastwards. Again Maximilian had to go to a *Reichstag*, which slowly assembled at Worms in April 1509. Again he eloquently demanded the army which he needed. This time he met with firm refusal. Not a man, not a *gulden*, for a war in which the estates took no interest and which was to be fought in alliance with France, so often described to them as the arch-enemy of the *Reich*. So the general attack on Venice took place without the assistance of the German ally, except that the Habsburg possessions around Trieste were recovered. Maximilian's one military effort, the siege of Padua (August to October 1509), with Tirolese, French, Italian and Spanish troops, ended in failure, and he returned to Germany humiliated. Alone of the four allies he had not achieved his purpose.

[1] Maximilian will hereafter be referred to no longer as king, but as Emperor.

To the *Reichstag* of Augsburg, in March 1510, Maximilian submitted yet another scheme for defence and internal order. The estates should provide for a standing force of 50,000 men for ten years, under a commander-in-chief and four commanders for four divisions of the *Reich*. A commission of representatives of the four areas should sit, with an imperial president, and decide when and to what extent to make use of this force in support of the law. Some such provision of a sanction was indeed what the *Reich* needed. But the estates had lost interest in central government and suspected that the force, if ever embodied, would be used for the Venetian war. They postponed the whole matter to the next *Reichstag*, and thus effectively buried it.

For the next two years Maximilian was the dependent of France. While Pope Julius was organising his Holy League with Spain, Venice and England, to drive the French from Italy, Maximilian, like Louis, played with the ideas of ecclesiastical reform which were so much in the air. He tried to persuade Louis that the reforming General Council should meet, not at Pisa, but at Trent or Verona. A national German Church, virtually independent of the Papacy, like the French, might be achieved. A German-born permanent legate should exclude the jurisdiction of the Holy See. Administrative and legal fees should no longer be paid to Rome, but should contribute to the support of the imperial government. When Julius fell seriously ill in August 1511, Maximilian, being again a widower, even entertained the bizarre project of putting himself forward for election as pope. Although she knew her father well, the Archduchess Margaret must have gasped when she read his letter informing her of this intention.[1] The level-headed lady replied that she would far rather see her father married to Mary Tudor than adding the problems of the Papacy to those which already harassed him. Also the almighty Fugger would not finance the project. And anyhow Pope Julius suddenly recovered his health and vigour. And Maximilian forgot his other ecclesiastical ideas in due course. The advantages of joining the Holy League were urged upon him by the pope and Ferdinand of Spain. For months he hovered between France and the League. Finally in 1512 he contributed decisively to the French expulsion from Italy by allowing the pope's Swiss mercenaries to descend on Lombardy through Tirol and by withdrawing the *Landsknechte* who formed the *élite* infantry in the French army. In

[1] The humorous tone of Maximilian's letter to Margaret of 18 September 1511 has thrown doubt on the seriousness of Maximilian's project. But another of his letters, of 16 September, to the *Landmarschall* of Tirol, Paul von Lichtenstein, of which we have only a copy, bears no traces of joking and deals with methods for raising the money necessary for Maximilian's election campaign for the Papacy. It is printed in Pastor's *History of the Popes*, vol. VI, appendix 90. See Schulte, *Kaiser Max. I als Kandidat für d. päpstlichen Stuhl* (1906); Nägle, 'Hat Kaiser Max. I im Jahre 1507 Papst werden wollen?', *Hist. Jahrb. d. Görres-Gesellschaft*, 1907; Ulmann (*op. cit.* vol. II, p. 440) thought that Maximilian was considering, as in 1507, only the acquisition of the temporal rule of the Papal States; contrary to the apparent meaning of the emperor's words.

November 1512 he solemnly adhered to Julius's Lateran Council, and was promised papal support in his weary struggle with Venice.

But Maximilian was unable to take advantage of the vacuum of power in northern Italy after the return of the Swiss to their homes. He was without resources. To the *Reichstag* of Trier-Cologne during the summer of 1512 he yet once more submitted plans for effective government. He asked for the revival of the Common Penny and the formation of a German militia as provided at Augsburg in 1500. The estates agreed in principle, but exempted the noble classes from the tax, since they served the *Reich* in other ways, and cut down the levy on the rest of the population to the equivalent of 0·02 per cent of capital. More than that, they said, their subjects would not stand. His other proposals were more favourably received. The *Reichstag* should meet annually. In each of the existing *Kreise*, used for elections to the *Reichskammergericht*, the estates should be under the obligation of joining in the 'hue and cry' against law-breakers, under a commander nominated by the Emperor, and should thus provide collective security. And an executive council of the *Reichstag*, consisting of eight or twelve members, resident at the imperial court, should supervise the scheme, deal with urgent matters and foreign relations, and act as conciliators in disputes which the parties were unwilling to submit to the *Reichskammergericht*. This plan represented a return to the deceased *Reichsregiment*, but under the Emperor's control. The estates substantially changed the proposal. To extend the system of six *Kreise* to the whole *Reich* (excluding the Bohemian, Swiss and Italian fringes), they now included the Habsburg and electoral areas. Saxony and Brandenburg; the four Rhenish electorates; the Austrias; Burgundy and the Netherlands; were each, together with some neighbours, to form a *Kreis*, making ten in all. But they insisted on the election of the commanders by the estates of each *Kreis* and rejected central control. They agreed to the council, but as a mere board of conciliators.

Nothing came of that scheme. Except for a poorly attended and abortive gathering at Worms in June 1513, no *Reichstag* met till 1517. The *Kreise* only came to life years later, after Maximilian's death. The princes of Germany were disillusioned. The movement for effective government was dead. The one surviving innovation, the *Reichskammergericht*, faced with a jungle of ancient claims and customs, through which new forces of princely administration were striving to break, was an irritation to the greater princes, but gave little protection to the weak. Germany was to experience shattering upheavals of social and religious rebellion before she settled down under the rule of those princes who succeeded in establishing areas of effective government and of those few towns that maintained the realities of republican independence.

Even after the *Reichstag* of Cologne of 1512 Maximilian flung himself, with resilient optimism, into the schemes of the Holy League. In 1513 there were to be convergent attacks on France by Spanish, papal, Swiss, English and imperial armies. Maximilian was to receive an English subsidy, with which he could equip the Swiss with cavalry and guns. His former dream, of 1496, was to come true. The western enemy was to be destroyed. And then, in happy union and under his command, the Christian Powers would devote themselves to the crusade against Islam. But neither Spain nor Pope Leo X went into the war with vigour. The Swiss did invade ducal Burgundy, but allowed themselves to be bought off (p. 207). From the *Reich* Maximilian could get no support. In August 1513 he appeared in the English camp before Thérouanne. But he came only as an expert military adviser, without an army, and found that Henry VIII, not wishing to fight France alone, preferred to sail home in October.

The Holy League dissolved; and Maximilian was once more left alone, to fight Venice with the resources of his resentful Austrian lands. But the accession of Francis I and the French re-annexation of Milan in September 1515 brought the League again into existence. Maximilian made his last effort to assert himself in Italy. With English money he hired some Swiss and German troops. He crossed the Adda and even entered Milan on 25 March 1516, for one day. But his Swiss could not be trusted to fight the Swiss in the French service. His funds were exhausted and his unpaid troops mutinied and dispersed, calling Maximilian a 'king of straw'. The Emperor hurried home over the Alps, as in 1496 and 1509. He was now without cash and did not know where to find it. He descended to painful expedients, deceiving the English envoys into endorsing drafts on banking-houses. When his grandson, the Archduke Charles of the Netherlands, since January 1516 king of Spain, allied himself with France at Noyon, 13 August 1516, Maximilian adhered to the alliance. It was the end of all his efforts in Italy. Lombardy was left to France. Out of the long war with Venice, interrupting German trade and wrecking the Austrian finances, all that he had gained was Riva and Rovereto and a few scattered villages and valleys.

A *Reichstag* met at Mainz in July 1517. A committee submitted a painful report of violence and anarchy. The iniquities of the black sheep among the knightly class were reaching their climax. Gangster knights made a widely organised business of banditry and ransoms, often with the connivance of princely officials. Franz von Sickingen, the most famous *Raubritter*, organised his private army, partly financed by France, and was able, without interference, to conduct a devastating war against the city of Worms for three years (1514–17), to the confusion of trade on the Upper Rhine. In 1518 he was to attack the city of Metz and then the territory of the Landgraf of Hesse. The *Reichstag* requested the Emperor to do something about the situation; but dissolved without adopting any resolutions.

By the next year the Germans had been thrown into a ferment of excitement by a new stimulus. The accumulated waters of their grievances against the Catholic framework of society, as they knew it, were suddenly released by Luther, the obscure professor in the little University of Wittenberg. Every element of discontent, nationalist, anti-clerical, social, economic, demanded action now that this friar, with lungs of brass and a slashing pen, had emerged and for the moment seemed to be the revolutionary leader so long desired. A *Reichstag* assembled in August 1518 at Augsburg to hear a papal legate and to be asked for the money for the crusade proclaimed by the Lateran Council. In his old age (59 was old age then) Maximilian would get his crusade, with the help of the pope's urgent demand. Cardinal Cajetan implored the *Reichstag*, in the interests of Germany herself, to organise military support for the Hungarians, Croats and Styrians, who were acting as the inadequate bulwarks of Christendom. The clergy should contribute a tenth of their income, the laity sums varying from 5 down to 2 per cent. The control of the proceeds was the Germans' own affair, the speaker was careful to say; none of it should be remitted to Rome. But the papal appeal came to Germany at the worst possible moment. The estates supplemented their reply, that they must consult their subjects, with a long list of 'the grievances of the German nation' against the Holy See.

To Maximilian, whose strength was failing, the important matter at Augsburg was to secure the election, as king of the Romans and future emperor, of his grandson, Charles, ruler of the Netherlands, Spain and Naples. This required much money. The two Hohenzollern electors, Joachim of Brandenburg and Albert of Mainz, were already pledged, in return for heavy cash payments and future pensions, to vote for Francis I, should there be a vacancy in the headship of the *Reich*. The francophil Lewis of the Palatinate had received Francis's promise of the restoration of his father's losses in 1505. The elector of Trier was a steady adherent of Francis, from whom he received a pension. A number of other influential German princes were also won for the French cause. To overtrump the French offers the emperor and his councillors informed King Charles that he must pay much more than he had expected, that only cash payments, not promises, would suffice, and that he should authorise them to borrow freely at their discretion. At Augsburg Maximilian succeeded in outbidding the French and in winning over the two Hohenzollerns and the Elector Palatine, who now received his long withheld investiture. The elector of Cologne was promised the moderate sum which satisfied him. The Bohemian vote, that of Maximilian himself and his friend Sigismund of Poland, as guardians of the young King Lewis, could now once more be used and was safe for Charles. That gave Charles five out of the seven votes. The Emperor and the four electors entered into a treaty to that effect on 27 August 1518. Only the elector of Trier stood out for Francis; and Frederick of Saxony, protesting against the whole business of auctioning the *Reich*, refused, in accordance with the Golden Bull of 1356, to enter into any bargains. To obviate the objection that a king of the Romans could not be elected while the existing king had not yet been crowned emperor, Maximilian undertook to demand his imperial coronation from the pope. Indeed, he made his participation in the crusade dependent on his coronation. But Leo X was unwilling to strengthen either of the foreign conquerors of Italy, the French king who ruled in Milan or, still more, the Spanish king who ruled the papal fief of Naples. He maintained the long-established papal opposition to a union of Germany and Naples in the same hands, and indicated his preference for the election of Frederick of Saxony, a prince respected and not too powerful.

The death of the Emperor closed the question of his coronation and, by creating a vacancy in the headship of the *Reich*, changed the situation. The electors held themselves released from their promises to Maximilian, and the auction between Valois and Habsburg was resumed.

After the *Reichstag* at Augsburg Maximilian had made his way eastwards towards the home of his childhood at Wiener Neustadt. He was now so penniless that his own Innsbruckers refused to house his retinue, since old bills were unpaid. At Wels he could travel no further. There he lay for six weeks, and died on 12 January 1519. He left the memory of a unique personality that has fascinated posterity; but he left the *Reich* in utter confusion and German opinion exasperated by the rumours that the venal electors were about to sell the monarchy to the king of France.

If Maximilian's reign as German king is a tale of frustration and increasing disorder, he has been called the founder of the Austrian State. He aimed at unification, the creation of a disciplined administrative service, and the separation of functions. He began, in his father's life-time, in 1490 in Tirol, where a council of government for 'Upper Austria', i.e. Tirol and the Habsburg possessions around the upper Rhine, already existed. With the goodwill of the estates he substituted nomination of the council by himself for election by them, and entrusted finance to a separate treasury commission of four members. But in 'Lower Austria', i.e Austria above and below the Enns, Styria, Carinthia, and Carniola, his unified, authoritarian system had to be imposed on the resentful estates of the several provinces. In 1493 he set up a council of regency for 'Lower Austria', and then a treasury, subordinated in 1496 to that at Innsbruck.

In 1498, when struggling against the limitations imposed on him at Worms, Maximilian created two organs of government for the whole *Reich* including his own lands—a *Hofrat*, as supreme court and executive council, and a *Hofkammer* supreme over all his finances. But any hope of disciplining the *Reich* was shattered in Maximilian's worst years, 1499–1502. He turned to the development of government in 'Lower Austria'. The regents became a permanent council at Linz, to which all, regardless of status, could bring their grievances. At Wiener Neustadt was established a *Hofgericht* as the central court, with twelve judges, mostly jurists with the mentality of the Roman Law. The treasury commission worked at Vienna.

These developments were opposed. The estates saw that an impersonal organisation, composed of men indifferent to local traditions, would gradually rob them of power and wealth. The Styrians objected that to them Linz was foreign soil. Maximilian overrode opposition, saying that he represented the new age and the way that the world was going. Let them be patient with his innovations and they would come to see their worth. His fatherly advice did not quell the opposition, and the cost of the Venetian war eventually made concessions necessary. Maximilian agreed to restore the traditional court of the *Landmarschall* in each province and to the codification of provincial customs. His organs of common government were suspended, except for the auditing treasury and the council, which was moved to Vienna and continued to supervise government in all five provinces. The estates began to accept the existence of some centralised government, but to demand a share in it, an innovation likely to produce a chaos of conflicting interests.

In his last year, when all his resources had been exhausted, Maximilian summoned an assembly, representing all his Habsburg estates, to Innsbruck. He wanted money for the redemption of his pledged sources of income. The estates had been fleeced for the Venetian war, which had seemed to them an imperial affair, and they now wanted a share in Habsburg and in imperial government. Maximilian proposed to establish a permanent imperial council (*Hofrat*) for the Habsburg lands and for the *Reich*, the two organs of 1498 having long ceased to function. The estates accepted the proposal in general and amended it. The *Hofrat* was to have eighteen members; four imperial officers, nine native representatives of the Habsburg lands, and five representatives of the rest of the *Reich*. The latter should be excluded when Habsburg affairs were discussed. All the finances of 'Austria' should be controlled by a permanent commission of the Habsburg estates. No war was to be made, nor Habsburg property alienated, nor new burdens imposed, without the consent of the estates. And all officials in 'Lower Austria' were to be under the control of the local estates. On those conditions the assembly would grant the sums needed for the proposed redemption.

Maximilian, though old and ill, would not accept such limitations of his authority. He rejected the division of the *Hofrat*, with its suggestion that Habsburg was a monarchy independent of the *Reich*, and with untiring persistence he argued the other demands. Whether owing to his diplomatic skill, or to divisions among the estates, or to the authoritarian fashion of the times, in the end he was granted 400,000 *gulden* with which to redeem his property, and he granted nothing, except that his Tirolese financial authorities should be assisted by native officials from 'Lower Austria'.

Maximilian exhausted his resources in the Venetian war and most of his governmental experiments were short-lived. But his council for 'Lower Austria' survived the reaction against centralisation after his death and was maintained by Ferdinand I. His central treasury at Innsbruck continued to work, with separate departments for receipt, expenditure, and audit. And he sought to apply principles, the collective responsibility of permanent commissions and the separation of functions, which were adopted by his successors and other German princes and accelerated the creation of modern states in Germany.[1]

A constant element in the background to central European life during Maximilian's reign was the Turkish danger. The lands of the Hungarian Crown had long struggled, with hardly any support, to resist the Moslem advance. A large union of forces was needed for the task. About 1500 it was not clear under what leadership such a union could be formed. It was Maximilian's constant endeavour, by diplomacy and occasionally by arms, to prepare the way for a union under Habsburg rule. Habsburg had a presentable claim to Bohemia and Hungary. If the estates of both kingdoms, like those of Poland, jealously maintained their right to elect their kings, their votes usually took account of heredity, succession treaties and the need of support. In 1438 the Emperor Albert II for the moment had united Austria, Bohemia and Hungary under Habsburg rule, with the hope of support from the *Reich* and the advantage that the Czech and Magyar kingdoms had German populations in their towns and mining villages. That union had dissolved. But by treaty in 1463 Frederick III was to be titular king of Hungary and, should the Hungarian Matthias Corvinus, the ruling king, die without male heirs, the succession was to go to Habsburg. And Frederick was careful to adopt Matthias, thus implying that the treaty was a fatherly concession.

When Matthias conquered Moravia and Silesia and then Austria, it seemed probable that the large union would be led by Hungary. His territories extended from Brandenburg to Serbia. But he died without a male heir in 1490, and his empire fell apart into its traditional units. Austria returned to Habsburg. But the Magyar nobles, who distrusted a German almost as much as a Turkish ruler, elected the king of Poland's

---

[1] For the controversy whether and to what extent Maximilian introduced Burgundian methods of government into Germany, see F. Hartung, *Deutsche Verfassungsgeschichte*, §21.

eldest son, Wladislaw Jagiello, king of Bohemia since 1471. The possibility opened that Bohemia and Hungary might become members of a great union under Polish leadership. No such union was created. The Polish nobles successively elected three brothers of Wladislaw. Moreover, these eastern monarchs, less even than Maximilian, had not the resources of revenue, troops, administration and diplomacy necessary for the efficient control of their kingdoms.

Maximilian's expedition into Hungary in 1491 resulted in Wladislaw's agreement that, should his line fail of direct male heirs, the succession should pass to Habsburg; an agreement accepted by a Hungarian diet at Buda in March 1492.

Thereafter Maximilian and Wladislaw remained allies. But a number of the Magyar nobles caused their diet to declare, in October 1505, that if the king died without a male heir, they would have no foreigner as his successor. Maximilian and Wladislaw replied with an agreement, of March 1506, that Wladislaw's daughter Anne should marry a grandson of Maximilian, and that his expected child, if a boy, should marry a granddaughter of Maximilian. To impose this settlement on the recalcitrant Magyar nobles Maximilian again invaded Hungary (p. 213). The birth of Wladislaw's son, Lewis, during the campaign of 1506, facilitated a treaty (12 November 1507) confirming the previous succession agreements and providing that Anne should marry that grandson of Maximilian who should become ruler of the Austrian lands.

The more stubborn of the Magyar nobles rejected the treaty and found a leader in John Zápolyai, whose sister Barbara in 1512 married the Polish king Sigismund. To counteract a possible Polish-Hungarian alliance Maximilian stimulated Ivan of Muscovy to threaten Poland and the Teutonic Order to reassert itself. But Wladislaw warned him that he must choose between friendship with Poland and the denunciation of the succession agreements. Maximilian dropped his anti-Polish allies, and the two Jagiello kings, of Poland and Bohemia-Hungary, met the emperor at Vienna in 1515. There the succession agreements were confirmed. Young Lewis was betrothed to Maximilian's granddaughter Mary. In the absence of his grandsons the 56-year-old Maximilian was himself conditionally betrothed to the 12-year-old Anne. In the next year he was relieved of a third matrimonial venture and the Archduke Ferdinand was duly married to Anne by procuration. Lastly Maximilian adopted Lewis as his son.

All this artificial construction of succession treaties, marriages and adoptions did not secure the Habsburg succession in Bohemia and Hungary. It was the shattering victory of the Turks at Mohács in 1526, and Lewis's death there, that drove the diets of the Bohemian lands and a part of the Hungarian diet to face realities and adhere to the great Habsburg empire which had come into existence. They conferred the two crowns upon Ferdinand, ruler of the Austrian lands and brother of the Emperor, who was king of Spain and the victor of Pavia.

Maximilian did not live to see the union which provided the power to protect the *Reich* and ultimately to repel the Moslem invaders from central Europe. But his persistent efforts to make possible a Danubian union under Habsburg rule justify the view of him as the father of the Habsburg monarchy of Austria-Bohemia-Hungary.

CHAPTER VIII

THE BURGUNDIAN NETHERLANDS, 1477–1521

THE unconfirmed news of the death of Duke Charles of Burgundy at the battle of Nancy (5 January 1477) created confusion in the Netherlands, restive at the cost of his wars. On 11 January 1477 Charles's widow Margaret of York and Mary, his only child, summoned the Estates General to Ghent. A fresh army had to be raised for defence against France; and if the duke was dead, as was the case despite contrary rumours, Mary had to be admitted as his heir by the provincial estates in each of the territories that composed the Burgundian Netherlands.

The forthcoming assembly of the Estates General was contemplated with misgivings at court, for in 1476 they had bitterly attacked ducal policy, and in summoning the present meeting relief from outstanding taxation was at once promised. Nevertheless, the general, unlike the territorial, estates were founded not on local custom but on the the institution of Duke Philip *le Bon*; and they had, up to the death of Duke Charles, served the duke's prerogative more than his subjects' liberties.

On 3 February Mary addressed at Ghent the estates, which, by recognising her as heir in all her father's lands, preserved the cohesion of the Netherlands; but they asked that she should grant 'certain general articles'. The *Grand Privilège* is the monument to the estates of 1477. To prevent the prince from pursuing a policy, domestic or foreign, other than one which satisfied each of his territories, it transferred to the estates, both general and local, the right to assemble themselves without summons. The declaration of war, an urgent matter in 1477, was made conditional on their approval. The *Grand Privilège* distinguished between the sovereign's interests and those of his subjects, who were to be allowed to trade with his enemies as Flanders had demanded since at least the fourteenth century.

Its purpose was to protect the regional liberties of each territory rather than to set up a general constitution. The supremacy of local jurisdiction was enthroned; and in accordance with the principle *de non evocando* no one was to be cited save before his local court. However, the *Grand Privilège* could not protect particularism without reforming the central power, which the estates wanted to modify rather than destroy. The economic advantages of unity were naturally appreciated; but the *Grand Privilège*, although it abolished the *Parlement* of Malines, did not deprive the Burgundian lands of a high court, for it invented a *Grand Conseil*.

The *Parlement* of Charles the Bold was staffed wholly by jurists, mostly from the duchy or county of Burgundy; the *Grand Conseil* was to be composed of lawyers and noblemen from all the duchess's lands, which were proportionally represented. The larger units, Brabant, Burgundy, Flanders, Holland and Zeeland were to provide two lawyers and two noblemen each, and the smaller territories either two or one representative. The proceedings were to be conducted in the language of the country from which a particular suit emanated. Moreover, the fact that the *seigneurs du sang* (lords related to the duchess) were to be admitted to the *Grand Conseil*, which was also to accompany the duchess, suggests that it was designed as a political council as well as a law-court.

Despite the article which permitted the estates in the last resort to distrain upon the duchess by withdrawal of obedience, the *Grand Privilège* was as much a federal as a feudal charter; and its *Grand Conseil* was to include members from Holland, Zeeland, Luxemburg and Burgundy none of which were represented when Mary granted the *Grand Privilège* on 11 February 1477. Although it restated traditional ideas of reform by forbidding the farming of judicial offices, and the appointment to ecclesiastical dignities *in commendam*, the motive was always to restrain the prince.

Even if Louis XI of France had not then been launching an invasion to recover the spoils of Duke Charles's overthrow, the *Grand Privilège* would still have been unpractical. It tried to place the ruler of the Burgundian lands in tutelage as the estates of Brabant had done to their duke in 1422; and the experiment, which failed in Brabant, had small chance of success when applied to what was already a European Power. Hainault obtained for conservation at Mons a French translation of the Flemish original of the *Grand Privilège*. The other Burgundian Netherlands obtained their own concessions, either when Mary was admitted as their particular countess or duchess (for example Flanders, 11 February 1477, the same day as the *Grand Privilège*, Brabant, *Blijde Inkomst*, 29 May 1477) or by procuration (for example Holland, 14 March 1477, whose charter is also called *Groot Privilegie*). In its collective sense the *Grand Privilège* was revolutionary. These charters accorded with that constitutional procedure whereby a new ruler entered contractual relations with each territory.

The reaction against Duke Charles ensured that the local charters reduced central and local regalian power to its minimum. Territorial self-sufficiency was everywhere proclaimed, in jurisdiction and appointment to offices. The charters cannot be dismissed as purely reactionary, for they were close to realities; and the *Groot Privilegie* of Holland was enlightened in its provisions regulating recovery of the drowned and digging for peat within dykes. Mary's charters, unlike the *Grand Privilège*, furnished the substance over which her son in 1495 and her grandson in 1515 had to negotiate. In essentials, Mary's charters resemble each other.[1]

From the 1470's to the 1490's some of the best names and wisest heads were attracted from the Burgundian camp to the side of France. In 1477 Louis XI had an opportunity to acquire the Low Countries, where nobles and officials disliked the gallophobia of the late duke and the estates saw in a French marriage for Mary the restoration of peace. Had he adhered to bribery and diplomacy Louis XI could scarcely have failed, but he would attempt two policies. One was the marriage of the duchess to the dauphin, the other was the armed conquest of Mary's inheritance. The result was that he achieved a minor success, while the main prize, the hand of Mary, fell to the house of Habsburg.

The conquest of the territories formerly ruled by Charles the Bold appeared deceptively easy. Despite sporadic resistance, Louis XI overran to the south the duchy and county of Burgundy, the latter an imperial fief, and to the north the Somme region, most of Artois and all the Boulonnais.

The personal efforts of Mary to broach negotiations with France in January 1477 having failed, the estates could not be kept out of diplomacy. Early in February an embassy to France was commissioned, led by the late duke's chancellor, Guillaume Hugonet, but including also representatives of the estates. The chancellor and the lord of Humbercourt, another servant of Duke Charles, were given a letter to the king written jointly by the duchess, by Margaret of York and by the lieutenant-general of the Low Countries, Adolf of Cleves-Ravenstein. No copy of it exists; but according to Commynes it asked Louis to deal with Hugonet and Humbercourt. The distinction between ambassadors and other members of a mission was well established; and the letter was probably a credence for the two ambassadors, rather than a contrivance to exclude the envoys of the estates. It proved, none the less, a maladroit combination of private and public diplomacy.

This embassy made no impression on Louis, who pushed forward his invasion; and about the middle of February 1477 the estates decided to raise a common army from the entire Netherlands, while sending to Louis a new mission made up of nobles, ecclesiastics and burghers, but no court officials.

Again Louis XI refused peace on terms other than the hand of the duchess for the dauphin. He was, however, polite to the burghers, to whom he handed the former credence on behalf of Hugonet and Humbercourt, for he meant to exploit the suspicion that the estates felt towards the officers of the late duke. In this he was successful. As soon as the embassy returned to Ghent, proposals for raising a common army were dropped and Hugonet and Humbercourt were arrested. Mary made a brave effort to save them; but they were both executed on 3 April 1477. The record

[1] P. van Ussel, *De regeering van Maria van Bourgondie* (Louvain, 1943), pp. 49–65.

of their trial is lost, vague accusations of treason remain; but they would not have suffered had they not been the agents of a fallen regime. Shortly after their execution Ghent procured letters of pardon excusing its participation in the affair. Mons, following the example of Ghent, arrested the receiver of the ducal estates, who was executed, despite the intervention of the duchess, on the sentence of a local court. A wave of unrest such as periodically swept the Netherlands broke over the towns in the next few months. At Brussels, the artisans were particularly violent; but the general picture was everywhere the same. The lesser trades led the attack on the magistrates and the rich who were identified with the government.

Among the deserters to France the most conspicuous were Anthony, eldest surviving bastard of Philip *le Bon*, styled *Le Grand Bâtard*, and Philippe de Crèvecœur, lord of Esquerdes, who became the king's lieutenant in Picardy, and henceforth identified his career with the extension of the French frontier in the north. However, local resistance in Hainault and elsewhere was growing, and the manner in which Louis XI waged war turned opinion away from any French marriage for Mary.

There had been innumerable suitors for the hand of Mary, but once the Valois alliance became impracticable the Habsburg alternative predominated. For what it was worth Mary was already affianced to Maximilian of Habsburg, the son of the Emperor Frederick III; and although Mary was under supervision from the commune of Ghent, the dowager Margaret of York became the champion of the Habsburg cause. Before March 1477 Burgundian agents were in Austria and brought Habsburg ambassadors to espouse Mary at Bruges on 21 April 1477 in the name of Maximilian.

Fear of French aggression was such that the estates welcomed a Habsburg alliance. Their meeting at Ghent had petered out, but Brabant, implementing the right conceded under the *Grand Privilège* for the estates to convene themselves, called the representatives of Flanders, Hainault, Holland-Zeeland and Namur to gather at Louvain in May 1477. The chancellor of Brabant, Jean de la Bouverie, told them that Mary had undertaken not to marry without the consent of the estates, who now approved her union with Maximilian, provided that he ratified the liberties which she had granted. An ambassador of the emperor expounded the marriage treaty, which was translated into French and Dutch for the benefit of the estates, who on this occasion fulfilled the role which the *Grand Privilège* had foreseen for them.

Margaret of York urged the emperor's ambassadors to make haste, for, while Maximilian duke of Austria was journeying westward slowly for lack of money, Ghent was preparing to produce a substitute for him in the person of Adolf of Egmond, the hereditary heir of Guelders, who had been imprisoned from before his father Duke Arnold's sale of Guelders to Charles the Bold in 1472. Through the agency of Ghent, Adolf was released and made an honorary citizen of the town, which planned to force him as a husband on Mary. The trades of Ghent provided a force which under Adolf's command attacked the French positions around Tournai, but disbanded, leaving him to be killed covering the rear (27 June 1477). Mary heard of Adolf's death without regret; but the episcopal city of Tournai remained a French thorn in the side of the Netherlands until the English conquest in 1513 and its final incorporation by Charles V in 1521. The urban militia of Bruges was routed by the French shortly after; and in judging the early popularity of Maximilian one must remember that he came to the Low Countries when their own efforts at self-defence had proved unavailing.

The marriage of the duke of Austria, aged eighteen, to Mary, aged twenty, was celebrated at the Prinsenhof within Ghent on 19 August 1477. There is little reason to regard it as necessarily sealing the fate of the independent Netherlands. They had already naturalised the Valois dukes, who had as large a stake in France as the Habsburgs in Germany, and were intellectually and physically more than equal to the Habsburgs. The nuptial contract was drawn in general terms, both parties adhering to written as against customary law. In the event of the death of one parent, the children alone were to inherit to the exclusion of the surviving parent's rights. But the marriage settlement was upset by letters patent of Mary (17 September 1477) settling on the duke of Austria her inheritance if she was to die without children. The estates after the death of Mary refused to countenance any amendment of the marriage contract; but momentarily constitutional vigilance was in abeyance. Maximilian had, of course, to confirm territorial charters, but he was never made to seal the *Grand Privilège*.

Maximilian was greeted as a defender against France; but though always a brave knight he never became a general. Moreover, the resources of Louis XI were superior to anything he could muster from the Netherlands. He was hampered by an unwarlike population, which compelled him to hire mercenaries, mainly Germans, at terrific cost. The wages of these mercenaries were seldom paid, and their rapine became the standing grudge of the peace-loving Netherlands against him. Maximilian's inability to negotiate or impose a peace by arms upon France hindered the reconstruction of princely authority in the Low Countries, where hardship always excited unrest. Louis XI played on this unrest by economic warfare. His troops destroyed crops in the upper Scheldt area to deplete the grain staple of Ghent, his fleets attacked the Flemish herring fisheries and intercepted vessels carrying grain from the Baltic to Holland. His influence with the banking houses of Florence prevailed on them to deny loans to the Burgundian court.

Hostilities followed the medieval pattern of raids and surprises, interrupted by two major truces from July 1478 to July 1479 and from August 1480 to March 1481. The single pitched battle, at Guinegatte

(7 August 1479), was a Burgundian victory, which if properly followed up might have led to the recapture of Arras. If the fighting delayed the recovery of the Netherlands from the crisis of 1477, it nevertheless proved that, although Artois and Picardy could not be reconquered, a line from Gravelines, on the Channel, to Luxemburg could be successfully defended against the French.

The former network of Burgundian diplomacy was renewed. The vital alliances were those with England (1478, 1480) and with Brittany (1480); the latter restored the duke of Austria to something of the position which Charles the Bold had held as leader of the feudatories of France.

In the northern and eastern lands, either recently conquered by Charles, like the duchy of Guelders and the bishopric of Liège, or indirectly controlled like the bishopric of Utrecht, whose bishop David was a bastard son of Philip *le Bon*, the crisis of 1477 released pent-up feuds of which Louis XI took full advantage. Maximilian was too taken up with fighting on the French frontier to pay much attention to Holland, Utrecht and Guelders until 1481; but his absence may have been advantageous to the preservation of Burgundian power, for its defence was left to its local partisans, and, however much withstood by particularist elements among the townsmen and gentry, the Burgundian State had influential champions, who had thrown in their lot with its survival. Thus in Holland, torn by a recrudescence of the old Hoek and Kabeljauw feuds, the Kabel-jauws were undisguisedly a government party. At Utrecht Bishop David was compelled in 1477 to grant concessions rather like the *Grand Privilège* on a local scale, but by May 1481 he had temporarily regained authority. In 1477 Guelders evinced a desire to return to its native dynasty; but on the death of its duke, Adolf, outside Tournai, his son Charles remained to be brought up at the court of Mary; and Jan van Egmond, a member of the house of IJsselstein, a cadet branch of the ducal family of Guelders, fought with varying success on behalf of the Burgundian cause in Holland, Utrecht and Guelders.

The two ecclesiastical territories of Utrecht and Liège were the gravest problems, especially the latter because of its proximity to France. In March 1477 Mary had to renounce the rights which her father gained over Liège by his conquest of 1468. The city of Liège had not recovered sufficiently from its sack at the hands of Charles the Bold; and its bishop Louis de Bourbon, an uncle and a councillor of Mary, hoped to regain authority by securing recognition of the neutrality of Liège from Burgun-dian and French belligerents. He was not strong enough to enforce this solution because he was challenged in his temporal power by the feudal house of La Marck, lords of much of the Ardennes, whom Louis XI used as the agents of French intervention throughout the Meuse valley. The consequent weakness of the bishop at least enabled Maximilian to regain some of the traditional Burgundian influence over Liège.

The birth of children to Mary, of whom two survived, Philip, born in 1478, and Margaret, born in 1480, reawakened loyalty to the dynasty, which contributed to the success of Mary and Maximilian in reviving the institutions of the Valois dukes under difficult circumstances. The Order of the Golden Fleece, which was symbolical of the European status of the ducal house, was restored by Maximilian in April 1478. In this Louis XI, who talked of assuming the sovereignty of the Order since his conquest of the duchy of Burgundy in 1477, was forestalled.

The administration was also rebuilt. Although the execution of Hugonet interrupted the series of the *chanceliers de Bourgogne*, the supreme officers of the dukes, that series was reopened by the appointment in March 1480 of Jean Carandolet. Significantly, he was a native of Franche-Comté, the county of Burgundy which, unlike the duchy of Burgundy, Louis XI never quite conquered. Franche-Comté continued, much to the discontent of the Low Countries, to supply the Habsburgs with law officers.

The *Grand Conseil*, set up under the *Grand Privilège*, came in practice to play the role of the former *Parlement* of Malines from which it took over many distinguished lawyers, Philip Wielant among them. Although it did not strictly follow the movements of the duchess and tended to become sedentary, it transferred with her from one territory to another in order to keep in reasonable proximity to her. It was certainly not inactive, and in 1479 alone gave 107 judgments, By hearing suits removed from local courts it undoubtedly broke the *Grand Privilège*; and in 1482 the enemies of centralisation wanted to clear the *Grand Conseil* of jurists.

The cost of the war and a prodigality that Maximilian early showed and never outlived caused him to pawn many of Mary's heirlooms; but the fiscal mechanism of the State remained. The central finance court that Charles the Bold erected at Malines never reappeared, so that the *Chambre des Comptes* at Lille and the *Rekenkamers* at Brussels and The Hague recovered their independence. But if the finances were geographically decentralised, administrative unity returned, for Charles with his admiration of French models had introduced the French division between the ordinary and extraordinary revenue. The destruction of his financial reforms brought back the sound Burgundian methods of Philip *le Bon* under which income from the domain and from taxation was administered by the same officials called *commis sur le fait des domaines et finances*.

Had the duke of Austria been more tactful and introduced fewer Germans to his court, the reconstruction of a central administrative edifice would still have conflicted with the spirit of the *Grand Privilège* and the letter of the provincial charters. In Brabant Maximilian ran into difficulties on reviving the *procureur general*, a guardian of the prerogative abolished by the *Blijde Inkomst* of 1477, and in Holland there was opposition to his appointment of officers who were not natives of the county.

He was criticised, more especially at Ghent, for conducting foreign affairs like an absolute sovereign by concluding a truce with France (1478) and an alliance with England (1480), without a word to the estates. In February 1481 increased taxation was met by demands for reduction of household expenditure and for the exclusion from the duchy and county of Burgundians, who were considered willing agents of absolutism.

Opposition was stiffening in the manner of 1477; but jointly Mary and Maximilian could probably have overcome it. But Mary died on 27 March 1482 as the result of a riding accident outside Bruges.

The death of Charles the Bold produced a reaction against centralisation, and the death of Mary not only renewed that reaction but also introduced a long constitutional crisis affecting the head of the State.

Unhesitatingly the estates recognised Mary's baby son Philip as *prince naturel*; but they denied the claim of Maximilian to become automatically regent (*mambour*) during Philip's minority. On their side they had the precedent of Brabant appointing a regency for the son of Duke Anthony who fell at Agincourt. In forcing upon Maximilian a treaty with Louis XI that made the king of France the guarantor of their supremacy, the estates were more revolutionary. The initiative came from the Members of Flanders (Ghent, Bruges and Ypres), led by Ghent, whose pensioner Willem Rym told the other provinces in April 1482 that together they should exercise *l'estat et gouvernment des pays*. Flanders won over the support of Brabant, where similar views were entertained in Brussels, Louvain and originally also at Antwerp. In October 1482 an association was formed between Flanders and Brabant ostensibly for defence, but really to exclude the duke of Austria and replace his power by a federation. Philip was to reside by turns in each of his lands; but for the time he and his sister Margaret were held by Ghent, which understood the value of their possession. Holland and Hainault refused to enter this association; but so long as they worked together Brabant and Flanders were strong, certainly stronger than the duke of Austria.

The Peace of Arras was concluded on 23 December 1482; but, months before, its terms were substantially settled with Louis XI by envoys of the estates regardless of Maximilian. Margaret of Austria, the daughter of Mary, was to marry the dauphin; and she together with her dowry, consisting of Artois and the county of Burgundy, were to be handed over at once to the French. The fact that legally the county of Flanders was part of the kingdom of France was uncompromisingly reasserted. On attaining his majority Philip was to do homage to the king for Flanders. In the meanwhile the jurisdiction of the *Parlement* of Paris in Flanders was restored. Louis XI exercised his rights as a suzerain by confirming all charters granted to Flanders since the death of Charles the Bold. The position of the estates in the other territories was safeguarded by an article which declared that if through the death of Philip their inheritance should fall to Margaret and the dauphin 'le gouvernement desdits pays demeure en l'estat qu'il sera trouvé'.

Louis XI dispelled fears of confiscation, which were a bugbear of the well-to-do since the dispossessions of Charles VII's reign. In Artois and Burgundy, fiefs and clerical benefices were not to be disturbed, and patents of nobility conferred since 1477 were recognised. The interest from 'rentes' sold by Duke Charles on the security of the ducal domain within the ceded counties was guaranteed. The fairs of Antwerp, which he had tried to ruin for the benefit of Caen, were now privileged by Louis, who gave assurances for the safety of the herring fleets.

The peace of 1482 reversed the 1435 Treaty of Arras. Louis XI retrieved the mistakes he made after the death of Charles the Bold, and shattered the Burgundian alliances which Maximilian had rebuilt, for England and Brittany were excluded from the peace. The treaty, which was printed in France and the Netherlands, attempted to place their relations on a more stable basis. Its value is best understood by associating it with the treaties of Senlis (1493) and Paris (1515).

The duke of Austria could only look on while his daughter Margaret was given up to the French and his son Philip was admitted count of Flanders in January 1483 to become the figure-head of an alternative government set up by the estates. Authority was exercised in Philip's name by a council composed of Adolf of Cleves-Ravenstein, Philip lord of Beveren, son of Anthony *le Grand Bâtard*, Louis of Gruuthuse and Adrian Vilain, lord of Rassenghem. It is significant that the first two were *seigneurs du sang*, related to the Burgundian dynasty, and the last two members of the urbanised aristocracy representing Bruges and Ghent respectively. For the next few years a broad section of the nobility, not only those living in the towns, opposed Maximilian and worked with the estates in the name of Philip for an understanding with France. The driving force behind Philip's government was Ghent; and what in 1483 and 1488 might seem to be 'Flemish separatism' is better understood if seen as the last attempt of Ghent to substitute its own power for that of the prince over an area wider than Flanders.

Since the Peace of Arras, Maximilian at least had a freer hand over the bishoprics of Liège and Utrecht, where Louis XI had abandoned his minor allies, the La Marck family in the former and the Hoek party in the latter.

Guillaume de la Marck, having made himself *mambour* (roughly the bishop's military and secular lieutenant), had led a revolt and killed the bishop Louis de Bourbon in battle (30 August 1482). Guillaume only just failed to coerce the chapter of St Lambert into adopting his son as bishop of Liège. However, Brabant provided Maximilian with an army of intervention, for the duchy traditionally regarded the Pays de Liège as its own sphere of interest. On 8 January 1483 the La Marcks were defeated by Maximilian's captain Philip of Cleves-Ravenstein (the son of Adolf); and John of Hoorne, whose family was associated with the Burgundian court, retained the bishopric of Liège. Although the power of the La Marck family was not destroyed, it was checked, and Habsburg influence at Liège rescued.

The duke of Austria himself took part in the hard fighting which finally in August 1483 restored Bishop David of Burgundy to his see at Utrecht. Maximilian was recognised as the lay 'advocate' of the bishopric, the status which his Burgundian predecessors held and which enabled them to exercise indirect control over the extensive lands of Utrecht.

Before this he had struck a blow against the party of the estates in Brabant, where on his orders representatives of Antwerp, Brussels and Louvain were arrested in May 1483. Four of them were executed on charges of treason, including the plenipotentiaries of Antwerp and Brussels at the Peace of Arras. The duke of Austria's high-handed action did not evoke a reaction in Brabant, which was growing suspicious of Flanders and tired of the retention of Philip at Ghent. Indeed, the unswerving loyalty of Antwerp towards the central authority dates from this event.

The duke of Austria had strengthened his position when Louis XI died (30 August 1483), leaving the throne of France to Charles VIII, aged thirteen, to whom Margaret of Austria was betrothed. So long as Louis lived, it was certain that the party which used Philip against his father Maximilian would be secure in the might of France. Not that intervention was henceforth abandoned; but Anne of Beaujeu, the regent for Charles VIII, had difficulties at home and could not send aid abroad in every direction. French military and diplomatic intervention in the Low Countries came to be increasingly delegated to d'Esquerdes, the former Burgundian, who was created marshal of France (21 January 1485).

The time seemed ripe to the duke of Austria to overthrow the alternative government around his son; and at the Antwerp fair in September 1483 with maximum publicity he proclaimed the dismissal of Philip's councillors. There followed a polemical exchange between them and him, each side raking up financial scandals against the other. Maximilian had overrated his power, and in May 1484 the Golden Fleece made the first of several attempts to mediate between him and the dissident Netherlands. The order was, characteristically, represented in both camps, and avoided a schism by recognising Maximilian as regent, but without concealing that it did so to preserve the inheritance of Philip. Mediation with Flanders broke down because of the intransigeance of Ghent, where Jan Coppenhole, until his death in 1492, was to use the struggle against Maximilian to make himself a civic tyrant.

Flanders did not shrink from civil war, and readily applied economic sanctions against the remainder of the Netherlands, Ghent prohibiting the export of grain, and Bruges building a blockhouse on the Scheldt to strangle the trade of Antwerp. The self-aggrandisement of Flanders drove opinion elsewhere toward the duke of Austria, who was supported by Holland. He was poor, and only limited objectives could be attempted by his mercenaries, so that raids were undertaken across the Scheldt, and the ransoms of prisoners and the captured cattle were sold by official auctioneers in Antwerp. Charles VIII had made a military alliance with Flanders (25 October 1484) and sent a virtual ultimatum to the duke of Austria (27 December 1484) summoning him to evacuate Flanders; but the French alliance could not save Flanders from being hemmed in, and on 28 June 1485 the partisans of court and commerce admitted the duke of Austria to Bruges.

The reaction had also set in at Ghent where the cry '*Vrient Oostenrijk*' was heard in the streets, and Jan Coppenhole fled to France. A moderate treaty with the Members of Flanders restored Philip to Maximilian and opened Ghent to him, but a few days of misbehaviour by his German mercenaries sufficed to produce an uproar in Ghent, where the trades in arms and under their banners occupied the old market. Maximilian was contemplating whether to destroy Ghent as his father-in-law had destroyed Liège; but Margaret of York and Philip of Cleves dissuaded him. Ghent was compelled to make a submission harsher than the foregoing treaty with Flanders. On 22 July 1485 the duke's *audiencier* publicly lacerated the charters which the town had received since 1477. The situation after the battle of Gavere in 1453 was substantially restored, for the trades were excluded and the duke reserved to himself the Renewal of the Law (the periodical reappointment of the magistrates), while the civic militia, the *Witte Caproens*, was abolished. The young Philip was removed to the shelter of Malines, the dower town of Margaret of York, who supervised his education.

The duke of Austria was victorious, but not strong, for despite the indemnity from Flanders and Ghent he was financially crippled. A few magnates, who in return for their services received offices, lands and pecuniary rewards, derived a greater relative advantage; and the years 1485–8 mark a stage in the transformation of the courtiers of Charles the Bold into the oligarchs of the time of Philip *le Beau* and after. The magnates had none the less a better knowledge than the duke of Austria of what the country wanted; and during his absence in Germany from November 1485 to May 1486 (for his election as king of the Romans on 16 February 1486), the council which he left behind composed of Philip of Cleves, Engelbert of Nassau and, with special reference to legal matters, the chancellor Jean Carandolet, won popularity mainly by preserving peace with France.

Maximilian returned with his father Frederick III, who came to live off the Netherlands while the Hungarians occupied Vienna. The king of the Romans, instead of devoting himself to the recuperation of the

Low Countries and above all to the restoration of their finances, immediately reopened hostilities with France. He attempted, until he had to leave the Netherlands ignominiously in 1489, to succeed where Charles the Bold had failed. Like Charles he sought to lead a coalition of French feudatories against the Crown and to conduct a grand invasion of France. Had Maximilian been more successful with his invasions in 1486 and 1487, he might have recovered the entire inheritance of Charles by gaining the full co-operation of the feudatories, who were only too anxious to utilise the weakness of the crown during the minority of Charles VIII. But it was in these years that Maximilian betrayed his inability to wage war, and that d'Esquerdes rendered invaluable service to France by the successful defence of her northern frontier. His failure wholly discredited the king of the Romans in the eyes of the Low Countries, where special taxation, such as *Ruitergeld* in Holland, was levied to pay for his mercenary armies, who fell instead to plundering the provinces. The nobility was left to conduct the war like a tournament; and a syndicate of nobles, who planned to surprise Béthune in August 1487, fell into an ambush in which Charles of Egmond, heir of Guelders, and Engelbert of Nassau were captured by the French.

By the autumn of 1487 warfare had reduced the central authority to the chaotic condition which followed the death of Mary in 1482. Rassenghem was rescued by sympathisers from the state prison of Vilvorde, in which he had been confined since 1485, and Jan Coppenhole returned from France to Ghent, where the magistrature was renewed in November 1487 in a sense wholly inimical to Maximilian, whose partisans had to flee to Bruges. Acting on behalf of Flanders, Ghent now reverted to the right conceded by the *Grand Privilège*, under which the estates could assemble themselves, and invited Brabant and Hainault to joint consultations. To forestall a rival gathering under the aegis of Ghent, Maximilian was driven to summon the estates to Bruges.

Philip of Cleves advised that the estates should be held in the fortress of Sluis, but the king of the Romans, ignoring the lesson of the rising in Ghent (1485) and an ugly scene at Brussels (1486) on the arrival of his father the emperor, took up residence in Bruges without armed protection. When at the last moment he prepared to introduce German mercenaries, the inhabitants, in terror at the prospect of a garrison of *Landsknechte*, shut the gates of Bruges (1 February 1488) trapping inside Maximilian and his court. Their action was unpremeditated, but had graver consequences than wrecking Maximilian's plan for holding the estates. The trades of Bruges, dominated by the lesser guilds, encamped on the market under arms. They scarcely knew what to do with the king of the Romans, but vented their grievances on his local partisans and officers. Among the latter, the treasurer, Pierre Lanchals, was executed. The politicians of Ghent seized the opportunity offered to them by the artisans of Bruges, and took control, removing the surviving courtiers of Maximilian, including the chancellor Jean Carandolet, to serve as hostages for Ghent in subsequent negotiations.

Bruges was frightened at its temerity, which startled German patriotism into life. The elector of Cologne pronounced spiritual censures, which threatened to bring grave economic consequences on Flanders, while by April 1488 Frederick III was leading an imperial army to his son's rescue. Within the Netherlands the method rather than the principle of restraining Maximilian was disapproved. The general assumption that the king of the Romans would only be released in exchange for a constitution on the lines of the *Grand Privilège* accounts for the ease with which Ghent transformed the estates summoned to negotiate Maximilian's freedom into a meeting which was to draft a statute to eliminate his power. In accordance with this development, the estates, which gathered at the end of February 1488 at Malines, the residence of Philip, now styled archduke, ended up in Ghent, where on 12 May they adopted 'The Union, Alliance and Confederation'. This instrument had been submitted at the Hôtel Ravenstein in Brussels to an aristocratic committee composed of Adolf of Cleves-Ravenstein, Philip his son, Philip of Beveren, Antoine Rolain, *grand bailli* of Hainault, and Jean de la Bouverie, recently chancellor of Brabant.

'The Union' abolished the regency of Maximilian in Flanders, and only allowed it to continue in the other territories under the *seigneurs du sang*. During Philip's minority the estates were to assemble annually, the first year at Brussels, the second at Ghent and the third at Mons; for the annual assembly was not to be twice in the same territory until it had been held at least once in the other two. The scope of the estates was defined as the correction of *toutes nouvellités* prejudicial to the individual territories; and because it was apparently more concerned with provincial than general liberties 'The Union' has been compared unfavourably with the *Grand Privilège*. However, it was meant to provide the permanent basis for a constitution, for the preamble to 'The Union' declared that in so far as it touched the lordship of the *prince naturel*, it was only to last for Philip's minority, but *en tant qu'il touche le police dureront a perpetuité*. Not only was the joint power (*la main commune*) of the provinces to be applied in negotiations with the German princes; but in a federal spirit an invitation to join 'The Union' was addressed to the bishoprics of Liège and Utrecht, and to unspecified '*pays voisins*'.

The king of the Romans was set free on 16 May 1488 after swearing to renounce reprisals on Flanders in a treaty, which embodied 'The Union' and became known as the Peace of Bruges. Although Philip of Cleves was left behind as a hostage in Bruges, and had to swear to fight against Maximilian for 'The Union' in the event of his breaking his oath, the king joined his father Frederick III and the imperial army at Louvain and repudiated the peace. He claimed that he was bound by an earlier oath to serve the emperor; but Maximilian's action was purely political and cannot be excused on moral grounds. Philip of Cleves, who took up arms against him, was better versed in politics than to have supposed that Maximilian would abide by his oath and too shrewd to have bound himself as a hostage unless he had been looking for a public issue on which to challenge the king.

Besides armed conflict, the Peace of Bruges, which was itself circulated in print, produced a literary conflict. Philip of Cleves put out a justification; but the most pungent manifesto was launched by Ghent with the collaboration of France under the pseudonym of *Philalites* in answer to a memorial which Maximilian addressed in July 1488 to the estates of Hainault.

The imperial army retired in July from before Ghent, which erected the *Rabot*, a fortified sluice, to commemorate the event; and in September 1488 Philip of Cleves entered Brussels, where he had the Peace of Bruges proclaimed. The opponents of Maximilian looked to be winning; and Henry VII received their envoys in August. The belief grew that the king of the Romans would accept an indemnity and depart from the Netherlands. 'The Union' of 1488 reconstructed the alliance of 1482–3 against Maximilian. With the notable exception of Antwerp the towns of Brabant were almost wholly on the side of Ghent, which was backed as in 1482–3 by a mixture of Burgundian aristocrats and lawyers.

Despite his qualities as a soldier and his connection with foreign dynasties, such as Portugal, Philip of Cleves was politically less important in directing the movement against Maximilian than Jan Coppenhole of Ghent, who came to Brussels in the autumn of 1488 to impose the authority of Ghent as he had already done on lesser towns.

In February 1489 Maximilian retreated to Germany, leaving as his lieutenant Albert duke of Saxony, an able leader of mercenaries and skilful at conducting the negotiations that throughout accompanied the civil war. Even before it faced so formidable an adversary as Albert of Saxony, 'The Union' was losing, for it had to win quickly if it was to win at all, since the towns of Brabant were overcrowded with refugee peasants. Moreover, although it claimed to act in the name of the Archduke Philip, the *prince naturel* was kept safely for Maximilian at Malines, where his presence was invaluable for drawing loyalism away from 'The Union'. The disturbances in Holland, where the leaders of the Hoek party joined hands with Philip of Cleves and took to the sea to exercise piracy, did not influence the course of events so much as France.

The Peace of Bruges restored the Peace of Arras, and 'The Union' was placed under the personal surety of Charles VIII; but French intervention against Maximilian was cautious, because of French designs on Brittany and French suspicions of Ghent. Long before the duke of Brittany died in September 1488, the regent of France, Anne de Beaujeu, and her council were determined to secure for the Crown the Breton succession; perceiving, therefore, that their military resources were insufficient to wage simultaneous war in Flanders and Brittany they reserved their might for Brittany. The Netherlands became a side-show in French eyes when, after the Peace of Bruges, they could not be used by Maximilian as a base from which to launch an invasion. The defeat of Maximilian, however, came to be seen as conducive to the supremacy of Ghent rather than of France in the Low Countries. The strained relations came to a head at a conference in February 1489 between d'Esquerdes and Coppenhole. In return for continued aid, France demanded the submission of Ghent in the form of the payment of a large sum to d'Esquerdes, ostensibly in settlement of a debt, and the transfer to him of two notabilities seized as hostages when Maximilian was taken at Bruges. The French received no satisfaction, while the alliance of Maximilian with Henry VII (February 1489) and the growing military success of Albert of Saxony in Brabant deterred them from committing themselves more deeply in the Netherlands. After months of negotiations, in which Engelbert of Nassau, who was still a prisoner in France, acted as Maximilian's diplomatic agent, a treaty was concluded at Frankfurt (22 July 1489) between Charles VIII and the king of the Romans.

The purpose of the French Crown was to bring about the neutralisation of Brittany, to prepare the duchy for penetration. In return for this Charles VIII was ready to facilitate under his mediation the return of Ghent and her allies to Habsburg obedience. The news from Frankfurt decided Brabant to submit and pay a fine to Albert of Saxony. Even Ghent, although undefeated, bowed to the Valois monarchy; and in accordance with the Frankfurt terms Flanders sent Gruuthuse, Rassenghem and Jan Coppenhole to negotiate at Tours. Maximilian despatched thither a numerous mission, of which the ambassadors of consequence were Engelbert of Nassau, *premier chambellan*, who since his captivity in France had gained for himself and his family a controlling position in Franco-Burgundian diplomacy, and Frans van Busleyden, *maître des requêtes*, the archduke's tutor, who now undertook his first major task.

The treaty of 30 October at Montils-lez-Tours abrogated the Peace of Bruges. The Members of Flanders were to pay within three years a huge indemnity, and in terms of any monetary revaluation which the government of the Low Countries might introduce. The Peace of Arras, which at Frankfurt was maintained, was now superseded, and, despite the protest of the Flemish delegation, the liberties granted since the death of Charles the Bold were to be reviewed at a personal interview between Charles VIII and Maximilian.

As the French knew, this was only a formal pacification, for Ghent was unconquered and Coppenhole and his party unreconciled, while Philip of

Cleves, though at his own request included within the peace, refused to recognise any authority that did not restore him to all his lands, offices and pensions, above all his captaincy of Sluis, to which he now retired. The restoration of authority in Flanders and Holland was largely wrecked by a revaluation of the currency under an ordinance of 14 December 1489. Since the death of Charles the Bold the coinage had declined in value, aggravating prices already at the mercy of war conditions, and the estates notably in 1488 had concerned themselves with proposals for reform. Technically the ordinance of 1489 produced a sound money, but it was also devised to enhance the value to the government of taxation and, as the reference in the treaty already showed, of the indemnity payable by Flanders. The debased coins in circulation lost anything up to 66 per cent of their value; and coming before Christmas, when leases, provincial and municipal *rentes* had to be paid, the ordinance caused hardship and litigation which lasted a decade. For more than a year the currency question caused recriminations with Ghent and contributed to keep in power Coppenhole, who was waiting for a turn in the international situation to reopen the struggle.

It was disastrous that, owing to his personal quarrel with Maximilian, Philip of Cleves was not reinstated, however exorbitant his demands. Thanks to his command of Sluis, Philip now became a more dangerous opponent of the regime than Coppenhole. From Sluis Philip expanded piratical operations, killing the trade of Bruges and severely interfering with that of Holland, where thanks to the resulting distress he succeeded in keeping rebellion alive. Politically the rekindling of revolt in Bruges was unimportant. The wealthy classes, knowing the contest to be hopeless, migrated from Bruges, which capitulated on 29 November 1490. At Ghent also the wealthy, among them Adrian Vilain, lord of Rassenghem, were coming to terms with the central government; but Cleves sent Rassenghem a personal cartel of defiance and caused his murder in June 1490.

The final revolt of Ghent, under the leadership of Coppenhole, might never have happened had not Maximilian resumed his quarrel with France, by implementing the plan, projected as long ago as 1486, of marrying the heiress of Brittany. On 19 December 1490 the king of the Romans married by proxy Anne duchess of Brittany. French intervention in the Netherlands inevitably restarted and Ghent, always ready to use France, was again in open revolt by May 1491.

The Valois scored an indecent triumph over the Habsburgs when in December 1491 Charles VIII married Maximilian's bride the duchess of Brittany and repudiated his daughter Margaret, to whom Charles was betrothed under the peace of 1482. The Estates General had to be gathered together in February 1492 at Malines to negotiate peace with Ghent. Philip of Cleves had rejected numerous peace offers since 1489, hoping to appeal to the estates over the head of the archduke's council.

But Philip in 1492 was out-moded. The Golden Fleece and the learned members of the archduke's council rejected his old-fashioned approach to a sovereign on terms of equality; and the estates, who were in close relation with the council, treated his apologia as a petition and surrendered their copies of it to the chancellor. Unlike 1488 the estates wanted to save the central power. The fact that the archduke, the *prince naturel*, would come of age in a few years, counted for much.

Philip of Cleves and Coppenhole had no political answer to the estates' request for them to choose between civil war and peace although they could still count on the government being embarrassed by other local rebellions. 1492 was one of the most difficult years since 1477, for a revolt broke out in Holland, and the precariousness of the Burgundian inheritance was proved by the return of Charles of Egmond to Guelders.

The movement in Holland and West Friesland was not a peasant revolt. It adopted for its banner not the plough or wooden shoe, the symbols of insurgent peasants, but cheese and bread to proclaim that the country was not to be eaten up by tax-farmers. The rising was a violent protest by rural communities and towns such as Alkmaar and Haarlem against the prevalent system which farmed taxation to syndicates of financiers, who advanced money to the government. The '*Kaas-en-Broodvolk*' were vanquished by German mercenaries under a banner of bread and beer and the rebellion was over by June 1492. Its chief importance was to bring about the decline of the Hoek party as a fighting faction, for the pacification led to stricter government in Holland so that the remaining Hoeks were absorbed among the allies of Guelders.

The loss of Guelders, which was not definitely reconquered until 1543, was the work of French diplomacy playing upon local particularism. Charles of Egmond was sent back to Guelders in February 1492, under the familiar French plan of raising up enemies for Burgundians or Habsburgs within the Low Countries. Charles had cause for grievance in that Maximilian had done nothing to secure his release from captivity since 1487, while the cadet branch of his family, Egmond of IJsselstein held the office of *stadhouder* of Holland from 1484 to 1517. Particularism is a frequently misapplied term, but it is applicable to Guelders, which in 1492 reverted to the medieval ideal of self-sufficiency under an hereditary lord. From the start the estates of Guelders were associated with Charles in the struggle that brought the country out of the wider Netherlands in which it had lived since 1473 and back to the condition of a fief.

After marrying Anne of Brittany, Charles VIII not only clung to Artois and Franche-Comté, the dower of the repudiated Margaret of Austria, but to wring concessions from her family detained Margaret as a hostage. The European situation, on the other hand, was changing in favour of the Habsburgs. The success of the French monarchy in Brittany, which Henry VII and Ferdinand of Aragon strove to reverse, brought attacks which had to be bought off with French concessions to England (Treaty of Étaples, 3 November 1492) and to Spain (Treaty of Barcelona, 19 January 1493). Maximilian allied with Henry VII and the Catholic kings of Spain; and his alliance with Spain is memorable for the overtures of a marriage between the Archduke Philip and a Spanish princess, which, although abandoned under the Treaty of Barcelona, ushered in the dynastic marriage of 1496.

By repudiating Margaret of Austria, the king of France destroyed his status in the eyes of the Burgundian lands through tearing up the Peace of Arras. In Artois and Franche-Comté, the dower counties of Margaret, that Burgundian loyalty, which had never perished, now became aggressive; and in November 1492 Arras rose against its French garrison, and to the cry of 'Vive Bourgogne' rejoined the Netherlands. Maximilian's invasion of Franche-Comté in midwinter succeeded more because of the co-operation which the towns gave him than because of the small battle at Dournon (19 January 1493) that he won over the French.

Confidence in the viability of the Burgundian State, accompanied everywhere, except in Guelders, by the decay of any ideological alternative, proved decisive in restoring peace. Ghent, although militarily unsubdued, submitted to terms equal to those imposed after its defeat in 1453 and 1485. Bitterness between artisans and peasantry culminated in the murder of Coppenhole (16 June 1492) by the captain of the peasants, nicknamed 'ploughman'. Despite this internal strife, Ghent was yet capable of inflicting a sharp repulse on Albert of Saxony, but, conscious that a town could not indefinitely defy a state, opened negotiations. The resulting Peace of Cadzand (29 July 1492) reduced Ghent from an autonomous to an ordinary town. Its jurisdiction was subordinated to the appellate powers of the *Raad van Vlaanderen*, and its right to create external burghers confined to narrow limits. In his capacity of count of Flanders, the prince secured a permanent influence over the annual reappointment of magistrates, who were to be drawn from the notables and not from the lesser guilds. As Pirenne has said, 'the prince was to control the town and the town its trades'. Although the plan of Charles the Bold to overawe Ghent by building a castle was not implemented until after the next revolt of 1539, the town remained unrebellious for a generation.

The waning of French intervention was obvious from events in the bishopric of Liège. After his short-lived triumph of 1485, Maximilian had connived at the putting to death of the *Mambour* Guillaume de la Marck by the bishop John of Hoorne. Such summary justice only relit the family feud between Hoorne and La Marck; and at the apogee of 'The Union' in October 1488, Charles VIII took Liège under French protection. A local civil war between the bishop and the La Marck party roughly kept pace with the major struggle between Maximilian and 'The Union'. The advantages of neutrality were slow to be appreciated; and it was not until the Peace of Donchéry (5 May 1492) that the warring factions and the estates were brought to accept neutrality and free trade for Liège. These principles for the status of the bishopric were recognised by Charles VIII in July 1492 and a month later by the archduke. The neutrality of Liège, however interesting for the development of international law, signified at the time a compromise solution which drew the Pays de Liège to closer relations with the Burgundian lands at the expense of French diplomacy.

The capitulation of Philip of Cleves came on 12 October 1492 after a lengthy siege of Sluis. At sea the government was weak; and its admiral Philip of Beveren acquiesced in ships of his own port Veere buying safe-conducts from the pirates of Sluis. Henry VII, however, was impatient at the damage they wrought on English trade, and under his alliance with Maximilian sent a fleet commanded by Sir Edward Poynings to help Albert of Saxony prosecute the siege. Philip of Cleves could not thereafter hold out indefinitely; but his submission was actually caused by the death of his father driving him to open negotiations for the preservation of his patrimony. Thanks to the solidarity of his fellow magnates, he was reinstated; but Philip was too wise ever to attack monarchical society again, and although he remained until his death in 1528 an exponent of peace with France he pursued it by more subtle means.

The re-establishment of normal relations with France was obstructed by Burgundian refugees at the French court; but the Peace of Senlis (23 May 1493) preserved the essentials of the Peace of Arras. France returned Margaret and her dower, Artois and Franche-Comté, which without the duchy of Burgundy constituted only a minor risk to French security. The Habsburgs, on the other hand, implicitly renounced war as a legitimate means for recovering the duchy of Burgundy; for while both parties reserved their rights under the Peace of Arras, they agreed to seek satisfaction 'par voye amiable' or 'par justice'. The permanent suzerainty and jurisdiction of the Crown of France was recognised in respect of all the French fiefs of the archduke; and pending his doing homage at the age of twenty, a condominium was devised for such strong points as Aire, Béthune and Hesdin, the military government of which was to be exercised by d'Esquerdes for Charles VIII while the civil administration rested with the archduke. Starting therefore from the medieval principle of divided jurisdiction an army of occupation was installed to protect the French northern frontier until 1498.

The clauses of 1482 favouring capitalists including the beneficed clergy were expanded. On both sides property owners were reinstated, but were denied the right to recover income disposed of by either state since 1470. The stability that characterised the relations between France and the Netherlands in the opening sixteenth century owed much to the economic provisions of 1493, which allowed for the holding of property on either side of the frontier and the abolition of safe-conducts for merchants. It is not surprising that the Peace, like the Peace of Arras before it, was published in print, seeing the number of individual interests which it involved.

Senlis heralded the end of Maximilian's regency. Frans van Busleyden and Thomas de Plaine, two of the most influential ministers of his son's reign, helped to negotiate it; and when Margaret of Austria, returning from France, was welcomed at Valenciennes, a play was performed in the pastoral style representing the country recovering from its plight.

The Emperor Frederick III died in August 1493; and the estates, who used Guillaume de Croy lord of Chièvres as their envoy, found Maximilian ready to accept the sum which they proffered as the price of Philip's emancipation. The ordinance of October 1493, which replaced Albert of Saxony by Engelbert of Nassau at the head of the archduke's council, marks the beginning of Philip's independent government. In keeping with Burgundian precedent, justice and finance were kept within the orbit of his household, but Maximilian's instructions for liaison between Philip's council in the Netherlands and his own in Austria remained inoperative.

Philip's accession did more than close the constitutional crisis persisting since 1482, for the inaugural charters under which his reign began resumed in each of the major territories prerogative power granted away by Mary in 1477. The *Blijde Inkomst* of 10 September 1494 on his reception as duke of Brabant only admitted usages current before 1477; although he agreed to grant additions, which the estates of the duchy unanimously proposed and his council deemed useful. The estates of Holland were forced to meet him in December 1494 at the inconvenient town of Geertruidenberg, where he all but abrogated the *Groot Privilegie* of Holland dating from 1477; but he was prepared to consider the suggestions of the province, and granted some additions in 1495. Philip rebuffed Flanders, where he had been acknowledged count in 1483, by sending proctors to take possession; and in Hainault, when he swore to be good lord *comme vray heritier et propriétaire du pays*, he revoked the privileges gained by Mons since 1477.

Thomas de Plaine, *président du grand conseil* (*grand*, implying its legal side) had so much to do with the negotiations in Brabant, Holland and Hainault, that he may have been responsible for the principle underlying the revision of the 1477 charters. The sovereign was not bound by his predecessor's concessions, and liberties were not an immutable birthright of subjects; but the additions which Philip issued aimed at introducing efficiency rather than absolutism, for joint responsibility could not always be enforced on the Members of a single territory. In December 1494 Holland was promised a new assessment of taxation and Philip's commissioners produced a survey (*Informatie*) contrasting population and property in the northern parts of Holland with what they had been in 1477. Taxation caused a suit between Dordrecht, claiming a reduced rate on the strength of its charters, and the other towns of Holland, who, maintaining that 'in public matters the minor must follow the major part', strove to compel Dordrecht to pay at the same rate as themselves. In 1497 an interlocutory sentence of Philip's council left Dordrecht in a strong position at the cost of the public fisc.

The foreign policy of the reign falls into two phases dividing at 1500. In the first, Philip found himself in a favourable international conjunction. French pressure, continuous since 1461, was diverted toward Italy; and the lord of Esquerdes, who died on Charles VIII's march to Italy, left his body to be buried at Boulogne as a protest against the new direction of French expansionism.

The basic problem in the foreign relations of the Netherlands, how to combine political peace with France and economic peace with England, that Maximilian, unlike the Valois dukes, disregarded, became capable of solution. French and English outlooks were represented within Philip's council, for if Chièvres and Frans van Busleyden leaned to France, the family of Bergen espoused the English cause out of regard for the trade of their town Bergen-op-zoom.

Philip began his reign by recognising the Peace of Senlis, and implemented its consequences by the Treaty of Paris (2 August 1498). In 1499 at Arras he performed homage for Flanders and Artois to the chancellor of France representing Louis XII.

Against Henry VII, Maximilian was committed to the diplomatically sterile and commercially disastrous support of Margaret of York's pretender Perkin Warbeck. While Warbeck's venture was in progress, Philip's government in 1495 set about persuading Henry VII to raise the economic sanctions, which he had imposed against the Low Countries; and on 24 February 1496 a trade treaty, generally known as the *Intercursus Magnus* was reached between them. Besides restoring the charges on English merchants to the rates of fifty years before, the treaty conferred on Philip absolute control of foreign affairs, by prohibiting unfriendly preparations against Henry VII within franchises, such as Malines, the dower town of Margaret of York.

In the second phase of foreign policy that began after 1500 the Netherlands were subordinated to the realisation of the archduke's inheritance in Spain. Initially the marriage (20 October 1496) of Philip to Juana, the daughter of the Catholic kings of Spain, and of Margaret of Austria to the infante in 1497, constituted a diplomatic success of Maximilian, and a renewal of the Burgundian connection with the Peninsula that ante-dated 1477; but when Don Miguel, the last male heir of Ferdinand and Isabella, died in 1500, the archduke became by right of his wife heir to the Spanish crowns, and when Isabella herself died (26 November 1504) he assumed the title of King of Castille.

Friendship with France and England was cultivated no longer for the sake of the Low Countries, but to secure the acquiescence of these Powers in Philip's succession to the Catholic kings. Toward France the archduke's attitude became servile, but at least it succeeded in keeping Louis XII until the summer of 1505 from seriously impeding his Spanish plans.

Philip undertook two visits to Spain. Firstly, he left the Netherlands in November 1501 only to return in November 1503, and secondly he sailed for Spain in January 1506 to die there 25 September 1506. The first visit was prepared by Chièvres and Busleyden who arranged the Treaty of Lyons (10 August 1501) with Louis XII. Philip's decision to travel to Spain through France was a triumph for the francophil party within his council. His entry into Paris recalled that of his great-grandfather in 1461, and formed the subject of a printed relation and ballad. As senior peer of France he attended the *Parlement* of Paris, demonstrating not only his feudal dependence on, but his personal status within, the kingdom.

The second visit to Spain was prepared by the treaty of Hagenau (8 April 1505) between Maximilian, Philip and Louis XII; but the king of France woke up to the implications of a Habsburg on his Somme and Pyrenean frontiers. Philip had to go to Spain by sea; and the virulent return of French intervention in the Low Countries dates not from the second regency of Maximilian after Philip's death, but from the latter half of 1505. Juridically Louis XII pressed the rights of the *Parlement* of Paris over the *ressort de Flandres*; diplomatically he supported the La Marcks at Liège and militarily he aided Charles duke of Guelders, whom France had never wholly dropped. The Spanish succession was a gamble by the court of Burgundy for stakes higher than those for which other powers contended in Italy, but the Netherlands financed it and bore the brunt of the reaction it evoked from France.

As in France and England so also in the Low Countries the business of government proved easier in the opening sixteenth century than for some generations, and very much easier than it became in the later part of the century, so that Philip's facile manners made him almost as popular as Louis XII. He strove for harmony even as a boy; and in 1492, before the attack on Sluis, he sent a message to Philip of Cleves, 'dittes a Monsieur Philippe qu'il ne me face faire chose dont je puisse avoir regret cy-après'. Subsequent admiration for the autocratic type has rendered his nickname *croit conseil* pejorative, but at the time it denoted a wise prince, who, unlike a Charles the Bold, was prepared to heed counsel.

Certainly the nobility increased its public influence; but at the same time, despite its cosmopolitan origin, it was growing to identify itself with the provinces. The members of the Bergen, Croy, Lalaing, Lannoy and Nassau families who surrounded Philip made his political council (*conseil privé*) resemble a gathering of the Golden Fleece. The state had much in common with an oligarchic republic like Venice.

The archduke returned not only to the pomp of his Burgundian fore-fathers, but to their residences. Confident in his subjects' loyalty, he spent 1498 at the Coudenberg, Brussels, and reconciled himself with the Flemings by going to the Prinsenhof, Ghent, where his son Charles was born in February 1500. The towns, with exceptions like Antwerp, laboured under the aftermath of civil war, and were grateful to receive state aid in the supervision of their debts, for between 1494 and 1500 most of the towns of Holland became bankrupt.

Because his outlook, unlike that of Charles the Bold, was peaceful, and because the central authority tended on the whole to be exercised through, rather than at the expense of, provincial institutions, measures, which in autocratic spirit could compare with those of Charles, were introduced without much difficulty. An act of resumption (Edict of 6 May 1495) reclaimed all regalian revenues and rights in Holland and Zeeland lapsed since 1477. Besides lands and offices that had been alienated, it included all tolls which had been farmed out; these were not only financially valuable (for example, those in the Scheldt estuary), but of political importance in the relations of the provinces with one another and with foreign Powers (for example, England).

The regime was not doctrinaire as regards centralisation. In 1496 the *Chambre des Comptes* at Lille and its equivalents at Brussels and The Hague were compulsorily reunited, as before 1477, in headquarters at Malines; and Philip told the estates of Brabant that what they called their *Rekenkamer* was in fact his. But by the end of 1498 the accounting bureaux were back in their provincial homes, for once the prince's power had been admitted he was ready to compromise with local feeling. Philip's two confidential ministers, Chièvres and Frans van Busleyden (died August 1502) had a head for business as well as diplomacy.

The creation of the *Grand Conseil* at Malines (22 January 1504) ostensibly did little more than provide a fixed residence for the prince's *grand conseil*, the legal section of his council; but the verbatim repetition of Charles the Bold's act of 1473 instituting the *Parlement* of Malines suggests that in founding a high court at Malines Philip was inspired by statecraft more than convenience. Philip's early death cut short the experiment of re-introducing legal centralisation, and the *Raad van Brabant*, to mention only the most important provincial rival of Malines, freed itself from the appellate jurisdiction of the *Grand Conseil*.

Official relations with the Estates General were satisfactory, and, because Philip, unlike his father and grandfather, often communicated with them personally, their suspicion of the court was diminished. In September 1501 he bade farewell to them and announced the appointment of Engelbert of Nassau as lieutenant during his forthcoming visit to Spain. The estates were a collection of provincial deputations, and notwithstanding the consequent delay and bargaining in securing an *aide* the government allowed these deputations time to refer back to their provincial mandatories, so that the reign of Philip and the minority of Charles were a period when, however grudgingly, taxation was raised with the consent of the individual provinces. The estates no longer, as during Philip's minority, shaped policy. Even when that policy was congenial to them (e.g. the Treaty of Paris in 1498), it was settled by Philip's council and only subsequently laid before them. After 1501 they displayed increasing restiveness over paying for his foreign policy; but they could always be relied upon to support Philip against interference from Maximilian.

In internal as in external matters, Philip completely freed himself from paternal control. Although when Maximilian summoned Philip in 1496 to Germany Busleyden was temporarily disgraced, he was quickly restored; and next year, 1497, Philip replaced Maximilian's old chancellor Jean Carandolet by Thomas de Plaine, another *franc-comtois*, but one wholly devoted to his interests. In 1498–9 and again early in 1503, while the king of the Romans was seeking to subdue Guelders, Philip and the estates clung to neutrality toward Charles of Egmond as a corollary of their alliance with France, even to the extent of permitting the passage of French reinforcements to Guelders.

Only in the summer of 1505, by which time Philip had displaced his father in the leadership of the Habsburg family, did he embark on the one campaign of his career, invading Guelders with Maximilian and forcing the capitulation of Charles of Egmond (July 1505), who was reduced to his pre-1487 status of a client hostage at the Burgundian court. The mildness of the settlement would not have been open to criticism if Charles had been properly guarded; but rather than go with Philip to Spain he managed to flee back to Guelders, where he could count on the full support of Louis XII.

So impatient was Philip to reach Spain, that he sailed from Flushing on 10 January 1506, although the outlook at home was more dangerous than at any time since 1493, for Louis XII controlled the entire length of the Meuse. Apart from the return of Charles to Guelders, French influence scored a success at Liège on the death of the bishop John of Hoorne. On 30 December 1505, Érard de la Marck, nephew of the one-time *Mambour* Guillaume, and the candidate of Louis XII, was elected to the bishopric by the chapter of St Lambert against the Habsburg nominee Jacques de Croy. For some months before he sailed, Philip was collecting money to pay for the expedition by mortgaging parcels of the domain, and by selling, in all but name, to Antwerp, Middelburg and Bergen-op-zoom the dues on the Scheldt resumed in May 1495.

The domain and tolls were considered mortgageable in an emergency like crown jewels; and in 1499 Philip ceded, as count of Holland, his rights over Friesland to Albert of Saxony in satisfaction of the debt owing to Albert in respect of his former military command. Although Margaret of Austria and Charles V recovered without undue difficulty what Philip had pawned, his liquidation of regalian assets to furnish money for Spain was a set-back to the policy pursued since 1494 of building up the prerogative. Two treaties with Henry VII interrupted Philip's voyage to Spain. The first (20 March 1506) was purely dynastic securing English support for Philip's rights in Castille. The second (30 April) was made after he had left England and was never ratified by him. It has acquired the name of *Intercursus Malus* because of the advantage it conferred on English trade. Taken together they afford evidence of the lengths to which Philip and his council were prepared to go in order to gain diplomatic and pecuniary support for his Spanish policy. That policy had already achieved unexpected success when Philip died suddenly in Spain on 25 September 1506.

The minority of Charles is a more realistic title for the period 1506–15 than the second regency of Maximilian. The emperor, as Max called himself after 1507, visited the Low Countries twice, in 1508–9 and 1513, and drew a monthly pension from them while retaining the appointment of officials in order to reap further profits. But the role, which Maximilian played during Philip's minority of embroiling the provinces in warfare, fell during Charles's to Margaret of Austria. The internal resistance to the waging of foreign wars, which had previously come from the towns and the estates, now sprang from within the *conseil privé*. Society was growing more unified; and the existence of a powerful pro-French party within the State explains the decline of French influence exercised from without. In any event the efforts of Louis XII to draw the towns on to the side of France failed in 1507 and 1513, while the nobles and lawyers no longer produced numerous deserters to France as in the time of Maximilian's first regency.

To call the party in the *conseil privé* and the Golden Fleece, which opposed Margaret's wars of reconquest and rebuffed in 1508 the emperor's attempt to set up Franche-Comté as a kingdom and to revive in 1511 the vanished realm of Austrasia, a national party would be too facile. Rather did this party see in peace with France the solution to difficulties at home, and wanted relations with England confined to trade without entailing dynastic—let alone military—alliances, while striving for the solution of the Guelders problem by marrying Isabella, Charles's sister, to Charles of Egmond. Chièvres, who developed from feudal lord and courtier into a European statesman, was the exponent of this outlook. The rival group within the *conseil privé* and Golden Fleece led by Jan van Bergen and Floris van Egmond of IJsselstein, which advocated a warlike settlement with Guelders and France, could claim to be equally patriotic, for the English alliance which they advocated had conferred no mean benefits in the past. The two factions, the pro-French led by Chièvres, whose family interests lay mainly in Hainault, and the pro-English headed by Bergen and IJsselstein in the north of Brabant and in Holland, might suggest a rivalry between north and south. But the aristocratic politics of the day did not proceed on these lines; and the Nassau family, whose centre in the Netherlands was at Breda, remained francophil up to and beyond the Treaty of Paris (1515). The one sense in which Chièvres and his supporters might qualify for the epithet patriotic is in their emphasis on the *prince naturel*. They were the party of *status quo*, aiming to preserve the conditions obtaining at Philip's death until Charles came of age to enter on his inheritance; and on this account they commanded the sympathy of the estates.

It is a tribute to the methods by which the restoration of monarchical rule was pursued under Philip that there was no reaction in 1506 comparable to that of 1477. The estates did not renew their former attempts to produce an alternative constitution; and the foresight of Margaret of Austria avoided later clashes, though the situation was often ugly. In 1508 the provinces swore to remain united and afford each other aid, ominously reminiscent of 1488, but Margaret produced the Peace of Cambrai as a sedative. Apart from their opposition to a war policy, the Estates General were conservative and divided by provincial jealousies. One of Margaret's first tasks was to arbitrate in a dispute over precedence between Brabant and Flanders, and in 1508 Bergen advised her to deal with the provinces separately rather than in a general assembly.

Together with that of Chièvres the personality of Margaret explains the ensuing political history. Her knowledge and patronage of the arts were too extensive for recapitulation; but politics interested her most, and after the death of her last husband, the duke of Savoy, in 1504, she was anxious to return and govern the Netherlands for either Philip or Maximilan. Her hostility to the Crown of France was no mere personal rancour deriving from her rejection by Charles VIII, but sprang from her Burgundian dynasticism, for while she knew that the Netherlands made the fortune of her family she thought of Dijon as its capital. At first she had little sympathy with the political traditions of the Low Countries. Her methods were exotic, and she relied on such men as Mercurino di Gattinara, whom she brought from Savoy trained in the cabinets of Italy.

The *conseil privé* with Chièvres at its head, whom Philip had left behind as his lieutenant, quickly supplied an answer to the constitutional question raised by the succession of Philip's son Charles count of Luxemburg, aged six, commonly called the archduke. On 6 and 7 October 1506 the councillors wrote begging Maximilian to accept the regency, indicating firmly that this solution would have to be submitted at once to the estates.

They followed the practice of Philip's reign in deciding policy and taking the estates into their confidence afterwards. Maximilian's decision of 27 October 1506 to maintain Philip's councillors in power enabled them to keep the administration running by retaining provisionally in office the staff of the *Chambre des Comptes* and of the *Raad van Vlaanderen*.

At the estates of October 1506 the council only won partial acceptance for the regency of Maximilian. Brabant and Holland agreed; but the Flemish deputation asked for time to consult its mandatories, while Hainault and Namur hesitated from fear of France. Louis XII hoped, perhaps expected, to become Charles's guardian. Not until the estates of April 1507 was Maximilian recognised as regent, no doubt because he commissioned meanwhile (18 March 1507) his daughter Margaret to take the oath for him as *mambour*. In doing so he granted her minimal independence, and not until 18 March 1509 could she elicit from him the powers of a regent. Her position was the more delicate in that she could only govern through the *conseil privé*, which retained the influence it acquired under Philip, and although theoretically an advisory body actually shared power with the head of the State. Margaret never gained control over the composition of the council during Charles's minority. When the old chancellor Thomas de Plaine died in 1507 she could not prevent Jean le Sauvage becoming *chef et président du conseil privé*, which under a minority was equivalent to being chancellor. Le Sauvage was not a *franc-comtois*, but a Flemish jurist conspicuous in dealings with France since 1494.

While there was hope of becoming Charles's guardian, Louis XII imposed a truce on the duke of Guelders and Érard de la Marck, bishop of Liège, but once Maximilian's regency was inevitable he again supplied them with arms and troops. Margaret turned to England, and in December 1507 Bergen, as the leading anglophil in the council, negotiated an alliance for her at Calais. But Henry VII was not the king to furnish military aid, so that Margaret's first attempt to challenge France and conquer Guelders failed, evoking in 1508 demands for peace from the estates of Brabant. By the Peace of Cambrai (10 December 1508) she brought about a coalition between the emperor and the king of France. The Netherlands gained a respite, for the duke of Guelders had to accept the terms and the coalition turned to war against Venice. Although Margaret trimmed the Peace of Cambrai by a pact with England, concluding (17 December 1508) a marriage treaty for Charles with Mary Tudor, the pro-French were inevitably strengthened, and the emperor, who was sensitive to such trends, made Chièvres *premier chambellan* to Charles. Margaret in vain sought for Bergen this vital post, which enabled Chièvres to preside over the bringing up of the *prince naturel*.

To the party of *status quo* Cambrai was to be a permanent peace like Senlis, but to the regent Margaret it was a temporary expedient. When, therefore, the succession of Henry VIII offered her a promising ally, she used the infractions of the peace by Charles of Egmond to wreck the negotiations with Guelders and to inflate the local conflict into an international one by a military alliance with England against Guelders in 1511. An English force arrived to help Margaret's troops besiege Venlo; but Charles of Egmond invaded Holland, and in November 1511 the siege had to be raised.

The introduction of English forces was a challenge to the party of *status quo*. In July 1511 the regent complained that councillors *de robe courte et longue* withdrew; and by the end of the year the captain of her land forces, Henry of Nassau, and the admiral Philip of Burgundy (youngest bastard of Philip *le Bon*) were pretexting sickness in order to be relieved of their commands. Although she persuaded the emperor to dismiss Le Sauvage, and make Gerard de Plaine, son of the late chancellor, *president du conseil privé* (November 1511), the party of *status quo* had demonstrated its power to frustrate official policy.

The regent extricated herself by a concession to the nobility and to all who saw in Charles the head of the state. In April 1512 she set up a princely household for the archduke. Flouting the emperor's wish to surround his grandson with a single set of permanent officials, she based Charles's enlarged household on the *état à demi-an*, which kept none but the highest officers continuously at court, while the rest performed duties for half the year, being replaced in the other half by a second set of officers. Margaret perceived that to please the nobility profits from court service must be spread widely. In Adrian of Utrecht, whom she chose as tutor for her nephew in preference to Erasmus, Margaret provided Charles with his future minister, who in the meanwhile exercised a formative influence on his religious and intellectual development. The regent was the readier to make these concessions, since she deemed the time ripe to reverse the Peace of Cambrai and bring the emperor, the kings of England and Aragon into a military coalition against France.

Already in July 1512 she told her father that the provinces existed on trade and peace, and, realising that they would resist positive participation in a war with France, she preferred to declare them neutral and wage war with foreign armies and funds. Neutrality was not new in principle but to extend it to exclude the Netherlands and Franche-Comté (the latter, Margaret's dower, already declared neutral August 1512) from major war was quite different from the neutrality of episcopal Liège. In April 1513 the emperor was induced to enter a Holy League with the pope, Henry VIII and Ferdinand of Aragon against France. The neutrality of the Netherlands was saved by a quibble, for Maximilian subscribed to the league only as emperor and not as guardian of his grandson, whose hereditary lands were thus excluded. Louis XII remarked that if Charles had been of age he would have been summoned as a vassal to defend France.

The regent's unusual formula for waging an aggressive war succeeded chiefly because the Swiss thrust at Dijon forced Louis XII to fight simultaneously on two fronts, while Henry VIII provided both an army and money for the emperor. Although many pro-English noblemen took service with Henry VIII, the main business of the Netherlands was supplying the armies; and Margaret was probably near the truth when she claimed in 1515 that they had made a million of gold in profiteering. Tournai, the fortified French enclave on the Scheldt, fell to Henry VIII (21 September 1513), and Margaret was glad to see him keep it, for Tournai committed Henry to a stake in the Low Countries, and England was the corner-stone of Margaret's policy.

A new household ordinance for Archduke Charles was promulgated at Lille in October 1513, which internationalised the *prince naturel* by sharing his guardianship between Maximilian, Henry VIII and Ferdinand of Aragon. This dynastic consortium, under which Charles was placed, thinly disguised an English alliance that was to prolong Margaret's tenure of the regency and weaken Chièvres and the pro-French group around Charles. Undertakings were exchanged at Lille that the marriage of Charles to Mary, Henry VIII's sister, should take place by May 1514; but the pro-French and pro-Castilian party entrenched in the *conseil privé* and the Golden Fleece delayed it beyond the stipulated date. When therefore, in August 1514, Henry VIII announced the marriage of Mary to Louis XII, the entire outlook was altered; and it became obvious that Margaret could not long retain her position as regent. Chièvres brought the archduke away from Malines, the home of dowagers and lawyers, to Brussels and new associations.

The estates of Brabant grumbled against paying any aide until Charles was declared of age; but when at the end of 1514 the Estates General offered the emperor a large sum in return for Charles's emancipation, Maximilian was as amenable as in 1493 under similar circumstances. Under his authority dated 23 December 1514, Charles came of age on 6 January 1515 before the estates at Brussels. Charles's majority was produced by a court intrigue and the readiness of the provinces to pay for the privilege of being ruled by a native prince.

The accession of Charles ushered in a Burgundian restoration. Jean le Sauvage was immediately created *chancelier de Bourgogne*, and proved to be the last occupant of the office, for on his death in June 1518 he was succeeded by Gattinara as Charles's personal chancellor, while the *audiencier* took charge of legal business in the Netherlands for which the chancellor had previously been responsible. But during his term of office, Le Sauvage exercised a supervision over all branches of government, as Nicolas Rolin had done in the fifteenth century. Again in conformity with Burgundian tradition, government was identified with the household.

This arrangement suited Chièvres and Le Sauvage, for the first as *premier chambellan* was head of the household department, which stood in closest relations to Charles, and the second as chancellor controlled the secretaries. The council was composed of lords and lawyers drawn from the Low Countries and Franche-Comté, with the exception of the Pfalzgraf, who was Maximilian's spokesman, and Gattinara, who was Margaret's. Although individual councillors, like Henry of Nassau, wielded great influence, on account of their wealth their political importance depended more on their position in the household. The highest decisions rested with Chièvres, Le Sauvage and Adrian of Utrecht, and with the two former after the last was sent on his invidious mission to Spain at the end of 1515.

Charles entered his lands on terms generally similar to the inaugurations of his father; but the stability of the regime in the intervening years turned Charles's entries into festive events rather than bargains about local liberties. In April 1515 he made additions to his *Blijde Inkomst* in Brabant, which, though expelling the gypsies, increased the personal freedom of his other subjects in the duchy. But he was not prepared to brook even the whisper of an extorted concession; and when after his reception at Ghent rumours spread that he had abrogated the Peace of Cadzand, Charles rebuked the town for its lenient treatment of the rumour-mongers and republished the peace in April 1515. The incident was significant of an unrest within the towns that became more marked as Charles's reign progressed, though already in 1514 there had been at Zierikerzee a riot against the magistrates. Discontent among the poor was growing, which at Brussels (1532) and Ghent (1539) culminated in sedition against the central government which backed the municipal ruling classes.

The reversal of Margaret of Austria's policy toward France was so striking as to create an exaggerated impression of the cleavage between Chièvres and her. Louis XII died on 1 January 1515, and the coincidence that his successor Francis I and Charles began to reign in the same month necessitated a fresh start. It is easy to condemn Chièvres in 1515 for surrender to France, but the situation in Liège, Guelders and Friesland invited French intervention, which, having delayed the moral and political development of a state in the Netherlands, threatened to postpone indefinitely their unification.

The embassy which Henry of Nassau led to Paris did homage in Charles's name for Flanders and Artois, attempting, though unsuccessfully, to do homage for Burgundy also. On 24 March 1515 the Treaty of Paris was made. Charles was to marry Renée daughter of Louis XII, but she was to be dowered with the inaccessible fief of Berry, and Henry of Nassau was to marry the heiress of Orange-Chalon, a house which for a century had steered between France and Burgundy. This feudal marriage, unlike most of the treaty, was fulfilled. An alliance of friendship was struck between Francis and Charles, who nevertheless received no protection against the duke of Guelders and the bishop of Liège, save in so far as the contracting parties undertook not to help each other's foes.

The treaty, which like every treaty with France was rapturously received, left the door open for an understanding with England, and following the analogy of 1496 and 1508 a settlement with England quickly succeeded one with France. In diplomacy the three Powers managed to keep pace with one another over the next few years. A political and trade agreement was concluded with England in January 1516; and when the Treaty of Noyon (13 August 1516) saved amity with France at the price of letting Francis substitute for Renée his own daughter less than a year old as a bride for Charles, negotiations for another treaty with England were begun within the month. At the very end of 1516 Maximilian paid what was to be his last visit to the Netherlands; but instead of removing Chièvres and Le Sauvage, as he had given Henry VIII to expect, the emperor ratified the Treaty of Noyon. The diplomatic activity of these years can only be understood against the background of Charles's approaching succession in Spain. On 23 January 1516 Ferdinand of Aragon died, bequeathing Aragon to Charles, whom he also named as regent in the other Spanish kingdoms. In March 1516 Charles was proclaimed king at Brussels.

The rich considered Spain a field of Burgundian expansion; and the Spaniards, whose numbers in the Low Countries had been growing, were well received compared with Maximilian's countrymen. Whereas the Golden Fleece blocked the emperor's attempt to convert it into an Austro-Habsburg order, the chapter of Michaelmas 1516 approved its extension to Spain, reserving ten stalls for Spaniards to be filled when its sovereign Charles visited his new realm.

Although conditions within the peninsula cried out for his presence, Charles delayed sailing for Spain until September 1517. It may be thought that Chièvres wanted to keep him a purely Burgundian prince for as long as possible; and in 1517 Henry VIII's ambassadors complained that Charles's councillors treated him more like a duke of Brabant than a king. On the other hand, Charles's government embarked early in 1515 on financial reforms that required time, besides having its attention fully engaged in Guelders, Utrecht and Friesland. The impatience of Philip in 1506 to get to Spain even at the sacrifice of security was not repeated.

In 1514 a more detailed survey (*Informatie*) than that of 1494 showed Holland to be wealthier and more populous than twenty years before; but when in 1515 a fresh tax assessment was made such opposition was aroused that by 1518 it had to be replaced. In Flanders any revision of taxation had to contend with an assessment more than a century out of date, which threatened to become an immutable quota. The reintroduction of amortisation (mortmain) on the clergy was in itself a measure sufficient to test the strength of the central power.

The 'Transport' of Flanders was a subsidy-book, which showed how much the Members, the smaller towns and the rural areas, paid whenever the county as a whole paid an *aide*. But the 'Transport' had not been revised since 1408, and changes in wealth rendered its modernisation urgent if it was to be made an instrument of taxation for a monarchic state. A commission for its revision was appointed in May 1515, whose report was only completed in October 1517.

The 1515 'Transport' brought in rather more than that of 1408; but whereas the towns had produced over 50 per cent of the whole, their share in 1515 sank to 44 per cent. The increase in the quota of the smaller towns and of the countryside was too general to be explicable otherwise than by a shift in industry. Bruges, which in 1408 contributed 15·7 per cent, made up only 14·4 per cent of the whole in 1515; but Grammont and Alost were raised from 7·4 per cent in 1408 to 8·6 per cent. Even more striking was the advance in the proportion of tax allotted to country districts around Ypres, Furnes and Courtrai, where rural cloth and linen industries were established.

The amortisation of clerical property was a step in the policy pursued throughout Charles's reign of bringing under state control ecclesiastical provisions, wealth and jurisdiction. In theory the dukes of Burgundy fixed their charge for amortising clerical property from liability to the *aide* at three times the annual value of such property; but until 1474 their mortmain ordinances, which varied from one territory to another, were not strictly enforced, and after 1477 few ecclesiastics complied with the law. In April 1515 an addition to the *Blijde Inkomst* forbade clergy outside Brabant from acquiring property inside the duchy without licence; but in May 1515 a census was ordered of all property acquired by the Church in Flanders during the last forty years, in other words since the mortmain ordinance of Charles the Bold (10 July 1474). This, and the letters sent in December 1515 to the prince's lieutenants in various provinces for the enforcement of amortisation, provoked opposition not only from the clergy, but from burghers who controlled pious foundations. The efforts of its opponents to appeal to Rome were treated by the government as tantamount to treason; but the standing of Charles with Leo X denied them much support from that quarter, and an edict of 19 October 1520 proceeded a stage further by forbidding within Brabant the conveyance of property to ecclesiastics save under licence.

His credit at Rome also enabled Charles to recover control over Utrecht in the Burgundian tradition of treating territorial bishoprics as appanages for the bastards of the dynasty. In 1516 bishop Frederick of Baden, whose neutral attitude toward the duke of Guelders was a matter of concern at Brussels, was induced to resign in favour of the admiral, the bastard Philip of Burgundy, who became bishop of Utrecht in March 1517. In Rome the affair was conducted at the highest level, to which regional parties, such as the estates of Utrecht or even the duke of Guelders, could not aspire. Pending the secularisation of the temporalities of Utrecht after his death in 1524, Philip could be relied upon to pay regard to the interests of the dynasty in the dangerous situation on the north-eastern side of the Netherlands.

In May 1515 George of Saxony sold to Charles his rights over Friesland for a fraction of the amount in respect of which Philip *le Beau* had pledged them to his father, Albert of Saxony. The sons of Albert and their competitor, Edzard Cirksena, count of East Friesland, failed to erect a territorial lordship over Friesland, because neither side could come to terms with Groningen. This town, on which all Friesland was said to depend, if not powerful enough to subjugate the province, could prevent any one else doing so except on terms acceptable to Groningen. Charles of Egmond readily agreed to its terms, and in October 1514 Groningen accepted him and soon after put itself under the protection of France. Charles of Habsburg and Charles of Egmond were brought into a direct clash for yet another land.

True to the tradition of playing the junior IJsselstein branch against the senior line of Guelders, Floris van Egmond, who succeeded his uncle as *stadhouder* of Holland in 1515, was appointed *stadhouder* also in Friesland for Charles of Habsburg. The fortunes of war fluctuated in Friesland through 1516 and 1517; but in the summer of 1517 a Frisian fleet swept the shipping of Holland from the Zuider Zee, and a horde of mercenaries landed in the service of Guelders at Medemblik, ravaging Holland southwards to Asperen. The estates had agreed in the autumn of 1516 to finance four *bandes d'ordonnance*; but inadequate financial and military preparation rendered them of little immediate service. The return to the military reforms of Charles the Bold was, however, a wholesome break with the dependence on mercenaries for which Maximilian was mainly responsible; and the revived *bandes d'ordonnance* mopped up the plundering bands of mercenaries in the lower Rhine during Charles's absence in Spain, and enabled him on his return in 1521 to conquer Tournai, which Henry VIII retroceded to Francis I in February 1519. For the time the duke of Guelders, who was running short of money, was more effectively contained by a treaty concluded at Ghent in June 1517 whereby Edzard Cirksena, count of East Friesland, became the client of the Habsburgs.

The estates held at Ghent in June-July 1517 showed what a strong position Charles had attained before he sailed to Spain from Flushing on 8 September 1517. The Pensioner of Ghent, whose predecessors were spokesmen of anti-monarchic opinion, now led the protests of devotion; and, amidst tears at his departure, the estates pressed on him an *aide*. In return political plans for the government during his absence were communicated to them. The council formed on 23 July 1517 preserved the nominal headship of the emperor. To Margaret of Austria was accorded ceremonial pre-eminence, but no specific authority over the council. In reality, however, she was freer than in 1507 or even after 1509, for, by declining to appoint a lieutenant, Charles left her a clear field, and the stamp for printing his name on official papers was entrusted to Margaret's keeping. Not until 1 and 16 July 1519, shortly after Charles's elevation to the empire, did he confer on her the powers of a regent.

During Charles's absence, Margaret achieved a promising (though impermanent) solution of relations with Liège. Two distinct problems existed, the status of the Pays de Liège within the Netherlands and the position of the bishop Érard de la Marck and his family between the Habsburg and Valois Powers. Since 1506 Érard had revealed himself as both an adroit diplomat and an able ruler, without whom Liège would scarcely have survived as a prince-bishopric. Charles's good standing at Rome facilitated his curtailment of the bishop's ecclesiastical jurisdiction in Brabant (July 1515), but in Girolamo Aleandro the bishop had a skilful intermediary with the Holy See; so that, on Charles's return from Spain in 1520, Aleandro and eventually Érard recovered a wide jurisdiction over the Low Countries for the repression of heresy. The estates of the Pays de Liège suspected any move toward closer ties with the rest of the Netherlands, clinging to neutrality as the guarantee of their regional independence. Already in January 1517 Charles, attempting to drive a wedge between the *Liégeois* and their bishop, summoned them to clarify their position as between Francis I and himself; but for a time it was easier for Habsburg to come to terms with La Marck, a deal between a major and a minor family.

Two treaties, one public, the other private, were agreed to at St Trond on 27 April 1518; the former was subject to ratification by the estates of Liège, the latter concerned the relations of Habsburg and La Marck. At the price of a pension and by dangling before his eyes preferment within Charles's patronage, Érard was induced to undertake not to dispose of his bishopric to any successor other than his nephew, and to pledge the La Marck family to serve Charles *envers et contre tous*. The estates of Liège were only brought to accept the public treaty on 14 November 1518, which although it did something to clear up confusions over jurisdiction to the advancement of commerce between Brabant and Liège, violated their ideas of neutrality by providing for military aid to the Brussels government. The La Marck family disregarded the secret treaty in 1521 when Charles fought his first campaign against Francis I; and subsequent trends delayed the incorporation of Liège into the Netherlands until the nineteenth century.

The death of Maximilian (12 January 1519) precipitated an imperial election, the Netherlands constituting the surety on which the Fuggers bought the Empire from the electors for Charles on 28 June 1519. The provinces, indifferent to the election of Max in 1486, were emotionally stirred at the elevation of his grandson in 1519, and the estates of Brabant anticipated with an *aide* the costs of his coronation.

Charles disembarked from Spain on 1 June 1520 at Flushing; and on his way to be crowned at Aachen told the estates that '*son cœur avait toujours été par deça*'. His will of 1522 is that of a Burgundian, directing that if Dijon was not reconquered at his death, he should be buried beside his grandmother in Bruges; in 1524 he paid 124 *livres* to the son of Georges Chastellain for a complete manuscript of his father's chronicle of Valois dukes. The provinces also beheld in him the bond of their unity; and when the question arose of a Habsburg family partition to provide lands for Charles's brother Ferdinand, public opinion, voiced by the estates of Brabant, resisted any dismemberment of the Low Countries, and helped to bring about Ferdinand's renunciation of claims upon them in return for his obtaining the Austrian lands.

CHAPTER IX

INTERNATIONAL RELATIONS IN THE WEST: DIPLOMACY AND WAR

A T the end of the fifteenth century the normal state among Christians was assumed to be peace, tempered by a readiness to repel the infidel. In practice nothing was more likely than war among Christians and, in order to leave them free to pursue it, overtures of peace to the Turk.

Chivalric writers still taught that war could be glorious, the scientific approach of Italian theorists lost sight of its horrors in deep interest, and both points of view admired the successful captain—one for his bravery, his *prouesse*, the other for the mark on events of his genius and energy, his *virtù*. The first thought war legitimate because it was noble, the other because force was an obvious and legitimate branch of negotiation.

The Church also, by supporting the institutions of chivalry and the knightly orders, had blessed weapons that were not always to be used against the oppressor or the infidel, and by admitting that it was permissible to wage a just war, she had in effect sanctioned all wars. The criteria of a just war, it was generally agreed, were that it should only be waged on the authority of a superior, for a just cause and with righteous intent, and the satisfaction of these conditions was not hard save to the most recalcitrant conscience. The Church, too, needed war to support her authority and punish those who defied it. And she was partly responsible for the view that in great causes war was a divine judgment, an extension of the judicial duel, where two armies instead of two rival champions fought to decide who was in the right. The condemnation of war was hampered, moreover, by the difficulty of distinguishing it from feud, which was tacitly admitted to represent a legitimate way of obtaining justice, as between either individual corporations, or countries. And the same lawyers who treated war and reprisal as one and the same thing added the theological defence that war was God's means of resolving discord into peace and harmony. Johannes de Legnano, who wrote in 1360 the first treatise to deal exclusively with the legal aspects of war, the *Tractatus de Bello, de Represaliis et de Duello*, stressed the naturalness of war, the necessary lance for humanity's imposthumes. The notion that the Prince of Peace blessed arms that were truly borne persisted through the increasingly scientific warfare of the early sixteenth century and caused guns to be named after the apostles, swords and halberds to be engraved with scenes from the passion and generals to kiss the earth before launching an attack in the name of their patron saints. In the best cause of all, war against the invading infidel, the armies and navies of countries which in this period were directly threatened by the Turks, Venice, Albania, Hungary, Wallachia and Moldavia, were continuously in action or at best in partial mobilisation during snatches of uneasy peace, and it was only in 1502 that the armies of Spain finally expelled the Moors from Granada. The spectacle of so much legitimate war blunted the sense of horror for war as a whole.

Every country, besides, had been shaped geographically by war and socially in part for war; the momentum did not easily run down. The nobility had been educated for war and in peace was at a loss. Land was no longer so profitable and the tourney was no adequate compensation for actual combat. For financial and emotional reasons the knight longed for war and foreign adventure, and the wars of Italy were encouraged and prolonged by a nobility whose functions at court had been taken over by professional administrators and whose estates were often incapable of supporting a large family. For the non-mercantile classes war offered the main chance of getting rich quickly, by loot and ransom. And once war had started, the same motives led to its continuing. 'What shall we do,' the French Marshal Monluc imagined a captain asking, 'What shall we do if we do not lay up money, and clip the soldiers' pay? When war is at an end, we must go to the hospital, for neither the king nor anyone else will regard us, and we are poor of ourselves.'[1]

In Spain the constant warfare against the Moors, the barren nature of much of the country and the fact that most trade and industry were in non-Christian hands, left a gentle class even more dependent on military adventure than the French, and the Spaniards were looked upon by contemporaries as a warlike people who thought honour reposed largely in the pursuit of arms. Similarly in Germany, especially in the south and west where industry and trade were ceasing to produce enough to cover imports of foodstuffs for a rapidly growing population, there were numerous nobles from small patrimonies, ridiculed in Italy for their exclusively military education, who were eager for war. Switzerland, who possessed the finest troops available and whose public gatherings were mainly concerned with drills and parades, depended on war to provide a market for almost her sole export—infantrymen.

No appeal to preserve the *status quo* during the second half of the fifteenth century would have been listened to, or have meant very much to countries like France and the Spanish kingdoms, for instance, whose frontiers were liable to wide fluctuations according to the result of a battle or siege or the falling in of a fief, or to those eastern countries whose boundaries were constantly shifting before the varying pressures of the Turkish advance. The period had seen the collapse of the semi-

[1] *The Commentaries of Messire Blaize de Montluc*, trans. Charles Cotton (London, 1674), p. 4.

independent empire of Charles of Burgundy, which stretched from the North Sea to the latitude of Lake Léman, Roussillon and Cerdagne pass to Spain, and the effective power of France advanced to the Mediterranean. In a Europe intricately meshed with feudal obligations and the counter-claims arising from centuries of dynastic marriages, the *status quo* was always liable to be altered by a fortunate demise or the disinterment of an ancient claim now judged ripe for enforcing. Nationalities were still vague, land was valued for the pleasures and profits of possession, not for the language spoken on it. Nations were not to be satisfied even with natural frontiers when such a conception did not yet exist.

A monarch's hunger for land, which he shared with other landowners, did not depend on the consent of his country before it could be gratified. 'Everyone knows', wrote Honoré Bonet at the end of the fourteenth century, 'that in the matter of deciding on war, of declaring it, or of undertaking it, poor men are not concerned at all.'[1] It was no less true a hundred years later, when royal hands had been still further strengthened by the grant of permanent taxes to meet grave emergencies. Foreign policy depended in no country on the estates, and where there was a really strong executive, as in France, they counted for little even where taxes were concerned; at no point was the course of the Italian wars seriously affected by the action of the belligerents' assemblies. Armies, too, were but a small fraction of the population and were composed largely of men either whose interests were identical with the ruler's, or who were hired by him. No case had to be laid before a country to woo it to arms, and as increasing reliance was placed in professional soldiery the bulk of the population was ignored. War was waged at the discretion of the king.

No economic compulsion drove the Powers into the Italian wars. Their initiator, France, was self-supporting. Her wine and grain made her independent of imported foodstuffs, nor was she dependent on imported raw materials, though she bought some metal for cannon. Her exports, wine, salt and grain, found ready markets and required no forcing. Her peasantry was so prosperous that they had no wish to leave their land and go soldiering. War for France was a luxury. Similarly the intervention of Spain was only incidentally to guard Sicily and the ships that brought grain to the Catholic kings. Maximilian did not join the Holy League of 1495 because his revenues were threatened by French successes. Henry VIII was not forced to join the Holy League of 1511 and invade Guienne to protect English commercial interests: like Charles, he was making a speculative grasp at certain luxuries. More imagined himself as inter-vening in the Council of the king of France, urging them 'to turn over the leaf, and learn a new lesson, saying that my counsell is not to meddle with Italy but to tarry still at home, and that the kingdom of France alone is almost greater than that it may well be governed of one man, so that

[1] *L'Arbre des Batailles*, ed. G. W. Coopland (Liverpool U.P., 1949), question 48.

the king should not need to study how to get more'. But this is a passage from *Utopia*.

The Powers of the west were ready to expand. England and France had recovered from the Hundred Years War, though the subsequent civil war left the former less immediately ready for an aggressive foreign policy than France, where the Crown had been strengthened by the acquisition of Guienne (1453), Burgundy (1477), Provence (1481), and Brittany (1491). By 1492 Spain was freed from internal commitments. And the tendency to expand was not delayed by any concept of national unification nor directed by one of natural frontiers. States looked beyond their borders as soon as the minimum internal order needed to support a war economy was gained. And no desire to make economic and national frontiers coincide determined the direction conquest should take, no desire to reach the natural lines of a mountain range or a river, nor to make frontiers correspond to language or custom. The obvious route for French expansion was north-east, across the plain to the Netherlands, to Brussels and Antwerp, so easily reached from Paris, and so rich. Instead, Charles VIII drove south, over the Alps and down the thin Italian peninsula to Naples, rich only in grain which France did not need, and where communications could only be ensured by a sea power she did not possess. Both the economic and political interests of the greater part of Spain lay more to the west in Portugal and the New World than in the Mediterranean, in spite of Aragonese expansion there, but even before there was any dynastic need to link Spain with Austria, she committed herself to being involved for three centuries in Italy. It is significant that the Nation States which have given their name to a popular view of this period fought their wars with the aid of foreign mercenaries, and that a queen of France proposed in 1501 to hand over the great duchies of Brittany and Burgundy in return for the betrothal of Charles of Habsburg to her daughter. National feeling and a national foreign policy were the consequence and not the cause of an age of dynastic wars. Again, treaties were not insuperable barriers to aggression. They were not broken lightly, it is true, for they were solemnised with the utmost gravity, and a breach of their letter involved the grave spiritual crime of perjury and brought dishonour as well as the more impersonal penalties of excommunication and interdict. It was necessary to find some legal flaw in the wording, or in the intention, of a treaty. It was necessary to prepare men's minds for the breach by an assiduous propaganda, using pulpit, university, street pageant, broadsheet, medal and song. Such a breach was made easier by uncertainty as to whether the successors to the original signatories of a treaty were themselves bound to it. More, again, put the matter clearly.

The more and holier ceremonies the league is built up with, the sooner it is broken by some cavillation found in the words, which many times of purpose be so craftily put in, and placed, that the bands can never be so sure nor so strong, but they will find some hole open to creep out at.... The which crafty dealing... if they should know it to be practised among private men in their bargains and contracts, they would incontinent cry out at it with an open mouth, and a sour countenance, as an offense most detestable, and worthy to be punished with a shameful death.

This implication of hypocrisy must not be taken too literally, however. Treaties could be broken by means of legal reinterpretation and papal approval, with no sense that personal convenience had been obtained illegitimately.

Apart from a minimum of internal stability, the prerequisites of war were money—of which the Powers, apart from the empire, had enough—and troops. Here there was a difficulty. The victories of the Swiss over the heavy Burgundian cavalry at Grandson and Morat (1476) had established heavy infantry as the decisive tactical factor in warfare. But this was true only of men trained on the Swiss model. Until the heavy infantry of Germany and Spain copied their tactics early in the sixteenth century, the Swiss monopoly was unchallenged. And it was consciously exploited. The free movement of mercenaries was checked: they were too valuable an export to be left unregulated by the State. And Switzerland was not simply a reservoir of troops, but a country with political and commercial aspirations of its own. Thus Louis XII lost Bellinzona to them in 1503 because he would not listen to their request for commercial liberties in the Milanese. His continued deafness to their demands finally cost him their alliance in 1509, and their troops came to be at the disposal of his enemies. The Confederation, in fact, in spite of its peculiar nature, and the looseness of the ties binding the cantons, had to be treated as an ally, not a contractor. This is not to say that rejection by the diet was final. Its own contracts were filled by its choice of the best troops, but many were left who could be hired, or, more accurately, bribed, independently. Thus in 1499, when Lodovico Sforza had been supplied officially with 10,000 troops to fight the French, Louis unofficially obtained 20,000 to fight Lodovico. On the whole, no Power had to give up its plans for war owing to the attitude of one of the *ad hoc* diets which regulated the military policy of the Confederation.

Confronting the Powers thus ready for war and able to wage it, there was the standing temptation of Italy, rich, divided, still with the glamour of the capital of the present spiritual and of the ancient secular world, linked already by feudal and family ties with Spain, the Empire and France.

To deal with these tensions, the latent impetus to war, the old international organs of arbitration were powerless. The Empire, it is true, had not lost all the prestige its propagandists had won for it. It was the highest secular dignity, the Emperor alone could create kings, he alone was addressed as Majesty. Charles VIII thirsted for an imperial title, and entered Naples holding the orb of the emperors of the east, accompanied by rumours of his coveting that of the west. But the Emperor was no longer invoked as an arbiter between nations. His decisions had seemed increasingly shaped to stress his own authority.

It was the same with the Papacy. Conservative men still looked to it to keep the secular rulers from one another's throats. 'It is the proper function of the Roman Pontiff, of the Cardinals, of Bishops, and of Abbots', wrote Erasmus in 1514, 'to compose the quarrels of Christian princes.' But though its universal sovereignty was not altogether contested, though Peter's Pence were still widely paid, though papal legates had acted frequently as mediators in the last phase of the Hundred Years War, its role as international arbiter was a declining one. Treaties might still be signed with an oath, inviting spiritual penalties, and the pope alone could dispense from their terms; but increasingly clauses were inserted that bound the parties not to apply for dispensation, or emphasised that the pope was acting not *ex officio* but as a private person. The control of the Papacy over warfare was still more definitely at an end. The prohibition of the second Lateran Council of 1139 against making slaves of Christian prisoners, confirming the Truces of God and forbidding trade in war materials with the infidel—all these measures were dead. Outside Italy papal censures were ignored though they troubled many individual consciences. The special nature of the spiritual power no longer seriously affected either preparations for war or the way in which it was waged.

The crucial test of the pope's influence over the warlike states was when he spoke as the head of Christendom in calling for unity against the Turk. The desirability of this unity was repeatedly granted by the Powers. 'It is the primary duty of Christian Powers to propagate the faith of Christ and to exterminate the enemies of the Christian name' urged the Treaty of London (1518) between Francis I and Henry VIII, and Francis, forced by lack of sea power to ally with the Turk in 1535, apologised for this action to the pope. The danger, moreover, was clear enough.

In 1456 the Turks had besieged Belgrade, in 1480 occupied Otranto, in 1521 they invaded Hungary and took Belgrade by storm. The countries who were most nearly threatened begged loudly for help. In 1499 and again in 1517 the Papacy called a crusade. Taxes were levied, consciences were stirred. When Ferdinand and Louis XII met at Savona in 1507 it was believed that it was to discuss the danger from the Turks. What in fact they were discussing was the partition of Italy. And on the fall of Aleppo, two years before the Treaty of London, Henry VIII spoke his mind to the Venetian ambassador who had begged his aid.

Domine Orator! You are sage, and of your prudence may comprehend that no general expedition against the Turks will ever be effected so long as such treachery prevails amongst the Christian powers, that their sole thought is to destroy one another.[1]

[1] *Four Years at the Court of Henry VIII. Despatches written by the Venetian Ambassador, Sebastian Giustinian*, ed. R. Brown (London, 1854), vol. II, p. 57.

And alongside cries for unity against the Turks active political traffic with the Turk continued on the part of Powers who feared them, or wished their support as allies against their fellow Christians—an example that had been already set by the rulers of the Morea. From 1490 to 1494 the Papacy received an annual payment from the Sultan Bāyezīd for keeping Jem, his brother and potential rival, a prisoner. This action of the pope's enabled the Turk to take a firmer line in his dealings with Christians in the Balkans, and with Venice. The sultan's tolerance of western merchants —by 1507 there were the agents of some sixty or more Florentine firms in Constantinople—made it difficult for the Italian states to look on him with proper horror. He was instead involved as an ally, Milan, Ferrara, Mantua and Florence combining in 1497 to bribe the Turks to help them in an attack on Venice. Though there was still a sentiment of the unity of Christendom as against the Turk, it is not surprising that the Papacy was unable to use it to turn the Powers from their wars of personal gain.

The common preoccupation was not with the Turk but with Italy, and it led to deepened political rivalry, not to unity, but though concentration for a long period on a common problem helped to define national antagonisms, at the same time it forced states to take more notice of one another; the tendency to expand led to increasing diplomatic exchanges, the common interest in Italy led to increased mutual watchfulness. A virtue of historians today is that they stress continuity; a foible, that they are tempted to over-stress it. In the history of diplomacy a definite change occurs in this period. The more swiftly armies could be mobilised, the better organised had the information services of the threatened states to be; as foreign policy became more complicated, more comprehensive, more subject to sudden change, each country, especially the weak, needed to be kept in touch with the intentions of the others. This could only be done by keeping permanent representatives at their courts. The growth of permanent embassies was also fostered by the preference for settling differences through diplomatic channels rather than by international arbitration; the Powers were more liable to get their own way. Besides, there was flattery implied in the presence of an ambassador as it so often reflected the fear of the weak for the strong. As the tempo of international relations quickened, the total time spent in negotiation grew. New alignments called for fevered diplomatic activity. Though there were a few lasting themes—English use of the Flemish alliance to counter French use of Scotland; Spain's reliance on England when plotting against France; English dependence on the Empire when threatened by France; Maximilian's longing for the Veneto—it was largely a period of flux. An alliance did not mean security, or that negotiations with other Powers could safely be dropped, as Henry VIII found in 1514 and 1517, when his allies were secretly preparing to change sides. There was urgent need for constant bargaining, information and vigilance.

The old casual diplomacy, in fact, no longer sufficed. The embassies which previously had accompanied the gift of a knightly Order, of the *rose d'or* or the *épée de Noël*, or had handled a marriage contract, a declaration of war or a truce, had been appointed for the occasion only and, on its completion, had returned and dispersed. There had been little continuity in diplomatic relations. Monarchs tried to see that their interests abroad were cared for by 'retaining' prominent officials at foreign courts by bribes. Louis XI paid such fees to the Chancellor of England as well as to the Master of the Rolls and the High Chamberlain, and was said to be more powerful in Germany than Maximilian himself. But such pensioners were only faithful when it suited them. Nor was it common for monarchs to be their own diplomats. Though interviews between sovereigns were often planned, they were seldom carried out. The assassination of John the Fearless of Burgundy on the bridge of Montereau in 1419 had provided a dismal precedent. When Louis XI met Edward IV in 1475 a wooden lattice was placed across a bridge of boats over the Somme, as close-set as the bars of a lion's cage, and through these the two kings embraced. The suspicion and precaution involved by these meetings robbed them of intimacy and frankness, and when meetings were arranged, as between Ferdinand and Louis XII at Savona in 1507, and Henry VIII and Francis I in 1520, they merely complemented the labours of standing diplomats and were no substitute for them.

For weak states to have permanent representatives abroad was the condition of their retaining alliances in which they were the dispensable partners. Venice owed her inclusion in treaties that could well have done without her to the pertinacious nursing of her interests by her ambassadors. Lodovico Sforza owed much to the skill of his permanent ambassador in France, the count of Belgioioso, who won round several of Charles's entourage to the Italian expedition. So urgent was the states' desire to be represented at a potentially dangerous court that Louis XII was nearly stifled by their competing importunities; all wished to see him at least once a day. They went hunting with him, feasted with him, in his absence paid court to his queen and his ministers; they even bribed his servants to report what he said while eating and drinking or going to bed. Or an exchange of ambassadors might serve to cement an alliance, and further understanding, between two powerful but suspicious rulers, especially if their agreement, like that between Henry VIII and Charles V in 1520, was a secret one.

One of the objects of standing diplomacy was to provide a news service to guide governments in determining their foreign policy. A preparation had been made for this in the early days of occasional diplomacy when Venice, by a decree of 1288, required her ambassadors to submit a report on all things interesting to the State within fifteen days of their return. From the mid-thirteenth century, too, she had had, in her commercial agents in the Levant, an example of the usefulness of regular reports. The *bailo* at Constantinople, the consul of Alexandria and the vice-consuls at Chios, Tunis and Naples, insensibly came to be concerned with politics as well as with trade and the legal position of Venetians abroad; they were expected to send regular political information whether it directly concerned the state of the market or not.

The tension which led to the proliferation of purely diplomatic standing representatives did not come till the second half of the fifteenth century, but there were some isolated examples which showed an appreciation of the virtues of continuous personal contact between states. Luigi Gonzaga of Mantua had a resident agent with the Emperor Lewis before 1341. In 1375 Milan and Mantua exchanged ambassadors to further their co-operation against the Scaligers of Verona. For more than seven years Filippo Maria Visconti kept a representative at the court of the king of the Romans, and for most of this period Sigismund was represented in Milan. Here too, the aim was to consolidate and keep alert an alliance.

The same aim prompted Francesco Sforza, aspirant to the duchy of Milan, to send his secretary Nicodemo da Pontremoli in 1446 to reside at Florence with his ally Cosimo de' Medici. He took part in negotiating the league of Milan, Florence and France, which, after considerable fighting, secured Sforza from Venice by the Peace of Lodi in 1454. This peace was followed by a period of some forty years in which the alignment of the five principal Italian states, Naples, the Papacy, Venice, Florence and Milan, was so nicely adjusted, and the response to any hint of expansion so immediate and regular (Florence, Naples, Milan checking Venice) that it has been seen as exemplifying the principle of balance in foreign policy—a phrase already used before the end of the century. The watchfulness and co-operation this required led to a rapid extension of standing diplomacy. By 1458 each of the four states had representatives at each other's courts. This development was confirmed by the position of Rome. There were precedents for retaining agents at the curia, for the importance of the Papacy as an ally, and the standing of the city as a news exchange, drew increasing numbers of ambassadors. From the dispatch of Marcolino Barbavara from Milan in 1445 numbers grew so fast that Pius II tried vainly to reduce them by threatening to degrade any who stayed longer than six months to the status of proctor, with a consequent loss of privileges. And as the transalpine states grew in power, and as they forced themselves increasingly on the notice of the Italian states, the practice of standing diplomacy spread to the north. When the shadow of aggression began to glide over Italy as France rose to her full height of warlike preparation, the states of Italy tried to repel or guide this menace by sending agents to reside there. From 1463 to 1475 there was a Milanese ambassador in France. Venice was represented in Burgundy from 1471 and, on the collapse of Burgundy, in France from 1485. When hostilities were near, or had actually begun, the process grew still further. Even the Papacy weakened, and sent two agents in 1495 to reside at Maximilian's court. Venice sent representatives to Spain and the Empire in 1495 and to England in 1496. Milan had standing agents in Spain from 1490, in England from about the same time, with Maximilian from 1494, and Belgioioso was with Charles VIII from 1493. Naples sent ambassadors to England in 1490, to Spain and the emperor in 1494. The practice extended still further as, forced into close and continual contact by their common preoccupation with Italy, the northern Powers came to maintain standing ambassadors at one another's courts. From 1495 Spain kept a representative in London. Louis XII was not only represented at Rome and Venice, but with the archduke, with Margaret of Austria and in Spain. By 1504 the attitude of the Papacy had changed from criticism to acceptance, and Julius II's master of ceremonies issued an order of precedence of Christian kings and dukes and their representatives.

This does not mean that by 1504, or even a generation later, standing diplomacy was the rule. Only the countries interested in Italy used it regularly. Scotland, Portugal, Poland, Scandinavia, Hungary and the German princes relied on the old occasional diplomacy, and even among the others the dispatch of a resident ambassador did not mean that the post would be maintained once it ceased to be profitable. The old reliance on spies had, after all been fairly effective. Henry VII was famous for the precision of his continental information, and this nearly all came from unofficial agents. A man like Thomas Spinelly, a Florentine in the pay of the English Crown from 1509, was not only a most valuable source of news, thanks to his access to information from the great merchant news centres, Antwerp, Bruges and Lyons, but could be used to handle matters that required secrecy. To bring these agents into the open, and to give them the title of ambassador, was not necessarily to increase their usefulness. But agents were eager to gain the prestige of official rank, and as the pressure of foreign relations increased, it became even more necessary to add to the class of secret agents men who were more responsible, and who could be used for open negotiation. Even France, who had previously been content with fairly steady representation at Rome, placed others at Venice from 1517, in Switzerland and Portugal from 1522, England from 1525 and the Empire from 1526. Special embassies were still used in conjunction with a permanent diplomacy. The resident ambassadors were concerned largely with investigation and report; neither their rank, as a rule, nor their credentials qualified them to negotiate matters of special importance. To deal with these, an ambassador of more standing was sent, and the resident remained in a subordinate position until he had gone.

Such ambassadors still travelled opulently on occasion, with an elaborate train comprising ecclesiastics, guards of honour, and a numerous secretariat of lawyers and scribes. The resident, though certain formalities were observed in the presentation of his credentials, lived humbly, sometimes with a colleague of equal or secretarial status, but often alone. Less officially than either of these classes of ambassador, important persons still undertook diplomatic missions, as did Beatrice d'Este, wife of Lodovico Sforza, when she went to Venice in 1493 to protest Milan's friendship. Nor was the herald without a place in the new diplomacy. Together with the *roi d'armes* he was especially *persona grata* at suspicious or hostile courts who accepted him for the chivalric prestige and the traditional immunity of his office. Heralds were not simply used as negotiators between armies in the field as at Fornovo or to bear defiance and declaration of war such as Montjoye took to Venice in 1509, but as ambassadors. Montjoye, sovereign king of arms of France, was indeed sent to many of the European courts and in 1500 to interview Bajazet in Adrianople, though in each case he came to demand or announce rather than to bluff or cajole.

And beside these official negotiations moved a shadow diplomacy of secret agents, spies and informers. Merchants and bankers were used particularly by the Italians, and the Medici were often better informed by their branch at Lyons, with its contacts at the court, than by their ambassadors. Venice favoured doctors, who were likely to be near monarchs at their least guarded moments. Charles V used members of religious orders as spies, and under Francis I a staff of secret agents was built up which comprised noblemen and women as well as obscure clerics and adventurers. Ambassadors did their best to gain informers at the courts to which they were accredited. Sebastiano Giustiniani gained so much information from the Papal Nuncio in England, Francesco Chieregato, whom he always referred to in his dispatches as 'the friend', that he begged the signory to offer him some preferment—cautioning that they should do this in cipher, lest the plot be discovered.

The large bulk of diplomatic writings show how closely governments were kept in touch with events abroad by their residents. Omitting formal documents like safe conducts and letters of credence, they fall into three classes: instructions, dispatches and reports. The first outline the purpose of the mission, tell the ambassador how to get to his destination, whom to contact there, and in what terms to put his government's case. As these instructions were sometimes shown on arrival as a proof of good will, the style tended to be formal. But ambassadors often carried secret instructions as well, guarded closely and shown only to some trusted individual, and these were often couched in vigorous and striking terms, suggesting the exact arguments to be employed.

From his arrival the ambassador was to send back regular accounts of his activities, and since information was one of the main profits of an embassy, he was expected to write as often as possible. Machiavelli sent back forty-nine dispatches in fifty days on his first legation at Rome, and though this is exceptional at least one a week was looked for, even from residents of long standing. Conversations with important persons were to be reported verbatim, together with every fact or rumour that could conceivably be of interest. The ambassador's impressions were valued too, his pen-portraits being the only way of enabling governments to imagine the men with whom they were dealing, the use of official portraits being limited. In a letter of advice to a novice ambassador to Spain, his young friend Rafaello Girolami, Machiavelli indicated the scope of the information required. He was first to send news of his arrival and an account of his interview with the king. Then he was to observe and report on everything that concerned the king and his country: whether Charles (the letter was written in 1522) was resolute or the tool of others; miserly or liberal; warlike or peaceful. Was a thirst for glory his dominant passion, or some other? Was he popular? Did he prefer Spain to the Netherlands? Who were the men who influenced him; what were their aims; were they open to corruption? What was the feeling towards Charles of the country at large?—all these and many other particulars, if well grounded and reported, would bring honour to an ambassador. Governments relied on their residents, moreover, for news about neighbouring states where they were not represented. When relations between Venice and England were broken, the Venetian resident in France had to send English news as well; when there was no agent in Turin, Venice received information about Savoy through Milan.

On his return a resident ambassador made a report, sometimes, especially in Italy, in writing. This was the invariable rule in Venice where the reading of a report by an ambassador in a full meeting of the senate was an important occasion. As the usual duration of an embassy was from two to three years, the practice meant that the senate was regularly informed as to the political, economic and social position of each country with whom it had dealings. The reports were expected to be full, the ceremony of presenting them was never scamped, and the reputation of envoys was considerably affected by their delivery.

In writings that passed between governments and their representatives, the vernacular was increasingly used from the beginning of the second quarter of the fifteenth century. By the end of the century, this was true even of the reports of papal nuncios. And foreign languages were increasingly learned by diplomats and statesmen. English and Italian ambassadors in France both commonly spoke French, and so did the Swiss. Princes showed their favour by receiving ambassadors in their own language, even if it were no more than a set speech learned for the occasion. French, owing to the diplomatic activity of Louis XI and his successors, and to its being the language of the German court under Maximilian, was beginning to insinuate itself as a second diplomatic language, although Latin was undergoing revival at the same time. Latin was used for international documents like treaties and safe conducts; it was used, *faute de mieux*, for international bargaining, and it was also used to imply a compliment—but whereas the vernacular was used to indulge the weaker party, Latin was used to flatter the stronger; it was also common to present a formal address in Latin, then to proceed in the vernacular. Though Latin, thanks to humanist stimulus, was more genuinely an international language than it had been for centuries of vernacular debasement and local pronunciation, its utility, in fact, no longer equalled its prestige.

In correspondence, of course, it suffered from the very qualities that commended it when spoken, for here privacy, not universal comprehension, was needed, and the uncertainty of posts and of diplomatic immunity led to the use of cipher to supplement the vernacular. Books were written on the subject. The *Polygraphiæ libri sex* of Abbot Johannes Trithemius was dedicated to Maximilian I. Usually only crucial passages were ciphered, but some chanceries, particularly that of Spain, favoured dispatches that were written entirely in code. Some of these were extremely complicated and difficult to break; they were likely to be tedious to compose (for example *enviando*, 'sending', was by one Spanish method encoded as 'DCCCCLXVIII *le* No γ malus 3 ') and impossible to decipher. The Spanish chancery found it necessary to simplify its codes in 1504.

The actual utility of dispatches, however frequently, fully and secretly written, depended on the posts, and these were still uncertain. There were private services, notably that run by the Tassis family in northern and central Europe; in France and Italy there were official postal services, but though the cheapest medium, they offered the least security. And special couriers were so expensive that there was a temptation to delay dispatches until a bundle was accumulated, thus destroying much of the value of the earlier ones. Once a post, a courier or a travelling merchant or friendly diplomat had been found, communication between France, Italy, and Germany was not unreasonably slow. Typical speeds were: Rome–Paris, twelve days; Rome–Venice, two to three days; Turin–Venice, six to seven days. Where a sea crossing was involved, times were less certain. Twenty to thirty days from Venice to London was usual and though a herald crossed from Seville to Venice in 1499 in fifteen days, it took thirty for the news of Isabella's death in 1504 to come to Rome.

Yet for all this activity, the host of couriers, the hundreds of dispatches, the resident ambassador was still far from being accepted as a normal, permanent element in European diplomacy. Writers of works *de legationibus* tended to ignore or minimise the part he played. His often obscure birth—it was some time before the education of gentlemen prepared enough of them for the duties of a resident—counted against him. Though diplomatic immunity was a long-standing principle of civil and canon law, and there had been few instances of the molestation of occasional ambassadors, the resident was not so safe. His social position did not protect him to the same extent, and because of his ceaseless search for information he tended to be looked on as a dubiously licensed spy. Wolsey opened French and Venetian dispatches and seized the papers and ciphers of the nuncio Chieregato, and Venetian agents in Constantinople were treated with open hostility on occasion; their lodgings were watched, they were insulted by the people and even imprisoned and tortured.

The contrast was most pointed in the chronic impoverishment of the average resident. Money was lavished on the special ambassador—magistrate, knight or bishop—to enable him to impress the prince he was visiting, but the greatest kings did not feel their reputation suffered if their resident—as was the case with Ferdinand's ambassador at London, de Puebla—lived in a miserable and disreputable squalor. Machiavelli's dispatches from France are full of complaints about the inconvenience of being forced to follow an itinerant king without having money for horses, to frequent a court while being unable to afford clean clothes and to write frequent dispatches without money for couriers.

The same indifference to their residents abroad was shown by the long periods during which governments sent no instructions, though letters expressing good will to the regime and containing news were essential to a diplomat as they were the means of his gaining good will and news himself. And to this silence was added the indignity that the residents' own dispatches were not always believed; Venice, for instance, was kept from enjoying all the benefits of her own diplomats by suspecting them of becoming corrupted by life abroad.

It was to be long before the gap between the status of standing and special ambassadors narrowed. Meanwhile the lot of the resident was felt to be unduly hard when neglect and distrust at home were added to the dangers of travel and the fatigues of court attendance abroad. Constant were the requests to be relieved, and severe measures had to be taken against newly appointed ambassadors who refused to go. The plea for exemption of Zachario Contarini, elected Venetian ambassador to Hungary in 1500, is a reminder that the changed diplomacy of the Italian wars still took place under familiar conditions. His request was only granted on the score that he had a sick wife and ten children, that he had been on ten previous embassies, three of them across the Alps, that in Germany the king of the Romans had lodged him in a house where there was a man dead of the plague, and that his father and two other relatives had died from the rigours involved in being an ambassador.

The tendency of the Powers to expand had made combinations necessary, but as there were no traditional friendships, no conventional axis, there was no trust or security, especially as all coveted one prize—Italy. The result was a cunning diplomacy, levity with regard to international agreements and an atmosphere of uncertainty, fear and mistrust. At the highest level, it would be hazardous to suggest that political morality was any worse during this period than before or since. Whenever it is convenient to break faith, excuses are to hand: King John's scrupulousness in returning to English captivity after the inadvertent breach of his parole after Poitiers was not, after all, characteristic of his age. At a lower level, among the diplomats, especially among the new residents, suspected and suspicious, unprotected by clear conventions of immunity, without the support of belonging to a definite, confident caste—here there was much that tempted men to be furtive, to adopt means that were crafty and oblique.

The fact that standing diplomacy was not yet taken for granted added to the air of uncertainty and suspicion. Princes who were glad to receive information about their neighbours resented attempts to discover their own. The aim of a diplomat was moreover to outwit, to deceive without being deceived—an aim formulated by Commynes from the behaviour of Louis XI, who not only boasted of the useful lies he had told, but preferred to use occasional ambassadors on the grounds that the promises of one might be disowned by the next. Ingenuity in cunning became almost comical with the use of disguises, concealed messages, and princes hiding one ambassador so that he could hear the false words of another. Nor were diplomats always servants simply of one state. Commynes, trusted adviser of the French Crown, was in the pay of Florence, who wished to reverse French policy, and the Florentine embassies for this purpose to the French court themselves contained elements hostile to their own government and favourable to Charles VIII. A general feeling of insecurity, coupled with the dissolution of international sanctions, produced an attitude to political affairs that has been named after the man who lived through it, learned from it, and codified it—Machiavelli.

From 1499 he was sent on a series of missions both abroad and to other Italian states, and the defiant amoralism of *The Prince* sprang directly from this contact with the ruthless and distrustful nature of contemporary diplomacy. Repeatedly snubbed or ignored as the representative of a weak state, he saw that a country was only respected when it was strong, and its strength had to be in arms. Repeatedly hampered by the hesitant policy of his employers, he saw that half measures were useless, neutrality a form of suicide. From the French gibe that Florence was *Ser Nihilo*, Mr Nothing, he saw that in the modern world money and arms alone counted, and in a life-and-death struggle a small man must sometimes hit below the belt. These lessons of the first mission to France in 1500 were confirmed by his meeting with the forceful Cesare Borgia in 1502. In the following year he passed them on to his fellow countrymen.

Florence was threatened by Cesare, by the Pisans, and by a French army on its way south to Naples, and was debating whether to arm or, as usual, to negotiate. Machiavelli took as his theme: without arms cities perish. Do not trust friends, today enmity is the norm; do not trust treaties, today princes are held only by the threat of war, 'for I tell you that fortune will not help those who will not help themselves, nor will the heavens— nor *can* they—sustain a thing that is determined to destroy itself'.[1] And subsequent missions, including three more to France, strengthened his opinion that Florence must be strong, and—just as a strong monarchy had made a fighting Power out of the fickle and light-minded French— must have a resolute leader, and finally that in this leader's policy there could be no place for scruple. These were the lessons of his career, and when after his dismissal in 1512 he determined to tell Italy through *The Prince* how to be strong, how to hold her own in a world of war, craft and crisis, he repeated them. Though idealistic about Italy as a cultural whole, he was realistic about Italy as a workable and defensible unit, and the Italy he wished to see unified had its base in Tuscany and the Romagna, where resistance would focus and prevent further partition. Here, if he modelled himself on the nearly successful Cesare, prepared resolutely for war, and remembered the sort of lessons provided by the unscrupulous contemporary governments, a prince might stop the collapse of Italy. Be honourable and tell the truth, he was to advise the young diplomat Rafaello Girolami, but if you cannot, then dissemble your lies, or at least be ready with a plausible defence. Similarly the prince must not sacrifice his country to his sense of honour, nor accept, for the sake of a code that no one else will observe, the contemptuous appellation of *Ser Nihilo*.

It was not only the small states who were forced to negotiate from weakness. The costs of war, already crippling in the fourteenth century, had risen again so steeply with changes in the equipment and composition of armies that no Power was always in possession of, for instance, sufficient artillery or the ready cash to pay mercenaries. Time after time bluff and ingenuity were used to fill in the space between a threat or a promise and the ability to implement them. The result was an exaggerated importance attached to the personal aspect of negotiation, the ability of one side to impress, or mislead the other. Guicciardini, in one of his *Ricordi*, says:

In sending forth ambassadors to treat with foreign courts, certain princes will freely make known to them their secret mind and the ends their negotiations are meant to serve. Others, again, judge it better only to impart what they would have the foreign prince persuaded of, thinking they can hardly deceive him unless they first deceive the ambassador who is to be the instrument and agent for treating with him. Something is to be said in favour of both these methods....

[1] *Parole da dirle sopra la provisione del danaio.*

But care must be taken that under the persuasive influence of Italian writers either the subtlety, or the realism, of Renaissance diplomacy is not exaggerated.

The credence given to the possibility of a crusade, or the effectiveness of a general council, may be taken to symbolise the continuation of a conservative approach to affairs that coexisted with a revolutionary change in method. It was still believed that dramatic personal intervention could be an effective substitute for prolonged expert negotiation, that eloquence was a substitute for common sense, that bribes could corrupt the enemy's agents, while his own gold was powerless. In many ways Renaissance diplomacy was obtuse and irrational. It must not be forgotten that in the world of Guicciardini and Ferdinand the Catholic *naïveté* still played its part.

Guicciardini saw the first generation of the Italian wars as a period of revolution, and wrote in another of the *Ricordi*:

Before the year 1494 wars were protracted, battles bloodless, the methods followed in besieging towns slow and uncertain; and although artillery was already in use, it was managed with such want of skill that it caused little hurt. Hence it came about that the ruler of a state could hardly be dispossessed. But the French, on their invasion of Italy, infused so much liveliness into our wars, that up to the year 1521, whenever the open country was lost, the state was lost with it.

And, indeed, the renewed superiority of defence over attack, a turning-point symbolised by Prospero Colonna's defence at Milan in 1521, was revolutionary, for it affected the entire nature of campaigns, slowing them down, emphasising strategy and political action at the expense of tactics, mere skill and bravery, substituting the desire to be victorious in a campaign for the urge to win a series of fights, and raising formidable problems of recruitment and supply. But if the French could make no impression on Milan, the same year saw the Turks break down one after the other the fortresses guarding the approaches to Belgrade. Above all, this was a period in which the old-fashioned and the advanced existed together; it was a period of real transition.

While some towns had learned the use of the bastion and the low, thick wall, others retained their towers and the tall thin curtain walls that meant so much to civic pride; the crossbow was still used side by side with the arquebus; artillery was dragged into action but was seldom properly exploited; tactics were being modified in the face of firearms and the use of field fortifications, but still on occasion sacrificed experience to blind over-confidence; professional troops, steady and skilled, fought with their own up-to-date weapons along with nervous amateurs, cheaply and often archaically equipped by the State; and dispassionate and scientific preparation might still be jeopardised by a chivalrous appeal to chance.

275

The pace of change was fast, because wars were almost constant, the effects of change were widespread, because unprecedented numbers of men were involved. And although many books on military matters were printed, these changes owed nothing to theoretical writers, but were forced by circumstances on intelligent commanders like Gonzalo de Córdoba and the marquis of Pescara. Most books simply repeated the lessons of classical military theorists, like Vegetius and Frontinus. Works that contained detailed technological advice like Leonardo's note-books, or Francesco di Giorgio's work on fortification, remained in manuscript. From the *De Re Militari* of Robertus Valturius, printed at Verona in 1472, books contained illustrations of new weapons, it is true, but these were often based on misunderstood descriptions of classical siege engines, and had little relevance to actual warfare in the field. Again, it was not until Battista della Valle's *Libro continente appertenentie ad Capitanii* appeared in 1528 that guns were included in the diagrams of troop formations derived from classical descriptions.

The outstanding example of a work dealing with war in a soberly realistic spirit is the *Nef des Princes et des batailles* of Robert de Balsac, seigneur d'Entragues. It was printed in 1502, and reflects the military experience of its author in the Armagnac and Breton campaigns of Louis XI, and in the Italian wars of Charles VIII. The conventional moralising tone of the first part of this work has caused it to be neglected, but the second part bluntly advises a prince how to succeed in war. It takes full account of artillery, giving close descriptions of siege work, and stressing the usefulness of light artillery and hand-guns in the field. He recommends the prince ruthlessly to adopt a scorched earth policy when it is needed, and urges the use of spies, both before and during a campaign. He emphasises the importance of flexibility in an army: all enemies cannot be fought alike, their special characteristics must be studied and the prince must dispose his own forces accordingly. He dwells on the dangers of indiscipline, and unlicensed booty, and suggests that the troops' morale should be kept up by the deliberate circulation of encouraging rumours. While recommending an exact keeping of faith in treaties, he warns the prince never to expect honesty of others, particularly during a truce. He concludes with a comment that owes less to classical precedent: 'most important of all, success in war depends on having enough money to provide whatever the enterprise needs'.

Actual analogies between Roman and contemporary war would emerge more fully in the next generation, when an emphasis on caution rather than valour was better appreciated, and when cavalry, by adopting missile weapons on a large scale, came to resemble the cavalry of the ancients, but there was already one topic on which the Roman was also a contemporary voice, discipline. Time after time success was jeopardised by lack of it. Looking back over the astonishing success of Charles VIII's march to Naples, and recalling the number of times when the army was on the point of breaking up, Commynes concluded that 'it must of necessity be acknowledged that God Almighty conducted the enterprise'. The difficulty was twofold. 'Mercenary troops were unreliable: they fought only for money, and when this was short they either became insubordinate, or disbanded. Native troops called up for an emergency were easier to control, but they lacked the training and stamina of professional troops, and were more liable to panic in combat. There were very few permanent troops, well trained, and prepared to fight for their country as well as for cash. Monarchs had personal guards, key fortresses were garrisoned, the personnel of certain services, like pay and artillery, were kept in being, but in case of war reliance was placed on native levies, volunteers, and mercenaries. The supply of cavalry was not a grave problem; the nobleman was educated for war. But tactics were not dominated any more by cavalry; the main problem was to secure good infantrymen.

The obstacles were part administrative, part temperamental. It was difficult to raise enough money to keep a large number of troops during periods of inactivity, and there was no body of trained men who could serve as the effective *cadre* of new units, to see that they were properly brigaded and drilled and equipped; and it was not always easy to persuade men of the advantages of a military career. Neither urban bourgeois nor prosperous peasant was willing to give up a modest but certain livelihood for the alternatives of death or a fortune in loot, as attempts to raise national armies in France and Germany repeatedly showed. Florentine writers deplored the debilitating effects of trade and luxury, and their complaints culminated in Machiavelli's denunciation of a way of life that had led to the separation of the two aspects of political life—civil and military—whose union had guaranteed the freedom, and had led to the greatness, of Rome.

In the *Art of War* (1521) he described the ideal condition: that war should be waged, not by hired foreign professionals, but by the citizens themselves, so that 'everyone may be ready to go to war in order to procure a good peace, and no one presume to disturb the peace in order to stir up a war'. But the avoidance of professional feeling could not be reconciled with effective training and discipline; by insisting that his model army should be thoroughly loyal, he made it impossible for it to be thoroughly efficient. The Florentine militia of 1506 incorporated many of his ideas: captains were frequently switched from command to command, for instance, to avoid personal loyalty detracting from loyalty to the State; the evils of militaristic rule were avoided by interposing political committees. A loyal Florentine noted in his diary that 'this was thought the finest thing that had ever been arranged for Florence', but the rout of the militia at Prato in 1512, on the return of the Medici, revealed the inadequacy of half-trained troops in modern war. Infantry which fell much below the standard of the best was useless, and the best—the German and Swiss pikemen, and the Spanish and professional Italian arquebusiers—owed their efficiency to the fact that they lived primarily for war. Spain and Switzerland were the only western countries which produced an infantry that was at once native and professional. Maximilian attempted first to raise a militia, and when this failed, to canalise the energies of the free-booting *Landsknechte* and foster their morale by building up their loyalty to the throne. What religion had done for the Hussites, and patriotism for the Swiss, the imperial ideal would perform for the *Landsknechte*. But neither the glamour of new military orders, no longer shunning the foot soldier, nor the efforts of his publicists, could shake the troops' conviction that their loyalty was to a captain of their own choosing rather than an abstraction more notable for fine sentiments than regular pay. Tactically, the *Landsknechte* improved until they rivalled the Swiss, but they remained a terror to their own country in peace time, in war were prepared to fight for the Empire's enemies, and on occasions such as the Sack of Rome in 1527 showed how fruitless had been Maximilian's attempts to substitute anything higher for their narrow *esprit de corps*.

France possessed the largest standing army among the western Powers, but apart from the artillery service, it was composed entirely of horse: the king's household troops and the *gendarmerie*, the first continually in service, the latter alternating garrison duty with long periods of leave. In time of war, the *ban* and *arrière-ban*—the levy of tenants owing military service for their fiefs—could be made to produce cavalry of variable quality, but the copious categories of exemptions from this service, and the preference of the military-minded for regular service with the *gendar-merie*, robbed this levy of much of its usefulness. There was no regular infantry. The *francs archers* still existed *in posse*, but their poor showing at Guinegate (1479) had proved them to be unreliable, and the Crown depended on *bandes* recruited by captains holding the king's commission wherever suitable men could be found to volunteer, and especially in Gascony and Picardy. Louis XII, faced by the defection of the Swiss in 1509, tried to organise a national infantry, and to resurrect the *francs archers* in 1513, but, as in Germany, only the least promising material was willing to serve, and problems of administration proved too great. For the rest of the period France relied on foreign mercenaries, when possible, the Swiss, when not, *Landsknechte*.

In artillery France had no serious rival, and the special importance her kings had attached to this arm was demonstrated by the expense to which they went to import metal and technicians, and by the grave risks run by the retreating army of 1495 to bring back their field and siege guns safely over the Apennines and the Alps.

In Spain, although the only permanent element in the army was a detachment of 2500 heavy horse, the *guardas viejas*, this was not the country's natural arm. Suitable horses were far outnumbered by mules, and the Moorish campaign of siege and skirmish had developed not heavy, but light horse, and siege cannon, not field artillery. There was a reserve of infantry, of which the town militias provided the most effective part, and though they proved unsuitable for long campaigns abroad the Italian wars soon attracted volunteers, and the material was there; within a generation the hardy and impoverished highlanders of Castile were found superior even to the Swiss. Indeed, thanks to the adaptive genius of the Great Captain, Gonzalo de Córdoba, who modelled part of his troops on the Swiss pikemen, part on the Italian arquebusiers, and took over the Italian device of using field fortifications to exhaust the enemy's attack before pressing home his own, the Spanish army was revolutionised by 1503, the year of his victory over the French at Cerignola.

The position in the cantons was contradictory. Though the hiring of mercenaries was so profitable, there was no permanent army or militia. The citizens drilled voluntarily with their own arms under local captains and ensigns, but these were the only men always ready to march. When the diet decided to hire troops, the cantons concerned fixed the number of men to go—the country's agricultural economy could safely be left in the hands of old men and the women—and called for volunteers. Once the troops were assembled, they chose their own commanders. This system had two serious drawbacks. The voluntary training was sound but quickly stereotyped; Swiss tactics stood still while other states learned to defeat them. And the severely qualified authority of the commanders led to indecision and on occasion to mutiny. But the excellent physique of the men, their confidence and national pride enabled them to make good use of the tactical superiority they possessed at the beginning of the wars.

Machiavelli admired and feared the Swiss whom he saw as the ideal citizen-soldiers, and his corresponding disparagement of the armies of Italy has hampered a just estimation of them. In fact, the Italian wars of the *Quattrocento* had not been bloodless, nor was Italy ruined by irresponsible *condottieri* who inherited this tradition, fighting with treacherous caution for purely selfish ends. The main *condottiere* bands had settled on their conquests, had, indeed, so far turned their swords into ploughshares that there was a serious shortage of experienced soldiers. Two states, Milan and Venice, had now a nucleus of permanent troops in the ex-*condottiere* bands settled in their territories. To these Milan added troops hired from captains enfeoffed by the State or related to the duke. Venice hired some of her cavalry and heavy infantry on a purely business footing because she preferred not to build up fresh military families, but she also had a large and well-armed peasant militia. In both cases armies were, in the main, bound to the State by ties other than cash. And in the states that depended almost entirely on mercenaries, like Florence, Rome and Naples, the commanders were often related to the ruling families, or enfeoffed by them, as were the Orsini and Colonna by a king of Naples afraid, like Venice, to arm his own barons. Italy's weakness was not that she relied on mercenaries, nor that her wars smacked more of the chessboard than the shambles; Italian troops had already shown at the Ponte di Crevola in 1487 that they could defeat the Swiss, her artillery was not so seriously inferior in quality to that of the French—whose instructor she had been—as her embittered historians suggested: it was in disunity, in divided command, in excessive reliance on political action that the weakness lay—as the fortunes of Fornovo showed.

Machiavelli's suggestion that to employ mercenaries was a mark of moral weakness and political folly was, after all, very misleading. Since the last campaigns of the Hundred Years War, the Hussite wars, and the conflict between Swiss and Burgundians, it was clear that armies needed a combination of arms, and no country was suited to produce them all. England, for instance, the most unified of states, and not the least wisely governed, was forced to rely on foreigners to fight for her. English horses were too squat and weak to support armour and barding, and Burgundian cavalry was hired instead. The infantry of the shire levies were used only to bow and bill, and German pikemen had to supply the essential stiffening of heavy infantry. The drawbacks were largely financial and in fact had little to do with morale; faulty methods of command would have cancelled out much of the advantage of a national army over a cosmopolitan one, and it would be hazardous to suggest that a soldier, except in defensive campaigns, fought for his country rather than for his pay. While the states of the west were, nevertheless, trying to lessen their dependence on mercenaries, and to develop standing armies, the reverse was true in the east. The fact that in Moldavia recruitment was based on land ownership, and that the call to arms against the Turk brought out landlord and tenant in an association familiar from the fields, kept discipline and morale high, and this cohesion was aided by the fact that there was no tactical split between classes: all travelled on horseback, and all fought on foot. But in Roumania, where the free peasant could only pay the tribute extorted by the Turks by selling the right in his property to the landlord, a rift occurred between the two classes. The peasants could no longer afford modern weapons, they were less willing to fight for an exploiting class, and the *boiars* no longer wished to arm them. As a result the government turned increasingly to mercenaries from Poland, the Baltic and the west.

In contrast to the Christian states, the Turks not only had a large and balanced standing army, but the whole machinery of state could be adjusted instantly from peace to war. The army was recruited from young Christian captives specially conditioned by a long educational discipline to be devoted to the sultan and his faith. The janissaries (infantry) numbered about 12,000, the *sipāhis* (cavalry) 10,000 to 12,000, but as each had to bring from two to six more horsemen with him the number was perhaps 40,000 to 50,000. To the *sipāhis* were added in wartime feudal levies that produced at least another 50,000 horse from Europe, another 30,000 from Asia, for territory had been granted on condition that the owners resided and kept order in peace, and brought troops when called to war. There were besides large numbers of irregular troops whose belief that death for the faith would lead to instant felicity made possible their use as cannon fodder. In numbers, training and devotion the Turkish armies were without peer. Fortunately for Christendom there were weaknesses. There was a disproportionate number of cavalry; so large a standing body was restless when there was no war; each sultan owed his throne to their support, and though half-worshipped he was also half victimised by their desire for action; the unity of the army under the sultan meant that it could not be split to fight on two fronts—when there was an attack in the east peace had to be made in the west, as in 1503, when the Persians invaded under Shah Ismā'īl and peace was made with Venice.

All these armies were accompanied by a host of camp followers, largely women and children, who foraged for food, cooked, tended the wounded and helped with the building of fortifications; the Germans had a special officer, the *Hurenweibel*, to deal with them. And the lives of still other civilians were closely linked to war; food was not, as a rule, provided by the military authorities, the men were expected to buy their own from the agents who obtained produce from the country as the army moved along. There were, besides, dealers who followed in the hope of making a profit by turning booty into cash. These civilians could seriously impede the progress of an army on the march; numbers can be gauged by those attached to the French army, which had entered Italy with some 40,000 men, and was still followed, after the long and arduous retreat of 1495, by some 10,000 non-combatants.

The most important technical changes in this period were those made in the art of fortification. The domination of battlefields by the pike affected the composition of armies, the increasing use of firearms affected their equipment and slowly influenced tactics, but, as Guicciardini showed, the fact that defence had once more overtaken attack altered the whole nature of campaigns—and, consequently, their financial and diplomatic background.

The success of French artillery earlier in the fifteenth century had revealed the weakness of tall, thin walls, which had withstood the plunging fire of wooden siege-engines, but were vulnerable to the horizontal fire of guns, especially when metal balls were used. A little had been done before the sudden challenge of 1494. A few French castles had been rebuilt with thicker walls, gun-ports had been provided for the defenders' guns, but most of these were merely round holes, and few (for instance, the Tour des Rondes at Blaye) showed a trace of the external splay that was to become habitual in the middle of the next century. But the most significant innovation, the bastion, had hardly been hinted at in practice. The need for effective flanking fire emerged as soon as breaches (which ruined the curtain defences, machicolations and *hourds*) became commoner than scaling attacks, and walls became too thick for the defenders to watch the ground immediately below them. The bastion was a solid construction projecting from the curtain, and of about the same height, sometimes curved, but presenting, as a rule, an angle to the field, with supporting guns capable of taking in flank any assault on the curtain, and covering the blind spots of the neighbouring bastion. Compromises had been made by cutting down towers and strengthening them with earth, and various designs had been sketched by Francesco di Giorgio, but the first true bastion to be built would appear to have been the Boulevard of Auvergne (1496) on Rhodes, an island forced to be in the van of progress by the threats of Turkish invasion. Italian architects, who had only played with the idea of the angle bastion before 1494, developed it rapidly after the shock of seeing defence after defence fall to the French. But for another generation the emphasis was on the modification of old fortifications rather than the building—at very great expense—of new ones. Citizens preferred to defend a breach with *ad hoc* internal works, ditches commanded by guns raised on the spoil thrown up on the inside. This technique had proved serviceable in France and defeated the fine imperial artillery at Padua in 1509. Only with the rebuilding of the fortifications of Verona in 1520 were large-scale works embarked on, and for another generation they were a feature only of places of great strategic importance. By 1520, too, the explosive mine, perfected in the first ten years of the wars, had been largely countered either by warning devices like bells placed on drums round the walls, by sinking vents to disperse the blast of the explosion, or by deepening moats.

Artillery underwent a great change in the last generation of the fifteenth and the first of the sixteenth century. By the end of the Italian wars it had achieved a form not substantially altered for 300 years. The period of wasteful experiment, as with huge guns with screwed-in breeches which could fire only a few times a day, was over by 1494. Princes like Ercole d'Este and James IV of Scotland were artillery enthusiasts, and Maximilian's interest, emphasised in the propagandist *Weisskunig* and *Teuerdank*, was emulated by Henry VIII. The constructional difficulties in building a long gun with a very wide bore had been recognised, and mere size was given up in the interests of portability and accuracy, qualities much enhanced by improved gun carriages and the invention of the trunnion. Indeed, a light artillery, which could keep up easily with armies on the march, and could be shifted about in the course of a battle, had been pioneered in Burgundy and was exploited by the French.

Against masonry guns were extremely effective; against men the effects were uncertain: in many engagements casualties were absurdly small in proportion to the shots fired, though at Ravenna—a battle whose fortunes were decided by guns, which dislodged the Spanish cavalry from its fortified position and forced an attack—a single shot was claimed to have struck down thirty-three men. Instead of stone balls which tended to shatter on impact, the use of iron balls was spreading. As yet there was no uniformity of type—the terms cannon and culverin are vague, and guns were built to the whim of a prince or founder. Francis I inherited seventeen different calibres, Charles V fifty. The supply and transport of ammunition was thus a complicated and wasteful task.

Portable firearms were no longer startling curiosities, and by the end of this period were the dominant missile weapon. The longbow had an effective range of some 250 yards, and could readily fire six shafts a minute; the killing range of the crossbow was from 220 to 250 yards, or, with square-ended armour-tearing bolts, 150 to 200 yards, and it fired one shaft a minute: the steel military bows had to be cocked with a windlass or cranequin. But, save in England, the latter was far more widely used, because against horse and armour weight and accuracy mattered more than range and speed. And this fact favoured the arquebus. Its useful range, even at the end of the wars, was hardly 400 yards, but its heavy bullet caused the crossbow to be relegated to sea warfare and siege work during the 1520's. Thanks to the introduction of the matchlock, it was no longer necessary to hold the gun (necessarily very small, but heavy, for its weight to absorb the recoil) in one hand and to dab the match against a touch-hole with the other; the marksman now had both hands steadying the arquebus at the moment of firing, and all his concentration on his victim, not half on the match. By the end of the period the wheel-lock had appeared, which made the arquebus into a tolerably effective cavalry weapon and opened the way for the development of the pistol. Stocks were made to rest against the chest or hip and sometimes to fit against the shoulder, and used as some of the heaviest were, with a rest stuck into the ground, a gun could be fired with reasonable accuracy. They were at first used mainly to defend fortified positions, but by 1512 had come out into the field, protected by pikemen, over whose heads they fired, and soon were used even without this defence as an independent arm to give covering or galling fire. The effect of gunfire was greater on formations, which had to be thinned against it, than on armour which had already been so far strengthened against crossbow quarrels that it was proof at least against spent or glancing bullets. The first great age of the gunsmith was also the finest age of the armourer.

During the first generation after the invasion of Italy by Charles VIII, armour underwent a stylistic revolution, caused by the blending of Italian with German and French tastes which resulted in the production (for the rich, at least) of suits in the Maximilian style, elaborately fluted and en-graved. It is interesting that in the age of gunpowder's most rapid de-velopment, the armourer was called upon to introduce changes not so much in the interest of increased protection, but of additional beauty and comfort. Monarchs like Charles VIII and Louis XII not only patronised armour but collected it, and the growing complication of the tourney, with its several types of combat, each needing special reinforcing or replacement pieces, provided a stimulus to the armourer just as powerful as war itself.

Armour, and the armourers' weapons, lance, pike, halberd and sword, continued to decide the fortunes of battle. At Cerignola (1503) the danger of attacking a fortified position protected by arquebuses had been shown. At Ravenna (1512) artillery had determined how part of the battle was to be fought, but not the way in which it was to be won. At Marignano (1515) artillery had gravely altered the course of events by galling columns of infantry brought to a standstill by cavalry charges. And at Bicocca (1522) and Pavia (1525) victory was determined by the use of artillery and, still more, the arquebus, at the former in a defensive position, in the latter in open country. But before these two battles gunpowder had stung tactics into contorted positions, the need of a careful overhaul of equipment not, however, being appreciated. The most dangerous threat still came from the massed column of pike.

The Swiss, whose defeat of the Burgundian cavalry at Grandson and Morat in 1476 had caused such general concern among military men, fought in compact squares of about 6000 men, eighty-five shoulder to shoulder, on a hundred-yard-long front, and some seventy ranks deep. The success of this formation depended on rigid discipline and strict drill. Nothing could be allowed to divert the pressure or resistance of the square till it was crippled or victorious; no prisoners could be taken, the wounded were ignored. A cavalry charge at such a square met first a solid hedge of steel, the pike heads of the first four ranks, then halberds, taking advantage of broken order to stab at close quarters or to grapple from the flank and hook a horseman down, then at the centre of the square broadswords which could swing at a man still mounted or be grasped below the hilt to thrust at those unhorsed. An infantry charge was met first by ranks of halberds which struck down the points of the pikes, then by row after row of pikes in front and in the flanks by swordsmen and crossbows and arquebusiers issuing from the centre and rear of the phalanx. Unlike another infantry that had defeated heavy cavalry, the English bowmen, the Swiss could attack, and because their morale was so high, they wore little armour and could attack fast and in firm order. In this case they were preceded by bows and guns which harassed the evolutions of the enemy and then retired to let the square come through, bristling with pikes and moving with a momentum irresistible unless thinned by heavy fire or disrupted by uneven ground. When numbers allowed, the Swiss used three squares in echelon to foil flank movements and to maintain a reserve, a practice triumphantly successful, but for the last time, at Novara (1513).

These tactics were soon copied, first by the princes of Germany and by the French, then by the Spaniards and Italians. The *Landsknechte* were the most faithful copy, but were less well drilled and led, partly because captaincies went to the highest bidder, not to the most efficient soldier, and they did not reach their peak until the second decade of the sixteenth century, by which time the front ranks were composed of veterans. The Spaniards and Italians accepted the Swiss example more cautiously and without losing their own characteristic of greater manœuvrability, for the Swiss manner had serious disadvantages. The squares were easy marks for missiles, and retained their dense composition even when firearms had become really effective. They were not suited to bad terrain, nor were they apt for siege work. They were cumbrous and inelastic in evolution, and were at their best when an enemy attacked in the old manner of battle against battle, like arm against like arm. In Italy they found more flexible armies, combining cavalry and infantry, undismayed by rough country, and making careful use of field fortification. Until the pike allied itself systematically with the arquebus the victory was with the more varied force that could harass and outflank it before delivering a death-blow. That the Italians were defeated by the direct tactics of the Swiss and the direct strategy of the French was largely the fault not of their armies but their commanders and their governments.

The need to counter Swiss-plan infantry led to a notably increased split between heavy and light infantry. Gonzalo de Córdoba, for instance, while increasing the armour of his pikemen, armed more and more of his other infantry with guns, and they acted increasingly on their own as these became more effective: the tendency throughout the wars was towards heavy shock troops on the one hand, fast light missile troops on the other.

The increasing prestige of infantry—Gonzalo's pikemen included noblemen, and the French infantry was led by the king himself at Marignano in 1515—did not mean that heavy cavalry ceased to be the aristocracy of war. At the siege of Padua in 1509 Maximilian proposed that the French men-at-arms should dismount and storm a breach with the infantry. The Chevalier Bayard's reply was: 'Considers the emperor it to be a just and reasonable matter to peril so much nobleness together with his infantry, of whom one is a shoe-maker, another a farrier, another a baker, and suchlike mechanics, who hold not their honour as do we gentlemen?' A proposal that French and German men-at-arms should fight dismounted but together produced an extension of this point of view. The Germans refused on the score that 'they were not such as went on foot, nor to go into a breach, their true estate being to fight like gentle-men on horseback'.[1]

Mounted on strong barded horses, armed with lance and axe or mace, the unvarying tactic of such heavy cavalry was a furious charge in bodies of from 400 to 500. The basic unit in the organisation was the lance, consisting of a man-at-arms and his entourage, varying in number from country to country. In France he was supported by an esquire, page and servant, and maintained two crossbowmen, all mounted, and on occasion charging together. As with the infantry there was a tendency for the heavy part of the unit, the man-at-arms and his supporters, to become separated from the lighter horsed bowmen.

The obvious usefulness of light horse in foraging and raiding aided this split, and it was completed by the effectiveness of the Spanish light horse and the Balkan *Stradiots* hired by Venice, whose mobility and recklessness provided the republic's main defence after the defeat of Agnadello in 1509. Favour then was given to a cavalry riding swift horses, armed with helmet and light body armour, sword, light lance or crossbow—the arquebus being hard to handle. Though an almost in-dispensable arm, however, it remained secondary to the heavy calvary, which alone was capable of halting a column of pike. The numbers of both declined relative to infantry, but this was in part due less to their decreasing tactical usefulness than to the fact that for social and economic reasons their supply was constant, while infantry could be recruited and equipped in increasing numbers.

For transport, communication and supply, ships were an essential complement to armies, and the fortunes of the warring Powers were affected by the extent to which they could secure them. There were few royal ships, little was done to establish royal navies. Just as the Swiss and Germans were called on to make up armies, the Italian sea-states were employed to complete fleets; as yet the difference between warship and merchant ship was small and both could fight together. Nor were the functions of galley and round ship considered so disparate that they could not be used together in both northern and southern waters, and both Atlantic and Mediterranean Powers used intermediate types of sail-and-oar ships.

Charles VIII had only twenty-one royal ships and two factors compli-cated the use of merchantmen: the jealous autonomy of the respective admirals of Brittany, Guienne and Provence, and the lack of native shipping in the Mediterranean, where almost all trade was in foreign hands. For the invasion of Italy, therefore, he had to hire ships from Genoa, and though he began building galleys at Toulon, Louis XII built royal ships at Brest, and Francis I created the port of Le Havre, France was

---

[1] *History of Bayard compiled by the Loyal Serviteur*, trans. L. Larchey (London, 1883), pp. 196–7.

never independent of hired ships and the political entanglements these involved.

Though Spain was equally poor in royal ships, and the mounting danger from corsairs did not revive the large-scale building of galleys until towards the middle of the next century, she was far better off in merchant shipping. The Crown paid a bounty on merchant tonnage and rigidly debarred ships potentially useful in war from being sold abroad, and Spain's interest in Sicilian grain and trade with North Africa left her with a large number of vessels suitable for requisitioning. Once requisitioned, however, they were shoddily organised. The fleets had no unity, poor morale. Captains undermanned in order to pocket the pay of the 'dead souls' they declared, and as they also carried merchandise as a legitimate private speculation, they preferred caution to the risk of losing it.

The fleets of Genoa suffered from the same disability. The State made contracts with private individuals to provide ships for government service. No compensation for damage or loss was paid, and pay was poor, so every effort was made to avoid combat with war fleets but to capture merchant vessels for the sake of prize money. Here, too—and it was the same with Tuscan and papal fleets—officers were allowed cargo space. In Venice this was true only of ships supplementing the State war-fleets, for Venice, alone of Italian Powers, had a fleet permanently in being. Constant threat from the Turks, whose war-fleet in 1495 numbered some 250 ships, had made this necessary, and after being caught with too few warships by the war of 1499, a fleet of from seventy to one hundred galleys, specially built for combat, was always available. Venice had the additional advantage that many of her nobles had had experience of the sea, her merchantmen were already armed, and that in her arsenal she had the largest and most efficiently run industrial plant in Europe.

Henry VII was more interested in peaceful trade than in war. He created the dockyard at Portsmouth with its dry dock—the first in England— and added eight ships to the three he inherited from Richard III, but he relied mainly on merchantmen and the bounties paid on ships of large tonnage. His successor's personal interest in the sea, his wish to pursue an expansionist foreign policy, the danger from Spain, soon united with the Netherlands, and from Scotland, who had built up a considerable fleet during the Wars of the Roses—these reasons were to bring Henry VIII's navy up to eighty-five: forty-six built, twenty-six bought and thirteen captured. To provide for them, more dockyard space was created at Woolwich and Deptford and the administration was centralised and made less haphazard. Admirals, for instance, were no longer responsible for victualling and equipping their own ships. But up to 1533 this fleet, save in actual wartime, was still dispersed on hire to private merchants.

Guns had been mounted on ships since the early fifteenth century, and, as on land, the tendency during the early sixteenth was to reduce size to make handling easier and fire more rapid, and to standardise bores to ease the provision of ammunition. The old-fashioned breech loaders were retained because of the speed with which they could be recharged, but increasing use was made of better-constructed muzzle loaders, swung inboard for re-loading on two-wheeled carriages which recoiled between chocks in the deck. The larger ships—France, Scotland, Venice and the Turks all had vessels of over 1000 tons, the last having two vessels of 1800 tons—carried one hundred guns or more, firing through ports in the fore and after quarters as well as from the deck and superstructure. The efficiency of these guns was not great. The weak powder thought safe to use on board could hardly push a medium ball more than a mile and with accuracy probably not more than 300 yards, but they were used almost entirely against rigging and men, and were only a supplement to the arms of the boarding parties. Though the best guns were hardly less effective than those of Nelson's day, they were not a deciding factor: the purpose of naval tactics was as yet to get men aboard, not to sink by gunfire.

Before their domination by broadside fire, in the middle of the century, tactics were simple, and required no complicated evolutions. Round ships attacked abreast, seeking the weather gauge and firing their heavy guns at close range before boarding. If the gauge was lost, the guns were fired to give smoke cover to an attempt to regain it. Once the ships had grappled, the fight was a purely military affair, though small boats might be dropped to assist generally and to bore holes at the water line. Galleys also attacked in line abreast—even more rigidly, as their weaker construction made fire possible only along the centre-line—and charged at the enemy's flanks in an attempt to break with their rams the outriggers supporting the oars. Tactics were not specifically naval. Nearly all commanders were military men, the proportion of soldiers to sailors aboard was 2 to 1. And signals were as simple as were tactics. An admiral could signal: enemy in sight, come aboard for conference, close up, attack—but there was nothing once battle was joined. From that moment the admiral had no further control over the *mêlée*.

Though the temper of war was changing, becoming more calculating and professional, chivalry still found a place. After the Hundred Years War, writers like Jean de Bueil in *Le Jouvencel* tried to show that real chivalry was no longer the concern of the individual in jousts and personal enterprises, but in military service, where impetuosity had to be subordinated to discipline while the individual could still show courage and devotion. Though the 'laws' of chivalry had never applied to other than noble classes, the increasing use of infantry still left a place for the hero, the man furious towards the cruel, gentle towards the humble, humane towards the poor, as his biographer described Bayard. In the storm of actual combat there had never been wide scope for fastidious ideals of fair play; book chivalry was seldom mirrored by battlefield chivalry. Yet from time to time chivalric conventions still cut across scientific warfare, over-riding tactical and strategic considerations. The complex machinery that brought two armies face to face might still be jettisoned by an appeal to single combat—as when Gaston de Foix challenged the Spanish viceroy before Ravenna. Important prisoners were still released on a noble whim—as Bayard was released without ransom by Lodovico Sforza. Commanders by sea and land were expected to be in the van, and lost control as a result as soon as an attack was launched. The impact of a solid charge might be broken by individuals racing for the honour of delivering the first blows. Rash counsel could still overcome caution, boldness shame wisdom—as when the defenders of Rapallo disastrously scorned to remain behind their fortifications in 1494. Quixotry might still be put before policy—as at Fornovo, where the French were allowed to recover from their passage of the Appenines, or Marignano, where Francis I let the shattered Swiss go unpursued. Nor did the use of fraud and stratagem mean that chivalry was dead. A distinction had existed at least from the fourteenth century between ruses that were legitimate and those that were not; an army could wear false colours, set ambushes and get the sun in its enemy's eyes, for instance, but it should not break truces or pacts. But how to decide what was allowable? By the early sixteenth century emphasis was laid on ending wars quickly as the aim of good men, a point of view that could soon lead a French commander to say: 'I am of opinion that towards an Enemy all advantages are good, and for my part (God forgive me) if I could call all the devils in Hell to beat out the brains of an Enemy that would beat out mine, I would do it with all my heart.'[1]

A test case in the European attitude to war is provided by the use of gunpowder. It was only in this period that the killing power of guns was properly appreciated; previously they had been hardly more effective than the trebuchets and ballistas of medieval siegecraft. They had been used, too, mainly for attacking fortifications: it was only now that the deadly effect of cannon playing over the open field of battle was understood. Renaissance Europe was confronted with what was, to all intents and purposes, a new weapon, and one of unprecedented ferocity and destructive power. It was challenged on humanitarian grounds, attacked because it was un-Christian, reviled because it enabled the base and cowardly to strike down the noble and brave from afar. The use of gunpowder ran counter to the teachings of the Church, and to the social code to which the majority of influential men subscribed. In spite of this the gun came to stay, became, indeed, ever more destructive during the period of maximum protest; while among the protests were heard other voices

[1] Montluc, *ed. cit.* p. 33.

that condoned, justified and admired it. The new weapon was accepted as other new weapons had been accepted, because it appealed to man's inventiveness, his admiration for military efficiency, and his national pride. The possession of large, up-to-date and powerful guns became an important part of national prestige; idealistic arguments made no headway against the crucial argument: guns helped rulers to win wars. The only Power which voluntarily crippled its military effectiveness by refusing to exploit firearms to the utmost was an infidel one. The Mamluk ideal of an aristocracy of horsemen led (at least until firearms could be handled with ease from the saddle) to the restriction of handguns to specially recruited units of black slaves, a restriction that put the Mamluk kingdom at a serious disadvantage in her wars with the Ottoman Turk.

Against the demoralising influence of war that both the practice and theory of popes and secular rulers in the south seemed to endorse, Christian humanists in the north set their face. More's Utopians scorned the spirit of conquest, the glory of war. Erasmus wrote again and again of the un-Christian nature of the wars of his day, their waste and brutishness. Whereas most of his *Adagia* occupied a fraction of a column of print, his commentary on the bitter tag *Dulce Bellum Inexpertis* had grown by 1520 into a long essay. Both he and More condemned conventional diplomacy as a means of settling international disputes; each league, each marriage, each exchange of ambassadors emphasised the split between the interests of nations, each treaty was itself a new *casus belli*. And the view was shared by Erasmus's contemporary Josse Clicthove who declared in his *De bello et pace* in 1523 that he was the citizen of no one country. 'I recognise only the name of Christian.'

But this was not enough. Wars could not be regulated by appeals to Christian duty. Control of war—as far as it could be controlled—came very gradually from the efforts of lawyers to codify the usages of war, accepting national sovereignty and appealing not to divine law but the *ius gentium*. The very licence of the time provoked the remedy. Certain aspects of war called urgently for regulation; reprisals, privateering, the rights of neutrals, the position of prisoners.

Their treatment was still arbitrary, and depended on the whim of individual captors, or their commander. A prisoner was the property, not of the prince, but of the man who had captured him—though English Articles of War enforced the payment of one-third of the profit from prisoners to the treasurer of the wars—and if the captive were a man of high rank his captor might sell him to a middleman who was better placed to extort a fitting ransom. The Swiss, like the Turks, preferred never to take prisoners and the Italian wars brought an abrupt change in the merciful habits of the peninsula, prisoners being imprisoned, set to forced labour, and, on occasion, tortured and blinded. It was usual for mercy to be accorded towns that had formally capitulated, and quarter to be granted to an enemy who was clearly defeated, but orders to this effect were not always obeyed, and the punishment of such disobedience in the cosmopolitan armies of the time was neither practical from a political, nor clearly justified from a legal point of view. Indiscriminate looting and pillaging wrought a havoc among civilians that was not to be checked until armies were better paid, provisioned and more amenable to discipline. From the late fourteenth century there had been isolated attempts made to restrict looting, in order to placate the civilian population, and to prevent armies disintegrating after a victory that might not, after all, be final. But the only effective prohibitions concerned war material vital to the State, notably guns and ammunition.

When the moral question of the Just War was raised at its acutest by the cruel progress of Spanish conquest in the New World it was discussed in terms of these practical problems, and as a result the dying sanctions of medieval internationalism—a compound of ideas derived from the chivalric code of what might and might not be done in time of war, the study of civil law, and the continuing pressure of Christian morality formalised in the canons of the Church—were slowly replaced by a body of international law.

CHAPTER X

FRANCE UNDER CHARLES VIII AND LOUIS XII

I N a changing world, France, at the close of the fifteenth century, found herself faced with problems different from those of the past. These were to force her governments to take the necessary measures to adapt their policy and were to have repercussions throughout society. The Hundred Years War, whose outcome assured France of national independence, had already freed her from threats arising from the existence of a Flemish-Burgundian state. After the war, the kingdom, which had been partly reconstructed in the reign of Louis XI, had to shape a course for its policy among the new nations that were being established, to put the State into working order at a time when its functions remained ill-defined, to work out a definitive status for the Church, which was still shaken by the upheavals of the Great Schism, and to restore its economy, on which the fate of the various social classes depended.

Louis XI's political mistakes had been offset by a sometimes incoherent capacity for action and by almost miraculous strokes of chance. He was succeeded by kings of feeble intellect whose enterprises were inspired by foolish ambitions and who were bound to be mastered by the most skilful of their rivals. Except in rare cases, moreover, there was no statesman at the French court capable of taking over the reins of government. Such were the conditions under which French policy, already jeopardised by the mistakes made by Louis XI, was about to move in a direction which influenced the future of Europe for years to come.

In the early years of Charles VIII's reign, although the king had legally come of age, government was in fact in the hands of his sister and her husband, Pierre de Beaujeu. Anne was like her father in some characteristics. She was responsible and diligent in studying state affairs, and earned from him the name of 'the least foolish woman in the world'. During those early years, a period of unrest among the aristocracy and among the people, the government felt the effects of her vigorous and far-sighted guidance. It is true that these good qualities were counterbalanced by short-sighted selfishness: her boundless greed and constant awareness of her own interests were later to bring the Bourbon-Beaujeu family and her son-in-law, the constable, into conflict with the interests of the king of France. But now, after seven years of tutelage, which he had borne with impatience, Charles VIII was about to exercise his authority for himself.

If we are to judge him according to the almost unanimous estimates of his contemporaries, he brought but indifferent abilities to his task. 'In body as in mind, he is of no great value', said Contarini; and Commynes bore out this opinion in describing him as 'very young, weakly, wilful, rarely in the company of wise men', and he added that 'he was endowed with neither money nor sense'. He had received very little education and was unable to understand Latin. His only appreciation was for 'moral and historical' works, and above all for the romances of chivalry which provided food for his imagination. He could sign his letters only with difficulty and was unable to write them himself; he took little interest in government affairs, and handed them over to advisers of no great ability who did not dissuade him even from his most hasty enterprises. Yet his intentions were good and he was anxious 'to lead a good life according to the commandments of God and to put the church and the administration of justice in order'. And indeed, immediately after the Italian expedition, he seemed desirous of bending himself to this task, when death cut short a reign for which some could foresee a glorious ending.

Charles VIII, whose degenerate children had been destined to die young, was succeeded by his cousin, Louis of Orleans, who, after a disturbing youth spent in the camp of the king's enemies, had grown wiser as with advancing years he drew nearer to the throne. He, too, was not very intelligent: he had a small head 'in which there was not room for much brain'; but he charmed his contemporaries with a certain warlike gallantry and provided matter for his eulogists by uttering words that bore the stamp of good will and wisdom. He reassured his subjects by giving evidence of a concern for economy, a desire to be compassionate towards the common people, to be fair in administering justice and to be wise 'in the manner of Moses'. All this might well delude readily-admiring courtiers, the notables of the 1506 Assembly who proclaimed him to be the 'Father of the people', and the hired writers who extolled his virtues. The truth must not escape us on that account: Louis XII was an overbearing king, and he undertook costly ventures which, conducted as they were, without foresight, ended in disaster. Besides, the members of his court did him no good service. His queens did not contribute to his popularity. His first marriage, to Jeanne de France, the daughter of Louis XI, who was very much out of favour, ended in divorce. The scandal created by this was intensified by the fact that an immoral and disreputable pope took part in it. A second marriage, with Anne of Brittany, brought the widow of Charles VIII back to the throne. She had shunned the limelight during her first reign, but afterwards grew bolder and intervened in government affairs, seeking the advantage of her Breton interests to the prejudice of those of the kingdom. Apart from a few favourites who never rose above mediocrity, the governing power was Georges d'Amboise, archbishop of Rouen, cardinal and papal legate. For ten years he enjoyed almost sovereign authority, directing

Italian policy and dictating to the Church in France, which he wished to reorganise within the framework of a national church. 'Ipse est vere rex Franciae', said a contemporary; but he, too, was a king who thought primarily of his own ambitions.

These two reigns, however lacking they were in men of genius and lasting achievements, left a favourable impression, because the nobility accomplished a few glorious exploits and the people recovered from the calamities of the previous century. There were no more devastating wars, no more famine, no more widespread and fatal epidemics; agriculture and trade prospered greatly. This was more than was needed to excite public opinion in the interval between two periods of poverty. Relations with Italy and the beginnings of the French Renaissance consummated the enthusiasm of scholars whose view of the period has prevailed ever since.

The heads of the French State were to decide on their policy in a Europe transformed by the disappearance of the medieval Empire and of the Papacy considered as a universal power. Louis XI had long been threatened by the appanaged princes, particularly by the duke of Burgundy, the most powerful of them; he had got the better of them in 1477 and in 1482 the Treaty of Arras left him with the greater part of the Burgundian patrimony. But there were still rivalries, and, as a consequence of the marriage of Maximilian of Habsburg to Mary of Burgundy, the heiress of Charles the Bold, the problems of French policy were linked to those of European politics. In the absence of an emperor seeking to impose his 'monarchy' on the Christian world, the heads of the neighbouring states would intervene in the feudal domains of France, thus threatening the territorial integrity of the kingdom. Two outstanding problems had to be solved, one concerning the provinces of Burgundy, and the other, Brittany. At this juncture, Maximilian and the king of England might be expected to intervene in both.

The Treaty of Arras had for the time being settled the question of the Burgundian inheritance and the fate of the unreliable provinces which tried to work out their destiny by remaining uncommitted to either France or the Empire. The uninterrupted development of their economic activity made them a tempting prey for neighbouring states. France had received Artois, Franche-Comté, Charolais and the county of Auxerre, but these made up the dowry of Margaret of Austria, then only two years old, who was to marry Charles VIII. This pacification was precarious and dependent on an event in the distant future, and it did not put an end to claims on these provinces from many quarters.

At the beginning of the reign, Brittany presented the most important question. The aristocratic reaction which made itself felt after the hard years of the reign of Louis XI was threatening to build up against the government a coalition grouped round Francis II, the duke of Brittany, who found support throughout society, all classes being equally ill-treated and discontented. The princes also relied on being allied to Maximilian of Austria and the king of England, Richard III, both of whom were prepared to commit themselves against the king of France. The threat was all the more serious because Francis II, who was no longer young, had no sons, and the fate of his province would depend on the marriage of Anne, his eldest daughter. The king had to resort to precautionary measures to prevent a hostile Power from taking up a position in this duchy, for it was deeply devoted to its independence and threatened the rear of the king's forces, whose attention was directed rather to the areas of the Scheldt and the Meuse. After the failure of a first coalition—the *Guerre Folle*—a new rising broke out in 1487-8, supported by contingents sent by Maximilian and the king of England. The royal army brought it to an end by its victory at Saint-Aubin-du-Cormier (1488), and the Treaty of Sablé enforced a solution that was satisfactory to the kingdom of France: foreign troops were to evacuate Brittany, and Anne was not to marry without the king's consent. And the possibility of this was now nearer because of the death of Duke Francis II and the accession of his daughter, who was then twelve years old, as duchess. The process of pacification, which seemed likely to be permanent, was further delayed by the resistance of the Breton nobility and the intervention of those princes who wished to marry the duchess. It was Maximilian who was successful, and the marriage took place, though only by proxy. The result was a most serious international dispute, and one likely to threaten the independence of the French kingdom (1490). It was this that was at stake in a new conflict. This time, it was Charles VIII who wanted to marry Anne of Brittany and he made ready to win her by force of arms. Victory for France led to the Treaty of Laval, in which Anne consented to marry her new suitor provided that he undertook to respect the autonomy of Brittany.

Having overcome the danger to which she was subject from Burgundy, France was freed from the threat from Brittany and, at the same time, the feudal lords, deprived of their principal leaders, inspired less apprehension. Abroad, the Emperor Maximilian, despite his claims on the Burgundian inheritance, was powerless to reopen the quarrel, and Henry VII, the king of England, while still demanding the French Crown, seemed to be unable to start afresh the hostilities which had been discontinued for forty years. French policy, freed from all immediate anxiety, was enjoying one of those rare periods of equilibrium when nothing compelled her either to take sides or to meet any enemy. But the coast was also clear for all the vagaries into which their imagination tempted the king and his advisers.

It was then that Charles VIII, carried away by his chivalric enthusiasm, undertook the Neapolitan expedition. He was thinking of reviving the rights of the dukes of Anjou to the kingdom of the Two Sicilies, questionable rights arising out of an occupation which had taken place in the remote past and had always been shaky. But he was urged to do this by entreaties from Italy—from Lodovico il Moro, duke of Milan. Beyond Naples, the king had visions of the conquest of Jerusalem and the crusade, and the restoration of the Christian empire at Constantinople, in the absence of the title of Roman Emperor which was no longer open for competition. These projects of wild adventure, these 'vanities and glories of Italy', as Commynes called them, were to put French policy out of true for more than half a century and use up her strength and wealth with no result save that of becoming the pawn of the governments of Italy. We should not, however, condemn this policy without taking into account the real interests which drew France in this new direction. Up to the time that the attraction of the New World was felt, trade with the East, the strategic points occupied on the shores of the Mediterranean, and the use of harbours which the annexation of Provence had incorporated into the kingdom had all deserved to hold the attention of statesmen and to encourage them to try to establish a strong position in the Mediterranean basin. They could not foresee that countries hitherto deprived of such advantages were to find other trade routes opening up and other sources of wealth within their reach.

From the beginning, the Neapolitan expedition entailed for France sacrifices which reduced her recent gains to nothing. On his own initiative, Charles VIII bought a promise of perpetual peace from England on payment of heavy indemnity (Treaty of Étaples); better still, he restored Roussillon and Cerdagne to Ferdinand of Aragon (Treaty of Barcelona), and Franche-Comté, Artois and Charolais to Maximilian, whose daughter was returned to him at the same time, since her projected marriage could not take place (Treaty of Senlis). France gave up without compensation the greater part of what she had gained from the Burgundian inheritance. The result was that her north-eastern frontier was in jeopardy for two centuries. Things being thus settled, Charles VIII could set out on his conquest of Naples—a short-lived one, for he was driven out by the Italian Powers in coalition and escaped, thanks to the drawn battle of Fornovo.

But the consequences of this conquest were not short-lived: the Powers who had an interest in the fate of Italy and the Mediterranean were to form a league against France; the answer to Charles VIII's expedition was the marriage of the Archduke Philip to Joanna of Spain, heiress to Aragon and Castile (1495). In this way, as a retort to Charles VIII, the union of the Habsburgs with the Spanish dynasty was being prepared, together with the immense power to be enjoyed by Charles V, which France would regard as a threat to her existence. Charles VIII was not disheartened by this setback and prospect: he was thinking of going to war again in order to make sure of Italy, when he died in 1498.

His successor, Louis XII, was no more far-sighted when he threw himself into similar ventures, with even greater ambitions, because of his claim to Milanese territory which he demanded as a descendant of the Viscontis. For half a century, the duchy of Milan was to be the cause of bitter rivalry between the Valois and the Habsburgs, being controlled first by one, then by the other, in the midst of fruitless wars and negotiations. Beyond Milan, French ambitions turned towards Naples, on which Spain also had designs; but there more than elsewhere, France was badly placed, as much by her geographical remoteness as by the weakness of her maritime forces compared with those of Ferdinand of Aragon and his successors, who were masters of the western half of the Mediterranean. France did not realise that the making of a great bid for sea-power was an indispensable condition for any policy of expansion in the maritime areas of the Levant.

French ambitions caused uneasiness even to the papal government. Although, by placing his forces at the disposal of Cesare Borgia, he succeeded in coming to an agreement with Alexander VI, Louis XII now had to deal with a far more formidable adversary in the person of Julius II, who was impatient of any curtailment of his independence. Having shown his tractability by being party to the League of Cambrai, which was directed against Venice, Louis XII saw a new league being formed against him, intended this time to drive the French out of Italy (1512). The situation was complicated by religious quarrels, by Gallicanism and plans for ecclesiastical reform. The military talents of Gaston de Foix and the victory at Ravenna did not produce the decisive results that might have been expected. By the end of 1512 the last signs of French rule had disappeared, and Milan had passed once more into the hands of the Sforzas. In 1513 another attempt to bring off a conquest ended in defeat at Novara, while the kingdom was invaded from all sides. Henry VII of England attacked the northern frontiers, thus showing the resurgence of English ambitions: as far as they were concerned, the Hundred Years War was not finally over. The Swiss advanced as far as Dijon and their retreat had to be dearly bought. The pope threatened to lay France under an interdict, and she had to yield to the demands of her enemies. When Louis XII died, the wise course for the new government would have been to minimise the consequences of all the battles that had been so rashly joined.

The extension of political activity, and the reorganisation of the State which was taking place during the same period in every country in western Europe, were characterised in France by the changes in her institutions which prepared the way for the administrative monarchy of modern times. From this point of view, the second half of the fifteenth century was rich in achievement.

In the feudal monarchy of the preceding centuries, authority rested on personal relationships and the performance of feudal services, and the power of the king varied from province to province and was purely nominal in the domains of the great feudal lords. In place of these arrangements, as a consequence of the ordeals of the Hundred Years War and the need for recovery after a period of anarchy, State administration and public services were to be substituted. The army, finance and the administration of justice were to be subject to rudimentary organisation under the supreme authority of the *Conseil du roi* and in the hands of a body of legal experts who were entirely devoted to the sovereign. These institutions were naturally not conceived according to very well-defined principles, nor were they very methodically brought into being. Neither Charles VIII nor Louis XII had any great gifts for government, and their courts contained more grasping rivals than statesmen. For all that, it is evident that a few reforms were effected during these reigns and some practices were adopted which, taken together, heralded the appearance of a new system.

At that time, a great change took place, a change which may be regarded as a transformation of the monarchical system itself. For more than a century the Estates General had met so frequently that they had become an essential organ of the monarchy: it was recognised that they had the right to authorise taxation and to nominate members of the *Conseil du roi* and, if the king was a minor, the regent. Government seemed, at times, to be evolving towards a parliamentary system modelled on that of England. The Estates General, meeting in 1484 in order to organise Charles VIII's government, appeared to be continuing this tradition. But matters subsequently turned out otherwise. Once his power was consolidated, the king shook off all forms of supervision and the Estates General were no longer summoned. Henceforward they were only occasional assemblies, whose powers were not clearly defined, and their advice was sought only in cases of extreme uncertainty.

The most permanent organ of government and the centre of the king's administration was now the *Conseil du roi* in which sat the great officers of the Crown, who were at the head of the chief administrative services. These were crucial years in the formation of the administrative framework of the monarchy of the *ancien régime*. From then on, the *chancellerie* and the *surintendance des finances*, with their staffs of *généraux des finances* and *trésoriers de France*, had a certain permanence which was ensured by tradition and sometimes by documents such as the great ordinance of reform of 1499. At the same time, these staffs were completed by the enrolment of new administrators of humbler extraction: they were less likely to change than the men of high rank who were at the mercy of court factions. In particular, these new administrators were the *secrétaires signant en finances*: these were given special tasks according to their competence and were later to become the *secrétaires d'état*. The supreme courts, which had gradually become separated from the king's court, were being constituted side by side with the *Conseil du roi*, with more precise functions established by ordinances. The existence of the *Grand Conseil* was recognised by the ordinance of 1498. The *Parlement* was still the supreme organ of the judiciary, and since the middle of the fifteenth century a number of regulations had completed the definition of its powers and procedure. Alongside it, the *Chambre des Comptes* and the *Cour des Aides* supervised the financial system.

In this way, the organisation of central government was being settled during the period of peace following the turmoil of the wars with England. The system seemed to be moving towards marked centralisation, but that did not exclude certain centrifugal tendencies. The kingdom was too extensive and the newly assimilated feudal states were still too autonomous to allow this centralisation to be complete or permanent. In place of the Estates General that were falling into abeyance, provincial estates were being organised; side by side with the supreme courts, which sat at the *Palais de la cité*, in Paris, others were being set up in the provinces with supreme powers which rendered appeals to the Paris *Parlement* unnecessary. This movement had begun in earlier reigns with the *Parlements* of Toulouse, Bordeaux and Grenoble, but during the reign of Louis XII the existence of those of Rouen, Dijon and Aix was ratified, while at Rennes a similar organisation was being initiated for the duchy of Brittany, which had some direct links with the Crown. At the same time, the kingdom was divided into four great financial districts, known as the *généralités*. These were the *généralités* of Languedoil, Languedoc, Normandy and Outre-Seine-et-Yonne, and to them the newly assimilated provinces of Picardy, Burgundy, Dauphiné, Provence, Brittany and Guyenne were soon added. This arrangement, which had been dictated by historical necessity, was destined to be reorganised in such a way as to become more homogeneous and more easily supervised by the central administration. But this improvisation foreshadowed reforms that were to be made later in financial administration. If we enter into the details of provincial organisation, we see that other changes were heralding the approach of modern times. While the towns had for several centuries been endowed with councils and genuine constitutions guaranteed by charters, the villages were now tending to organise themselves into *communautés d'habitants*. In order to facilitate the apportionment and collection of the *taille*, more and more villages held meetings and set up a rudimentary form of municipal administration. In addition, a few privileges of franchise were being granted, especially in connection with the administration of justice. These were the earliest developments of local powers which were subsequently to become more active.

The same tendency could be observed in legislative matters. The kings, wishing to overhaul and unify the code of law which prevailed in the kingdom, undertook in the first place to record in writing local customs which were for the most part handed down orally and through tradition. The 1454 meeting of the Estates General had ordained that all provinces of the kingdom subject to customary law should carry out this work, and the task of recording and revising was one of the jurists' chief occupations in the reigns of Charles VIII and Louis XII. It was evident that later the systems would need to be co-ordinated, thus creating a uniform code of law throughout the kingdom; but this project was never completed. The consequence was that, here again, differences prevailed, and, at the same time, the various traditions of customary law were strengthened.

In this way, the system which was to be peculiar to the government of the realm up to the end of the *ancien régime* was being created—a centralised system which yet allowed of regional autonomy.

Two novel instruments, which were firmly established during these two reigns, were now at the disposal of the Crown: finance and the army. In both cases, Charles VII's ordinances had laid down the broad principles. But from these tentative beginnings, a system of specific rules was developed which placed two indispensable tools in the hands of the sovereign.

The ordinary revenue, coming from the royal domain, was no longer sufficient to supply the ever-growing needs of the State. In addition, various other sources had been tapped. At first, they had been regarded as available only in special circumstances, but they subsequently provided the royal treasury with its most stable and easily collected income. Of these, the *taille* yielded the highest sums and it was the most readily available to the king. It was a direct tax, levied annually, and had originally to be granted by the Estates General, who also decided on the total amount to be raised. At their meeting in 1484 they had reaffirmed this principle, but, from the end of the reign of Charles VII, there was no longer any need for them to intervene, and the total sum was fixed annually by the *Conseil du roi* on the basis of anticipated expenditure. Louis XI had raised the *taille* to the exorbitant figure of 3,400,000 *livres*; after his reign, the government had to restrain its demands so as not to rouse the Estates General of 1484 to opposition. The rate was, therefore, reduced by more than half, and the new figure fluctuated very little despite expenditure arising out of the Italian wars. But this restraint was made possible only because it was counterbalanced by a system of loans, of mortgages on the royal domain and of other financial expedients, so that at the end of his reign Louis XII, despite his reputation for economy, was compelled to raise the rate of direct taxation, which eventually exceeded the rate imposed by Louis XI. This organisation of the finances, brought to perfection at the end of the fifteenth century, put at the king's disposal an extremely flexible fiscal system and resources on which later kings drew in large measure when placed in difficult circumstances. These resources were primarily devoted to the upkeep of the royal army, in which paid soldiers were replacing once and for all the contingents that had been provided as part of feudal dues. The *compagnies d'ordonnance*, raised under Charles VII, made up the chief component of the armies which fought in Italy. These heavily-armed companies of cavalry were made up almost entirely of noblemen. Louis XII added to them an artillery force which was both powerful and mobile and could be transported across the Alps to Italy. This costly achievement contributed largely to the success of the royal armies on the battlefield. They were victorious in the Italian expeditions until the whole military system had to be remodelled as a result of the use of portable firearms, the transformation of defence procedure and the introduction of new tactical methods.

At the same time, a new service was making its appearance in the royal administration. This was the diplomatic service, which had first been tried out by Louis XI in imitation of Italian governments. Since 1484 it had become customary for the king to be represented at Rome by a cardinal in permanent residence, and embassies extraordinary negotiating with foreign governments grew in number. From the beginning of the sixteenth century the Italian wars and relations with Switzerland were to extend this diplomatic activity, and in later reigns it would be put on an organised footing.

It is in the reigns of Charles VIII and Louis XII that we must seek the origin of the administrative and doctrinal changes which were a feature of the religious history of France for several centuries. The last of the disturbances caused by the Great Schism were still being felt in a Church that was seeking to regain its balance, and the endeavours of reformers wishing to restore dogma and discipline could be observed.

The religious crisis, which had thrown Christendom into confusion for more than a century and in which conciliar authority was at odds with that of the pope, had appeared in France in the form of Gallicanism. This movement, faithful to conciliar doctrine, accorded to the pope only an honorific primacy. Within the French kingdom, the Church was to be administered as a national unit and governed according to its particular customs and the decisions of its own councils under the direction of its bishops. The pope was deprived of all jurisdiction, and at the same time the levying of tithes and collection of annates and other dues extracted by the Pontifical Chamber when benefices were conferred were forbidden. Gallicanism, which had been inspired by certain renowned theologians of the fifteenth century, was not a doctrine which had been defined once and for all. Among its supporters, there were obvious differences corresponding to the particular interests actuating the various groups. Gallicanism among the clergy, being more absolute, was different from that of the king—the latter tending above all to safeguard the rights of the monarch—and also from that of the *Parlement*, that is of the lawyers, who primarily showed respect for juridical principles.

In 1438 the Pragmatic Sanction of Bourges had, without the pope's agreement, fixed the status of the Church of France. It had stipulated that benefices should be filled by free election or by the patrons designated to grant them, and that papal taxes should be abolished, together with appeals to the court of Rome in ecclesiastical actions. This enactment was condemned by the popes who had endeavoured, since the end of the Great Schism, to restore their own absolutism. Meanwhile, the kings, drawn this way and that by opposing political motives, hesitated between applying the Sanction and rescinding it. Louis XI, who was particularly fickle, had abolished it when he wished to make use of the pope, only to resuscitate it in the form of ordinances of Gallican inspiration when he was at loggerheads with Rome. Charles VIII's government was equally changeable. In 1484 the Estates General demanded that the Pragmatic Sanction be restored, but shortly afterwards there was more talk of negotiating with the pope for a concordat.

This policy of shifts and delays might have gone on quietly for a long time had the Italian wars not brought fresh fuel to the quarrel. In the belief that he was strengthening his position there, Charles VIII presented himself in Italy as a reformer of the Church. Opposing the Papacy, which had been discredited by the scandals of Alexander VI's court, he let it be said that he intended to depose the pope, and he held before him the threat of a general council. At Tours, in 1493, he had called together a commission which was to prepare a programme of reform; and his departure for Italy assumed the character of a crusade against both the Turks and Rome. But these fruitless projects faded at the very moment he was in a position to realise them: he swore an oath of allegiance to Alexander VI who soon made game of him by refusing to invest him with the kingdom of Naples.

As for Louis XII, he made use of Gallicanism as though it were a means of striking at the Papacy. This he did in view of the perplexities of Italian politics, in which Pope Julius II led every coalition directed against France. To considerations of ecclesiastical discipline were added the personal ambitions of Cardinal d'Amboise, who was constantly playing a part parallel to the king's. The cardinal, who was always helping himself to benefices, was assisted by a large and insatiable family. His ambitions turned towards Italy, and he was the chief architect of Louis XII's enterprises in that country. He had visions of putting the crowning touch to these by becoming pope himself. When he was disappointed in this ambition, he wanted at least to strengthen his hold over the Church in France by setting up a national church over which he would have ruled with all the powers of a pope. This system came into being with the legatine bull which made Georges d'Amboise the pope's representative with unlimited powers to carry out the reform of the Church in France (1501). This arrangement might spread alarmingly and jeopardise the unity of the Church; and it foreshadowed the eventual constitution of the Church of England. Moreover, it disturbed real Gallicans, for they saw in it not the restoration of traditional liberties but the threat of subjection to the king in place of subjection to the pope.

The development of this policy brought about a violent conflict which Louis XII did not scruple to kindle in the last years of his reign, with the collaboration of Cardinals Briçonnet and de Prie. As a reply to threats from Julius II, Louis XII called an assembly of jurists at Lyons in 1510: they were to draw up a judicial ordinance, based on Gallican principles, to effect a partial revival of the Pragmatic Sanction. Shortly afterwards, an assembly of clergy meeting at Tours asserted that the king had the right to defend his kingdom in any circumstances and to appeal to a council to suspend the necessity for submission to the pope. As the conflict became more serious, Louis XII, with the support of a small group of cardinals, wished to try his luck with an ecumenical council which was summoned in 1511 by a decree issued by the dissenting cardinals. The council opened at Pisa, attended by very few participants, most of whom were French. This deprived the council of its universality. Its meetings had scarcely begun when it had to escape to safety at Milan, then at Lyons, where it broke up after making a few gestures inspired by traditional conciliar doctrines. This failure was due both to military reverses in Italy and to Julius II's counter-offensive: at the same time as the council of Pisa, the pope had convened a papal council whose authority was immediately acknowledged by most Christian states (1512).

This conciliar policy, whose aim was to reform canon law and Church discipline, ran the risk of being misunderstood by the mass of the people. The government wished, therefore, to play upon public opinion through juridical and literary propaganda which would penetrate every section of society. Writers addressed every kind of reader. Jean Lemaire de Belges published an historical treatise entitled *La différence des schismes et des conciles*, in which he gave a tendentious view of the history of the popes. Jean Bouchet wrote the *Déploration de l'Eglise militante*. Pierre Gringore addressed the common people in a broad farce with the title *La chasse du cerf des cerfs* and in *Le jeu du Prince des sots* which portrayed Church and pope surrounded by personifications of the vices. Jurists and canonists influenced the educated public by republishing the text of the Pragmatic Sanction together with legal commentaries by Cosme Guymier, buttressing it up with all the arguments of Gallicanism. M. Bertrand, of Toulouse, published a *Tractatus de bello inter summum pontificem...*, and Jacques Almain, one of the theologians of the Sorbonne, wrote innumerable dogmatic treatises—*Exposition de la puissance ecclésiastique*, *De dominio naturali*, *De auctoritate Ecclesiae*. These were replies to those who defended the absolutism of the pope and to Thomas de Vio (Cajetan, the Dominican general) whose treatises were submitted to the faculty of theology with instructions to censure them. These polemics roused the passions of the opposing parties.

Such polemics were none the less relatively mild, though they were often couched in violent language—for religious feeling was too strong for the polemists not to wish to exercise some discretion. The king realised that his subjects desired peace, and, after the failure of his Gallican council, he saw, as a result of fresh military disasters, that he must come to an understanding with his enemies. The Lateran Council had condemned the 'council' of Pisa. A papal bull had anathematised the French kingdom, thus making it liable to be laid under an interdict. Louis XII was rendered powerless by repeated failures and had to give in; and the death of Julius II now facilitated the making of peace. When the cardinals who had promoted the schismatic council had become reconciled with the new pope, the king threw in his lot with the Lateran Council and sent a solemn embassy to it. All this was to bring the conflict over Gallicanism to an end. But the council had instituted proceedings against the Pragmatic Sanction and the king's government was summoned to appear in order to prove its innocence. In 1515 Francis I found himself compelled to negotiate a compromise, unless military success made it possible for him to reopen the controversy and impose his will.

This long period of militant Gallicanism had sorely tried the Church in France. Far from finding protection in the Pragmatic Sanction, it had been subjected to arbitrary interference from popes and kings alike. The rules laid down by the Sanction for the conferment of benefices had never been observed. For consistorial benefices (bishoprics and abbeys) elections were ordained and responsibility for the selection of prelates was handed over to the chapters of canons or monks of the appropriate order. But the kings had compelled acceptance of their candidates, either by commending them to the electors, or by getting them elected through resorting to intimidation or violence. This was so in every feudal domain in which princes attempted to secure appointments for their favourites. The electors were more or less submissively resigned to accepting the sovereign's creatures; if they did resist, there were endless legal actions between the canonically elected candidate and his rival. Such actions resulted in a loss of reputation for both candidates and kept anarchy alive in the dioceses. In the reigns of Charles VIII and Louis XII, fifty-five episcopal sees came under dispute in this way within the province of the Paris *Parlement* alone. The Pragmatic Sanction had laid down equally strict rules for minor benefices—curacies, canonries and chaplaincies. The customary patrons of these were also stripped of their powers, either by the pope at times when the king was trying to come to an agreement with him, or by the king himself, who made improper use of his regalian right.

In this way, all orderliness had disappeared from the life of the French Church. Those who opposed it wrongly blamed the Pragmatic Sanction for this decline, for these irregularities had their origin precisely in infringements of its instructions. Episcopal sees and abbeys were set aside for members of great families and for dignitaries of the State who wished to find a lucrative career without having to give up their secular activities. Some families, who were more particularly devoted to the Church, monopolised provincial benefices which seemed to be set apart for them. Such were the Briçonnets, the Salazars, the Ponchers; such also the d'Amboise family, whose members at one time occupied simultaneously five dioceses and several abbeys. Moreover, since the most lucrative benefices did not satisfy them, they did not scruple to indulge in pluralism, contrary to all canonical rules concerning incompatible benefices. And wealthy holders of benefices arranged among themselves barter and exchanges together with settlements of incomes, trafficking in dues paid to ecclesiastical courts and other financial agreements, all these being so many simoniacal practices. What is more, these dignitaries did not make a rule of carrying out their duties. Spending their lives at court or in their great houses, in the army or in embassies, they visited their dioceses only to take them over or, in some cases, to be buried in their cathedrals. Instead they delegated their powers to vicars-general and to agents appointed to collect their revenues. In monastic benefices, the procedure was different but the results were identical, because no one imagined that these great dignitaries could ever submit to a monastic rule: they held their abbeys *in commendam* and entrusted their administration to deputies. These worldly clergy had not lost their faith, but were imbued with a secular spirit, and were more concerned with humanism and art than piety. Even if they did not shock them by their dissolute morals and by the violent conflicts between the bishops and the canons and monks who owed them obedience, these clergy disappointed the faithful by abandoning their traditions.

The lower clergy, all the innumerable canons, curates, chaplains and vicars, showed the same lack of order, which persisted despite the requirements of the Pragmatic Sanction. Very many of these benefices were occupied by eminent dignitaries who used them to supplement their income. The remainder were set apart for ecclesiastics of humbler origins, for university graduates and law-officers, who were no more anxious than their superiors to carry out their duties. In the end, it fell to the general body of priests in charge to perform these duties. They were men of no education or ecclesiastical training, ignorant of dogma and liturgy, sometimes ignorant even of Latin and capable only of going through rites whose inner meaning escaped them. They also lost dignity because of the poverty in which they lived, for they were deprived of the greater part of the normal income of their church by the titular incumbents, and were very often reduced to living on perquisites which were not collected without causing clashes with their parishioners. How many more of these priests, having no incumbency, lived haphazard on alms or casual and undependable fees?

The monasteries were afflicted with the same disease. Their revenues were reserved to the commendatory abbot, while the monks were reduced to such extreme poverty that some of them were brought to the point of suing their own abbot. Buildings fell into ruin and life was no longer ordered according to the rule. The ablest among them gave up communal life and lived as if in private within the monasteries, while others indulged in the most worldly pleasures, like dancing and hunting, and did not abstain from more serious forms of dissipation. In this way, the orders were breaking up and the wandering monk is a figure who often appears in the society of the times.

These members of the lower clergy, whose origins were in the common people and who shared their kind of existence, were neither more nor less depraved than the rest of their contemporaries. But, like their superiors, they were not distinguishable from the general body of the faithful and had lost sight of the meaning of the religious life.

Those who were concerned to bring about a change maintained that the Pragmatic Sanction was responsible for this decline. Later, in order to get acceptance of the concordat, Chancellor Duprat was to assert that it was necessary to reform the system of legislation. But in reality, all these irregularities arose from the fact that the Pragmatic Sanction was held in contempt and that the king and higher clergy interfered illegally in Church affairs. So ingrained indeed was habit that, even when the concordat was in force, morals were unchanged and irregularities grew more serious.

However, with the appearance of certain personages who visibly exerted their influence in the times of Charles VIII and Louis XII, there were signs that a change for the better might take place. The so-called *rigoristes* did their utmost to bring about a return to order and to observance of canonical rules, to restore monastic discipline and the study of theological subjects, and to encourage among the clergy the tradition of mysticism which had gone on uninterrupted in the fifteenth century in Flanders and the Rhineland. Some attempts at reformation had been made during earlier reigns: certain abbots had striven to regain proper control over the Benedictine monasteries and the mendicant orders. But these reforms gave rise to quarrels in which every institution tried to maintain its independence. This spirit of reform also inspired the Estates General of 1484, which resulted in the Synod of Sens (1485) and the assembly of clergy at Tours (1493) publishing decrees of reform. These ordained that discipline should be restored and were in fact a mere reminder of the requirements laid down by the Pragmatic Sanction.

Charles VIII and after him Louis XII were prompted by good intentions, as was also Cardinal d'Amboise who had control over all the clergy in the kingdom. But the temptation to make use of the Church and her riches for purely temporal ends was too strong, and only a few individual reformers were able to take up the work of restoration. The most famous of these reformers were the Franciscan preacher Olivier Maillard, the hermit Saint Francis of Paola, who founded the order of Minims, and Jean de Rély, bishop of Angers. At the same time, a mystic from the Low Countries, Jean Standonck, who was filled with a desire for asceticism and also with eagerness to apply the canonical rules to the letter, re-established the Congregation of Montaigu and enforced the discipline with relentless rigour. Jean Mombaer, who also came from the Low Countries, reformed the monasteries of Château-Landon and Saint-Victor. All these were supported by the judicial authorities, for their reforms sometimes necessitated the use of force. This made these undertakings dangerous and hardly compatible with the religious spirit which should have inspired the clergy.

A renewal of Christian thought was no less indispensable as a result of the decline in university studies, for these were bogged down in scholastic philosophy and the study of commentaries through which they were losing sight of the thought of the great writers of antiquity and the Middle Ages. On the model of the Italian Renaissance, there was taking shape a movement in which great attention was paid both to ancient philosophy and to the text of the scriptures, with the intention of restoring these writings to their original form and of fathoming the thought of their authors.

The founder of this movement was Jacques Lefèvre d'Étaples, who was active during the half-century before the French Reformation came to light. The centre of his activity was the college of Cardinal Lemoine where he taught and attracted all those who, like himself, were concentrating on a study of the scriptures. Lefèvre had been trained on the methods of the Italian humanists with which he combined the mystical thought of the Rhineland. He began his career with a study of Aristotle, and had published an edition of his works. But he mistrusted the philosophy of the ancients and soon came to regard it only as a stepping stone towards Christian thought. So he turned to a study of the Scriptures, considering that they should be edited according to the methods of classical scholarship. His tremendous toil led up to the publication of the *Psalter* in 1509; this included a commentary to elucidate the literal meaning and a mystical interpretation of the text. In 1512 he published the *Epistles* of Saint Paul, which concerned some of the fundamentals of Christian dogma: they were to be interpreted by the reformers in such a way as to provide the doctrine of justification by faith. Lefèvre was satisfied with a very simple commentary on the thought of Saint Paul, and did not broach the disconcerting questions of salvation, grace and predestination.

The work of Lefèvre, whose career had been eminently successful, opened up new vistas of theological interference with traditional dogma. His work was still imbued with medieval mysticism and respected established practices, but it also prepared the way for the changes to be brought about by the reformers.

Lefèvre had been the first to pay due respect to humanism, and little by little it gained esteem in all the literate sections of society, in the monasteries and in the Paris colleges. A number of open-minded men bent themselves also to a study of antiquity, of Greek and of the works of the Italian humanists. Robert Gaguin and, later, Guillaume Budé were among the foremost of those who renewed these studies. But Erasmus was the most renowned of them: by residing more than once in Paris and corresponding with scholarly circles, he became one of the most influential mentors of the Parisian humanists. While the influence of Erasmus may have been comparable to that of Lefèvre, their attitudes towards morality and traditional religion were different. There was a marked contrast between Lefèvre's mysticism and Erasmus's Christian wisdom and his respect for a religious ideal which made light of formal observances and strict conformity.

Under their two-fold influence, there appeared edition after edition of classical texts, with commentaries inspired by increasingly precise knowledge of the thought of the ancients. Teaching at the Sorbonne and the College of Navarre was revolutionised, and in this way the 'Pre-renaissance' was initiated, and Paris, in the reign of Louis XII, like Oxford and Basle and other Rhenish towns, became one of its most active centres. It was a powerful movement and swept along the most eminent scholars, but as yet it affected only a limited and select group. The religious and intellectual outlook of the great majority still belonged to the Middle Ages. Books of popular piety, devotion to images and relics, pilgrimages, and an acute sense of suffering and death maintained in men's minds a formalism which was expressed in religious art by the themes of the Crucifixion, the Entombment and the Dance of Death.

The common people, who remained outside the stream of the intellectual revival, were still primarily concerned with the material anxieties of their corporate life and their daily bread. In this sphere, too, the reigns of Charles VIII and Louis XII are a period apart, rich in new beginnings. The Hundred Years War had brought in its train disasters comparable to those of the harshest epochs of the early Middle Ages. Depopulation and ruin of the countryside, and economic crisis aggravated by epidemics had even affected the towns. Since the middle of the fifteenth century, recovery had been difficult, and the looting carried on by troops and the wars of the reign of Louis XI had prevented the appearance of any movement of revival.

When Charles VIII came to the throne, the decline in population was still very marked. In the provinces most seriously affected, the countryside was deserted: their inhabitants had been annihilated or had left them for districts where there was less danger. Many documents refer to villages that were abandoned never to be occupied again. Much land had become a wilderness once more: forest and scrub had invaded the arable ground, and some stretches of country which became waste were not to be cultivated again until the nineteenth century. The boundaries of the domains themselves had disappeared and properties got badly confused. Feudal dues and the revenue accruing from the ownership of land had disappeared with the boundaries within which their collection was authorised. It was not uncommon to find that people no longer knew to which lord a particular estate belonged, so that the very foundations of the feudal system, which had been worked out in such minute detail before, were shaken. And this state of affairs was not limited to a few isolated districts. On the contrary, it was the fate of those areas which, in the past, had been most prosperous: the Ile-de-France, Normandy and Gascony, which suffered particularly from soldiers' looting, were becoming a wilderness once more. Even the towns were not spared these disasters. There was no reconstruction of buildings that fell into ruin, and, although the peasantry took refuge in them, all witnesses testify that their population was small and labour expensive.

There were to be increasing efforts towards recovery for more than half a century, during which domestic peace remained undisturbed after the end of the Italian wars and fiscal exactions were less severe. At the same time, a series of strokes of good fortune spared the country the fatal epidemics and bad weather which caused widespread famine. The population increased and villages were slowly rebuilt during this period of relative prosperity. At the end of the fifteenth century, people reappeared in the places that had been abandoned and began to till the soil again. Often the new inhabitants came from far afield. There were many strangers in the towns, and not a few in the country districts, and at the same time there was much migration from one province to another.

The lords, who depended on the cultivation of their domains for their income, tried every conceivable means of attracting new tenants. For them, what was most important was to put the land under the plough again, even if it involved making sacrifices. The most outstanding of these were the emancipation of the serfs, and concessions of every kind granted to freemen. Rather than develop their estates entirely for themselves, which was made hazardous by the scarcity of labour, the lords preferred to grant perpetual leases on payment of a fixed annual rent which never exceeded four *sous* an *arpent*. This amount was insignificant even in the currency of the time, and was to become more so later on as the value of money depreciated. The system of tenancies with a fixed time limit, whose terms were liable to revision, was also abandoned, and the lords, who could claim all untenanted lands as their own, apportioned them like the others in the hope of reconstituting their estates and attracting to them a larger population. There were other advantages, too, such as temporary exemption from feudal burdens, and the loan of tools and seed. The result was that, after the close of a particularly difficult period, the peasantry enjoyed once more a semblance of prosperity. Some of them, indeed, who were especially favoured, achieved genuine affluence, bought up vacant lands and built up great holdings, made up of pastures and mixed farming. These newly-rich peasants were to go on rising in the social scale until they took their place among the bourgeois aristocracy, along with certain of the town-dwelling artisans and merchants. Ownership of property in the hands of former tenants who now held it in hereditary right was confirmed, but it was at the mercy of fluctuations in the value of money and their long-term consequences.

Now, while it is clear that at the end of the fifteenth century the metallic value of money declined as it had done almost uninterruptedly for several centuries, it is also evident that its purchasing power increased appreciably. The lord, who was sure of a fixed revenue from his feudal domain, was undoubtedly adversely affected, because he received less cash for an unchanging rent which had been stipulated in money of account; but his receipts allowed him to buy an ever-increasing quantity of goods, with the result that a balance was maintained and he was secure in a certain affluence which seemed likely to subsist in the future. The tenant, too, gained advantage from this state of affairs, because he was protected against any arbitrary raising of his dues, and especially against excessive exactions of the *taille* to be paid to his lord. And the real agricultural prosperity of the times provided the tenant with adequate means of livelihood. There is no doubt that in this period the welfare of the rural population was at a standard rarely attained in our history. But all this was to be subjected, in the first thirty years or so of the sixteenth century, to the challenge of renewed invasion and a period of monetary upheavals more intense than ever.

In the towns, there were similar achievements in reconstruction. Industry and commerce were coming to life again as security returned, and were undergoing a transformation as a result of relations being established with new countries. Contacts with Italy brought new forms of trade as well as commercial methods that had not been used before. The Mediterranean countries were being opened up, as a result of the annexation of Provence to the royal domain, and soon afterwards it was the turn of the Atlantic coast on which maritime activity had been growing since the discovery of the New World. The increase in population was particularly noticeable in the towns. After Louis XI, who had called upon foreigners to come and populate the industrial centres, the movement became broader, particularly with the arrival of Italian artisans and merchants. Once they had taken up permanent residence, they found their way into all classes of French society in the sixteenth century. In this way Lyons became an international centre, continuously inhabited by a cosmopolitan population of Flemings, Germans from the Swiss Cantons and the Rhineland, and above all Italians. This renewal of activity was very marked in the traditional guilds, but brought to them at the same time a spirit hitherto unknown.

While some aspects of medieval life were fading away, it seemed that the life of the craft guilds was being renewed. Guilds were found only in certain regions; they were almost unknown in the western provinces and even in the big industrial towns like Lyons, which was still faithful to the principle of freedom in the crafts. But they now spread, thanks to the artisans themselves and to the authority of the king, who found opportunities to make use of these organisations. Successive kings greatly increased the number of guilds by issuing sets of rules for them and ratifying the regulations governing the trades already established. The guilds thus became public bodies, and they had a share in municipal life and provided the constables of the watch. They could also be relied upon to pay any exceptional taxes or to meet demands for forced loans. It was the secret schemings of municipal policy, particularly in financial matters, that favoured the growth of the guild system and enlisted the kings' active sympathy. At the same time, the spirit of the guilds was undergoing a change: the crafts, concentrating now far more on their professional activities, were giving up the political agitation in which they had often indulged in earlier reigns. Domestic quarrels within the guilds were less frequent, and disputes between masters and journeymen less serious. This was no doubt a result of the relative stability of the economic situation which, for a time, blunted any clash of interests.

But beneath this apparent peace, signs of disorder could be detected. As they grew richer, masters were more and more inclined to accentuate the differences between the journeymen and themselves. While the masters received public honours and material rewards, together with pre-eminence in municipal administration, the workers formed more and more associations in the guise of brotherhoods and *compagnonnages* (journeymen's guilds). These contained seeds of a hostility that was to result in violent conflicts and repressive measures when economic circumstances deteriorated. Such tendencies were even more easily discernible in the crafts which had risen out of new techniques. Silk manufacture, introduced from Italy, took root at Tours, where it was supplied by silkworms bred in the southern provinces. If one may not yet speak of large-scale industries, there were, none the less, groups of artisans—spinners, throwsters, weavers and dyers—who used expensive raw materials. These necessitated the use of complicated equipment; considerable capital was therefore involved, and the operatives were under the constant direction of merchants responsible for the co-operation of individual workers whom they provided with tools and raw materials.

The printing industry, dependent as it was on the manufacture of paper, absorbed even more labour and capital. It had been introduced in the reign of Louis XI and had since spread rapidly. After the first printing-houses had been established, in Paris in 1470, and in Lyons in 1473, the number of presses in the two cities increased greatly. These towns were to become the chief centres of the book trade in the sixteenth century. In Lyons there were fifty-three printing-houses at the end of the fifteenth century and more than a hundred in 1515. A considerable number of workers were employed, when one includes those engaged in the indispensable auxiliary activities—paper-making, type-founding, illuminating, engraving and binding. At first, these workers had come from Germany, like the materials they used, but they were later recruited locally. Rapid progress was made and the industry spread through every province: in the latter years of the century, there were presses in more than thirty towns and a very large number of books were being printed at that time.

More than any other industry, printing called for big advances of money: the equipment, involving the use of type and presses, was costly in itself. The wages of the specialised workers—compositors and proof-readers—were high, and the sum that had to be advanced for the publication of a book exceeded the outlay necessary in any other trade, particularly as arrangements had to be made for the distribution of books. Printers were both booksellers and publishers and had therefore to attend fairs and find export markets. The great printers of the period, Jodocus Badius, the Marneffes and the Estiennes, needed to be both scholars and captains of industry. In addition, the new industry brought other changes to the world of labour. Printers' journeymen, and proof-readers in particular, often came from far afield, attracted by the important printing-houses in the large centres. There they formed groups in which frequent disorders made for conditions favourable to the spread of new ideas.

In the same way, trade, encouraged by more settled conditions, was developing along lines hitherto unknown. While wars were raging, the great trade routes had avoided France, but from now on we see her resuming her place in international commerce. The great trading centre was Lyons. Fairs had been established there by Charles VII in 1420, but were held regularly and became really active only after 1489. Then, however, they began to enjoy considerable success, for privileges were granted to the merchants who attended them and some of these settled permanently in the town. The great volume of business transacted there was due to the proximity of large trading-towns in foreign countries (Geneva and the Rhine towns) and to trade with Italy, which had increased as a result of the wars and continued to expand up to 1567. Each of the four annual fairs, which lasted for a fortnight, was preceded and followed by periods of privilege and delay for the settlement of accounts. They maintained almost constant activity in this city which, served as it was by good navigable waterways, was a halting-place on the routes linking the northern countries to the Mediterranean.

To a lesser degree, other towns enjoyed similar activity. The practice of holding several fairs spread to all parts, and 400 grants of privilege were made in the reign of Charles VIII alone. Like the chief towns of the kingdom (Rouen, Tours, Troyes, Dijon and Montpellier), Paris had its fairs, at Saint-Denis and Saint-Germain-des-Prés. These fairs were real international markets for certain products needed in industry—salt (in which a few maritime countries had a virtual monopoly), alum (which was indispensable in the manufacture of cloth), silk, spices, and metals (in which France had but poor natural resources), especially copper, which was needed in the casting of artillery and was imported from mines in Bohemia and Upper Germany.

Together with this increasing trade went considerable movements of money, transfers of precious metals and all kinds of coinage, which were difficult to transport owing to the dangers attendant on travel. The scarcity of money was not conducive to the ever-growing needs of commerce. Like other countries, France suffered, at the end of the fifteenth century, from this shortage of precious metals, and this necessitated the use of credit and the intervention of banks. Banks were not unknown in France from the thirteenth century onwards, if not earlier. But political crises had suspended their activities which, until now, had been primarily concerned with money-changing and short-term loans. After the Hundred Years War, they reappeared, controlled by Italians, when the Medici established a branch of their bank at Lyons. Others followed, and they became more numerous as the sixteenth century approached. These companies, most of them with headquarters at Lyons, multiplied by setting up branches in the main towns of the kingdom, especially in Paris, which was decidedly subordinate to Lyons.

All these companies were in the hands of foreigners—Italians, from Florence or Lucca, like the Capponi, the Gadagnes and the Bonvisi, or Germans whose activity was controlled by banks in Augsburg or Nürnberg. French banks were few and far between and traded only incidentally in money; and even then they did so only in conjunction with their merchant activity, so that it is difficult to draw the line between banking proper and large-scale trading in general. They kept almost entirely in their own hands banking business 'at the court of Rome', where they acted as intermediaries and lent money to the recipients of benefices and to litigants who had dealings with the papal administration.

This trading involved somewhat complex operations on which the business of the fairs and international commerce were based: bills of exchange, payments by transfer and balancing of credits, and deposits and loans. It was thus possible to settle accounts to which the lack of circulation of currency would otherwise have brought insurmountable difficulties. Even governments had to seek the help of bankers, when their enterprises demanded the advance of large sums. Charles VIII's campaign in Italy was financed by loans granted by Italian bankers at Lyons. This state of affairs continued, and from then on every political undertaking was accompanied by an undercurrent of financial transactions, as the imperial election of 1519 showed.

It was in this way that certain families amassed great fortunes which were the basis of their power. And these were very different from the landed fortunes of former times. The mercantile bourgeoisie, which had ties with the administration, made great strides in the reigns of Charles VIII and his successors. It was certainly not without predecessors, of whom the best known is Jacques Cœur, but the growth of this new class was hardly noticeable before the end of the fifteenth century, when the de Beaunes, the Bohiers, the Huraults and the Briçonnets made their mark. They were merchants, financiers and administrators of the royal treasury all at once, and without their aid the state could not exist. They took advantage of this to have themselves appointed to the great offices of Government and Church, and they aspired to raise themselves to the level of the great landowners and even to gain access to the nobility.

This emphasis on money, and the fact that it was indispensable in certain industries and in large-scale trade, mark the advent of capitalism in the economic life of France. In the silk industry, the capitalist who bought and imported the raw material had it processed by a number of workers, whose equipment he himself owned; and afterwards, when its manufacture was complete, he marketed the cloth. Differences became more marked between the merchant who possessed the capital, ran risks and enjoyed the profits, and the worker to whom he paid a wage. The same distinctions were to be found in the printing trade. Very often, the same merchant who possessed capital lent money at interest. This might be against the laws of the Church, but he resorted to all kinds of merely formal precautions which concealed the true nature of his transactions. In this way, he became the creditor of the artisans and peasants whose land he eventually held as security. This was the beginning of vast changes in the ownership of landed property.

The capitalists made loans even to the king; his needs were great and he contracted more debts every day. But his credit was so low that he had to borrow with the great personages at court standing surety for him, and at rates of interest much higher than those in use among business men. It was not unknown even for newly-rich bourgeois to buy the administrative offices which the government was beginning to use as a source of revenue. Public services and even part of the power of the State were thus passing, as though they were part of their inheritance, into the hands of ordinary subjects. First the king put financial offices up for sale, then judicial offices; at first he did so diffidently and with all kinds of precautions: sales were disguised as loans, which the king never repaid. This practice continued to develop, particularly in and after the reign of Louis XII, as the needs of the treasury increased and administrative services became more numerous. These were practices new in the economic life of the nation, and they closely affected its social structure. The changes they produced became clearly manifest with the renewal of business activity following the end of the English wars.

CHAPTER XI

THE HISPANIC KINGDOMS AND THE CATHOLIC KINGS

THE year 1492 was an *annus mirabilis* for Spain. Granada was taken and the eight centuries of war with the Moslems brought to an end. The Jews were expelled from Spain, and the New World was discovered. Castile, which all through the Middle Ages had been secluded in the centre of the peninsula, suddenly emerged as a world Power. The rise of Castile was rather a matter of luck and accident than of thoughtful planning. But when opportunities came the Castilians rose to the occasion and seized them as successfully as they could, the chief limitation being the economic factor. Fate put enormous wealth into the hands of a nation with high ambitions and lofty ideals, but with little economic sense. No wonder the great empire which emerged was beset with financial problems. The real wonder is that it lasted so long.

The population in the peninsula under the Crown of Castile was not large. A count taken for military purposes in 1482 gave a total of 7,500,000. But the count was very rough and the figure seems much too high. Another count, taken in 1530 for tax purposes, gave only 3,433,000, but this did not include Galicia (perhaps with 600,000 people) or the kingdoms of Granada and Murcia, also densely populated. A third tax-count in 1541 gave about 6,272,000. Considering that 1530–70 was probably a peak period, the figure for 1482 ought to be much lower than for 1541, but should probably be over 4,500,000. As for the states of the Crown of Aragon, the approximate figures are: Aragon 270,000 (1495), Valencia 270,000 (1510) and Catalonia 307,000 (1512).

The people of Castile were mainly engaged in agriculture or led a nomadic pastoral life. Most of the arable land was owned by the nobility, the military orders, the Church, monastic orders, and the Crown, or was the common land of towns and villages. The taxes were borne by peasants, the noblemen being exempt. Cereals were the most important crop, though they were often insufficient and wheat had to be imported. Ferdinand thought he could supply Castile with corn from Sicily, and thus increase sheep-rearing and wool production for the Flemish market. Charles V, who wanted the peasants for soldiers, supplied Castile with wheat from the Netherlands, Denmark and Germany. The peninsular states of the Crown of Aragon imported corn from the other Mediterranean states, Sicily and Sardinia; Valencia sometimes had it from Roumania or Turkey. The Castilians thought Aragon might provide a market for their corn, and its export to Aragon was declared free (1480). New land in

Murcia was devoted to growing wheat for Aragon. But the shepherds, who wanted the land for grazing, rose in opposition. After Isabella's death and subsequent friction between Castile and Ferdinand, the Castilian Cortes tried to stop exports of corn to Aragon. In spite of good harvests they insisted on this again in 1518, and finally in 1525 exports were banned completely. The ban was in the end lifted by Charles (1537). Aragon, and sometimes Catalonia, relied on imports from Languedoc and Provence. The Basque provinces were supplied from Nantes with wheat from Brittany and the west of France. The wheat supply to the Indies was another liability. It had to be brought from Germany, Flanders, France and the Barbary states.

Though the harvests of 1509–20 were better than those of 1503–7, the Castilian wheat-crop was always insufficient. As from 1502 the Crown had to control the price, though the official prices were not always observed. The price-index for wheat, if taken at 100 in 1511, had reached 273 by 1530, although the influx of American silver had not yet affected it. The peasantry was in destitution and hunger. According to official texts the peasants were head over ears in debt and were compelled to sell corn still on the threshing ground to the middlemen who profited by their poverty. Not until c. 1535 did changes begin which were to last some thirty years. Thanks to American silver, new buyers of land appeared, but it was then used for vineyards, not for wheat, and by mid-century the price of wine was going up.

For the economy of Castile, sheep rearing was far more important. The nomadic shepherds and their movements were under the control of the Mesta (*Honorable Consejo de los Pastores de estos Reinos*), a national guild of sheepowners dating from the thirteenth century. According to incomplete figures, the average number of sheep for each year from 1512 to 1521 was c. 2,840,000. Most of the pasture lands of the south, where they wintered and which the sheepowners rented, belonged to the military orders, whose estates Ferdinand and Isabella had annexed to the Crown. The Mesta was extremely wealthy, and whenever Charles found himself in difficulties he appealed to it for help. The Mesta acted as banker for the Crown, in 1518, 1519, 1525, 1526, 1528 and in later years. In return many laws were passed favouring sheep rearing as against agriculture, and forcing land to be left uncultivated for the benefit of the flocks. National economic life and much of the royal finances were centred in the flocks. Besides occasionally lending to the Crown, the shepherds paid an annual rent for the pasturages that nominally belonged to the military orders, but were in fact under the direct control of the Crown. Charles V often farmed out these pasturages and the collection of their rents was accepted by foreign bankers as surety for loans. Thus in 1525 they were granted to the Fuggers in return for advances made to Charles for his election as emperor.

The royal policy of protecting the wool trade had the same reason behind it. Under Ferdinand and Isabella an order of 1462 was still enforced by which one-third of the wool had to be reserved for the Castilian weavers. Charles later tried to raise the proportion to half, but the measure, intended to develop home industry, was opposed by the exporters and by the Mesta and had to be withdrawn. Genoese merchants controlled perhaps 40 per cent of the wool trade, and this led them to play an active part in Spanish trade and banking. Castilian wool was shipped to Italy from Màlaga and Cartagena; wool from Aragon, the Maestrat and the Castilian hinterland of Valencia went from Tortosa and Valencia. Exports to Flanders were the most important, the great wool markets being at Burgos and Medina del Campo. In 1494 Ferdinand and Isabella granted the merchants of Burgos the privilege of organising their *Consulado*, a guild for the conduct of home and foreign trade on the model of the Catalan *Consolats de la Mar* (Valencia 1283, Mallorca 1343, Barcelona 1347). The Burgos *Consulado* had the right to fix freight and maritime insurance rates. Shipping in the Bay of Biscay was brought under its control, and an agreement was made with Bilbao (1495), the port which actually provided most of the shipping. Seven or eight thousand pack mules went between Burgos and Bilbao carrying twelve to fifteen thousand woolpacks every year (roughly 900 tons). One fleet or two, as required, sailed every year from Bilbao to Antwerp.

Seville was meanwhile emerging as the great centre for trade with the Americas. The *Casa de Contratación* to control all trade with the Indies was established there in 1503 and later on (1543) a *Consulado* modelled on that of Burgos. Seville, moreover, with a monopoly of trade with America, both export and import, attracted all foreign merchants, expanding rapidly in the sixteenth century and becoming the largest city in Spain (25,000 inhabitants in 1517, 90,000 in 1594).

In the Catalan-speaking countries the picture was different. Valencia, and even more Barcelona, were now in decline after a brilliant past. Their political expansion had grown out of the expansion of their Mediterranean trade: the Balearics, Sicily, Malta, Greece, Sardinia and Naples, one after another came under Catalan rule or influence (trade settlements on the coasts of North Africa, the Black Sea and in Ethiopia). This early Catalan nucleus of empire, was the contribution that Ferdinand brought as his patrimony to the formation of the later empire, along with the legacy of Catalan-Aragonese friendships and enmities on the diplomatic chessboard of Europe. On the other hand, the later empire failed to use the experience of the Catalans in empire-building, in the administration of overseas territories (except for borrowing their institutions of the *Consolat* and the viceroy) and their economic good sense. There were two reasons for this: the nationalistic tendency of the Castilians to regard the empire as their own possession, with the royal support of this view; and the decline of Catalonia.

The biological roots of this decline go back to the fourteenth century and may be found in the exhaustion of a small people after their Mediterranean expansion, the Black Death, and losses among the nobility in the expeditions to Sardinia in the third quarter of the fourteenth century. Catalonia was also affected by the European economic crisis at the end of the century, and a number of adverse conditions developed in trade, finance and banking, to which the Catalans often failed to make adequate adjustment because of their too rigid traditional methods. After the Barcelona banking crisis of 1381–3 the financial capital of the Crown of Aragon shifted to Valencia, which throve on its agriculture (based on rice and sugar), the attraction of the Aragonese wool exports, and the facilities which it afforded to Genoese capital and merchants.

After 1430 dissensions developed in Barcelona between the merchants and craftsmen on the one hand and wealthy citizens and landowners on the other, and in the country districts between the feudal landowners and the peasantry. These problems were aggravated by the neglect of Alphonso V, who left his peninsula domains to settle in his newly acquired kingdom of Naples (1432–58). The various attempts by the authorities and the merchants to redress the situation might have succeeded had they been supported by a sympathetic and coherent royal policy such as that of the past sovereigns of the house of Barcelona.

The devaluation of the coinage in 1458, while it was welcomed by the merchants as a measure to foster trade, was resented by the landowners and *rentiers*. These sabotaged the measure, causing such animosity between the social classes and such unrest that the stage was set for a major drama. This was the Catalan Revolution (1462–72), led mainly by the Barcelona merchants, against John II, the father of Ferdinand, from which Catalonia emerged utterly exhausted, although the final settlement between the king and the country was satisfactory as regards the national and democratic liberties for which the Catalans had fought. Social unrest continued with the revolt of the peasants (*remences*) against the feudal landowners. Many merchants left Barcelona during the war and settled in Valencia, but the final blow came with the establishment of the Inquisition in the teeth of Catalan opposition (1484–7). Then most of the merchants, Jews or converted Jews, left the country with their capital and goods, so that the municipal authorities could fairly describe Barcelona as 'completely lost and destroyed'.

A moderate revival of Catalan trade with North Africa occurred in the early sixteenth century, with the expeditions against Mers-el-Kebir, Oran, Algiers and Tripoli in the years 1505–10; Cardinal Jiménez de Cisneros played a large part in organising the expeditions, but substantial Catalan financial help, armed contingents and shipping were engaged. While the occupied cities were annexed to Jiménez's archdiocese of Toledo, the Catalans gained the right to trade with the new territories (1512) and preferential terms for their textile exports to those lands. During the first half of the sixteenth century Catalan trade continued with Sicily, Naples, North Africa, and Egypt, but it was only a shadow of what it had been. The Mediterranean, infested with Turkish and Berber pirates, had lost much of its importance by the removal of the centres of European economic life to the north and west. The exclusion of the Catalans from trade with America deprived them of their last chance of redress. After this, towards the middle of the century, Barcelona sank into obscurity.

The marriage of Ferdinand and Isabella (19 October 1469) took place during the period when Catalonia was outside the authority of the bridegroom's father, John II, who was not recognised again until 1472. The Arab kingdom of Granada was not conquered until 1492, and Ferdinand, after Isabella's death, when he was in Castile as sole governor to administer the realm, but not as king, conquered the kingdom of Navarre in 1512. Thus all the peninsula except Portugal later came under the authority of one man, Charles V.

The union of the Crowns of Castile and Aragon under Ferdinand and Isabella is therefore an important landmark in this evolution and its constitutional aspects deserve examination. The marriage of Ferdinand with Isabella was planned by the crafty John II of Aragon, who closely watched developments in Castile in connection with the succession of Henry IV. Court gossip insisted that Princess Juana, the queen's daughter, was not the child of King Henry (known as *El Impotente*) but of a Portuguese nobleman, Beltran de la Cueva, after whom Juana was contemptuously called *La Beltraneja*. The party of the nobles and prelates opposing Henry made capital of this gossip in their intrigues. The king, who under pressure from the opposition had sometimes admitted the illegitimacy of Juana, stated on his death bed that she was his own daughter. (In our own day Dr Marañon, after collecting all the available medical evidence, has concluded that she probably was the daughter of the king.) The opposition party, however, managed to get her declared illegitimate and supported Prince Alfonso as the heir to the throne. He and Henry were sons of John II of Castile (1406–54), but Alfonso and the future Isabella the Catholic were the children of his second wife, Isabella of Portugal. This Portugese queen was insane, like Juana the Mad, the daughter of Isabella and mother of Charles V. She was probably responsible for the streak of abnormality that ran through the Spanish Habsburgs. Prince Alfonso died young (1464). As soon as John II of Aragon heard the news, he dispatched agents to Castile and began to cast his toils round Isabella in order to obtain her for his son. First, though the agreement of Toros de Guisando (1468) seems now to have been a fake, Henry recognised Isabella as his heir. Then the other suitors were discarded. These were the French duke of Guienne, brother of Louis XI, and Alfonso V of Portugal. The marriage of Isabella to Ferdinand was the final outcome of John II's many intrigues, his league with the archbishop of Toledo, Alphonso Carrillo, and his bribery of Castilian notables, particularly those to whom the custody of the young princess (then about 18) had been entrusted, their role now being to advise her to marry Ferdinand. In all these negotiations John II was helped by the most prominent Jewish families of Castile (the Benvenistes and Abraham Seneor) and of Aragon (La Cavalleria), who were linked by common business interests and who believed that the young sovereigns would protect their race against the anti-semitism that had been mounting in Castile since 1391.

John II, of the Castilian illegitimate line of the Trastamaras, though a sovereign of the Crown of Aragon, had always considered himself a Castilian prince, no less than his Castilian second wife Juana Enriquez. Among his perennial anxieties were his large estates in Castile and Estremadura coveted by rival nobles. In addition, all the thrones in the peninsula were occupied by himself and his sisters. His brother, Alfonso V, had been a sovereign of the Crown of Aragon and brought under it a new kingdom, Naples, and John was his heir. His sister Maria had been the first wife of John II of Castile and was the mother of the reigning Castilian king, Henry IV. His other sister Eleanor was the wife of Edward I of Portugal. He himself, by his first marriage to Queen Blanca of Navarre had become king consort of this kingdom too and kept its crown after her death. All this was more than enough to inflame an ambitious man like John II with the desire to bring all these kingdoms under his rule or that of his young son. There were also considerations of power and diplomacy. Foremost among these was his rivalry with Louis XI of France and the need to build up in the peninsula a force to match that north of the Pyrenees.

The surprising fact about the union of Castile and Aragon is the absence of any agreement on the matter between sovereigns or cortes, apart from the marriage contract between the young couple, Ferdinand who was eighteen, and Isabella who was nineteen. The contract was signed by Isabella's representatives and Ferdinand on 7 January 1469 at Cervera, the headquarters of John II's army in his campaign against Catalonia. Two objectives were met by the contract: the Castilian demand for guarantees against interference by Ferdinand and the Aragonese in the government of Castile; and John's determination to have Isabella for his son at any cost. The contract provided that Ferdinand should live with Isabella in Castile and neither leave the country nor take their children out of Castile without her consent. All letters and deeds must be issued and signed by the queen and king jointly, in the kingdoms of either. No person must be appointed by the king to the royal council of Castile or to any other office, other than a Castilian national, and with the advice and agreement of the queen. All cities and fortified places in

Castile must take an oath of allegiance to the queen alone. The king must not enter upon any war, or make peace or any alliance with any other king or lord without the queen's advice and consent. In token of the 'confederation' with the kingdom of Castile, and to augment her dowry, Ferdinand was to hand over to her two cities (mentioned in the text) in each of the kingdoms of Aragon, Valencia, and Sicily, plus a third city in each to be chosen later by her (nothing is said about Catalonia, as the country was then up in arms against John II). Ferdinand was to give Isabella 100,000 gold florins within four months of the contract, and in case of trouble within Castile Ferdinand would personally lead 4000 spearmen to suppress the trouble.

The docility with which Ferdinand and his crafty father had accepted these terms was explained on the death of Henry IV of Castile (1474). Then Ferdinand sprang a surprise by claiming that he, and not Isabella, was the legitimate heir as the only male descendant of the house of Trastamara. This being a Castilian affair was submitted to Cardinal Pedro Gonzalez de Mendoza and to the archbishop of Toledo, Alonso Carrilloz. The main points of their award were as follows: in all laws, coins and seals Ferdinand's name should precede Isabella's, but the arms of Castile should precede those of Aragon. The revenue of Castile should be used to defray all the expenses of its administration and what remained should be shared by the queen and the king in a form to be decided between themselves. The same condition should apply to the income from Ferdinand's side. Names of candidates for vacant bishoprics should be submitted to the pope jointly by king and queen, although the queen alone should suggest the names. Decisions of the courts should be signed by both, should they be in the same place. If they were in different provinces, each would administer justice in the province where he or she was, but if either was in a place along with the royal council he or she would hear cases from all the provinces. All this, however, could apply at that time only to Castile, as John II was still alive and Ferdinand did not become king of Aragon until 1479.

Leaving aside these technicalities, the fundamental structure of the union of the Hispanic kingdoms and later of the Habsburg empire or *Monarquia*, as it was called, was that of a loose confederation. Its main points were: each of them retained its own parliament, political institutions, laws, courts, armed forces, taxation and coinage. None was constitutionally subject to any of the others, and the subjects of any were aliens in the others. No system of extradition of criminals existed until much later, and there were customs barriers between Castile and Navarre, and between Castile and Aragon. The powers of the monarch were neatly defined by a later political writer, Solórzano Pereira: 'the Monarch who keeps all these countries together is sovereign of each rather than king of all'. Although some writers occasionally referred to the 'King of

Spain', constitutionally the title did not exist. The monarch used the various titles corresponding to each of his states. There were seventeen provinces in the Netherlands all recognising the same prince, but each by a different title and vesting him with different powers.

The monarch was represented in each state, as its sovereign, by a viceroy. The viceroy in the Habsburg monarchy had its origin in the medieval Catalan-Aragonese union. On account of the federal nature of this union the sovereign was represented in the state in which he did not happen to be by his heir, or a prominent member of the royal family as his lieutenant. In the fourteenth century a vicar-general appeared in Athens and later a viceroy in Sardinia. Christopher Columbus was the first to receive the title of *Visorey* for the Indies. On the death of Ferdinand, his widowed queen, Germaine de Foix, continued as vicereine of Valencia, and his natural son Alfonso de Aragon, archbishop of Saragossa, as viceroy of Aragon. The viceroy in the states of the Crown of Aragon in the early days of Charles V was expected to be a member of the royal family, and when Philip II annexed Portugal a promise to the same effect was given. But conditions gradually changed and viceroys were first chosen from the Catalan and Aragonese high nobility and later from the Castilian nobility. From the days of Charles onwards there were viceroys in each country of the monarchy—Aragon, Valencia, Catalonia, Sicily, Naples, Sardinia and Navarre, plus those in Peru and New Spain (that is, Mexico) in America. The Netherlands had a governor-general.

The monarch was surrounded by a constellation of councils for the government of the various states, Castile, Aragon (with the Italian possessions) and the Indies. The councils were not territorial but personal—in the sense that they did not sit in the country they administered but always accompanied the person of the sovereign. Thus the federal traditions of the Crown of Aragon, firmly established since the union of Catalonia and Aragon (1137) prevailed over the Castilian system of annexation and centralisation, displayed throughout the changing relations between the kingdoms of Leon and Castile, after their final union in 1230, and in the expansions of Castile over western Andalucia, Granada and America. The Burgundian tradition was also federalist, and this probably explains Charles V's consistent respect for the federal structure.

The Indies were regarded as Castile's own possessions, and administered in accordance with Castilian, and not federalist, tradition. The sovereign there was the king of Castile and the viceroys represented him as such. There was never any attempt to set up self-government or representative institutions; the colonies were administered from Castile by the *Consejo de Indias*. Isabella had definitely stated in her will that since those countries had been discovered and conquered 'at the expense of my kingdoms and settled with nationals of these kingdoms, it is right that all their trade and traffic should belong to my kingdoms of Castile and Leon and be conducted from them; and everything brought from the Indies should go to them and be for them'. Only natives of the kingdoms of Castile could settle or trade with America, and trade and shipping were conducted exclusively through the port of Seville. This rule was kept, in spite of temporary concessions by Ferdinand (1505), after Isabella's death, to the subjects of all his states, and by Charles to the German bankers, the Welsers and the Fuggers. A petition by the city of Barcelona (1522) to be allowed to trade with America was not granted.

The other case of extension of Castilian rule was that of the conquest of the Arab kingdom of Granada. The terms of the treaty of surrender (25 November 1491) were generous. The kingdom was put under the authority of a Castilian governor, but the inhabitants were allowed to retain their Moslem religion, their laws and judges, their ancient usages, language and dress, the enjoyment of their property, and were given a guarantee that taxes would not exceed those they had paid to their Moorish sovereigns. But these terms, observed as long as Hernando de Talavera, archbishop of Granada (1493–1507), conducted the attempted conversion of Moslems, were soon abandoned. The slow rate of progress that worried Isabella caused Francisco Jiménez de Cisneros to be sent to join the archbishop and accelerate it. Under pressure mass conversions then took place. This pressure, and the public burning of Islamic religious books, finally made the Moors revolt. Then came the expulsion from the kingdom of Granada of all Moslems over the age of fourteen who did not accept baptism (12 February 1502). They were not allowed to go to North Africa or to the states of the Crown of Aragon (though Ferdinand allowed many of them to take refuge in Valencia); they could only go to Egypt or leave Castile by her frontier with Biscay. The new converts, known as the *Moriscos*, came automatically under the loving care of the Inquisition. By a later decree of Charles V (1525) they were forbidden to use Arab names, or to wear jewellery with Arabic designs: only crosses and Christian images were allowed. They were forbidden to make marriage contracts in accordance with their ancient laws. In 1556 the enforced use of Castilian was decreed, the Arab language being banned under very severe penalties. This and other harsh later measures precipitated the new revolt of 1571, the dispersal of the Moors over the Castilian countries and their final expulsion from Spain in 1610.

The outline of the federal monarchy given above requires qualification in two respects to make clear how it worked in practice. Though in principle no state was in any way subject to another, the American treasure, and the fact that the army was recruited mainly in Castile, where the monarch and the Castilian courtiers and advisers surrounding him resided, gave Castile a position of hegemony. This was reinforced by the nationalistic ambitions of the Castilians, who continually sought civil and ecclesiastic posts in the other countries. It was thus that the Catalans and Aragonese were soon eliminated from the administration of their Italian possessions. But although royal policy encouraged this trend, and even Isabella was reported by Guicciardini to have said 'Aragon is not ours and we must go and conquer it', no attempt was ever made during the reigns of Ferdinand or Charles upon the freedom of any of the other states, in striking contrast with later policy. Even Navarre, conquered in 1512 and annexed to the Crown of Castile in 1515, was left her independence and political institutions, Ferdinand following this time the Catalan-Aragonese pattern of confederation. The other important influence towards centralisation in the empire was an institution, and an extremely powerful one, common to most of its countries—the Inquisition, governed from the court by the *Consejo de la Santa y Suprema Inquisición*, and not infrequently used for political purposes (below, pp. 334–8).

The union brought about by the marriage of Ferdinand and Isabella had to face a number of crises. The first was on the death of Henry IV of Castile (1474), when Alfonso V of Portugal took up the claim of Princess Juana *La Beltraneja* to the Castilian throne, and invaded the country. Then, as in previous years when a Portuguese party was influential in the Castilian court, the shape of a united Spain hung in the balance. Was Castile going to incline towards the Atlantic or towards the Mediterranean? Geographically and culturally Portugal and Castile were closer than Castile and the Catalan-speaking countries. The union of Castile and Portugal might then have been successful and Spain might have been spared much internal strife to come, generated by the union of Castile with the Catalan states; whereas union was bound to fail in the days of the Philips, when Portugal with her colonial empire had become stronger. But whereas Portugal had defeated the Castilian army at Aljubarrota (1385) and so preserved her independence, now the Castilian victory at Toro (1476) maintained the separation between the two countries.

The union of the Crowns of Castile and Aragon went through another crisis on Isabella's death (1504). By her will she appointed her mad daughter Juana queen of Castile (*señora natural propietaria de estos reinos*). Ferdinand, therefore, in spite of all the previous elaborate agreements, was dispossessed of the crown, and Isabella again separated Castile from Aragon. Only if Juana should be abroad or be unwilling or unable to govern (as was in fact the case) would Ferdinand be recalled as 'governor and administrator', and only if he condescended to take an oath to govern the kingdom well and not dismember it. Philip of Austria, Juana's husband, was recognised as king consort. These unwise measures soon brought the results that might have been expected. An anti-Ferdinand party, led by Philip, was supported by the grandees. Despite Ferdinand's offer that Castile should be ruled jointly by Juana, Philip and himself (24 November 1505), when Juana and her husband landed from the Netherlands, Philip was soon supported by a large Castilian army, and father and son-in-law decided that Ferdinand should withdraw to his own kingdoms (27 June 1506). Thus all the efforts for the union of the Hispanic countries were foiled again.

The Cortes of Aragon (1502) and those of Catalonia (1503) had taken an oath of allegiance to Juana, but with the proviso that the oath would become null and void if the king should have legitimate male issue. The condition was the more remarkable because Isabella, although still alive, was already ill (she probably died of cancer of the uterus) and no issue could be expected from her. The resourceful Ferdinand, who liked neither Philip nor the prospect of a foreign dynasty ruling Spain, decided to marry again, as a move in a new political and diplomatic game. As a protection against Philip and his father the Emperor Maximilian (Philip was already claiming the kingdom of Naples on the pretext that Castilian troops had contributed to its conquest) Ferdinand had made a nimble *volte face* and signed an alliance with his bitterest enemy, Louis XII of France (Treaty of Blois, 12 October 1505), promising to marry the French king's niece, Germaine de Foix. When Philip landed in Spain from the Netherlands the marriage had already taken place (18 March 1506), following negotiations conducted by the Catalan Joan d'Enguera, bishop of Lerida. Ferdinand and his new queen moved to Naples. To ensure his possession of that kingdom he dismissed Castilian officials there, replacing them with trusted Catalans. His own nephew, John of Aragon, was substituted for the Castilian viceroy Gonzalo de Córdoba, the Great Captain.

The whole situation suddenly changed again with the unexpected death of Philip (25 September 1506). A regency council was formed, presided over by Cardinal Jiménez de Cisneros. The unruly Castilian nobility raised their heads once more, and those who had supported Philip now wanted his father, the Emperor Maximilian, to intervene. Jiménez and the regents, however, asked Ferdinand to come back, confident that he would know how to deal firmly with the restive nobles. But Ferdinand was in no hurry, wishing first to consolidate his Italian possessions and have a meeting with his new friend Louis XII (June 1507). Not until the late summer did Ferdinand come to Castile and set about the task of pacifying the rebellious and winning back the confidence of the people. Finally, in the Cortes of Madrid (October 1510) the ex-king took the oath as administrator of the realm on behalf of his insane daughter.

The hopes of an heir from Germaine de Foix were dashed after the birth of a male child who lived for only a couple of hours. In the last period of his life the old king's love and solicitude turned to his younger grandson, Ferdinand, the future ruler of Austria, who seems to have been preferred in his grandfather's heart and schemes to his brother Charles, the future Holy Roman Emperor. When the grandfather died Cardinal Jiménez closely watched the friends of young Ferdinand and their plottings against Charles, in which Ferdinand was encouraged by his father's stepmother Germaine. When Charles went to Saragossa to obtain recognition as king from the Cortes of Aragon (1518), he had to face a separatist movement based on the recognition of Ferdinand as Charles's heir (as against his future children) to the throne of Aragon.

The last state brought into the union of the Hispanic kingdoms was Navarre. John II of Aragon, through his first marriage with Blanche, queen of Navarre, had possessed this kingdom until his death. The rights to the Crown had passed through his daughter by his first wife, Eleanor, married to Gaston IV de Foix, to her son Gaston and his children. Of these the son, Francis Phoebus, died young and without issue, and the Crown passed to the daughter Catharine, wife of John d'Albret. The Foix branch, however, considered the d'Albrets as intruders and claimed that the rights had passed from Eleanor's son Gaston to his brother John. Now the latter, married to Mary, sister of Louis XII of France, was the father of Germaine de Foix, Ferdinand's second wife. In other words Ferdinand was in a strong position, through his wife, to make a serious claim to the kingdom of Navarre. Other circumstances further complicated this dynastic tangle. First, there were internal divisions and rival parties within Navarre. Moreover, while the rivalry between Ferdinand and Louis XII had been running high, the French had supported the Foix against the d'Albrets, but when Ferdinand married a Foix there was no point in doing so any longer and Louis changed his protégé. The Navarrese problem was also reflected in the diplomatic chessboard. When Ferdinand sought the friendship of the French king by the Treaty of Blois, Navarre was for the time being put on one side. But when Ferdinand was once more firmly established in Castile (1510), the French alliance was no longer of any use to him. By this time Ferdinand was entering upon the last and most brilliant phase of his diplomatic activities, and competing with France for hegemony in western Europe. The position of Navarre on the Pyrenees between the realms of the two rivals became of vital strategic importance to both of them.

Events were precipitated by the death of Gaston de Foix, Germaine's brother, at the battle of Ravenna (11 April 1512). Ferdinand found that his wife unexpectedly inherited claims to Navarre: he was determined to make full and quick use of the fact. As usual, he prepared his *coup* carefully. While secretly gathering a Castilian and an Aragonese army, he continued his negotiations with John d'Albret of Navarre, in order to lull him, realising that after his (Ferdinand's) marriage with a Foix the king of France had been drawn closer to the d'Albrets. Moreover he prevailed upon Henry VIII to send an army to Guienne, ostensibly to recover the ancient English possessions but in fact to threaten France and to prevent her from helping Navarre and so avoid involving himself in a major war. On the pretext that the Navarrese king was schismatic because he had adhered to the council at Pisa, summoned at the instigation of Louis XII against the pope, Ferdinand obtained from Julius II, his ally in the Holy League against France, a bull of excommunication (21 July 1512) depriving the d'Albrets of their rights and freeing the Navarrese from their allegiance to them. Meanwhile Ferdinand's spies had obtained information of negotiations between Louis XII and John d'Albret. Skilfully piecing together the various pieces of information received, he drafted a résumé of an imaginary treaty between his rivals, pledging themselves to attack Castile. He used this text (17 July 1512) as justification for his own attack on Navarre, pleading self-defence. The next day the French and the Navarrese signed the real treaty at Blois, by which John d'Albret engaged himself to support the king of France against attacks from Ferdinand and Henry VIII.

On 21 July the duke of Alba at the head of a Castilian army invaded Navarre from the west and a few days later an Aragonese army entered from the south. By early September Navarre lay conquered by force and cunning. Ferdinand hesitated on the political future of his new kingdom. It was first annexed to the Crown of Aragon, but in order (according to Zurita) to prevent the Navarrese from uniting with the Aragonese and pressing for more freedoms and exemptions, Navarre was finally annexed to Castile (Cortes of Burgos, 1515). But in this Aragonese, and not Castilian, traditions were observed. The king of the new dynasty was represented in Pamplona by a viceroy; but the cortes, the permanent council of deputies that represented parliament between sessions, the internal administration, laws, coinage, taxation and finance under the *cámara de contos*, all remained unchanged; the only change was that a council of Navarre was organised, on the model of the council of Aragon, to be at the king's side with help and advice on the ruling of the newly acquired kingdom.

The great achievement of Ferdinand and Isabella was to give shape to the chaotic Castile they had found and to create the new institutions on which the government of the peninsular states was to rest. The medieval administration was transformed by a long and gradual process into that of a Renaissance state, expanded and adapted to become the instrument of government of a world-wide monarchy. It is reported that Philip II once stopped before a painting of Ferdinand and murmured, 'To him we owe it all'.

The central principle round which all the reforms revolved was the concentration of power in the Crown. The degree of concentration was stronger in Castile than in Aragon in accordance with the political traditions of each and the attitude of the inhabitants and local authorities, though in most cases resistance was useless and the royal authority prevailed, as was exemplified by Ferdinand's introduction of the Inquisition into Catalonia in spite of three years of resistance. The Crown first fought the unruly and self-seeking nobles always ready to revolt and snatch *mercedes* (concessions of land or grants of money) from an increasingly depleted royal patrimony. To restore the latter was the first task of Ferdinand and Isabella. The same aim promoted their annexation to the Crown of the grandmasterships of the three military orders, along with their very extensive estates.

Ferdinand and Isabella did not object to the large numbers of titled people, provided they quietly acknowledged the royal power and agreed to raise its economic position. There were seven dukes in Castile at their accession, fifteen at the end of their reign, and twenty-five grandees in the early days of Charles V. But the policy of curbing the power of the nobility, continued by Charles V, was not pursued. The income of the nobility in the early sixteenth century was estimated at 1,400,000 ducats. As for the lesser Castilian nobility, the *hidalgos*, they were legion. The earliest estimate we have of *hidalgos* (exempt from taxation) and *pecheros* (taxpayers) for the allocation of the subsidy of 1541 gives totals of 108,358 and 784,578 respectively. These figures being for householders, the total for each class might be 540,000 *hidalgos* to some 3,923,000 commoners.

The action taken by Ferdinand and Isabella was directed against the high nobility. Very skilfully and properly, Ferdinand and Isabella brought the matter before the Cortes of Toledo of 1480, but left the initiative to the representatives of the cities. They petitioned that the royal revenues should be restored to their legitimate proportions, and that to prevent higher taxes having to be levied, grants made to nobles without sufficient cause should be revised and revoked. The queen's confessor, Hernando de Talavera, was entrusted with working out the revision, and as a result an annual revenue of 30,000,000 *maravedis* passed from the nobles into the royal treasury. But Isabella was not satisfied about the results as is shown by an unusual clause in her will. Conscious of her duties as queen to the royal patrimony, she ordered the nobles to restore to the Crown anything granted them or retained by them that was not their due. Many grandees, such as the dukes of Alba and Medina Sidonia, the marquis of Villena and others, found themselves after the queen's death faced with her unwelcome orders to hand back to the royal patrimony grants given or confirmed by her in her lifetime. Many castles, strongholds of rebellious nobles, were systematically demolished, and the Cortes of 1480 banned the building of new ones, as well as the waging of private war. Alongside these forceful means the Catholic kings developed a policy of attracting noble families to the royal court. While they were gradually removed from political offices in the government of the country, their places being filled by *letrados* (jurists of humble birth), the nobles were allowed to retain their privileges (e.g. exemption from torture and from imprisonment for debt) and their titles—new titles even were granted. At the same time the nobles were encouraged to give their children an elaborate education, often by Italian tutors, who thus helped to spread Renaissance ideas in Castile. The royal family set the example; Isabella learnt Latin, as well as her daughters, Isabella of Portugal, and Catherine, Henry VIII's queen.

Another important step towards the strengthening of the power of the Crown and the royal patrimony was the annexation of the estates of wealthy military orders. In 1476, when the Grand Master of the Knights of Santiago died, a bull was obtained from Rome conferring the office on King Ferdinand, agreement on the part of the pope being required on account of the mixed nature, ecclesiastical and military, of the orders. Ferdinand, however, with great circumspection, allowed a knight elected by the order to take the office and waited till his death in 1499 to implement the papal concession in his own favour. Meanwhile he had assumed the grandmastership (*Maestrazgos*) of the Orders of Calatrava (1487) and Alcántara (1494). The elections to the grandmasterships had always caused contention between the great nobles. The king's assumption of the grandmasterships of the three orders prevented quarrels and in addition brought to the royal patrimony considerable revenues from their estates. The papal bull in fact had awarded the revenues of the orders to Queen Isabella, and in her will she bestowed them on Ferdinand. Not until 1523 did another bull grant to Charles V in perpetuity the offices of grandmaster and the management of the estates of the orders. Unfortunately, financial pressure on Charles V was always heavy, and about 1529 an opposite trend begins to appear, namely mortgaging, selling and dismembering the estates of the orders and their revenues. In 1519 the collection of all revenues from the orders was farmed to Gutiérrez de Madrid, himself a royal treasurer, for the sum of 133,000 ducats.

To keep order in the country districts, and incidentally to keep the restless nobles in hand, the Catholic kings adapted an ancient institution, the *Hermandad* (brotherhood). In the Middle Ages it had been a federation of cities, with a council that met regularly, a seal and a militia, with a set of rules covering the duties of its members, its working and functions, punishment of crimes, and prosecution of offenders. It was in short a *regnum in regno*. The sovereigns, dependent on the support of the cities, as we have seen in the Cortes of 1480, had already in the Cortes of Madrigal (1476) obtained the reorganisation of the *Hermandad* under royal control. An assembly of representatives of the towns and cities of the kingdom of Castile laid down a constitution for the new *Hermandad*. A *Junta*, or council, of provincial delegates was set up under the presidency of a representative of the sovereigns. The *Hermandad* received full power to prosecute and punish robbery, arson or rebellion against the royal authority, crimes then removed from the jurisdiction of the ordinary courts. The old armed forces of the *Hermandad* were revived as a kind of rural constabulary. All towns had to pay tribute to maintain the *Hermandad* and its forces, and within each town everyone, citizens, clergy and nobles, had to make his contribution. Squadrons of archers patrolled roads and the countryside, dealing ruthlessly with criminals. Mutilation or death were the usual punishments. The nobles were bitterly hostile, but their complaints went unheeded. The working of the *Hermandad* was a complete success. It suppressed crime and disorder and protected travellers and trade. The nobility desisted from the practices that had brought Castile to anarchy. Above all, the royal power stood strengthened and universally respected. In twenty years the *Hermandad* had achieved its aims. An ordinance of 1498 suppressed its council or *Junta* and the taxes for its upkeep. The severity of its punishments was mitigated, and appeals from its decisions to the ordinary courts of justice were allowed.

After the sovereigns had used the cities against the nobility, they proceeded to bring them too under the control of the Crown. The medieval principle of municipal autonomy was a thing of the past by the fifteenth century. The municipal councils were riddled with corruption, dominated by persons who trafficked in municipal offices, which were bought, sold or leased not only in the city where the dealer lived but in cities far afield where his activities extended. This was the situation which Ferdinand and Isabella found and which they strove to remedy. Redress was achieved in suppressing these corrupt practices; unfortunately municipal freedom was suppressed as well. Vacancies in municipal offices were now filled not by election but by lot, the names being drawn out of a bag which contained only the names of persons acceptable to the royal authorities. Royal officials were now appointed to the municipal councils. Foremost among them was the *corregidor*, appointed by the Crown from 1480 to the council of every city in Castile. Merriman described the *corregidores* as the 'omnicompetent servants of an absolute King'. They had to keep a close watch on municipal finances, on the common lands of the municipality, and to study the best method of increasing their revenues. Relations between Moors and Christians, gambling, local tolls and excise, the administration of justice, etc., all came under the *corregidores*. Through them every man in the realm was brought under the direct surveillance of the central power.

The cortes themselves lost most of their character as representative national assemblies, even allowing for the fact that the cortes of Castile, in contrast with those of Aragon, Catalonia and Valencia, had never enjoyed much power either financial or legislative. Ferdinand and Isabella summoned the cortes of Castile at irregular intervals: four times before 1483 and twelve after 1497, the first four times because the sovereigns needed them as allies against the nobility, as is shown by the Cortes of 1476 and 1480 referred to above. But once the royal power was absolute the ally was no longer needed. The fourteen years without cortes (1483–97) show how little necessary they were by then. If they were again summoned after 1497, it was only to recognise heirs to the throne or to make grants for wars in Italy. None of the members of the Castilian cortes sat in his own right. The king summoned whom he liked, and when he liked, although traditionally certain persons would expect to receive the summons. The nobles and clergy gradually ceased to attend, since the cortes were summoned only to grant funds, and they were exempt from taxation. There remained only thirty-six representatives of the cities, two from each of eighteen cities—a figure, it has been said, which was too large for a council but not large enough for a national assembly.

Relations between the Catholic kings and the Holy See were determined by two principles: mutual support for political interests, and the surrender of ecclesiastical affairs to the royal power in Spain and the Indies. Relations were particularly friendly in the days of Alexander VI (1492–1503), the Valencian Rodrigo Borja (or Borgia, in the Italian spelling), a period of considerable Hispanic influence in Rome. King and pope understood one another well and followed similar policies, which resulted in a strengthening of both royal and papal power. With his bull *Inter caetera* (3 May 1493) Alexander VI granted in perpetuity to the kings of Castile all continents and islands to be discovered overseas not belonging to any other Christian sovereign. Next day, by another bull, *Eximiae devotionis*, a dividing line was drawn one hundred leagues to the west of the islands of Cape Verde and the Azores to separate the discoveries of Castile and Portugal. When the French Charles VIII sent his forces to Italy to conquer Naples and threaten the papal states, Alexander VI, at the end of 1494, conferred upon Ferdinand and Isabella the title of 'the Catholic Kings', as a reward for their services to religion, covering a diplomatic move to encourage Ferdinand in his efforts to form an alliance against the king of France. The alliance, known as the League of Venice, was finally signed (31 March 1495) between the Venetian republic, the Emperor Maximilian, the duke of Milan, Ferdinand and the pope 'for the peace and tranquillity of Italy, the welfare of all Christendom, the defence of the honour and authority of the Holy See and the rights of the Holy Roman Empire...'. This was the beginning of the chain of events that brought the kingdom of Naples once more under the king of Aragon.

The bulls of Alexander VI and Julius II left the ecclesiastical affairs of the Indies almost entirely in the hands of the sovereigns. It was incumbent upon the Crown to send missionaries and build churches; in return it received all tithes (1501) and held the *derecho de presentación*, the right to submit to the pope nominations for bishoprics and all ecclesiastical offices in Spanish America. Bishops designated by the Crown took possession of their sees often before the pope's confirmation. Thanks to the *regio patronato*, the king was the immediate authority on ecclesiastical matters in America. Only on one point was Rome adamant. Ferdinand and Isabella petitioned for the right to nominate a supreme patriarch of the Indies, with power to settle many affairs without recourse to Rome. The dangers were obvious and the Holy See refused to yield. When in 1524, in the days of Charles V, Pope Clement VII appointed a patriarch of the Indies, the title was only one of honour and carried no real power.

This regalian policy was consistently applied in the Hispanic kingdoms themselves, tending in many respects, dogma apart, to the formation of a sort of national church. Two main lines were followed in connection with the clergy and the religious orders—submission and reform. The great prelates, who had been as unruly as the great nobles, felt the consequences of measures taken to keep the nobility well in hand. As a result of the *derecho de presentación* gradually only prelates loyal to Ferdinand and Isabella were appointed to vacant sees. After some discussion this right was granted in 1482 by Sixtus IV, the same pope who had recognised the new Inquisition and the annexation of the military orders.

The religious orders, and particularly the secular clergy, were no better in Spain than in other countries during the period preceding the Reformation. Pope Alexander VI in 1494 granted the Catholic Kings full powers to reform all communities of nuns and friars in their kingdoms. Cardinal Jiménez de Cisneros was entrusted with the task. Jiménez stands out as one of the most extraordinary men of this period. A man of ardent zeal and unbounded energy, he combined in a strange fashion the humility of a Franciscan and the strong will of a statesman. He was the reformer of many orders and of the secular clergy themselves. For their education and perfecting he founded the University of Alcalá (1498), and he twice ruled Castile as regent, in Ferdinand's absence (1506–7), and again on the death of the latter, pending the arrival of Charles from the Netherlands (1516–17) on the death of Philip. From 1492 he was Isabella's confessor, but, great as his influence on the queen must have been, he was not the sole inspirer of the policy of the Catholic Kings. Most orders were then divided into two branches: the 'observants', who strictly kept the original rules, and the 'conventuals', whose discipline had become relaxed. Jiménez worked indefatigably to enforce on all the strict observance of the rules. The Franciscans, Jiménez's own order, were the first to be reformed, the process being completed by 1506, and the Dominicans, Benedictines and Hieronymites followed. These orders, particularly the Franciscans, grew to extraordinary numbers. From them came most of the missionaries to the Indies. From among the Franciscans and Dominicans a select group was formed, cultured and deeply religious, in sympathy with Erasmus, whose ideas in later years influenced certain aspects of the Counter-Reformation.

The Spanish sovereigns received considerable financial help from the Church in their kingdoms. Pope Sixtus IV (1471–84), considering the

campaign against Granada a crusade against the infidels, granted indulgences to the faithful making financial contributions (1482). The concession
continued with intermissions, even after the war with the Arabs had
ended. It was renewed for Charles V in his wars with the Turks, until
it became permanently established. Priests, *ministros de la Cruzada*,
visited every parish, urging the people to accept the benefits offered by
a bull granting them indulgences and the privilege of eating meat during
Lent, in exchange for a donation rated at 68 *maravedís*. The Cortes of
Castile (1518, 1520, 1525, 1548) complained of the methods used:
people were forced to attend church sometimes for two consecutive days;
they had to listen to endless sermons and they had to neglect their work,
until they agreed to buy an indulgence. The system was extended to all
the kingdoms in the peninsula and Italy. It was first used in America in
1523, though not definitely established until 1538.

During Ferdinand's regency (1510–15) a council (*Consejo de la Cruzada*)
was established to fix the appropriate contribution for each bishopric and
collect it. As in the case of the estates of the military orders in the days
of Charles V, one finds the ubiquitous German bankers Fugger and
Welser (1530) and the Genoese Salvaggio and Lomellino (1538) in control
of the revenues of the crusade as surety for money advanced to the
Crown. Of the 68 *maravedís* paid one-fourth was retained by the Church,
and the remaining 51, after deducting collection expenses, went into the
royal treasury, whence it was used for any purpose except the non-
existent crusades. Everyone was expected to possess an indulgence.
An allocation among bishoprics (1523?) estimated at over 1,420,000 the
number of people under the Crown of Castile who were expected to have
one, though this figure probably referred to householders. The receipts
were estimated at 450,000 ducats in the years 1523–5.

The clergy paid a special contribution, the *subsidio*, agreed by Pope Leo X.
This tax was levied upon all clergy receiving rents from ecclesiastical
establishments and on all churches and monasteries (there were 470
monasteries in Castile in 1532). As usual, the collection of this tax was
often farmed to the Genoese bankers, Centurione and Grimaldo. The
subsidy of 1536 for arming twenty-two galleys against the Turks was
estimated to yield about 193,000 ducats.

The Inquisition is the most representative institution of the union of
political and religious power in the hands of the Catholic kings. To give
it its proper place in the royal plans for the reorganisation of the country,
it is useful to remember that the bull establishing it to deal with converted
Jews in 1478 came between the bull for the annexation of the estates of
the military orders to the Crown in 1476 and the act passed in the Cortes
of 1480 for the restitution to the royal patrimony of *mercedes* granted to
the nobility. Given the problems which were then exercising the royal

minds, it seems, therefore, that the mission of the Inquisition was not intended to be purely spiritual. If its purpose was to be strictly religious, the Church would have been the competent authority, as it had been in the medieval inquisition, and it would have been difficult to account for Ferdinand and Isabella's insistence upon wresting control from the pope.

The Jewish problem had been serious in Castile since the terrible pogroms of 1391. What made it more acute during the fifteenth century was the number of converted Jews or new Christians who occupied prominent positions in the country but were trusted neither by their own brethren nor by the Christians, who accused them of keeping the old faith under cover of the new. To maintain the purity of their faith severe measures were taken in the synagogues against renegades. On the other hand, many *conversos*, in order to justify and defend themselves in the eyes of the Christians, became violently anti-Semitic. From Jews and *conversos* came eminent writers and physicians and most of the merchants. Many noble families had entrusted Jews with the management of their estates, and not a few bishops followed their example, employing Jews for the collection of their diocesan revenues. Kings had also farmed out their taxes, minting, dues, trading licences, salt monopolies, etc., to the most prominent Jewish families of Castile. Their positions had thus made the Jews unpopular in many quarters, while they must have been very much in the royal mind when the sovereigns were reorganising the administration. This does not mean that the Catholic Kings had not been uninfluenced by religious motives—this would have been unlikely, living in those times and surrounded by ecclesiastics—or by the desire to unify the people or settle the social problem of the *conversos* and the rising tide of anti-Semitism.

Negotiations ably conducted by Cardinal Rodrigo Borgia (the future Alexander VI) obtained from Sixtus IV a bull establishing the Inquisition (November 1478) in accordance with the king's desire. In the medieval inquisition in France and in Aragon the inquisitors had been subject to the bishop's authority; in the new one they were subject to the king. It was, in fact, a royal inquisition of the Crown of Castile. Gradually the Crown came to supervise the appointment of inquisitors and instructions issued by them to control and regulate salaries, and to be able to command that confiscations should be paid into the royal treasury. The Inquisition was not established in practice until 1480, an indication that it had met with resistance.

Panic and a general flight of *conversos* were the first results of the Inquisition in Seville, where it began to operate ruthlessly in the autumn of 1480. Reports reached Rome, and Sixtus IV, realising the dangers, withdrew his previous concession (January–April 1482). He now tried to bring the Inquisition back to the medieval model; he appointed the inquisitors himself and refused Ferdinand's petition to introduce his royal Inquisition into the kingdom of Aragon. Moreover, deploring excesses committed through greed of gain, the pope granted a general pardon to *conversos* and then laid down the inquisitorial procedure: this had to be in public and with a right of appeal to the Holy See. Ferdinand replied with an angry letter (13 May 1482): he had been told of the pope's decision but he could not believe it to be true, because it was the duty of His Holiness to conduct the Inquisition in a proper manner; and even if the *conversos* had really been given these concessions by the pope, he was not prepared to accept them. He insisted, therefore, that the Inquisition should be established *secundum beneplacitum et voluntatem meam in his Regnis et terris meis.*

These negotiations with Sixtus IV should be viewed in relation to others on Italian affairs. The Turks had taken Otranto in 1480, and Ferdinand was the chief promoter of the league that expelled them in the following year. But the situation was quite different in 1482, when Venice was opposed to Ercole d'Este, duke of Ferrara, son-in-law of King Ferrante of Naples and a cousin of Ferdinand the Catholic. Sixtus IV not only supported Venice, which on 2 May attacked Ferrara and invaded it in the summer, but solicited the aid of Louis XI, offering him in return support for his claims on Naples against the house of Aragon. Ferrante turned to Ferdinand, but the latter, though not ready to make a military expedition abroad, threatened Venice with commercial war and the pope with armed intervention against the Papal States. The pope was so daunted that he promptly moved to the side of Naples and Ferrara. Abandoned by the end of the year by all her allies except Genoa, Venice still tried to get the French to intervene. The *volte face* of Sixtus IV in Italian affairs under Ferdinand's threat probably also explains his change in the matter of the Inquisition. On 10 October 1482 the pope capitulated completely to the king. On 23 February 1483 he wrote to Isabella that a commission of cardinals was studying her petition that she and her husband should be quite free to appoint inquisitors and a judge of appeal: he assured her that he had never entertained any suspicion that this affair had been prompted by any *bonorum temporalium cupiditate*. It is nevertheless to be noted that in Spain, particularly in Aragon, witnesses in cases before the Inquisition repeatedly stated or reported the belief that its purpose was to deprive the accused of their wealth, and they blamed Isabella rather than Ferdinand.

Ferdinand's attempts to introduce the Inquisition into Aragon met with strong opposition. In Aragon itself it culminated in the murder of the inquisitor, Pedro de Arbués, in the cathedral of Saragossa (1485), an outrage that naturally led to the prosecution of the leading Jewish families, though those nearer to the king escaped almost unscathed. In Catalonia all the authorities, lay and ecclesiastical, including the members of the old inquisition, opposed Ferdinand and his new Inquisition for three years (1484–7). There was something repugnant about the institution to the Catalan democratic tradition. Meanwhile Jewish and *converso* merchants escaped to France with their goods and capital, a serious blow to Catalan trade. But in face of the hostility of Rome and the inflexible determination of Ferdinand the Catalans had to surrender. The Inquisition was also introduced into Sicily, Sardinia, and the American colonies. It was the only institution that, ruled from a council sitting at the monarch's elbow, was able to exercise its authority over all the territories of the monarchy.

Fray Thomas de Torquemada was appointed inquisitor-general for Castile by the papal bull of 2 August 1483, and for the Crown of Aragon on 17 October. His successor Diego de Deza, archbishop of Seville, was appointed for Castile (1498) by Ferdinand and Isabella, and later confirmed by the pope. Nine months later he was appointed inquisitor-general for the Crown of Aragon. On the death of Isabella, when the two Crowns separated, each acquired its own inquisition and inquisitor. Cardinal Adrian of Utrecht, the future Pope Adrian VI, became once more the common inquisitor (1518). When Sixtus IV finally recognised the royal Inquisition (1483) the royal council, or rather *Consejo de Castilla*, had already been organised. Another council for the Inquisition of Castile was set up on the same model, and later a council for the Inquisition of Aragon, although the two often had a common president. Both later joined the *Consejo de la Santa y Suprema Inquisicion*.

The outcome of the Jewish problem was the final expulsion of the Jews (1492). This measure was not a sudden step. As early as 1480 Isabella had intended to expel the Jews from Andalusia. When the Inquisition got into its stride, local expulsions were ordered: Jews were expelled from the bishoprics of Seville and Córdoba (1 January 1483); no Jews could remain more than three days in Cuenca (12 December 1483); all young Jews were expelled from Burgos (March 1486); no Jew might spend the night in Bilbao (12 August 1490); and so forth. These measures were taken during the campaign against Granada, and prominent Jews like Abrevanel and Abraham Seneor had contracts to supply the Christian army. But after the fall of Granada the Jews were no longer needed. Obviously religious fanaticism played its part in the expulsion ordered three months later (30 March 1492): the Muhammadans had been expelled, it was now the turn of the Jews. A similar event took place some years later, when, as thanksgiving for his victory at Pavia against the French (1525), Charles V expelled all the Jews who had remained in Naples. Probably some 35,000 families left the kingdoms of Castile: few quitted Catalonia, as there were not many left there. It is not their numbers that matter; it is the suffering and misery inflicted on human beings. On the other hand through the Inquisition, through the expulsion of the Jews and later of the Moslems, the religious unity of Spain was preserved.

While she thus acquired the role of champion of the Roman Catholic Church, she had to pay a heavy price in other directions. The expulsion of the Jews, the only citizens with economic ability, sealed the fate of the Castilian empire before it was born. The Inquisition has to be judged not only on what it did in the way of persecution but on what it prevented being done, at a time when the Renaissance was spreading the principle of free discussion which fostered the development of science and thought.

To Ferdinand is due the inception of the system of councils which has been considered typical of the government of the Habsburg monarchy. The medieval royal council of the kings of Castile was modified in the Cortes of Madrigal (1476) and received its final reorganisation in those of Toledo (1480). The radical changes were: the nobles were superseded by *letrados* or jurists (one prelate, three nobles and eight or nine lawyers); it became a permanent body sitting in the royal court. In other words, from being a council of the nobility for advising the king, it became a bureaucratic body of civil servants for the execution of the royal policy.

Ferdinand also found himself with the old royal council of the Crown of Aragon, well organised in the days of Peter IV of Aragon, with the chancery, the treasury, and the office of the royal chamberlain. After some temporary arrangements the council was reorganised in 1494. It had a vice-chancellor at its head, five regents or councillors (usually doctors of law), a prothonotary as head of the chancery, and his lieutenant, the advocate of the fisc, representing public or Crown interests, a treasurer-general who had no vote on matters of justice, and four secretaries, each at the head of an office to deal with the affairs of Aragon, Valencia, Catalonia and the Italian territories respectively. The vice-chancellor and the five regents had to be natives, two from each of the three peninsular provinces of Aragon. The treasurer-general need not be a national, and royal policy later was to appoint a Castilian. Other councils were organised, to which reference has already been made: the council of the *Hermandad*, founded in 1476 and lasting only until 1498; the council of finance (1480 in its embryonic form, but not a fully fledged council until much later); the council of the Inquisition (1483); and the council of the military orders (1489).

Of these councils those of Castile, Aragon and the Inquisition were *supremos*, that is, they were not subordinate to any other or to any authority except the king. The councils of the Indies and Italy were later added to this category. The complicated problems of precedence were meticulously discussed and determined: the councils of Castile and Aragon were of equal status and in processions walked to right and left of the king; the council of the Inquisition followed immediately behind him, and then came the other councils. The councils advised the king on policy regarding their respective countries or jurisdictions, proposed their nominees for appointment as royal officials, made decisions subject to the king's approval, on matters of royal government as distinct from that of the national government of the country, and also acted as courts of legal appeal.

The finances, considered as part of the patrimony of the sovereign rather than as the resources of the country, were managed by the *Contadores Mayores* and the *Contadores de Cuentas*. The system persisted until the return of Charles to Spain after the defeat of the *Comuneros*. He then appointed Henry of Nassau, who had been *chef et surintendant des finances* in the Netherlands, to control the Castilian *Contadurias* at the head of a committee of six members (1523). Though the Emperor Charles referred to this body as a 'finance council', the name did not exist officially in Castilian legislation prior to 1568. In the period of Ferdinand's regency a group of men from the *Contadurias* was put in charge of the revenue of the Crusade. From this evolved the *Consejo de la Cruzada*.

In the days of Ferdinand and Isabella the royal council of Castile also dealt with the affairs of the Indies. It seems that in the early days of Charles a sort of committee within the council of Castile specialised in Indian affairs; at least there is a vague reference to 'those of the Indies' in a paper contemporary with the Cortes of Corunna (1520). But the council of the Indies as such did not appear until 1524.

We may turn from the internal administration of the Hispanic kingdoms to a wider field and glance briefly at Ferdinand's diplomatic activities. The culmination of years of intrigue, the harvest from seeds sown in many fields, only took place in the last period of his life, after the queen's death and when he was only regent of Castile, although king of Aragon.

Most of Ferdinand's international activities were a development of the Catalan-Aragonese diplomacy of previous centuries. His Mediterranean policy of relations with North Africa and opposition to the Turks was the line followed of old. Intervention in Italy and conflict there with French interests had begun with the Catalan landing in Sicily in 1281, and these remained the two chief problems in Ferdinand's international relations. France was more formidable than the Italian States, and most of Ferdinand's diplomatic moves aimed at the encirclement of France: the alliances and marriages of his daughters with the English king and the emperor's son are examples of this. Castile had led a more isolated existence throughout the Middle Ages, and her only important contribution to foreign policy was her relations with Portugal.

During the reign and after the defeat of King Alfonso V of Portugal (1476 and 1479), the relationship between the two kingdoms was one of friendship, based chiefly on marriage alliances. Isabella, Ferdinand's eldest daughter, was married first (1490) to Alfonso, grandson of the defeated king, and after his death to Manuel, duke of Bejar (1497), who had become king. Isabella died in childbirth, and her baby son, who might have united the Crowns of Aragon, Castile and Portugal, died two years later (20 July 1500). Meanwhile Prince John, the only son of the Catholic kings, husband of Margaret, the Emperor Maximilian's daughter, had also died (1497), and shortly afterwards his wife was delivered of a stillborn child. The only hope of succession was now in the marriage of the king's daughter Juana the Mad with the Emperor's son, Archduke Philip the Handsome. This, however, made it likely that the Hispanic kingdoms and their possessions would pass to a foreign prince, a prospect not relished by the Catholic kings, but destined nevertheless to be realised. So when Manuel, still bent upon the union of the whole peninsula, approached Ferdinand and Isabella for the hand of their fourth daughter, Maria, the petition was granted (October 1500). And when Maria died (1517) he again married into the Spanish royal family, this time Eleanor, the elder daughter of Juana and Philip, and sister of Charles V. Maria's son John III, the Portuguese king, never fulfilled his father's constant ambition, but all these marriages and later ones had the final result of placing Philip II in a strong position to claim the throne of Portugal.

These friendly relations with Portugal involved respect for the agreement of Alcaçovas (4 September 1479) by which Alfonso V had renounced his claim to Castile and brought about a division of the African and Atlantic possessions of both kingdoms. While the Canary Isles were recognised as Castile's, Portugal was recognised in the islands of Cape Verde, Madeira and the Azores, and in the territories of Fez and Guinea in Africa. In 1494, two years after the conquest of Granada, the pope granted the Muhammadan territories in North Africa east of the kingdom of Fez to the Catholic Kings. During the early period of Ferdinand's rule as administrator of Castile (1506–11) expeditions were launched against North Africa. Peñon de la Gomera was conquered (1508) and later (1509–10) Oran, Bugia, Tripoli, Tenes and Algiers. These were allotted to the Crown of Aragon and to Catalan trade. Then at the General Cortes of the confederation (Monzon, 1510) a crusade to Egypt and Jerusalem was discussed for which the states of the Crown of Aragon voted five hundred thousand pounds.

Mediterranean relations had brought Ferdinand into opposition with the Turks, separated from the territories of Naples only by the Straits of Otranto. Their common enmity against him was finally to bring the French and the Turks into an alliance, to the scandal of Christianity.

While the Castilian medieval tradition had on the whole been one of friendship with France, a contrary Catalan tradition now became, under Ferdinand, the policy of all his kingdoms. With France he wanted first to settle accounts for her annexation of the Catalan counties of Roussillon and Cerdagne. John II, Ferdinand's father, in his financial difficulties during the Catalan Revolution, had pawned those counties to Louis XI for 300,000 crowns, and when he could not pay, the French king foreclosed. When Charles VIII of France became involved in war in Brittany (1485–91), Ferdinand began to get him into his toils, inducing the Emperor Maximilian and Henry VII of England to take sides against him. In the spring of 1488 the English king proposed a close alliance between the two countries, and the marriage of his eldest son Arthur to Catherine, the daughter of the Catholic kings. Opposition to France was one of Ferdinand's conditions for acceptance.

The war with Brittany passed without making any considerable military demands upon the confederates. But, conscious of how he was encircled, Charles VIII when planning his expedition against Naples first tried to break the circle by conciliating Ferdinand with the return of the counties of Roussillon and Cerdagne (Treaty of Barcelona, 1493) and inducing him to consider himself the enemy of all those at war with France. Obviously Ferdinand could not comply with this condition if Charles really wanted to seize Naples. So he began to forge another alliance against the French king—the League of Venice, the partners in which were the Republic of Venice, himself, Pope Alexander VI (Rodrigo de Borgia), the Emperor Maximilian, the duke of Milan and his cousin Ferrante, the dethroned king of Naples (1495). Ferdinand's plans were successful. His army defended and occupied Naples, and Charles VIII withdrew. But then Ferrante died and was succeeded by his old and weak uncle Federigo (1496). Ferdinand saw an opportunity to recover the kingdom of Naples, which his own uncle Alfonso V had not included with Sicily and the Crown of Aragon in his will in favour of John II. His first move was to woo the French king, encircled as he was by England and the Empire. In the winter of 1496 to 1497 a double marriage linked the royal and the imperial families: Princess Juana was married to the Archduke Philip (October 1496), and the Archduchess Margaret to Prince Juan (April 1497). Meanwhile negotiations for the marriage of the prince of Wales, Arthur, to Princess Catherine were renewed.

Charles VIII therefore welcomed a suspension of hostilities in Italy, and then by means of secret negotiations he was inveigled into a plan of Ferdinand's for the partition of Naples between them (1497). The plan was confirmed by his successor, Louis XII (1498). War between Venice and the Turks gave Ferdinand a pretext for sending his army to the vicinity of Naples (1500). King Federigo had appealed in vain to Ferdinand for help, and now, realising where the danger came from, rashly allied himself with the Turks. Here was the excuse Ferdinand had been waiting for. His army and the French king's invaded the kingdom of Naples (1501–2) and they divided it between them. The final act of the drama was easy to foresee: quarrels between the victors. Ferdinand again applied his diplomacy, to secure at least the neutrality of the Empire, Venice and the

Holy See; the rest was accomplished by force of arms. The French were defeated and had to recognise in a treaty (March 1504) Ferdinand's possession of Naples.

Ferdinand's diplomacy was supple enough to allow him to conciliate the French after fooling or defeating them, and to maintain the English connection. After Isabella's death he had to protect himself in face of Philip's ambitions and possible threats from the Empire, and this drew him closer to France. When the clouds passed, his next care was to recover the Adriatic ports of the kingdom of Naples, which had remained in the power of Venice. Taking advantage of the rivalry of other Powers against Venice, he entered into a new alliance—the League of Cambrai (1508) —with Pope Julius II, Florence, the emperor, Louis XII and himself. The Adriatic ports were easily retaken. France's position in North Italy was now becoming too strong for the comfort of the old allies. Besides, Ferdinand was now well established as regent of Castile and no longer needed France. The result was the Holy League against France (1511–13), between Venice, the pope, the emperor, Ferdinand, and his son-in-law Henry VIII. As usual Ferdinand managed to choose the winning side. He did not obtain any more advantages in Italy, but he succeeded in manœuvring the French into a position that aided him in his conquest of Navarre. At the end of his life Ferdinand was still able to reinforce the English alliance (October 1515) directed against Francis I of France. This policy had borne fruit in the war of Brittany and, more particularly, in the moves for the conquest of Navarre. Charles V maintained the alliance, which culminated in the marriage of Philip and Mary Tudor. After that the two countries parted company.

Friendship with the Empire, also originally intended as a move against France, brought such developments for Spain as Ferdinand could never have foreseen. His heir, Charles, was to be in a position in both hemispheres that was entirely without precedent. The isolated Castile of the Middle Ages now rose to world power and unparalleled splendour. But at the same time insoluble problems accumulated around her, making exhausting demands on her resources and forcing her to endless sacrifices. Charles reaped the harvest sown by Ferdinand. But the old king, though it was he who laid the foundations of the empire, could scarcely have visualised its later dimensions. At the time of Charles's accession and his early election as emperor, people were fortunate in being able to see only the brighter aspects of the future.

CHAPTER XII

THE INVASIONS OF ITALY

WITHIN twenty years of Charles VIII's invasion, Italians had begun to speak regretfully of the happy days which preceded the coming of the French. They looked back on the years before 1494 as an age of peace and prosperity, when endless opportunities were open to men of talent, and when life in court and city was marked by a round of novel and refined pleasures. Their view of the past was nostalgic, yet the second half of the fifteenth century may rightly be considered the heyday of Italian civilisation. During the forty years which lay between the Peace of Lodi (1454) and the French invasion, the rulers of Italy had done much to establish peace and order within their dominions and friendly relations with their neighbours. Quarrels between the various states were of less significance than the common interests which united them. Petty wars did not place serious hindrances in the way of the pursuit of wealth or the cultivation of the arts. Although the challenge to Italy's commercial supremacy was already formidable, the merchants had money to spend on pictures, books and building, whilst the princes used their earnings as mercenary captains to make their capitals centres of the art and learning of the Renaissance. The individual contribution to civilisation made by each state at a time when it was still independent and at peace bore fruit in the splendours of the early sixteenth century. A reverse side of the picture is the growing interest shown by foreign Powers in Italian affairs. The claims of the houses of Anjou and Orleans to Naples and Milan were frequently brought into prominence through the evil habit contracted by Italian rulers of seeking French aid in their own quarrels. The rapid development of Spain as a Mediterranean Power was a danger to Italian independence as yet not fully realised. Imperial suzerainty over northern and central Italy remained a factor in politics which gained practical significance from the tension between Venice and the house of Austria with regard to Italy's eastern frontiers. Meanwhile a steady stream of seekers after learning crossed the Alps, numbering among them not only poor scholars, but men of rank and influence in their own countries. Other visitors came as diplomatic agents to the chief courts or on commercial business. All helped to create in their own countries an impression of Italy as a treasure-house of the arts, rich yet divided and militarily weak— a prize worth winning, and not impossible of attainment.

The first half of the fifteenth century in Italy had been a period of warfare, expansion and consolidation from which had emerged five more or less equal Powers. Milan, Venice, Florence, the Papacy and Naples

343

varied considerably in size and character, but the balance of their political influence was roughly maintained. Out of a collection of cities, each with a strong separatist tradition, the Visconti dukes of Milan had created a single state held together by solid benefits arising from an efficient central government. After the death of the last Visconti (1447) an experiment in republicanism ended in failure, and Francesco Sforza, the leading *condottiere* of the day, became duke of Milan. His claim rested less on his marriage with Visconti's illegitimate daughter than on the will of the citizens who proclaimed him duke, and on the recognition by the Italian Powers that a continuation of the Visconti system was in the general interest. A strong and united duchy facing the chief passes between France and Italy was a bulwark against foreign invasion, and at the same time a check on the territorial expansion of Venice. With the Peace of Lodi, which left Cremona, a long-standing object of Venetian ambition, in Milanese hands, Sforza's fighting days were over. He retained, however, a military organisation superior to that of any other Italian state save possibly Naples. The cavalry of the ducal household, with a force of infantry and some artillery, formed the nucleus of a standing army, whilst the *condottieri* were for the most part relatives and vassals, raising their companies locally, and recognising Milan as their *patria*. Milan prospered under her Sforza dukes. The agricultural resources of the duchy were developed by irrigation, and the planting of mulberries fostered the rapidly expanding silk industry. Building went on at the two chief monuments of the Visconti era, the Duomo of Milan and the Certosa of Pavia. To them were added the Castello Sforzesco and Francesco Sforza's great hospital in Milan, as well as churches and public buildings throughout the dominion. Having failed to obtain investiture with the duchy from the Emperor, the Sforza were at pains to cultivate the good-will of the people, the source of their title to rule. There was an undercurrent of discontent amongst an opposition which called itself Guelf, but the duchy remained for the most part united and at peace until Lodovico Sforza became the guardian of his nephew Gian Galeazzo. With his assumption of power (1480) Milan entered upon the period of her greatest glory and also upon the beginning of her troubles.

The acquisitions of Venice on the Italian mainland during the first half of the fifteenth century had broken down her old isolation. With frontiers stretching from the Alps to the Po, and from the Adda to the Isonzo, she became a vital factor in Italian politics. Machiavelli ascribes her decline to the mainland dominions which forced her to add hired *condottieri* to armed forces hitherto consisting of a navy manned by her own citizens. In fact, both in the handling of her captains and in the government of her subject cities she was both skilful and successful. The *condottieri* respected an employer who was stern but just, and punctual in payment, and for the most part they served her loyally. Levies from the subject cities provided an infantry which acquitted itself with credit against the armies of the League of Cambrai. Venice prided herself on treating the cities of her territory as colleagues rather than as subjects. The lower classes in particular benefited by the high standard of Venetian justice and by light taxation, raised indirectly on the purchase price of goods imported from the East. If the nobles resented the presence of the Venetian governors in cities where they themselves claimed the first place, they too recognised the advantages of Venetian rule, and acquiesced in it. In Venice itself, the monopoly of political power enjoyed by the nobility gave them exceptional opportunities for advancement. Yet wealth was spread evenly among the dominant class, as government control prevented any single family from amassing a great fortune. The non-nobles found an outlet for their administrative activities in the management of their own trade guilds, and through their employment in the civil service. It was the policy of the government to protect the interest of every class, from the merchant and the industrialist to the workers in the state arsenal and the rowers in the galleys. The citizens on their side were bred in a tradition which regarded the republic of St Mark as the greatest which the world had ever seen, save for that of Rome, and which set the good of the State above that of the individual. Venice's chief weakness lay in the jealousy and suspicion which she aroused among her neighbours. A new-comer on the Italian mainland, her gains were made at the expense of other Powers. Pope, Emperor, Milan, Mantua, and Ferrara were all the poorer for her advance and all feared her unabated greed for territory. Her overseas interests and her struggle with the Turks made her reluctant to join Italian combinations, and she acquired a reputation for selfish absorption in her own affairs. Her very efficiency added to her unpopularity with states less practised in the art of goverment. At this time rivalry with the Turks was weakening her hold on the Levant and endangering the safe passage of her merchant ships, whilst with the discovery of the Cape route to India a mortal blow to her monopoly of the spice trade was looming on the horizon. Nevertheless, when Philippe de Commynes visited her in 1494 she was to outward appearance at the height of her prosperity, a city of splendid buildings and lavish entertainment, wise in government and strong in the unity of her citizens.

During the ascendancy of the early Medici (1434–94) the government of Florence was skilfully adapted to the character and ideals of her citizens. All were united in their devotion to the republic, yet such was the rivalry between classes and families that popular government failed to function effectively. The dominant class in the city was composed of members of the greater guilds (*arti maggiori*), merchants associated with the textile industry, having commercial interests throughout Europe. Through their possession of seven out of nine places in the chief magistracy (*signoria*), they were in a position to control Florentine policy. They failed to do so owing to their own quarrels, which kept the government weak and divided, and provided opportunities for the less favoured classes to air their discontents. The Medici, whilst remaining in law private citizens, gave to the government the element of strength and continuity which it had hitherto lacked. Certain changes in the constitution facilitated their control over the State. The abandonment of election by lot in favour of appointment by a select committee, in the bi-monthly elections of the *signoria*, went far to secure that the chief magistracy was always composed of their friends. The institution in 1480 of a Council of Seventy, with functions which included choosing from among their own number the committees dealing with finance and foreign affairs, marked a further concentration of power in the hands of a ring of Mediceans. Important as were these changes, they depended for their efficacy upon the support of a substantial proportion of the ruling class which willingly accepted the leadership of first Cosimo, then Piero and then Lorenzo de' Medici. Their supremacy was, in fact, popular with the majority of citizens. Association with the great banking firm proved profitable to the merchants. An abundant food supply in the city, money freely spent for charitable purposes, and gaieties in which all shared, kept the lower classes content. Scholars and artists benefited by generous patronage, and the Medici palace became a treasure house which visitors from many lands came to admire. Owing to their extensive banking connections, and their genius for diplomacy, the Medici raised Florence to a position of influence in striking contrast with her military weakness. Lorenzo in his later years became the guardian of the peace of Italy, to whom other Powers looked for help and counsel. He was the friend and equal of princes, yet in Florence he had learned from his childhood to speak, write and act as a citizen and servant of the republic. The title of the Medici to rule was that they enhanced the fame of Florence and preserved, at least in name, her liberty, but from first to last their position was precarious.

From the time of the return of Martin V to Rome after the ending of the Great Schism, the aim of the Papacy had been to bring all Italian territory subject to papal suzerainty under its direct rule. In fulfilment of this purpose it encountered opposition from many quarters. The city of Rome remained republican at heart, even while it recognised the prestige which it gained as the seat of the Papacy. The great Roman families, with representatives in the college of cardinals, houses in the city, and vast estates outside, had abundant opportunities to hamper papal policy, and did not fail to use them. Cities such as Perugia and Bologna, and despots ruling as Vicars of the Church in Romagna were all but independent. Papal suzerainty over Naples was little more than a useful weapon in the hands of malcontent Neapolitan barons or rival claimants to the throne. For the extension of their authority the popes depended largely on their own relatives, whether clerics whom they made cardinals, or laymen on whom they bestowed lands and offices. Sixtus IV, in particular, made nepotism a fine art. Riario and della Rovere nephews were created cardinals, or made lords of cities. Girolamo Riario at one time came near to mastering all Romagna, and even aspired to the conquest of Ferrara. These designs were thwarted by the consistent opposition of the major Italian Powers, whose interest it was to retain their own influence in Romagna by acting as the patrons of the local rulers. In spite of all these hindrances, the spiritual authority of the Papacy continued to favour the development of the temporal power. Italian rulers, half-pagan and strongly anti-clerical, were nevertheless conscious of the evil effect of interdict and excommunication on their none too secure hold over their subjects. Despots and republics within the states of the Church had no thought of repudiating papal suzerainty; their aim always was to make a settlement with the Papacy, which would guarantee as far as possible their stability and freedom of action. Thus the papal claims remained intact, awaiting the opportunity for their assertion.

Naples in the fifteenth century was still a feudal kingdom, bearing the marks of the organisation imposed on it by its Norman conquerors. It was a land of great estates held by nobles of French, Spanish and Italian origin, whose aim was to live as little kings within their own dominions, independently of the monarchy. Its two outstanding rulers of the century, Alfonso and Ferrante of Aragon, did their utmost to increase monarchical power. Alfonso claimed the throne on the death of Joanna II (1435), but it took him seven years to establish his authority. He and his successor reorganised the finances, increased trade with the help of Florentine capital, and imposed heavy taxes. Opposition to their harsh rule was relentlessly crushed and rebellious barons were punished by death, imprisonment or exile. Alfonso (d. 1458) was a typical Renaissance prince, a builder and a lover of learning, who filled his court with men of talent from northern and central Italy. Ferrante (d. 1494) followed his father's example, less from personal taste than from his appreciation of the political value of patronage of the arts. Being illegitimate, he could lay no claim to Sicily, which on his father's death passed with the Crown of Aragon to his uncle John. Naples was won only after a long struggle with the French claimant, René of Anjou. With a kingdom confined to the mainland of Italy, his heir married to a Sforza, and his daughter to the duke of Ferrara, he entered the family circle of Italian princes. Naples under her Aragonese kings tended to be a disturbing element in Italian politics. There was constant friction with the Papacy over the question of suzerainty. Ferrante refused to add tribute to the white palfrey which he presented annually to the pope in token of his vassalage. He was the traditional ally of the Roman nobles, whilst the pope espoused the cause of the oppressed Neapolitan baronage. Ferrante's warlike and ambitious son, Alfonso duke of Calabria, seized every opportunity to extend his power in Italy and he did not forget that his grandfather had been named by Filippo Maria Visconti as his successor in Milan. Venice and Naples were rivals in the Adriatic, where the former strove to obtain possession of some Apulian ports. These local quarrels were an incentive to the external enemies of the Aragonese dynasty. Invitations to the Angevin princes to press their claims were made by both Venice and the Papacy, whilst the Angevin party in Naples and in exile never ceased to urge the coming of the French. The kings of Aragon were for the time being fully occupied in Spanish affairs, but the hope of uniting the island and the mainland parts of the old Sicilian kingdom made them prompt to take advantage of the difficulties of their cousins in Naples. In August 1480 Turkish forces occupied Otranto and Ferrante appealed in vain to the Italian Powers for help in their ejection. The danger passed with the death of Mehemmed II in the following year, but it had afforded an alarming example of Italian vulnerability.

Chief among the smaller states was Ferrara, ruled over by the house of Este, which also held the imperial fief of Modena. Ferrara lay within the states of the Church, and, although Borso d'Este received investiture as duke in 1471, the popes did not abandon their aim of bringing the city under their direct control. Venice also tried to extend her territory at Ferrara's expense. In the face of this double threat the Este looked for protection to Milan, and continued to do so when the duchy fell to the French. Ferrara owed her continued independence not only to her allies but also to the long-standing and popular rule of the house of Este. A marquis of Este became lord of Ferrara at the close of the twelfth century and his successors remained there for four hundred years. In comparison with this ancient race of rulers the Sforza and the Medici were upstarts. It was the Este who set the tone of Italian society in which the traditions of chivalry mingled with those of a free city, and public ceremonies were flavoured with classical culture. The court of Ferrara was a worthy setting for the work of Ariosto, the supreme poet of the Renaissance. Mantua was a small and poor state, a prey to the ambitions of its powerful neighbours, Milan and Venice. It was able to maintain itself owing to its strong position, amid marshes and lakes on the river Mincio, and to the fighting qualities of its Gonzaga lords. In 1403 the reigning lord had been created marquis of Mantua by the Emperor Wenzel, and the connection with the Empire was strengthened by the marriage of two of his successors to members of German princely families. The policy of the Gonzaga was determined by their profession as mercenary captains. They fought at various times in the service of the chief Italian states, and their earnings enabled them to transform their castle in Mantua into a vast Renaissance palace, to which successive generations added new features. The Gonzaga were intimately associated with the Montefeltro dukes of Urbino. Friendship between the two families began when

Federigo da Montefeltro came to Mantua as a pupil in the school of Vittorino da Feltre, and was cemented by marriage alliances. Federigo is an outstanding example of the soldier-scholar of his times. He founded a great library and built a palace at Urbino which during the foreign invasions became a place of refuge for more than one exiled family, and the scene of the discussions on the doctrine of courtesy embodied in Castiglione's *Il Cortegiano*. Owing to a marriage arranged by Sixtus IV, the duchy of Urbino passed on the death of Federigo's son to the della Rovere family. Bologna in the latter part of the fifteenth century was still a republic, where, in theory, the papal legate shared with the city magistrates in the government. In fact the real power lay with Giovanni Bentivoglio who, as first citizen, was able to impose his will on the republic, and to reduce the legate's authority to a shadow. Bentivoglio was a *condottiere* of Milan, and with Milanese support did much to maintain the cities of Romagna in freedom under their native lords in defiance of the papal claims. The palace which he built was as splendid as that of Mantua or Urbino; it was razed to the ground by his enemies after Julius II took possession of Bologna. Perugia and Siena followed the fashion of the times in placing the government of the republic in the hands of a leading citizen family, as the surest guarantee of their peace and independence. All these lesser states had their local schools of painting, and their special literary interests; all contributed to the rich variety of Italian civilisation; all were effective obstacles to Italian unity.

Throughout these years the principles laid down in the Italian league of 1455 remained a factor in the maintenance of peace. In an attempt to build up a system of defence against aggression whether on the part of an Italian or a foreign Power, the league outlined an elaborate machinery which never materialised and imposed terms on its members which were broken almost as soon as they were made. It did not succeed in preventing war, but it gave expression to the conviction that both common interests, and those of each state, demanded peace and unity within the borders of Italy. It remained an ideal to which statesmen appealed, and which the smaller states hailed as the guarantee of their continued existence. After the formal renewal of the league for another twenty-five years in 1480, the preservation of peace depended largely on the close understanding between Milan, Florence and Naples, and on the untiring efforts of Lorenzo de' Medici to smooth over occasions for dispute. When the Papacy and Venice launched an attack on Ferrara, the intervention of the three Powers preserved the city for the Este. It was largely owing to Lorenzo de' Medici that war between the Papacy and Naples was localised and brought to a speedy end. His death in April 1492, at a time when relations between Milan and Naples were deteriorating, and when Charles VIII of France was succumbing to the lure of Italian adventure, precipitated the crisis.

When the government of France passed from the capable hands of Anne of Beaujeu into those of Charles VIII, conflicting counsels were urged upon the young monarch. Among those who pressed him to enter Italy as the champion of the Angevin claims to Naples was Antonello di San Severino, prince of Salerno. A leader of the rebel baronage in the rising of 1486, he had fled from Ferrante's vengeance to the French court, where he painted a vivid picture of the sufferings of the Angevin party in Naples, and the enthusiasm with which its members would rally round Charles. Although the latter's title to the throne does not bear examination, he was, by the will of René of Anjou, the recognised representative of the Angevin cause. Nurtured during his sickly childhood on the romances of chivalry, Charles saw himself as a conquering hero, who, having won Naples, would use it as a base for a crusade against the Turks. With a fine French army waiting to prove itself, he believed that the expedition would contribute to the glory and unity of the nation. Among Charles's counsellors, Guillaume Briçonnet, a finance officer, and Etienne de Vesc, seneschal of Beaucaire, were eager in their support. On the other hand, the older men, such as Philippe de Commynes, bred in the tradition of Louis XI, saw the Italian expedition as a war waged for mere glory which would not serve French interests. Charles, who, as a Florentine envoy noted, habitually changed his mind according to the advice of the last person with him, continued to halt between two opinions. But for the fresh encouragement which came from Italy, the invasion might never have taken place.

From the time that Isabella of Aragon married Gian Galeazzo Sforza, duke of Milan, she made repeated complaints to her father and grandfather in Naples that she and her husband were in all things subordinate to the regent, Lodovico, and that she was deprived of her rightful position as first lady of the court by Lodovico's wife, Beatrice d'Este. Alfonso of Calabria caught at an opportunity for asserting himself in Milan, and an attack from Naples appeared imminent, As Lodovico's fears increased, he resolved to use the threat of French invasion as a means of self-protection. In April 1493, after efforts at reconciliation had failed, he came out openly as the ally and supporter of France. Relying on past precedents, he probably thought that the threat would not materialise, and that he could use it as other Italian Powers had used it, for his own purposes. It was his misfortune that on this occasion the French came. The Milanese alliance opened Charles's passage into Italy, and the scales were now weighed down on the side of invasion. A further incentive came with the appearance at the French court of Cardinal Giuliano della Rovere. In the election which followed the death of Innocent VIII, he had been defeated by Rodrigo Borgia, now Pope Alexander VI. Alive to the embarrassment which Charles VIII's coming must cause to his feared and hated rival, he urged the invasion with characteristic vehemence. Charles

hoped to persuade Alexander to invest him with Naples, but there was always the possibility that, with della Rovere at his side, his crusading spirit might be directed towards the summons of a general council, which would depose the pope. Before setting out for Italy, Charles secured the acquiescence of Ferdinand of Aragon and Maximilian, king of the Romans, by means of the treaties of Barcelona and Senlis. The first handed back Roussillon and Cerdagne to Spain, the second restored Franche-Comté and Artois to Burgundy. Thus the achievements of Louis XI, which strengthened the frontiers of France at the Pyrenees and to the east, were thrown away for the shadow of Italian conquests.

As the French invasion of Italy grew imminent, the chief Powers had to make up their minds on which side to range themselves. Milan's choice was already made, but both the Papacy and Florence hesitated as to the course they should take. Alexander realised that opposition to France would imperil his position as head of Christendom, but he knew himself to be incapable of defending his temporal possessions against Naples. He decided that the nearer danger was the more formidable, and recognised Alfonso as king on Ferrante's death, at the same time admonishing Charles not to disturb the peace of Italy. In Florence, alliance with France was based on long tradition, and fortified by commercial ties, but the key-note of Lorenzo de' Medici's policy since 1480 had been friendship with Naples and discouragement of French intervention. The choice between two parts of a policy which could no longer be united fell to Piero de' Medici, the stupid boy of the family. With more courage than wisdom he decided to stand by his Neapolitan friends. Resolute resistance to France on the part of Venice might have changed the course of events, but the republic according to her custom adopted an attitude of strict neutrality. Giovanni Bentivoglio of Bologna told the Milanese envoy that his master should consider well this coming of the French into Italy, saying that in his own opinion Italians should find some better means of taking vengeance on their enemies than that of allowing barbarian peoples to come between them. Bologna, lying astride the Via Emilia, could have been a formidable impediment to the southward march of the French. Despite his wise words, Giovanni wavered between fear of offending Milan and hope of obtaining a cardinal's hat for his son from the pope, until the course of events had gone beyond his power to influence them. This absorption in local and personal interests is typical of the attitude of the smaller Powers. It marks the fundamental weakness of the Italians which spelt victory for the French.

Alfonso of Aragon had inherited from his father a sound plan of defence, and adequate forces to put it into operation. The Neapolitan fleet under the king's brother Federigo was to blockade Genoa, whilst the bulk of the army was to take up its position in Romagna, and thus, with the co-operation of Piero de' Medici in Tuscany, prevent the French from crossing

the Apennines. Disaster occurred at every point. Delay in mobilisation enabled the duke of Orleans to get into Genoa before the arrival of the Aragonese fleet. When the French fleet appeared before Rapallo, which had been occupied by a Genoese exile with Aragonese aid, Federigo withdrew rather than risk contact with it, leaving Rapallo to its fate. In Florence, Piero de' Medici's support of Naples roused antagonism among all classes, not least among the operatives in the cloth industry, who were suffering from lack of work, owing to the French embargo on Florentine goods. When Charles VIII reached Piacenza after his progress through Milanese territory, he was met by the representatives of the junior branch of the Medici family, who assured him that Florence was wholly French in sympathy. On his arrival in Tuscany, Piero de' Medici went secretly to the French camp, and threw himself on Charles's protection. The fortresses of Sarzana, Pietrasanta, Leghorn and Pisa were handed over to the French and the way to Florence lay open. This marked the end of Piero's supremacy. A week after he had fled from the city as an exile Charles VIII entered (17 November 1494), to be received with every sign of honour, as the man foretold by Savonarola's preaching, sent from God to regenerate Italy. Before he left Florence, a treaty was signed by which the city recognised Charles as the protector of her liberties, and agreed to contribute financially to his Neapolitan enterprise. From henceforth, Florence was, in all but name, the vassal of France until the French were driven from Italy in 1512. Meanwhile, Neapolitan forces in Romagna, under Alfonso's heir, Ferrantino, withdrew before the French contingent advancing along the Via Emilia, and the Orsini, in their strongholds north of Rome, did nothing to impede the invader's triumphal course. Charles entered Rome, as he had entered Florence, without opposition, and left it having received, by treaty with Alexander, the right of passage through papal territory. Deserted by his allies, Alfonso resigned the Crown in favour of his popular young son Ferrantino, yet he too failed to stay the advance of the French, and on 22 February 1495 Charles entered Naples. Shortly afterwards, the two strongholds of Castel dell'Uovo and Castel Nuovo surrendered. Ferrantino fled to Ischia, and practically the whole kingdom was in the hands of the French. Charles had won Naples without fighting a single battle. The superiority of the French artillery had proved itself in assaults on outlying fortresses, and the ferocity of the sack which followed their capture had aroused terror of the consequences of resistance. As the armies of the allies melted away, the larger cities, seeing no hope of succour, in turn opened their gates to the enemy.

Various factors account for the loss of Charles's acquisitions in Italy almost as rapidly as they had been won. Among them is the behaviour of the French in Naples. Lands and offices went to Frenchmen, and their Angevin supporters were offended at faring no better than the

adherents of Aragon. Supplies were short, the administration was corrupt, whilst the army of occupation earned an evil name by its brutality, its licence and its dirt. Insurrections began before Charles left Naples, and soon Ferrantino and Federigo of Aragon were at their head. They had slipped across from Sicily which was to form the base for the re-conquest of the mainland. Ferdinand the Catholic was determined to prevent the establishment of French rule in Naples. His troops were mustered in Sicily under Gonzalo de Córdoba to be transported to Naples, and to re-establish Ferrantino on his throne. His diplomacy brought together opposing elements in the League of Venice. The league was concluded on 31 March 1495, the contracting parties being the pope, the emperor, Spain, Venice and Milan, and their object the mutual defence of their states against aggression. In form, the league resembled the various pacts for the maintenance of peace made between the Italian Powers during the past forty years. It was welcomed as a sign of the ending of dissensions which had let in the French, but the real significance of a combination which included Spain and the Empire was that Italy had lost control over her own destinies.

On 6 July 1495 the forces of the league led by Francesco Gonzaga made contact with the French in the Taro valley as Charles was on his homeward journey. The battle of Fornovo was claimed by both sides as a victory, but the far heavier losses suffered by the Italians, and the fact that Charles got away safely into Lombardy, prove that the advantage lay with the French. Yet the Italians fought vigorously and Gonzaga's encircling movement all but succeeded. Lack of discipline and failure of the various elements in the allied army to co-operate, together with the unrivalled efficiency of the French *gendarmerie*, decided the day. 'Our chief satisfaction', wrote the Milanese envoy in Bologna,' is that the French have found in Italy forces that can face them, and have learned that Italian arms are no less sharp than theirs.'[1] This, and the capture of the entire French baggage train encouraged Gonzaga to order from Mantegna the *Madonna della Vittoria*, in commemoration of his exploits on the Taro. The inclusion of Milan in the League of Venice gave Louis of Orleans the opportunity to assert his claim to the duchy, as the grandson of Valentina Visconti. From his grandmother's dowry town of Asti, where he had remained since Charles first came to Italy, he occupied Novara, and was closely besieged by the forces of the league. Charles, however, had no desire to further his cause, and was as anxious to get home as Lodovico Sforza was to see the last of him. To the indignation of those in both camps who desired to go on fighting, they came to terms in the Peace of Vercelli (10 October 1495) by which Novara was restored to Milan, and

---

[1] 'Quello che piu piace alla brigata è che Franzesi hanno pur trovato in Italia chi li ha facto volto et facto provare che le arme Italiane non sono mancho pungente che le loro.' Letter of July 1495, Milan, Archivio di Stato: Potenze Estere, 187.

Lodovico promised his support to Charles in the event of a new French expedition. Meanwhile the French viceroy, Montpensier, carried on a losing struggle in Naples. By the spring of 1496 Ferrantino was in full possession of his capital. Montpensier and many of his troops succumbed to the epidemic called by the French *le mal de Naples*. The chief preoccupation of the few that were left was how to get home. Charles VIII continued to make plans for a fresh expedition until his death on 7 April 1498 ended his dreams of conquest.

In no Italian state had the coming of the French more momentous consequences than in Florence. Without it, Girolamo Savonarola might have been known only as a great preacher, an exponent of the Christian faith, and a denouncer of vice. His political importance, as the champion of the French alliance and the new Florentine constitution, began with the advent of Charles VIII, and the fall of Piero de' Medici. In the days of crisis men of all classes hailed him as the herald of a new era of freedom, peace and prosperity, and owing to his influence the revolution was effected without bloodshed. The Grand Council, on the Venetian model, which with its 3000 members gave effective rights of citizenship to a greater number of Florentines, came into being largely through his advocacy. It won the approval of the publicists, and was at first generally popular. Pisa had revolted from Florence when the French took possession of the fortress, and in friendship with France lay the best hope of its recovery. Disillusionment soon followed. The Pisan war constituted a heavy drain on Florentine resources, and the situation worsened when the French commander, sympathising with the Pisans, handed over the fortress to them. When Florence refused to enter the League of Venice, pressure was put upon her by sending help to Pisa, whilst the pope forbade Savonarola to preach, and finally excommunicated him. Faction, the curse of Florence, deprived the Grand Council of its competence. Savonarola's insistence that his political programme represented the will of God, which it was sin to disobey, together with the extravagances of his followers, roused opposition in many quarters, intensifying the enmity between citizens which he had sought to heal. News of the death of Charles VIII, deferring hope of assistance from France, came at a time of reaction against religious revivalism and of acute financial crisis. So, in return for leave to levy tithes on the clergy, Florence handed over Savonarola to the papal commissioners and to his death (23 May 1498). His fall was marked by no change of policy. The republican constitution and the French alliance remained in being, and the war against Pisa continued until the city fell to Florence in 1509. During the last Republic (1527–30) the spirit of the friar lived again. Religious fervour combined with patriotic ardour to inspire the Florentines in their final struggle for liberty.

With the departure of the French, Lodovico Sforza appeared to have got all he wanted at comparatively little cost. Gian Galeazzo died in

October 1494. Whether his death was due to his uncle's poison or to the effects of his own excesses on a weak constitution, remains an open question, although the latter alternative is more probable. Thereupon Lodovico was proclaimed duke by an assembly of leading citizens, and in the following year imperial ambassadors solemnly invested him with the duchy. He was the first Sforza to obtain imperial investiture, Maximilian's habitual need of money making him ready to sell the privilege which Frederick III had steadfastly refused. Having made his peace with Charles VIII, and with nothing to fear from Naples, Lodovico was free to spend time and money as his personal interests dictated. At the court of Milan, every aspect of Renaissance life found expression. It numbered among its members painters, architects, sculptors, musicians, scholars, and soldiers. All were experts in their own sphere, and added distinction to it by their work. All played their part in the masques, tournaments and banquets which marked great occasions, as also in the simpler pleasures which enlivened the leisure hours of the court. Discussions on topics of literary and artistic interest, improvisations in song accompanied on the lyre, games and practical joking offered a rich variety of entertainment. Immersed in this gay and highly civilised life, Lodovico neglected his army and his fortresses, and paid no heed to warnings of danger to come. Despite his genuine interest in schemes for the well-being of his subjects, heavy taxation and arbitrary rule caused a rising tide of discontent within the duchy, and his policy during the French invasion had left him without a friend in Italy. When, with the accession of Louis of Orleans to the throne of France, the blow fell, Lodovico found himself without means to resist it.

Louis XII's obsession with the idea of Italian conquest is curiously inconsistent with the keen appreciation of the needs of France and the French people discernible in his home policy. A man of simple tastes, domestic, peace-loving, economical, he was nevertheless tenacious of his rights. Convinced of the justice of his claim to Milan, he regarded his failure to conquer it during Charles VIII's expedition as a disgrace to be wiped out. His plans for a descent on Italy were warmly supported by his chief adviser, Georges d'Amboise, archbishop of Rouen, whose ambitions soared not only to a cardinalate but to the Papacy, and immediately after the king's accession preparations were put in hand. The reaction of the Italian Powers to the prospect of a second French invasion shows how demoralising were the effects of Charles VIII's expedition. Before 1494 they were confident that the French would not come; after Charles's withdrawal they flattered themselves that the French would not stay; the chief thought in their minds was how Louis's intervention could best be used to their individual advantage. Alexander VI at once entered into negotiations with the new king, whom he saw as a valuable ally in his projects for the extension of the temporal power of the Papacy, and the advancement of his family. His son Cesare Borgia

13-2

was now bent on exchanging an ecclesiastical for a secular career. He was on the look-out for a wife and a principality, and Louis agreed to supply both in return for the facilitation of his divorce from Jeanne de France and his union with the widowed queen, Anne of Brittany. In 1498 Cesare, with a retinue of outstanding magnificence, left Italy on a French vessel, no longer cardinal of Valencia but duke of Valentinois, taking with him to France the dispensation for Louis's second marriage and a cardinal's hat for d'Amboise. His proposed bride was Carlotta, daughter of King Federigo of Naples, who had been brought up at the French court, but Federigo, to his honour and also to his undoing, supported his daughter in her persistent refusal to marry the ex-cardinal. Instead, Cesare married Charlotte d'Albret, sister of the king of Navarre, and returned to Italy with Louis's invading army. From Milan he set out with the prestige of the French name, a contingent of French cavalry and some Swiss infantry, on his first campaign of conquest in Romagna. Florence welcomed Louis's coming, which put an end to her isolation in Italy and gave new hope of recovering Pisa, but it was only after protracted negotiation that an alliance was signed between France and Venice. Hatred of Lodovico Sforza, who had made peace behind her back at Vercelli, and Louis's promise that in the event of victory her western frontier should be extended to include Cremona and the Ghiaradadda, at length turned Venice from her traditional policy of neutrality to active support of the invaders. No one but Federigo of Naples, whose throne Louis claimed, and some rulers in the Romagna who feared Cesare Borgia, ranged themselves on the side of Milan.

In the face of the formidable array of forces piling up against him, Lodovico Sforza appeared at his worst. Beatrice d'Este was no longer at his side to resolve his doubts and hesitations by her quick brain and common sense; he seemed incapable of decision and all his preparations were begun too late. His chief hope lay in his friendship with the Emperor, but Maximilian's capacity to help was as usual unequal to his desire. The repudiation by the Swiss of the alliance made by certain cantons with Milan, and the conclusion of a ten years' treaty with Louis, permitting him to recruit infantry within Swiss territory, were prompted by Maximilian's quarrel with the Confederation in which Lodovico became involved. At home, Lodovico reaped the fruit of his mistakes. The sound financial system which he had inherited was thrown into disorder by his lavish spending. Owing to the favouritism which he showed to Galeazzo San Severino, a brilliant tournament winner and an incompetent general, two experienced commanders were alienated. Gian Giacomo Trivulzio was a member of the Guelf nobility whom Lodovico should have been careful to placate. When he found himself supplanted in the army by San Severino he espoused the cause of the Duchess Isabella, and went off to Naples to lay her grievances before her father. Here he entered French service and now returned to Milan at the head of Louis's invading army. The count of Caiazzo, who had led the Milanese contingent at Fornovo, also took offence at his younger brother being preferred to himself and deserted to the French at the first opportunity. San Severino failed to hold Alessandria, which was the bulwark of the Milanese defence; as one city after another yielded to the French, resistance became hopeless, and in September 1499 Lodovico withdrew to the Tirol, where he and his two little sons were hospitably received by Maximilian. His hope of a speedy return lay in the Castello of Milan which he left, fortified and provisioned to hold out for a year, in the charge of a castellan in whom he placed implicit confidence. The betrayal of the Castello to the French by this 'new Judas' twelve days after the duke's departure came as a crowning misfortune.

Nevertheless, Lodovico's prospects were not unfavourable. The Swiss cantons, dissatisfied with their treatment by the French, agreed to supply him with 10,000 men, with whom he was able to set out for Milan, in the following spring. Here, the dictatorship of Trivulzio, the leader of one faction of the nobility, was bitterly opposed by his rivals. Taxation was heavier than it had been before, the cession of Cremona to Venice aroused general indignation, and there was a revival of devotion to the ruling family in which Lodovico's unpopularity was forgotten. On the news of his approach, the Milanese rose and seized the city gates. With every child who could speak shouting *Moro*[1] in the streets, Trivulzio abandoned the city, and Lodovico entered amid frantic rejoicing. From this moment his cause declined. The French clung tenaciously to the Castello and to other strong places in the duchy. Whilst their army was reinforced, Lodovico's resources diminished. On 8 April 1500 a fiasco, unworthy to be called a battle, at Novara sealed the fate of the house of Sforza. The Swiss laid down their arms, refusing to fight against their fellow countrymen, and Lodovico was captured by the French when attempting to escape. His remaining years were spent as a prisoner in France, 'confining within narrow walls him whose aspirations and ambitions all Italy had been hardly wide enough to contain'.[2]

Having won Milan, Louis XII aimed next at Naples. He would have been wise to accept Federigo's offer to hold his kingdom as a fief of France, but he preferred the hazardous course laid down in the Treaty of Granada (November 1500) by which he and Ferdinand of Spain agreed to conquer and partition the dominion which each coveted. The unfortunate Federigo was kept in ignorance of the bargain until the invasion had begun, and, believing that Gonzalo had come to his aid, he prepared

---

[1] Lodovico was known popularly as *Il Moro*. He adopted both the mulberry and the Moor's head as his devices.

[2] 'Rinchiudendosi in una angusta carcere i pensieri e l'ambizione di colui, che prima appena capivano i termini di tutta Italia.' Guicciardini, *Storia d'Italia*, bk. IV.

to give battle to the French. When he found that Ferdinand was against him, he knew that his cause was lost, and after the capture and sack of Capua by the French he submitted unconditionally to Louis, choosing to trust an open enemy rather than the kinsman who had betrayed him. He was treated generously, being sent to France, and given the duchy of Anjou in compensation for his lost kingdom. Louis was now possessed of the northern half of Naples, including the capital, whilst Ferdinand held Apulia and Calabria. The latter was abler and more unscrupulous than his partner and had greater advantages, both military and political. Very soon disputes between the allies led to war, and war ended in the ejection of the French from their portion of the kingdom. Trouble arose over certain districts which had not been mentioned in the partition treaty, especially over Capitanata, lying between French Abruzzi and Spanish Apulia, to which each side laid claim. Its importance lay in its fertility, and in the profits derived from the tolls levied on the cattle going to and fro between their summer and winter pastures. The French took up arms to enforce their claim and at first had some success. Gonzalo retired to Barletta where he remained besieged throughout the winter of 1502–3, maintained by supplies brought by sea from Spain and Sicily. In the spring reinforcements poured in, and he was able to take the field; here his victory at Cerignola opened his road to the capital. The French retired to Gaeta until they were strong enough to make a southward drive on Naples, but they were delayed by various causes, and it was mid-winter when the two armies faced each other on either side of the Garigliano. Gonzalo contrived to get across the river secretly by means of a bridge of boats, and took the French by surprise. After a fierce battle they retreated in disorder to Gaeta, and on 1 January 1504 this, their last stronghold in Neapolitan territory, yielded to the Spaniards. The whole kingdom was now reunited under the Crown of Aragon. In Italy Aragonese rule in Naples was no innovation. The French kings were foreign invaders, but the Aragonese were accepted sovereigns who had adapted themselves to Italian ways. Thus the transference of the throne from the illegitimate to the legitimate line aroused little apprehension. Inhabitants of the kingdom had yet to learn the difference between the easy-going Catalans and Valencians, who had surrounded the first Aragonese king of Naples, and the Castilian officials who came to extend to their new acquisition the centralising policy of Ferdinand and Isabella in Spain. Few native rulers grasped that a Mediterranean Power, long established in Sicily and Sardinia, had a vital interest in controlling Italy and effective means of so doing, or that the roots previously struck by the Aragonese on the mainland rendered them more formidable enemies of Italian independence than the French could ever be.

Among Louis XII's allies, none gained more from his coming than the Papacy which, during his reign in Milan, succeeded in bringing practically all the states of the Church under its direct rule. The first stage in the process was the work of Cesare Borgia. In three breathless campaigns he made himself master of Romagna, driving the native lords from their cities, and establishing order and unity in the province. He organised an army owing allegiance to himself alone, set up a central court of justice, and did his best to secure that all classes subject to him benefited by his rule. Finding his plans for extending his power in Tuscany thwarted by Louis XII's alliance with Florence, he was contemplating deserting France for Spain, when his career was cut short by the death of Alexander VI (August 1503). His outstanding characteristics were utter ruthlessness, personal magnetism and a certain flair for good government. These led Machiavelli to see in him a potential saviour of Italy, but the man who by his treachery, cruelty, and self-seeking earned the detestation of his neighbours was ill-fitted for such a role.[1]

Cesare Borgia's achievements ended the day of small states in Romagna. Few cities, after his fall, showed any inclination to receive back their ruling families, and Giuliano della Rovere who, after the brief pontificate of Pius III succeeded to the Papacy as Julius II, reaped the fruits of his work. Julius was a man of vast ambitions and boundless energy. His aims were first to recover all the territories of the Church, and then to place himself at the head of an Italian confederation which should drive out the foreigner. Louis XII reluctantly promised aid for the pope's immediate enterprise, and after two years of preparation Julius set out from Rome on a campaign of conquest, forcing all but the most infirm of the cardinals to accompany him. On his approach to Perugia, Baglioni, the local despot, came out to place the city in his hands. There followed the flight of Giovanni Bentivoglio from Bologna and the triumphal entry of the papal forces. This great city was a prize which had eluded Cesare Borgia. Here Julius held his court during the winter of 1506-7, well satisfied with his achievement. He returned to Rome on the disquieting news of the rebellion of Genoa against the French and its suppression by Louis XII in person. Julius was not alone in his alarm at such a demonstration of French power. Maximilian complained that Louis coveted the Empire for himself and the Papacy for Amboise, and announced his intention to come to Italy to receive the imperial crown and to assert his suzerain rights over both Genoa and Milan. Ferdinand of Spain came to meet Louis at Savona, where under cover of a courtesy visit the two monarchs reached an understanding with regard to their future policy in Italy. In 1508 Maximilian asked passage for his army through Venetian territory and, on being refused, came notwithstanding. His forces were defeated in Friuli and he had to agree to a truce which left the Venetians

---

[1] Pepe, *La politica dei Borgia* (1946), denies that Cesare's rule in Romagna was in any way beneficent, but the evidence of his reforms, and the opinion of contemporaries such as Guicciardini cannot lightly be disregarded.

in possession of Fiume, Trieste and other cities, hitherto Habsburg. Thereupon both Maximilian and Louis decided to end their quarrels in order to combine against Venice. Margaret of Austria and d'Amboise were sent to Cambrai as their plenipotentiaries, to draw up terms of peace, and to make provision for a league which should despoil Venice of all the territories which she had won at the expense of Italian Powers during the last hundred years. Maximilian's share was to extend as far west as the Mincio, including the important city of Verona. The cities between the Mincio and the Adda were to be restored to Milan. Naples was to receive back Brindisi and other Apulian ports occupied by Venice when she helped to drive Charles VIII from Italy. Mantua and Ferrara, which had both suffered losses, were included in the League of Cambrai, and promised that their former possessions should be returned to them.

Julius II's quarrel with Venice was both ecclesiastical and territorial. She had taken advantage of Cesare Borgia's fall to increase the number of cities which she held in Romagna, and had ignored the pope's peremptory demands for their restoration. She had refused to bestow the temporalities of bishoprics upon papal nominees who were not Venetian subjects. There is a story of a war of words between the Venetian ambassador and Julius II, in which the latter declared 'I shall not rest until I have made you, as you were, humble fishermen', to which the ambassador replied 'Holy Father, if you are not careful, we could far more easily make you a little clerk'.[1] Julius's first intention was merely to use the threat of the League of Cambrai to induce Venice to submit to his demands, and he only joined the allies on the eve of the outbreak of hostilities. On 10 May 1509 Louis XII crossed the Adda in force and a few days later at Agnadello, in the territory ceded by France to Venice ten years before, the one important battle of the war took place. Owing to lack of co-operation between the two chief commanders, a part only of the Venetian army faced the concentrated power of the French. The infantry, in particular, fought with great gallantry, but the odds against the Venetians were overwhelming and they suffered a major defeat, which was followed by the loss of their entire dominion. One after the other the cities hastened to make terms with their new masters, and there were those in the Venetian Senate who advocated the final abandonment of their mainland territories and a return to the sea. Venice, however, had two great advantages; one was the jealousy and suspicion rife among her enemies, the other the recognition by the subject cities of the benefits enjoyed under her rule. Typical of the turning of the tide is the part played by the Vicentine noble Luigi da Porto whose war memoirs in the form of letters give an illuminating picture of the times. He and his family welcomed

---

[1] Da Porto, *Lettere Storiche* (ed. Bressan, 1857), p. 30. 'Io non mi rimarrò che non vi abbia fatti umili e tutti pescatori, sicome foste.' 'Vieppiù agevolmente vi faremo noi, Padre Santo, un piccol chierico, se non sarete prudente.'

Maximilian on his occupation of Vicenza, saying that their object was to be on the winning side, but when the opportunity came they helped to restore their city to Venice; Luigi then fought under Venetian banners until disabled by a wound. In 1510 Julius II changed sides. When he had ousted the Venetians from their cities in Romagna he had only to win Ferrara in order to have the papal states under his control. The dukes of Ferrara relied upon France to maintain their independence, and Julius's attack on Ferrara became an episode in his war with the French. The events of the next two years include a treaty imposed by the pope on Venice, which she refused to consider as binding, an unsuccessful campaign against Ferrara, and the temporary restoration of the Bentivoglio to Bologna by French arms. Whilst a schismatic council, summoned to Pisa under French auspices and later transferred to Milan, carried the struggle into the ecclesiastical field, Julius laboured until he had brought all the enemies of France together in the Holy League. Ferdinand of Aragon, having recovered his Apulian ports from Venice without fighting for them, readily joined the league and sent the viceroy of Naples to besiege Bologna. Gaston de Foix came from Milan to its defence. He had succeeded in raising the siege when news that Brescia, through the action of some leading citizens, was again in Venetian hands called him back to Lombardy. Brescia was re-conquered and mercilessly sacked by the French. Gaston then returned to face the army of the league at Ravenna. The battle of Ravenna (11 April 1512) proved a desperate struggle between two evenly matched forces in which the losses on both sides were exceedingly heavy. At one point the Spanish and papal troops all but got the upper hand, but the French cavalry, effectively supported by Ferrarese guns, finally won the day. Gaston de Foix, a young man of outstanding military genius, was among the killed and the loss of their leader turned the joy of the victors into sorrow. The French were in no condition to face the new crisis which came upon them in the following month with the descent of the Swiss upon the Milanese.

The part played by the Swiss in the Italian wars was the outcome of their economic ties with the duchy of Milan and also of their national industry as mercenaries. If easy access to Milan was important to the trade of the urban cantons, to the forest cantons it was vital, as the duchy was their main source of corn and wine. When the king of France, the chief employer of Swiss infantry, became duke of Milan, the Confederation hoped to profit both as traders and fighters. In fact, the relations between Louis XII and the Swiss were marked by one quarrel after another. Ill-feeling was aroused by disputes over trade, over the occupation of Bellinzona by men of the forest cantons, and over the payment of Swiss infantry and their unauthorised employment against Genoa. As a result of the tension the Franco-Swiss alliance was not renewed in 1509. Under the leadership of Matthias Schinner, cardinal bishop of Sion, the Swiss prepared to act as an independent Power in Italy. This warrior-patriot was a man after Julius II's own heart, and through their combined efforts the Swiss, as members of the Holy League, became the chief instrument in the expulsion of the French. With Maximilian's permission, Schinner's forces entered Italy by the Brenner Pass bringing with them Lodovico Sforza's elder son, Massimiliano. The French were taken by surprise and withdrew without a contest. With the army went the council, which had been deliberating over the election of an anti-pope, and now passed into oblivion at Lyons. In 1513 the French attempted to fight their way back, only to be routed by the Swiss at Novara. Massimiliano was recognised as duke by the Holy League, and the Swiss remained in control of the duchy. In France, the failure to hold Milan aroused little regret; it was viewed rather as a relief from an unprofitable burden. Machiavelli ascribes Louis' undoing to the mistakes which he made in Italy, but a greater mistake than any of these was his decision to go there at all.

The expulsion of the French, which set a Sforza upon the throne in Milan, also brought the Medici back to Florence. The republic had gained little from its alliance with Louis XII. French military aid in the Pisan war was not worth the large sums which were paid for it, and was offset by the help which the enemies of France gave to the Pisans. When in 1509 Pisa was at last obliged to yield, Florentine arms alone were responsible for the victory, all other forces being engaged in the war between the League of Cambrai and Venice. The election of Piero Soderini as *Gonfaloniere di Giustizia* for life gave the republic a permanent head, but it did not heal party strife or rescue Florentine finances from the chaos into which they had fallen. Soderini's refusal to join the Holy League exposed Florence to the attacks of Julius II, and caused discontent within the city which played into the hands of the Medici party. The end came in August 1512, when Spanish forces assaulted Prato, the Florentine militia engaged in its defence ran away, and Prato was taken and sacked. A few days later, Soderini was deposed and the Medici were invited to return. The leading members of the family at the time were the two younger sons of Lorenzo de' Medici, and his grandson and namesake, Lorenzo, the son of Piero. In 1513 Cardinal Giovanni, already the moving spirit among them, became Pope Leo X. The Medici, as virtual rulers of Florence, succeeded to the dominating position in Tuscany which Cesare Borgia was trying to acquire at the time of his fall; thus a great block of territory stretching from sea to sea across central Italy was under the control of a single family. If any one of their number possessed Cesare's gifts, he had a unique opportunity to unite Italy under his leadership and drive out the foreigner. Such were the circumstances which inspired Machiavelli to write *Il Principe* and to dedicate it first to Giuliano and later to Lorenzo di Piero de' Medici. Yet both lacked the ability and the motive for such a task. The amiable and popular Giuliano would have been content to live in Florence as a private citizen, and at the instance of Leo X he soon yielded his place as head of the State to his nephew. Lorenzo had energy and ambition, but he was a poor soldier, and his craving for the outward signs of lordship made him ill-fitted for the government of a republic. Leo X's chief concern was the advancement of his family and, second to this, the increase of papal power. In pursuit of those aims he was as ready to make terms with foreign rulers as to expel them. He drove Francesco della Rovere from Urbino and made Lorenzo de' Medici duke in his place. He even talked of placing Giuliano on the throne of Naples, yet he was by nature a *dilettante* and his energies were dissipated by the delights of life in Rome, where under his patronage the Renaissance reached its zenith. Throughout Italy the departure of the French was the signal for a return to the old ways, and amid the gay and cultivated life of the courts the brief respite from foreign invasion was allowed to pass without heed for the future. The third French expedition entered an Italy unprepared and divided.

In August 1515 Francis I crossed the Alps at the head of an army which comprised the flower of the French nation. Great nobles such as Bourbon and Alençon were in the front line, the incomparable cavalry were 3000 strong, and although the bulk of the infantry were German mercenaries they were supported by Gascons. Like Charles VIII, Francis made Constantinople his ultimate aim, yet his motive was neither the chivalrous romanticism which had inspired Charles, nor Louis XII's determination to secure his legal rights, but glory for himself and France. He was a typical Renaissance monarch, who demanded a wide field on which to deploy his varied gifts of mind and body. The Venetians were once more allies of France, and their forces under Bartolomeo d'Alviano, who had been taken prisoner at Agnadello, played a crucial part in the campaign. Another former enemy in French service was the famous engineer and mine-layer Pedro Navarra, who had helped to take many castles for the Aragonese in the Neapolitan wars, and was now in charge of the French artillery. Against the French were ranged the combined forces of the Holy League. Leo X negotiated with both sides but decided in the end to support his allies; he sent a force under Lorenzo de' Medici to Piacenza, and lent troops to the Milanese. A contingent from Naples was hurried north and took up its stand at Verona, which was still held by Maximilian. The brunt of the defence of Milan lay with the Swiss, whose hold upon the duchy was by no means secure. The treaty signed between Massimiliano and the Confederation offered a unique opportunity for the economic and political development of the Swiss, if they had been far-sighted enough to allow time for the duchy to recover its prosperity before pressing their financial claims to the full. The first consideration of a nation of mercenaries was, however, prompt payment for their services, and Schinner's efforts to restrain their rapacity met with little success. Massimiliano's extravagance further increased the financial burden imposed on an exhausted people, until it was said openly that French rule was preferable to the present regime. Among the cantons, also, a French party appeared, which preferred the old system of bribes and pensions from France to independent action on the part of the Confederation. Thus discontent in Milan and dissension among the Swiss paved the way for defeat in the field.

Francis I was expected to enter Italy either by the Mont Cenis Pass or by that of Mont Genèvre, and the Swiss were stationed at Susa to intercept him as he descended into the plain. His appearance by the unfrequented passage of the Col d'Argentière turned the Swiss position and forced them to fall back on the capital. The French, having routed the Milanese troops at Villafranca, encamped at Marignano, a few miles south-east of Milan, and here on 14–15 September a two-day battle was fought. Again and again the weight of the Swiss infantry was hurled against the French and was repelled at heavy cost. To Gian Giacomo Trivulzio, fighting the last of his eighteen battles, it seemed no mere human contest but a struggle between giants. The French were beginning to yield when Trivulzio caused confusion in the Swiss ranks by flooding the meadows where they fought, and the arrival of d'Alviano and his Venetians decided the day. Venetian forces further contributed to the French victory by tying down the Spaniards to Verona. The papal contingent remained throughout motionless at Piacenza.

The battle of Marignano marked the end of an epoch. Its immediate effect was the elimination of the Swiss as an independent factor in Italian politics. The task of holding the duchy of Milan had shown itself to be too great for the loosely constructed Confederation, even before the legend of Swiss invincibility was shattered. Marignano proved the falsehood of Machiavelli's dictum that the French were no match for the Swiss. After an abortive attack on Milan in the spring of 1516, Schinner came to terms with France in the Eternal Peace of Fribourg. The Swiss had to surrender Domodossola, controlling the Simplon Pass, but they kept Bellinzona and the Ticino valley, together with the greater part of Lake Lugano, and the Locarno end of Lake Maggiore. Thus the frontiers between Switzerland and the Milanese were fixed substantially as they remain today. The treaty revived the system of pensions which bound the Swiss to the service of France. Henceforth their role in European conflicts was simply that of mercenaries; their policy as a nation was, as it still is, one of strict neutrality. The effects of the battle were also decisive for the Italian States. Francis I became duke of Milan, and Massimiliano retired on a pension to a life of ease in France. There was no further hope that Milan could retain its independence. Although there was to be one more Sforza duke, he owed his position to the Emperor Charles V, and his reign was the prelude to direct Spanish rule. Leo X made his peace with Francis I, yielding to him Parma and Piacenza, cities long in dispute between Milan and the Papacy, and receiving in return Francis's guarantee that the Medici should remain in Florence. After the death of both Giuliano and Lorenzo de' Medici, Florentine affairs were directed mainly from Rome, thus weakening still further the illusion that Florence was a free republic. In December 1515 Leo X and Francis I met at Bologna. The outcome of their conversations was the settlement of the relations between the French Church and the Papacy after nearly eighty years of discord. Although the pope gained by the abolition of the Pragmatic Sanction of Bourges (1438), he conceded to the Crown the right of nomination to French bishoprics and abbeys, and submitted to a limitation of his powers of provision. The Concordat of Bologna bore the marks of an agreement between victor and vanquished; in it Gallican liberties and papal prerogatives were alike sacrificed to the royal supremacy. For Venice, Marignano paved the way for the final settlement of the issues raised by the League of Cambrai. In 1509 Maximilian had offended the citizens of Verona by his dilatoriness in taking possession of the city, but once occupied he could not be persuaded to relinquish it. He was now faced with the necessity of coming to terms with Francis I, and agreed to hand it over to him, on the understanding that it should be returned to Venice. With the recovery of Verona, Venice was once more in possession of the bulk of her mainland territory. Recent acquisitions, such as Cremona and the towns taken from Maximilian beyond the Isonzo, were lost, as were the cities which she had held in Romagna and Apulia, but the greater part of the Lombard plain was in her hands. It remained Venetian until the coming of Napoleon, and as long as the Republic of St Mark lasted was the freest and most prosperous part of Italy. Paradoxical as it may seem, the Power that gained most from the French victory was Spain. So long as the Swiss remained in Milan they reaped the advantage of any counter-moves against the French. Now Spain stood out as the sole effective rival to France in Italy. In the course of three successive invasions Italian independence had been destroyed. The next phase was to be a struggle between two major European Powers for predominance, in which the Italian States strove to preserve some measure of freedom by playing off one against the other.

The failure of Italy to stand up to invasion should not be attributed primarily to military incapacity. Far more serious than any weakness in her armed forces was the fervid local patriotism which divided state from state. The evils of separatism were further intensified by the internal divisions which undermined the stability of every government and increased the fears and suspicions with which each state regarded its neighbours. The first shock of Charles VIII's invasion fell on armies less well-equipped than the French, especially in the matter of artillery, and unaccustomed to the rapidity and ruthlessness with which the seasoned forces of the enemy swept obstacles from their path. In the course of the war the Italians showed remarkable initiative in adapting themselves to new methods. Cesare Borgia, with the help of Leonardo da Vinci, provided himself with an efficient artillery, and before the end of the period Alfonso d'Este had made the Ferrarese guns superior to all others. Recruiting of infantry had increased considerably before the invasions, and its development was pressed on. At Città di Castello, the Vitelli brothers, all of them notable *condottieri*, trained their infantry on the Swiss model. The wars show many instances of skill and bravery on the part of individual Italians. Among them is the famous combat between thirteen Italians and thirteen Frenchmen at Barletta in 1503, when the French, who had boasted of their superiority, were completely defeated. The memory of this feat of valour lived on, and became the theme of a novel written by an Italian patriot in the early days of the Risorgimento. Although the Italians produced no military genius equal to Gonzalo de Córdoba or Gaston de Foix, they had among them distinguished generals. The great Roman families of Orsini and Colonna were trained from boyhood in the profession of arms, and fought all over Italy. Prospero Colonna contributed to the defeat of the French on the Garigliano, and later, in the service of Charles V, showed himself a worthy disciple of Gonzalo. Bartolomeo d'Alviano was an Orsini by adoption, who practised the French method of swift attack. His defeat at Agnadello was due to the failure of his colleague to support him, and of the Venetians to ensure unity of command. During his captivity in France he acted as a loyal servant of Venice, helping to renew her alliance with the French and returning to win glory at Marignano. Pedro Navarra, although an alien by birth, spent his active life in Italy and first won fame as a mine-layer in the service of the Florentines at the siege of Sarzana in 1488. If the legend of the *condottieri* as incompetent, treacherous, greedy, and intent on avoiding battle still persists, its falsehood is apparent. War, like much else in Renaissance Italy, was practised as a fine art by men who studied their profession, and were eager to distinguish themselves in it. There were traitors among them, but there were those who were faithful to their employers against their own interest. The transference of a captain from one side to another was prompted not for the most part by love of money but by the desire for a more important field of activity, or readiness to take offence. Italians fought well and courageously in the principal battles of the period, but separatist interests prevented them from fighting as a united army. Relations between Milan and Venice were so far from friendly at the time of the battle of Fornovo that Caiazzo was suspected of deliberately holding back the Milanese forces on his employers' orders. The suspicion was apparently unfounded, but the fact that it was widely believed at the time could not fail to injure the allied cause. When appeal was made to Florence to join the league for the expulsion of the French for the sake of the good of Italy, the line taken by the republic was that its concern was not with the good of Italy but with the recovery of Pisa. Whilst state was divided against state, the rulers had everywhere to reckon with enemies within the gate. The instability of Naples, with a baronage divided into opposing factions, agreeing only in their desire to weaken the monarchy, is obvious. Elsewhere Italy was a land of city-states, each conceiving of itself as a Roman republic in miniature, and claiming sovereignty for its citizens. The title of the despots to rule was, in the first instance, authority conferred on them by the people, and although several had supplemented popular election by obtaining investiture with their city from pope or emperor, their continuance in office depended upon the goodwill of their subjects. Even in so well-established a monarchy as Milan, there was a republican party traditionally opposed to the Sforza dukes, which, when discontented with the government, welcomed the coming of the French. Rulers with no legal title, who were merely leading citizens, were even less secure. There were other wealthy families in Florence who considered themselves as well-fitted as the Medici for the first place in the city and awaited an opportunity to turn against them. During the war against Venice the ties which bound subject cities to the republic were those of convenience rather than of loyalty. The patriotism of the citizens was concentrated within their walls, and the welfare of their own city was their primary consideration. Italians intent on the hard task of maintaining the independence and integrity of their states sought aid from the foreigner or opposed him, as their needs dictated. When Francesco Gonzaga, as a captain of the Church, was engaged against the French in 1510, his wife Isabella d'Este acted as his regent in Mantua. She gave instructions to castellans in Mantuan territory to give passage to French troops coming to the defence of her brother in Ferrara, and to excuse themselves on the ground that they had yielded to superior force. In her eyes France was the friend and Julius II the enemy; she is a typical representative of a nation that was, as yet, incapable of united political action.

CHAPTER XIII

EASTERN EUROPE

FOR the thirty-five years before its transformation under the effects of the battle of Mohács, Europe east of the frontiers of the Empire and north of the lines reached at that date by the Turkish armies fell into two parts, sharply distinguished politically and even psychologically: on the one hand, the Russian lands which the grand dukes of Moscow were welding into a compact, disciplined and self-regarding world on its own; on the other, the vast and complex area comprising the kingdoms of Poland-Lithuania, Hungary and Bohemia—for the connection between Bohemia and the Empire was during this period purely technical, whereas it was intimately joined with Hungary and in close relationship with Poland. These three kingdoms were linked together, albeit loosely and, as the future was to prove, transiently, by dynastic ties; the Crowns of Hungary and Bohemia were united, and that of Poland held by brothers or uncles of the Hungarian king, all these rulers belonging to the Polish-Lithuanian house of Jagiello. The principality of Moldavia alternated between semi-independence and vassalage, now to the Porte, now to Hungary, now to Poland.

It is permissible to confine our account of the easternmost of these two divisions to a very few words, for the rise of Moscow and the growth, round the Muscovite nucleus, of the Russian State, in which the whole history of this area resides, were processes which had begun long before 1490 and were not completed until long after 1526: the period described here constitutes only a term in a steady progression. It was, indeed, a brilliant one. Ivan the Great, grand prince of Moscow from 1462 to 1505, was among the most conspicuously successful of all his line. He may, indeed, be regarded as the real founder of the Russian State. His absorption of Novgorod, with its vast territories, a task accomplished by gradual stages between 1465 and 1488, not only brought him an immense access of strength but also settled for all time the question whether Moscow or Lithuania should be the ultimate heir to Kiev. Perm, subjected in 1472, was a territorially even larger addition, although strategically less important. Vyatka, Tver and Ryazan followed in and around 1485. Meanwhile Ivan had shaken off the last relics of the Tatar yoke in 1480; thereafter the various Tatar hordes were sometimes his enemies, but as often, his clients and allies; in any case, no longer his masters.

What was new in Ivan's reign was not the increases in territory and independence which he brought to his throne—here he was only carrying on the work of more than one predecessor—but the conscious and confident claim made by him in justification for his aggression.

As he enlarges his territories and consolidates his position, Ivan begins, partly under the influence of his wife Zoë (Sophia) Palaeologue, to put forward larger claims still, to be the heir of Kiev, of Byzantium and even Rome. He takes the arms of the two-headed eagle and the title of *Samoderzshets* (αὐτοκράτωρ) and 'Sovereign of all Russia'. He proudly rejects the Emperor Frederick's offer to confer on him the title of king: 'We have wanted it from no one, and do not want it now.' 'We, by the grace of God, are sovereigns in our own land from the beginning, from our first forefathers, and we hold our appointment from God.' When Casimir of Poland complains in 1501 that Ivan is seizing his patrimony, he answers: 'What do they call their patrimony? The Russian land is our patrimony from our ancestors of old.' In 1503 he again describes as his 'patrimony' 'the Russian land which is in the hands of Lithuania— Kiev, Smolensk and the other towns....Our patrimony is not only those towns and districts which we now hold, but all the Russian land of old, from our forefathers also.' And this dynastic claim is linked with and reinforced by a religious one. Since the fall of Constantinople, Moscow is the 'Third Rome', even the 'Second Jerusalem'. The metropolitan of Moscow is not yet patriarch, but there is no question of his deriving his appointment from Constantinople, or of being anyone but a Russian. The wars with Lithuania and Poland are waged in part for the recovery of 'the patrimony of St Vladimir' and Alexander of Lithuania's attempts to propagate the Union of Florence among his Orthodox subjects suffice Ivan for a *casus belli*.

Under these conditions there could be no question of lasting peace between Moscow and Poland-Lithuania: Ivan himself told his ally, the khan of the Crimean Tatars, that there could be no peace, 'only pauses to draw breath'. These words accurately define the history of Ivan's relations with his western neighbour, the main events of which are given below, in another connection. Although fortunes fluctuated, the balance of advantage, in the long run, was with Ivan; and it is worth mentioning that this was not due only to force of arms. The Russian towns under Lithuanian sovereignty were not impervious to the Muscovite and Orthodox appeal, and several of them—Peremysl, Serejsk, Kozelsk—changed their allegiance voluntarily. Novgorod itself, while specifically rejecting the claim to be a 'patrimony', had contained a large party which thought union with Moscow more natural than the Lithuanian alternative.

Ivan's death in 1505 naturally slowed down the rate of Muscovite expansion, and the only important gain in the west made by his son and successor Basil (1505–33) was that of the fortress of Smolensk; besides which he rounded off Moscow's conquests nearer home by incorporating the rest of Ryazan, and destroying the liberties of Pskov. But the objectives of his policy were exactly those of his father, as they were to be also those of his son, Ivan the Terrible. His internal policy, too, was in the direct line. Ivan had taken away the Bell of Novgorod, symbol of its self-government, Basil took away the Bell of Pskov. The process is one of steady centralisation and subordination to a single will, exercised through a bureaucracy which is still primitive, but now beginning to take definite shape.

The fortunes of the countries west of Moscow require, and deserve, more detailed description, both on account of their greater complexity and because, unlike those of Muscovy, they form a distinct chapter in the history of each country. The intimate connection established in 1290 between Poland, Hungary and Bohemia might, indeed, have seemed at the time only a part of a process of development destined to continue and eventually to result in the emergence of some sort of real unity in this area which possessed so many common features and common interests. History shows it to have been the precursor of an act of violent disintegration which threw Bohemia and part of Hungary into a western system centring on Vienna, the rest of Hungary into the eastern world dominated by the Porte, and left Poland as the sole surviving independent representative of the earlier grouping. And as we shall see, this disintegration was not altogether a reversal of the provisions made for the future during the period itself, but, so far as the eastward extension of the Habsburg power is concerned, the fulfilment of them. Nevertheless, it is still legitimate to speculate how far the triumph of the centrifugal over the centripetal tendency represented the inevitable triumph of the stronger natural forces or how far it was brought about by trivial and personal motives which might as easily have acted in the opposite direction. It is the possibility which the story offers for this speculation that lends it its peculiar and painful interest.

It is, however, undeniable that the position which obtained in 1490— Jagiellos on all three thrones, Habsburgs as serious claimants to two of them, temporarily behind in the race but with far the larger reserves of strength—was largely due to what may legitimately be called chance: the incidence of birth and death in half-a-dozen families. Up to the opening of the fourteenth century Poland, Hungary and Bohemia had developed on lines which were parallel and natural, if anything may be called natural: under dynasties of native stock, whose members followed policies which were always based on their nations and usually consonant with the national interests and wishes. Then, while the Polish Piasts survived (and if their rate of reproduction, too, fell below replacement level, this was all to Poland's advantage, for since Boleslav III's seventeen children there had been far too many Piasts), the Árpáds and the Przemyslides died out almost simultaneously, leaving Hungary and Bohemia to be scrambled for by competing European dynasties. The male lines of both families to which the prizes fell died out in their turn, that of the Hungarian

Angevins after two generations, and that of the Luxemburgers in Bohemia after three, and it was purely the thought taken by royal fathers for their daughters, as expressed in the series of compacts concluded by the two families with one another and with their Habsburg neighbours, that brought the Habsburg, Albert III, on to both thrones in 1437.

Now the luck which had been so benignant to the Habsburgs turned against them, for Albert died in 1439, after a reign of less than three years, and left no son, although his wife was pregnant. Meanwhile the Poles had saved themselves in curious fashion: the rule of the foreign king, Louis of Hungary, who was brought to Poland when the direct male line of the senior branch of the Piasts closed with Casimir the Great (distant cousins survived, but could not win support for their claims), was so unpopular (and memories as disagreeable survived of the Czech king Wenzel II), that when he died leaving only daughters, of whom the one destined for Poland was betrothed to another Habsburg, the nation revolted, broke the engagement and married the little princess to the stern Lithuanian, Jagiello: a foreigner too, but lacking the far-flung international engagements of the more fashionable dynasties. Jagiello proved successful as Jadwiga's consort. He had, however, no issue by her, a daughter who died early by his second wife, and again no children by his third. By the wife of his old age (a Lithuanian lady unrelated to any European dynasty), he became father of three sons of whom two survived him, thus re-establishing a national dynasty which could not only exclude any other claim to the Polish Crown but itself export kings to other countries in need thereof.

The first such invitation to be received by any Jagiello prince—that addressed to Jagiello's younger son, Prince Casimir, in 1437 by a party among the Czech nobles—did owe something to questions of suitability, for Casimir's sponsors were those Czechs who objected to Albert for his German birth and his Catholic connections. But even so, what commended Casimir to his partisans was the absence of these defects in him, not any positive qualities; none of them thought of creating a Polish-Czech union. And when, in 1439, the Hungarians elected Jagiello's elder son Wladislaw (*Úlászló*) as soon as Albert died, this was simply and solely because he was at hand, and more or less adult by the standards of the time (he was sixteen years of age), and with the Turkish danger pressing as it was they simply dared not wait for the birth of Albert's child, who might not even be a boy. It is true that among the promises which Wladislaw made to his electors was the defence of Hungary with both the Hungarian and Polish armies; but the Habsburgs could probably have raised an equally effective force. Then Wladislaw was killed at Varna in 1444 leading an army in which, in fact, hardly any Poles were present, and Albert's son Ladislas Postumus got the two thrones after all; but when he died unmarried in 1457, the establishment in both countries of national kingdoms under Matthias Corvinus and George Podiebrad respectively was assuredly, to both, the most popular of all possible solutions.

And for a time it seemed likely to prove permanent. Both Habsburgs and Jagiellos (not to mention other, less important, dynasties) maintained their claims to the two thrones, under titles complicated by the fact that Casimir Jagiello, who succeeded his brother, married Elizabeth of Habsburg, Albert's daughter and sister of Ladislas Postumus, and claimed the crowns for her Jagiello children as heirs to her Habsburg brother; while the Emperor Frederick claimed them in virtue of the old compacts concluded in 1362–4 between his family and Charles IV of Bohemia. But Frederick was notoriously inactive, and the Bohemian Crown made no special appeal to him: in the end he himself, as emperor, invested George with the insignia of royalty. If he pressed his claim more vigorously in Hungary, this was chiefly because he was urged to do so by a party of Hungarian magnates hostile to Matthias, and in 1463 he relinquished his immediate claim in return (amongst other things) for a promise that he or his heirs should inherit if Matthias died without male heirs. As for Casimir, his children were also in their infancy, and he was too much occupied in Prussia and Lithuania to turn south at that moment. He preserved excellent relations with George, to the extent of refusing the pope's invitation to join a crusade against him on the ground that 'he did not understand how an anointed and crowned king could be dethroned'. If his relations with Matthias were less cordial, he at any rate usually found it prudent to keep his hands off that competent man's property, although intervening later, on his son's behalf, in Silesia.

The failure of the two national kingdoms to outlive their founders is due to those founders' own fault—that of Matthias in incomparably the greater measure: for if George was not innocent of certain rather dubious intrigues, they never reached sufficient maturity to make them dangerous. But Matthias had the gift of doing nothing, good or bad, that was not significant; and great king as he was in many respects, he brought neither peace nor union to the Danube. He had begun by buying off the emperor, cultivating the friendship of George, whose daughter he married, and fighting lustily against the Turks, but he soon let himself be seduced by dreams of western conquest, the naked ambition of which his country's historians vainly try to disguise as long-term strategic moves intended to gather strength for more energetic prosecution of the war against the Turks. His rule never produced the smallest feeling of solidarity between the inhabitants of Hungary and those of the Austrian and Bohemian provinces which he conquered, and the accession of Casimir of Poland's eldest son, Wladislaw Jagiello, to the Bohemian throne in 1479 was the direct result of Matthias's attacks on Podiebrad. For George had originally meant his own elder son to succeed him, but in his extremity, in order to secure the support of Casimir of Poland against Matthias and the pope, he in 1469 offered Casimir the succession to the Bohemian Crown for his eldest son. When George died, two years later, no serious candidates came forward for the throne except Wladislaw and Matthias, and while Matthias insisted on the validity of his election, the national party elected the fifteen-year-old Wladislaw, just as an earlier diet had elected his father, for his negative qualities of not being (it was expected) dangerous to Bohemia's independence or her religion; safeguarding themselves in both respects by binding Wladislaw to observe the *Compactata* and assure religious peace in Bohemia, and to grant no offices in the state to foreigners.

Meanwhile Matthias in his turn had failed to beget an heir to the Hungarian throne, either by Catherine Podiebrad or by the beautiful but uncomfortable Beatrix of Aragon whom he married in 1476, after Catherine had died. His only issue was the bastard, John Corvinus, his son by the daughter of a burgher of Breslau. In his last years he devoted much of his time to endeavouring to assure that John should succeed him. He offered Maximilian (now married to Mary of Burgundy) the return of the Austrian provinces which he had seized between 1477 and 1485 if Maximilian would renounce the treaty of 1463 and accept John as king of Hungary; John was then to marry Maximilian's daughter. Agreement was reached in principle, although not sealed, in the autumn of 1489, and Matthias then exacted an oath from the royal free towns and from many dignitaries of Hungary, lay and ecclesiastical, that they would accept John; he also secured the adoption of the *Lex Palatinus* (a measure which, although failing of its immediate purpose, was to retain its importance for many centuries) which gave the Palatine the first vote on the succession 'should the royal seed die out' and made him guardian of a minor king and viceroy during an interregnum, then making his own creature and adherent, Imre Zápolyai, Palatine.

But on 6 April 1490, as he was on his way to a meeting from which he expected the definitive agreement with Maximilian to result, Matthias died, suddenly and prematurely. Imre Zápolyai had predeceased him, and his successor had not yet been appointed. The smaller nobles, who in their day had secured the election of Matthias, were for his son, but the magnates, other considerations apart (and to do them justice, many of them felt John's illegitimacy to be a real stumbling-block), had found Matthias's strong rule much less to their taste than unconsolidated conditions which allowed them to rule their own areas as petty kings.

Besides John, there were three possibilities: Maximilian, and two of Casimir of Poland's sons, Wladislaw, already king of Bohemia, and the surviving brother next in age to him, Jan Olbracht. Both Maximilian and Jan Olbracht were strong and able men, and both had their partisans, but more of the great lords favoured Wladislaw, precisely because he was notoriously neither strong nor able. A harmless and friendly creature with neither taste nor understanding for politics, he had earned in Bohemia the nickname of King *Dobře* (King 'All Right'—*dobře* meaning 'good') from his habit of assenting with that word to any proposal put before him; and 'a king whose plaits they could hold in their fists', as one of them cynically put it, just suited the Hungarian magnates. There was long argument, much bribery and some fighting, but Wladislaw's partisans had taken the precaution of raising the money to keep temporarily in being and in their service, the real force in the vicinity, Matthias's 'Black Army', then stationed in Silesia. John Filipec, bishop of Nagyvárad, whose strong advocacy of Wladislaw's cause may have owed something to his own Moravian origin, hurried to Silesia with the funds which had been hastily collected and brought back the army. John Corvinus's partisans were soon defeated. John, who lacked either his father's energy or his ambition, renounced his pretensions in return for the title of duke of Slavonia and the prospective Crown of Bosnia (when available). Jan Olbracht was not anxious to press his claim against his elder brother when the latter became the other candidate, a position reached in the course of 1491. Maximilian, after reoccupying the lost Austrian provinces, had invaded Hungary with a mercenary army, but he was unable to pay his soldiers and they dispersed. He now agreed by the Treaty of Pressburg (7 November 1491) to recognise Wladislaw as king in return for recognition that the Austrian provinces were his, and the promise of the succession for himself or his issue if Wladislaw died without male heirs.

It is true that the agreement was never ratified in Hungary. The Habsburg connection was very unpopular in that country, and among the many promises which Wladislaw had been forced to give when offered the throne, was one to make no agreement with Frederick or Maximilian without the consent of the diet. When Wladislaw brought the Treaty of Pressburg before the diet in 1492, the lesser nobility refused to accept it; but Wladislaw personally always considered it binding on himself, and sixty-seven magnates signed a solemn declaration that, if Wladislaw died without male heirs, they would vote for Maximilian or his heirs. Maximilian contented himself with this, and Wladislaw's throne was now secure against any foreign pretender.

In the same year Casimir of Poland died. Now it was Wladislaw who stood down in favour of his brother, the clear favourite of the Polish electors, and Jan Olbracht became king of Poland, although, unlike his father, not also grand duke of Lithuania. During Casimir's rule there had been considerable discontent in Lithuania over his alleged neglect of Lithuanian interests in favour of Polish (especially when he failed to give Novgorod effective support against Ivan) and Casimir had been obliged to promise that a separate person should rule as grand duke of

Lithuania, residing in Vilna. This prize now fell to the third surviving brother, Alexander. The fifth brother, Frederick, was a cardinal; the fourth, Sigismund, was left for the time without any special provision.

Hungary and Bohemia were now practically under single control, so far as foreign policy was concerned, for although the diets of both countries safeguarded themselves by various resolutions, to be described, these could not affect the dynastic agreements which formed so large a part of the real foreign policy of those days. Wladislaw and Jan Olbracht agreed, at a meeting which took place between them on 5 May 1494, mutually to intervene with all their forces should the subjects of either rebel, or dissipate the royal revenues. The agreement did not bind its two authors to a common foreign policy, but they concerted together on that subject, both at the meeting in question and on later occasions, and it is not impossible to make a single narrative of the foreign relations of Poland and Hungary-Bohemia during the next twenty-five years; even if that narrative will reveal discord as well as agreement, and many events in which only one of the parties was concerned. As preliminary to the story we may mention here that while Wladislaw ruled in Hungary and Bohemia during the whole twenty-five years, Jan Olbracht died on 17 June 1501, and Alexander, who had succeeded him in Poland while retaining the grand duchy of Lithuania, on 19 August 1506. Sigismund then began that long rule over both Poland and Lithuania, which was to end only in 1548.

Once Wladislaw and Jan Olbracht were settled on their thrones, the story became for a time relatively simple, and except in one direction, affecting Poland almost exclusively, relatively uneventful. The Balkans were, for once, quiet. It is true that the local Turkish begs in Bosnia and Serbia made several raids on Hungary's frontiers in the first years after Wladislaw's accession, but the fortifications were then still in reasonable condition, and the frontier captains—John Corvinus, the Frangepáni in Croatia and the famous old warrior, Pál Kinizsi—beat them back without loss of territory. Fortunately for Hungary, the Sultan Bāyezīd was of a mild and peaceable disposition and not inclined to undertake big adventures; his only serious European war—that in which he was engaged with Venice at the turn of the century—was probably undertaken from defensive rather than aggressive motives. Hungary on her side could not think of taking the offensive—in 1500 she refused an invitation from Venice to do so—and, when the Venetian war was ended, concluded a seven years truce with the sultan, which was renewed in 1510 and again in 1513. By this time the war-like Sultan Selīm had succeeded his father, but was, during the first years of his reign, too fully occupied in the south and east to trouble Hungary.

The Turkish capture, in 1483-4, of Kilia and Akkerman, and the establishment of Ottoman suzerainty over the Crimean Tatars (as also, intermittently, over Moldavia) had created a situation which the rulers of Poland regarded as permanently dangerous to themselves and calling for reversal, and Casimir had sent three expeditions across his southern frontiers between 1483 and 1489, but they had not been successful. In 1489 he had concluded a truce on the basis of *uti possidetis*, and Jan Olbracht renewed this for a further three years in 1494. He did not mean this to be final, and employed the respite in preparing to launch a grand attack to recover the two fortresses and cut the line between the Turks and their Tatar satellites when it expired. This, again, was unsuccessful. Olbracht had initiated conversations with Wladislaw with a view to joint action, but in the course of them indiscreetly proposed that the *voivode* (viceroy) of Moldavia, Stephen, whom he regarded as unreliable, should be deposed in favour of the fourth Jagiello brother, Sigismund. Wladislaw in any case regarded Moldavia as Hungary's vassal, and refused to take action against him, so that Olbracht was obliged to withdraw his proposal, but it had been betrayed to Stephen. When, then, the truce expired and the expedition was launched in 1497, Poles and Lithuanians co-operating but Hungary standing aside, Stephen, who believed the operation to be directed against himself, declared himself to be the sultan's vassal and attacked the Polish force, which had to retreat; neither did the Lithuanians attain their objective. The Turks and Tatars raided Poland heavily in retaliation. Olbracht had to patch matters up with Stephen, recognising his independence, and negotiate another truce with the sultan; this was finally concluded in 1501, the sultan granting it the more readily because it averted the threat that Poland might join forces with Venice, which was then at war with the Porte. The Venetian delegates had, indeed, urgently begged the Poles to join in the crusade proclaimed by the pope when those hostilities opened. After this Poland, like Hungary, regularly renewed the truce with the sultan until 1521, when Casimir refused to do so.

Poland was almost continuously at war with Moscow, as the consequence of the Muscovite policy of expansion mentioned above. Almost the first sequel to the division between Poland and Lithuania which followed Casimir's death was that Basil, allying himself with the Crimean Tatars, invaded Lithuania. Alexander was obliged to sue for peace, and to ask that this should be sealed by a marriage between himself and Ivan's daughter, Helena; which Ivan granted, but only on condition that Alexander recognised all his recent conquests and his title of 'Sovereign of all Russia'. This did not bring lasting peace or stability, for more frontier areas transferred their allegiance to Ivan, who accepted them and in 1500 declared war again, using as pretext Alexander's support of the movement for union between the Greek and Roman Churches. This time the war went on (outlasting Alexander's succession to the throne in Poland) until 1503, when Ivan granted peace again, once more on the basis of recognition of his gains. The position was now changed by the deaths of both Ivan and Alexander. The Tatars, too, had been so thoroughly worsted that they had actually changed sides, becoming Poland's allies. This encouraged Sigismund to take advantage of the confusion caused in Muscovy by Ivan's death and to demand the restoration of Ivan's conquests. Both countries moved their armies (the Russians actually leaving their bases first), and the Poles at first had the better of the fighting; but the rebellion of one of their leaders, a Christianised Tatar named Glinski, disorganised their movements, and on 8 October 1508 Sigismund concluded a 'perpetual peace' with Muscovy, recognising Ivan's acquisitions. His chief profit was that he was now able to turn on Stephen of Moldavia, who had invaded Galicia; although he had to recognise Hungarian suzerainty over Moldavia.

During most of this period Poland had had few dealings, either friendly or inimical, with the Empire, or with any of its components; while in Hungary a remarkable situation had developed under the stress of the internal dissension in that country, which was of dimensions sufficient to affect the international position by threatening the stability of the throne. As we have seen, the smaller nobles had hoped to see John Corvinus succeed his father as king, and did not altogether renounce that hope even after 1492. John, indeed, proved ineffective as rival to Wladislaw, being apparently quite content to accept the settlement made with him and to serve Wladislaw loyally (the only time he appears to have considered rebellion was when he had been disgracefully cheated of some of his estates). But anti-Wladislaw feeling lived on, and the leadership of this party was seized by the Zápolyai family, now risen to extraordinary power. Imre Zápolyai's brother Stephen was elected Palatine in 1490, and held that office for ten years, during which he added substantially to his already enormous fortune. He, in turn, died in 1500, but his energetic and ambitious widow, *née* duchess of Teschen, made no secret of her intention to place one or the other of her sons on the throne.

The question of the Hungarian succession, meanwhile, remained in a ridiculous position of stalemate, largely produced by Wladislaw's feebleness of character. In 1475, at the age of twenty, he had married by proxy Barbara, daughter of Albert Achilles of Brandenburg, but had never sent for his bride. In 1478 he had met Matthias's young second wife, Beatrix of Aragon, at the conquest of Olmütz, and they are said to have been struck by one another's charms, which in both cases were more than considerable, and as soon as Matthias died, Beatrix proposed that Wladislaw should marry her, providing her simultaneously with a handsome husband and a crown. The Cardinal-Primate Bakócz married the pair secretly in Beatrix's lodgings, Wladislaw protesting the while that the act was invalid, since he was already married. He was now safely tied up without prospect of begetting lawful issue in any manner.

In this situation Maximilian had every interest in keeping Wladislaw on the throne, while Wladislaw for his part turned for support and encouragement against his over-ambitious subjects to the man who at least was willing to wait for his death. By 1510 Maximilian had, as a contemporary chronicler wrote, 'long ceased to be the King's enemy and became instead his friend and counsellor'. Ambassadors from the emperor travelled to Buda in quick succession, bringing the king advice and help, and incidentally building up a pro-Habsburg party among the Hungarian magnates; in which task they achieved considerable success.

In 1499 the threads of Polish and Hungarian relations with the Empire became entangled in curious fashion, and with paradoxical results. Up to this date the Teutonic Order had for many years given no trouble to Poland, and had also received no encouragement from the Empire. The grand master during Casimir's closing years, Tieffen, had been the Polish king's uncomplaining vassal and loyal collaborator, and he had duly done homage to Jan Olbracht after Casimir died. But not all the members of the Order had been contented with this relationship, and, when Tieffen died in 1498, they decided to try to strengthen their position and to gain support in the Empire, and offered Tieffen's succession to Frederick of Saxony, one of the leading princes of the Empire. Frederick refused to do homage.

A Jagiello family conference, attended by Wladislaw, Sigismund (who had been staying with his brother in Buda) and the cardinal, Frederick, met in Pressburg in December 1499. The plan was evolved of seeking alliance with France, and sealing it by the marriage of Wladislaw to Anne de Candalle, niece of Anne of Brittany, and of Olbracht to her younger sister, Germaine. Louis XII accepted the proposal, and on 18 July 1500 a French embassy in Buda signed with Poland and Hungary a general and perpetual alliance against the Turks and against all enemies, present and future, the pope, the emperor and the king of the Romans excepted.

This done, Jan Olbracht turned on the Order, demanded the homage and prepared to mobilise. Since, under the circumstances, neither the emperor nor the imperial diet, who were, moreover, deeply divided by their mutual quarrel, were willing to help him, the grand master yielded and agreed to take the oath. Before he had done so, however, and also before Olbracht's marriage could take place, Olbracht died. The grand master now delayed paying homage to Alexander. Thus the only immediate result of the affair was the odd one that Wladislaw found himself presented with a French wife; for, the pope having at last cut his Gordian knot by declaring both his marriages invalid, he sent for his bride and duly married her.

This did not affect Wladislaw's relations with Maximilian, but Poland was now at odds with the Empire, for Frederick persisted in his refusal to do homage, and Maximilian, irritated by Olbracht's action, encouraged him, and after Alexander had appealed to the pope and secured from him a letter enjoining obedience from the Order, Maximilian got the pope to withdraw the letter. Meanwhile, the queen of Hungary had given birth to a daughter, named Anne like her mother. In 1504 John Corvinus died, leaving two little children, a son, Kristof, and a daughter, Elisabeth. The duchess of Teschen saw her chance: she quickly betrothed her younger son, George, to Elisabeth Corvinus and, descending on Wladislaw, demanded the hand of the little princess for her elder son, John, now occupying the important office of *voivode* of Transylvania. The match was pressed by Sigismund, whose heart at this time was entirely in the anti-German policy.

The whole business seems to have been forced on Wladislaw by his more energetic brothers, but at least he could summon up the determination not to give way to the Zápolyais. He put them off and appealed to Maximilian. Extraordinary scenes took place in 1505. John Zápolyai now linked his cause with that of the lesser nobles, as the cause of national independence against the Habsburgs. The diet of February threatened Wladislaw with deposition, but did no more than threaten: a second diet, to meet in July, was expected to bring matters to a head. Before this met, Wladislaw asked Maximilian for armed support, which the imperial diet voted; but the German soldiers were late, whereas Zápolyai, who had brought 2000 soldiers with him, was punctual, and the diet passed a resolution, sparing Wladislaw himself (as Zápolyai had previously agreed with the queen) but laying every evil from which Hungary had ever suffered at the door of her foreign kings and swearing never again to receive one.

Next year the queen gave birth to a boy, Louis, and the immediate crisis passed over, Maximilian contenting himself with concluding an agreement that the two children should marry two of Maximilian's own descendants. Thus relations between Hungary-Bohemia and the Empire remained as cordial as ever, but Poland, where Sigismund was crowned king on 24 January 1507, was not in this group and still at odds with the Teutonic Order. Frederick was still refusing homage, and the Order had, at the Congress of Marienburg (August 1506), produced a plan for abolishing the allegiance of East Prussia to the Crown of Poland and uniting it with Royal Prussia, the united province then to be held by the grand master as a fief of the Polish Crown. Protracted negotiations went on, Hungary trying to mediate, while Sigismund was unwilling to precipitate the issue at a moment when he wanted all his forces for his enterprise against Basil. The conversations dragged on during the whole course of Poland's war with Muscovy and the first two years of the perpetual peace. Then Frederick of Saxony died (14 December 1510), and the Order elected for its new grand master the obscure and needy, but enterprising and ambitious, Margrave Albrecht of Hohenzollern-Anspach, who promptly opened up negotiations, not only with Maximilian, but also with Basil. Learning of this, Sigismund turned to the Hungarian opposition, took to wife Zápolyai's sister, Barbara, and concluded with the Zápolyais a secret pact for mutual assistance against all enemies, meaning thereby the Habsburgs. This was in 1512; and late in the same year, Basil attacked Lithuania.

Fighting went on throughout 1513; meanwhile, Maximilian had learnt of Sigismund's treaty with the Zápolyais, and, seeing in this a threat to his whole dynastic plans for acquiring Hungary and Bohemia, himself sent an ambassador to Moscow (December 1513). The ambassador (exceeding his instructions) concluded a far-reaching offensive alliance, but this proved unpopular in Germany, where several of the princes were reluctant to attack Poland for the sake of Habsburg family aggrandisement; then, on 8 September 1514, the Polish-Lithuanian armies defeated the Russians crushingly at Orsza. Thereupon Maximilian decided to come to terms with Sigismund, who was himself ready to compromise, since the prospect of seeing Russia, the Empire and the Order allied against him was more than he cared to face. After some negotiation, a preliminary agreement on the question of the Order was signed at Pressburg on 20 May 1515, and a definitive treaty at Vienna on 22 July. By the preliminary agreement, the emperor recognised the Treaty of Thorn, while Sigismund agreed that Poles should not be recruited into the Order, and that all conflicts arising within the next five years between Poland and the Order should be submitted to arbitration by the emperor and the king of Hungary. The full congress saw the final settlement of the question of the Hungaro-Bohemian succession. The little King Lewis (who had already been crowned in 1508) was married to Maximilian's granddaughter, Mary, while Anne Jagiello was betrothed to one of Maximilian's grandsons, Ferdinand, the emperor himself standing proxy and promising to marry the child himself if Ferdinand proved recalcitrant (the marriage in fact took place in 1521).

It is hardly possible to over-estimate the importance of this transaction. As the event proved, it brought the Crowns of Hungary and Bohemia to the Habsburgs only eleven years later. Some Hungarian historians argue that this was a direct consequence of the agreement, for Louis XII might never have egged the sultan on to attack Hungary had he not regarded it as a satellite of the Habsburgs; and it was certainly little else from 1515 onward. It also transformed, for a long period to come, Poland's relations with the Empire, for Sigismund now dropped his anti-German policy, the more easily for the providential death of Barbara Zápolyai. On 12 April 1518 Sigismund married Bona Sforza (a marriage arranged by the Germans), so that the extension of Italian influences in architecture, art and letters, which was so marked a feature of Polish life in the following years, admittedly owing much to Queen Bona's personal influence, may also rank as a consequence of the Congress of Vienna. So, undoubtedly, may Sigismund's refusal to annex West Pomerania, which he could have done soon after, and his rejection of an offer made to him by the national party in Sweden of the Crown of that country.

The sufferers were the Zápolyai party in Hungary, the Teutonic Knights, and Muscovy. John Zápolyai at the time took his defeat gracefully, and, to do him justice, stirred up no trouble in the next few years. The Order reopened its wearisome negotiations with Poland. The grand master seems to have received some secret encouragement from the emperor, for he used a very bold tone, and demanded as price for agreement, not only the return of Royal Prussia, but compensation for fifty years' occupation by Poland On 10 March 1517, he concluded an offensive and defensive alliance with Moscow, and the next year asked the emperor for military support if Poland refused to accept his conditions; also approaching Denmark, with more success. In December 1519 Sigismund declared war, and there was heavy fighting; but on 5 April 1521 a four-year truce was arranged through the mediation of the emperor and the king of Hungary, who were to decide before its expiration whether the grand master should or should not take the oath. Before the term had expired, the whole position had been changed through Albrecht's acceptance of Luther's advice that he should turn Protestant, marry, and transform his ecclesiastical state into a secular one. Since the emperor was hostile to the Reformation, this could not be done except in conjunction with Poland, and Sigismund, who was anxious to be done with the wars, both on internal grounds and in view of the renascence of the threat from Turkey, accepted Albrecht's proposals. A treaty was concluded in Cracow on 8 April 1525. Albrecht received East Prussia under fealty to the Polish Crown. The right of the successor to the newly created duchy was vested in himself and his three brothers, and their successors; if their line died out, the duchy was to revert to Poland. Three days later Albrecht did public homage in the market-place of Cracow.

The fighting with Moscow had meanwhile proceeded intermittently, Basil having succeeded in recovering the alliance of the Crimean Tatars. Neither party could gain a decisive advantage, and an armistice was signed on 2 September 1520, followed by a five-year truce on 14 September 1522. Concluded on the basis of *uti possidetis*, this left Moscow in possession of the fortress of Smolensk—a small but strategically very important gain. The truce was renewed in 1526.

The family compact between Wladislaw and Jan Olbracht had related to domestic affairs only in so far as it provided against actual rebellion, and against the squandering (by the king's subjects) of the royal revenues. It may be remarked that the former case did not arise, or at least, not so openly as to be used as a *casus foederis*, while the latter went on constantly, but was, again, never made a justification for fraternal intervention.

There is no record of the two brothers, or their successors, ever going beyond this in the co-ordination of their domestic policies. Still less did the other political factors ever combine or even concert together; we do not even find the diets of Bohemia and Hungary joining forces against their common ruler. Nevertheless, institutions and conditions in all three countries developed during this period along closely similar lines, a fact which is only partly to be explained by like causes producing like effects and must inevitably have been due largely to mutual influence and imitation. Unfortunately the detailed comparative studies which would make possible the treatment of the three countries' internal histories from this most interesting angle have yet to be written and it is not possible to do more here than briefly to indicate the main developments in each country separately.

Poland, whose constitutional structure had been much more primitive and its development more belated, was in fact largely engaged in over-taking Hungary. Now she was rushing through certain stages of an evolution which Hungary had already left behind. One writes 'Hungary', for whatever the facts may be regarding the origin of the Polish *szlachta*, it is certain that at any rate by the thirteenth century this numerous class of lesser nobles, politically and socially, bore a much closer resemblance to the Hungarian *köznemesség* of the day than to the Bohemian noble classes; the resemblance would be more apparent still if the Hungarian clan had been more closely and more intelligently investigated. The status of the *szlachta* was then clearly further assimilated to that of the *köznemesség* by the Charter of Kassa granted to the Polish nobles in 1374 by the Hungarian king, Louis; this being in the main a close adaptation of the Hungarian Golden Bull of 1223. By a short time after this, the *szlachta* had become a homogeneous class through the final disappearance of the lower category of the *wlodykes* and the mutual assimilation between the different Polish provinces; and the rights of its members to various personal freedoms and immunities had been confirmed again and again. The existence of these rights clearly limited the king's power in the sense that he could not undertake any enterprise, at home or abroad, which was incompatible with those rights, but beyond that the *szlachta* had no voice in the determination of policy. The only body consulted by the king was his council, a small body composed of a few high officials; and he was not even bound to seek its advice, still less to accept it.

But in the fourteenth century the growing class-consciousness of the *szlachta* begat in it a wish for a bigger voice in the control of affairs, and a number of factors combined to enable it to make its wishes felt. Particularly the development of military technique made the old *insurrectio* almost useless; the king required for his campaign better-trained armies, native or foreign, which had to be paid; but he could not take from the *szlachta*, without their consent, more than the immutable two groschen per hide conceded in the Kassa Privilege. This put the *szlachta* in a strong bargaining position, for the king really needed its consent to loosen the purse-strings before he could undertake any major enterprise. His position was further weakened by the uncertainty of the Polish succession: every Polish king from Jagiello onward had to bargain with his subjects if he wished to be sure of the throne for himself and his heirs.

Thus the fifteenth century saw the *szlachta* rise rapidly to the position of partner with the king in the conduct of the state's affairs. The beginnings of something like a general representative system go back as far as 1404, when the king, requiring an extraordinary levy, deputes members of the council to deliberate with the body of the *szlachta* in each of the districts. In 1454—to mention only the principal stages—the king, in the Charter of Cerekwice, reaffirms the principles of the *szlachta* of Great Poland and promises not to alter these, and not to call on the 'insurrection'[1] without consulting the district *seymniki*, or local assemblies of the *szlachta*: these promises are afterwards extended to other parts of Poland and certified in the Charter of Nieszawa. By 1493 at the latest the technical arrangements had taken form, and Poland possessed a three-fold representative system, the local *seymniki*, the provincial *seyms*, composed of delegates from the *seymniki*, and thirdly, the national *seyms* composed of three 'orders', the king, the council and the chamber of deputies, this last consisting of delegates from the district *seyms*.

In theory nothing of this affected the prerogative of the king, for the *seym* had to be consulted only when it was being asked for something which it was admittedly entitled to refuse.[2] The famous statute *nihil novi* of 1505 did not alter this: here again the king was simply reaffirming earlier pledges. Even after this the king carried through many important transactions, including the settlement with the Teutonic Order and the regulation of the status of the towns and of the Jews, without consulting the *seym*. But the existence of the *seym* obviously made it very much harder for the king to override the *szlachta's* rights by unilateral action. Moreover, as conditions became more complex, the range of matters which the king could decide without asking for supplies shrank steadily. The *seym* was further apt to make the grant of each concession dependent on counter-concessions which reduced that range farther still.

The new developments increased the power of the smaller nobles at the expense not only of the king but also of the magnates. The latter were not, indeed, legally a separate class, but a small clique of big families had

[1] The wording of the Charter runs only 'Nullas novas constitutiones faciemus neque terrigenis ad bellum moveri mandabimus absque conventione commune in singulis terris instituenda.' It seems clear to the present writer that 'bellum' must be understood as war outside the frontiers of Poland, for the obligation of the *szlachta* to defend the country against invasion was never questioned.
[2] The Privilege of Mielnik, of 1501, which would have obliged the king to accept the decisions of the senate, was afterwards regarded as not legally binding.

in fact come to form the entourage of the court and to share between them the great offices whose holders formed the old council, now the senate. The chamber of deputies, which was composed exclusively of the smaller nobles, formed a natural counter-weight to the senate and even held in its hands the *ultima ratio* thanks to the requirement of unanimity for any decision taken in the *seym*; although in practice no important decision was ever held up by the veto of an individual or small group.

The *szlachta* also increased their power very greatly during the period at the expense of the towns, and in particular, of the peasants. The Polish peasant was not badly situated in the early fifteenth century. Many of the villages owed their origin to colonisation, possessed a measure of guaranteed self-government in their own affairs and paid fixed dues which, with the fall in the value of money, had become as derisively small as the nobles' contribution to the treasury. The landlords, before they turned to commercial farming, had no interest in sweating their peasants to lay up larger stores of produce than could be consumed. Above all, the peasants still possessed the right of free migration, which was cardinal, since, in an age where the demand for labour exceeded the supply, no landlord dared impose exorbitant conditions; his peasants could simply leave him and take service elsewhere on better terms. Later in the century conditions began to change owing to a variety of causes, of which the possibility now arising of exporting cereals through Danzig was one, although not perhaps so decisive a one as is sometimes said. But for this and other reasons, including the transformation of the national defence service from one in which they took personal part to one for which they paid, the landlords were turning into commercial farmers, strongly interested in securing cheap and abundant labour for the lands which they were now beginning to farm directly, on an ever-increasing scale. The diet of 1493 confirmed the earlier provisions under which a peasant quitting his farm could do so only on certain dates and must leave land and inventory in good order, besides providing a new tenant. But now a series of laws were passed (1496, 1501, 1503, 1510, 1511) forbidding either the peasant or his sons (at first the prohibition applied only when there was more than one son) to leave without his master's consent, and making more summary the procedure whereby anyone who did so could be retrieved. Simultaneously, the peasant's legal status was depressed. The old self-government was abolished, the landlord's bailiff replacing the former village headman. The peasants had long been subject to the patrimonial jurisdiction of their landlords in many respects, but the possibility of appeal to the royal courts had been open to them in certain cases. This was greatly restricted by laws of 1496 and 1501, and in 1518 Sigismund finally renounced the right of deciding an appeal by a peasant against his master where the latter was a private man (on the Crown and Church lands appeal was still possible). Dues and *corvées* were increased, and the landlords, although not legally entitled to do so, were now able to encroach largely on the former peasant land for the benefit of their own farms.

The towns still retained their self-government and their rights and the king negotiated separately with them for supplies. They were thus not directly affected by the development of the *seym*, in which only Cracow was, by usage, represented. But that development naturally increased the political weight of the *szlachta* also against that of the towns; and several other of the privileges extorted by the *szlachta* and notably that of exemption from customs dues (enacted in 1406 and re-enacted in 1504, 1541 and on other, later occasions) were also to the disadvantage of the towns. Local manufacture could not compete with the duty-free imports from Germany. The position of the towns was further worsened by the cessation of the old transit trade from the East when the Turks established themselves on the north coast of the Black Sea.

In Poland the evil effects which many of these developments produced later were not immediately apparent. The Polish kings of the Jagiello era were a competent set, who held their country together well enough. The survey which we have given of Poland's foreign relations shows that her actual losses (given the still existent possibility of a favourable outcome of the compromise with the Teutonic Order) were small. Against them, Sigismund incorporated Masovia in Poland in 1526, on the death of the last princes of the Piast dynasty, who had reigned there till that date. The Polish-Lithuanian relationship underwent fluctuations: after the kingdom and the grand duchy had again come into one hand on the death of Jan Olbracht, the Poles attempted to enforce a new union (that of Mielnik) which stipulated the joint election of the king and the grand duke. As Poland was not bound to elect a Jagiello, this would have meant that the family's hereditary right to the grand duchy vanished. The Lithuanians, however, refused to ratify the union, although they afterwards accepted Sigismund as their grand duke, notwithstanding that he was also king of Poland. The question was raised again only at a later date.

Affairs in Hungary proceeded more turbulently than in Poland, for while in the latter country the developments of the 1490's were a natural sequel to those of the 1470's, and they in turn to the decades before them, there had intervened in Hungary the dynamic reign of Matthias Corvinus, who had been much closer akin, both in the objectives of his policy and in its methods, to the princes of the new age who were his contemporaries in central and western Europe, than to his Slavonic neighbours. While respecting the forms of the Hungarian Constitution, he had largely disregarded it in practice, so that his rule came near to an enlightened despotism and both the social and political development of Hungary tended to follow western patterns.

His death was followed immediately by a strong reaction which was not, perhaps, so completely lacking in all reason as later Hungarian historians have been inclined to maintain. The chief beam in the Hungarians' eye had been the taxation levied on them by Matthias for the upkeep of his 'Black Army'. It is rightly said that, had the force been kept in being, Hungary might have avoided the disaster of Mohács. But Matthias did not organise his standing army primarily for use against the Turks, nor use it for that purpose. He only used a few mercenaries on the southern frontier to supplement the *banderia*, and confined himself there (after the first years of his reign) to defensive operations for which these light forces sufficed. When he expanded his mercenary army into a large force, and levied heavy taxation for its upkeep, this was in the interest of his western campaigns, which brought his Hungarian subjects no advantage and to which they were not legally bound to contribute. Of his other measures, while many were to the ultimate benefit of the nation, many again were undoubtedly oppressive in their immediate effects.

Nevertheless, his rule was still popular, not only with the peasants, who long mourned him, but also with the lesser nobles whose favour he, like Casimir of Poland, had courted, less by making them positive concessions than by the heavy hand with which he dealt with the magnates. It was a small clique of rich men, lay and ecclesiastical, who put Wladislaw on the throne with the help of that very standing army which was such a thorn in their flesh. The first requirement made by these men of the new monarchy was that it should be weak; and having secured a man whose general character answered that requirement, they proceeded to limit the royal power drastically. Wladislaw was made to reinforce his coronation oath with a written 'Inaugural Diploma' in which, besides repeating the general and usual undertaking to respect all rights, privileges, immunities, etc., he had to give specific undertakings regarding various points of foreign policy (*inter alia*, as mentioned above, to make no agreement with Frederick III or with Maximilian 'without the express, free and voluntary consent' of the prelates and barons) and also of internal policy (the consent of the bishops and barons was required before new coinage could be issued and for various other purposes). He also had to agree to rescind Matthias's 'innovations', in particular the Florin Tax out of which the Black Army had been kept up. The diet was to meet regularly, and the king had to give a month's notice before convoking it, and to notify in advance what were the subjects he proposed to lay before it. In 1507 the principle was finally established that no decree issued by the king was of legal effect unless confirmed by the council of state, and a most important bolt-hole was blocked in 1504 when it was declared illegal for any county to offer the king any subsidy or contribution, contrary to the ancient liberties of the kingdom, without the consent of the entire diet.

The royal power, thus closely limited even in law, was in practice reduced to zero by Wladislaw's personal feebleness. The Crown could still have wielded very great power by thrifty husbanding and wise employment of the important revenues which it should have derived from the crown lands, the mines and the other *regalia*. But Wladislaw let the control of these slip into the hands of the court clique, who plundered them for their private advantage so mercilessly that the yield from them, by the time it reached the treasury, was only a half, at times only a quarter, of what it had been in Matthias's days. Some of them were farmed out to Hungarian or foreign speculators in return for advances of ready money; when these were spent, the wretched king resorted to selling the books and pictures from Matthias's collections. At times he literally had to beg for charity in order to keep his court supplied with food and drink.

The complete elimination of the Crown as an effectual political factor left the field open for a bitter struggle between the lesser nobility and the magnates. On paper, the smaller men had the better of the contest. The magnates had begun by limiting the membership of the council to four high officials, four bishops and four barons: the diet forced through a measure adding to this number sixteen representatives of the lesser nobility. The small nobles were, of course, in a great majority in the diet, which all nobles were entitled, and indeed, obliged to attend. In 1495 the jurisdiction of the counties was affirmed to extend also to the magnates' estates; it was laid down that the *föispán* (lord-lieutenant) was elected by and responsible to the county diet (in the election of which all nobles in the county had a voice) and that no one in the county was exempt from his jurisdiction. And in 1514 the small nobles achieved a remarkable theoretical affirmation of their position. The diet of 1498 had resolved on a general codification of Hungary's constitutional law. This made little progress for some years, but was then taken in hand by the jurist Verböczi, himself by origin a member of the small nobility, although second to none in the art of self-enrichment. Verböczi's *Tripartitum*, as his work was called, appeared just after the peasant rising to which we shall come shortly and records the changes for the worse in the peasants' status enacted after the rising. It emphasises the complete monopoly of freedom and political rights enjoyed in Hungary exclusively by the nobles —the '*populus Hungaricus*' by contrast to the '*misera contribuens plebs*'. Going on, it stresses very strongly the complete equality of status between all members of the *populus*. They enjoy 'one and the same liberty'; all laws and usages apply equally to them all, except only that the wergild is higher in the case of a 'lord'. But that derives 'not from freedom but from office and rank'. The same work developed the famous theory of the Holy Crown as a mystic entity symbolised by the physical crown itself, but in the political sense consisting of two members: one the crowned king, the other the corporate *populus* of which again every nobleman was a member. They are mutually complementary and inseparable, for nobles elect the king, and the king is the source of nobility; and the decision of neither is valid without the consent of the other. Verböczi's book (which claims to be a codification of Hungarian customary law and probably rests to a far greater extent that is commonly believed on genuine ancient tradition) never received legal sanction, but was nevertheless invoked for centuries as the authoritative statement of the Hungarian Constitution, and its appearance greatly strengthened the position of the smaller nobles, not only against the peasants and the burghers, but also against the magnates, who, it is worth emphasising, not only (as in Poland) did not form a separate class under the constitution, but were also not a homogeneous body in other respects. Most of them were new men: the father of the primate-chancellor, Bakócz, was a villein by status and a candle-maker by profession: the later treasurer, known to history in three languages as Fortunatus, Szerencses or Glück, was a baptised Jew. The great power which a few men exercised in these years was due simply to the chaotic conditions which enabled those possessing the opportunity and the talent to fish successfully in the troubled waters to draw enormous hauls out of them. But this possibility in fact placed in the hands of the magnates a *de facto* power which outweighed that constitutionally enjoyed by the lesser nobility, so that the affairs of Hungary during these years were controlled by the magnates and the direction of them depended on the course of the unremitting intrigues which went on between their rival factions. The very rights of the small nobles were no real source of strength to them, for the obligation to attend the diet strained their resources heavily: they could not afford to leave their farms for long periods, and the magnates could literally starve them into submission by prolonging the debates on controversial questions.

The condition of the Hungarian peasants moved downward in the same way as that of the Polish, although at first more slowly. The diet of 1492 still confirmed the peasant's right of free migration, limiting it by the indirect method of reducing his temptation to do so, which it did by the method of lowering all standards to the lowest admissible anywhere: all landlords, including the king, were bound to impose all admissible dues and these were also extended to the free districts and market towns previously exempt from many of them; in 1498 also to the royal free boroughs. In 1504 peasants were forbidden hunting or fowling. Then in 1514 came the extraordinary and horrible incident of the Dósza rising. The cardinal primate, Thomas Bakócz, aspired to the Papacy and wished to acquire merit therefor. At the instance of the pope, Leo X, he preached a crusade, for which some 100,000 peasants and other members of the poorer classes volunteered. Since no person of high rank was ready to take command of this multitude, Bakócz entrusted the leadership of it to a Szekel professional soldier named George Dósza; then, taking fright, tried to disband the crusading army. Thereupon Dósza turned his followers against the 'lords'. He was defeated and taken prisoner after severe fighting, in which his followers had committed frightful excesses; he himself was put to death by indescribable tortures. Thereupon the diet condemned all the peasants of Hungary, those of the royal free boroughs alone excepted, to 'real and perpetual servitude', further imposing on them dues and *corvées* far heavier than anything previously in force.

Although more sensational and less gradual, the Hungarian anti-peasant legislation was not severer than that of other countries, and left its victims in no worse state, but Hungary could afford it less because of her exposed situation; and this applied even more to the question of defence. The abolition of the Black Army put the country back on the *banderia* system unless foreign invasion occurred, when the *levée en masse* could still be proclaimed. When, then, the Florin Tax had after all to be reimposed, the lords bound to provide *banderia* claimed exemption from it. Thus, one way and another, little tax was raised and few *banderia* kept in being. The only part of Hungary where the defence system was not utterly neglected was the southern frontier zone, where the garrisons were maintained by the king and, in practice, usually paid for out of subsidies granted by the pope, or Venice.

In Bohemia, to which Moravia, Silesia and Lusatia were reunited *de facto* after 1490 (the Hungarian diet pertinaciously reserving its rights and maintaining its claim to an indemnity which, however, was never paid), the chief special problem was the religious one. The measure of peace established between Catholics and Utraquists by the Treaty of Kutna Hora was still very incomplete: the Utraquists steadily refused to surrender the *Compactata*, or any of the main doctrinal or organisational points which divided them from the Catholics; while, although many efforts were made to mediate, the pope as consistently refused to continue the *Compactata*. It was an armistice, not even destined to be of long duration, since hostilities were to flare up again with the spread of Luther's teachings. Meanwhile, the sect known as the 'Unity of the Brotherhood', which, for some reason, Wladislaw treated with a degree of favour, and which had several powerful patrons among the nobility, and also among the higher Utraquist clergy, made steady and rapid progress. In 1496 the more radical party in it, known as the Amosites, seceded: the majority, under a Brother Lukas, gradually moved over to less ascetic doctrines: their members were now allowed to participate in worldly affairs by occupying any kind of office. Considerable numbers of Czech nobles now joined the sect, which came to hold an important middle place between the two main antagonists.

The Bohemian nobles naturally took the same advantage of King *Dobře's* weakness as did the Hungarian. In 1500 they produced a complete constitution, which gave the diet the power to vote taxes, regulate the application of the yield of them, and fix the number of effectives necessary for the national defence. The king had the right of disposing of the army only in case of foreign attack. The provincial officials were elected by the nobles and took the oath to the constitution. The king even lost his right of pardon, the members of the supreme court were irremovable and their verdicts irrevocable. In 1508 the estates took over the king's debts, but on condition that it managed the royal revenues.

Bohemia was thus, in all but name, an aristocratic republic. As in Hungary and Poland, the nobles regarded themselves as the sole repositories of personal rights or political power: the constitution enunciated the principle that they alone were free, the other classes of the population were destined to servitude and any benefits enjoyed by them were of grace and not of right. The position of the peasants underwent the same deterioration in Bohemia as in the neighbouring countries. The considerable class of free or half-free peasants which had survived up to the Hussite wars had been abolished after them by the adoption of the principle that 'whoever was not a lord, must have a lord'. In the first years of Wladislaw's reign the diet decreed that no peasant might leave his holding without his lord's consent; the lords agreed mutually not to receive migrants from other estates. In 1497 the peasants' servitude was legally affirmed, and re-enacted in the constitution of 1500. As elsewhere, the lords were turning increasingly to direct farming and agricultural industry, and the dues and *corvées* heaped on the peasants increased accordingly.

The nobles also pursued an offensive against the towns, the conflict here being often sharpened by religious and national antagonisms. The towns came under the surveillance of the nobles and their liberties were revised downward or cancelled. The burghers were forbidden to trade in the country districts, and merchants were even arrested on the roads. The constitution of 1500 excluded them from representation in the diet. The burghers, however, who represented a considerable force, defended themselves with spirit in a struggle which at times amounted to actual civil war. In 1508 they recovered the right of representation and in 1517 a truce (the so-called Treaty of St Wenceslas) was concluded under which the towns renounced the monopoly, granted under a decree of George Podiebrad, of brewing and selling beer, while the nobles recognised their autonomy and confirmed their right to representation on the diet.

The great difference in the social structure of Bohemia, as compared with Poland or Hungary, was the absence of a large and vigorous class to correspond with the Polish *szlachta* or the Hungarian *köznemesség*. Under the western influences which were strongest in Bohemia of all three countries, a small number of great families (in Moravia, in 1480, there were only fifteen of them) had secured recognition as a separate hereditary class, whose members were not only nearly absolute sovereigns on their own estates, but also enjoyed the sole title to all the main offices of state. The smaller nobility, known collectively as the *rytierstwo* (*Ritterstand*, Order of Knights), held a position midway between the magnates (*pani*) and the unfree classes.

The reign of Wladislaw saw the knights on the offensive, in Bohemia as in the other countries, not only against the unfree population but also against the magnates. In 1487 (Bohemia) and 1492 (Moravia) they secured admission for a certain number of their representatives to the supreme courts. In 1497 King Wladislaw laid down an agreed proportion in which the two estates were to partition the principal offices of state between them. This represented a gain for the knights, who now secured a share in these offices, but still left the magnates in the majority and in possession of all the more important offices. The Bohemian oligarchy (whose real power was, of course, increased here also by the impotence of the king) thus enjoyed legally, and in even greater measure, a supremacy which its Hungarian opposite numbers exercised only *de facto*.

The Bohemians were not superior to the Hungarians in the use which they made of their opportunities. Here, too, the internal history of the period is one of a sordid scrambling for spoils between rival cliques. If the selfishness and anarchy brought less fatal results to the country, this was because of its better fortune in lying further from the Turkish armies. Having extracted from Wladislaw an undertaking that they should not be bound to provide soldiers for use outside their own frontiers, the Bohemian estates were able to watch, with detachment and even complacency, the gathering of the storms which were to overwhelm Hungary.

King Wladislaw died in Buda on 13 March 1516. The ten-year-old Lewis had already been crowned in both Hungary and Bohemia, and in neither country did the magnates of the court cliques raise any objection to his succeeding, only to the suggestion that the emperor and Sigismund, who had been appointed his joint guardians, were in any way entitled to intervene in the countries' affairs, which they took entirely into their own hands. The situation in Bohemia developed into a struggle for power and wealth between two cliques, headed by the two men whom Wladislaw had appointed to be his son's tutors: Zdeněk Lev of Rožmital, first burgrave of Prague, who represented the Utraquist party, and Bretislav Svihovsky of Rosenberg, leader of the Catholics. Rožmital was the stronger at first, but his depredations caused such discontent that there was real joy when the young king, arriving in the country for the first time in 1522, replaced him by John of Württemberg, and appointed as regent Duke Charles of Münsterberg, a grandson of George Podiebrad. Rožmital, however, was strong enough to get the decision reversed, and the history of the country during its few remaining years of independent existence was simply that of the internecine struggle between the leaders and followers of the Catholic and Utraquist factions.

The position was at least as bad in Hungary, where the court clique, the most influential member of which was Lewis's cousin, the Margrave George of Brandenburg, plundered the revenues mercilessly, and withal kept up an extravagant estate, so that less money than ever remained for the national needs. Lewis actually disbanded his own *banderium* and several of the magnates followed his example. Opposition to this régime came only from the rival magnates who wanted their share of the spoils, for the smaller nobility was leaderless again; John Zápolyai had severed his connection with them and retired to Transylvania, where, indeed, he was consolidating a local near-principality of his own. The representatives of the lesser nobility were even excluded from the royal council. Then the situation in the Balkans grew menacing again. In 1520 Sulaimān the Magnificent succeeded his father Selīm, and at once turned north. In 1521 he sent envoys to Lewis demanding tribute. This being refused, he prepared to march on Buda, but it was necessary first to reduce the fortresses on the Save and the Danube. Sabác and Belgrade were taken after heroic defences, which their garrisons waged without help; for the Palatine and Zápolyai, summoned by the king to lead relief forces, moved so slowly that the operation was over before they arrived.

Now the country awoke to the need of defence, and, remembering the great days of Matthias, the diet of December 1521 enacted a law which accepted the principle of a general tax for the establishment of a standing mercenary army; but this was to replace, not to supplement, the earlier system. At the same time, the lords were relieved of the obligation of maintaining *banderia*, and the lesser nobles of obeying the *levée*. Little of the tax, incidentally, was ever levied, and of that little a substantial part vanished into the pockets of the Palatine and other officials, or of Szerences, who managed and manipulated many of the king's financial affairs.

Hungary was again granted an undeserved respite through Sulaīman's decision to take Rhodes before following up his campaign in the north; but instead of strengthening her defences, Hungary seized the opportunity to invade Wallachia and establish her suzerainty there.

Messengers were sent abroad to beg for help. The imperial diet of Nürnberg was impressed by the fall of Belgrade, and sent a commission to Vienna to discuss matters with the Archduke Ferdinand (now married to Anne Jagiello) and the Bohemian and Hungarian representatives. But the great conflict between the Habsburgs and France had just broken out. The Germans had few men to spare and only granted Ferdinand 3000 men, whom he sent down to Croatia. Renewed entreaties in 1523, 1524 and 1525 brought no better results. As for Lewis's own Bohemians, Rosenberg's Catholic party was willing to give a little help, but the diet, which had, as we saw, safeguarded its constitutional rights, answered to Louis's appeal that 'if he sent a cartload of such letters, written in gold, they would not obey'. The only real help—and that on a minute scale—

came from the pope; the latter sent a nuncio to Hungary (Baron Antonio Burgio) who himself raised and paid for a small force of mercenaries from Moravia. Sigismund of Poland, too, wanted to help: he refused to renew the truce with the sultan, and sent a small force to Hungary, but the Turks, with Tatar help, ravaged Ruthenia, Volhynia and Podolia cruelly, and he needed all his soldiers for himself. It was in connection with these raids that the organisation of the Cossacks, as a special defence force for the southern and south-eastern frontiers of Poland and Lithuania, began to take shape; the first bill of enrolment for the Cossacks dates from 1524.

In Hungary the years 1525 and 1526 were largely filled with a violent struggle between the rival cliques of the magnates, and the lesser nobles, each party blaming the other for the state of the country. In 1525 the small nobles succeeded in forcing through the appointment of Verböczi to be Palatine, but he was overthrown next year; and truth to tell, he had been no more constructive than his opponents. And in that year there came the famous advances by Francis I to the sultan, which sealed the fate of Hungary.

At the beginning of 1526 quite certain information reached Buda that the sultan was preparing to move, and in April he began his slow march northwards with an army of 100,000 men and 300 cannon. The Hungarian diet of that month ended in its members disclaiming responsibility if the king did not raise and apply the resources which, they said, the country could produce, while the king replied that the resources were insufficient and he was not to blame if disaster occurred. The sultan himself moved slowly, but sent the Grand Vizier Ibrāhīm ahead to attack the fortress of Petervaradin, which guarded the passage across the Danube. It was stubbornly defended, but fell at the end of July. A few days earlier the general *levée* had been proclaimed, and Lewis himself set out from Buda with a force of 3000 men, all that was then available in the capital. He moved down the right bank of the Danube, marching slowly to give time for the *banderia* and the detachments from the different counties to join him, but made things worse by sending out confused and contradictory orders. Zápolyai, who arrived with his Transylvanians too late to take part in the decisive battle, was afterwards freely accused of having delayed purposely; but the fact is that he received four sets of orders, the first of which commanded him to invade Wallachia, while the later instructions to link up with the king's army reached him too late. The same thing happened to Kristof Frangepán, commanding the Croat levies, which were reinforced by the German troops; but he and Zápolyai begged the king not to join battle before they arrived. The Hungarians with the king refused to move without him, and this allowed the sultan to cross the Drave unimpeded at Eszek. It was to prevent defections that, when the king learned that the Turkish army was drawn up in front of Mohács, he determined to give battle without waiting for his reinforcements, although his entire army consisted only of some 16,000 Hungarians and half as many Polish, German and Czech mercenaries. On 29 August this little force was drawn up south of Mohács, awaiting the Turks' advance. To encourage his followers, the young king, with his entire government, led the very centre of the line. Paul Tomori, the archbishop of Kalocsa, on whom the command had been forced, believed that by attacking the sultan's Roumelian advance-guard quickly he could disperse them before the main army came up. The main force was, however, nearer than he expected, and when the Hungarians drove the Roumelians back, themselves disorganised by the fighting, they found that they had run clean into the sultan's guns. About 15,000 of the little force fell, including many of its leaders. Lewis himself was wounded. Two of his aides-de-camp got him away from the field; but as they were crossing a marshy stream, the king and one of his two attendants were drowned. The other reached Buda to tell the country that its army was lost and its king dead.

CHAPTER XIV

THE OTTOMAN EMPIRE (1481–1520)

SULTAN MEHEMMED II (1451–81) had striven throughout his reign to realise one dominant aim: the consolidation of the Ottoman State. In 1453 he had conquered Constantinople which, impoverished and greatly depopulated during the last years of Greek rule, was to become once more, under his guidance, the proud capital of an empire. The sultan repaired the ancient walls and peopled the empty spaces of the city with groups of Muslims, Christians and Jews taken from all parts of his realm. Public buildings were erected, like the great mosque which he founded, with its baths and hospital, its accommodation for travellers, and its colleges where students were trained in the law of Islam. Constantinople was transformed into Istanbul, an imperial city which, reflecting in itself the rich and complex character of the Ottoman State, bound together the provinces of Anatolia and the Balkan lands as Adrianople, the former capital of the empire, could not do.

Consolidation was also the objective behind the ceaseless campaigns of the sultan. In 1459 the last remnants of independent Serbia were converted into the Ottoman frontier province of Semendria, the strong bridgehead of Belgrade, besieged in vain by Mehemmed in 1456, being left however to the Hungarians. Bosnia was overrun in 1463–4. The Bosnian aristocracy largely embraced Islam and played henceforth a great role in the defence of the frontier and in the attacks launched against Hungary and Austria. In Greece, the principality of Athens, held by a Florentine family, the Acciaiuoli, and the Greek Despotate of the Morea, ruled by the Palaeologi, were subjugated in 1458–60; while in the Aegean Sea the islands of Thasos and Samothrace, Imbros and Lemnos were taken over in 1455–6, and Lesbos in 1462. During a long war with Venice (1463–79) Negroponte fell to the sultan in 1470; but it was not until the Albanians, the allies of Venice, had weakened in their resistance after the death of their leader, Scanderbeg, in 1468, that the Ottomans secured a firm hold on the Adriatic littoral through the capture of Croia and Scutari in 1478–9.

The Black Sea became an Ottoman lake. Genoese Galata, a suburb of Constantinople, had been forced to submit to Mehemmed in 1453, Genoa being thus severed from her maritime empire in those waters. In 1461 Ottoman control was established over the southern shore of the sea, where Amastris, a centre of Genoese interests, together with the Turkish emirate of Kastamuni, including its port of Sinope, and also the Greek 'empire' of Trebizond yielded to the sultan. The northern shore was secured in 1475 when the Ottoman fleet seized the old Genoese emporium of Kaffa in the Crimea. Even the khan of the Krim Tatars now became a vassal of the Ottomans. In Anatolia most of Karaman, a Turkish principality which had long been a dangerous foe in the rear of the Ottoman State, was taken over in the years after the death of its ruler, Ibrāhīm Beg, in 1464. Princes of the old ruling house continued to resist in the mountainous regions of the land, thus necessitating further Ottoman campaigns, as in 1470 and 1474; but, although the tradition of independence remained alive for more than a generation after these events, Karaman was henceforth an integral part of the sultan's dominions.

In spite of these achievements the work of consolidation was not complete when Mehemmed died in 1481. In Europe the Ottoman hold on the Christian principalities of Wallachia and Moldavia was not yet assured. Wallachia, ravaged by the Ottomans in 1462, had given less trouble than Moldavia which, led by its able ruler, the *voivode* Stephen (1457–1504), had defeated the Ottoman frontier warriors of the Danube provinces on the River Racova in 1475. Although this reverse had been avenged in 1476 when Mehemmed had routed the Moldavians at Valea Albă, the Ottomans had still to win control over the estuaries of the Danube and the Dniester, in order to establish safe land communication with the Crimea. On the north-western frontiers of the empire, the Hungarians retained Belgrade and parts of Bosnia; while the Venetian fleet had at its disposal a number of strong bases on the Adriatic and in the Morea.

To the east, tension had grown in the later years of Mehemmed's reign with two neighbouring Muslim Powers—with Mamluk Egypt over the buffer state of Albistan, ruled by the house of Zu'l-Kadr and regarded by the Mamluks as their protectorate, and with Persia because the state lately founded there by Uzun Hasan was a serious threat to Ottoman Anatolia. Originally the chief of the Turcoman tribes known as the Ak Koyunlü, who had dominated the region around Diyarbekir, Uzun Hasan (1423?–78) had started on a career of conquest which, in the years after 1453, had made him master of western Persia, Azerbaijan, and Kurdistan. As the ally of Venice during her war with Mehemmed, he had invaded Anatolia, only to be repulsed at the battle of Terjan in 1473. None the less, the Ottoman frontier towards the Ak Koyunlü State remained ill-defined in 1481, and so, too, the frontier towards Mamluk Syria.

Mehemmed had raised to the status of a law the old Ottoman custom that a sultan, on ascending the throne, should eliminate all possible rivals by having his brothers and their male children put to death; but he had left the problem of the succession itself undecided. When he died on 3 May 1481 two sons survived him, Bāyezīd and Jem, each of whom, in accordance with the Ottoman procedure that princes, from an early age, should learn how to govern, had charge of a province in Anatolia. Bāyezīd, the elder son, was at Amasia, and Jem at Konia, the old capital of Karaman. A conflict between them was unavoidable. It would be resolved in favour of the prince fortunate enought to win the allegiance of the janissaries and the great officials of state. The high dignitaries were divided amongst themselves but several of them, including the beglerbeg, that is the governor-general, of Anatolia and, according to some of the sources, the agha in command of the janissaries, were married to sisters or daughters of Bāyezīd and were therefore staunch advocates of his claim. It is true that no less a figure than the grand vizier was the head of Jem's party, but this man, Mehemmed Pasha, was a most unpopular personality.

Sultan Mehemmed had died at Maltepe, not far from Scutari opposite Istanbul, at the commencement of a new campaign. The grand vizier concealed the sultan's death and sent messengers to Amasia and Konia, hoping that Jem would arrive before Bāyezīd. To prevent the janissaries still encamped at Maltepe from crossing to the capital, he returned to Istanbul and ordered the landing-places on the shores of the Bosphorus to be closed and all available shipping to be seized. His efforts were in vain, for the secret filtered out and the janissaries, rising in revolt, secured ships on the Anatolian shore, crossed the strait from Scutari, and slew him. At the same time the messengers bound for Konia were caught and held on the command of the beglerbeg of Anatolia. In order to ensure the accession of Bāyezīd, his partisans raised to the throne one of his sons, Korkūd, until Bāyezīd himself should arrive from Amasia. Thus, when Bāyezīd reached Istanbul on 20 May 1481, he was at once proclaimed sultan.

Jem, driven to armed resistance, gathered in Karaman and among the Turcoman tribes of the Taurus mountains, the Varsak and the Torghud, a powerful force which enabled him to take the old capital of his fore-fathers, Brusa, where he assumed the title of sultan. His troops, however, were no match for the janissaries. Defeated at Yenishehir in the neighbourhood of Brusa (20 June 1481), he sought refuge in Egypt with the Mamluk Sultan Kā'it Bāy (1468–95). Just at this time Kāsim Beg, of the dispossessed house of Karaman and hitherto an exile in Tabriz at the court of Uzun Hasan's son Ya'kūb Beg (1478–90), had invaded his ancestral lands but had been driven into Cilicia. He and Jem joined forces in the spring of 1482 and made a vain assault on Konia in June. Jem, despairing of success, fled to Rhodes where he found asylum with the Knights of St John (26 July 1482).

The knights, knowing how eager Bāyezīd was to gain possession of so dangerous a claimant to the Ottoman throne, sent Jem to France in September 1482. They undertook to keep the prince in safe confinement when Bāyezīd promised to refrain from all hostilities against Rhodes and, after further discussion in December 1482, to pay them a yearly pension of 45,000 Venetian ducats. To secure control of Jem, the Christian

Powers and even the Mamluk sultan began a long series of negotiations and intrigues, in the course of which the knights agreed, in 1486, to place him under the control of Pope Innocent VIII, who, once he had the prince in his care (1489), came to an understanding with Bāyezīd in November 1490 and received thereafter the pension formerly paid to the Knights of Rhodes. In 1494 emissaries from Pope Alexander VI alarmed Bāyezīd with the news that Charles VIII of France, then on the point of invading Italy (ch. xii), might well make use of Jem in a crusade against the Ottomans; but the sultan's fear was soon dispelled, for, although the pope was indeed forced to hand over Jem to Charles VIII in January 1495, the prince died in February of the same year.

Almost fourteen years of Bāyezīd's reign had passed under the constant danger that a coalition of Christian Powers, using Jem as their instrument, might invade the Ottoman empire. Neither in the west nor in the east could the sultan commit his forces to a definite line of action. There were, indeed, various armed enterprises, but these were either raids due to the initiative of governors in the frontier provinces or campaigns strictly limited in scope. As long as Jem was alive, the Ottoman military machine was never irretrievably engaged in a great war.

In Europe along the frontier marked by the rivers Sava and Danube, from Bosnia to the Black Sea, Muslim and Christian border lords waged against one another a ceaseless guerilla warfare which the central authorities on both sides were impotent to hold in check. The Ottoman begs of Bosnia and Semendria must have regarded the death of Sultan Mehemmed as a specially favourable opportunity, for in 1481 their raids into Hungary became so menacing that, in reprisal, the Hungarian governor of Temesvár, Pál Kinizsi, laid waste the province of Semendria in November of that year. In the spring of 1483 the sultan repaired and strengthened the frontier defences along the river Morava. At the same time, he established full Ottoman control over the Herzegovina. Of all the Bosnian lands, only a small area in the north, guarded by the Hungarian-held fortress of Jajce, remained outside the Ottoman dominions. Neither Bāyezīd nor the Hungarian king, Matthias Corvinus (1458–90), was eager for a serious conflict, and hostilities ended in 1483 with a truce for five years, later extended until 1491.

The death of Matthias and the ensuing dissension amongst the Hungarians over the choice of a new king (ch. xiii) induced the Ottomans to attack once more when the truce came to an end. Hostilities took the form of massive raids directed not only against Hungary, but also against Croatia and the Austrian lands—Styria, Carniola, and Carinthia. The great incursions of 1492 brought swift and terrible ruin to the Christians. None the less, one raiding column, as it returned laden with plunder and captives, was trapped by the men of Carinthia near Villach, where a desperate battle was fought in which 10,000 Muslim warriors and 7000

Christians are said to have been slain; while other raids into Hungary were repulsed at Szörény and at the pass of the Red Tower in Transylvania. The incursions were renewed in 1493 with increased ferocity, Croatia and lower Styria being ravaged once more and the Croat nobility almost annihilated at Adbina on 9 September. There were further attacks on Styria and Temesvár in 1494, to which the Hungarians retaliated by devastating the region around Semendria in November. Peace was restored in 1495 when the sultan, worried by recent developments in Italy, concluded a truce with Hungary for three years.

While Jem was a captive in Christian hands, Bāyezīd himself made a notable campaign against Stephen, prince of Moldavia (p. 396). On 15 July 1484 he took the fortress of Kilia on the Danube estuary; and on 9 August, after the khan of the Krim Tatars, Menglī Girāi, had brought a large force of horsemen to his aid, he seized Akkerman at the mouth of the Dniester. Stephen now turned to Poland for assistance, recognising Casimir IV as his overlord at Kolomea on 15 September 1485; but, although in November of the same year, near Katlabug in southern Bessarabia, he succeeded, with the help of a Polish contingent, in repelling the Ottoman frontier warriors of the Danube led by Malkoch-oghlü Bali Beg, he could not recover Kilia and Akkerman. Poland, harassed by the Tatars of the Volga, was unable to give him effective aid. In 1487, therefore, he sent tribute once more to the sultan. Poland herself made peace with Bāyezīd in 1489 in the form of a truce which was prolonged in 1492 and again in 1494, on this latter occasion for a further period of three years.

In the east, the unsettled conditions along the Taurus frontier led to a war with Egypt which claimed an ill-defined protectorate over Cilicia and the neighbouring principality of Albistan. The latent hostility between the Ottomans and the Mamluks was brought to a head by the intrigues and alliances, now with Egypt and now with the Ottomans, of the local dynasties which ruled in this 'no-man's land'. To the west in Cilicia, in the region around Adana and Tarsus, the Ramazān-oghlü were vassals of the Mamluk sultan. The Mamluks even laid claim to the lands beyond the Taurus because in 1464, on the eve of the Ottoman conquest (p. 396), Ishāk, a prince of the old ruling house of Karaman, had belatedly placed himself under the protection of Egypt. To the east of Cilicia the buffer state of Albistan dominated the route down the Euphrates. Because of its great strategic importance, the Mamluks had long striven to maintain a firm hold over this principality, but with no enduring success. Throughout Cilicia and Albistan, powerful Turcoman tribes, the Varsak and the Torghud, ever eager for warfare and plunder, added to the instability of the Taurus frontier.

Friction between the Mamluks and the Ottomans had arisen in 1465 when, on the death of Arslān Beg, prince of Albistan, two of his brothers,

Budak and Shahsuwār, had fought against each other for the throne. At first Budak had been successful with the help of the Mamluk sultan Khushkadam (1461–7), who had also encouraged the princes of Karaman in their conflict with the Ottomans. In 1467, however, Shahsuwār had appealed for aid to Mehemmed II, who was himself married to a princess of Albistan, and, having received from him investiture as ruler of the land, had driven out Budak Beg. For some years Shahsuwār defied the efforts of Kā'it Bāy, sultan of Egypt, to evict him, but in the end he was captured and then executed at Cairo in 1472. Budak Beg now returned to Mar'ash, the chief town of the principality, to rule there as a vassal of the Mamluks. In order to have a free hand in dealing with Albistan, Kā'it Bāy had refrained from aiding the Karaman-oghlü in their resistance to the Ottomans and had assured Mehemmed that, far from wishing to exert full control over Albistan, he had acted only because of a personal grievance against Shahsuwār. It was, however, clear that he meant to exclude the Ottomans from all influence in the land, a policy which was successful until 1480 when Mehemmed, free to intervene once more, established 'Alā ad-Daula, a younger brother of Budak Beg, as prince of Albistan.

Ottoman relations with Egypt became worse after the death of Sultan Mehemmed, for Kā'it Bāy, as we have seen, aided Jem against Bāyezīd in 1481–2. The Ottomans complained, too, that the Mamluks were inciting the Turcoman tribes to make incursions into Karaman and that pilgrim caravans bound for Mecca were being molested in the Cilician passes.

Serious warfare did not begin until 1485 when Karagöz Pasha, the Ottoman governor of Karaman, marched into Cilicia and seized Adana and Tarsus. In retaliation, Kā'it Bāy had Karaman raided by the Turcomans and sent to Cilicia a force of Mamluks which took the Ottoman troops by surprise. Reinforcements came to their relief under Hersek-oghlu Ahmed Pasha, beglerbeg of Anatolia, now appointed to be general in command of the campaign. Karagöz failed to co-operate with the beglerbeg, stood aloof from the fighting and thus by his inaction caused the defeat and capture of Ahmed Pasha. On hearing of these reverses, Bāyezīd made careful preparation for a new campaign. In 1487 the Grand Vizier Dā'ūd Pasha occupied Cilicia without resistance, the Mamluks withdrawing before his superior forces, and then, on the advice of 'Alā ad-Daula who had taken the Ottoman side, set out to punish the Varsak and Torghud Turcomans. In the next year 'Alī Pasha assumed command in Cilicia with a strong army which included the *sipāhis*, i.e. the feudal cavalry, of Rumeli and Anatolia as well as a large contingent of janissaries. To repel this threat, a Mamluk army, reinforced by troops drawn from Damascus, Aleppo and Tripoli and by Turcoman warriors under the Ramazān-oghlü and the Torghud chieftains, advanced towards Adana. Near this town a battle was fought on 17 August 1488, after which 'Alī Pasha had to retire from Cilicia. This further Ottoman defeat caused 'Alā ad-Daula to desert to the Mamluks; whereupon his brother Budak Beg, since 1480 an exile in Damascus, fled to Istanbul. Bāyezīd ordered the troops of Amasia, Kaysari, and Karaman to restore him to the throne of Albistan; but this attempt failed in 1489, Budak Beg being captured and sent to Egypt. In 1490 'Alā ad-Daula, supported by a powerful Mamluk army, invaded Ottoman territory and laid siege to Kaysari. Unable to take the strongly fortified town, the Mamluks ravaged the surrounding lands until lack of supplies and the approach of a large Ottoman force compelled them to withdraw.

Both sides were now willing to make peace. The attention of Bāyezīd was diverted once more to Hungary where Matthias Corvinus had died in April 1490; while Kā'it Bāy was eager to end an expensive war financed only by the imposition of harsh measures which aroused discontent in Egypt. In these circumstances, an agreement was soon reached in 1491. After six years of inconclusive warfare, Egypt was recognised in her possession of Cilicia but the revenues of Adana and Tarsus were to be devoted to the sanctuaries of Mecca and Medina.

To all appearance, Sultan Bāyezīd had met with a major reverse in failing to take Cilicia. And yet in no phase of the war had he exerted the full weight of his military power—for Jem was still alive. The forces which he had sent to Cilicia had consisted, for the most part, of *sipāhīs* from the provinces of Anatolia, with detachments of janissaries and *sipāhīs* from the Balkan lands to aid them when need arose. Compared with this limited use of the Ottoman might, the Mamluks, in their war effort, had gone to much greater lengths. The campaigns of 1488–9 had absorbed a large proportion of their resources. Even so, the situation on the Taurus frontier in 1491 was in no wise more favourable for the Mamluks, despite their victories in Cilicia, than it had been before the war. One fact was clear: the time was approaching when the Ottomans would seek in earnest to solve the problems of this frontier. When the critical moment came, the Mamluks would have to meet all the formidable strength of the Ottoman war machine.

The death of Jem in 1495 set Bāyezīd free at last to pursue a more enterprising policy; but before he could make use of this new freedom he had to meet a threat from Poland. The Polish king Jan Olbracht (1492–1501), unwilling to accept the fact that from the Crimea to the Danube the Ottomans and the Krim Tatars together blocked Poland's access to the Black Sea, hoped to break this barrier with Moldavian aid. The *voivode* of Moldavia, Stephen, who had sworn allegiance to Poland in 1485 after the loss of Kilia and Akkerman but, disappointed by Poland, had later paid tribute once more to the sultan, had no wish to be a Polish vassal in fact as well as in name. Moreover, the Hungarians, too, claimed a protectorate over Moldavia and might be expected to resent Polish intervention.

These complications did much towards the failure of the Polish campaign of 1497 which aimed at the conquest of Kilia and Akkerman but became, in fact, an invasion of Moldavia when the *voivode*, doubting the true intentions of Jan Olbracht, appealed for aid to the sultan. The Poles, after an unsuccessful assault on the Moldavian fortress of Suceava, were compelled to retire through lack of supplies and the approach of winter. Their withdrawal became a wild retreat when the Moldavians defeated them at Kozmin in the Bukovina (26 October 1497).

Bāyezīd, angered by this Polish attack on his vassal, ordered the great frontier warrior Malkoch-oghlü Bali Beg, the governor of the Danubian province of Silistria, to invade Poland. In the spring and summer of 1498 Bali Beg, reinforced by Moldavian and Tatar horsemen, laid waste Podolia and then Galicia as far as Lemberg; but a second incursion launched against Galicia in the late autumn of the same year came to grief in bitter snowstorms on the Carpathians. Abiding memories of Bali Beg's terrible retreat have survived in Roumanian folk ballads. The door was closed against further raids when in April 1499 Jan Olbracht made peace with the *voivode* of Moldavia. Bāyezīd, however, being now on the verge of war with Venice, had no desire to prolong hostilities and therefore consented to renew the former truce with Poland.

After the death of Jem, Bāyezīd could not ignore the growing pressure from those of his advisers who urged that it was time to renew the assault against the Christians. In the end, it was Venice which had to face a major Ottoman offensive, despite the fact that relations between the sultan and the *signoria* had remained tranquil since 1482 when Bāyezīd, anxious to maintain peace in the west during his conflict with Jem, had confirmed on more favourable terms than before the Venetian trade privileges within the Ottoman empire. The war, when it came, arose not so much from precise and determinable grounds of dispute as from tensions inherent in the general alignment existing between the two Powers. Ottoman domination on the Adriatic shore would remain incomplete so long as Venice held, in Dalmatia and Albania, important territories like Sebenico and Spalato, Zara, Budua, and Antivari, Dulcigno and Durazzo. The same was true of the Morea where Venice was mistress of Lepanto, Modon, and Coron, Navarino, Napoli di Romania, and Monemvasia.

To defend these possessions, Venice made use of Greek, Cretan, and above all Albanian mercenaries, who were no less bent on plunder than the Ottoman frontier warriors whom they opposed. 'Incidents' were therefore common enough. Moreover, there was friction at sea where Christian pirates using Venetian harbours and Muslim corsairs from the Ottoman coasts and islands were both numerous and active. Venice was alarmed at the growth of the Ottoman fleet, for in the years after 1496, at ports in the Aegean and the Adriatic, the sultan built many vessels of war and manned them by recruitment among the corsairs.

War became imminent in 1498-9 when hostilities flared out with a growing intensity along the frontiers from Dalmatia to the Morea. Venice complained of Ottoman raids on Sebenico and Spalato; while Bāyezīd was angered to learn that Venetian mercenaries had ambushed 500 Ottoman soldiers near Napoli di Romania. In November 1498 Venice had decided to send Andrea Zanchani to Istanbul with the tribute which she owed for the island of Zante and with the assurance that she had no desire for war. Zanchani's mission of March 1499 failed, however, to avert the approaching conflict. The sultan was apprehensive about the alliance which Venice had just made with Louis XII of France against Lodovico Sforza, duke of Milan (ch. XII). Sforza had sent emissaries to Istanbul with the information that France, if the invasion of Milan were successful, intended to prepare a crusade against the Ottoman empire, an argument which other Italian states hostile to Venice also urged on the sultan. Bāyezīd, believing that the Venetians would be gravely hindered by their Italian commitments, began the war in the summer of 1499.

On 12 August the Venetian fleet was defeated off the island of Sapienza, not far from Modon, when attempting to prevent the Ottomans from sailing to Lepanto in the Gulf of Corinth. Although reinforced by a French squadron, the Venetians fared no better in further minor engagements off Belvedere and Chiarenza (23-5 August) and withdrew to shelter under the guns of Zante, leaving the mouth of the gulf unguarded. Lepanto, besieged by the sultan on land and now deprived of all relief from the sea, surrendered on 29 August. Meanwhile, in order to divide the Venetian forces, Mikhāl-oghlü Iskender Pasha led the frontier warriors of Bosnia on a great raid into the Friuli. In June he laid waste the lands between Trieste and Laibach and then, reinforced after the fall of Lepanto, crossed the Isonzo and the Tagliamento in the last days of September and ravaged the Venetian lands as far as Vicenza.

In 1500 the Venetian fleet, ill-manned and ill-equipped owing to the financial difficulties of the *signoria*, failed once more to defeat the Ottoman naval forces operating off the coast of the Morea, where the great fortress of Modon, invested by land and sea, fell to the sultan on 9 August. Six days later Coron and Navarino surrendered to the Ottomans. Throughout this campaign the frontier warriors raided the Venetian territories in Albania and Dalmatia. Venice, desperate for allies, sought to win the aid of the Hungarians through the offer of large subsidies and at length succeeded in bringing them into the war, although a formal alliance, which also included Pope Alexander VI, was not completed until May 1501. In the meantime the Venetian fleet, with the help of a Spanish squadron which carried a force of veteran soldiers under the command of the famous Gonzalo de Córdoba, seized the island of Cephalonia in December 1500. The league between Venice and Hungary failed to check the Ottoman raids along the Adriatic shore, where, in the summer of 1501,

Mehemmed Beg, the governor of Elbasan, took Durazzo. In October of the same year Venetian and French ships sailed to the Aegean and made an unsuccessful attack on the island of Lesbos. This, however, was almost the last notable event of the war; for Venice found the conflict too expensive and was longing for peace, a desire which the sultan was the more inclined to welcome since affairs in Anatolia were beginning to demand his close attention. None the less, desultory warfare continued for most of 1502. Venice won a last victory when she captured the island of Santa Maura on 30 August; while the Hungarians, whose share in the war had been limited to ineffectual raids into Serbia and Bosnia, made an incursion into the Ottoman provinces of Vidin and Nicopolis.

Peace was now in sight. The main articles were approved on 14 December 1502, although the formal ratifications were not completed until August 1503. Venice abandoned all claim to Lepanto, Modon, Coron, Navarino and Durazzo; agreed to continue the payment of tribute for Zante; and promised to evacuate Santa Maura. In return, she retained Cephalonia and recovered her commercial privileges in the Ottoman empire. The delimitation of the frontiers on the Adriatic was reserved for further discussion, as the result of which Venice yielded to the sultan certain disputed lands near Cattaro in 1504, and, in 1506, the fortress of Alessio in Albania. The war, if unspectacular, had been a great triumph for Bāyezīd. On the Adriatic, and in the Morea where Venice now held only Napoli di Romania and Monemvasia, he had brought the consolidation begun by Mehemmed II much nearer to completion. Still more notable, since it foreshadowed their future mastery of the Mediterranean, is the fact that the Ottomans, aided by the Muslim corsairs, were becoming a formidable Power at sea. The peace was not confined to Venice alone. On 20 August 1503 the Hungarians obtained from the sultan a truce for seven years which embraced the other Christian states implicated directly or indirectly in the war. Bāyezīd was eager to be free of all complications in Europe, since he had to deal with threatening events in the east.

During the years of the Ottoman war with Venice a new power had arisen in Persia. Shaikh Safī ad-Dīn (1252–1334), who claimed descent from 'Alī, the son-in-law of the prophet Muhammad, had founded a religious order, known after him as the *Safawiyya*, at Ardabil in Azerbaijan. This mountainous region had long been a refuge for followers of the Shī'a, i.e. of various sects which all claim the caliphate for one or the other amongst the descendants of 'Alī. The *Safawiyya*, led by the family of its founder, had developed, from the time of Shaikh Khoja 'Alī (1392–1429), a widespread religious propaganda with the result that Ardabil became a much frequented centre of pilgrimage. Shaikh Junaid (1447–60), ambitious to add political power to his religious authority, forged out of the *Safawiyya* a military instrument which earned for him the enmity of neighbouring princes, so that he had to flee to Anatolia. In the years 1449–56 he taught and preached with great success in Karaman and in the province of Tekke around Antalia, in the Jebel Arsūs in northern Syria among the Varsak and Torghud Turcomans of Cilicia and the Taurus, and in Janik and Kastamuni, a mountainous area in northern Anatolia. From 1456–9 he disseminated his propaganda intensively from Diyarbekir where he found shelter with the ruler of the Ak Koyunlü, Uzun Hasan (p. 396), whose sister he married in 1458. The son of this marriage, Shaikh Haidar, later received the hand of Uzun Hasan's daughter, 'Ālemshah Begüm, who became the mother of Ismā'īl, the future shah of Persia. Events continued to favour the rising power of the *Safawiyya*, for after the death of Ya'kūb Beg (1478–90), the son and successor of Uzun Hasan, dynastic quarrels brought about the rapid collapse of the Ak Koyunlü régime. There was now in western Persia and Azerbaijan a political vacuum which the *Safawiyya* alone was strong enough to fill. In 1499 Ismā'īl, by this time the head of the order, set out on a war of conquest which, through his victories at Shurur (1501) and Hamadan (1503) over the divided princes of the Ak Koyunlü, made him the master of Persia.

The Safawid propaganda in Anatolia, pursued with unbroken vigour after the death of Shaikh Junaid, had won a success so remarkable, especially amongst the Turcomans, that it was the Anatolian followers of the *Safawiyya* who formed the main military strength of the new state in Persia. In this connection, the names given to some of the most powerful Turcoman tribes in the service of Shah Ismā'īl are illuminating, such as the Rūm-lü (i.e. men from the Amasia-Sivas region, which was called Rūm), the Karaman-lü, and the Tekke-lü.

The Ottomans, who were sternly orthodox Muslims, abhorred the teaching of the *Safawiyya* as heretical. They rightly regarded the movement, however, as far more than a religious danger: for them it was also a grave political menace. Even in normal times, the authorities in the Anatolian provinces had difficulty in restraining the Turcoman tribes who were ever prone, as nomads always are, to bring trouble to the settled populations in the villages and towns. The tribes won over by the Safawid propaganda had become the blind and fanatical servants of a foreign master held by them to be endowed with divine attributes. There was a real danger that the *Safawiyya*, if it were allowed a free hand to organise the Turcomans, might undermine Ottoman rule over entire provinces in Anatolia. Nor was this all. The Shī'a beliefs were strong in those regions where Mamluk and Ottoman pretensions were in conflict. How, then, would the Mamluks react if the Ottomans sought to crush the Safawid movement in the Taurus lands? Intervention of this kind would mean a radical alteration in the balance of forces along the frontier and might drive the Mamluks, despite their adherence to the orthodox faith, into an alliance with the Shī'a State in Persia. If this were to happen, the Ottomans would be confronted with a major crisis.

Even before the peace with Venice, Bāyezīd had been alarmed at the progress of the *Safawiyya*. In 1502 he ordered numerous followers of the Shī'a to be deported from Tekke to his recent conquests, Modon and Coron, in the Morea and rejected a protest from Shah Ismā'īl who complained that his adherents in the Ottoman lands were being hindered from going to Persia.

Once he had established his power in western Persia, the shah began to intervene on the Taurus frontier. 'Alā ad-Daula, prince of Albistan, had given refuge to Murād, the Ak Koyunlü lord of Fars and Persian Iraq, whom Ismā'īl had routed near Hamadan in 1503. Moreover, he had tried to seize the region of Diyarbekir, which Ismā'īl claimed for himself as the successor of the Ak Koyunlü, and had refused to bestow his daughter in marriage on the shah. In 1507–8 Safawid forces defeated 'Alā ad-Daula, conquered Kharput and Diyarbekir, and occupied Kurdistan. Ismā'īl had been careful to assure the Mamluks and the Ottomans that he had no hostile intentions towards them. None the less, both Bāyezīd and the Mamluk sultan Kānsūh al-Ghaurī (1501–16) garrisoned their frontiers in strength to restrain the shah and keep the border Turcomans under control.

The danger of a conflict with Persia receded in 1510, for Ismā'īl had to turn his attention to the east where the Uzbeg Khan of Transoxania had overrun the Persian province of Khorasan. This diversion brought little relief to the Ottomans, since in the next year a great revolt broke out in Tekke amongst the adherents of the *Safawiyya*. Their leader, a certain Shah Kuli, who had long been active in Tekke, preached the end of Ottoman domination, declaring that Ismā'īl was the incarnation of the Godhead, and he himself the Mahdī or 'rightly guided one' who would restore the rule of the true believers. In the spring of 1511 the rebels defeated the beglerbeg of Anatolia near Afiun Karahisar, plundered Kutahia, and then advanced towards Brusa. The Grand Vizier 'Alī Pasha, with an army which included 4000 janissaries, joined the forces of Amasia commanded by Bāyezīd's son, Ahmed, and drove Shah Kuli towards Kaysari. Near this town, in June 1511, a battle was fought in which both 'Alī Pasha and Shah Kuli were slain. The rebels, routed and leaderless, fled to Ismā'īl, who had some of them put to death for excesses committed during their escape to Tabriz. The shah sought in this manner to disclaim responsibility for the revolt, since he could not afford to provoke the Ottomans while the Uzbeg war was still in progress. Bāyezīd, however, was not free to attack Persia, even had he wished to do so, for, owing to the quarrel between his sons over the succession to the throne, the Ottoman empire was on the verge of civil war.

Three sons of Bāyezīd were alive in 1511, each of whom, in accordance with the Ottoman custom, had been given charge of a province in Anatolia.

Korkūd, the eldest son, had been appointed governor of Tekke. Alarmed at the growing influence of his brothers and worsted in a dispute with the Grand Vizier 'Alī Pasha over certain lands in Tekke, he had sailed to Egypt in 1509, hoping to find there support for his claim to the throne. Although well received at Cairo, he was unsuccessful, for the Mamluk sultan Kānsūh al-Ghaurī, being then at war with the Portuguese in the Red Sea and the Indian Ocean, had no wish to offend Bāyezīd. Korkūd, therefore, had no choice but to seek reconciliation with his father who in 1510 restored him once more to Tekke. Each of the princes desired a province as near as possible to Istanbul, since, in the event of a conflict for the throne, to arrive there first might mean the difference between success and failure. In this respect, Korkūd won the advantage over his younger brothers when, in exchange for Tekke, he obtained from Bāyezīd the province of Sarukhan, centred around Manisa, which was much closer to Istanbul. Nevertheless, despite the fact that he had been sultan for some days after the death of Mehemmed II in 1481 (p. 397), he had little chance of succeeding Bāyezīd. Amongst the great officials of state and the janissaries he had the reputation of being a scholar and poet ill-fitted for the Ottoman throne, an impression which his undistinguished share in the quelling of Shah Kuli's revolt did nothing to diminish. In the events which now ensued Korkūd had but a minor role.

The issue was, in fact, to be fought out between Ahmed, the governor of Amasia, and the youngest of the three princes, Selīm, who had charge over the remote province of Trebizond. To all appearance it was Ahmed who would, in due course, become sultan. Bāyezīd seemed to incline towards him rather than towards Selīm, a predilection shared by a powerful group of high officials. Selīm, however, had one great advantage over Ahmed: because of his warlike and resolute character he was beloved of the janissaries. In the end, it was their approval, even more than the boldness of his own schemes, which brought him to the throne.

Selīm had prepared with great foresight for the hour of crisis. In Trebizond he had built up an armed force which he led on raids into Safawid territory with such effect that the shah had complained to Bāyezīd in 1505 and again in 1508. In spite of these protests, Selīm made further incursions in the region of Erzinjan, whereupon Ismā'īl, in 1510, threatened to retaliate but was placated when an envoy arrived bearing gifts from Bāyezīd. Not content with securing troops well trained in warfare and loyal to his person, Selīm made good use of his influence at court to arrange the appointment of Iskender Beg, reported to have been his son-in-law, as commander of the Ottoman fleet; if the course of events were to favour Selīm, Iskender Beg might be able to prevent Ahmed from crossing the straits to Istanbul. To create a further obstacle for Ahmed, Selīm had his own son, Sulaimān, made governor of Boli, a province in north-west Anatolia controlling the communications between Amasia and the capital; but the plan failed, for Ahmed, seeing the danger to himself, induced the sultan to revoke the appointment. Selīm now made the daring resolve to transfer his activities from Trebizond to the Balkans. He prepared for this enterprise by requesting and obtaining for his son, Sulaimān, the province of Kaffa in the Crimea, an excellent point of departure for a campaign across the Danube, all the more since he succeeded at the same time in winning the alliance of Menglī Girāi, the khan of the Krim Tatars, who promised to provide him with horsemen.

The time for action had come. Without seeking Bāyezīd's consent, Selīm sailed with his troops from Trebizond to Kaffa where he enrolled more men and increased his fleet. He ignored his father's command that he should return to Trebizond, declaring that he had left it because of his desire to make war on the Christians and, for this purpose, wished to be given a province in Europe. The extent of his request is not clear. He seems to have asked for Semendria, but Bosnia and Silistria are also mentioned in some of the sources. When Bāyezīd rejected this demand, Selīm sent his ships to the Danube estuary and, with an army composed largely of Tatar horsemen, crossed the river in March 1511.

At Adrianople, where the court was then in residence, the partisans of Ahmed strove to impress on the sultan the gravity of Selīm's offence; but Bāyezīd, loath to begin a war against his son and worried over the revolt of Shah Kuli which had broken out in Anatolia, resolved in the end to grant what Selīm desired. In a formal agreement he conferred on Selīm the province of Semendria and promised furthermore that he would not abdicate in favour of Ahmed. This concession of a great government on the middle Danube to a prince reputed to be himself a warrior and an avowed advocate of war against the Christians was in full accord with the wishes of the border chieftains of Serbia and Bosnia, for example the Malkoch-oghlu, who were resentful of the peaceful attitude which Bāyezīd had maintained towards the Christian states since 1503.

For the moment Selīm was content with his success; but while he was moving towards Semendria, news arrived that Shah Kuli had defeated the beglerbeg of Anatolia and that the Grand Vizier 'Alī Pasha, who was a staunch friend of Ahmed, had been ordered to lead a strong force of janissaries and other troops against the rebels. Selīm suspected, and with good reason, that 'Alī Pasha, if he were able to crush the revolt, would use the powerful army under his command to secure the throne for Ahmed. Even before attacking Shah Kuli, the grand vizier had tried to win over to such an enterprise the forces which he himself had brought from Istanbul, an attempt which had failed, however, before the determination of his janissaries not to be dissuaded from their preference for Selīm. In the meantime, to forestall the danger which would arise when Ahmed and 'Alī Pasha had united their armies, Selīm marched once more on

Adrianople which yielded to him without resistance, for Bāyezīd, thinking his son meant to dethrone him, had withdrawn in haste towards Istanbul. When Selīm continued his pursuit, the sultan, under the urgent pressure of his advisers, made a stand at Tchorlu. Here, on 3 August 1511, the janissaries of Bāyezīd, however strong their inclination towards Selīm, fought loyally for their lawful master and by their discipline proved more than a match for the Tatar horsemen who swarmed around them. Selīm, completely defeated, had no choice but to flee to his ships on the shore of the Black Sea and to sail back to Kaffa. Some sources relate that he had not intended to give battle to his father and that only the rumour of Bāyezīd's death had made him hasten towards Istanbul in order to secure the throne. Whether he was the victim of a deception and believed this rumour, or else started it himself from motives of policy is not clear; but there can be no doubt that Ahmed's followers were doing their utmost to bring about his downfall. A Venetian observer wrote at this time that it was the great dignitaries who 'dominate and lord it over the land' and that few of them wanted Selīm as their master, since he was a man who would pursue his own road and not submit to their control.[1]

Meanwhile, both Shah Kuli and 'Alī Pasha had fallen in the battle fought near Kaysari in June 1511. Ahmed, though deprived of his surest advocate, could still count on the aid of numerous and powerful friends at court. Moreover, the death of the grand vizier had left him in command of the strong forces which had suppressed the rebellion in Anatolia. He therefore led them towards the capital, hoping that he would be able to cross the straits despite the possible resistance of the Ottoman fleet now under Iskender Pasha. When, however, in September 1511, his allies at court sought to bring him across the water to Istanbul, the janissaries, more than ever ill-disposed towards him because of the ineptitude which he had shown during the campaign against Shah Kuli, rose in revolt and sacked their houses. The warning was unmistakeable: the janissaries would not have Ahmed as sultan.

This event was decisive. Now that his partisans were silenced, Ahmed had but one course left to him: to strengthen and extend his power in Anatolia and prepare for armed resistance. He brought much of western Anatolia under his own control and proceeded to take over Karaman as well, and this without asking for his father's consent. It was in fact an open revolt made manifest when he defied the order of the sultan to withdraw at once from Karaman to his own province of Amasia.

Angered by Ahmed's behaviour, Bāyezīd agreed to restore Semendria to Selīm who, since his defeat at Tchorlu, had been gathering new forces

[1] Marino Sanuto, *Diarii* (Venice, 1879–1903), XIV, 293 (Andrea Foscolo to Piero Foscolo, Pera, 28 March 1512): '...loro son quelli che domina e signorizano el paexe'; also *ibid.* XII, 515–16 (the same to the same, Pera, 21 July 1511): 'Pochi da conto voria veder dito Selim signor, perchè è di sua testa e faria quello li paresse; ma le persone di bassa man e homeni armigeri tutti lo desiderano...'.

at Kaffa. For a time his alliance with the Krim Tatars had seemed to be in danger as a result of the intrigues which Ahmed instigated at the court of the khan but, in the end, Menglī Girāi proved faithful to his word. Tatar horsemen rode once more with Selīm when he crossed the Danube in the last days of January 1512. His cause was already won. Ahmed was reported to be seeking an alliance with Shah Ismā'īl. This alone, by arousing the fear of a possible Safawid intervention, was enough to bring Selīm to the throne. It was evident that a campaign in force would have to be made against Ahmed without delay. In March 1512 the janissaries demanded that Selīm be recalled to lead them. To acquiesce meant to abdicate, but the old sultan was compelled to agree. At this moment, Prince Korkūd, the governor of Sarukhan, made his own bid for the throne. He came to Istanbul and went to the barracks of the janissaries, hoping to win their aid on the plea that he had once been their sultan. They refused to help him. Meanwhile Selīm was approaching with all haste and on 19 April encamped outside the capital. One week later he became sultan. Bāyezīd was allowed to retire to the town of his birth, Demotika, but died on 26 May 1512 before he reached his destination. Of him Machiavelli wrote that, benefiting by the great achievements of Mehemmed II, he was able to maintain the empire by the arts of peace rather than war; but that, if Selīm had been a sultan like Bāyezīd, the Ottoman State would have been ruined.[1]

Selīm could not feel secure as long as his brothers and their sons were alive. To do away with them was, therefore, his first concern. The danger was urgent, for news arrived that Ahmed's son, 'Alā ad-Dīn, had seized Brusa. In the summer of 1512, while the fleet watched the shores of Anatolia, lest one of the princes should seek refuge abroad as Jem had done, Selīm drove Ahmed's forces from Brusa back to Amasia and thence towards the Persian and Syrian frontiers. On his return to Brusa he ordered the death of five nephews who lived there (November 1512). Soon afterwards the same fate befell Korkūd who was captured in Tekke whither he had fled from Sarukhan in the hope of escaping across the sea. Meanwhile Ahmed had recovered Amasia where he passed the winter in preparing for a new advance against Selīm. His cause, however, was desperate, since Shah Ismā'īl, still occupied by his war against the Uzbegs (p. 406), could give him no effective aid. In the spring of 1513 Ahmed began his last effort to win the throne. Although he defeated the vanguard of Selīm's forces at Ermeni Derbend, the end came on 24 April when at Yenishehir not far from Brusa he risked all on a decisive battle. His men broke and fled before the might of the janissaries and the wild

---

[1] Machiavelli, *Discorsi sopra...Tito Livio*, Lib. i, cap. 19: 'Baiasit...potette godersi le fatiche di Maumetto suo padre; il quale...gli lasciò un regno fermo, e da poterlo con l'arte della pace facilmente conservare. Ma se il figliuolo Salí, presente signore, fosse stato simile al padre, e non all'avolo, quel regno rovinava.'

assault of Selīm's Tatar horsemen. Ahmed was taken in the rout and killed at once on the order of Selīm.

Ahmed's death did not diminish the tension between the Ottomans and the Safawids. In 1512 Ismā'īl had commanded the governor of Erzinjan to lead several thousands of the Anatolian followers of the *Safawiyya* into Persia. This action had given rise to frontier hostilities in the course of which the forces of Erzinjan had seized the town of Tokat. Now in 1513 the shah welcomed at Tabriz a son of Ahmed, Prince Murād, who had escaped from the battle at Yenishehir. These events convinced Selīm that war against Ismā'īl was unavoidable. As a precaution lest revolt should break out in his rear, while he himself marched against Persia, he ordered punitive expeditions to be made throughout Anatolia, in which 40,000 adherents of the Shī'a faith are said to have been slain or imprisoned.

On 24 April 1514 Selīm began the long march to Persia, advancing through Yenishehir and Akshehir to Konia and then to Kaysari. Here he asked for supplies of food and reinforcements of men from 'Alā ad-Daula, prince of Albistan, who returned an evasive answer and did nothing to restrain his Turcomans from molesting the Ottoman columns. From Kaysari the sultan moved to Sivas where he held a muster of his entire army and left behind a strong force to garrison the frontier regions. As he advanced through Erzinjan and Erzerum, he found the lands before him ravaged of all fodder and provisions by the Persian commanders, so that his men suffered severe privations which were only partially alleviated through the arrival of stores transported by sea to Trebizond and thence laboriously overland on camels. Despite the grumbling of the janissaries, Selīm pressed forward until at last the shah was constrained to give battle in defence of Tabriz. The two armies met at Tchaldiran on 23 August 1514. On the Ottoman right were the Anatolian horsemen under Sinān Pasha, the beglerbeg of Anatolia, and on the left the cavalry of Rumeli commanded by their own beglerbeg, Hasan Pasha; while at the extremity of each wing were the guns linked together by iron chains. The janissaries, protected by the baggage and the camels, held the centre, the sultan himself standing behind them with his viziers and his household cavalry. The Ottomans, exhausted after their arduous march, had to face what must have been a maximum concentration of the Safawid forces. In the number of his horsemen the shah was probably not inferior to Selīm; but he had no artillery and no infantry comparable to the janissaries. Hoping to overrun the Ottoman guns and take the janissaries in the rear, Ismā'īl attacked on the extreme left and right of the battlefield. His cavalry broke through the *sipāhīs* of Rumeli, only to be decimated by the fire-arms of the janissaries; while the assault against the horsemen of Anatolia was shattered because Sinān Pasha ordered his forces to fall back behind the guns which thus obtained a clear field of fire.

This crushing victory opened for Selīm the road to Tabriz which he entered on 5 September. He intended to winter in the neighbouring region of Karabagh where ample fodder and supplies could be found; but the janissaries threatened to revolt and compelled him to withdraw, through Kars and Erzerum, to winter quarters around Amasia and Ankara, where the army was dispersed in November 1514. Tchaldiran did not lead to the conquest of Persia but was none the less a decisive battle. Never again, not even when Selīm was involved in his perilous war with Egypt, did Shah Ismā'īl dare to attack the Ottomans.

Tchaldiran had made Selīm the master of Erzinjan and Baiburd which he now united with Janik, Trebizond and Karahisar to form, under the command of Biyikli Mehemmed Pasha, a strong frontier province in the north-east of the empire. To consolidate his hold on this region, Selīm, while still in winter quarters at Amasia, ordered Mehemmed Pasha to besiege the great fortress of Kamakh not far from Erzinjan. It did not fall, however, until May 1515, after the sultan himself had arrived there to hasten the siege. The conquest of Kamakh meant that the hour of reckoning had come for 'Alā ad-Daula, whom Selīm had not forgiven for his hostile behaviour during the campaign of Tchaldiran. Already in November 1514 Selīm had appointed as governor of Kaysari a nephew of 'Alā ad-Daula, Shahsuwār-oghlü 'Alī, and sent him to raid into his uncle's territories. In June 1515 Sinān Pasha, at the head of 10,000 janissaries, defeated and slew 'Alā ad-Daula together with four of his sons. The principality of Albistan was now conferred on Shahsuwār-oghlü 'Alī, who was to rule over it as an Ottoman vassal.

At the same time Selīm was extending Ottoman control over Kurdistan where the native feudal lords, jealous of their independence, resented Shah Ismā'īl's attempt, since 1508 (p. 406), to rule them through governors chosen amongst his own Turcoman chieftains. After Tchaldiran, Diyarbekir had revolted of its own accord against the shah. Moreover, twenty-five of the Kurdish begs had appealed for aid to Selīm who had thereupon sent a prominent Kurdish noble, Idrīs, later famous as an Ottoman historian, to receive their homage and organise the resistance against the Safawids. Idrīs and the Kurds, although not unsuccessful in the field, were unable, without further assistance, to relieve Diyarbekir, which was closely besieged by the main Safawid forces in Kurdistan. Once the campaign against 'Alā ad-Daula had ended, Biyikli Mehemmed Pasha, then at Baiburd, was sent with several thousand men to join Idrīs and raise the siege, a task which he achieved in October 1515. Nevertheless, the Safawid commander in Kurdistan, Karakhan, continued to resist stubbornly until at last he too was defeated in 1516 at Koch Hisar, after Mehemmed Pasha and Idrīs had been reinforced by Khusrev Pasha, the governor of Karaman. Urfa, Mardin, and Mosul now fell to the Ottomans, so that almost all Kurdistan was in their hands. Idrīs, receiving from Selīm full authority to regulate the future status of the new conquests, wisely refrained from any attempt to impose everywhere direct Ottoman control. He divided the land into twenty-four governments, of which five were to be completely autonomous under Kurdish chieftains, and a further eight likewise under native families, but with the right of supervision reserved to Ottoman officials; the other eleven areas becoming Ottoman provinces of the normal kind. This far-sighted policy secured for the sultan the continued allegiance of the Kurds.

The events of 1514–15 had altered profoundly, and to the detriment of Egypt, the balance of forces along the Taurus frontier. The Mamluk sultan Kānsūh al-Ghaurī had hoped in 1514 for an Ottoman defeat which would enable him, at little cost to himself, to improve his position on the Taurus. If he had not instigated 'Alā ad-Daula's hostile behaviour towards the Ottomans, he had clearly approved of it; for when Selīm, while on the march to Persia, sent an ambassador in all haste to Cairo, with the urgent request that Egypt should restrain 'Alā ad-Daula, Kānsūh had given a polite but unsatisfactory answer. Later it emerged that he had secretly congratulated the prince of Albistan, bestowing on him a robe of honour and urging him to persevere in his unfriendly attitude towards the Ottomans. Alarmed at the danger which threatened 'Alā ad-Daula after Tchaldiran, Kānsūh al-Ghaurī complained to Selīm about the appointment of Shahsuwār-oghlü 'Alī as governor of Kaysari, alleging that this province was a part of Albistan and therefore within the Mamluk sphere of influence. This protest, delivered to Selīm in April 1515, as he was marching to the siege of Kamakh, had no effect. As we have seen, once Kamakh had fallen, 'Alā ad-Daula was defeated and slain in June of the same year. Kānsūh al-Ghaurī was now compelled to take decisive action. When emissaries from the shah arrived in Cairo to ask for Mamluk aid against a possible renewal of the Ottoman attack on Persia, he promised, in such an event, to appear on the Syrian frontier with all his forces.

The belief that a mere demonstration in force would set a limit to the Ottoman advance and that no actual warfare would ensue was nothing but wishful thinking. The Mamluks indeed must have been aware of their own weakness compared with the Ottomans. The feuds of the great amirs amongst themselves and with their sultan, feuds in which their respective Mamluks were involved, were bound to have a disastrous effect in a time of crisis. As soldiers, too, the Mamluks, now less well trained than of old, had lost much of their former excellence. Moreover, their contempt for the use of fire-arms and their blindness to the value of artillery, so vividly shown at Tchaldiran, revealed them as a force which, in military technique, had already become rather obsolete. Equally grave was the fact that the populations of Egypt and Syria were wholly estranged from the Mamluk regime, indeed even hostile to it—and with good reason.

413

The contemporary historian, Ibn Iyās, emphasises time and again the rapacity of the Mamluks. Exorbitant taxation and unbridled licence amongst the soldiery had long been normal evils of their rule. Kānsūh al-Ghaurī, having lost the large revenues of the Indian trade because of the Portuguese blockade in the Red Sea, had to resort to harsh financial measures, with the result, as Ibn Iyās wrote, that each day of his reign seemed to the common people to be like a thousand years.[1] The Mamluks, in their hour of need, could expect no aid from their subjects.

Although aware of Kānsūh al-Ghaurī's intention to support the shah, Selīm was determined to resume the offensive against Persia, which he regarded as the more dangerous foe. He therefore sent Sinān Pasha, now grand vizier, to Kurdistan. Sinān set out on 28 April 1516 and, at Kaysari on 13 June, joined forces with the beglerbeg of Rumeli and the agha of the janissaries. He was compelled, however, to halt in Albistan when, on 4 July, spies brought him the news that Kānsūh was advancing towards Aleppo and that the Mamluk governor of Malatia had been instructed to deny the Ottomans passage through his province.

Already on 21 April Kānsūh had issued orders for a campaign on the Taurus frontier. From 9 May Mamluk detachments marched daily into Syria, the sultan himself, with the main force, moving out of his camp at Ridaniyya near Cairo on 24 May. He took with him almost all the funds available in the state treasury and most of the valuable war material gathered by his predecessors. Arriving at Gaza on 5 June and at Damascus two weeks later, he reached Aleppo on 10 July. Here emissaries whom Selīm, still hoping that the Mamluk intervention might be averted or at least deferred, had dispatched from Istanbul on 4 June, awaited him with the assurance that their master had no wish for a conflict with Egypt. Kānsūh reproached them vehemently for the seizure of Albistan and threw them into prison.

Meanwhile, Selīm had crossed from Istanbul to Scutari on 5 June. Marching through Kutahia (20 June) and thence through Afiun Karahisar and Akshehir to Konia (1 July) and Kaysari, he joined Sinān Pasha with strong reinforcements on 23 July. At this moment, an ambassador sent by Kānsūh al-Ghaurī from Aleppo arrived, warning Selīm not to proceed against Persia and, as one Ottoman source relates, requesting that Albistan be restored to Egypt. Selīm's answer was brief: insistence on these demands would leave him no choice but to invade Syria.

This unexpected defiance must have brought sudden disillusionment to Kānsūh al-Ghaurī. In a last effort to avoid war, he ordered the Ottoman emissaries imprisoned at Aleppo to be set free and sent one of his amirs, Mughul Bāy, to Selīm. It was already too late. On 28 July Selīm had entered the plain of Malatia where he was well placed to move

[1] Ibn Iyās, *The Ottoman Conquest of Egypt*, transl. W. H. Salmon (Oriental Translation Fund, New Series, vol. xxv), London (1921), p. 58.

towards either Aleppo or Diyarbekir, as need should arise. Here he was joined by the troops of Kurdistan led by Biyikli Mehemmed Pasha. When, on 3 August, it became known that Kānsūh al-Ghaurī had asked the shah for aid, Selīm was forced to make an immediate decision. On 4 August, in consultation with his viziers, he resolved to leave Persia alone and to turn at once against Syria. Some days later he must have received in audience the Mamluk envoy Mughul Bāy. In his anger that Kānsūh had chosen a soldier as ambassador, Selīm had the amir's retinue slain and sent the amir himself ignominiously back to Aleppo. Advancing from the north-east the Ottomans reached 'Aintab on 20 August, the day after the Mamluks had marched out to meet them, leaving most of their baggage and treasure in the citadel of Aleppo, since it was evident that the decisive battle would be fought somewhere near the city. The two armies met at Marj Dābik on 24 August 1516.

There is no good evidence for the total strength of the Ottoman forces, but their battle order is clear: in the centre stood Selīm with the grand vizier and the janissaries; on his right were the Anatolian cavalry and, beyond them, Turcomans from Albistan and Cilicia commanded by Shahsuwār-oghlü 'Alī and by Mahmūd Beg, a prince of the Ramazān-oghlü; on his left, the horsemen of Rumeli and then the Kurds under Biyikli Mehemmed. To oppose the Ottomans, Kānsūh al-Ghaurī had perhaps 60,000 men, of whom 12,000 to 15,000 were Mamluks. The rest were contingents from Egypt and Syria composed in part of Bedouin, Turcoman, and Kurdish horsemen. The Mamluk order of battle is not known in detail, but the sultan himself held the centre, the troops of Aleppo being on his right, and those of Damascus on his left wing.

Even now, Kānsūh al-Ghaurī could not refrain from acting as a partisan in the feuds which divided his forces. Wishing to spare his personal Mamluks, he ordered those who had belonged to his predecessors to make the first assault. These veterans, about 2000 in number, followed by the horsemen of Aleppo and Damascus, drove back the Kurds and the Turcomans on the extreme left and right of the Ottoman formation, only to be cut down by the fire of the enemy guns and of the janissaries. At this critical moment when a resolute advance might yet have won success, Kānsūh al-Ghaurī and his own Mamluks remained inactive. As the Ottomans launched a violent attack on the Mamluk centre, Khā'ir Beg, the governor of Aleppo, who had long been in traitorous communication with Selīm, spread the rumour that Kānsūh was slain. The Mamluks wavered and, after a brief resistance, fled. In the turmoil Kānsūh al-Ghaurī met his death. At Aleppo, where in the weeks before the battle their excesses had aroused bitter resentment, the fleeing Mamluks found the gates closed against them, a disaster which meant the loss of the state treasury and all the war material lodged in the citadel. Syria could no longer be defended. Nothing was left to them save to continue their flight first to Damascus and then to Egypt.

Syria yielded to the Ottomans without further resistance. Selīm entered Aleppo on 28 August. One month later he reached Damascus where he decided to rest his tired army. Ottoman governors were now appointed to each of the more important cities like Aleppo, Tripoli, Damascus, and Jerusalem; while a strong garrison was stationed at Gaza to watch the route into Egypt across the Sinai desert. As yet Selīm was uncertain about the wisdom of continuing the war. His main purpose had been achieved. No more need he fear an alliance between Egypt and Persia, now widely separated by a Syria firmly held in Ottoman hands. It was true that he could count on enough time to invade Egypt, for Shah Ismā'īl would not attack during the harsh Anatolian winter but wait at least until the spring of 1517. Nevertheless, an assault on Egypt would be a dangerous enterprise. There was first the desert to be crossed where water would be scarce and the Arab tribes eager to harass the Ottomans; and then, no doubt, the Mamluks would resist desperately in defence of their last stronghold. After much thought and despite Khā'ir Beg's plea for continued war, Selīm sent an ambassador to Cairo, offering peace if the new Mamluk sultan, Tūmān Bāy, who had been raised to the throne on 16 October, would consent to govern Egypt as an Ottoman vassal.

Before the result of this mission could be known, it was learnt that Tūmān Bāy, though hard pressed by the discontent of the Mamluks and by lack of funds and equipment, had dispatched about 10,000 men under the amir Jānberdi al-Ghāzālī to reconquer Gaza. To meet this threat, the Grand Vizier Sinān Pasha marched from Damascus on 1 December with 5000 men, including a contingent of janissaries, and joined the garrison of Gaza just as the Mamluks were emerging from the Sinai desert. Feigning a retreat, he moved northward by night, turned swiftly to the south, and forced Jānberdi to stand and fight on 21 December. The fire of the janissaries drove the Mamluks from their strong position on the edge of a steep wadi. Sinān Pasha crossed, re-formed his men, and launched a fierce assault which ended in the rout of the Mamluks.

Meanwhile, Selīm, with all his forces save for the garrisons left in Syria, had moved southward from Damascus on 14 December. The Mamluk attempt to recover Gaza and the news, received towards the end of the month, that his ambassador to Cairo had been slain convinced him that Egypt would have to be conquered. He joined Sinān Pasha at Gaza on 3 January 1517 and six days later began the march through the desert. Although repeatedly harassed by the Arab tribes whom Tūmān Bāy had roused against them, the Ottomans were on Egyptian soil by 17 January and, after a further march of two days, reached Belbeis about thirty miles to the north-east of Cairo. Through the treachery of the Mamluk amir Jānberdi al-Ghazālī it was discovered that Tūmān Bāy had constructed at Ridaniyya a fortified emplacement defended by ditches and by all the guns which he could muster. On 23 January Selīm took these defences in the rear and destroyed them by artillery fire. None the less, the battle was not won until the repulse of a desperate Mamluk assault, during which the Grand Vizier Sinān Pasha was killed. Four days of stubborn street fighting ensued in Cairo (27–30 January), before the Mamluk resistance was broken. On the night of the 27th Tūmān Bāy, with about 7000 men, surprised and overcame the Ottoman detachments stationed in Cairo after the battle of Ridaniyya; but defeat was inevitable when, in the following night, Selīm brought his artillery into the city in order to batter down the Mamluk barricades. After a last stand near the citadel, Tūmān Bāy escaped with a mere remnant of his forces. With some aid from the Arab tribes he continued to harass the Ottomans until at last he was beaten once more on the banks of the Nile in March 1517. Soon afterwards he fell into Ottoman hands and on 13 April was executed in Cairo.

The conquest of Syria and Egypt meant a great increase in the prestige of the Ottomans, already renowned as the foremost warriors of Islam in war against the Christians. Now for the first time an Ottoman sultan was honoured as the Servitor of the two Sacred Cities, Mecca and Medina, a title which made him pre-eminent amongst the rulers of the Muslim world. In Egypt, Selīm contented himself with leaving an Ottoman pasha and a strong garrison at the head of affairs, the old Mamluk order with its own laws and its own system of military fiefs and administration being allowed to continue; whereas in Syria he created provinces organised on the lines found elsewhere in the empire, although here, too, Mamluk laws and local customs were confirmed to a large degree. At the same time he recognised the privileges of the Arab chieftains, of the Druze and Christian lords of the Lebanon, and of the Turcoman dynasties on the Taurus frontier, for example the Ramazān-oghlü. Nevertheless, despite these arrangements, there was unrest for some years in the former Mamluk dominions, until in the reign of Selīm's son, Sulaimān, the Ottoman regime was reorganised in a more stable and permanent manner.

On 10 September 1517, having appointed the former Mamluk amir Khā'ir Beg as pasha of Egypt because of his intimate acquaintance with conditions there, Selīm began the long march from Cairo back to Anatolia. By 7 October he was outside Damascus, where he spent the winter in making further arrangements for the administration of Syria and in dealing with the revolt of an Arab chieftain, a certain Ibn Hanush. While Selīm was still at Damascus, he received an ambassador from Persia, who had come to compliment him on the conquest of the Mamluk realm. Throughout the Ottoman campaign Shah Ismā'īl had remained quiet, in part because he feared to risk another defeat, but also because troubles in eastern Persia had claimed his attention. His dispatch of an ambassador to Syria implied that he had no wish for further hostilities with the Ottomans. Nevertheless, around Tokat in Anatolia, adherents of the Shī'a, led by a certain Shah Welī, had started a new rebellion which was crushed in 1518 by Shahsuwār-oghlü 'Alī, the Ottoman vassal prince of Albistan. In the meantime, Selīm, having entrusted Damascus to the former Mamluk Jānberdi al-Ghazālī, had arrived at Aleppo in March 1518. Here he received the news that the new pasha of Damascus had defeated and killed the Arab chieftain Ibn Hanush. After remaining in Aleppo for two months the sultan resumed the march towards Istanbul which he reached on 25 July, just over two years since he had left it in 1516.

With the Christians there had been peace since 1503. Venice, in 1513, had obtained the renewal of her commercial privileges in the Ottoman empire. After the conquest of Syria and Egypt she sought from Selīm a confirmation of the rights which she had secured in those countries under the Mamluk sultans. This was achieved in the agreement of 17 September 1517, Venice promising to pay to the Ottomans the annual tribute of 8000 ducats which she had given to the Mamluks for the possession of Cyprus. The Hungarians and the Poles were also able to remain at peace with the sultan despite the ceaseless unrest along the frontiers. In 1519 Selīm renewed with them the truce which had been extended on several occasions since 1503. This maintenance of peace in the west cannot be taken to mean that Selīm had no aggressive intentions for the future. In 1515 he had begun the creation of a great arsenal at Istanbul. Now, in the years 1518–20, he pressed forward with the building of a new and more powerful fleet. It seems that he had in mind an attack on Rhodes which Mehemmed II had failed to take in 1480; but before he could set out on such an enterprise, he died on 20 September 1520 near Tchorlu while travelling from Istanbul to Adrianople.

Even in his own time his character gave rise to widely differing judgments. To the superficial observer he was, by reason of his severity, little more than a tyrant. Yet, with all his warlike ardour and fierce anger which earned for him the name, compounded both of fear and admiration, of Yavuz Sultan Selīm, i.e. the Grim Sultan, he was also a patron of learning and literature, himself writing poetry in Persian. The Venetian Luigi Mocenigo who saw him victorious in Cairo at the summit of his fame and splendour retained an abiding impression of his greatness.[1] In five years of relentless warfare Selīm had solved the grave problems which his father had bequeathed to him. Now he handed to his own son Sulaimān an

---

[1] Paolo Giovio, *Commentario de le cose de Turchi* (Venice, 1541), fol. 25v–26r: '...mi diceva il clarissimo Miser Luigi Mocenigo...che essendo lui al Cairo Ambasciadore, appresso à Soltan Selim, et havendo molto ben pratticato, che nullo huomo era par ad esso in virtù, iustitia humanità, et grandezza d'animo, et che non haveva punto del Barbaro....'

empire vastly increased in size, enriched with new resources, and able to resume the offensive against the Christians on a scale more formidable than ever before. The Ottoman poet and historian Kemālpashazāde, Selīm's companion on the Egyptian campaign, wrote, with no exaggeration, in a lament on the death of the great sultan, that in a brief space of time he had achieved much and, like the setting sun, had cast a long shadow over the face of the earth.[1]

[1] See E. J. W. Gibb, *A History of Ottoman Poetry*, vol. III (ed. E. G. Browne, London, 1904), p. 19.

CHAPTER XV

THE NEW WORLD

I. THE PORTUGUESE EXPANSION

HISTORIANS have chosen the discovery of America as a convenient date for dividing modern times from the Middle Ages, a conventional point for changing editors and attitudes. Yet the history of science, the history of ideas, and perhaps especially the history of the expansion of Europe all serve to remind us that the division is an arbitrary one. The world of Ptolemy did not suddenly become the world of Mercator. On the contrary, a traditional cosmography was gradually adjusted in the light of widening experience, and even Columbus's remarkable discovery forms part of a long process that has its origins deeply hidden in the Middle Ages. Behind his venture across the Atlantic lies the whole range of the Portuguese discoveries of the fifteenth century leading up to the finding of the sea-route to India. At their head stands the conquest of Ceuta in 1415, when the Portuguese established their first overseas possession and thus launched the movement of European expansion. This expansion in turn is the inversion of the Muslim conquest of the Iberian peninsula. The main phases of peninsular medieval history thus provide the background of the discoveries—the collapse of the 'Ummaiyad caliphate after 1002, which opened the centre of the peninsula immediately and the south ultimately to the Christian advance; the conquest of Lisbon in 1147, the first Atlantic seaport where the Gothic north met the Mozarabic south; the capture of Seville and the opening of the straits of Gibraltar to the trade of northern and southern Europe; the intervention of the peninsular states in the affairs of Muslim North Africa; the expansion of Italian commerce from the Mediterranean into the Atlantic, and the confluence of Italian and northern European enterprise and capital in Portugal.

The medieval economic history of Portugal is still imperfectly known, yet it is abundantly clear that the undertakings of the Infante Henry cannot be viewed independently of that commercial and maritime experience in the winning of which he displayed so fruitful an interest. Between the capture of Ceuta in 1415 and the death of the infante in 1460, the Portuguese had acquired a certain leadership in nautical science, in naval construction and in the methods of exploration and colonisation. They had settled and brought under cultivation the uninhabited Azores and Madeira groups, hitherto only casually visited by Europeans. They had edged their way in the newly-invented caravel down the west African coast to within eight degrees of the Equator, or possibly somewhat beyond, and they had engaged in trade with successive races of natives, Berbers, Azenegues, Jaloffs and Mandingas. In these activities they were followed by the seamen of the Andalusian fishing-ports to the west of Seville, who occupied the Canaries.

The transformation of the Reconquest into a movement of expansion in Africa may have been in the minds of statesmen in the twelfth century. Even before taking Seville, Ferdinand III intervened in Morocco, and by 1280 Tunisia was a Catalan protectorate. Soon after, Castile and Aragon defined their zones of influence by treaty. A limited European expansion in Africa dates thus at least from the thirteenth century. At what precise moment the infante of Portugal and his collaborators raised the sights to a wider and more significant expansion, it is difficult to say. The occupation of the Azores and the Madeiras in the first half of the fifteenth century is plainly something outside the scope of the limited expansion of the Reconquest (though the methods by which they were colonised were those that had been learnt during the resettlement of the peninsula); so too were Henry's schemes for reaching the mysterious Christian ruler Prester John, at first thought to be in Asia, but later identified with the ruler of Abyssinia. In Henry's time the remote fable of Prester John and the marvellous tale of Marco Polo were brought into perspective, and from their fusion emerged the idea, which was to become an aim of Portuguese national policy, of finding a sea-way to the East. It would, of course, be wrong to ignore the complexity of Henry's motives. The possibility of leading a new crusade against Islam, the hope of finding a Christian ally in Africa, the quest for geographical knowledge, the desire to capture the spice trade, the aspiration to spread the gospel— all these purposes were present, and in differing proportions at different times. Occasionally the desire to crusade outweighed all other considerations, and the conduct of a religious war in Morocco was placed before the pursuit of the discoveries. Owing to the limited resources at the disposal of the Portuguese kings, any major campaign in Morocco for long required at least a temporary interruption of the sea-voyages, and this and the weakness of the kings who preferred to seek expansion in Morocco, Afonso V and the unhappy Sebastian, with whom the dynasty of Avis foundered in the wreckage of the Moroccan policy, have tended to obscure the fact that the existence of a strong sea-power in north-west Africa could well have thwarted the whole scheme of the discoveries, and that the subjugation of the Moroccan seaports was therefore almost essential to its success. In the last quarter of the fifteenth century the finding of a sea route to India clearly emerged as the main objective of Portuguese overseas policy: it remained so until the catastrophic knight-errantry of Sebastian changed the whole course of Portuguese history.

It is hard to fix the start of this preoccupation with the Orient. We know that Henry's brother, the future regent Dom Pedro, spent four years in foreign travel between 1425 and 1429, that he fought against the Turks, and that in Venice the doge presented him with a copy of Marco Polo and an unidentified *mappa mundi*. These gifts were of more than symbolical importance. The growing European demand for spices and the high duties levied by Egypt on the transit of oriental goods naturally placed a new value on the discovery of a direct route to the East, but we have no precise information of the channels by which such economic forces came to bear on the Portuguese movement of discovery.

Already the legend of Prester John had been cut down to size. In the fourteenth century, European travellers had reached Abyssinia, and in the fifteenth several Abyssinian missions came to Europe—one was in Lisbon in 1452. Ten years earlier the infante had instructed one of his followers to sail to Africa in search of news of the land of Prester John and of India. Successive captains pressed down to the Guinea coast vainly seeking tributaries of the Nile and even that 'terrestial paradise' which Columbus half a century later thought to lie at the source of the Orinoco. The diligent inquiries that Cadamosto made among West African natives about their religion and their neighbours were evidently framed in the hope that they would have news of a Christian ruler, yet none was forthcoming. When the infante died in 1460, his expeditions had still reached only as far south as Sierra Leone. His nephew, the Infante Dom Fernando, completed the exploration of the Cape Verde Islands, but died in 1470. The king, Afonso V, inclined towards knightly deeds against the infidels of Morocco and displayed little interest in the long series of voyages which seemed only to lead to endless dickering with African savages. Yet the discoveries were not entirely neglected. An effective temporary expedient was put into practice. The trade of West Africa was leased by the Crown to a wealthy Lisbon merchant, Fernão Gomes, who undertook in return to explore a hundred leagues of coast a year for five years, beginning from Sierra Leone. It was naturally hoped that India would be found to lie within this range, and such expectations were supported by the statements of the geographers Ptolemy and Fra Mauro. No chronicles exist of the voyages carried out under this contract, but Fernão Gomes's captains entered the Gulf of Guinea, passed Nigeria and reached the Cameroons. However, when the contract expired in 1474, it was not renewed, and the conduct of the discoveries was taken over by Afonso's energetic and capable son, the future John II, who succeeded to the throne in 1481. The resumption of royal control was marked by new and stringent laws to protect the Crown's rights. Ruthless measures were taken against intruders in the African trade; the fort at Arguim was strengthened and a new one built at Mina. The establishment of this station was at once followed by the two voyages of Diogo Cão begun in 1482, when he reached the Congo and explored part of the coast of what is now Angola, and concluded in 1486 or 1487, by which time he had reached Cape Cross in south-west Africa. These voyages took the Portuguese much farther south than they imagined would be necessary before turning north-east again for Prester John and the Indies. In view of the great distances involved John II both considered alternative means for reaching India and sought to verify the exact whereabouts of Abyssinia and India by sending expeditions overland. He seems to have consulted an Italian geographer, Paolo Toscanelli, about the problem of reaching India by sailing to the west. The only evidence for this, it is true, is the letter that Toscanelli later sent in reply to Columbus's inquiry, but there is no good reason to repudiate it. It is generally assumed that John rejected Toscanelli's advice. What seems more probable is that John did in fact send or license expeditions to the west, but that ships either were lost or returned without reaching land. In any case, when, probably in 1484, Columbus put his scheme before John, the Portuguese council rejected it, either because they lacked confidence in Columbus himself, or because they had now evidence that the true route to India was by way of Africa.

In 1486 the Portuguese received promising news from a native of Benin, who reported the existence of a great king called Ogané. This ruler confirmed the authority of the chiefs of Benin and sent them a cross to wear. He was never seen, but ambassadors kissed his foot which he put out from under a curtain. He lived twenty moons east of Benin. Ogané seemed undoubtedly to be Prester John, and the twenty moons were Fra Mauro's 300 leagues. This news seems to have decided John to test the information he had by sending single explorers overland to Abyssinia and India. One of these, Pero da Covilhã, a member of John's bodyguard who had served as a spy in Spain and Morocco, successfully reached Cananor, Calicut and Goa, returning to Cairo after about four years, where he met other emissaries of John II to whom he made his report. His companion Afonso de Paiva, commissioned for Abyssinia, died on the way, and Covilhã was therefore instructed to proceed from Cairo thither. He successfully made the journey, settled in Abyssinia, and there spent the rest of his life, being visited some thirty years later by members of Dom Rodrigo de Lima's expedition. Although opinions differ about whether Covilhã's news of India reached John II before Vasco da Gama set out, it seems quite probable that it did.

Meanwhile Bartolomeu Dias had been sent out to carry on the great quest by sea. His three ships left Lisbon in August 1487, carrying a number of negroes who were to go inland with samples of spices and precious metals and ask the way to Prester John and India. After coasting as far as Angra Pequeña, he was at length driven out to sea by storms, and only after these had subsided did he turn east and, failing to find land, ran north to discover what he called the Bahia dos Vaqueiros. This was the first time a European ship had entered eastern waters. Although Dias advanced a little farther and would himself have gone on, his men grew restive and in view of their lack of supplies insisted on returning, passing on the way the Cape of Good Hope which they had previously missed. Dias's return to Lisbon took place at the end of 1488. The news that he had successfully rounded the African continent and laid open the way to India caused John II to order the preparation of a suitable expedition to crown the great enterprise.

For reasons that are not altogether clear, a long delay occurred before this fleet could sail. It is probable that, at the same time as Dias sailed to reach India by the Cape, another Portuguese expedition led by Francisco Dulmo attempted to find the sea route to India by crossing the Atlantic, but that the attempt failed. At about the same time Columbus despaired of persuading John to provide the facilities he sought and retired to Castile to ply Isabella and Ferdinand with his theories. Although timber had been cut for the Indian fleet and an admiral appointed to take charge of it, the expedition was still not ready when at the beginning of March 1493 Columbus suddenly appeared off Lisbon after having completed his extraordinary feat. Although John received Columbus courteously, he does not seem to have been able to conceal his mortification at having, as it was supposed, failed to be the first to reach India; and while he gave the discoverer facilities to clean and refit the *Niña*, he had already determined to resist the claims of Ferdinand and Isabella by alleging the Treaty of Alcaçovas and the bull *Aeterni regis* of 1481, which assigned all discoveries south of the Canaries and west of Africa to Portugal.

Columbus's voyage was therefore followed by protracted negotiations between Portugal and Spain. The Spaniards began by obtaining papal support for their case with the bull *Inter caetera* of 3 May 1493, the Portuguese by giving orders for the preparation of a fleet which was to sail across the Atlantic under the command of Dom Francisco de Almeida. Only in June 1494 was the state of suspense ended by the conclusion of the Treaty of Tordesillas, which established the famous line of demarcation running north and south three hundred and seventy leagues west of the Cape Verdes. This arrangement reserved for Portugal the discovery of Brazil, whose existence is said to have been suspected by John II, while it allowed Castilian ships to run across the Atlantic secure from the stronger Portuguese fleet. The negotiations were conducted on the eve of Columbus's second voyage when the discoverer was preparing a grand fleet with which he hoped suitably to impress the rulers of Japan, China and India. John II, who had made a better bargain than he knew, died just over a year later in October 1495. If Columbus had succeeded in reaching India on his second voyage, the long-cherished aim of the Portuguese discoveries would have had to be relinquished, for the Castilians could have barred them from the Orient just as they barred the Castilians from Africa. But Columbus's second voyage brought no real evidence that he had reached or was approaching the Indies, and, by the time he returned in the middle of 1496, his undertaking was bathed in disillusionment. He himself continued to affirm that the lands he had discovered were a little way from Asia, but there were now few who shared his belief.

It was in these circumstances that the new ruler of Portugal, Dom Manuel, put the question of the continuation of the discoveries before his council in the first year of his reign, in December 1496. Some of the members, aware of the cost of the Moroccan campaigns and the need for some conservation of forces in face of the greatly strengthened power of Castile, now united with Aragon and, doubtless disquieted by the supposed Castilian discovery of the outer isles of Asia, were inclined to abandon the great enterprise, but others were in favour of pursuing it, and Dom Manuel was with them. A new expedition would sail for India by the traditional route as soon as possible. The admiral appointed by John II had died, and his son Vasco da Gama, whose leadership, firmness and courage were unquestioned, was given the command. Vasco da Gama's four ships left Lisbon in July 1497; after three months at sea without sight of land, they touched shore not far from the Cape of Good Hope, and early in 1498 made contact with the outposts of Muslim civilisation in East Africa at Mozambique, where a pilot was obtained. They called at Mombasa, and at Malindi, where Gama was hospitably received and met Indian seafarers whom he thought were Christians. The fleet left Malindi on 24 April, sighted India on 15 May and sailed into a harbour near Calicut two days later.

In reply to Gama's announcement of his arrival the samorin of Calicut sent a welcome, and Gama went ashore with thirteen companions to present King Manuel's letter. He was taken into what he supposed was a church, prayed before a goddess he thought was the Virgin Mary, and was attended in the streets by an enormous throng with drums, trumpets and volleys of shot. Having pushed his way through to the palace, Gama was taken before the samorin and explained the long story of the Portuguese quest, offering Dom Manuel's friendship. Unfortunately the presents he had for disposal, consisting of cloth, coral, sugar and honey, were considered quite unsuitable for the samorin. Gama thus lost some face, but was permitted to trade.

At this moment the states of the Malabar Coast were governed by several Hindu princes of whom the chief was the samorin of Calicut. Their foreign trade was conducted by Arabs or by native Muslims. These merchants, seeing in the Portuguese undeniable rivals in the Indian trade, set out to make things difficult for them. A large bill for customs duties was presented to the Portuguese, and their goods seized, together with some men. These men were duly recovered, but Gama decided to depart, receiving a final letter from the samorin expressing interest in further trade. At length on 10 July 1499, after an absence of two years, the first of Gama's ships reached Lisbon again. Gama himself was given a triumphal reception. He had crowned a century of effort, and brought back samples of most of the Indian wares that had become the chief incentive of the great movement of expansion. Unlike Columbus, who had demonstrated his theories to his own satisfaction, but failed to satisfy his employers' more material interests, Gama had proved the rightness of the infante and of John II and had proved it in such a way that the concessions made to the Castilians in the Treaty of Tordesillas had not been infringed, and indeed seemed to be trifling. Small wonder that Dom Manuel lost no time in assuming the titles of 'Lord of the Conquest, Navigation and Commerce of Ethiopia, Arabia, Persia and India'.

No sooner had Gama returned than King Manuel sent forth a new fleet to India. It consisted of thirteen ships and was commanded by Pedro Álvares Cabral, a young courtier who was accompanied by such tried discoverers as Bartolomeu Dias and Duarte Pacheco. One ship became separated off the Cape Verde Islands; the rest sailed south-west until they found signs of land and on 22 April 1500 discovered the Brazilian coast in what is now the state of Espírito Santo, naming it the Land of the True Cross. It has been much discussed whether this discovery of Brazil was accidental or by design. There is no evidence that Cabral experienced bad weather or adverse winds that might have taken him unwillingly so far west: both Bartolomeu Dias and Vasco da Gama would probably have recommended him to stand well out from the African coast, and his course is not far west of the route still recommended for sailing ships seeking the Cape of Good Hope. It has been maintained that Manuel already knew of the existence of land across the south Atlantic and that Cabral was instructed to visit it. There is, of course, no reason why Manuel or anyone else should not have suspected the existence of this land: the accounts of Cabral's journey are tantalisingly inconclusive on this point.

A ship was sent home with the news and the rest of the fleet continued to India. Four of them were lost with all hands but the rest duly arrived at Calicut. Cabral had wisely brought suitable presents for the samorin, but the Muslim traders took effective measures to prevent the Portuguese from obtaining the goods they sought; and, when Cabral seized a Muslim ship with a load of spices, his trading post was attacked and his factor and his assistants were killed. Cabral then seized ten Muslim ships and departed for Cochin and Cananor where he completed his cargo. Only six of his thirteen ships reached Lisbon in July 1501, though their cargoes fully repaid the cost of the whole expedition.

It had already been decided that regular trading operations should be begun and that a fleet should leave Lisbon annually in March. The news of Cabral's difficulties caused a new discussion to be held about the wisdom of pursuing the Indian enterprise, but the majority was now in favour of it, and it was decided to send out forces that could, if necessary, fight it out with the Muslims: once they were eliminated, the Hindu rulers would have no recourse but to trade with the Portuguese. Thus in 1502 Gama set out with fifteen ships, to be followed by a second fleet of five. A number of these were intended to hold off Muslim ships sailing between the Red Sea and India and to provide naval protection for the factories at Cochin and Cananor: the rest formed the usual trading fleet. On his way out Gama stopped at Kilwa and extracted a handsome tribute in gold from the native ruler, while his first act in India was to bombard Calicut as a punishment for the murder of Cabral's factors. By now the Portuguese were committed to intervention in Indian affairs: they were already friends of the ruler of Cochin and enemies of the samorin of Calicut, and in the following years their trading activities were interpersed with the building of forts and the conduct of campaigns on behalf of their allies. The expedition of Dom Francisco de Almeida, the first viceroy of India, in 1505, led to the establishment of forts in East Africa and at Cochin, Anjediva and Cananor, where the Portuguese defended themselves with a stone fort and found large quantities of pepper and other goods.

The appearance of the Portuguese in eastern waters was at once followed by the creation of an Egyptian fleet, which attempted to clear a way to India with disastrous effects on itself, for it was decisively defeated by Francisco de Almeida at Diu in February 1509. The same year saw the appointment of Afonso de Albuquerque as governor of India, and in the following six years the foundations of Portuguese power in the East were laid. The whole of the traffic of the Orient was to be controlled from a small group of fortified ports which would serve as military bases and trading centres. The first and most important of these was Goa, which Albuquerque wrested from the sultan of Bijapur in 1510 and which now took the place of Calicut as the headquarters of all Portuguese operations in the East. Two years later Malacca was seized, and became an advanced post for trade with Java, Siam and Pegu: its command of the Malay Straits gave the Portuguese control over most of the commerce between the Near and Far East. Their command of the sea routes of the Indian Ocean was still incomplete, since the attempt to take Aden failed, but in 1515 the capture of Ormuz gave them the key to the Persian Gulf. A strict and fairly effective licensing system was applied to all ocean shipping moving east and west of India, and it was to this domination of the carrying trade that the Portuguese mainly owed their power and prosperity. During these years, the Portuguese became one of the strongest trading nations in Europe: Lisbon was marvellously enriched: Dom Manuel became an absolute monarch: adventurers flocked to Lisbon to make their fortunes by holding the gorgeous East in fee.

So resounding was the Portuguese 'discovery' of India and so great the effort required to support it that the acquisition of Brazil was at first little regarded. An atmosphere of disillusionment hung over the lands beyond the Atlantic from the time of Columbus's second voyage until the conquest of Mexico. The continent of Asia was not found, and the quantity of gold recovered from the Caribbean Islands was small. With the breaking of Columbus's monopoly, Castilian seamen continued to seek the elusive passage to India, gradually probing the coastline north and south and establishing that the mainland reported by Columbus in 1498 was in fact a continuous land-mass and that it offered no immediate contact with Asia. Even in the year or two before Cabral's expedition, Columbus's successors had reached the coast of what is now northern Brazil from Venezuela, and although the evidence is confused and not contemporary, it is likely that Vicente Yáñez Pinzón's Mar Dulce, which he reached at the same time as Cabral reached 'Vera Cruz', was the mouth of the Amazon. In the previous June another Castilian expedition, possibly commanded by Hojeda, had made a landfall at what is thought to have been the Assú delta (Rio Grande do Norte), and this expedition may have been that of Vespucci's first voyage. It seems probable that the Castilian expedition of 1499 was the first to sight what is now Brazilian territory, that Pinzón was the first to coast along a considerable stretch of Brazilian shore, but that Cabral was the first to strike Brazil as a separate discovery and the first to land.

The maps of Cantino and Canerio show that an enormous length of coastland was discovered between 1500 and 1504, though records of individual expeditions are confusing. On the return of Cabral's messenger-ship, King Manuel sent three caravels to explore Brazil, and they met the remains of Cabral's fleet on its return from India at the Cape Verdes. It was probably this expedition that sailed down the Brazilian coast from about eight degrees south to thirty-two degrees, when it was forced back by cold and storms according to António Galvão (c. 1550) and which is referred to by Vespucci as his second voyage. Of the long journey from eight degrees to thirty-two degrees south Vespucci says merely that nothing of value was found 'save endless dye-wood trees and cassia and the tree that makes negrol and other marvels that cannot be described'. The very brevity of this description suggests that the main purpose of the expedition was to sail as far south as possible in quest of a western sea route to India. The fact that none was found and that Cabral's 'island of Vera Cruz' was shown to be a continuous mainland affords Vespucci's chief claim to have given his name to America. He certainly did not discover it; but he may have been the first to demonstrate that it was a new continent.

The voyage of 1503 referred to by Damião de Góis and described by Vespucci explicitly aimed at the discovery of a south-western passage, and succeeded in establishing a fort in southern Brazil and in loading a cargo of dye-wood for Lisbon. On the return of this expedition, the Portuguese Crown seems to have decided that the south-western sea route was still a desirable but not an immediate objective. It was plain that this coast, inhabited only by scattered tribes of primitive Indians, some of whom were cannibals, offered little attraction to a trading nation with the exception of the large quantities of dye-wood— from which it was now to take the name of Brazil—and such fancy goods as monkeys and parrots. Manuel therefore adopted the same procedure as Afonso V had done in Guinea: the dye-wood trade was leased to a *converso* merchant, Fernão de Loronha or Noronha, on condition that ships were sent to explore 300 leagues of coast a year for three years.

As early as 1503 a French ship from Harfleur, aided by two Portuguese, reached the middle Brazilian coast. Although immediate steps were taken to prohibit the export of maps and charts, to prevent Portuguese seamen from sailing in foreign ships, and to obtain from the pope a confirmation of Portuguese rights under the Treaty of Tordesillas, the French now knew all they needed to know, and despite numerous protests continued to cut dye-wood and trade with the Brazilian natives. Intrusions, conflicts and protests continued for some years, until finally it became abundantly clear that Portugal must either occupy Brazil or share it permanently with the intruders. In 1526 John III began to send armed fleets to drive off the French, and soon after to settle and fortify the points at which trade was conducted.

This running conflict with the French coincided with a difference of opinion with Spain. Although the lands disposed of by the Treaty of Tordesillas had not been demarcated, no serious quarrel about the delimitation of the Portuguese and Spanish areas had occurred in the quarter of a century that followed it. At this time the Spaniards were engaged mainly in setting up an administration in Hispaniola and in exploring and dominating the neighbouring islands, far from the Portuguese sphere. Portuguese seamen who strayed into the Caribbean might be arrested, and so might Spaniards seeking the south-west passage who came ashore in Brazil. But it was only the defection of Magellan to Castile and his success in reaching the Philippines by the south-westerly route that raised again the question of ownership of access to the true India. Under the dispensation of Tordesillas the Spaniards could claim what they reached by sailing westwards and the Portuguese what they found by going to the east. It was now necessary to draw a line corresponding to that of Tordesillas in the east. The main bone of contention was the Spice Islands, the much-coveted source of some of the most valuable of oriental products. After several years of haggling it was agreed by the Treaty of Saragossa in 1529 that the islands should remain with Portugal, but that an indemnity of 350,000 ducats should be paid to Spain. Thus the whole world, newly discovered and still to be explored, was divided between the two peninsular Powers.

2. THE SPANIARDS IN THE NEW WORLD, 1493–1521

THE settlement of Spanish America began with Columbus's second voyage. The first voyage had been a successful reconnaissance, carefully planned and ably executed. Making, by good fortune, the best of the North Atlantic wind system, Columbus had sailed from the Canaries to the Bahamas before the north-east trades, and back to the Azores in the zone of the westerly winds of winter. He had discovered the two largest islands of the Antilles, Cuba and Hispaniola. He claimed, and believed until his death, that he had found islands lying off the coast of eastern Asia, and possibly part of the mainland too. We cannot be sure whether these claims agreed with Columbus's original intentions and promises, nor whether Ferdinand and Isabella entirely accepted them— some intelligent contemporaries certainly did not. But beyond doubt Columbus had discovered an extensive archipelago of hitherto unknown islands which yielded some gold and were inhabited by a peaceful and tractable, though extremely primitive, people. Whether these islands were really within striking distance of the settled parts of Asia remained to be seen; but they were certainly worth careful investigation.

The first voyage, though successful, had been expensive. Columbus had lost his flagship and had been compelled to leave half his men behind in Hispaniola to face an uncertain fate. The plunder he had secured was negligible in proportion to the cost of the enterprise. It was now essential to follow up the discovery and to produce a return on the investment. Immediately upon receipt of Columbus's first report, and even before his arrival in their presence, the sovereigns commanded him to begin his preparations for a second voyage. Shortly afterwards, they embarked upon negotiations with the Papacy and with Portugal, in order to secure a monopoly of navigation and settlement in the seas and lands which Columbus had discovered.

The negotiations with the Papacy presented little difficulty. Alexander VI was himself a Spaniard, already under heavy obligations to the Catholic monarchs and looking to them for support in his endeavour to create a principality in Italy for his son. His predecessors had conferred on Portugal the monopoly of exploration and missionary activity in West Africa, and Alexander was more than willing to do as much for Spain. He issued a series of four bulls, each successively strengthening and extending the provisions of the previous ones, in accordance with successive demands made by Ferdinand and Isabella, upon Columbus's advice. The first two granted to the sovereigns of Castile all lands discovered, or to be discovered, in the regions explored by Columbus. The third, the famous *Inter caetera*, drew an imaginary boundary from north to south a hundred leagues west of the Azores and Cape Verde Islands, and provided that the land and sea beyond the line should be a Spanish sphere of exploration. The fourth, *Dudum siquidem*, extended the previous grants to include 'all islands and mainlands whatever, found or to be found... in sailing or travelling towards the west and south, whether they be in regions occidental or meridional and oriental and of India'; further, all grants previously made in the regions mentioned were cancelled, even if they had been followed by actual possession. Whatever the international force of these enactments—and Catholic opinion was divided in the matter—the four bulls constituted for Spaniards the basic legal claim of the Spanish Crown to the lands of the New World.

The counter-claims of Portugal, however, could not easily be brushed aside. John II, suspicious of Italian exaggeration, had never accepted Columbus's interpretation of the discoveries. To him the 'Indies' were another group of islands in the Atlantic, and at first he laid claim to them as such under the terms of the Treaty of Alcaçovas of 1479. Clearly Portugal would not go to war over the possession of a few distant islands inhabited by naked savages, gold or no gold; but *Dudum siquidem* gave serious cause for alarm. The generosity of its terms, and the specific reference to India, implied a threat to plans which the Portuguese had cherished for years. All the resources of diplomacy and of geographical reasoning were used, therefore, to limit the effect of the bull. John II, having failed to move the pope, opened direct negotiations with Ferdinand and Isabella. He accepted the bull of demarcation, *Inter caetera*, as a basis for discussion, but asked that the boundary line be moved 270 leagues farther west. The Spanish monarchs, secure in the delusions which Columbus had fostered concerning the western route to India, agreed; both sides must in any case have realised that so vague a boundary could not be fixed with accuracy, and each thought that the other was deceived. Both sides, moreover, were anxious to avoid open conflict. The Treaty of Tordesillas was duly signed in 1494, a signal diplomatic triumph for Portugal, confirming to the Portuguese not only the true route to India, but the whole of the South Atlantic with the imaginary land of Antilla and the real land of Brazil; though probably that was not known, even in Lisbon, at the time.

Columbus was back in the West Indies long before the treaty was signed. He left Cadiz in September 1493 in command of a large fleet, ships, caravels and pinnaces, seventeen sail in all. The composition of the fleet, no less than the instructions which the admiral carried, indicated the purpose for which it was sent. It contained no heavily armed fighting ships; it carried no trade goods, other than the small truck normally taken to West Africa for barter with savages. Its chief cargo was men—

twelve hundred people, priests, gentleman-soldiers, artisans, farmers—and agricultural stock—tools, seeds and animals; a whole society in miniature. The immediate object of the voyage, then, was not to open a new trade or to conquer oriental kingdoms, but to settle the island of Hispaniola, to found a mining and farming colony which should produce its own food, pay for the cost of the voyage by remitting gold to Spain, and serve at the same time as a base for further exploration in the direction of India or Cathay. There had been no lack of volunteers. The talk of gold in itself was enough to attract them. For men-at-arms, unemployed through the decline of private war and the fall of Granada, the Indies offered adventurous service, plunder, and the possibility of landed ease. For humbler folk there was the hope of escape from the harsh uplands of Castile, overrun by the privileged flocks of the Mesta, to a place where soil and climate were kind and native labour cheap and plentiful. The fleet was fitted out under the orders of Juan Rodríguez de Fonseca, archdeacon of Seville, who was to have a long and influential connection with the Indies. Columbus complained bitterly of Fonseca, whom he thought obstructive and dilatory. Sea-going commanders are often impatient of the red tape of dock-yard administration, and the two men seem to have disliked one another personally. In fact, the fitting-out was done with great efficiency and remarkable speed: five months was a very short time for the preparation of so large a fleet in fifteenth-century Spain. Fonseca's only serious mistake was failure to provide the colony with enough food for the first year; over-optimism about the extent to which Europeans could live off the country in the tropics was a common feature of these early explorations, and was one of the chief causes of the difficulties which Columbus encountered.

The fleet made a prosperous passage and a good landfall, at Dominica, and passed along the beautiful arc of the lesser Antilles, through the Virgin Islands, past Puerto Rico, to the north coast of Hispaniola. There Columbus's good fortune ended. The settlement of Navidad, planted on the first voyage, had been wiped out; in selecting as a site for his second settlement the unprotected, unhealthy shore which he named Isabela, Columbus made his first serious blunder. Isabela never prospered. It would have taken a leader of commanding genius to maintain discipline among those early Spanish settlers—touchy, adventurous and greedy as they were—to compel them to clear the forest, build houses, and plant crops, instead of roaming about the island in search of gold or of slaves. Great explorer and sea commander, brilliant navigator though he was, Columbus had neither the experience nor the temperament of a successful colonial governor. He was, moreover, a foreigner and the son of an artisan tricked out with an empty title and a new coat of arms. It soon became a question whether he and his officers could keep his men in hand until the relief fleet arrived.

The search for India could not be delayed, however, and after sending some of the most troublesome away to explore the interior, Columbus again set sail with three caravels, to explore the south coast of Cuba and to discover Jamaica. On his return to Isabela, he found his people weakened by sickness and at open enmity with the natives. The Tainos, unwarlike gatherers of roots and shellfish, lacking all but the most rudimentary agriculture, armed with feeble tools and weapons of wood or stone, had been exasperated to the point of war by incessant demands for food and women. Columbus turned upon the Indians, hunted them through the forest with armed men and savage dogs, and imposed upon them a poll-tax of gold dust which they could not pay. The captives in this pitiful warfare were enslaved. Columbus shipped some hundreds to Spain, where most of them died. The remainder were released and sent back by the orders of the queen, so that even the slave trade brought no profit. Meanwhile, at Isabela, the surviving Indians left their land untilled, and famine threatened the Spaniards who remained in the wretched fever-ridden camp.

Matters were in this state when, in the spring of 1496, Columbus sailed for Spain to deal with the complaints which had been carried there by malcontents from Isabela. In his absence, but with his approval, his brother Bartolomé, whom he left in charge, organised the removal of the settlement from Isabela to a better site on the south coast. There, in 1496 or 1497, the colonists began to build the town of Santo Domingo, which was to be for half a century the capital of the Spanish Indies, and which survives as a thriving city today.

The Catholic monarchs still trusted Columbus. With their support and at their expense he returned to the Indies in 1498; but this time there were few volunteers and men had to be pressed, or released from prison, to sail with the admiral. Columbus sailed to the south of his former course, to discover the island of Trinidad and the mouths of the Orinoco, by far the largest river then known to Europeans, whose great volume of fresh water proved the new-found coast to be part of a mighty continent. By ill-luck he missed the pearl-bearing oyster-beds off the Venezuelan coast, but sailed directly north from Margarita, by a remarkable feat of navigation, to Hispaniola, to the new city which his brother had founded.

At Santo Domingo Columbus found half his settlers, under the *alcalde* Francisco Roldán, in open revolt against the authority of Bartolomé. Columbus could not, or did not, suppress the revolt by force, but bought off Roldán and his followers by concessions—pardon, restoration to office, and free land grants. Besides consenting to these humiliating terms, the admiral made at this time another and more significant concession to the rebels, the division of the Indians of the island among the Spanish settlers as servants and estate labourers. This *repartimiento* system later became general in a modified form throughout the Spanish

Indies. Forced labour, together with smallpox and measles, accelerated the decline in numbers of the native peoples of the Greater Antilles; but for the time the arrangement served its turn in pacifying the leaders of the rebellion, and Columbus was able to suppress subsequent minor Spanish revolts with a severity probably overdue. The damage was done, however. Where Columbus's policy had been weak, malcontents returning to Spain were able to represent it as tyrannical. In the spring of 1499 the sovereigns appointed Francisco de Bobadilla to supersede Columbus and to investigate the complaints against him. Bobadilla sent the admiral home in irons. Though his sovereigns restored his title and property and treated him with all courtesy to the end, Columbus was never again allowed to exercise his offices of admiral and viceroy or to interfere in the government of his island of Hispaniola.

The real beginnings of settled government in the Indies date from the arrival of Bobadilla's successor, Frey Nicolás de Ovando, knight commander of Alcántara, who governed Hispaniola for six years with a severity far harsher than Columbus had ever dared to exercise. Discipline, indeed, was what the settlers chiefly needed. As for the Indians, Ovando secured a royal decree in 1503 giving legal form to the *repartimientos* begun by Columbus. From the subjugated Indians the invaders exacted tribute and forced labour in return for conversion and protection. Against the wild Indians they waged relentless war. Probably the Tainos were doomed already, and Ovando's severities only hastened their extinction. Nevertheless, during his time, Spanish landholders achieved a modest prosperity, pasturing great herds of pigs and horned cattle upon open ranges, and growing yams, cassava, and even a little sugar cane, which they ground in horse- or water-mills. Oviedo gave the number of mills in his time as twenty-four, which represented a considerable capital investment. The production of gold from the streams of Hispaniola also increased steadily, and reached in the second decade of the sixteenth century a quantity sufficient to attract the interest and the cupidity of Ferdinand and his advisers.

Lack of labour was the chief hindrance to the development of Hispaniola. The settlers resorted to slave-raiding in the Bahamas in order to replace the dying Tainos, and a little later negro slaves began to be imported in small numbers from the Portuguese factories in West Africa; but there was never enough labour. To men of the temperament of the early Spanish settlers land was useless without hands to work it; even gold mining was tedious work which called for unskilled labour. It was lack of labour, as much as greed for gold, missionary zeal, or simple restlesness, which drove many Spaniards on from Hispaniola to settle in other islands and mainlands, where the native population might prove more numerous and more hardy. Hispaniola became, as its founders had intended, the base for further exploration and the source of bacon, dried beef and cassava bread to victual the exploring expeditions which sailed out in ever-increasing numbers during the government of Ovando's successor, the old admiral's son Diego Colón.

In 1509 Juan de Esquivel began the settlement of Jamaica, or at least of the area round New Seville, near what is now St Ann's Bay, where Columbus had beached his worm-riddled caravels five years before. Jamaica yielded no precious metals. It supported a small population of Spaniards who lived by cattle-ranching, but was never of much importance in Spanish times. The much larger enterprise of settling Cuba was undertaken in 1511, by Diego Velásquez, who had been lieutenant-governor of Hispaniola under Ovando. Velásquez, like Ovando, was a disciplinarian and an administrator of considerable ability. With a small force of personal followers he put down native resistance and occupied the whole island within three years. He showed unusual skill and foresight in selecting the best localities for the establishment of Spanish settlements; during the first five years of his governorship he founded seven towns, and though both the names and precise sites of several of them changed more than once, they all survived in the districts where they were founded. Cuba produced considerable quantities of gold, and being both more fertile and less mountainous than Hispaniola it offered better opportunities for ranching, tobacco farming and sugar planting. As in Hispaniola the labour for mines and farms was procured in the early years by the *repartimientos* of the native population. Cuba attracted many settlers from Hispaniola, and for a time at least Velásquez succeeded in making himself practically independent of the governor of the older colony.

The fourth major island settlement, that of Puerto Rico, which began in 1512, was less immediately successful. Intrusive groups of Caribs from the Lesser Antilles had already established themselves in Puerto Rico, and offered a much more formidable resistance to the Spaniards than the natives of Hispaniola had done. The attention of the first governor, Juan Ponce de León, was moreover divided between the island itself and the peninsula of Florida, where he made an unsuccessful attempt to settle in 1514. The settlement of Puerto Rico, in consequence, was slower, more sanguinary and less complete than that of the other islands, and the colony never attracted large numbers of Spaniards in the sixteenth century.

While the Greater Antilles were thus being subdued and settled, other longer, more dangerous and more speculative expeditions were sailing from Hispaniola to explore the mainland coasts of the Caribbean. Even during the admiral's lifetime, his monopoly of exploration of 'islands and mainlands' had been infringed several times, with the connivance of the Crown. In 1499 Vicente Yáñez Pinzón, former captain of the caravel *Niña* and companion of Columbus, in a notable and courageous voyage, had coasted northern Brazil and found the delta of the Amazon.

Alonso de Hojeda, also an old companion of Columbus and a constant source of trouble to him, in the same year had followed up the admiral's third voyage to the Gulf of Paría, explored the coast of Venezuela and discovered the valuable pearl fishery of Margarita. With him had sailed Amérigo Vespucci, whose ready pen and sound geographical judgment were to bring him a fame which for a time eclipsed that of Columbus himself. The little island of Cubagua became the site of the Spanish settlement of New Cadiz, founded to exploit the pearl fishery. For about twenty-five years, until over-fishing destroyed its source of wealth, New Cadiz was one of the most prosperous places in the Caribbean, and the centre of a thriving and very brutal trade in slaves to serve as divers.

More permanent, and more significant for the future, were the settlements in Central America, on the isthmus coast which Columbus had found on his fourth voyage and where the Columbus family later held their only mainland possession, the little duchy of Veragua. The shores of the Gulf of Darien had been visited in 1500 by Rodrigo de Bastidas, accompanied by Columbus's old pilot and cartographer Juan de la Cosa. In 1504 de la Cosa carried out a more thorough exploration, in which Amérigo Vespucci also took part. Their reports decided the Crown in favour of mainland settlement, and, despite the protests of Diego Colón, two licences were issued, one to Diego de Nicuesa for the settlement of Veragua, the other to Alonso de Hojeda for what is now the north coast of Colombia. The two expeditions, which sailed at the end of 1509, numbered together over a thousand men, but hunger, sickness and poisoned arrows soon killed all but a few score. This was the most serious loss which the Spaniards had suffered in America up to that time, and one of the earliest casualties was Juan de la Cosa, whom Spain could ill spare. Reinforcements eventually arrived, under the command of one of the judges in Hispaniola, Martín Fernández de Enciso; but the real leadership devolved, by common consent, upon a popular desperado, Vasco Núñez de Balboa. Balboa had the advantage of local knowledge, having sailed with Bastidas in 1500; he was decisive, unscrupulous, and no respecter of persons. He shipped Enciso back to Hispaniola (Hojeda had gone already), turned Nicuesa adrift to drown, and assumed command of the whole enterprise. Balboa was the first of the great *conquistadores* of the American mainland, and Oviedo, who knew him well, is a convincing witness of his courage, his ability, and—by the admittedly savage standards of that time and place—his humanity. He founded the city of Darien; he achieved an ascendency over the Indians of the isthmus by a combination of force, terror, conciliation and diplomacy; he collected from them great quantities of both food and gold, but at the same time compelled his own people to make provision for the future by building houses and planting crops. Most important of all, in 1513, following up an Indian report, he led an expedition through the dripping forests of the isthmus to the shores of the Pacific.

Balboa's discovery not only revealed to Europeans the existence of the 'South Sea'; it revealed also how narrow a strip of land separated the two oceans, and so gave a new encouragement to those who hoped to find a strait through Central America and a westward all-sea route to the East. It was partly that hope which prompted the exploration of the Caribbean coasts of the isthmus, and, as soon as boats could be built, the Pacific coast also. The conquest of Central America was thus in a sense an incident in the race between Spaniards and Portuguese to reach the East. In the same year (1513) that Balboa crossed the isthmus, the first Portuguese ships reached the Moluccas. In the same year (1519) that Cortés landed in Mexico, Magellan sailed on the voyage which was to reveal both the true western route to the East, and the daunting size of the Pacific. Magellan's voyage also revealed that the Spaniards had lost the race; but in Central America they had a reward of a different sort. Though they failed to find a strait, they founded a great empire.

Both as a discoverer and as an architect of empire, Balboa deserved well of his comrades and his king; but, like Columbus, he suffered from the tale-bearing of enemies who returned to Spain. The king was understandably concerned over the loss of Nicuesa and Juan de la Cosa, and resented the affront to his authority in the person of Enciso. Balboa's report on the discovery of the Pacific, supported by samples of pearls and gold, arrived too late to affect the royal decision; the first royal governor of Darien, appointed in 1513, was not Balboa, but Pedro Arias de Avila, the terrible old man whom his contemporaries called *furor Domini*. Pedrarias drove on with great energy the work of exploration and settlement, but abandoned entirely Balboa's policy of conciliating the Indians and undid much of Balboa's constructive work. He and his captains ruled, exploited and devastated the isthmus for sixteen years. Balboa himself fell victim to Pedrarias's jealousy; he was tried on a charge of treason in 1519 and beheaded.

The appointment of Pedrarias as governor of Darien, though disastrous in itself, marked a new determination on the part of the Crown to control the activities of its subjects in the Indies. Ferdinand had already set aside the claims of the Columbus family on the mainland; he now made it clear that authority in those settlements was to reside in officers appointed by the Crown and not in self-appointed leaders. Already in the islands there was a recognised organisation for carrying the royal will into effect. A court of appeal had been established at Santo Domingo in 1511, a fore-runner of the *audiencias* of school-trained lawyers which were later to exert so profound an influence on the government of the empire; and although the authority of Diego Colón did not extend to the mainland, the appellate jurisdiction of the *audiencia* did. In the same year, 1511, a standing committee of the council of Castile had been appointed in Spain to advise the king on the government of the Indies. Its chairman was Juan Rodríguez de Fonseca, whose bureaucratic methods had so irritated Columbus. On the financial side, the *Casa de la Contratación* had been established at Seville as early as 1503 to regulate trade with America; and as each new settlement was founded, royal officials were appointed to protect the financial interests of the Crown. It was in such a capacity that Oviedo accompanied Pedrarias to Panama.

One of the most urgent tasks of the young administration was to regulate the relations between conquering Spaniards and conquered Indians. The reaction against the reckless exploitation of the natives in the islands began with a Christmas sermon preached by Fray Antonio de Montesinos at Santo Domingo in 1511, which gave great offence to Spaniards in the island and caused a considerable stir in Spain. Montesinos was sent home by his fellow Dominicans to plead the cause of the Indians at court, and after much deliberation the king's advisers produced the Laws of Burgos of 1512, the first European colonial code, which among a mass of detailed regulation enunciated three clear principles: the Indians were free men, not slaves; they were to be converted to Christianity by peaceful means, not by force; and they were to be made to work. The *repartimiento* or *encomienda* system introduced by Columbus and regularised by Ovando was to be continued, but the demands of labour and tribute made upon Indians by Spaniards were limited, and the *encomenderos* were to carry out their side of the bargain (protection and religious instruction) and to observe a whole series of rules designed to prevent ill-treatment. This definition of native rights was, for the Dominican agitators, unsatisfactory and inadequate; but at least the Crown had admitted by a formal enactment that the Indians had rights, and thereafter the royal conscience was not allowed to slumber. Montesinos, having made his protest, relapsed into silence, so far as is known; but other religious took up his work, urging better treatment and greater liberty for Indians and closer control over the Spaniards. Most prominent among these followers of Montesinos was the great Dominican missionary and polemist, Bartolomé de las Casas, whose writings and sermons were to influence the colonial policy of Spain for over half a century.

At the time of Balboa's death at the hands of Pedrarias, therefore, there existed a rudimentary system of colonial administration and the beginnings of a native policy. Both the system and the policy were soon to be applied on a scale undreamed of, to peoples more numerous and better organised than any the Spaniards had yet encountered in America. Scattered through tropical America, mainly in highland areas, were a number of distinct peoples who, though lacking wheeled vehicles and beasts of burden, and using tools of wood or stone, had nevertheless achieved a remarkable skill in some of the arts, in sculpture and building, and in handicraft industries, including the working of soft metals. Their basic crop was maize, a cereal more productive and more sustaining than the cassava of the islands; and they had brought the hoe-cultivation of maize to a high level by means of well-organised systems of communal work. Their principal settlements, adorned with stone or adobe temples and community-houses, were large enough to be called cities. In two centres at least (the valley of Mexico and the central plateau of the Andes) warlike tribes had established themselves as overlords, exacting tribute and forced labour from subject peoples over a wide area; and had set up political organisations bearing a superficial resemblance to empires or kingdoms in the Old World sense. Among Spaniards the wealth and power of these peoples lost nothing in the telling; and for pious Christians their religions had a horrible fascination, combining, as in some cases they did, messianic legends of familiar beauty with revolting rites of human sacrifice and ritual cannibalism.

None of these ancient city-builders of the New World was a sea-faring people. Their chief centres were all well inland, and for that reason the Spaniards for some years remained unaware of their existence. Even the great Maya cities of Yucatán were difficult of access from the sea. The first of the ancient 'empires' to be discovered, attacked and subjugated was that established in Central Mexico by the Aztecs, an intrusive and warlike people whose capital city, Tenochtitlán, was built upon islands in the lake of Texcoco. Over-crowding on these islands had driven the Aztecs to expand; and by a series of wars and alliances in the century before the arrival of the Spaniards they had extended their influence west and south nearly to the Gulf Coast, where Spaniards engaged in coastal exploration found the evidence of their activities and heard stories of their power.

The isthmus, Castilla del Oro, had been settled from Hispaniola. The men who explored and invaded Mexico came from Cuba, and the leading spirit in the work of preparation was the able and ambitious governor, Diego Velásquez. Velásquez's people had for some time been slave-raiding in the Bay Islands off the Honduras coast, and there perhaps found evidence of trade with the more developed cultures of the mainland. Small expeditions were sent from Cuba in 1517 and 1518 to reconnoitre the coast of Yucatán and the Gulf of Mexico. In 1519, as a result of their reports, Velásquez fitted out a much larger fleet with a view to trade and exploration, and appointed as its commander Hernán Cortés, who had been his private secretary, and was financially a partner in the enterprise. Cortés was personally popular and the project attracted a force of about 600 volunteers, a large number for that sparsely settled country. Velásquez and Cortés did not trust one another, and probably Cortés from the start contemplated the conquest of an independent kingdom. He left Cuba in clandestine haste, and upon landing lost no time in repudiating Velásquez's authority. From that moment the enterprise was Cortés's own.

The conquest of Mexico is the best known and best documented of all the Spanish campaigns in the New World. There are four surviving eye-witness accounts, of which two at least are of unusual literary and historical merit. Cortés's own letters are graphic and detailed, though inevitably affected by political considerations and by a natural tendency to represent all decisions as Cortés's own. The corrective is to be found in the *True History* of Bernal Díaz del Castillo, which tells the story from the point of view of a loyal and intelligent non-commissioned officer who happened to possess a remarkable memory. But besides being well-known and well-told, the story of the conquest represents perfectly and characteristically the three main strands in the psychological make-up of the *conquistadores*—their wolfish greed for gold, for land, and for slaves; their passionate longing to strike down the heathen and to win souls for Christ; and, more subtle but not less compelling, their love of great deeds for their own sake. It was this last feeling, this pride in doing great deeds, which made the rank and file applaud actions of their leaders which they knew to be imprudent, which held them together in the face of disaster and led them, almost without thinking, to attempt the seemingly impossible. They thought of themselves not as imitators but as equals and rivals of the heroes of ancient times; and certainly there are no stories in classical legend or medieval romance more marvellous than this conquest of a great, if semi-barbarous, empire by a handful of down-at-heel swordsmen.

Cortés landed near what is now Vera Cruz and began operations by two symbolic acts. The first was the destruction of the ships in which he had come. By so doing Cortés prevented malcontents returning to Cuba, freed the sailors to march with the army, and satisfied the *conquistador's* love of a dramatic gesture with a classical analogy. The second was the ceremonious founding of a municipality. To the magistrates of the 'town' of Vera Cruz Cortés resigned the commission he had received in Cuba; from them, as representatives of the Spanish Crown in Mexico, he received a new commission, and wrote at once to the emperor for confirmation of it. Having thus legalised as best he could his assumption of an independent command, he led his army up the long and rugged climb from the steamy jungles of Vera Cruz to the high plateau of Central Mexico.

To the modern traveller Cortés's route seems almost perversely difficult; it included two high passes, that between Orizaba and the Cofre de Perote in Vera Cruz State, and the Paso de Cortés between the twin snow peaks Popocatépetl and Ixtaccíhuatl. Neither pass carries a usable road today. The route was dictated largely by political considerations, by the need to travel as far as possible through friendly territory. Between Vera Cruz and Tenochtitlán were many *pueblos* which paid tribute unwillingly to their Aztec overlords; and one town, with its surrounding countryside, which was still holding out against the Aztecs. By a mixture of force and diplomacy Cortés was able to quicken the resentment of Cempoala and neighbouring *pueblos* into active revolt; and after sharp fighting he achieved an offensive alliance with the recalcitrant town of Tlaxcala. These friendly towns helped the Spaniards with food, with porters, with fighting auxiliaries, and, most important of all, with information. In Cempoala Cortés first heard of Quetzalcoatl, the god-hero of Toltec mythology, whose return to earth was expected by Mexican augurers about the time that the Spaniards landed. From the redoubtable warriors of Tlaxcala, Cortés must have learned much about the military strength and weakness of the Aztecs. Embassies arrived in the camp, bringing presents whose value and workmanship revealed the wealth of Mexico to the greedy eyes of the waiting Spaniards. They brought also threats and unconvincing pleas of poverty, in a hopeless attempt to dissuade Cortés from advancing on the capital. Cortés wisely sent the best of this glittering treasure home to the emperor (though some of it was intercepted by French privateers and never reached Spain). From the threats he divined the mixture of defiance and superstitious dread in the mind of the Aztec war-chief and saw the use which could be made of Montezuma's fears. Cortés's greatness largely consisted in his power of appreciating the psychological factors in the situation, and in the skill with which he built up his own prestige alike among his allies and enemies. His chief difficulty at this stage was in restraining the allies, whose notions of war were less subtle and more direct. He succeeded in this delicate task; the advance of the army was orderly and swift, and in due course the Spaniards, escorted by their Aztec hosts, marched along the causeway into Tenochtitlán in a peaceful display of martial pageantry. The Spaniards were lodged in a great community-house, or palace as they called it, in the city, while the auxiliaries camped outside, on the shore of the lake. It was remarkable evidence of Aztec powers of organisation that, in a country where all transport was on the backs of porters, so many extra mouths could be fed at such short notice.

Peace was short-lived. The first interruption was the arrival at Vera Cruz of a powerful force under Pánfilo de Narváez, one of the original conquerors of Cuba, who had been sent by the governor to apprehend Cortés. Cortés rushed down to the coast, out-manœuvred Narváez, and by a mixture of threats, bribes and promises enlisted the men from Cuba under his own command. In his absence, however, the zeal of his lieutenants in destroying heathen temples, and their incessant demands for food, had exasperated the Aztecs to the point of war. Montezuma, a discredited captive puppet in Spanish hands, could do nothing to restrain his people. A new war-chief had been elected, and Cortés's return with reinforcements precipitated the outbreak. His only mistake in the whole campaign was his re-entry into Tenochtitlán, trusting to his own prestige and to Montezuma's authority. Montezuma was stoned to death by his own people, and Cortés had to fight his way out of the city along the broken causeways by night, losing in that one night a third of his men and most of his baggage. The auxiliary tribes remained loyal to the alliance, however. The army was able to retire on Tlaxcala and re-form for a more thorough and less spectacular advance. Cortés had boats built for fighting on the lake, and laid siege to the city, cutting off its fresh water and its food supply, systematically looting and destroying it building by building and shovelling the rubble into the lake as he advanced towards the centre, until at last, in 1521, the surviving Aztecs surrendered. In the beautiful Spanish city which Cortés began to build upon the site, hardly a trace of Indian building remains. The place was built over as completely as the Roman cities of Europe, and the lake is now an arid dusty plain.

The speed of the Mexican campaign, and indeed the speed with which the *conquistadores* seized all the chief centres of American civilisation, compares with the speed of Portuguese commercial expansion in the East; but the Spanish conquest achieved far more enduring results and its success is even harder to explain satisfactorily. Generalship counted for much; but the Indians too had able leaders, and showed themselves capable at times of adapting their tactics to new conditions: they learned, for instance, to use rough ground for ambushes instead of fighting in dense masses in the open, as was their custom. The possession of fire-arms was an important, but probably not a decisive, factor. A ship carries its armament wherever it goes; but on land cannon had to be dragged over mountains and through swamps by human strength. The army with which Cortés invaded Mexico possessed only a few small cannon and thirteen muskets. Horses were perhaps more important than guns; but the Indians soon lost their fear of horses and even learned to ride them. Cortés had sixteen horses when he landed. For the most part his men fought on foot with sword, pike and crossbow. They had the advantage of steel over stone; but they were not a well-equipped European army fighting a horde of helpless savages.

The Spaniards had unbounded courage and the discipline of necessity. They had the superior toughness and endurance of a race whose principal food is wheat over a race whose principal food is maize. Being few in number they lived off the country, whereas their enemies could not easily supply large armies in the field for more than a few days. They were able to exploit some of the legends and superstitions of their adversaries in such a way as to paralyse opposition, at least temporarily. They were fighting a dominant warrior tribe which collected tribute by force or by threats and did little for its subjects in return. They had the help, therefore, of large numbers of Indian allies who, having never heard of King Log and King Stork, gleefully attacked their former overlords or rivals. Without the Tlaxcalans, Cortés could not have pulled down the buildings of Tenochtitlán. Finally the Spaniards had the advantage of their truculent missionary faith and the sublime confidence it gave. The Indian believed that his religion required him to fight and, if he must, to die bravely; the Spaniard believed that his religion enabled him to win.

Cortés showed genius, not only in holding his own men together, but in securing at least the passive loyalty of the conquered Indians. He worked so wisely that there was never afterwards any serious trouble with the natives of the plateau region. Cortés's own men, in fact, gave him more trouble than the Indians. The loot of the conquest proved disappointing; it could hardly have been otherwise, so high were the soldiers' expectations. Cortés was blamed for it, and even accused of hiding treasure for his own profit. Fortunately for Cortés, Indian society already made economic provision for rendering tribute and services to an overlord. By distributing Indian settlements in *encomienda* among his followers, Cortés enabled a new Spanish aristocracy to step into the place which the Aztecs and their allies had formerly occupied, and a new priesthood to supplant the custodians of the ancient temples. He prudently assigned a due proportion of tributary villages to the Crown; and retained for himself an *encomienda* comprising some 23,000 tributary heads of households, a princely fief. Meanwhile he found employment for the more ambitious among his officers in exploring and conquering the Maya lands in the south and in attempting to subdue the wilder tribes to the west. Alvarado, Olid, Sandoval, in imitation of Cortés, added great semi-independent provinces to the kingdom of New Spain. Many of them rivalled Cortés in courage and surpassed him in ruthlessness; none equalled him in generalship and wisdom. By 1524 this southward drive from Mexico met the northward drive from Darien, and the leaders fell to fighting. Cortés had to take the field again. His last campaign, the terrible wasting expedition to Honduras, was fought against Spaniards, in one of the savage civil wars which seemed the inevitable outcome of every great *conquista*.

The rule of the *conquistadores* was quarrelsome and brief. They had gone to America at their own expense, endured great hardships, risked their lives and fortunes, such as they were, without help from their government at home. Most of them looked forward to a pensioned retirement. Left to themselves, they would probably have settled in loose communities, employing the feudal forms which already were anachronisms in Spain, exploiting the Indians as the needs of the moment dictated, and according verbal homage but little else to the Crown. The rulers of Spain never for a moment thought of allowing such a state of affairs to persist. In the late fifteenth and early sixteenth centuries the Crown, with considerable bloodshed and expense, cut the claws of the great feudal houses, of the knightly orders and of the privileged local corporations. A growing royal absolutism could not tolerate the emergence of a new feudal aristocracy overseas. Private commanders like Cortés, Pizarro, Belalcázar and Nuño de Guzmán, who depended for their power upon their personal following, if they escaped the knives of their rivals, were soon displaced by royal nominees. Lawyers and ecclesiastics took over the direction of the empire; cattle ranchers, mining capitalists and the exporting merchants of Seville exploited its riches. In Mexico, indeed in most parts of Spanish America, the great age of the *conquistadores* ended when the principal settled areas were deemed secure. There was nothing further for them to do. Forests and empty prairies were not to their taste. Some succeeded in settling down as ranchers or *encomenderos*; some met violent ends; some like Bernal Díaz, lived on in poverty. Not one was trusted by the Crown with real administrative power. Cortés himself spent his last years in bored and litigious retirement. He was not the stuff of which bureaucrats are made.

CHAPTER XVI

EXPANSION AS A CONCERN
OF ALL EUROPE

THE discoveries of the fifteenth and early sixteenth centuries were remarkable, among other peculiarities, for the way in which geographical scholarship burst the bonds of nationalism in a strongly nationalistic age. The explorer was in almost the same class as the mercenary soldier, the painter, the sculptor or the goldsmith of that period. His approach to his problems and his technical skill were moulded by his national background; but they were at the disposal of whichever prince or country would pay for them. The Cabots were Venetians in the service of the English king; Columbus the Genoese would have served the same king most willingly, or the French or the Portuguese, instead of the queen of Castile; Verezzano the Florentine carried the French flag to the mainland of America; Magellan the Portuguese sailed in the service of Spain. In a slightly later period Henry Hudson the Londoner set out from Amsterdam in the service of the Dutch East India Company on his voyage of 1608, while later still the English Hudson's Bay Company owed its origins to the persistence and the experience of two French Canadians, Médard Chouart, sieur des Groseillers, and Pierre Esprit Radisson.

These men drew on a common fund of cartographical knowledge and of geographical surmise. There was much that was cosmopolitan, even if it was not international, in the 'Period of Discovery'. But cosmopolitan as the scientific and navigational skills might be, the direction to which they submitted and the finance to which they owed their successes, were markedly nationalistic. The purposeful organisation and the protection from intolerant ignorance, which the royal house of Avis brought to the explorers in Portugal, were a most important factor in putting that small country at the head of the movement. But Portugal was not unique in her possession of a royal house interested in the navigators and the fabulous new world of which they spoke and wrote.

Against the background of the internal struggles of the western monarchies for power and revenue, the fact that the kings readily turned to organise the cosmopolitan genius for exploration of the period calls for little remark. It was, in some sense, no more than one aspect of the general patronage of the arts and sciences which was to be expected of a prince of that day. But such patronage had a significance of its own. For it fitted into the dominant mercantilist concepts and practices of the period.

In what has come to be called mercantilism may be seen, almost from the first emergence of trade as a matter of national concern (at the end of the thirteenth century or thereabouts), a rising preoccupation with a single purpose. It was the aim of each state to make itself economically independent of potential enemies and doubtful friends. The single aim was sought in a multiplicity of ways, varying from state to state and from period to period. The manifestations of the policy may be seen in charters and privileges, monopolies and protections, controls over exports and imports, encouragements for shippers, and embargoes on luxuries. For most countries an over-riding consideration was the accumulation of bullion by means of a regulated balance of trade. The manifestations fluctuate; the aim remains constant. In consequence 'Mercantilism is so broad and so loose a term that it seems to defy definition'. It is, as nearly as it may be defined, 'a term which may be applied to those theories, policies, and practices, arising from the conditions of the time, by which the national state, acting in the economic sphere, sought to increase its own power, wealth, and prosperity'.

It was quite inevitable that events so revolutionary in their nature and so pregnant with economic possibilities as the discoveries should deflect the concepts and the practices of mercantilism into new patterns. The underlying purpose, the achievement of an economically self-sufficient and independent kingdom, had to be attained by revised arrangements in a new and wider world, a world too in which so much actual and potential wealth had been revealed as to alter all of the old balances.

Consequently the intensely nationalistic direction which had organised the discoveries, and which controlled the results of those discoveries, became by its very nature an international factor of the greatest weight. This was in part the result of the somewhat fortuitous circumstance that the early discoveries gave the wealth and power implicit in them to the Roman Catholic powers of Spain and Portugal, and that by 1580 the official title to enjoyment of both the Spanish and the Portuguese portions of the discoveries had passed to the house of Habsburg. Since the national and mercantilist ideals of all the other states of western Europe came to a point in the desire to be free in religion, in policy, in finance, from the power of Philip II, these aims became, in effect, desires to be free from power and wealth conferred by overseas possessions.

In part, however, the reorientation of the European concepts of trade and diplomacy was bound to be affected, whether the Habsburg domination were an element in the situation or not. If trade, shipping and a sea-faring population, the control of the primary commodities for manufacture, consumption and warfare, and the amassing of a hoard of bullion, were the prime objects of statecraft (as they were), then the revelation of new sources of all of these things was bound to stimulate new ambitions and new rivalries. The exploitation of the newly-revealed resources was bound to produce a new range of values, new balances of wealth and power, even without the Habsburg dominance. Yet not only the old political pattern but much of the old trade pattern remained largely unaffected by the new trade routes, new sources of wealth and of treasure.

Since it was the shrinkage of the Mediterranean trade system in the fifteenth century which gave much of the impetus to the discoveries, it may seem paradoxical to maintain that the Mediterranean and its sea-borne trade still remained the most important single element in the active commercial and maritime life of western Europe throughout the sixteenth century. But, despite the disappearance of the great Italian galley-fleets from northern ports, and the decline both of the shipping and of the general power of Florence, Venice, Genoa, and the other Italian ports, trade in general between the north and the Mediterranean increased instead of decreasing in the sixteenth century. The spices and other products of the Levant-overland contact with India and the Far East were interrupted by the Turks and Arabs, and reappeared at the termini of the new trade routes which the discoveries had opened up. But the other products of the Mediterranean trade, the cottons, wines, raisins and dates; the fine silks of Florence and the silks and glass of Venice; the sugar, cotton, silk of Sicily and North Africa; the oil, olives, wine, almonds and oranges of Iberia, the woad and wine of Toulouse, and the iron from northern Spain; all of these things flowed in larger and swifter streams. They provided some of the vital raw materials for manufactures; they catered for a more middle-class standard of comfort; and they were less conspicuously exotic and luxurious than the products of the eastern trade which the Turk had interrupted.

There came a period when even these trades were at a standstill until the battle of Lepanto reduced the menace of piracy. But for most of the sixteenth century it is true that the trade of the Mediterranean was of greater mercantile significance than that of the outer world, the Atlantic and the Indian Oceans.

Nevertheless even these trades shifted in their emphasis on localities, and that partly because of the reorientation which the discoveries brought with them. Admirably as Portugal had organised and supported the voyages to the Indian Ocean and to the Indian mainland, and so to the Spice Islands and (by accident) to Brazil, that small kingdom had neither the men, the experience nor the wisdom to regulate the settlement and trade which followed from the discoveries. The great wealth of the East Indian spice trade was hers, as long as conditions were maintained at a level which would make interlopers unprofitable. But controls and monopolies were almost inevitable in the fifteenth and sixteenth centuries, and although Turkish interruptions put an end to Mediterranean traffic in 1512 and produced a European spice famine, this merely served to accentuate the rivalry with which Portuguese East Indian trade was threatened. By the middle of the century restrictions and controls had emphasised the vulnerability of this source of wealth.

In 1514 it had been established that for Portugal colonial trade was a royal monopoly, and it was organised by royal factors on behalf of the royal family; the *Vedores da Fazenda*, set up in 1516, prepared the outward cargoes, split up and sold the return cargoes of spices and silks, and recruited troops and administrators. The chaos and overwork which resulted were not cured when, under Spanish influence, the *Vedores* were replaced by a *Conselho da Fazenda*. The East Indian trade was forced through a small number of entrepôt ports—Goa for the main spice trade of the islands and the Indian mainland, Ormuz for Arabia and the Persian Gulf, Macao for China, and Malacca for Sundas and the Moluccas—and thence was sent for Europe in closely regulated shipments, strictly limited in the number of ships and directed only to a single mart town. Trade to the west coast of Africa and trade between the different colonial areas was largely in the hands of licensed individual merchants (many of them officials), and individuals could also engage in the main trade from Goa to Lisbon on payment of heavy dues (about 30 per cent *ad valorem*). But the unmistakable feature of the Portuguese development of the trade placed within that country's power was its authoritarian but chaotic over-organisation.

Such restrictions invited the interloper, especially in view of the part which trade played in diplomacy and the weak hold which the Portuguese had on the outskirts of their supposed domains. Here the discrepancy between means and ambitions was clear, and the weak hold of the Portuguese, dependent to a large extent on early prestige and on a miscellany of treaty rights agreed with local rulers, was not capable of withstanding a European challenge.

The placing of the produce of the trade upon the European market was organised (if that be the correct word) in such a manner as to accentuate the inevitable tendency to both private and national rivalries for so rich a source of wealth. Despite the failure to establish effective government in her dependencies and to put into effect the plans of Almeida and Albuquerque, Portugal enjoyed a brief period of intense prosperity in the early years of the sixteenth century. It was a period marked by a flourishing commerce and by the complete dominance of Lisbon in the colonial trade. Originally the eastern produce had been 'uttered' through the Portuguese factory at Antwerp from 1494 onwards. But from 1549 the trade was directed to Lisbon, and from there it found its way to Antwerp by ordinary commercial channels, running the gauntlet of the administrative interferences. The great bankers of the period, especially the Fuggers, controlled the trade by the power which they wielded over the revenue of the royal house of Portugal. The result was that the spices were still marketed through Antwerp, but that administrative interference, the intervention of the *Vedores da Fazenda*, the system of entrepôts in the East and the monopoly of Lisbon in the West, all added to the costs which the merchant-bankers had to face before they began to enjoy the trade. The selling-prices ultimately bore no relation to those which could have been obtained under a more competitive system, or by non-Portuguese interlopers.

The system invited challenge both by its weakness and by its wealth. But it did nothing to bring to Portugal ability to defend its treasure. For Portuguese public revenue the climax was reached when in the financial crisis of 1569 Sebastian was unable to meet his bills and was forced to suspend payment at Antwerp. The more general picture of the failure to exploit is given by John Wheeler in his *Treatise of Commerce* at the end of the century. 'First, for the Portingall, we know, that like a good simple man, he sayled everie yeare full hungerly (God wot) about 3 parts of the earth almost for spices, & when he had brought them home, the great rich purses of the Antwerpians, subjects of the King of Spain, ingrossed them all into their own hands, yea oftentimes gave money for them before hand, making thereof a plaine Monopoly.' Wheeler, as secretary of the Merchant Adventurers of England, was not without prejudice where Antwerp was concerned, but his picture of the way in which the Portuguese spice trade served to enrich Antwerp and to give to that city a dominance in European trade is not overdrawn.

The Spanish possessions in the New World differed from those belonging to Portugal in that they required settlement rather than trade to produce wealth. That, at least, was the first conclusion to which the Spaniards came, and Columbus on his third voyage set out the conditions of colonisation. But the agricultural produce which was the first fruit of Spanish colonisation was of little value in a Europe which was itself predominantly agricultural. It was not until the rapid penetration of the *conquistadores* revealed the great mineral wealth at Spain's disposal that the Spanish possessions became anything like as important in the European economy as were those of Portugal.

Ferdinand and Isabella rehabilitated their impoverished domains, fought their wars and reconstituted royal authority, by means of absorbing the grand masterships of the great military orders, by restrictions on the privileges and revenues of the nobles, by harmony with the urban elements of the *Hermandad*, taxation of the clergy, taxation through the cortes of Castile, and the *alcabala*. The period of the Catholic monarchs was one of magnificent achievement, but it was not a period from which the monarchy emerged solvent even though the system of finance in Castile was more advanced than in any other European country, and Isabella had achieved serious retrenchment. The queen was forced to pawn her jewels to raise loans for the war against the Moors in 1489 and, though in her last will she ordered that the unallocated revenues of her kingdom should be used for debt redemption, this was not carried out and Spain came into the sixteenth century as a monarchy whose resources were deeply pledged and whose revenues could ill support the drain which any attempt to govern effectively, let alone to play a leading role in Europe, would entail.

Revenue was largely derived from the kingdom of Castile. In Aragon and its dependencies the cortes were so troublesome that they were seldom summoned, and they contributed little by way of taxation. Revenue from the New World played as yet no recognisable part either in restoring royal authority in Spain or in increasing the power of Spain in Europe. Not until the 1520's did the volume of imports of precious metals from the New World reach and sustain a flow which made it a serious factor in the economic and political situation of Spain and of Europe. Significant quantities of gold had begun to arrive by the start of the century. The amount of the period 1503–5 was almost doubled by the period 1511–15, but the epoch-making increases did not begin until the 1560 period. Then the increase was more largely in silver than in gold, although gold imports also rose very considerably. By 1516 the revenue derived from his overseas possessions brought to Charles V about 35,000 ducats a year. Rapid short-term fluctuations (to 122,000 ducats in 1518 and down to a mere 6000 in 1521) make it advisable to allow more weight to long-term trends than to the figures for any particular year, or even for a period of five years. For the ten-year periods from 1538 to 1548 and from 1548 to 1558 the average yearly revenue was about 165,000 ducats, a vast increase on the 35,000 with which Charles V had started his reign. Even this figure was soon to be passed as the great silver mines were brought into production. Royal revenue derived from this source increased rapidly to over a million ducats a year, and for most of the reign of Philip II it gradually increased to between two and three millions a year.

These were revenues which exceeded those which the Habsburgs drew from their possessions in the Low Countries. But they were only a small proportion of the wealth derived from the New World. The royal *quinto*, the fifth part of the metallic production, was often modified and at times remitted. It paid for the cost of an increasingly elaborate administrative system in Spanish America, and it paid also for the administration of the Spanish West Indian islands. Even when the *quinto* was swelled by other sources of revenue—by customs duties, sales of offices, salt, tobacco and other monopolies, tithes and other semi-ecclesiastical dues, the *alcabala* levied in the colonies, benevolences and even outright confiscations—the revenues were still often largely absorbed by the costs of administration. It was reckoned that about 50 per cent of the revenue was absorbed in this way in the fifteenth century, that towards the close of the seventeenth century about 80 per cent was so taken up; and there are years in which no revenue was remitted even from the most productive areas because it had been completely absorbed by the salaries of the viceroys and other officials.

When the amount of the revenue received in Spain has been swollen by all exactions and by the determined manner in which the mercantilist administrators extracted the bullion from the colonies and tried to keep it in Spain, and when it has been diminished by the smuggling, the piracy and the peculation to which such a trade was inevitably subject, it remains clear that Spain in the sixteenth century was receiving such quantities of bullion as to upset the balances of Europe. This was a factor in the diplomatic machinations of the period which gathered weight during the second half of the sixteenth century and which at times predominated in the seventeenth. When Charles was elected king of the Romans in 1519 it was the support of the Fuggers which enabled him to buy votes. There was only too much justification for Jakob Fugger's reminder that 'It is well known that Your Imperial Majesty could not have gained the Roman Crown save with mine aid'. The loan which the Fuggers then made was secured against the revenues of Tirol and of Spain, and it was upon the revenues of the great ecclesiastical orders of knighthood in Spain that the Fuggers had based their main business with the Habsburgs for more than a century. By contrast, as the financial crisis of the Schmalkaldic War loomed up in 1551–2, the Fuggers, who were already too deeply committed and who could not extract revenue from Spain or the Netherlands, began to turn to the gold and silver expected from 'India' as the only acceptable security for reluctant loans. When Anton Fugger stepped in and made a loan to the emperor at Villach in 1552, the last time when the Fuggers held the emperor's fate in their hands, the loan of 400,000 ducats which saved Charles from accepting the harsh terms put to him at Passau was secured entirely on Spain. Anton Fugger was in this partly inspired by loyalty to the house of Habsburg; but partly by the fact that the shipments of New World bullion to Spain were by this time getting into spate and that it had just proved possible to get large cargoes of American silver from Spain to Antwerp. The transference of such bullion from Spain to the financial centre of Antwerp was an essential part of the manœuvre, and the stoppage of this trade by Philip II entailed enormous losses for the bankers.

The extent to which the war-like capacity of the Habsburgs was based on credit advanced by great bankers against the European revenues of the house, or on actual bullion brought into Europe from the overseas territories, is impossible to estimate, for the confusion of the accountancy system adds to the difficulties. Certainly it is possible on important occasions to demonstrate that without the lure of New World bullion the credit-basis of Habsburg war-finance would have been infinitely less elastic.

The royal house, however, even when it raided the trade of ordinary merchants, normally touched only a small portion of the total trade to the

New World. In addition to that brought in as royal revenue the flow of bullion through the ordinary channels of commerce was enough to produce the purely economic results which could not well be avoided in such a period. Here the facts and the theories become intermingled. The sheer quantity of new bullion must in itself have produced great and lasting changes in society. On the other hand, the royal houses of Europe were all concerned to profit, if possible, by manipulations of the coinage, and the period is one of general but uneven debasement. Such machinations caused suspicions and inequalities in merchant practice and make any assessment of prices and price-trends doubly difficult, whilst the increased use of merchants' bills enhanced the amount of currency or pseudo-currency in circulation to an extent which exaggerated the consequences of the increase of bullion.

The first impact of the bullion was on Spain itself. There the imports of treasure have been tabulated (Earl J. Hamilton, *American Treasure and the Price Revolution in Spain*, p. 34) in five-year periods, in *pesos* equal to 42·29 grams of pure silver.

1503–5	371055·3	1551–5	9865531·0
1506–10	816236·5	1556–60	7998998·5
1511–15	1195553·5	1561–5	11207535·5
1516–20	993196·5	1566–50	14141215·5
1521–5	134170·0	1571–5	11906609·0
1526–30	1038437·0	1576–80	17251941·0
1531–5	1650231·0	1581–5	29374612·0
1536–40	3937892·0	1586–90	23832630·5
1541–5	4954005·0	1591–5	35184862·5
1546–50	5508711·0	1596–1600	34428500·5

The decade 1590–1600 was the peak until the middle years of the eighteenth century; although actual production of silver increased in the New World during the seventeenth century, it did not rise enough to overtake the increasing costs of administration, and imports into Spain showed a steady decline. Such an increase in bullion over a century as is indicated by these figures had two major results. In Spain itself, and spreading from Spain to the rest of Europe through the ordinary channels of commerce and finance, it affected the relation of bullion and coin in circulation to other goods, and so produced a price-rise. Outside of Spain it produced a policy of jealous emulation, to make the possession of some share in this bullion a necessary part of the policy of any power which would aspire to independence of Spain or to rivalry with her.

The normal economic effects of the flow of bullion were complicated by the fact that from 1519 onwards silver began to play a more important part, and completely outweighed the imports of gold during the latter half of the century. The result was that the comparatively stable relations of the two metals were upset, and the problems of adjusting bi-metallic currencies to a far more rapid and voluminous flow of the two metals were added to the difficulties of the statesmen and financiers of the age.

Since the statesmen were, on the whole, slow to appreciate that the troubles arose in large part from the sheer increase in the amount of bullion in circulation, and since they all, at various times, attempted to solve their local problems by adjustments of the mint standards (often on a provincial rather than on a national basis), the price-rise of the period is beset with subsidiary causes, with expedients which accentuated its influence, and with a wide but confusing spate of theorising. Such factors make the absolute influence of New World treasure difficult to estimate. Yet it is quite clear that the period from about 1550 to about 1600 was the period in which Spain had to adjust her economy, if possible, to the new flow of bullion after the less remarkable shipments of the first half of the century had started the processes. There, in Spain, prices began to move upwards in the years around 1519–20 and continued steadily upwards for the rest of the century, to finish five times as high as they had been at the start of the century.

From Spain the movement flowed outwards and reached its climax in western Europe towards the end of the century, but never affected prices so disastrously as those of Spain. In France by the end of the century the peak figures were only about two-and-a-half times those at the start; in England the movement started perhaps a little later than in France (about 1550) and did not reach a climax until the middle of the seventeenth century, when prices ruled at a level which was more than three times that at the start of the sixteenth century. Holland in her turn felt the influence and was forced to attempt a remedy of the consequences of the New World treasure. Charles V had decreed that all traffic with his possessions overseas should flow through Seville, so that although the Netherlands were under Habsburg rule they participated in the treasure only as a result of normal commercial intercourse, on much the same terms as did France or England. But Antwerp's importance had been vastly enhanced by the increased traffic in spices which had followed after the Portuguese discoveries and she was the undoubted centre of the financial world of the sixteenth century. There the great bankers had their principal houses; there the conditions of the loans which dominated the diplomacy of the period were laid down. It was by shipments of specie from Spain that the Habsburg credit at Antwerp was maintained, and the intense commercial activity of that city inevitably enhanced the natural results of the bullion shipped there. The high point of the commercial predominance of Antwerp was about the middle years of the century, and by that time the general level of prices there was higher than in France or England. The contemporary description of Guicciardini puts the cost of house-room at Antwerp higher than anywhere else in Europe except in Lisbon, and English representatives found the cost of living there twice as dear as in France.

Suffering though she was (according to modern diagnosis) from a surfeit of precious metals, Spain strove strenuously to keep them from being exported. This has been denied, but there can be no serious doubt that Spanish policy was mercantilist in its broadest sense, in that commerce was used as a means of bringing political and diplomatic pressure to bear on other states; and it was mercantilist in its narrower, bullionist, sense in that strict measures were enacted to secure the accumulation within that country of as large a hoard of bullion as possible. The normal trade with the Spanish colonies was reserved to Spain and the export of gold and silver to foreign countries was forbidden. Such measures proved not only useless but disastrous; they enhanced in Spain the dearth of goods in relation to bullion which was the chief result of the bullion shipments. Thus by the middle of the sixteenth century the rise of prices in Spain was ascribed in part to the export of goods to the colonies; the remedy was to forbid exports of Spanish goods since the colonies had enough raw materials to satisfy their own needs. So trade and industry in Spain suffered a loss of markets, her economy rapidly became unable to answer even her own requirements, and more and more Spain came to be dependent on a trade system in which she bought her requirements from the rest of Europe, and paid the bulk of the purchase price in New World treasure. The practices which applied to Spain herself applied even more to the New World possessions, where the ban on trade with aliens was evaded in many ways, often by the intervention of a Spaniard to 'colour' the goods as though they were his own. Ships from the Hanseatic cities brought to Seville textiles and other goods from the Baltic and from England, and as the pattern of seventeenth-century trade developed, French vessels came to dominate the Seville-New World market, closely followed by the Genoese and the Dutch. By 1691 it was estimated that each year the French traded about twenty million *livres*-worth of goods to Seville, of which about twelve million went to the New World. Of the return cargoes the French took about fourteen millions, the Dutch share was about ten millions and the English about six or seven millions.

So, despite the policy pursued, the Spanish government was unable to contain within that country either the good or the evil results of the new flow of treasure. Both the sheer bulk of treasure and the changes in the relative supplies of gold and silver had their reactions outside of Spain. From the Spanish point of view this meant that the picture of the outcome of the Portuguese spice monopoly was now repeated. Whereas the Portuguese had toiled 'full hungerly' about three parts of the world in order to bring home spices to enrich the great rich purses of the Antwerpers, the Spaniard now felt that 'All that the Spaniards bring from the Indies, acquired after long, prolix and hazardous navigations, and all that they harvest with blood and labour, foreigners carry off to their homelands with ease and comfort'.

The results of such an expansion of the effects of the treasure were by no means entirely bad. But they were disruptive. Thereon has been built one of the strongest arguments for the thesis of the 'profit inflation' in European economic history. It is the mark of a 'profit inflation' that prices are running away from costs of production, so that the class which organises and lives by the sale of goods (the entrepreneur) reaps the profit and there is, according to the length and depth of the inflationary movement, a change in the balance of society in which the entrepreneurs become more wealthy and powerful at the expense of the landowners on the one hand and of the wage-earners and producers on the other hand. Circumstances in Spain led to the new purchasing power going in the first instance to the aristocratic and ruling classes, so that they bid up wages and created in that country an 'income inflation' rather than a 'profit inflation'. The new bullion reached the other countries of western Europe, however, by the avenues of trade and finance, and there the merchants selling to the treasure-glutted Spanish market made the enormous profits which are the hall-mark of the economic history of the period. There the great fruits of the economic progress of the period accrued to the profiteer rather than to the wage-earner or the landowner. The 'profit inflation' is held to have lasted in England from 1550 to 1650, and in France from 1530 to 1700, with wages in England and France declining in purchasing power as the period wore on.

This result of the spread of the New World bullion not only produced a noteworthy change in the balance of society. It also produced a rapid and stimulating growth of capital and a corresponding spirit of enterprise in the merchant and manufacturing elements in the western states. Not least among the manifestations of this spirit was the widespread growth of new industrial techniques and of new methods of financing them. This is the age of the so-called 'Industrial Revolution of the sixteenth century', and there can be no reasonable doubt that the new bullion played its part in inspiring and in financing the technical improvements, the enlargements of the unit of production and the marketing expansions of the age. There was an 'atmosphere of buoyancy, exhilaration and freedom from economic cares' which led to crisis and to hardships, but which was also a requisite for the economic and the cultural vivacity of the sixteenth century.

The nationalist reactions to the Habsburg possession of the sources of the new bullion fitted in well with this spirit, and much of the anti-Habsburg nationalism of the period has no other theme than that of disputing the wealth of the New World with the Spaniards. It was a theme made more urgent by the accession of Philip to the throne of Portugal in addition to that of Spain, in 1580. Thus both portions of the New World (as divided between Spain and Portugal by the bull *Inter Caetera* in 1493, or subsequently and more effectively by the Treaty of Tordesillas) came into the possession of the same threateningly predominant Power.

Western Europe felt, as the younger Hakluyt wrote, that the threat of 'the peril that may ensue to all Princes of Europe if the King of Spain be suffered to enjoy Portugalle with the East Indies is soche as is not on sodden to be set down'.

The Spanish economy was such that, in any case, she was forced to rely on the rest of Europe for manufactures both for herself and for her colonies, and so to allow her treasure to find its way to the markets of Europe. Her predicament was enhanced by two serious defects which were natural and geographical, not the result of her own mercantile system. These were her lack of naval stores and her lack of West African possessions. Burghley was convinced in the Armada year that Spain, without masts, boards, cables, cordage, pitch, tar and copper from the 'Eastlands' (the Baltic), could not transport the smallest army of invasion. Therein lay a grave weakness, which made it essential that Spain should stand in good credit in Antwerp, the seat of the Baltic trade, and which laid her open to raids such as crippled her when sixty Hansard ships were captured at the mouth of the Tagus. This lack of naval stores was a general problem in the Age of Mercantilism, one from which England suffered as much as Spain, and which made the Baltic States and the merchants who dominated their trade unduly important in the diplomacy of the period. More peculiar was the dependence of the Spanish empire on extra-Spanish trade for slave labour.

Christopher Columbus as the first coloniser had brought, on his third voyage to the West Indies, a strange mixture of would-be settlers. Despite the close scrutiny of the *Casa da Contratación* at Seville, many undesirables accompanied him and still more followed him. Emigration as a means of solving the problems of the European economy was both unnecessary and undesirable in terms of the problems set by the sixteenth-century statesmen. Spain, for example, had a population of only about eight millions at the end of the century, France of perhaps sixteen millions, England about five millions; Portugal had only about a million, and the Netherlands less than three millions. These figures were indeed tending to mount in the course of the century, especially in the denser centres of population—in the cities from which most of the exiguous statistical material derives. It is difficult to ascertain from actual evidence whether the sixteenth century was a period of increase or decrease in population in western Europe. On the whole it was probably a period of increase, but not of such increase as to make the peopling of the newly-discovered empty spaces of the world by Europeans either desirable or possible. Any such movement towards large-scale emigration would in any case have been clean contrary to one of the major tenets of the statesmen of the period; for next after bullion sturdy infantry soldiers were the main defence of a country, unless it happened to be an island, in which case seamen were the objects of attention.

Neither in fact nor in theory, therefore, could the peopling of the New World be accomplished by the Old World. There arose a conflict of purpose between a desire to send out only suitable colonists and an acceptance of the colonists who offered. In fact numbers were small, women emigrants were scarce and generally unprincipled, and men were anxious to make fortunes and return to spend them rather than to make homesteads and enjoy them. From the start the Spaniards had recourse to native labour. The Indians of New Spain could be got to work so cheaply that poor young men from Old Spain could not get work, 'For the Indian will live all the week with less than one groat, which the Spaniard cannot do, nor any man else'. Even if working men could have been provided in adequate numbers, competition with Indian labour on a wage basis, still more competition on a basis of forced labour or of slavery, made emigration unattractive save for those who did not propose to engage in heavy labour.

The exhaustion of the Carib and Indian labour and the recourse to negro slave labour had been a constant preoccupation of the Spanish authorities from the start. The first shipment of negro slaves was made in 1503 and was followed by a constant traffic. Until 1515 they were bought from the Portuguese at Lisbon; then they were shipped direct from the Guinea Coast, and from 1517 onwards the trade was worked under a system of permits, or *asientos*, allowing alien merchants to supply this defect in the Spanish imperial economy. The *asiento*, however, merely gave a monopoly of this vital trade to the concessionaire; it did not supply labour in the quantity or at a price to satisfy the colonist. So a slave trade in despite of authority developed, which was certainly a smuggled trade and was at all times little distinguished from piracy.

The most celebrated incidents in the early years of this trade are the three voyages of John Hawkins of Plymouth. His first voyage, of 1562, left him the wealthiest man in Plymouth, his second voyage of 1564 left him the wealthiest man in England, and his third voyage of 1567 led to the fight at St Juan d'Ulloa and to the intensification of the privateering raids on Spanish commerce which developed into open naval warfare between England and Spain.

Hawkins's ventures are outstanding, but they are not unique. The underlying factors were that Spain could not supply her colonists with goods or with labour; neither could she create such a barrier of sea-power and administrative efficiency as to exclude other Powers from the dominions which she claimed. There was a reputable colony of English merchants in Seville and other Spanish ports whose business was to trade to Spain the goods which the colonies required, for onward shipment in the annual Spanish *flotas*; there were many voyages to the Guinea Coast made by both French and English merchants; and the Spanish possessions and shipping in the Caribbean were the constant prey of

French privateers, many of them Huguenots. Organised and fitted out by the great *armateur* of Dieppe, Jean Ango, the French had throughout intercepted the Spanish treasure. In particular the great Jean Fleury early developed the plan of lurking off Cape St Vincent or the Azores for the returning Spanish fleets; there in 1522-3 he intercepted the first treasures sent by Cortés from the conquest of Mexico, and thence the French derived a series of charts by use of which they preyed increasingly on Spanish trade to the New World. Hawkins hoped at one stage to profit from these French depredations, half a century old and still in constant practice by this time, by selling protection to the Spaniards in return for trading privileges. The negotiation came to nothing, and the wealth of the Indies, in this instance as in so many others, merely added to the many causes which were setting the Powers of Europe at logger-heads during the sixteenth century.

Thence arose deep disputes on problems of international law. For French and English and Dutch in their turn, as they claimed a right to trade across the seas and a right to explore where Spaniards and Portuguese had not yet penetrated, were all compelled to put forth a doctrine which, whatever the form of words used, challenged the right of the Habsburgs and the competence of the Papacy. The denial came to much the same concept of freedom of trade and navigation, whatever the nation which uttered it. For the English the classic exposition (out of many which were put forth) came in a protest that the English were excluded from commerce with the West Indies *contra jus gentium*. The papal title to possession was not accepted; the use of the air and of the sea was claimed as common to all mankind, and the Spaniards were told that 'Prescription without possession availeth nothing'—their claims would only be accepted where they were re-enforced by effective occupation. The French, in similar terms, protested that 'In lands which the King of Spain did not possess they ought not to be disturbed, nor in their navigation of the seas, nor would they consent to be deprived of the sea or the sky'.

These were profound challenges, based on legal doctrine. The effective motive in the matter was the wealth of the Indies and the challenge presented to merchants, explorers, governments and patriots by the exclusive claims and the inefficient administration of the Spaniards. Too much, however, can easily be made of the inefficiency of Spanish colonial administration, for in face of the difficulties of travel, the novelty of the problems, the lack of trained staff and the inroads of opponents, they made a most notable contribution to the art of colonial government and retained an outstanding proportion of the profits of empire. It was the administration of metropolitan Spain, rather than of the colonial empire, which provoked the challenge, by its attempts to preserve the bullion imports within a Spain which could not supply the colonists with their wants. Such a policy could not be maintained in the face of competition from other states which commanded the resources to supply the demand and the sea-power to deny the prohibitions. Two considerations bring out this incompatibility; by the second half of the sixteenth century the high prices, high wages and general attractions found in Spain drew regular trains of Frenchmen across the Pyrenees to earn some capital from the treasures of the Indies. These 'fleas living on Spain' were not only French, though it was estimated that there were ten thousand French workmen in the kingdom of Valencia alone in 1548; Italians and other peoples shared in the immigration despite the fears of depopulation and the difficulties conjured up by their own governments, and contemporary accounts describe a Spain in which it would be hard to find artisans if strangers were not admitted. The evidence is not statistically accurate, but it leaves a clear impression that Spain herself offered terms of employment which attracted aliens and allowed them to drain her treasure. The new treasure had created a labour market in Spain which neither her own nor her rivals' legislation could confine within her boundaries.

A second factor to be borne in mind in considering the Spanish position as the monopolist of the new treasure is that at the time of Hawkins's second voyage, in 1565, Elizabeth of England was by no means firmly opposed to Spain. The serious threats to her position at that time came rather from France and Mary Queen of Scots, with French support, than from Spain—so much so that one of the terms which Philip had imposed on France at Cateau Cambrésis had been an acknowledgment of Elizabeth's right to the English throne. Yet Elizabeth allowed herself to share in Hawkins's outfit and in the profits of the venture; and until the Spanish attitude hardened in the succeeding years there was great hope that Hawkins might be held to have given merely an encouraging exhibition of the way in which English shipping and merchant competence could supplement and take a place within the Spanish concept of empire. Behind Hawkins's ventures lay a considerable body of diplomatic interchanges, from which it might have emerged that Spain would grant an *asiento* to the English to trade in return for facility to use English shipping to defend Spanish lands and trade against French and Moorish privateers.

These are but two outstanding aspects of the general lack of balance and of feasibility in the Spanish concepts. The incompatibility of ambitions and achievements was a common feature of Spanish imperialism, as of Portuguese; enough in itself, by its economic working, to have roused the desires of the rest of the world. When, however, such incompatibility was coupled with a severely nationalistic application of mercantilist concepts, with the attempt by Spain, not only to retain the treasure as a source of power but also to manœuvre her wider trade policy, with treasure at its centre, so as to gain dominance over the economic life and general policy of her neighbours, then the temptations to interrupt the flow of treasure gained momentum. Examples could easily be multiplied of the way in which trade policy was envisaged by Spain as a means of bringing pressure to bear on her neighbours. Exclusive possession of the newly-discovered outer world was easily taken for granted, as when Philip, not as yet himself directly concerned, nevertheless gave his opinion that English trade to the Guinea Coast should not be permitted in 1555, that being a region plainly known to be in the occupation of the king of Portugal 'so as the sayed navigation might not bee maynteyned withoute soch notable inconvenyence as wer not expedyent to bee adventured'. From feelings of exclusive possession, inexpediency and possible trouble, Spanish policy ranged to definite and purposeful intervention, as when for political reasons corn was forbidden to be exported to England in the shortage of 1555, or when in 1562 the new Spanish ambassador to London received his instructions. Elizabeth's poverty was to be fostered with all care; thus she would be forced to grant concessions in the Anglo-Flemish trade in order to get the customs revenue which could only be obtained when that trade was flourishing; and thus, being kept dependent on Spanish goodwill for the bulk of her revenue, she might be compelled to alter the religious establishment of her country.

The outward spread of the new bullion, the impact of the new range of prices, and the revision of the ratios of gold and of silver, all combined to make government finance even more difficult than formerly in all the countries trading with Spain and the Netherlands (which meant the whole of western Europe) and so to make the governments even more susceptible to the kind of economic pressures which Spain tried to exercise. The Netherlands were the centre of the financial world; there, at Antwerp, the emperor, the kings and queens of France and of England and the multitude of German princes, all raised the loans on which they depended for the internal stability and the external independence of their regimes. They could not conceivably ignore or overlook the financial conditions and concepts which dominated the money-marts of the Netherlands, and they were almost forced to work out some sort of thesis which would enable them to understand their contacts with this trade and to regulate those contacts in their own interests. Denied direct access to the new bullion at its source by the claims, and to some extent by the practices, of Spain, they turned with vigour to denials of the claims, to evasions of the rules, and to regulations of their own trades so as to mulct the Spaniard at the last.

This is the period in which both France and England are preoccupied with theories and precepts for regulating coinage, for manipulating rates of foreign exchange, for encouraging exports and for discouraging imports. There are, too, significant contributions to economic theory in attempts to encourage 'invisible exports' in the shape of shipping, marine insurance and banking. But the chief result of the situation was a deep study of the problems of coinage, and an emphatic reiteration of the already accepted concept of the balance of trade as a means of drawing the required bullion from one country to another. The best known, but by no means isolated, feature of these movements is the proposition of a 'Quantity theory' of the results of the new bullion by Jean Bodin. 'Je trouve que la charte que nous voyons vient pour trois causes. La principale et presque seule (que personne jusques icy n'a touchée) est l'abondance d'or et d'argent, qui est aujourd'huy en ce royaume plus grande qu'elle n'a esté il y a quatre cens ans', wrote Bodin in 1568 in his *Response au Paradoxe du Sieur de Malestroit*—a paradox in which debasement of the coinage was put forward as the cause of the rise of prices. Almost equally well-known, but not so easily to be understood (for the events were shrouded in some of the mysteries of diplomacy, many of the confusions of economic theory, and much personal vain-glory) were Thomas Gresham's efforts to gain for Queen Elizabeth a share of the treasure which she needed.

Gresham's career as the 'éminence grise des finances anglaises' can be taken as exemplifying the way in which the affairs of the whole of western Europe, and of Elizabethan England in particular, turned on the current of New World bullion, via Seville and Antwerp, by the middle of the sixteenth century. Of the outstanding events in his career, which key up this picture, the chief is his voyage to Seville in 1554, in search of bullion. He had been sent to Antwerp in 1552 to negotiate substantial loans from the Fuggers. He was successful, and the loans were repaid within a year, after which the needs of the emperor absorbed all the Fuggers' capacity, and in 1554 Gresham was glad to accept a loan from the Fuggers and from some Genoese, the money to be collected in Spain. Here may be seen the manner in which even England shared in the bullion flow by means of loans on the Antwerp bourse; and the limitations imposed by Spain and the precarious balance of the Spanish economy. For Gresham in Spain so used the rates of exchange and so upset the credit of the Spanish bankers, that the banks at Seville had to suspend payments and he was at one time afraid that he had precipitated a general financial crisis.

The second typical event in the career of Gresham came when, in 1565, he set to work to manipulate the rates of exchange, the comparative soundness of English coinage, and the deserved reputation which he had gained for strict business probity, in order to secure loans for Elizabeth on better terms than could be got by other monarchs. For this purpose he used the technique of mobilising the overseas credits of English merchants in order to pay off outstanding loans without setting the rates of exchange against himself, and his manœuvre was accompanied by a compensating grant of favour to those English merchants. This was the time at which the age-old privileges of the Hansard merchants in England were overridden, to the advantage of the Merchant Adventurers. There was in all of this an unmistakable emphasis on the economic unity of the State of England, the subordination of individual interests to those of the

State—and the reluctant dependence of that State on the markets, the credit and the bullion, of the Netherlands.

England, as the other countries of western Europe, found it essential to share in the wealth of the New World, and found the Antwerp marts a satisfactory way of so doing. It was a way supplemented by interloping voyages to the Spanish Main, by direct trade with Spain, and by indirect relations between the participants, each of whom attempted to keep as large a share of the bullion as possible, but each of whom was forced on occasions to allow remittances which transferred the bullion from one to the other. In effect mutual toleration ruled between Spain and her opponents to such an extent that both sides accepted the Netherlands as 'the Indies of England' and wrote of Spanish coin as the best circulating medium of France. With such close financial and trading links serving the purpose of bringing the Spanish bullion to the other countries of the West, the regulations by which each such country tried to secure, and to retain, a portion of the specie took on a new and urgent importance.

Such a system was peculiarly open to political influences, and the overriding religious purposes of Spanish policy in the Netherlands in the end broke down the system by ending the religious tolerance on which it had been based. Overmuch can be made of the advent of the duke of Alba in the Netherlands in this connection. For Cardinal Granvelle had fomented religious disputes there since his appointment in 1561, and had worked there with great effect for an intolerant religio-economic regime which would exclude heretics from trade and from the marts, and so would reduce heretic princes to conformity. The success with which he had managed to exclude English cloths from trade, on the pretext of plague in London, was plainly attributed to 'Spaniards and priests', amongst whom the 'first worker' was without doubt the cardinal, 'whom ys hattid of all men'. Alba, however, certainly perpetuated the policy of Granvelle, though there were occasions on which he showed himself less bigoted and more of an economist than the cardinal. It was with Alba's appointment that Gresham decided that English traders and financiers ought to quit the Netherlands, where men were so ready 'one to cut another's throat for matters of religion'. He himself left Antwerp in 1568. The mart of the Staple Company migrated to England after a series of unsatisfactory expedients in an attempt to find an alternative to Bruges. And the cloth mart of the Merchant Adventurers was at that time transferred from Antwerp to Hamburg, thereby removing from the Netherlands one of the key trades of sixteenth-century Europe and at the same time detaching the great and rising city of Hamburg from its allegiance to the Hanse League. Such changes inaugurate a new epoch in the trade pattern of Europe, quite apart from their peculiar importance in the economic history of England, where the export trade in wool never recovered from its divorce from the manufacturers of the Netherlands and where the already booming trade in the export of woollen cloths was confirmed in its dominant position by these changes. More important, probably, than the technically economic results of the changes were the political and diplomatic adjustments which they entailed.

Such an interruption led to a newly nationalistic organisation of the English economy, an organisation in which piracy in the Channel played an increasingly important part, giving to England that share of the treasure which she could not now get by loans and by trade in the Low Countries. The former type of piracy, nearly allied to trade, the 'piraterie à l'aimable, commerce interlope plutôt' of the early English voyages to the West Indies, gave way to the endless English robberies which provoked Councillor Viglius, after Granvelle left the Netherlands, to his heartfelt complaint 'O Lord God, we live in peace, but we sustain more damage than we should do if we had open war....The pilleries do continue still. There is no justice executed.' In 1568 a major diplomatic incident was touched off when Elizabeth decreed the arrest of a shipment of Genoese bullion, *en route* from Spain, destined to succour Alba's troops. The ships had sought refuge at Plymouth, and there Elizabeth took the treasure into 'protective custody', after which there was virtually open war at sea and the treasure route from Spain to the Netherlands could only be used by large and well-armed *flotas*, such as the Medina Celi fleet of 1572 or the larger and ineffective *flota* of the following year. English pirates were astride the route by which Spanish New World treasure reached the entrepôts of the Netherlands.

English intervention in the route by which the Netherlands 'uttered' the New World bullion was to be of vital significance to England's economy and to her diplomacy. It was to lead to that speculative mania which marked the Elizabethan period and which gave the background to the social and educational changes of the time. It was to divert much enterprise from more normal and possibly more productive commercial and agricultural pursuits; and it was to lead to a forthright challenge to Habsburg power in the Narrow Seas which, being settled, opened a new era in European history.

In these developments England was alone only because of the facts of her geographical situation. France and Portugal were alternative treasure-routes between Spain and the trade-centres of western Europe. Much went by bills of exchange and other means, and it must be accepted that the harrying of the Channel route certainly did not bar the transport of bullion by that means; but it did make it more perilous, more expensive, and less reliable.

Perhaps more important is the fact that it coincided, within a few years, with the dominance of Spain over Portugal, and the control of the spice-trade by Philip II. Hitherto the new overseas routes to the spices of the East had created crises in the spice-trade of the world, and had at times given to Portugal and to Antwerp a financial predominance which Antwerp exploited and which Portugal abused. The new conditions had never ended the older Mediterranean routes to the spices, however. Now, from 1580 onwards, the king of Spain was in control, at a time when relaxations in the monopoly of the Portuguese trade had combined with an Arab revival to give to Portugal once more a predominance which that country had earlier allowed to slip after the brief spurt of the first quarter of the century. This newly-predominant trade Philip purposefully directed away from the Channel, away from the English pirates and from the Netherlands merchants, and into the Mediterranean. In 1585, for example, he offered the contract for the Portuguese pepper trade to Venice, then to Milan, Genoa and Florence. That these cities decided not to accept the terms is evidence of their belief in the continued vitality of the Mediterranean trade to the Levant, as they knew it. Philip's policy in this instance failed, partly from suspicion of the Habsburgs. But it represented a long-term change in the weight of economic balance. Now, at last, may be seen that shift in the balance which the new trade-routes had not brought in their first flush. Now, in the last decade of the sixteenth century, not at any earlier date, may be seen the decline of the Mediterranean before the Atlantic—despite the fact that the defeat of the Armada and the consequent dominance in the Channel of the English and their satellites made pepper of Levantine origin cheaper in Europe than pepper of Portuguese origin in the immediately subsequent years.

It was, therefore, in the last generation of the sixteenth century that the impact of the New World upon Europe began to assume serious proportions and to produce lasting and fundamental changes in the balance of European interests. The gathering momentum of the changes, against the constant factor of Habsburg predominance, led to a re-phrasing of the anti-Habsburg mercantilist doctrines of the opposition countries. The first result was in a desire to alienate the Portuguese possessions from Philip. English thought fell naturally into grooves which led to the fostering of rebellion in Portugal. Thus Spain would be deprived of the treasure of the West, of her trades and merchandise, of her mariners, of victuals too. Thus, by breaking the Spanish domination and claiming a share of Portuguese trade (a share ultimately confirmed by the marriage of Charles II and Catherine of Braganza) 'may we retayne the grete masse of tresure that workes the grete effects of the worlde'. So wrote the younger Hakluyt in 1580. He was but putting into phrases the commonplace sentiments of his contemporaries.

The concept of the 'Balance of Trade' was by this time generally accepted. Disputes were not over the reality of the problem, but over the details of the means by which the desired result, the increase of bullion by a favourable balance, might be achieved. In England by 1575 an able state paper had stated the concept, had defended it, and had even struck the balance for that year. The 'Somme of the inplussing in value of the owtcarried above the inbrought commodities' was £255,214. 13s.

The 'Balance' became a strong argument (not only in England) for persistent attempts to establish a new and 'colonial' trade system, in which the overseas commodities should not be got from Spain, either by direct trade or through the Netherlands, but by direct access to colonies within the allegiance. The advantages, and the potential fruitfulness, of overseas lands were cried up. The temperate parts of North America, in particular, seemed to promise everything which could be desired, even the timber and other naval stores for which the Baltic had hitherto been the only source of supply. By settlement there, it was argued, England could rid herself of dependency on Spain for oils, 'sacks', raisins, oranges, lemons, skins; of dependency on France for woad, salt and wines, and of dependency on the Baltic lands for flax, pitch, masts and tar, 'and so shoulde we not so exhaust our treasure, and so exceedingly enriche our doubtfull friends, as we doe, but should purchasse the commodities that we want for halfe the treasure that now we do'. Here was the hard core of the English thesis, as it was developed in the last quarter of the sixteenth century. The Hakluyts were to a large extent responsible for giving such views publicity. But it would be wrong to imagine that they represented nobody but themselves. They had behind them a large number of influential statesmen, seamen, financiers and economists, and the movement overseas, half-way between piracy and settlement, absorbed so large a portion of the fluid capital of the period that it certainly retarded and possibly altered domestic agricultural and manufacturing changes. Even the inhospitable lands of Newfoundland were worked into the theme, with a heavy emphasis on fishing as a nursery for seamen, on salt as a commodity which could be manufactured instead of being bought, on the masts and spars which might be got from the forests, and on the low cost of the goods which would need to be taken out from England.

Equally clear were the objectives of the French or of the Dutch, and equally clear the need to defy or evade the Spanish government if anything was to be accomplished. French attempts, based largely on the interests and enterprise of the fishing population of the Breton coast, were directed more to the northern territories of the American continent than were the English. They were attracted to the Grand Banks of Newfoundland, and they were fishermen rather than explorers or settlers. As early as 1510 the cod fishery was methodically organised, with a central market at Rouen. Yet the Norman Gonneville spent six months ashore in Brazil in 1505, and after him a succession of French captains practised a mixture of trade and piracy on the coasts of Brazil.

It was the Florentine Verezzano who firmly settled the French in their peculiar approach to the problems of the New World, with his 1524 cruise along the coast of North America from North Carolina to

Newfoundland. His last voyage was intended to discover some way round the continental land-mass which he acclaimed. He did not succeed, but he paved the way for Jacques Cartier and for the French expansion under Francis I, when Pope Clement VII had so interpreted the famous bull of Alexander VI as to cover only the territories already discovered by Spain and Portugal, and so to leave France free to embark on discoveries without risk of a papal embargo which Francis could ill afford. Cartier's voyages of 1534 and 1535 were therefore royal voyages, undertaken by the orders, and on behalf, of the French king. He was to find some rumoured islands and land where there was wealth of gold, and he was to find the strait which would lead him to the land of Cathay. He explored Newfoundland and moved on to Labrador, landed in the Gaspé basin and took possesion for the French, on his first voyage. On his second expedition, in 1535, he proved that the St Lawrence was a river, not a strait, and he travelled up it to Montreal and Quebec and spent the winter in misery there. Such enterprise was followed by definite plans for settlement. Cartier's voyages had attracted no attention in Spain or Portugal, but the plans which arose from his descriptions of the fertility of the soil in the Lower St Lawrence basin led to the formulation of a concept of international law which should protect the French settlements from Spanish claims. Here Francis laid down the doctrine that not discovery but occupation and settlement gave title to overseas territories. Such a formula had the consequence that lands which were settled were accepted as rightly the property of Spain or of Portugal, and the Treaty of Crespy-en-Lannois in 1545 forbade French intervention in the Spanish colonies or in Brazil. French efforts, however, continued in Canada and in the south; Fort Coligny was established near Rio de Janeiro in 1555, and Jean Ribault started a series of French attempts to settle a French colony in Florida in 1562.

The French emphasis on colonisation rather than on exploration and trade was even more marked in Canada than in the south. But there it was upset by the wealth of furs which, it soon became apparent, might be got by trade with the Indians. Cartier's voyages were followed by a charter for colonisation, with Roberval as viceroy and lieutenant general, instructed to convert the Indians to Christianity and to find a route to the Indies, a mission which produced Cartier's voyage of 1541–2, the settlement of Charlebourg Royale, the emigration of several hundred men and women, and obvious failure. Cartier's *Brief Récit*, however, kept the attractions of Canada before the minds of Frenchmen, and when France's conquest of her internal troubles left her able to venture constructively into the overseas territories once more, Canada occupied most of her attention.

By that time (the consolidation of power in the hands of Henry IV and Sully marks the turning-point here as elsewhere) the diplomatic conventions had been still further enlarged so as to permit of action by France or by other Powers. For as early as the treaty of Cateau Cambrésis it had been agreed that 'West of the prime meridian and south of the Tropic of Cancer ... violence done by either party to the other side shall not be regarded as in contravention of the treaties'. This concept of 'No peace beyond the line', giving freedom to the adventurers to plunder, attack or settle, without disturbing the peace of Europe, was again written into the Treaty of Vervins of 1598. So Spain's acknowledgment of Henry IV's right to the French throne carried with it an implicit acknowledgment of the right to attempt settlement or trade overseas. France, moreover, was now dominated in her trade policy by a coherent theory of economics, in which the self-sufficiency of that great and wealthy country was the central theme and the need to maintain the economic independence which such natural wealth gave was the main purpose.

Though Newfoundland and Canada took so much of her attention, the peculiar circumstances of France made for emphasis on the East India trade as a source of desirable luxuries, and on the Levant route to that trade as consonant with the history and practices of French trade and diplomacy. A French East India Company was founded in 1602; a renewed treaty with the Porte in 1604 gave promise of a reinvigoration of the trade of Marseilles, and there was talk of some sort of canal to link the Red Sea and the Mediterranean at this time. But the East Indies trade on these lines did not flourish. New activity by the Algerian pirates, and lack of French experience, made this route unable to compete with the Cape route as the latter was being developed by Dutch and English competitors with the Portuguese. The French desires for a flourishing East India trade were not fulfilled until a new approach, borrowing experience from the Dutch, was made under Colbert in the latter half of the seventeenth century.

In this approach to the East Indian trade Sully reflected a very general French attitude. But the more theoretical economists of the period, as represented by Barthélemy de Laffemas, by the discussions in the Commission of Commerce, and by Montchrétien's *Traicté de l'économie politique*, were not so preoccupied with a Levant-East Indian trade. For them Canada and the north promised support for shipping, and fishing both for cod and for herring. There a New France could be raised. There the Indians could be Christianised. There French manufactures might be sold and there the raw materials needed by France might be produced. There, too, a sturdy race of Frenchmen might find homes. Into this picture comes Samuel de Champlain, geographer royal, and his voyage of 1603 up the St Lawrence, his second voyage of 1604 and the start of French settlement in Acadia, the charter to de Monts and the Canada Company of 1608, and Champlain's foundation of Quebec in that year. From that time onwards the French hold on the Lower St Lawrence was precarious but durable.

The Dutch, meanwhile, had reaped the advantages of the trade of the New World without finding it necessary to participate actively in the voyaging and trading either to the east or to the west. Much of their energy was absorbed in their religious disputes and in the long struggle with Spain; and they were able by virtue of their geographical position and of their commercial acumen to make their country, and their great city of Antwerp, the entrepôt for the spices of the East and the bourse for the treasures of America. The North Sea herring trade, too, brought them into profitable commercial touch with Portugal and the Mediterranean, and their Baltic trade in timbers, flax, tar and furs made them indispensable to the other states of western Europe, in particular to England.

Their natural maritime outlet was to the north rather than to the west or to the east, and their first attempts to find for themselves a place in the contacts of Europe with overseas lands took the shape of attempts at a north-east passage to India, not of rivalry in the Atlantic and Indian Oceans. Even so, it is usually held that such attempts were not necessary until Philip II joined Portugal to the Spanish Crown in 1580 and began to close access to Iberian ports to Protestants and rebels. Until then the Dutch had free and profitable access to the spices of the East, and much of the wealth of Antwerp, and of the Baltic trade of the Dutch, depended upon their spice trade with Lisbon. Their exploratory ventures took them north and west, not south and east. The Dutch visited Nova Zembla in 1584, and in 1594 they sent an expedition of four ships to the Arctic. It requires considerable special pleading to maintain that the Dutch navigators and geographers knew the details of the Indian Ocean route to the Spice Islands and sailed that route under Portuguese command (as they sailed across the Atlantic to Brazil and the West Indies) before Philip imposed his embargo, but that the reason why they changed their tactics and began to fit out undisguised Dutch voyages in defiance of Spanish authority after the embargo was that hitherto the navigation of the Indian Ocean had been thought too difficult and dangerous.[1]

In any case, it is universally accepted that the fitting out of an argosy of four ships in 1594, to sail to Java and to return in 1597, marks an outstanding change in the Dutch approach to the business of overseas trade. The voyage was indeed the outcome of a long and careful collection of evidence by the Dutch. It depended in particular on the knowledge amassed by Jan Huygen van Linschoten, who had spent several years at Goa in the service of the Portuguese archbishop there, and who on his return to Europe published his *Reysgeschrift* and his *Itinerario*, giving a geographical description of the world and including all the knowledge which he possessed, both at first hand and from conversations with

[1] This is the view put forward by B. H. M. Vlekke in *Nusantara, A history of the East Indian Archipelago*, pp. 91–104. The more orthodox view is summarized in J. S. Furnivall, *Netherlands India*, pp. 20–1.

sailors and merchants, of the routes to India and America. In 1594, too, Cornelis de Houtman returned to Amsterdam after several years spent in Lisbon. There he had acquired considerable knowledge of the Portuguese East Indies trade, of its possibilities and of the difficulties into which the Portuguese were running. There was already in Amsterdam a considerable weight of knowledge, and maps of the closely guarded Portuguese routes had already been printed and sold in Holland. (It is interesting to note that this necessary feature of a wider approach to overseas trade and navigation seems to have been concentrated in Holland from the start; as late as the middle years of the seventeenth century French pilots were navigating the St Lawrence with the help of charts printed in Holland.) A *Compagnie* of Amsterdam merchants financed Houtman for a voyage in 1594, and its safe and comparatively successful outcome stimulated a succession of similar voyages, fourteen fleets from Holland making the journey in the next five years.

Such voyages were, to varying degrees, the outcome of the enterprise and enthusiasm of the civic corporations of Holland, not of strictly private capital. They produced a new price-crisis in the European markets, a new fury of speculation, a new and competitive, price-cutting, source of spices, and a new desire for organisation, control and monopoly. The outcome was the co-ordination of the local chambers into the Dutch United East India Company, with a monopoly of the Dutch spice trade and with a united capital of 6,424,588 florins, to which the Estates General added a further 25,000 florins.

For the Indonesians the Dutch East Indies Company brought a new regime, in which the Dutch showed themselves determined to claim suzerainty as a means of excluding European rivals from the growing areas, and determined to use that suzerainty to exact the production of the spices which their closely organised control of the European market led them to demand. For Europe as a whole the irruption of the Dutch in this form into the East Indian trade marked a new epoch in that it brought a newly purposeful trading approach to the commerce of the overseas lands and in that, coinciding with the foundation of the English East India Company in 1600, it brought to Europe a new rivalry, of the Protestant and maritime nations, for the trade and navigation of the New World.

INDEX

Aachen, 258

Abelard, Peter, 2, 4

Aberdeen, University of, foundation, 111

Abrevanel, Jewish contractor for army supplies in Spain, 337

Abyssinia
Catalan trade settlements in, 318
European journeys to, 422, 423
ruler of identified with Prester John, 421

Acciaiuoli family, ruling Principality of Athens, 395

Achillini, Alessandro, humanist philosopher, 101

Acton, Lord, xxiii, xxiv, xxxiii, xxxiv

Adana (Cilicia), in fighting between Mamluk and Ottoman Turks, 400, 401

Adda, river, 32, 217, 360

Adelphus, Johann, German humanist, 188

Aden, failure of Portuguese attempts on, 427

Adrian Florents, of Utrecht (later Pope Adrian VI)
at University of Louvain, 113
tutor to Archduke Charles, 251
mission to Spain (1515), 253
inquisitor-general in Castile and Aragon, 337

Adrianople, 408
captured by Ottoman Turks (1361), 32
Ottoman capital before 1453, 395

Adriatic coast, Ottoman hold on, 395

Adriatic Sea, Venetian-Neapolitan rivalry, 348

Aegean Islands, Ottoman capture of, 395

Aemilius Paulus, his triumph re-enacted by Lorenzo the Magnificent, 147

Aeschylus, 114

Afiun Karahisar (Anatolia), 414
Safawid revolt (1511), 406

Afonso V (the African), king of Portugal, 339, 421
invasion of Castile (1474), 325
and division of Portuguese and Castilian possessions, 340
crusades in Morocco, 422, 423

Afonso of Portugal, marriage to Isabella, daughter of Ferdinand and Isabella, 339

Africa, caravan trade with Europe, 47
Portuguese voyages and settlements, 49, 420–5, 427

division between Castile and Aragon of north-west, 421
slave trade to West Indies, 434, 457

Africa, North
Catalan trade settlements, 318
Jiménez and revival of trade, 319–20
Portuguese-Castilian division (1494), 340
expeditions under Ferdinand the Catholic and Castilian administration, 340

Agnadello, battle of (1509), 360, 363, 366

Agricola, see Husmann, Rudolf

Agriculture, 20–37 passim
expansion and contraction between fourteenth and seventeenth centuries, 20–1, 25, 35
native, in Spanish America, 439
effect on, in England, of overseas enterprises, 465

Ahmed, son of Sultan Bāyezīd
commands against Safawid rebels (1511), 406
rivalry with Selīm and civil war, 406–11; his death (1512), 411

Ahmed Pasha, beglerbeg of Anatolia, in campaign against Mamluks, 400

'Aintab (Syria), in Mamluk-Ottoman war, 415

Aire, Franco-Burgundian condominium (1493), 242

Akkerman (Moldavia), seized by Ottoman Turks (1484), 375, 376, 399

Ak Koyunlü, Turcoman tribe, 396, 405, 406

Akshehir (Anatolia), in Mamluk-Ottoman war, 411, 414

'Alā ad-Daula, prince of Albistan, 413
established in Albistan by Mehemmed II, 400
desertion to Mamluk alliance, 401
defeated by Safawids, 406
in Ottoman-Persian war, 411; defeated and killed (1515), 412, 413

'Alā ad-Dīn, son of Ottoman prince Ahmed, put to death by Selīm, 410

Alba, Fadrique de Toledo, 2nd duke of, 329
invasion of Navarre (1512), 328

Alba, Fernando Alvarez de Toledo, 3rd duke of, his regime in the Netherlands, 462

Albania
effects of Turkish occupation, 33
yields to pressure of Ottoman Turks, 395
in Venetian-Ottoman war, 402, 403

INDEX

Alberico, Filippo, Italian humanist in England, 107

Albert II, emperor, king of Hungary and Bohemia, 221, 371

Alberti, Leon Battista, Italian architect, 131
his reinterpretation of classical architectural grammar, 128
and artistic theory, 150–1
his *De Re Aedificatoria*, 160

Albertini, Francesco, his antiquarian work, 99

Albistan, disputed between Mamluk and Ottoman Turks, 396, 399, 400, 413, 414
see also 'Alā ad-Daula, Shahsuwār-oghlü 'Alī

Albret, Charlotte d', marriage to Cesare Borgia, 356

Albret, Jean d', *see* Jean (d'Albret), king of Navarre

Albuquerque, Afonso de, Portuguese governor in India, 427, 448

Alcalá de Hénares, University of, 122, 123, 125
biblical scholarship, 124

Alcaçovas, Treaty of (1469), and partition of discoveries between Portugal and Castile, 340, 424, 431

Aldus, *see* Manutius, Aldus

Aleandro, Girolamo, cardinal, 104, 105, 119, 257

Aled, Tudur, his sententious verse, 192

Alemán, Melchior, as court painter to Isabella of Castile, 168

'Ālemshah Begüm, wife of Shaik Haidar and mother of Ismā'īl, shah of Persia, 405

Alençon, Marguerite de Valois, duchess of, and Clément Marot, 183

Aleppo, in Mamluk-Ottoman war, 415, 416

Alessandria, falls to French in invasion of Louis XII, 357

Alessio, ceded by Venice to Ottoman Turks (1506), 404

Alexander VI, pope (Rodrigo Borgia), 125, 297
character, 77, 78, 83
and Savonarola, 78–9, 354
partition of the New World (the 'Alexandrine bulls'), 79, 332, 430–1
relations with Ottoman Turks, 80; imprisonment of Jem, 265, 398
relations with Louis XI, 80
and conciliar movement, 82, 302, 350
Euhemerist tradition in paintings commissioned by, 141–2
introduces Italian artists into Spain, 169
and French invasions of Italy, 200; the League of Venice (1495), 332, 341, 353;

support for Naples against Charles VIII (1494), 350–1; allows passage of French troops, 352; encouragement for Louis XII's invasion (1499), 355–6; benefits from, 358–9

Spanish sympathies, 332, 430
and reform of religious in Spain, 333
establishment of Inquisition in Spain, 335
death (1503), 359
and offer of grandmastership of Teutonic Order to Frederick of Saxony, 379
and alliance with Hungary and Venice against Ottoman Turks, 403

Alexander I, grand duke of Lithuania, king of Poland, 222
attempt to force union with Rome on Orthodox subjects, and war with Russia, 369, 376–7
and Teutonic Order, 378–9

Alexander, natural son of James IV of Scotland, 13

Alexander of Aphrodisias, 101

Alexander of Villedieu, his text-books in use till sixteenth century, 96

Alexandria, 46, 267

Alfonso II, king of Naples
his territorial ambitions, 348
threat to Milan provokes French intervention, 350
recognised as king by Alexander VI, 351
resigns crown to Ferrantino, 352
see also Italy (the invasions)

Alfonso V (the Magnanimous), king of Aragon and Sicily, 319, 321
separation of Naples and Sicily in his will, 341
his rule in Naples, 347

Alfonso X (the Learned), king of Leon and Castile, establishes association of herdsmen, 29

Alfonso, prince of Castile, son of John II, 320

Algiers, 319
Castilian ownership, 340
pirates of, 467

'Alī, son-in-law of the Prophet, 404

'Alī Pasha, Ottoman commander (later grand vizier), 400–1
killed in suppressing Safawid rebellion, 406, 408, 409
and rivalry between Ahmed and Selīm, 407, 409

Aljubarrota, battle of (1385), 325

Alkmaar (Holland), in revolt of 1492, 240

Allegri, Antonio, *see* Correggio

Allenby, Lord, xxviii–xxix

Almain, Jacques, Gallican propagandist, 303–4

Balboa, Vasco Nuñez de
and Spanish settlements on American
mainland, 436–7
his disgrace and execution, 437
Balearic Islands, 318
see also Mallorca
Balkan peninsula, geography and economy
before 1500, 33–4
Balsac, Robert de, seigneur d'Entragues,
his *Nef des Princes et des Batailles*, 276
Banbury, grammar school at, 106
Bandello, Matteo, Italian writer, 178
Banks, banking
and Papacy, 93
Louis XI influences Florentine bankers
against Burgundian court, 228
development of, 313–14
banking houses: Bonvisi, Capponi,
Gadagne, 313; Medici, 313, 346;
Centurione, Grimaldo, Lomellino, Sal-
vagio, Welser, 334; *see also* Fugger
Italian banks finance Charles VIII's
invasion of Italy, 314
crisis of 1381–3 and decline of Barcelona,
319
American trade concessions to, 324
and crusade revenue, 334
Maximilian uses revenue of Tirol as
security, 451
royal revenues and bullion from New
World as basis of credit, 451
Antwerp as financial centre, 451, 453
Gresham's financial mission in Spain, 461
see also Expansion (overseas), its effects
in Europe; Fugger
Baptist of Mantua, *see* Mantuan
Barbara, queen of Poland, wife of Sigismund I, 222
Barbara, daughter of Albert Achilles,
margrave of Brandenburg, marriage
(by proxy) to Wladislaw II of Bohemia
and Hungary, 377
Barbarelli, Giorgio, *see* Giorgione
Barbari, Jacopo di, and Dürer, 154
Barbaro, Ermolao, Italian humanist, 105
his anti-Ciceronianism, 98
his attack on scholasticism, 100–1
Barbavara, Marcolino, Milanese representative at papal court, 267
Barbosa, Arias, Spanish humanist, and study
of Greek at Salamanca, 123, 125
Barcelona, 48, 318, 319
financial and mercantile decline, 319–20
excluded from American trade, 324
Barcelona, Treaty of (1493), 241, 296, 341,
351
Barclay, Alexander, adaptation and imitation of Brant and Mantuan, 189

Barletta, French siege of (1502–3), 358, 366
Bartolomeo, Fra, Italian painter, 137
Barzizza, Gasparino, Italian humanist, 103
Basil IV, Tsar of Russia, 369–70
invasion of Lithuania, 376
Polish wars, 379–80, 381
Basle, 124, 154, 155, 205
printing at, 115
admitted to Swiss Confederation, 206
Basle, Peace of (1499) and implicit accep-
tance of Swiss independence, 206
Basle, University of, 68, 119
Bastidas, Rodrigo de, exploration of Gulf of
Darien, 436
Battagio, Giovanni di Domenico, Italian
architect, 128
Bavaria, Albert IV, duke of, 206, 209
in Swiss war of 1499, 206
Bavaria-Landshut, George 'the Rich', duke
of, and war of Landshut succession, 211
Bavaria-Landshut, Elizabeth of, wife of
Rupert, Count Palatine, 211
Bavaria-Munich, Albert and Wolfgang,
dukes of, and war of Landshut succession, 211
Bay Islands (Caribbean Sea), Spanish slave
raids, 439
Bayard, Pierre du Terrail, seigneur de
quoted to illustrate contempt for infantry,
285
as type of chivalry, 288, 289
Bāyezīd I, Ottoman sultan, 78, 269, 375, 407
payment to Papacy for confinement of
Jem, 265
tolerance of western merchants, 265
disputed succession with Jem, 396–8
attacks on eastern Europe, 398–9, 402
wars against Egypt, 400–1
war with Venice, 402–4
and progress of *Safawiyya*, 406
civil war and succession of Selīm, 408–10;
abdication and death (1512), 410
Bayonne, 43
Bazzi, Giovanni Antonio, *see* Sodoma
Beatrix of Aragon, queen of Hungary and
Bohemia, second wife of Matthias
Corvinus, 373
marriage to Wladislaw II, 377
Beauce, 25
Beaufort, Lady Margaret, countess of
Richmond and Derby, 110
Beaujeu family, 292
Anne de, *see* Anne de Beaujeu
Pierre de Bourbon, seigneur de, *see*
Bourbon, Pierre, duke of
Beaune family, 314
Behaim, Bartholomew and Hans, engravers,
163

INDEX

Boccaccio (*cont.*)
treatment of myth in *Genealogy of the Gods*, 144
and Pistoia's *Panfila*, 175
Corbaccio, 179–80
Bodin, Jean, French political writer, 26, 63
his 'quantity theory' of coinage, 461
Boece, Hector, Scottish poet and humanist, 111
Bohemia, 11, 196
weakness of monarchy, 8–9
German and Czech colonisation, 35–6
adverse effects of Hussite wars, 36
mining in, 39; German towns developed from mining camps, 39
Habsburg interests in, 221–2
succession of George Podiebrad, 370–2
of Wladislaw II, 372
religious dissensions, 389, 391
growth of power of the aristocracy, 389–90
social structure, 390–1
disputes at succession of Lewis II, 392
see also Hungary
Bohier family, 314
Boiardo, Matteo, Italian poet, 149, 174
Orlando Innamorato, 74, 173
Boleslav III, king of Poland, 370
Boli (Anatolia), Ottoman province, 407
Bolivia, effect of discovery of silver mines, 39
Bologna, 47
and papal control, 346; conquest by Julius II, 81, 147, 349, 359
republican government in later fifteenth century, 349
failure to resist French invasion (1494), 351
French restoration of Bentivoglio, 361
and Holy League, 361
Bologna, University of, 17, 67, 96, 105, 108
Bombasio, Urbano, Italian humanist, 96
his Greek grammar, 100
Bona (Sforza), queen of Poland, second wife of Sigismund I, 380
Bonet, Honoré, French writer, on the ruler as sole initiator of war, 261
Bonvisi family, Italian bankers, 313
Börde (Germany), 24
Bordeaux, 43
Borgia family, 2
and paintings commissioned by Alexander VI, 141–2
Borgia, Cesare, 81, 273, 297
co-operation with Louis XII in invasion of Italy, 355–6
marriage to Charlotte d'Albret, 356
military achievements and character, 359; his use of artillery, 366

Borgia, Rodrigo, *see* Alexander VI, pope
Bosch, Hieronymus, Netherlands painter, 168
enigma of his imagery, 164
Boscoli, Pier Paolo, 97
Bosnia, incorporated in Ottoman empire, 33, 395, 396, 398
Bosworth, battle of (1485), 1
Botoner, William, of Worcester, 106
Botticelli, Sandro, 88, 138, 168
the *Primavera* contrasted with Raphael's treatment, 133
influence of Savonarola, 138
Bouchet, Jean, Gallican propagandist, 303
Boulonnais, overrun by Louis XI in 1477, 226
Bourbon, Anne, duchess of, *see* Anne de Beaujeu
Bourbon, Louis de, see Liège, bishops of
Bourbon, Pierre de Beaujeu, duke of, 292; patron of Lemaire de Belges, 183
Bourdichon, Jean, French painter and miniaturist, probable debt to Perugino, 158
Bourgneuf, bay of, 25
and salt fleets, 41
Brabant
the *Blijde Inkomst* of 1477, 225; modified by Archduke Philip (1494), 243
represented on *Grand Conseil*, 225
summons estates to approve marriage of Mary of Burgundy to Maximilian, 227
joins Flanders in opposition to Maximilian's regency for Archduke Philip, 231; arrest and execution of Maximilian's opponents, 233; and the 'Union' of 1488, 237; military successes of Albert of Saxony, 238
traditional interests in Liège, 231
reception of Archduke Philip as duke, 243
Margaret of Austria arbitrates in dispute with Flanders, 249
acceptance of Maximilian as regent for Archduke Charles, 250
and Archduke Charles's coming of age, 252
expulsion of gipsies, 253
Brabant, Anthony, duke of, 231
Bramante (Donato d'Angelo Lazzari), Italian architect, 127, 128, 130, 132, 133, 160
design for St Peter's, 130
and cultural primacy of Rome, 131
Brandenburg, 23, 25
Brandenburg, Albert Achilles, elector of, 377
Brandenburg, Albrecht of, *see* Mainz, Albrecht, archbishop of

479

INDEX

Caux, 25
Cavaillero, Estevan, humanist influence in
his *Prosodia Grammaticae*, 125
Caxton, William, 58, 106, 108, 191
his literary conservatism, 53, 54
his *Reynard the Fox*, 187
Cellini, Benvenuto, Italian artist, 178
Celtis, Conrad, German humanist, 120
and literary academies in Germany, 117–18
his medieval studies, 118
Cempoala, Mexican town, assists Cortés, 441
Cents Nouvelles Nouvelles, Les, 12, 184
Cephalonia (Aegean island), in Ottoman-Venetian war, 403, 404
Cerdagne, county of, ceded to France by Aragon and returned by Treaty of Barcelona (1493), 296, 340–1, 351
Ceresara, Paride da, adviser to Isabella d'Este, 145
Cerignola, battle of (1503), 279, 358
effective use of firearms, 284
Cervantes, Miguel de, Spanish writer, 170, 180
Cervera, 321
Cesariano, Cesare, his edition of Vitruvius, 130
Cesena, 95
Ceuta, Portuguese capture of (1415), 420
Chacón, Francesco, court painter to Isabella of Castile and censor, 168
Champagne, 25
fairs of, 40
Champlain, Samuel de, and French settlement in Canada, 467
Charlebourg Royale, French settlement (1541–2), 466
Charles V, Emperor (Charles I, king of Spain), 38, 167, 223
creation of his empire by dynastic marriages, 1, 10, 296; his empire a cause of war in Italy, 7
on papal fiscality, 89
patronage of Titian, 153, 169
acquires territory of Ulrich of Württemberg, 198
Maximilian's plan for his marriage to Claude de France, 210, 213
negotiations for election as king of the Romans (1518), 218–19
and charters granted by Mary of Burgundy, 225–6
recapture of Tournai (1521), 228
his minority in the Netherlands (1506), 248–52
plans for marriage to Mary Tudor, 250, 252

independent government of the Netherlands, 252–8
expulsion of gipsies from Brabant, 253
succession to Ferdinand the Catholic in Aragon (1516), 254; departure for Spain, 256
revival of the *bandes d'ordonnance*, 256
election as emperor (1519), 257–8
loans from house of Fugger, 257, 451
popular identification with unity of Netherlands, 258
love of Burgundy expressed in his will of 1522, 258
use of religious as spies, 269
Machiavelli's enquiries about in letter to ambassador in Spain, 270
and import of corn to Spain, 316, 317
and wealth of sheepowners' guild, 317
and Spanish wool trade, 318
American trade concession to bankers, 324
regulations affecting Moriscos, 324
rivalry of his brother Ferdinand, 326–7
and military orders in Spain, 330
expels Jews from Naples, 337
and 'finance council' in Spain, 339
and Spanish rule in Milan, 365
revenue from overseas possessions, 450–2
and Seville's domination of Spanish overseas trade, 453
Charles II, king of England, 464
Charles IV, king of Bohemia, 372
Charles V, king of France, 6
Charles VII, king of France, 1, 6, 26
and royal control of finance and army, 300, 301
Charles VIII, king of France, 1
and Church reform, 92, 302, 307, 350
invasion of Italy (1494), 160, 182, 244; Maximilian's intervention (1496), 202–3; recruitment of Swiss, 204; not determined by natural line of French expansion, 261–2; his ambitions in Italy and beyond, 295–6; invited by Milan as protection against Naples, 296, 350; financed by Italian bankers, 314; formation of the League of Venice (1495), 332, 341; plan for partition with Ferdinand of Aragon, 341; encouragement at home and in Italy, 350–1; initial success, control of Florence and capture of Naples, 352; his failure (League of Venice and battle of Fornovo, 1495), 353–4; Peace of Vercelli (1495), 345–5; effect of the invasion in Florence, 355
and humanism in France, 182
in Commynes's memoirs, 184, 196
death (1498), 203, 296, 354

483

Cremona, 47
secured to Francesco Sforza by Peace of
Lodi (1454), 344
Venetian designs on, and invasion of
Louis XII, 356
surrendered by Venice after battle of
Marignano (1516), 365
Crespy-en-Lannois, Treaty of (1545), 466
Crestone, Giovanni, his Graeco-Latin dic-
tionary, 100
Crétin (Crestin), Guillaume, French poet,
183
Crèvecœur, Philippe de, lord of Esquerdes
desertion to Louis XI, 227, 233, 235
negotiations with Coppenhole (1489),
238
military governor for Charles VIII in
Franco-Burgundian condominium, in
Burgundy, 242
his death and last protest against Charles
VIII's Italian ambitions, 244
Crinito, Piero, Italian humanist, and scienti-
fic criticism of texts, 99
Cristofano, Francesco di, see Franciabigio
Croatia, Ottoman attacks on, 398
Croia, captured by Ottoman Turks (1478–
9), 395
Croke, Richard, English scholar, 110
teaches in Germany, 119
Cromwell, Thomas, 2
Croy family, 245
Croy, Guillaume de, sieur de Chièvres, 244,
246, 249, 252, 254
and independent government of Philip of
Burgundy, 243
and Treaty of Lyons (1501), 245
opposition to Margaret of Austria's
French policy, 248, 253
tutelage of Archduke Charles, 250
Croy, Jacques de, 247
Crusades
remains of crusading spirit in fifteenth
and sixteenth centuries, 10
the Fourth Crusade, 33, 46
appeals and plans for, 59, 76–7, 218, 264,
340, 376; the appeal in Hungary in
1514 and the peasant rising, 388–9
the papal fleet, and naval operations, 76,
80
death of the crusading ideal, 80, 94
Brotherhood of the Holy Crusade, 94
taxation for, 94, 264
grant of indulgences for contributions,
333–4
Ferdinand of Spain's plans for Egypt and
Jerusalem, 340
Portuguese campaigns in Morocco and
African expansion, 421

Cuba, 439
discovery and exploration by Columbus,
430, 432
Spanish settlement of, 435, 436
Cuenca, exclusion of Jews, 337
Cusanus, see Nicholas of Cusa
Cuspinianus (Johannes Spieshaym), German
humanist, 117, 118
Cyprus, Venetians pay tribute for, 418
Czechs, colonisation of Bohemia, 36

Dalmatia, in Venetian-Ottoman war, 402,
403
Damascus, in Mamluk-Ottoman war, 416;
Ottoman occupation, 416
Dante Alighieri, 1, 3, 71, 147
Bruni's admiration of as ideal citizen, 16
influence in France, 182; French transla-
tion of Inferno, 182
Danube, river, 36, 396, 399
Danzig, 44, 45
export of cereals, 384
Darien, founded by Balbao, 436
Gulf of, exploration, 436
Daucher, Adolf, German sculptor, possible
Venetian influence on, 159
Daucher, Hans, German sculptor, and
mixture of Gothic and Italian styles, 159
David of Burgundy, see Utrecht, David,
bishop of
David, Gerhard, Flemish painter, 156, 168
Degli Agostini, Nicolo, Italian poet, 173
De la Bouverie, Jean, chancellor of Brabant
and marriage of Mary of Burgundy to
Maximilian, 227
and 'Union' of 1488, 236
De las Casas, Bartolomé, Dominican mis-
sionary and writer, and rights of Indians
in New World, 438
De la Chesnaye, Jean, French writer, his Con-
damnation de Banquet, 186
De la Cosa, Juan, Columbus's pilot, explora-
tion of Gulf of Darien and death, 436,
437
De la Marck, family of, and Liège in
Habsburg-Valois relations, 232–3, 245,
247
De la Marck, Érard, see Liège, Érard de la
Marck, bishop of
De la Marck, Guillaume
revolt against Louis of Bourbon, bishop
of Liège, 232
put to death by John of Hoorne, bishop of
Liège, 241
De la Sale, Antoine, 60
Le Petit Jehan de Saintré, 2, 184
Della Torre family, tomb in the Louvre,
147

INDEX

Literature (*cont.*)
in Italy: modification of troubadour poetry, 70; political disunity and localisation of literature, 171–2; reaction from Petrarchism, 172; fusion of epic and romance, 172–4; Boiardo and Ariosto, 173–4; Odasi and Folengo, 174; classical influence in the theatre, 174, 175; *sacre rappresentazioni*, 175; comedy, 175–7; Ariosto's dramatic work, 176; historiography, 177–8; the novella, 178

in Spain and Portugal: persistence of medieval tradition, 178; under Ferdinand and Isabella, 178–9; predominance of Castilian, 178–9; lyric poetry, 179; prose, 179–80; *Amadis de Gaula*, 180, 181; the Palmerin romances, 180; *La Celestina*, 180–1; vernacular chronicles, 181; Nebrija and Encina's poetic theory, 181; drama, 181–2

in France: the medieval tradition and Italian influences, 182; the *Grands Rhétoriqueurs*, 182–3; Burgundian chroniclers, 183; Marot and Lemaire de Belges, 183–4; prose, 184–5; drama, 185–6; Provençal literature, 186

in Germany: lyric poetry and the *Meistersinger*, 186; moralising plays, 187; satire, 187–8; translations of Latin literature, 188; Reuchlin as preparatory to Luther, 188; Luther and German prose, 188–9

in the Netherlands: the *Rederijkerskamers* and morality plays, 189 (*see also* 62, 69, 170)

in England: traces of humanism, 189; didactic works, 189; persistence of medieval tradition, 189–90; popular poetry and moralities, 190; prose, Berners and Malory, 190–1

in Scandinavia, 191

Gaelic literature, persistence of native traditions, 191

Brythonic Celtic in Brittany, Cornwall, Wales, 191–2

outside Western Europe, 192

Lithuania
sympathy for union with Moscow, 369
separation of grand duchy from kingdom of Poland, 374–5, 385
invasion of Ivan the Great, 369, 376–7

Livery companies of merchants, 54

Livy, 58, 70
influence on Renaissance writers, 97, 111, 178

Llanos, Fernando, Spanish painter, 169

Locarno, 207

Lodi, Peace of (1454), 267, 343, 344
Loire, river, 25
Lombardi, Antonio and Tullio, sculptors, 135
Lomellino, house of, Genoese bankers, 334
London, population of, 42
London Chronicle, 54
London, Treaty of (1518), 264
Longueil, Christopher de (Longolius), humanist scholar, 113–14
Lorch am Rhein, 195
Loronha, Fernão de, 429
Lotto, Lorenzo, painter, 139, 148
Louis XI, king of France, 1, 6, 183, 292, 321, 351
encourages mining, 26
and French Mediterranean trade, 48
and papal absolutism, 82
employment of Commynes, 184
invasion of Netherlands (1477), 224–31 *passim*
plans for marriage of Dauphin Charles to Mary of Burgundy, 226, 227
and Order of the Golden Fleece, 230
and Peace of Arras (1482), 231–2, 294
death (1483), 233
bribery of foreign officials, 266
meeting with Edward IV (1475), 266
character and abilities, 293
taxation, 300
initiation of diplomatic services, 301
attitudes to Pragmatic Sanction, 302
encouragement of foreign merchants and artisans, 310–11
his claim to Naples, 336
Louis XII, king of France, 12, 104, 158, 186, 245, 266, 286, 298
relations with the Church and Papacy: with Alexander VI, 80; the 'conciliabulum' of Pisa (1511), 82–3, 207, 215, 303, 304, 361; use of Gallicanism against Papacy, 302–3, 304; church reform, 307
and freedom of thought, 103
Perreal's portrait, 158
cedes Bellinzona to the Swiss (1503), 206, 263, 361
Treaty of Blois (1504), 210, 213
and the Netherlands, 229, 244, 245, 248, 250
marriage to Mary Tudor, 252; to Anne of Brittany, 356
death (1515), 253
use of resident ambassadors, 268
attempt to organise national infantry, 278; development of artillery, 301
patronage of armourers, 284
taxation, 300

506

INDEX

Margaret of Austria (*cont.*)
  and neutrality of the provinces, 251
  and Holy League, 251-2
  reversal of her French policy under Archduke Charles, 253-4
  during Charles's absence in Spain, 257
  and the problems of Liège, 257
Margaret of Navarre, *see* Alençon, Marguerite d'
Margaret Tudor, queen of Scotland, wife of James IV, 10, 190
Margaret of York, widow of Charles the Bold, duke of Burgundy, 224, 226, 234
  supports marriage of Mary of Burgundy to Maximilian, 227
  supports Perkin Warbeck, 244
Margarita island, in Columbus's Caribbean explorations, 433
Margarit i Pau, Joan, cardinal, bishop of Gerona, and new learning in Aragon, 125
Marienburg, 44
  Congress of (1506) and duchy of East Prussia, 379-80
Marignano, battle of (1515), 285, 289, 364, 366
  effective use of artillery, 284
Marj Dābik, battle of (1516) in Mamluk-Ottoman war, 415
Marneffe family, printers, 312
Marot, Clément, French poet, 182, 183
Marot, Jean, French poet, 183
Marseilles, and East India trade, 467
Martin V, pope (Oddo Colonna), 346
Martinez de Toledo, Alfonso, his *Corbacho*, 179-80
Martorell, Johanot, Catalan writer, his *Tirant lo Blanch*, 180
Mary, queen of Bohemia and Hungary, wife of Lewis II, 380
Mary of Burgundy, *see* Burgundy, Mary duchess of
Mary, queen of Castile, first wife of John II, 321
Mary Tudor, queen of France, wife of Louis XII, 215, 250, 252
Masip, Vicente Juan, and Italianising school of painting, 169
Masovia, annexed by Sigismund I of Poland, 385
Mathematics, Italian and German revival of, 68
Matthias Corvinus, king of Hungary, 37, 221, 372-3
  death (1490), 373, 401
  his marriages, 373
  negotiations with Maximilian, 373

and constitutional development of Hungary, 385
  his 'Black Army', 386
  and Ottoman Turks, 398
Mauro, Fra, geographer, 422, 423
Maya cities, Yucatán, 439
Maximilian I, king of the Romans and emperor-elect, 1, 7, 8, 248, 265, 268, 295, 326
  his papal ambitions, 13, 215
  and humanism, 17-18, 117
  his *Der Weisskunig*, 161, 282
  patronage of the arts, 161-2, 187
  succession to Frederick III (1493), 194
  character and appearance, 198-9, 210
  in Austria: acquisition of Tirol (1490), 199; organisation and unification, 203, 219-21
  and the Swiss war with the Swabian League (1499), 198, 206, 356
  and reform of the *Reich*, 199-216 *passim*; *see also* Empire, Holy Roman (reform of the *Reich*)
  in the Netherlands: invasion of Franche Comté and Peace of Senlis (1493), 198-9, 241, 242-3, 351; imprisoned at Bruges (1488), 200, 235-6, 238; marriage (by proxy) to Anne of Brittany, 200, 239, 295; plans for invasion of Burgundy (1498), 203-4; and duchy of Guelders, 204, 227-8, 229, 240, 247; and Ghent, 227-8, 230-1, 232, 233-4, 235-6, 239, 241; French war (1477-82), 228-31; alliance with England and Brittany (1478, 1480), 229, 232; and bishopric of Utrecht, 232, 233; and bishopric of Liège, 229, 232-2, 241-2, 247, 250; administrative reforms, 230-1; Peace of Arras (1482), 231-2, 241; regency for Archduke Philip, 231 ff. (*see also* Netherlands, minority of Archduke Philip); failure of expedition against France (1486, 1487), 236-7; retires to Germany (1489), 237; quarrel with Philip of Cleves-Ravenstein, 238-40, 245; alliance with England and Spain, 240-1, 341; and Archduke Philip's independent government, 243; and Margaret of York's support of Perkin Warbeck, 244; and minority of Archduke Charles, 248, 249-50, 252; and Charles's coming of age, 252; ratifies treaty of Noyon, 254
  and Italy: invests Lodovico Sforza with duchy of Milan, 200, 355; marriage to Bianca Maria Sforza, 200; and the League of Venice (1495), 200-1, 261, 332, 341, 353; support for his Italian

509

Navarre, 6, 323
conquest by Ferdinand of Aragon, 320,
325, 327–8, 342
retained by John II of Aragon after death
of Queen Blanca, 321
Navarre, Collège de, 308
Navidad, failure of Columbus's settlement,
432
Nebrija, Elio Antonio de, and humanism in
Spain, 121, 122, 123, 126, 179, 181
Nef, J. U., on silver mining, 1460–1530, 37
Negroponte, falls to Ottoman Turks (1470),
395
Niels of Sorö, Danish monk, his *Rimkrönicke*, 191
Nemesianus, 104
Neoplatonism
overcomes early Renaissance secularism,
74–5
as influence on Renaissance artists, 129,
134
see also Florence; Plato, Platonism
Netherlands
popular mysticism, 12
geography and economy, 24–5; herring
fisheries, 41; textile industry, 42
population, 42, 456
cultural development, 61–2; vernacular
literature, 62, 69, 189; influence of
humanism, 111–15; see also Arts of the
Renaissance (Northern Europe)
reaction after death of Charles the Bold
(1477), 224–5; recognition of Mary of
Burgundy, 224, 225
French invasion (1477–82), 224–32;
French successes, 226; embassies to
Louis XI, 226–7; desertions to France,
226, 227, 248; alliance with England
(1478, 1480) and Brittany (1480), 229;
attempt of Louis of Bourbon to secure
neutrality of Liège, 229; local defence
against the French, 229; Peace of Arras
(1482), 231–2; recognition of Louis XI
as guarantor of supremacy of the
estates, 231; French suzerainty over
Flanders recognised, 231; termination
of alliances with England and Brittany,
232
constitutional and administrative
changes: the *Grand Privilège* and local
charters of Mary of Burgundy, 224–6,
230, 235, 236; the *Grand Conseil*, 224–5,
230; abolition of *Parlement* of Malines,
224–5, 230; independence of the
Chambre des Comptes and *Rekenkamers*, 230; revival of the *procureur
général*, 230; opposition to centralisation, 230–1; revocation of privileges by

Archduke Philip, 244; Philip's creation
of the *Grand Conseil* at Malines, 246;
the position of the *Conseil privé* in the
minority of Archduke Charles, 250
marriage of Mary of Burgundy to
Maximilian I, 227, 228
the minority of Archduke Philip: death of
Mary of Burgundy (1482) and recognition of Philip as *prince naturel*, 231;
opposition in the estates to regency of
Maximilian I, 231 ff.; the estates set up
alternative government, 232; Maximilian recovers control in bishoprics
of Liège and Utrecht, 232–3; his successes in Brabant (1483), 233; civil war,
233–4; the magnates profit from Maximilian's success, 234; reopening of
hostilities with France, 235; Maximilian's failure and collapse of central
authority, 235; fresh outbreaks against
Maximilian, 235–6; Maximilian imprisoned in Bruges (1488), 236; the
'Union' of 1488 and Peace of Bruges,
236; campaign and successes of Albert
of Saxony, 237, 238; lack of support
against Maximilian from France, 237–
8; Treaty of Montils-lez-Tours (1489),
and abrogation of Peace of Bruges,
238; Philip of Cleves's quarrel with
Maximilian, 238–9, 242; revaluation
of currency impairs Maximilian's
authority in Flanders and Holland,
239; submission of Bruges (1490), 239;
revolt of Ghent (1491), 239; renewal of
French intervention (1491), 239; revolts
(*Kaas-en-Broodvolk*) in Holland and
W. Friesland, 240; loss of Guelders,
240; Maximilian's invasion of Franche
Comté (1493), 241, 351 (*cf. also* 198–9);
end of French intervention, Peace of
Senlis (1493), 242–3
independent government of Archduke
Philip (1493), 243–8; centralisation of
justice and finance, 243; revocation of
privileges granted by Mary of Burgundy, 243–4; taxation assessment in
Holland (1494), 243–4; friendly relations with France, Treaty of Paris
(1498), and England (*Intercursus
Magnus*), 244; effect on foreign relations of Philip's marriage to Joanna of
Spain, 244–5; renewal of French intervention (1505), 245; growing influence
of the nobility and their identification
with the provinces, 245–6; modified
centralisation of authority, 246; relations with the estates, 246–7; consent
of provinces to taxation, 247; indepen-

Pollaiuolo, Italian artist
his influence on Dürer, 154
his tomb for Sixtus IV, 168
Polo, Marco, 2, 421, 422
Polotsk, 44
Pomerania, 23, 24, 25, 381
Pomponazzi, Pietro, Italian scholar, 88, 97
and new approach to Aristotle, 101
Ponce de Leon, Juan, government of Puerto Rico and attempt at settlement in Florida, 435
Poncher family, 305
Pontano, Gioviano, 97
Ponte di Crevola, battle of (1487), 280
Pontormo (Jacopo da Carucci), 138, 152
Pontremoli, Nicodemo da, secretary to Francesco Sforza, 267
Popocatépetl, Mt. 440
Population, 50, 456
urban, in fifteenth and sixteenth centuries, 42–4, 46, 47
decline and recovery in France, 26, 308–9, 310–11
of Spain in sixteenth century, 316, 318
and colonisation of New World, 456–7
Portinari, Tommaso, 157
Porto, Luigi da
on Julius II's quarrel with Venetian ambassador, 360
in Venetian war with Maximilian, 360–1
Portsmouth, dockyard of Henry VII, 287
Portugal
dynasticism in, 9
geography, 28
humanism in, 125–6
battle of Toro (1476) and failure of possible union with Castile, 325
marriages of Manuel I and Philip of Spain's claim to, 339–40
union with Spain under Philip, 455, 468
population, 456
overseas expansion: motives behind voyages of discovery, 2–3, 421; maritime trade in fifteenth and sixteenth centuries, 49; partition of the New World with Spain, 79, 332, 340, 424, 429–30, 430–1, 455, 458, 466; blockade of Red Sea against Egypt, 414; medieval background to expansion, 420–1; Crown leases of colonial trade, 422, 429; the sea route to India, 421–8; exploration of West Africa, 430; naval and military protection for Indian posts, 427; the Brazilian voyages, 428–30; slave trade with West Indies, 434, 457; royal monopoly and licensing system in

the East, 448; weakness of eastern trade organisation, 447–8; the European market, 448–9; the spice trade, 463–4; English fight for share in colonial trade and support for revolt from Spain, 464; see also Africa; Brazil; Magellan
Portuguese language, 179, 182; see also Literature, vernacular (in Spain and Portugal)
Posts, 271
Poynings, Sir Edward, naval assistance at siege of Sluis (1492), 242
Pragmatic Sanction of Bourges (1438), 7, 12, 85, 186
abolition (1516), 86, 365
later attitudes to in France, 302–3
use in Gallican propaganda, 303–4
condemned by fifth Lateran council, 304
effects of its failure, 304–5, 306
Prato, Spanish capture of (1512), 277, 362
Preaching, fifth Lateran council and control of, 93
Pressburg, Treaty of (1491), 374
Prester John, legend of, 421, 422, 423
Prie, René de, cardinal, and Gallicanism, 303
Printing
exaggerated views on immediate effect of the invention, 4, 53
as indication of popular piety, 89–90
ecclesiastical control, 92
and dissemination of classics, 95–6, 100, 115–16
at the Sorbonne, 103
in France, 104, 312
early signs of humanist influence in England, 106
as evidence of literary taste, 112
the Brethren of the Common Life, 112
at Louvain, 113
in Germany, 115–16
in Scandinavia, 121
as evidence of humanism in Spain, 122
first Danish, 191
introduced to Iceland, 191
first Breton, 191
first Welsh, 192
as stimulus to German nationalism, 194
Pripet marshes, 22
Proclus, Linacre's translation of De Sphaera, 109
Provence, acquired by France (1481), 262
Prussia, 25
Przemyslide dynasty, in Bohemia, 370
'Pseudo-Phalaris', Aretino's translation, 106
Pskov, 44
subjected by Tsar Basil IV, 369, 370
Ptolemy, geographer, 2, 420, 422

INDEX

Trade and commerce (*cont.*)
wine trade, 41; French with England, 27
timber and timber products, 41–2, 456
wool, 29, 42, 317–18, 319
luxury goods, 42
Mediterranean trade in fifteenth century, 45–8; in sixteenth century, 447, 464
Italian sea-trade to north-west, 47
caravan trade with Africa, 47
Portuguese in fifteenth and sixteenth centuries, 49; establishment of eastern trade, 422–7, 447–9; organisation of the European market, 448–9; Philip II diverts spice trade from English Channel, 464
German expansion, 1350–1550, 66
Fugger-Höchstetten control of copper, 197
French expansion in fifteenth century, 310–11; Lyons and foreign trade, 312
Castilian monopoly of American trade, 324
Ottoman Turks and cessation of Black Sea trade, 385
effect of Christian reconquest of Iberian peninsula, 420–1
Brazilian dye-wood trade, 429
slave trade, 434, 436, 457–8
naval supplies from the Baltic, 458
Netherlands herring trade, 468
Dutch East Indian trade, 468–9
see also Expansion (overseas), its effects in Europe
Tramellio, Alessio, Italian architect, 128
Transylvania, ethnic groups in fifteenth century, 37
Trastamara family, its position in Hispan ruling houses, 321, 322
Treaties, respect for, and excuses for breach of, 262–3
see also names of treaties
Trebizond, 46, 411
Greek empire of, incorporated in Ottoman empire (1461), 395
Ottoman province, 407, 412
Trevelyan, G. M., on cultural conservatism in fifteenth-century England, 52–3
Trier, archbishop of, as secular ruler, 195
Trieste, taken by Venice (1508–9), 214; confirmed to Venice by Maximilian, 360
Trinidad, discovered by Columbus (1498), 433
Tripoli (North Africa), 319
Castilian ownership, 340
Tripoli (Syria), in Mamluk-Ottoman war, 400; Ottoman occupation, 416

Trissino, Giovanni Giorgio, Italian writer, 175
Trithemius, Johannes, abbot of Sponheim and Würzburg
and humanist scholarship, 117, 120
on ciphers (*Polygraphia*), 271
Triumphal processions, modelled on antiquity, in Renaissance Italy, 147
Trivulzio, Gian Giacomo, 136
leaves Lodovico Sforza to serve Louis XII, 356–7
his victory at Marignano (1515), 364
Troitsa, 21
Troubadours, Italian modification of their poetry, 70
Troyes
cathedral, 160
fairs, 313
Tuat, oasis of, 47
Tūmān Bāy, Mamluk sultan, defeat and death in Mamluk-Ottoman war, 416, 417
Tunis, 267, 421
Turcoman tribes, Ottoman recognition of their privileges, 417
see also Ak Koyunlü; Karaman-oghlü; Ramazan-oghlü; Rum-lü; Tekke-lü; Torghud; Varsak
Turks, *see* Egypt, Mamluk empire of; Ottoman Turks
Turmair, Johann (Aventinus), and German historiography, 118
Tver, subjected by Ivan the Great, 368

Ulm, cathedral of, 160
'Ummaiyad caliphate in Spain, its collapse and European expansion in Africa, 420
Union of Florence (1438–9), and war between Ivan the Great and Alexander of Lithuania, 369, 376–7
Unity of the Brotherhood, religious sect in Bohemia, 389
Universities
German: increased numbers of students, 4; humanism in, 67–8, 116–17; preponderance of secular foundations, 196
Italian contrasted with northern in early Renaissance, 15
failure of medieval programme for Church reform, 51
decline after mid-fifteenth century, 51–2
humanism and the medieval tradition, 96–7
introduction of Greek, 100, 104–5
foundations in Scandinavia, 121
and diffusion of Roman law, 197
in Spain, 122–4
see also under names of university towns

528

Wladislaw II (Jagiello), king of Poland, and
establishment of Jagiello dynasty in
Poland, 371
Wladislaw V (Postumus), king of Hungary
and Bohemia, 371
Wolsey, Thomas, Cardinal, archbishop of
York, 13, 110, 272
Worcester, William, *see* Botoner, William
Worde, Wynkyn de, English printer, 191
Worms, 159, 202
attacked by von Sickingen (1514–17), 217
Worms, *Reichstag* and Edict of (1495), 199–
202, 203, 204, 214–15, *see also* Empire,
Holy Roman (reform of the *Reich*);
(1521), 105
Württemberg, Eberhard (Barbatus), duke of,
and Swabian League, 198
Württemberg, Ulrich, duke of, overthrown
by Swabian League, 198
Würzburg, abbey of, 117

Ya'kūb Beg, shah of Persia, 397, 405
Yañez, Fernando, Spanish painter, 169
Yaroslav, 21
Yenishehir (Anatolia), 411
defeat of Jem (1481), 397
defeat of Ahmed by Selīm (1513), 410–
11
Ypres, and opposition to regency of Maxi-
milian for Archduke Philip, 231
Yucatán
Maya cities of, 439
Spanish exploration of the coast, 439

Zaccagni, Bernardino, Italian architect,
130

Zanchari, Andrea, Venetian ambassador to
the Ottoman Turks, 403
Zante, in Venetian-Ottoman war, 403;
Venice pays tribute for, 404
Zápolyai, house of, and opposition to
Habsburgs in eastern Europe, 377, 379,
381
Zápolyai, Barbara, *see* Barbara, queen of
Poland
Zápolyai, Imre, Palatine of Hungary, 373
Zápolyai, John, *voivode* of Transylvania
(later king of Hungary)
and opposition to Habsburgs, 222, 379,
392
in Ottoman attack on Hungary, 392, 393
Zápolyai, Stephen, Palatine of Hungary, 377
Zara, held by Venice, 402
Zealand, island, 22
Zeeland
represented on the *Grand Conseil*, 225
and marriage of Mary of Burgundy to
Maximilian, 227
resumption of regalian revenues and rights
by Archduke Philip, 246
Zierikerzee (Zeeland), 253
Zoë (Sophia) Palaeologue, wife of Tsar Ivan
the Great of Russia, 369
Zuccaro, Federigo, Italian painter, 144
Zug, Swiss canton, 204
Zuider Zee, 256
Zu'l-Kadr, ruling house of Albistan, 396
Zuñiga, Diego Lopez, Spanish scholar, his
attack on Erasmus and Lefèvre
d'Étaples, 124
Zürich, Swiss canton, 204, 205
Zurita, Jerónimo de, 328